A LEVEL
PSYCHOLOGY

Cara Flanagan

Letts
EDUCATIONAL

First published 1994
Reprinted, 1994, 1995, 1996

Letts Educational
Aldine House
Aldine Place
London W12 8AW

Tel: 0181-740 2266

British Library Cataloguing in Publication Data
A CIP record for this book is available from the British Library.

ISBN 1 85758 233 0

Acknowledgement
Photographs on pp. 28, 29, 31 by kind permission of
Weidenfeld & Nicholson Ltd.

Printed and bound in Great Britain by
WM Print Limited, Walsall, West Midlands WS2 9NE

Letts Educational is the trading name of BPP (Letts Educational) Ltd

PREFACE

Psychology is a subject full of interest. In pursuing it as an academic subject, I hope it manages to enlarge your understanding of the world and provides you with a useful examination pass. This book was written with both these aims in mind.

I acknowledge the Associated Examining Board, the Northern Examinations and Assessment Board, and the Oxford and Cambridge Schools Examination Board for permission to use their exam material. These boards cannot accept any responsibility for the answers or methods given in this book.

I am most indebted to Phil Banyard, who read through the whole manuscript, as well as answering my persistent queries and supporting me with idle psychological chitchat. I hasten to add that any mistakes remaining are mine entirely. The officers-in-charge of psychology at the examination boards have all been most helpful and patient with my queries; my thanks to Rupert Masters, Miss Heritage, Mrs Wagstaff, Elizabeth Dolman and Emma Talbot. My thanks also go to those at home, Rob and Philippa, Jack and Rosie, for the sacrifices and allowances they have had to make for me; to Dennis and Geraldine, who have done much unpaid research on my behalf; and to Wayne Davies, who stepped in at the end, offering me much needed advice.

Cara Flanagan

CONTENTS

SECTION 1: STARTING POINTS

SECTION 2: PSYCHOLOGY TOPICS

SECTION 3: TEST RUN

BIBLIOGRAPHY

APPENDIX: GENERAL THEMES

INDEX

STARTING POINTS

In this section:

How to use this book

    Structure of the book

    Using your syllabus checklist

Syllabus checklists and paper analysis

    Examination board addresses

Studying and revising Psychology

    The difference between GCSE and A/AS-level

    Study strategies and techniques

    Coursework

    Revision techniques

The examination

    Question styles

    Examination techniques

    Final preparation

HOW TO USE THIS BOOK

STRUCTURE OF THE BOOK

The key aim of this book is to guide you in the way you tackle A-level Psychology. It should serve as a study guide, work book and revision aid throughout any A-level/AS-level Psychology course, no matter which syllabus you are following. It is not intended to be a complete guide to the subject, but should be used as a companion to your textbooks, which it is designed to complement rather than duplicate.

We have divided the book into three sections. **Section One, Starting Points,** contains study tips and syllabus information – all the material you need to get started on your A-level study – plus advice on planning your revision and tips on how to tackle the exam itself. Use the **Syllabus Checklists** to find out exactly where you can find the study units which are relevant to your particular syllabus.

Section Two, Psychology Topics, the main body of the text, contains the core of A-level Psychology. It has been devised to make study as easy – and enjoyable – as possible, and has been divided into chapters which cover the themes you will encounter on your syllabus. The chapters are split into units, each covering a topic of study.

The **Chapter Overviews** direct you towards the key points of the chapter you are about to read. The **Chapter Roundup** at the end of the chapter links the text just covered to other themes of study within the book. To reinforce what you have read and learned, there are **Illustrative Questions** with worked answers at the end of each chapter. All questions are taken from papers recently set by the examination boards. The tutorial notes and suggested answers give you practical guidance on how to answer A-level questions, and provide additional information relevant to that particular topic. There is also a **Question Bank**, with further examples of A-level exam questions for you to attempt, and notes highlighting important points and possible pitfalls.

In **Section Three, Test Run,** we turn our attention to the examination you will face at the end of your course. First, you can assess your progress using the **Test Your Knowledge Quiz** and analysis chart. Then, as a final test, you should attempt the **Mock Exam**, under timed conditions. This will give you invaluable examination practice and, together with the notes specially written by the author, will help you to judge how close you are to achieving your A-level pass.

The appendix lists general topics which run through the book.

USING YOUR SYLLABUS CHECKLIST

Whether you are using this book to work step-by-step through the syllabus or to structure your revision campaign, you will find it useful to use our checklist to record what you have covered – and how far you still have to go. Keep the checklist to hand when you are doing your revision – it will remind you of the chapters you have revised, and those still to be done.

The checklist for each examination – A or AS – is in two parts. First there is a list of topics covered by this book which are part of the syllabus. Although the checklists are detailed, it is not possible to print entire syllabuses. **You are therefore strongly recommended to obtain an official copy of the syllabus for your examination and consult it when the need arises.** The examination board addresses are given after the syllabus checklists.

When you have revised a topic make a note of the date in the column provided and, if there are questions elsewhere in the book, try to answer them, putting the date or dates in the final column.

The second part of the checklist gives you information about the examination, providing useful details about the time allocated for each paper and the weighting of the questions on each paper. The different types of questions which may be set are explained in detail later in this section under the heading The Examination.

SYLLABUS CHECKLISTS AND PAPER ANALYSIS

ASSOCIATED EXAMINING BOARD
A-level (0651)

Syllabus topic	Covered in Unit No	Completed on (date)	Questions attempted
1A Perspectives on psychology			
Nature of psychological enquiry	see Appendix for		
Issues in psychology	detailed references		
1B Cognitive psychology			
Sensory systems and perception	1.1		
Attention	1.2, 1.3		
Memory processes	1.5		
Language and thought	1.2, 1.6, 4.1		
1C Social psychology			
Social perception	2.1, 2.2, 2.3		
Attraction and prejudice	2.4, 2.5		
Social influence in interaction	2.8, 2.9, 2.10		
Pro- and antisocial behaviour	2.6, 2.7		
1D Comparative psychology			
Genetic and evolutionary determinants of behaviour	8.1, 8.2, 8.4		
Learning and behaviour in the natural environment	8.2, 8.3, 8.4		
Laboratory studies of learning and behaviour	1.4, 9.3		
Animal communication and social behaviour	4.3, 8.4		
2A Experimental design and research methods			
Choice of appropriate methods	10.1, 10.2, 10.4		
Design of studies	5.3, 10.2		
Analysis of data	10.3		
2B Bio-psychology			
The nervous system and behaviour	7.1		
Awareness	7.1, 7.2, 7.3		
Motivation and emotion	7.4, 7.5		
Anxiety and stress	7.6		
2C Development psychology			
Early socialisation	3.1, 3.4		
Cognitive development	3.2, 4.1		
Social behaviour and individual differences in development	2.4, 3.3, 3.4		
Adolescence, adulthood, senescence	3.4, 3.5		
2D Individual differences			
Personality and intelligence	5.1, 5.2, 5.3, 5.4, 5.5		
Normal and abnormal behaviour	6.1, 6.2, 6.6		
Psychopathology	6.4		
Therapeutic approaches	6.2		

Broad and traditional syllabus, with little on applications.

Paper analysis

Paper 1   *3 hours*   40% of the total mark

Divided into 4 sections:

Section A Perspectives on Psychology	3 questions
Section B Cognitive Psychology	4 questions
Section C Social Psychology	4 questions
Section D Comparative Psychology	4 questions

Section A is compulsory, candidates should answer one question.

In sections B to D, candidates should answer 3 questions in total, but not more than 2 from any section.

Paper 2   *3 hours*   40% of the total mark

Divided into 4 sections:

Section A Experimental Design and Research Methods	1 question
Section B Bio-psychology	4 questions
Section C Developmental Psychology	4 questions
Section D Individual Differences	4 questions

Section A is compulsory, based on a real or hypothetical psychological enquiry.

In sections B to D, candidates should answer 3 questions in total, but not more than 2 from any section.

Paper 3   *coursework*   20% of the total mark

4 psychological investigations, to include: one repeated measures, one independent measures, and one correlational study.

The written report should be between 1200 and 2000 words, excluding diagrams and appendices, and should cover: planning and carrying out an investigation, treatment and interpretation of results.

ASSOCIATED EXAMINING BOARD
AS-level (0998)

Syllabus topic	Covered in Unit No	Completed on (date)	Questions attempted
A Research methods			
Choice of appropriate methods	10.1, 10.2, 10.4		
Design	5.3, 10.2		
Analysis	10.3		
B Cognitive processes			
Learning and memory	1.4, 1.5, 7.1, 9.3		
Language	1.2, 1.6, 4.1, 4.3		
Thought and artificial intelligence	1.2, 1.6		
C Biological foundations of behaviour			
Basic neural processes and genetic influences on behaviour	6.4, 7.1, 8.1		
Cortical functions and perceptual mechanisms	1.1, 4.1, 7.1		
Awareness	7.1, 7.2, 7.3		
Motivation and emotion	7.4, 7.5		
D Individual development			
Early socialisation	3.1		
Cognitive development	3.2, 4.1, 9.3		
Social behaviour and individual differences in development	3.3, 3.4, 3.5		
Atypical development	6.5, 9.3		
E Social behaviour			
Social interaction and social skills	2.1, 2.2, 2.4, 2.9, 4.2		
Social influences and persuasion	2.3, 2.8, 2.9		
Pro- and antisocial behaviour	2.6, 2.7, 2.10		
F Work and the individual			
Employment and unemployment	3.5, 9.1		
Selection and training	3.5, 9.1		
Work performance and quality of working life	7.6, 9.1, 9.2		
G Adulthood: Adjustment and abnormality			
Coping with life events	3.5, 7.6		
Conceptions of abnormality	6.1, 6.2, 6.3, 6.4		
Treatments and therapeutic approaches	6.2, 6.6		

More emphasis on applications than A-level. Omits some traditional areas, e.g. intelligence, animal behaviour.

Paper analysis

Paper 1   *3 hours*   80% of the total mark

Divided into 7 sections:

Section A Research Methods	1 question
Section B Cognitive Processes	4 questions
Section C Biological Foundations of Behaviour	4 questions
Section D Individual Development	4 questions
Section E Social Behaviour	4 questions
Section F Work and the Individual	4 questions
Section G Adulthood: Adjustment and Abnormality	4 questions

Section A is compulsory, based on a real or hypothetical psychological enquiry.

In sections B to G, candidates should answer 3 questions in total, but not more than 2 from any section. It is permissible to answer from 3 sections.

Paper 2   *coursework*   20% of the total mark

2 psychological investigations, the written report is the same as for the A-level.

NORTHERN EXAMINATIONS AND ASSESSMENT BOARD
A-level (For examination in 1995)

Syllabus topic	Covered in Unit No	Completed on (date)	Questions attempted
Cognitive and linguistic development			
Perception	1.1		
Language	1.6, 4.1		
Cognitive development	3.2, 9.3		
Intelligence	5.1, 5.3, 5.4		
Acquisition of knowledge and skills			
The learning of skills	9.1, 9.3		
Mechanisms underlying learning	1.3, 1.5, 1.6, 9.1		
Individual characteristics of learners	1.6, 3.5, 9.3		
Information processing and computer approaches to learning	1.1, 1.2, 1.5		
Development of social behaviour			
Theories of social development	1.4, 3.3, 3.4, 5.2		
Infant–caregiver interactions	3.1, 8.3		
Interpersonal behaviour	2.1, 2.4, 2.5, 2.7, 2.10, 3.1, 3.3, 3.4, 7.5		
Adulthood	3.4, 3.5		
Applications of psychology			
Learning in the classroom	5.3, 9.3		
Atypical development	6.1, 6.2, 6.3, 6.4, 6.5, 6.6, 9.3		
Design and analysis of investigations			
Methods of investigation	10.1, 10.2, 10.4		
Statistical techniques and experimental design	10.3		

Emphasis on applications, e.g. education; however some areas of psychology not represented, e.g. personality, attitudes, attribution theory, sleep, motivation, stress and animal behaviour. This is changed in the new syllabus for 1996.

Paper analysis

Paper 1   *3 hours*   Section A   10% of total mark
one compulsory question, set on statistics and design
Section B   30% of total mark
part (i) Cognitive and Linguistic Development   4 questions
part (ii) Acquisition of Knowledge and Skills   4 questions

Candidates will be required to answer 3 questions from Section B, at least
one from each part (i) and (ii).

Paper 2   *3 hours*   Section A   10% of total mark,
style as for Paper 1.
Section B   30% of total mark
part (i) Development of Social Behaviour   4 questions
part (ii)
Option P: Learning in the Classroom   4 questions
or
Option Q: Atypical Behaviour   4 questions

Candidates will be required to answer 3 questions from Section B, at least
one from each part (i) and (ii).

Coursework   20% of the total mark
5 psychological investigations, which must include at least: one observational study or
survey and one experiment.
The written report should include details of: planning investigations, implementation,
interpretation and evaluation.

NORTHERN EXAMINATIONS AND ASSESSMENT BOARD
A-level and AS-level (For examinations in and after 1996)

Syllabus topic	Covered in Unit No	Completed on (date)	Questions attempted
Perspectives in psychology			
The study of psychology			
The biological approach			
Behaviourist and cognitive approaches	see Appendix for references		
Person-centred approaches			
Methods and debate in psychology			
Research methods and data analysis			
Methods	10.1, 10.2		
Issues	10.4		
Data analysis	10.3		
Drawing conclusions/representing data	10.3		
Contemporary topics in psychology			
Human relationships	2.4, 3.4		
Psychology and work	2.9, 9.1		
Substance abuse	6.5		
Human ageing	3.5		
Paranormal phenomena	7.2		
The psychology of atypical behaviour			
Definition and classification	6.1, 6.3		
Treatment	6.2, 6.6		
Emotional disorders	6.4		
Research in atypical psychology	10.1		
Social psychology			
Attitudes	2.3, 2.5		
Social influence	2.8, 2.9		
Groups	2.9		
Social cognition	2.1, 2.2		
Applied social psychology	1.5, 2.5, 2.8, 2.9		
Child development			
Issues	3.1, 3.2, 10.1		
Cognitive development	3.2, 4.1		
Social development	3.1, 3.4		
Moral development	3.3		
Cognitive psychology and its applications			
Perception	1.1		
Attention	1.4		
Remembering and forgetting	1.5		
Language	1.3, 4.1		
Thinking and problem solving	1.3		
Artificial intelligence	1.2		
Health psychology			
Health and illness	9.4		
Psychological aspects of illness	7.7, 9.4		
Lifestyles and health	9.4		
Stress and illness	7.6		
Coping and stress management	7.6		

Syllabus topic	Covered in Unit No	Completed on (date)	Questions attempted
Psychology in education			
Learning and its assessment	5.3, 9.3		
Reading	9.3		
Social dynamics in the classroom	2.1, 2.5, 3.4, 9.3		
Assessment and modification of behaviour	2.3, 6.2, 10.1		
Special needs	6.5, 9.3		

Paper Analysis: modular assessment

A-level

The modular scheme can be taken as 5 modules plus 1 from another biological science; (the 2 compulsory modules must be included), or a psychology module can be included as part of another science A-level. A certificate will be awarded for each module.

2 compulsory modules: Perspectives in Psychology, Research Methods and Data Analysis

4 optional modules selected from: Contemporary Topics, Atypical Behaviour, Social Psychology, Child Development, Cognitive Psychology and its Applications, Health Psychology, Psychology in Education.

Assessment: end of module tests. 80% of total mark.

Coursework: 6 assessments, one from each module taken, including one full investigation. Each assessed for: designing, implementing, interpreting and communicating. 20% of total mark.

AS-level

Identical to the A-level, except fewer modules.

2 compulsory modules: as above.
1 optional module: selected from list above.

Assessment: end of module tests. 80% of total mark.

Coursework: 3 assessments, as for A-level. 20% of total mark.

Paper analysis: end of course assessment

A-level

5 compulsory modules: Perspectives in Psychology, Research Methods and Data Analysis, Social Psychology, Child Development, Cognitive Psychology and its Applications.

1 optional module selected from: Contemporary Topics, Atypical Behaviour, Health Psychology, Psychology in Education.

Assessment: two 3 hour papers. 80% of total mark.

Coursework: as for modular assessment. 20% of total mark.

AS-level

Modules: as for AS-level, modular assessment
Assessment: one 3 hour paper. 80% of total mark.
Coursework: as for modular assessment. 20% of total mark.

OXFORD AND CAMBRIDGE SCHOOLS EXAMINATION BOARD
A-level (9674) and AS-level (8501)

Syllabus topic	Covered in Unit No	Completed on (date)	Questions attempted
A- and AS-level			
Themes			
Methodology	10.1, 10.2		
Perspectives	see Appendix		
Ethics	10.4		
Core Studies			
Cognitive	1.2, 1.5, 1.6		
Social interaction	2.4, 2.6, 2.8, 2.9		
Developmental	2.7, 3.1, 3.2, 3.3		
Social cognition	2.2, 2.3, 2.5		
Abnormal	6.1, 6.2, 6.3, 6.4, 6.6		
Physiological	7.1, 7.2, 7.5		
Comparative	4.3, 8.2, 8.3, 8.5		
Culture and identity	2.5, 3.4, 5.3		
A level only: specialist choice			
Psychology and education	Mainly 9.3. Also in: 1.6, 2.1, 2.2, 2.3, 2.4, 2.9, 3.2, 3.4, 4.1, 4.2, 5.3, 5.4, 6.2, 6.5, 9.1, 10.1		
Psychology and health	Mainly 9.4. Also in: 2.1, 2.3, 2.8, 7.6, 7.7		
Psychology and the environment	Mainly 9.2. Also in: 2.7, 7.6, 8.4, 9.1		
Psychology and organisations	Mainly 9.1. Also in: 2.9, 3.5, 5.3		

Broad but limited range of specific *core studies*; interesting use of prescribed journal articles to enable study in depth rather than superficial overview in breadth; includes applications of psychology.

Paper analysis

A- and AS-level

Paper 1	*3 hours*	A-level: 40%, AS-level: 80% of total mark

Covers the core studies: Cognitive, Social interaction, Developmental, Social cognition, Abnormal, Physiological, Comparative, Culture and identity.

Section A: 20 short answer questions, all compulsory

Section B: answer one out of two stimulus questions on Ethics

Section C: answer one out of two stimulus questions on Methodology and Perspectives

Paper 2   *coursework*

A-level: 10%, AS-level: 20% of total mark
2 pieces of structured practical work

A-level only

Paper 3   *coursework*

10% of total mark
  (a) one project
  (b) one centre-set assignment applying concepts
      to an everyday event

Paper 4   *1 hour*

10% of total mark
Research methods, paper given to candidates one week before exam, to research their answer.

Paper 5   *3 hours*

30% of total mark
Specialist choice, select 2 applications of psychology:
  Education, Health, Environment,
  Organisations.
3 stimulus-response structured essays, applying specialist material, 2 questions will be set on each specialist choice.

EXAMINATION BOARD ADDRESSES

AEB

The Associated Examining Board
Stag Hill House, Guildford, Surrey GU2 5XJ

Tel: 01483 506506

NEAB

Northern Examinations and Assessment Board
12 Harter Street, Manchester M1 6HL

Tel: 0161 953 1180

Oxford and Cambridge

Oxford and Cambridge Schools Examination Board

(a) Purbeck House, Purbeck Road, Cambridge
    CB2 2PU

    Tel: 01223 411211

(b) Elsfield Way, Oxford OX2 8EP

    Tel: 01865 54421

STUDYING AND REVISING PSYCHOLOGY

THE DIFFERENCE BETWEEN GCSE AND A/AS-LEVEL

Psychology as a subject is probably new to you, unlike some of the other A-levels you may have chosen to study. In particular, A-level psychology relies heavily on empirical (experimental) data and draws on a variety of academic disciplines.

A **quantitative difference**: generally speaking, A-levels involve more than GCSEs: more hours in the classroom, more work at home, longer essays, longer examinations, and there may be more examinations.

A **qualitative difference**: the most important change from GCSE work is that A-levels require a thoughtful and critical approach rather than simply churning out a previously learned set of facts. The emphasis is on understanding, applying a body of knowledge (facts) to novel situations, organising material into a coherent whole, evaluation and comparison. The words which are used in A-level questions indicate the kind of thinking expected, for example: assess, discuss, justify, analyse, consider, contrast.

This approach is also reflected in the kinds of question which are set; the examiner aims to prevent the use of prepared essays which only demonstrate the candidates ability to learn. There is no right answer, there are legitimate answers which must be argued for. Facts are important as a means to the end, not an end in themselves, as at GCSE.

Therefore **opinions** are a feature of A-level study. You must learn to form your own which are based in fact. Reading psychological material will help you form opinions; arguments and discussions with classmates and teachers will help too, as will writing essays. Psychological journals are a good source of recent empirical data, and some are specifically written with students in mind.

An **eclectic approach** is one which chooses the best from a variety of sources; it is a feature of advanced studies. While the syllabus may appear to be neatly divided into sub-areas, this is by no means true. Each Chapter Roundup in this book shows the considerable overlap between the sub-areas. It is important not to limit your thought according to artificial divisions of the body of psychological knowledge. Intelligence is shown by combining information from these different areas.

There is a greater **element of choice** at A-level, you can select those topics which interest you and pass over the ones that don't. The only compulsory topic is research and design.

The **coursework** is much more rigorous than at GCSE level, in line with scientific practice.

AS-levels

AS-levels offer an alternative to A-level. They enable students to study more subjects while maintaining the depth of study. This means that less time is spent studying the subject, the examination is shorter and the coursework less, but the syllabus remains as broad and the questions are as difficult. It is possible to study an AS-level in one year or to take two years. AS-level students can be taught in parallel with an A-level class.

STUDY STRATEGIES AND TECHNIQUES

Many of the ideas discussed below are drawn directly from psychology, since psychology is the study of behaviour. There are many books on study techniques and the Open University broadcasts useful television programmes.

1. **Enjoy it**: it should be remembered that you do best at things you enjoy (and vice versa).

2. **Revision techniques** are closely related to study skills:
   - in the act of studying you are also learning and revising,
   - the notes you make during study will later be used for revision,

- in both, successful techniques are related to means of improving memory,
- see the following section on 'Revision Techniques'.

3 **Hierarchical organisation**: the key to both understanding and remembering the material is a logical framework for organising the facts. **Ausubel** called this **'advance organisers'**, **Bruner** talked of **categories** and **coding systems**. A teacher or a book such as this one may provide you with 'advance organisers', frameworks such as chapters and subheadings which order the material and help make sense of it. Alternatively, you may devise your own coding system. Either way, sensible organisation serves to make the material more meaningful, which is also linked with making it more memorable. It is essential!

4 **Speed reading**: learn to skim through long texts and select relevant data. Some books usefully give key words in bold, italic, or underlined text which helps speed reading enormously. There are also methods for reading which improve recall (variously called the SQ3R or PQRST methods):

- survey or preview the chapter,	S	P
- list questions to actively involve yourself,	Q	Q
- read the text,	R	R
- recall or self-recite,	R	S
- review or test yourself.	R	T

5 **Essay plans**: an important skill for writing timed essays; practising the skill under non-stressful conditions helps reduce stress in exams.
How to answer an essay question:
- 'free associate' to every *significant word* of the question, in an effort to understand it,
- brainstorming: write down everything you can think about in the broad area,
- go through each topic area in the psychology syllabus (e.g. chapter headings in this book) to see if there is anything relevant to the question,
- re-read the question,
- cross out anything which is irrelevant to the question,
- organise and place what's left in a logical order,
- you now have a structure for your essay,
- write the essay.

6 **Writing notes**: the purpose of notes is to record *highly condensed* material from which you can revise later. Organising material also makes it more meaningful and helps memory.
Some ideas for condensing and organising data:
- use advance organisers,
- use abbreviations, your own or standard ones (ψ stands for 'psychology'),
- highlight keywords,
- record information in diagrammatic summaries, flowcharts,
- write numbered lists,
- flexibility helps for re-organising: use a loose-leaf file, a card index, word processor or database.

Class notes: many students start with the intention of copying up their class notes after each lesson. This is probably a waste of time, unrealistic and usually not done. A more pragmatic solution might be to read the notes after each lesson, writing in additional comments or side headings and using a highlighter to mark key words. This helps to consolidate the day's learning and to make the notes more useful later.

Book notes: brevity is difficult. Either make notes then do the same as with class notes or force yourself to only write after each section of the book using the PQRST method (above).

Essay notes: keep the notes you make when planning essays and use them for revision.

Cross-syllabus notes: essays often require material from several areas of the syllabus, therefore it helps to 'limber up' by making notes that connect different topics across the syllabus. It also makes you organise the material differently, thus improving your memory of the information.

Personal glossary: keep a list of key words and key empirical data, for later revision and to enhance memory.

⑦ **Handwriting and expressive skills**: if you know that these are likely to cause problems for you, practise them!

⑧ **Set targets** and **work plans**: success is related to motivation. Find ways to increase yours (worker motivation, satisfaction and morale are discussed in Chapter 9). It helps to have:
- realistic targets so that you can have a sense of achievement, otherwise you end up feeling the work is a never-ending task,
- rewards which are task or time related, such as 'after each hour I can have a snack' or 'after finishing the essay I can go out for the evening',
- a study timetable with a record of how much you did and a list of things to do,
- a pleasant place to study; you can then associate studying with a sense of relaxation,
- good equipment: a good file for keeping notes, pens, sharp pencils, highlighters,
- a card index or a ring binder, as the contents can be reorganised.

⑨ **Wider reading**: it is important to go beyond your teachers' notes and to use more than one book, as each person and book are inevitably biased. Be sure to include recent material; psychological journals are useful.

⑩ **Individual differences**: different people find different strategies more effective. Therefore part of the two year course, leading up to the final stretch of revision, should be a time to develop your best techniques.

⑪ Don't leave everything to the last minute!

COURSEWORK

Coursework is stressful in a different way to exams. Because you have a large amount of time you may feel pressured to go to extraordinary lengths to produce a brilliant piece of work. This is not necessary: your aim should be maximum gains for minimum effort.

Maximum gains

❶ It's **the report that gets the marks**, therefore make sure you put as much effort into that as into the research itself.

❷ Experimental research and design is a **compulsory question** on the written paper; conducting your research and writing the report helps enormously when tackling this question.

❸ The writing of the introduction for your report takes research and thought, all of which will lead to a **greater understanding** of that part of the syllabus, so you have killed two birds with one stone. Spread your projects across the syllabus.

❹ A successful project is by no means one which produces the expected result; all results are significant and, in any case, **a flawed project** can lead to a worthwhile discussion.

Minimum efforts

❶ **The best design is a simple one**: one hypothesis, one group of subjects. Many students try to do too much which leads to poor methodology and confused reporting.

❷ **Don't re-invent the wheel**: there are marks for good design or for minimal teacher guidance, but not for originality of design or materials. Don't design your own questionnaire, survey or test, unless that is your project in itself. A good one takes a lot of time to write, try out, re-write, standardise, and so on. There are thousands of them around, some are restricted in their use, but many are generally available. It's not just the stimulus material which can be borrowed: why not borrow the whole design? Replicate a previous study, or adapt some features of the design. Use a book which gives 'recipes' for student projects.

❸ **Find short cuts for collecting data**: data collection can also be very time consuming. A good study looks at a 'good', possibly random sample, but this is difficult with your resources and therefore it is not expected. If you want a large sample:

- use data which have already been collected, such as IQ or exam results (but you must respect confidentiality),
- use assemblies or other class/tutorial time (many psychological studies would provide excellent material for group discussions),
- ask an expert to conduct the experiment for you, for example ask your school/college's educational psychologist to help. This may also enable you to use restricted tests.

4 **Enjoy it**: choose topics of interest to you. However, you may be tempted to choose some obscure subject which does not lend itself to student investigation, and therefore spend a lot of time with little to show. Be advised by your teachers and only do research where you can find enough reference material to write a good introduction and discussion.

Ethics and public relations

Ethical considerations are paramount to any research: be familiar with ethical guidelines (see 10.4). In particular do not use any drugs or alcohol, do not use any restricted psychological tests and only use children or animals under close supervision.

You are in a position of responsibility when acting as an experimenter. Do not treat your subjects trivially even if they are friends or family. Remember, for many people you may be their first and last close encounter with psychology. Do nothing which will bring psychology into disrepute.

Writing the report

Your report should look like a journal article, and the total length should be between 1200 and 2000 words. The presentation should be neat, clearly labelled and orderly; typed scripts are easily readable but not compulsory. Folders are nice but more importantly the pages should turn so that they can be read easily.

There is no single 'correct' format but the following is a useful guide (it is based on the AEB structure):

1 **Title**: not too short and vague but also not too long; something which gives the reader a good idea what the study is about.

2 **Table of contents**

3 **Abstract**: about 150 words, a brief summary of your study, not using note form. The abstract gives the reader a chance to find out the bare essentials without going any further. Include where possible:
- *a one sentence summary*, giving the topic(s) to be studied and, possibly, the hypothesis, some brief theoretical background, similar research findings.
- *subjects* and *setting*: who, when, where, how many, what groups.
- the *method*: what design, what experimental treatment, what questionnaires, surveys or tests used.
- the *major findings*, which may include a mention of the statistics used and the significance levels, or simply one sentence summing up the outcome.
- *what does it all mean?* Mention the implications of your findings and suggestions for further research.

4 **Introduction**: about 600 words. This explains where your hypothesis has come from.
- *Introductory paragraphs*: outline the general theoretical background, don't turn this introduction into an essay.
- Move on to *specific psychological theory and research* which is directly relevant to your study. Even one or two studies will be sufficient. Don't spell out all the details of a piece of research unless it is one you are replicating, and don't include material more appropriate to the discussion or you won't have anything left.
- The *aims* should not appear out of thin air; the preceding review of psychological research should lead logically into your aims. Write them to help yourself; many candidates simply don't know what they're aiming to find out.
- *Hypothesis*: the aims are formally stated by the alternate and null hypothesis (is it one or two tailed?)

5 **Method**: the precise details of what you did; most importantly a *defence* (not just a statement) of your design decisions and sufficient information for the project to be *replicated*. Include:

- details of research method and design (independent, repeated, matched pairs),
- subjects: population, sample and sampling method,
- situation and experimenter(s): what, where, who,
- variables: independent, dependent, subject, confounding variables,
- data collected and level of measurement,
- controls: experimental and/or control groups: allocation, function, counterbalances for order, practice, etc,
- apparatus/materials: stimulus materials (e.g. pictures) psychological measures (e.g. tests, scales), physical measures (e.g. stopwatch, tape measure); for researchers: tape/video recorders, cameras; for subjects: pens, paper, etc. (full details may be given in appendices),
- procedure, standardised instructions (full details may be given in appendices).

6 **Results and findings**:

- *Raw data*: present in tabular form in an appendix, doesn't need as much detail as giving the names of all subjects,
- *Descriptive statistics*: numerical and graphical (see Chapter 10), all graphs and tables should have clear titles, axes should be labelled, column headings should be clearly explained, all graphs should be drawn on graph paper,
- *Inferential statistics*: present a summary of the data in the main text and the mathematical calculations in an appendix, state the test(s) to be used, *justify* the choice of statistical test, state the observed and critical values, significance level and conclusion drawn (i.e. accept/reject null hypothesis),
- Short cuts: use a computer or calculator program *but* only omit the mathematical workings from your project; still include all other data and methods of representation.

7 **Interpretation and discussion**: this section has the greatest potential for gaining marks and is where most marks are lost. The aim is to comment on the theoretical significance of your findings, with reference to the introduction.

- State the *outcome(s)* of your study (again), this time in psychological rather than statistical terms.
- Explain the outcome in terms of your *hypotheses* and/or aims.
- Discuss the outcome in terms of *theory/related research*, relating this to the introduction; this should not be a second literature review but some theory/ research may be more pertinent here than in the introduction. If your results agree with previous theory/research the discussion will be brief, if your results are different look for alternative explanations.
- Mention any *additional outcomes*, such as matters raised by subjects during debriefing.
- Criticise and *suggest remedies* related to your design (what you intended to do) and your methods (what you actually did). Even a well-designed study will have flaws; don't nit-pick.
- *Wider implications* and ideas for follow-up research?

8 **Conclusions**: end by reiterating your findings.

9 **References**: an essential part of any report, to confirm that your statements are based on 'fact' rather than common sense. References are written in a standard form (see the references at the back of this book for examples):

- Give the reference in the main text in the form: Brown (1982) or (Brown, 1982).
- If there are more than two authors, list them all, or write Brown et al. (1982).
- List all references in alphabetical order at the back of your report.
- For a journal artical the standard form is: author name(s), year, article title, journal title, volume (and issue number), page numbers.
- The journal title and volume number should be in italics, or underlined if italics is not possible.
- For an article in a book: author name(s), year, article title, book author, book title, publisher and, if possible, the particular pages in the book.

- For a book: author name(s), year, book title, publisher and, if possible, relevant pages in the book.
- Book titles should be in italics or underlined.

⑩ **Appendices**: contain additional material such as: standardised instructions/ debriefing details for subjects, raw data, statistical calculations, questionnaires, observation checklists, surveys, test mark schemes for any surveys, test stimulus materials (pictures, photographs), details of any pilot studies,

⑪ **Copying**: if a textbook says exactly what you want to say, copy it BUT use quotation marks and state the source. Never risk copying someone else's project, it may mean disqualification for both of you.

Common faults

- The introduction is too long. Remember it is *not* an essay, but a review of relevant theory and research which explains why the current research was conducted.
- The reasons for using a particular research design are not given – usually because the student hasn't designed the research themselves and therefore simply doesn't understand the principles.
- The results are presented unimaginatively; a mass of bar charts or lists of numbers don't help the reader see what you've found out.
- The statistical presentation indicates that the student doesn't understand what they are doing.
- The discussion is too brief, and doesn't offer insightful understanding into the results. It's not enough to say just that the samples were too small or that there was a difference between boys and girls.

REVISION TECHNIQUES

How do psychologists explain forgetting? What advice might psychologists in this field give students revising for an examination? (AEB, 1989)

An answer from a psychologist would draw on evidence from memory research which has demonstrated that these activities can aid memory.

- organisation: gives meaning to the material, e.g. making notes,
- memorising category headings and numbered lists: related to chunking (see 1.5),
- visual images: drawing a diagram to condense or represent information,
- acoustic images: memorising out loud, as in learning lines for a play,
- imagery and acoustic links: e.g. the keyword method (see 1.5),
- elaboration: discussions with friends or writing an essay,
- practice: rereading notes,
- method of loci (often the basis of systems to improve your memory, see 1.5),
- meaningful connections: acronyms, acrostics, rhymes,
- avoiding forgetting: rest periods help to consolidate learning.

Other ideas, related to study skills generally:

❶ Set a **revision timetable**, with realistic goals and, very importantly, small rewards for reaching them.

❷ Work for **short spells** with adequate breaks: you may not feel tired but a change of activity will make you much more effective.

❸ **Make notes** of your notes every time you revise, improving them in line with what you found was successful (skill feedback), re-organising and re-evaluating (making them more meaningful).

❹ Use a **personal glossary** or **summary cards** to revise from.

❺ Revise with **friends** (as long as you can stay on the task), criticise each other's essays. Stress is reduced by the presence of others.

6 Study **past papers**, not for question-spotting, but to see how the questions relate to the syllabus, and to write essay plans. This is a kind of mental 'limbering up' by tackling novel questions.

7 Read the **chief examiner's reports** to see how previous candidates fared; in Section 2 of this book, the comments on the practice questions have drawn on these reports.

THE EXAMINATION

QUESTION STYLES

Short answers

At present, only the Oxford and Cambridge exam sets short answer questions. These are based directly on the core studies set in the syllabus. For example:

> Give a psychological definition of obedience. (2 marks)
>
> In what ways does Nobles criticise the Western idea of self-concept?
> (4 marks)

Remember that the number of marks gives some indication of the expected length of answer.

You do not have to read through the whole paper before you begin because all the questions are compulsory. There is no reason why you have to answer the questions in the order they are set. Some people prefer to do the questions they know best first. Be sure to put some answer down for all the questions: every mark counts.

Stimulus question format

The question starts with a paragraph or more for you to read (the stimulus). This is followed by related questions. This approach is used by NEAB and AEB for their compulsory research and design question. It is also a popular style for the Oxford and Cambridge examination throughout the syllabus. Be sure to read all of the stimulus thoroughly before attempting any of the questions.

Differentiated questions

A question which is broken down into parts, often where each is given an individual mark, is a differentiated question. Some questions are differentiated just by using two terms such as 'describe' and 'evaluate'. Here are two examples:

> *Describe and assess* evidence from psychological research into the effects of media violence on children. (25 marks)
>
> (a) Critically consider how gender roles are acquired. (15 marks)
>
> (b) Using research examples show how gender roles affect our behaviour and our perception of others' behaviour. (10 marks)

Many of the question styles use this method of prompting the candidate to explore different aspects of the topic. Some candidates disregard the individual marks for the parts of the question and write a general answer. This undoubtedly loses marks because you are not answering the question.

Essay questions

This traditional approach to A-level exams is becoming less popular. It may help you, when answering such a question, to make up your own differentiated sections and answer the question according to this plan.

Open book

The research question for the Oxford and Cambridge exam is given to students a week before they are required to write their answer. It is important to strike a balance between doing no preparation and feeling panicked into trying to work non-stop for that week when you will probably work badly due to stress.

EXAMINATION TECHNIQUES

1. Where you have a choice of what questions to answer, you *must* read through the whole paper *slowly* before making your decision. It may help to write down ideas for each question to see how much you actually know. Where questions have parts, it is vital to read all the parts; often candidates select a question because they can answer part (a), only to discover, when it is too late, that they don't know anything about part (b).

2. *Read the rubric carefully*: when the paper says 'answer 4 questions' that's what you should do.

3. Work out an *exam strategy*: for example, how much time you will spend on each question, or which questions to answer first, your best or worst. You must stick to your time ration for each question, as running out of time and doing a very short last question can really drag your mark down. Some people like to answer the question about which they feel most confident first. Others will leave this until the end because they know they can complete it in a shorter time.

Question strategies

1. *Answer the question*:
   - Avoid the 'machine gun' approach of writing down everything that comes to mind in the hope that some of it may be relevant. This will only gain a limited number of marks because it has no organisation and much of it will be irrelevant.
   - Don't 'memorise' a set of essays which are likely to come up and write them regardless of the questions asked. Examiners can spot such answers all too easily.
   - State the obvious and make your answer relevant: what seems obvious to you might not be to anyone else, and the examiner can't assume that you understand how the question and your answer are related. If the question seems ambiguous, state your understanding of it.

2. Don't ignore *features of the question*, for example:
   - When the question asks for evidence for *and* against a theory, often candidates only present one side; or if the question says '*or*' they give both kinds of evidence.
   - Beware of using non-human evidence for questions which specifically say 'human'.
   - Take note of 'special' words such as 'consider' or 'assess' (see list of key words below).
   - When the question is split into parts, use the marks for each part to give you an idea of how much to write.

3. Write an *essay plan*: see 'Study strategy and techniques' section, for ways of writing a plan. An essay written without a plan tends to wander and will lose marks for organisation and coherence. A plan means you can relax as you write because you've put all the key points down and won't forget them.

4. Write *structured* essays: it is not necessary to write an introduction and conclusion in an examination *unless* they make the essay more readable. The introduction can spell out the essay's structure. The point of the conclusion is to clearly state your critical grasp of the topic. Don't waste time with a trite conclusion.

5. *Don't waffle*: a one page essay may receive the same marks as one that covers many pages; the examiner may miss important points which are buried in a mass of trivial detail. A common piece of unnecessary padding is historical background, which may have been included in lessons to make them more interesting, but is inappropriate in

an exam (for example, many candidates write about Binet and nineteenth century IQ testing when answering questions on intelligence). However, a sense of historical order is important in presenting certain arguments which have developed over time, as new researchers have entered the fray.

6 Avoid *'common sense' answers*: psychology aims to be an objective, empirical science. You must convince the examiner that your answer is drawn from what you have learned, not from everyday knowledge.

7 Use *specific references* where possible. If you know the author's name and date, use them. If you're not sure, say so or leave the reference out; a mistake looks worse then an honest approach. The names strengthen the answer but arguments are more important and an examiner will be able to identify standard pieces of research without the specific reference.

8 *Write briefly*: at around 45 minutes per essay, you only have time to record the key details of each argument or piece of research. Some questions explicitly ask for such detail (e.g. 'describe a study of...'), otherwise you must find a balance between detail and condensed information.

9 A balance between *description* and *evaluation* makes a good answer. Strong evaluation skills are the chief distinction between a good and poor candidate.

- 'Description' can be demonstrated through clear understanding, construction and coherence of the essay.

- 'Evaluation' uses techniques such as criticism, analysis, selectivity, comparison and relevance, as applied to theories, concepts, applications and empirical evidence. Also important are an eclectic approach across the syllabus and drawing on wider reading.

  Theories can be criticised in terms of their quality, coherence, comprehensiveness (in terms of known evidence), alternatives, falsifiability, ability to generate empirical research, and cultural specificity.

  Empirical evidence can be criticised in terms of its purpose, type of subjects used, any special apparatus, nature of experimental (or other) procedure, findings, conclusions. A good idea is to use the same headings as for presenting your coursework.

Key words used in questions

Terms which indicate description	
consider	demonstrate knowledge and understanding of the topic area.
define	explain what is meant by a particular term or concept.
describe	present evidence of your knowledge.
examine	present a detailed, descriptive consideration.
explain	convey your understanding, coherently and intelligibly.
outline/state	offer a summary description in brief form.

Terms which indicate evaluation	
(critically) analyse	demonstrate understanding by examining the separate elements of the topic area.
(critically) assess	make an *informed* judgement about how good or effective your information and arguments are.
criticise	critically appraise the strengths/weaknesses.
(critically) evaluate	make an *informed* and systematic judgement regarding the value of the topic area.
justify	consider the grounds for a decision.

Both description and evaluation	
compare/contrast	consider similarities and/or differences between the named topic areas.
critically consider	as 'consider' above, but also show an awareness of the strengths and limitations of the material presented.
distinguish between	demonstrate an understanding of the differences between the named topic areas; may be done by description and critical contrast.
discuss	describe various approaches to the topic area and evaluate them. It is useful to select different or contrasting points of view. You may choose to discuss each view separately or to contrast them point by point.
discuss... in terms of	discuss with reference to particular criteria.

Coping with stress

In Chapter 7 techniques for reducing stress are listed. Some of these are appropriate in an examination:

1. Increasing your sense of control: positive thinking, e.g. 'It's too late to worry now, just get on with it'.

2. Writing essay plans: frees available cognitive resources for constructing the essay rather than trying to recall everything which might be relevant.

3. Avoiding ego defence mechanisms such as denial: recognise the feeling of stress and intellectualise your problem.

4. Relaxation and rest periods: have a break and think pleasant thoughts unrelated to the exam, use self-hypnosis.

5. Social support: think about comforting people or things.

6. Physical exercise and emotional discharge: go for a run before the exam, stretch your legs, find some means of discharging tension during the exam (which doesn't disturb anyone else).

FINAL PREPARATION

- Check the time, date and place for the examination.
- Check you have the necessary equipment.
- Take some physical exercise before the exam to relieve tension and clear the mind.
- Arrive in good time.
- Practice relaxation techniques while waiting for the exam to start, look forward to the conclusion of your studies.

PSYCHOLOGY TOPICS

In this section:

Each chapter features:

■ *Units in this chapter*: a list of the main topics to follow.

■ *Chapter overview*: key ideas which are covered in the chapter are introduced.

■ *The main text*: this is divided into numbered topic units for ease of reference.

■ *Chapter roundup*: links to connected themes in other chapters.

■ *Illustrative questions*: typical exam questions, with tutorial notes and our suggested answers.

■ *Question bank*: further questions, with comments on the pitfalls to avoid and points to include in framing your own answers.

COGNITIVE PSYCHOLOGY

Units in this chapter:

Chapter overview

Cognitive psychology broadly covers all internal mental processes; it is the study of how the mind works. It therefore covers the whole of psychology.

Historical perspective

Cognitive psychology appeared when Wundt opened the first psychology laboratory in 1879. This signalled the separation of psychology from philosophy, though, like philosophy, the methods used by Wundt were chiefly introspective and concerned with conscious experience.

Early psychologists, such as Watson, Tolman and Pavlov, rejected the use of hypothetical mental processes, and emphasised observable facts. This approach grew into **behaviourism** and marked the first attempts to describe the mind from a psychological rather than philosophical viewpoint. Considering the differences now between behaviourists and cognitive psychologists, it is interesting to reflect on their shared ancestry.

Cognitive psychology was reborn in the 1950s, influenced by various developments such as the advent of the computer, Chomsky's linguistic theories on languages and work on attention and memory by Broadbent, Miller and others. In addition, behaviouism was going out of fashion, as many psychologists felt it provided only part of the picture.

Research today in cognitive psychology centres on three areas: laboratory studies of normal behaviour, investigations of brain damaged subjects and computer simulations.

The **Gestalt approach** is important in many areas of cognition. It first appeared in 1930s Germany, though many of its founders fled to America before World War II. The emphasis was on the whole (*Gestalt*) rather than the constituent parts ('the whole is greater than the sum of its parts'), in opposition to structuralism, functionalism and behaviourism. Its most notable contributions have been accounts of how sensations give rise to perceptions, particularly visual ones. These are collectively called the Laws of Prägnanz (meaning) because these principles give meaning to all we see (see 1.1). The principles also explain how a melody remains recognisable despite changes in instrument, key or variations. Contributions to learning suggest that is not a process of association between stimulus and response, but one of restructuring the whole situation, often involving insight (see 1.6). When thinking about thinking, the Gestalt psychologists introduced the concept of functional fixedness (*Einstellung*) which blocks creative thinking (see 1.3). The classic problem is 9 dots arranged in 3 rows; try to join them without lifting the pen off the paper. The difficulties can be explained in terms of the Laws of Prägnanz. This also demonstrates the principles of perception.

Critics point to the descriptive and imprecise nature of the theory. The Gestalt approach as such no longer exists, but its influence is felt in many areas where holism is emphasised.

1.1 PERCEPTION

The study of perception combines the mechanics of the physical systems with the influence of mental processes. Perception is the act of giving coherence and unity to sensory input.

The five senses are: vision (sight), audition (hearing), olfaction (smell), tactition (touch) and gustation (taste). Additionally we have proprioception (internal senses), which are: kinaesthetic (muscular movement) and vestibular balance.

Some generalisations can be made for all the senses:

- They each have a **sense organ**, which contains **sense receptors**.
- These specialised cells convert energy, such as sound, into a nervous impulse, which is transmitted to a specific part of the brain.
- The sense receptors have an **absolute threshold**, which is the level of stimulation required for the stimulus to be detected.
- There is also a **difference threshold** which is the minimum stimulation necessary to distinguish a difference between two stimuli. **Weber's Law** is the statement of this **just noticeable difference**.
- **Afterimages** are sensed after a stimulus is removed, and created by over-stimulation of the receptors.

THE VISUAL SYSTEM

Physical basis

In the human eye, the **retina** – the light-sensitive lining of the eyeball – is composed of thousands of receptors, or **photo-sensitive cells** called **rods** and **cones** because of their shape. These are present in enormous quantities; something like the whole population of the United States is roughly equivalent to the number of rods and the population of greater New York represents the cones. Rods are the more primitive cells and respond under low illumination to shades of black. **Colour** is detected by 'mixing' the signals from three different types of cone cell: red-, blue- and green-sensitive.

The nerve fibres of the retinal cells are bundled into the **optic nerve** which is connected to the **visual cortex**, lying towards the back of the base of the brain. The pioneering work of **Hubel and Wiesel (1962)**, experimenting with cats, showed how cells in the visual cortex react to incoming data. They found that a particular cortical cell fired only when a line of a particular orientation (for example, \, | or /) was detected. Later they found cells that were equally sensitive to specific inputs, such as a stationary or moving dot, or the direction of movement.

Absolute and relative perceptions

Brightness or **illumination** is the simplest of the visual sensations. Whatever the general level of illumination, the most important fact is *differences* in illumination rather than absolute brightness. An example of this is **dark adaptation**, the eye compensating for low lighting.

The detection of **motion** is complicated by three things.

1 The problem of **constancy**: the system must distinguish between retinal image changes that result from head movements and of those changes that are due to the stimulus object moving. The brain integrates this eye–head system with the image–retina system to provide constancy.

2 The time 'gaps' in the system. The phenomenon of apparent motion (as used in motion pictures - see later in this unit) shows us that change does not need to be continuous in order for movement to be seen. The cells of the retina 'don't notice' a time gap of very limited duration.

3 A curious fact about the visual system is that it is dependent on constant small movements of the eye, such as **saccades** or more random ones called **nystagmus,** in order to see *any* images. **Pritchard (1961)** stabilised the retinal image by mounting a tiny slide projector on a contact lens. Any movement of the eye was tracked by the image on the screen so that the retinal image was fixed. Within a few seconds the normal image begins to fade and after a minute the observer sees nothing at all. Clearly the photoreceptors need constant stimulation to produce a response, otherwise they **adapt** to the image and cease transmitting to the visual cortex.

Gregory (1990) comments that 'all eyes are primarily detectors of movement', and that movement is detected by changes in brightness (on/off).

Depth perception is also due to a synthesis of cues rather than absolute data. Binocular vision provides some information but we also rely on many learned features, such as shadow or one object being in front of another. Depth is discussed further under perceptual constancy.

The information processing approach

1 **Bottom-up** or **data-driven processing** describes the perceptual (or any cognitive) system as being primarily determined by the physical stimulus, e.g. 'driven' by the retinal images. The perceiver deals with information by starting at this level and working their way up to more abstract, cognitive operations. An example of this approach is the **direct perception model** or **ecological psychology** of **J.J. Gibson (1966, 1979)**. This suggests that the stimulus inputs are far richer than is often appreciated and can explain the process of perception without reference to higher cognitive mediation.

2 **Top-down** or **concept-driven processing** takes the view that sensory information alone is not enough to explain the processes of perception. If perception were independent of cognition, expectations should not influence what we 'see'. There is good evidence, however, that expectations *are* important as can be seen from visual illusions and empirical evidence on perceptual set (see p.30).

The two processes, bottom-up and top-down, need not be seen as competitive but rather as complementary. It may be that bottom-up processes represent innate sensory mechanisms whereas top-down depend on learned experience, or that their relative importance varies with particular circumstances (see 9.3).

3 **Neisser's analysis-by-synthesis model (1976)** represents an attempt to show how the two systems might interact. Perception starts with feature analysis (bottom-up), for example, four legs might be a dog. The next step is to employ a top-down approach looking for other expected features, in our case, a wet nose and a hairy body. If these are not found, disconfirming the original hypothesis, a new model has to be generated, going back to bottom-up.

4 **Marr (1982)** put forward the **computational theory of vision** to account for the way ambiguous and often incomplete information is processed. His approach combines neuropsychology and mathematics (the design of a computer program which could solve this problem). Building up an image involves three steps:

- the primal sketch: the pattern of light falling on the retina, using data about edges, blobs, textures;
- $2\frac{1}{2}$ D sketch: the primal sketch converted to an image from the observer's point of view, using further data such as depth and orientation of visible surfaces;
- 3D model: the image independent of the observer; this must be compared with stored representations to arrive at recognition.

Marr's computer program could recognise simple outlines but required additional information to cope with ambiguous stimuli. One limitation of this theory is that it is concerned mainly with bottom-up processing and takes little account of how top-down processes might be involved. Also, the fact that a computer program could accomplish the same task as the eye and the brain does not mean that the methods are the same.

Form recognition

How does a young child extrapolate from one example of a tree to understand the general concept 'tree'? How can we program a computer to recognise all examples of the letter 'A'? How do we recognise an object as the same even when it has been distorted? We can see that this area of perception is of both practical and theoretical interest. What are the possible explanations?

1 There are **templates** in the visual system which recognise certain shapes. Unless we have an almost infinite number of templates to handle all eventualities, this model would work only at the simplest level.

2 **Prototypes,** or abstract forms, represent the basic elements of the stimulus they represent. These could be fewer in number than templates, but the details of how such systems might work remains imprecise and it is not clear whether all categories of stimulus could be represented in this way.

3 The **feature detection model** is a hierarchy starting with the most simple features and ending with the detection of complex patterns. Undoubtedly feature analysis plays a critical role but several deficiencies suggest that it too cannot explain the whole process. For example, empirical work on perceptual set demonstrates the importance of context, yet these effects are ignored in feature detection. Also the interrelationships between features is given little emphasis; in contrast, a **Gestalt** approach would predict that the whole stimulus is perceived before its parts. **Navon (1977)** showed that decision speeds with large letters was unaffected by conflicting local letters suggesting that global processing is prior to feature analysis. Feature detection has been incorporated into more complex models, such as the **analysis-by-synthesis model** described on p.26.

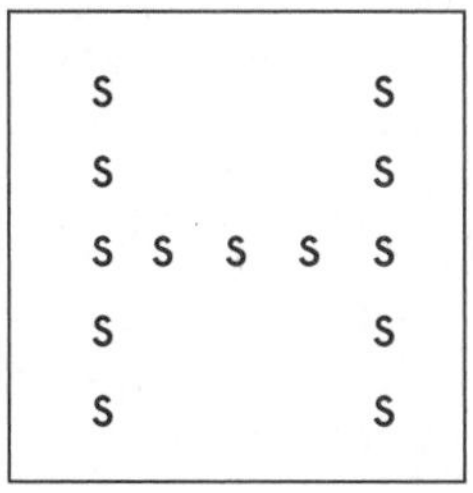

Fig. 1.1 Decision speeds with large letters are unaffected by local letters

THE DEVELOPMENT OF VISUAL PERCEPTION

Perceptual capabilities of the infant

There are a number of key problems or questions in this area of research:

● Perceptual capabilities can be either innate or learned. Nativists and empiricists, respectively, take these opposite positions.

● What impetus lies behind a particular capacity? Is it socially or physically 'driven', such as recognising the human face or depth perception?

● There is also the problem of how to test a somewhat immobile and unresponsive subject, as in the case of the neonate (newborn baby).

Physically, the neonate's eye is reasonably well developed in terms of being sensitive to colour, brightness and movement. Their **visual acuity** (perception of fine details) is limited by a focal length of about 20 centimetres, a useful distance for studying their mother's face while they are being fed. There is some debate about whether babies are born with the ability to recognise the pattern of a face but, by 12 weeks, they recognise particular faces and respond with a smile. Such social smiling is vital as the beginnings of **socialisation**.

Depth perception in 20 day old babies was demonstrated by **Bower (1970)** who observed that they put their hands in front of their face when they were exposed to a fast approaching disc. Bower also explored size constancy, successfully training three-month-old babies to discriminate between cubes of the same actual size but different retinal size (because they were further away).

These studies illustrate some of the techniques used to test infant subjects – avoidance response, and discrimination in terms of how often a baby turns its head towards an object. Another method is to study the infant's eye movements, which tend to fix on objects of interest. **Fantz (1961)** used such a method to show that infants prefer patterns to colour or brightness, and that the preference for more complex patterns over less complex ones is a function of age.

Nature or nurture

The Nativist position is that we are born with certain capacities to perceive the world in certain ways, though they may be incomplete or immature at birth. Empiricists maintain that all is learned through experience. Such extreme positions are simplistic and we now see that the answer is one of interaction; research throws interesting light on the development of innate capacities when combined with environmental influences. Evidence comes from five sources: neonates (newborn babies), formerly blind adults whose sight has been restored, studies of visual distortion, cross-cultural and other studies of visual illusions, and animal experiments.

1. The famous **visual cliff** experiment by **Gibson and Walk (1960)** showed that babies of six months perceived depth, though by this age they may have learned, rather than been born with, such an ability. **Bower's** work, mentioned above, showed depth and size constancy in very young babies. At a higher perceptual level, **Fantz (1961)** found that neonates looked longest at drawings of human faces, suggesting that some patterns might be innately recognised. It may be that the innate predisposition is for pattern complexity rather than a face *per se*. **Fantz**, however, found a preference for a 'real' face rather than one with scrambled features.

2. There are adults whose sight has been restored after they have been blind from birth due to, for example, cataracts. About 100 such patients have been studied and in general they seem to see little at first, being unable to name even simple objects or cope with perceptual constancies such as size. S.B., a patient studied by **Gregory and Wallace (1963)**, was never fully able to use his newly acquired sight. Overall, this evidence supports a more empirical view of perception, but requires cautious interpretation. Such patients may have undergone physical and psychological trauma when their eyesight was restored, and they have learned to rely on other sensory modalities. One interesting aspect of innate vision, observed in these studies, is an ability to distinguish figure from ground (see 'Perceptual organisation' on p.29).

3. What happens if you wear goggles which turn the world upside down? **Snyder and Pronko (1952)** did such an experiment and found that subjects learned to cope easily. However, what seems to be learned is not perception but rather appropriate motor behaviour. Nevertheless, a totally innate system would not allow such a development to take place.

4. If processes such as depth perception and perspective, which are involved in producing visual illusions, are innate then we would expect all normal human beings to see them in the same way. Cross-cultural comparisons are one means of finding out if this is the case. **Deregowski (1972)** reviewed studies which suggested that some Africans find it hard to interpret 3D drawings.

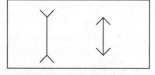

Fig. 1.2 *The Müller–Lyer illusion (right) may work because of our experience of perspective: the inside corner of a room forms the same image as the 'outgoing' arrow, and the outside corner of a building forms that of the 'ingoing' arrow*

Segall *et al.* (1963) observed that Zulus, who live in a comparatively non-perspective, circular world (round nuts and no distant horizons), are less susceptible to the **Müller–Lyer illusion**, which may well be the result of our experience of seeing corners and perspectives (see Fig. 1.2). Such findings support an empirical view but should be treated with caution since differences may have arisen because of the novel paper drawings and inter-cultural misunderstandings.

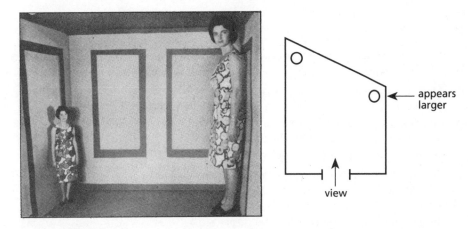

Fig. 1.3 *Ames room*

The **Ames Room** is another illusion which illustrates the effects of learning on perception, though not in a cross-cultural context. The room is constructed awry: one corner is actually much further away and the ceiling made correspondingly higher, so that the room appears to be a normal rectangular one. A person standing in the far corner appears smaller because the alternative explanation – that the two people are the same size but the room is strangely shaped – is unconsciously rejected as too improbable. This alone shows how learning has profound effects. If the person in the far corner is very familiar, the size effect disappears and the room is seen as distorted; the same happens if you make yourself familiar with the room by walking around it, which can be tried at the Science Museum in London.

⑤ What are the effects of visual deprivation? This kind of research uses animals as subjects, not surprisingly. **Blakemore and Cooper (1970)** restricted kittens' visual experiences to five hours a day in a drum painted with vertical or horizontal stripes. When they tested the visual cortex they found only cells which responded to the orientation to which they had been exposed. **Wiesel (1982)** sewed one eye of a kitten shut; if this is done early enough and lasts for long enough the eye becomes blind. These studies suggest that experience is necessary to maintain the innate system. **Held and Hein (1963)** showed that the effects of visual deprivation are tied to sensorimotor experiences. When one kitten is allowed to walk in a 'kitten carousel' its sensorimotor co-ordination develops normally whereas a yoked control, kept in a basket and not allowed to walk, has no such co-ordination.

VISUAL PERCEPTION AS AN ACTIVE PROCESS

Perceptual organisation

The **Gestalt** approach (see 'Historical Perspective' at start of chapter) emphasises the importance of the whole rather than the constituent parts or elementary sense experiences. One well-known example of this is Rubin's vase, which demonstrates the **figure–ground relationship**. How can we predict what is seen from sensory data alone? What are the laws of perceptual organisation?

One example is the principle of **proximity**. Elements which are seen close together, in space or time,

Fig. 1.4 *Rubin's vase demonstrates the figure–ground relationship*

tend to be perceived as a whole. This enables us to draw patterns with dots (e.g. dot-matrix printing) and also explains the phenomenon of **apparent motion** (see later). A related principle is that of **closure**: where gaps exist we tend to fill them in to produce complete and/or recognisable figures. Other principles are: **continuity, symmetry,** and **similarity**.

The importance of the Gestalt view is that it emphasises perception as an active process, one where the perceiver imposes structure largely on the basis of past experience, which can be explained in terms of set (see below), and learned cues for constancy.

Perceptual set

Set is the tendency to respond in a certain manner, in line with expectations built on past experience. A number of factors have been shown to influence perceptual set:

1. **Stimulus variables** – features of the stimulus itself, such as visual illusions. In the **Moon Illusion**, the moon on the horizon is larger than the moon overhead, despite the fact that the retinal images are the same. This occurs because many cues for greater distance occur when the moon is viewed over terrain, and this greater distance is interpreted as being caused by a larger object.

2. **Situation variables** are variables arising from context, such as ambiguous figures. **Bruner and Minturn (1955)** demonstrated how 13 is seen as the number 13 or the letter B depending on whether it appears in a list of numbers or a list of letters, i.e. the context. Other ambiguous figures used by psychologists include the **ratman** and **Leeper's Lady**. The contextual effects of language have been demonstrated by **Carmichael** *et al.* **(1932)** who showed that the label used for a picture affected the way the picture was perceived and remembered.

Fig. 1.5
Leeper's Lady

3. **Perceiver variables** are those related to internal states such as motivation or emotion. Perceptual **defence** is probably the best known example of the effect of emotion on perception. **McGinnies (1949)** found that the more 'emotional' a word (as measured by a galvanic skin response), the longer it took to recognise an unpleasant word. **Worthington (1969)** found a positive relationship between emotionality of words and perceived brightness. Another avenue of research looked at the relationship between perceived brightness and motivation. **Gilchrist and Nesburg (1952)** showed that hungry subjects thought that slides of food appeared brighter than other scenes. The effect of emotion on perception of race was shown by **Pettigrew** *et al.* **(1958)**. Subjects, who were Afrikaner, English, coloured, Indian or African, were shown pairs of photographs of members of the other ethnic groups, stereoscopically for 2 seconds. If the pair was black and white, the subjects showed 'manifest fusion'; they saw *either* black or white. This suggests that judgements by emotionally involved subjects tend to be extreme.

Perceptual constancy

The perceptual world needs to remain the same despite the fact that actual retinal images may be different. **Shape, size, colour, movement,** and **location** all show constancy because knowledge of the 'real' object means we persist in seeing it that way despite changed retinal images which may distort the image.

Depth perception and visual illusions show how the visual system integrates learned cues to produce an accurate perception. Distance is suggested by a variety of cues, such as one object being in front of another, familiarity with the actual size of objects and perspective cues. The **Ponzo Illusion** (Fig. 1.6) is a good example of how depth cues (the oblique lines seeming to show perspective) lead to mistakes in size constancy (the parallel lines look different in length because one appears to be farther away and therefore, while having the same retinal image, should actually be longer).

Brightness is a clue to depth – demonstrated by the **Pulfrich Pendulum** effect. If one eye is covered with a shade to reduce brightness, a pendulum swinging in a straight line at right angles to the observer is 'seen' as swinging in an ellipse because the differences in brightness between the two eyes are misinterpreted as differences of depth. The importance of this example is that it might be more innate than learned.

Fig. 1.6 Ponzo illusion and railway lines

Visual illusions: Surprises of active processing

The unconscious 'mistakes' of perception have been shown to throw light on the normal processes. Visual illusions are not really mistakes but are normal, relatively consistent phenomena, subject to regular rules. Illusions are distinct from hallucinations or delusions. They are the results of unconscious overextension of simple rules, similar to a child using 'goed' rather than 'went'. Illusions are usually associated with an element of surprise; however, many commonplace visual techniques, such as using shadow to imply 3D in pictures, are also 'illusions'.

Illusions can be put to practical as well as theoretical use. As in the case of optical brakes – parallel lines that become progressively closer to slow drivers down when approaching roundabouts.

Another more familiar application is the use of **apparent motion**, as seen in motion pictures, television screens and neon lights. Two distinct phenomena are at work. First **persistence of vision**, which is the inability of the retina to detect rapidly changing intensities, so that anything changing faster than 50 flashes per second appears steady. Not surprisingly the lines on a television screen are refreshed at 50th of a second intervals. Second the **phi phenomenon**, which occurs when two (or more) stationary lights flash with an optimal rate of 150 milliseconds between them. The gap is sufficiently small to fool the retinal system into thinking that they were one object. Such an illusion is what makes moving pictures move.

OTHER SENSORY SYSTEMS

Hearing

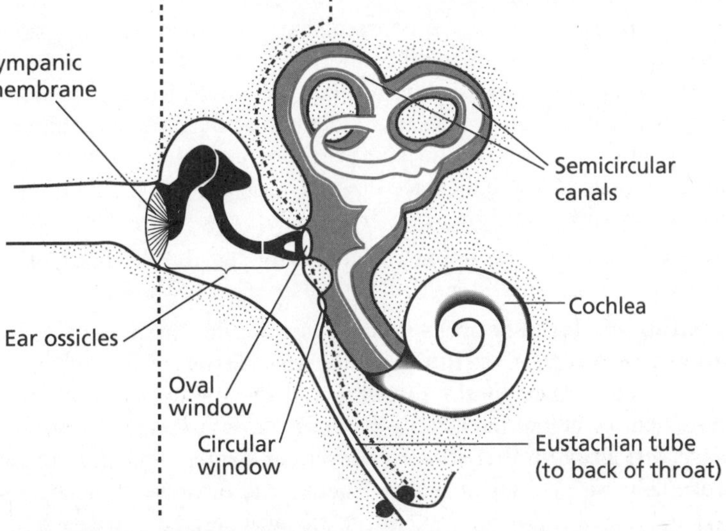

Fig. 1.7 Cross-section through the ear

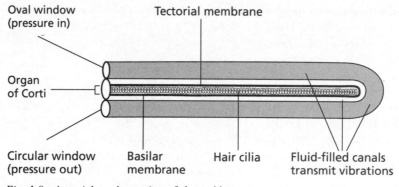

Fig. 1.8 A straightened-out view of the cochlea

Sound waves are collected and amplified by the funnel shape of the **outer ear**, the **tympanic membrane** or **ear drum**, the **middle ear bones** or **ossicles** (known as the **hammer, anvil**, and **stirrup** because of their respective shapes) and the **oval window**.

Vibrations on the oval window are transmitted to the three fluid-filled cavities of the **cochlea**. The **basilar membrane** bends in response to these vibrations; this movement is communicated to the **tectorial membrane** by the stiff **hair cells** which lie in between the membranes (which together are called the **Organ of Corti**). The inner ear also contains the **semi-circular canals**, which are concerned with balance. These **inner ear** structures turn vibration into neural impulses which are transmitted mainly to the **auditory cortex**, located in the temporal region of each hemisphere. Damage to this part of the brain does not result in total deafness because some sound is perceived at a sub-cortical level. There is some cross-over but primarily each ear is joined to its contralateral side. Some fibres connect to superior colliculus and the optic nerve and eye muscles for orientation to sound.

The physical dimensions of sound are **frequency** (the number of waves per second) and **amplitude** (the amount of energy in each wave). The perceptual equivalents of these physical properties of sound are **pitch** and **loudness**, together producing pure tones, as in a tuning fork. **Timbre** is the result of a richer mixture of sound waves, which explains the difference between the same tone played on a flute or violin.

Feature detection in hearing

1. **Loudness** is recorded by the number of cochlear cells which respond. Information is transmitted to spatially coded cells in the auditory cortical surface which are located at right angles to those cells responding to frequency.

2. **Pitch perception** is a combination of:
   - **Frequency theory**: the temporal coding of pitch, the basilar membrane vibrates in synchrony with a sound and causes the hair cells to transmit neural impulses of the same frequency. However, they cannot fire much above 300 vibrations per second, whereas sounds can be up to 20,000 Hz. In part this is resolved by the **volley principle**, a group of neurons may fire synchronously producing a volley of impulses. However, this still cannot explain very high frequencies.
   - **Place theory**: the spatial coding of pitch, an anatomical explanation which accounts for higher pitch detection. The basilar membrane is thinnest and stiffest at the base of the cochlea and thickest at the apex. A vibration striking the oval window sets up a travelling wave down the membrane, the point at which this wave peaks varies with frequency. Low frequencies peak at the wider, floppier end.

3. **Timbre** is detected by the unique anatomically coded pattern which is produced via the basilar membrane and identified by higher areas of the brain.

4. **Localisation of sound sources**: humans can localise high and low frequencies well:
   - **differential loudness** or **intensity differentiation**: the sound is louder for the closer ear because the head creates a sound shadow, which produces accurate localisation for higher pitches. Low pitches have wave lengths wider than the head.
   - **phase difference**: different arrival times at the near and far ear cause the eardrums to vibrate out of phase. This is true for low frequency sound.

5. **Feature detection**: there are cells in the auditory system which respond to **specific features** rather than variations in frequency and amplitude. For example, the

start/stop of a sound and changes in pitch/intensity. This suggests that the auditory system, like the visual system, is most responsive to changing rather than continuous stimulation. The evidence from studies on attention also shows that changes attract notice.

Auditory illusions

Illusions in hearing, like visual ones, are useful in revealing the mechanisms by which we derive perceptions from incomplete physical details. Auditory illusions are related to perceptions of speech. However, unlike visual illusions, auditory illusions are not limited to ambiguous patterns; changes are impossible to predict and vary between individuals.

Warren and Warren (1970) studied several auditory illusions and confusions:

- **phonemic restoration** (described in 4.1): a sentence is tampered with so that a bleep occurs instead of a particular phoneme. The subject still 'hears' the phoneme even when they know it's missing.

- **lack of temporal structure**: when subjects hear a hiss, tone and buzz successively they cannot accurately report the order of the sounds. It seems that this restriction may be an important part of being able to detect signals from background noise.

- **verbal transformation effect**: if subjects hear a word such as 'tress' in a continual loop and in the absence of any context, they 'hear' a succession of illusory forms, e.g. one subject heard 'tress' as dress, stress, Joyce, florist and purse.

- **age differences and contextual cues**: younger adults employ a post-contextual strategy to decipher verbal messages. They wait until the end of the sentence, when all cues for context are available and then 'hear' the message. Older subjects appear to use different, concurrent strategies, which may be related to their poorer short term memories, and therefore they make fewer mistakes and respond more quickly on the verbal transformation task.

Taste, smell and touch

Touch and taste rely on a set of specific receptors, like in the visual system. The skin contains receptors for pressure, pain, warm and cold. Taste is built from a combination of bitter, sour, sweet and salty sensations, and there may be others. Smell may equally be the product of specific receptors responding to a large set of primary sensations.

A FINAL THOUGHT

Agnosia, literally not knowing, is a curious defect which may occur in any of the perceptual/ cognitive systems. An agnosic can sense objects and forms but is unable to recognise and interpret their meaning. For example, agnosics may have normal visual acuity but cannot say what they are seeing. This raises the question, what constitutes perception? Is it physical sensation, seeing the whole or is it knowing?

1.2 INFORMATION PROCESSING APPROACHES

The arrival of computers and information processing in the 1950s lead quickly to their adaptation as a metaphor for human cognitive processes. **Allport (1980)** has commented that 'the advent of artificial intelligence is the single most important development in the history of psychology'.

Information processing has led on to Artificial Intelligence (AI) and cognitive science.

- AI originally was part of *computer science* rather than psychology, the first 'intelligent' machine was developed by Babbage in the 19th century.

- *Information processing* was very influential at the 'birth' of cognitive psychology. Information processing theories of cognitive functions were the norm.

- By the 1970s information processing had gone the same way as behaviourism had before it. Its *limitations* were realised and it was superseded as the dominant theme by approaches which included emotional and motivational influences.

- Today AI and psychology are fused under the banner of *cognitive science*. The ever increasing power and complexity of computer systems means that, in terms of theory and application, AI is very active in cognitive psychology.

AI concerns any computer-produced output that would be judged as intelligent if it were produced by a human. In looking at AI it is important to distinguish between:

- programs written to produce the same behaviour (*output*) as humans (applied AI), and

- those written to work the same way (*process*) that people do (simulation, theory or 'pure' AI).

APPLIED AI: PRODUCING INTELLIGENT TOOLS

Work in applied AI includes developing programs (and acronyms such as MARGIE which stands for Memory Analysis, Response Generation and Inference on English) for:

1 *specialised tasks*, such as pattern/shape recognition, speech recognition, image analysis, automatic programming (programs which write programs);

2 *interactive, language programs*, e.g. ELIZA (**Weizenbaum, 1966**) one of the first conversational systems, simulates Rogerian non-directive counselling so that the user engages in apparently realistic conversation as with a psychotherapist;

3 *expert systems* databases to assist an expert in his decision making, or enable someone to act as an expert, e.g. medical diagnoses (MYCIN), configuring computer systems (XCON);

4 *computer-aided instruction* (CAI) explains mistakes to the student rather than just telling them they are wrong, e.g. WHY for teaching geography. LOGO was developed by **Papert (1980)** as a method of teaching problem-solving through using computers. Such an approach was based on Piaget's notion that people learn primarily from their own interaction with the environment.

5 *CAD/CAM* (computer-aided design and manufacture) to drive machines that will be able to cope with changing environments

6 *games* such as chess, backgammon, bridge.

PURE AI: SIMULATING HUMAN BEHAVIOUR

Supporters of AI feel that intelligence can best be understood by trying to reproduce it through computer simulation.

Analogies between the computer and the human mind

1 **Computer terminology** which has been usefully applied to human cognition: **input, output, storage, central processing unit (CPU), peripheral processing, information processing, bottom-up** and **top-down processing, network, data structures**. Most of the terms are self-explanatory, a few are given here:
   - **buffer storage**: a temporary storage area,
   - **serial processing**: processing one thing at a time,
   - **parallel processing**: simultaneous execution of a number of tasks,
   - **multiprogramming** (or **multiprocessing**): what may seem like parallel processing is still serial, the computer is in fact doing bits of each program in bursts,
   - **distributed systems**: have many independent interconnections.

2 **How are they similar?** Both require capacity for: storage, input and output, and processing. A neat twist is using the model of the human mind as a means of explaining how computers work, something which will be familiar to many students who have been taught how computers work.

❸ **Examples of information processing models**: filter models of attention (see 1.4), cell assembly and multistore models of memory (see 1.5), connectionist theory of reading (see 9.3), problem-space theory (see below).

❹ **How are they different?**

	Computers	Brains
processing speed	nanoseconds	milliseconds
processing	mostly serial	mostly parallel
storage capacity	vast for digitally coded information	vast for visual and linguistic information
material	silicon and electricity	carbon and electrical/chemical activity
co-operation	obedient	autonomous control, subject to social conformity
learning capacity	simpleminded	naturally impressive
best feature	number-crunching, can do lots in little time, good 'employee', easy to maintain, predictable, cheap labour: cost-efficient	can make judgements, inferences and generalisations easily, has speech, language, vision, emotions, can think

(adapted from Solso, 1991)

Computer simulations

Simulations test models of perception, language, learning and problem-solving.
Newell and Simon (1963, 1972) have made a number of contributions to the study of problem-solving and cognition generally:

- *Protocol analysis*: a research methodology to test computer simulations. A *protocol* is a record of what a person is thinking when engaged in a task (usually a problem-solving one). These can be compared with the *traces* of a computer program trying to solve the same problem, a trace is the record of a computer's activity.

- *The General Problem Solver* (GPS): a computer program which could solve a limited selection of problems, and through protocol analysis could be used to explain human problem-solving behaviour.

- *Heuristic methods* are means to solve a problem which do not guarantee a solution but, if they succeed, save time and effort, e.g. rules of thumb. [Algorithms are rules that will definitely solve a problem, e.g. a knitting pattern.]

- *Problem-space theory*: the *problem-space* is the total set of alternative possibilities which exist between a person's *initial knowledge state* and their *goal knowledge state*. The shortest route is selected using heuristic methods.

- *Means–end analysis* was one of the most important heuristic methods:
  - note the difference between current and goal state (problem-space),
  - create a subgoal to reduce this difference,
  - select an operator which will solve the subgoal.

- *Operators*: generate the alternative paths and are stored in long term memory.

Empirical evidence

- If a person can structure a problem into various subgoals their overall performance should improve, **Egan and Greeno (1974)** gave subjects five and six disc versions of the Tower of Hanoi. Those who had previous experience with three and four disc versions were better than a control group.

- If subjects are given subgoals this should facilitate their problem-solving. **Simon and Reed (1976)** gave subjects a version of the missionaries and cannibals problem with five missionaries and five cannibals. On average it takes 30 moves to solve the problem but when subjects were given a hint to use a different strategy this resulted in significantly improved performance.

● Rubik's cube presents a particular difficulty that at any time there is no way of estimating how near the goal you are. **Korf (1985)** derived 238 macro–operators (a short sequence of moves) which positioned a small cube without disturbing the position of already correctly positioned cubes.

Strengths of Simon and Newell's approach:

● an early and influential program (GPS) and theory, with predictive success.

Weaknesses of Simon and Newell's approach:

● has only been applied to narrow range of problems, though potentially may have wider scope,

● protocol analysis: difficult to measure the goodness of fit between the protocol and the trace. To what extent does a person's commentary relate to what they are actually doing?
(See also Mair, 1.1)

Do computer models increase our understanding of thought?

Advantages of the computer modelling approach:

● it allows testing of theories and/or models,

● it requires that every process is spelled out in detail,

● it has produced widely applicable theories and architectures, e.g. connectionist networks have been used in perception, learning, memory and reading,

● analogies and metaphors are frequently used in science to advance theoretical understanding (e.g. Rutherford's planetary model of the atom),

● the computer metaphor is closer than previous ones, e.g. a mill or a telephone exchange.

Disadvantages of the computer modelling approach:

● the same behaviours can be produced by a number of models,

● computers only deal with one class of goal-oriented thinking,

● it is misguided because computer models are only models, they do not capture the essence of human thought, such as emotional and motivational influences.

CAN MACHINES THINK?

The issue of how relevant computer simulation is to human thought is a philosophical one, touching on the mind–body problem. Variations of the question are 'do machines see or do they just simulate seeing', 'do they understand language or just simulate language?' The following are appeals to common sense:

● the behavioural evidence suggests that a robot does think,

● simulations of weather systems do not rain, so in the same way machines do not think.

Weak and strong AI

Searle (1980) suggested that weak AI is acceptable, it is the position that the computer is a useful tool in studying the human mind. However, strong AI – the view that computers have mental states and therefore that they are an artificial intelligence – is untenable in Searle's view. He contends that computers can simulate human thought but they cannot duplicate it.

Arguments against strong AI

❶ **The Chinese Room**, used by **Searle** to argue against strong AI. If a person is placed in a room with some Chinese symbols and a book giving the English meanings for each symbol then that person might be able to communicate with a Chinese speaker outside the room by computing new sets of symbols. This behaviour is achieved without any understanding of the symbols, only a knowledge of the rules.

The person in the Chinese room is a simple metaphor for a computer program: data in, data out, the process in between is governed by a knowable set of rules. The crucial difference is of syntactic versus semantic processing, following rules but having no understanding.

However, this argument is not testable.

2 **The Turing Test** (or imitation game) proposed by **Turing (1950)** as a means of proving the existence of strong AI. If a person cannot distinguish the behaviour of a computer from that of a human on the same task, then the machine is shown to be intelligent. Turing described the following scenario: the machine should take the role of a player in a game where an interrogator questions two people to discover which is a man (the other is a woman). However, one of the players tries to fool the interrogator. If the machine can fool the interrogator as successfully as a person, Turing would regard this as evidence of intelligence.

ELIZA (see p.34) has been cited as a possible candidate for strong AI. Weizenbaum's secretary was sufficiently taken with the machine's realism that she asked Weizenbaum to leave the office so she could 'talk' privately with the 'therapist'. The program succeeds because it has a variety of stock phrases which fit into most situations, not because it has any understanding.

PARRY (**Colby** *et al.* **1972**) may be an even more suitable candidate. It simulates the response of a paranoid patient. Colby asked psychiatrists to interview PARRY and recorded the conversation. This is shown to a 'judge' as a 'real' conversation. The texts were found to be indistinguishable and therefore might appear to pass the Turing test. Psychiatrists, in their defence, say diagnosis of paranoia involves face-to-face interviews. The problem may also lie in the subjective nature of psychiatric diagnosis.

There are no reports that the test has been passed by any machine.

3 **Carbon or protoplasm chauvinism: Searle** and others (e.g. **Norman, 1980**) have taken the view that human functioning is an interaction between a pure cognitive system and a biological system which is driven by survival and protection needs, based on carbon molecules. The latter significantly governs the former and means that only organisms with these drives can truly have mental states.

Torrance (1986) has called this carbon chauvinism, suggesting that such a view is overenthusiastic support of your own stuff (carbon or protoplasm).

4 **Mechanistic view** of human nature. **Dreyfus (1979)** has suggested that AI misses the point of human intelligence altogether. Phenomenological approaches are more appropriate, e.g. the Gestalt view that the whole is greater than the sum of the parts. Computers lack the essence of what makes human human, chiefly emotions.

A chess grandmaster has suggested that the reason expert players refuse to take on computer versions is because they don't want to see the game reduced to inhuman calculation.

Arguments favouring machines

1 In some respects they are **superior** to humans, e.g. far larger memory capacity, and can correlate facts in a second.

2 **Automatic programming**: can a computer which can program itself be considered intelligent? Consider the act of cooking a cake, who is doing the thinking: the microwave which 'knows' when to stop cooking, the cook who makes the cake or the person who wrote the original recipe. We might consider that all three have some intelligence, at least in terms of feedback.

3 **Bionic brain**: when considering Searle's idea that intentionality is a key aspect to thinking, **Pylyshyn (1980)** posed an alternative riddle: if you gradually replaced each cell in your brain with an integrated chip, at what point would you cease to be human or to have intentionality?

4 **Now or never**: a distinction should be made between whether machines can think *now* or *yet*, it may simply be that given sufficient power they can pass the tests and perform on a par with humans. For example, fuzzy logic is a recent development (see 1.3, 'Concepts and Concept Formation').

Conclusion

The solution is perhaps that the problem is irresolvable, though the issue will continue to be debated as intelligent machines proliferate.

Moral considerations

Apart from whether machines can think, the question is do we want them to? Do we want to be controlled by machines? **Weizenbaum (1976)** claims that computers encourage a dehumanising, mechanistic view of human behaviour and should be excluded from certain areas of psychology, such as human interaction. In his attack he argues that dehumanising behaviour was at the root of the Nazi atrocities and that we must take special care.

However, computers are only quantitatively and not qualitatively different from any other technological development, and control may be the central issue.

1.3 THOUGHT

Thought is what exists in the mind as representation – an internal process in which information is transformed. Complex thought (intelligence) is the greatest characteristic of our species. It was a very popular topic among early psychologists and was investigated through introspection. When behaviourism become popular, thought was rejected as a topic of study because it was not directly observable. The advent of computer models reintroduced it as a legitimate study, though it remains mainly theoretical rather than practical. It is a particularly wide concept, and it is therefore better to address specific aspects:

- *concept formation*: discerning features common to a class of objects and discovering rules which relate these features,
- *logical thinking*: reasoning consistently and validly,
- *problem solving*: thought directed towards discovering a solution for a particular problem, a particular interest for AI,
- *creativity*: results in a novel perspective of a problem, not restricted to pragmatic outcomes,
- *decision-making*: a special case of problem-solving, and estimating probabilities,
- *imaginal thinking*: using visual images.

Other aspects of thought, which are discussed elsewhere: *complex learning*, *human intelligence*, *memory*, *attention*.

Cognitive style is the difference between individuals in terms of the cognitive approaches they tend to use, e.g. convergent and divergent thinking, use of imagery, field dependence or independence, reflectivity and impulsivity.

Attempts to explain how thinking arises include:

- minute movements or tensions of the vocal chords (**Watson**),
- that it is as an association of ideas (**Locke** and **Hull**),
- that thinking occurs when we are finding ways to satisfy our biological needs. A drive state produces an internal image of what is required and thinking is the means to realising that image (**Freud**),
- that thinking is how we adapt to the environment. Thought is the conscious activity associated with disequilibrium, assimilation and accommodation (**Piaget**),
- that thinking occurs to resolve discrepancies when they occur. Behaviour usually is governed by 'automatic pilot', but any discrepancy calls for attention and thought to resolve it (**Dewey**).

CONCEPTS AND CONCEPT FORMATION

The organisation of thinking:

1 **Defining-attributes**: the traditional view of a concept is that it has a set of attributes (features), which are all necessary. There are distinct boundaries between concepts, and

membership is all or nothing. An example is the hierarchical network proposed by **Collins and Quillian (1969)**. Concepts are organised hierarchically so that any concept has the attributes of all those above it in the hierarchy. They account for the fact that some concepts *don't* have all the attributes as those above it (e.g. an ostrich is a bird even though it can't fly) by saying that there can be exceptions.

2. **Fuzzy boundaries**: one object may belong to different concepts. The particular concept addressed at any time is determined by the context. **Labov (1973)** showed subjects a picture of a container with a handle and a description of how to imagine it (as if it had coffee, mashed potatoes or flowers in it). When subjects were asked to name the object they said cup, bowl or vase, depending on their initial image. Therefore context influences conceptualisation, concepts have fuzzy boundaries.

This calls for a different formulation of concepts than the defining attribute. It is also related to developments in computing and mathematics, fuzzy logic is a calculus for dealing with boundaries which are not sharply defined.

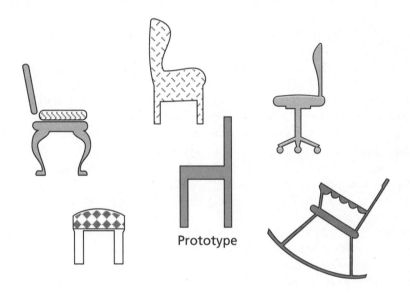

Fig. 1.9 Chairs with prototype

3. **Prototype (characteristic-attribute) theories**: a prototype is a set of characteristic attributes (there are no defining attributes) or the best example of the concept (the exemplar). Membership is determined by the *similarity* of an object's attributes and the category's prototype, therefore category boundaries are fuzzy.

4. **Defining and characteristic attribute theory**: for example, **Rosch (1975)** proposed:
   - *classical concepts:* all the examples of the concept share the same features, e.g. a bachelor is simply an unmarried, adult male,
   - *probabilistic concepts:* members of the set share *many* of the same properties, e.g. birds don't all fly. Most of our concepts are like this,
   - such *concepts are hierarchically organised:* superordinate (fruit), basic (apple) and subordinate (Golden Delicious),
   - *typicality gradient:* when you are asked to give an instance of a concept you search the basic level first, the most typical. This can be related to stereotypes and expectations,
   - *economy:* the basic level holds the most obvious aspects of any concept. **Berlin (1972)** found that the terms used to describe trees at the basic level were fairly universal between languages (birch and maple) whereas the super and subordinate terms differed.

5. **Schemata and scripts**: the alternative to the single concept approach. Schemata or scripts contain knowledge about stereotypical situations and account for our ability to make inferences in complex situations. They are structured clusters of concepts.
   - **Bartlett (1932)** used schemata to explain how people's memories are shaped by expectations (see 1.5 'Memory as an active process');

- **Piaget (1967)** used schemata to explain the changes which occur in children's cognition (see 3.2);
- **Schank and Abelson (1977)** proposed that **scripts** are plans for action; they encode expectations about others and directions about how to behave yourself. There are situational (social situations, like a restaurant), personal (expectations and behaviours), instrumental (goal directed behaviour, such as getting to school) scripts.

Concept formation

Some concepts are probably inborn, e.g. time and space. Others have to be formed, though the strategies for doing this are innate and may to some extent reflect cognitive style.

1 **Assimilation and accommodation (Piaget)**: schemata are adapted to fit in with experience through these twin process (see 3.2).

2 **Exemplar strategy**: when children encounter a known instance (exemplar) of a concept they store it and use it later as a standard. Then any new object is compared with the exemplar and included if it is similar enough. This works for typical but not atypical examples.

3 **Prototype formation**: – abstracting verbal and visual information. **Reed (1972)** presented subjects with a simplified set of faces, varying features such as nose length or eye spacing. When they were asked to classify the faces the most common strategy used was to abstract a prototype and compare each image against this. It seems that children are only able to do this after the age of six **(Solso, 1991)**.

4 **Hypothesis testing**: – **Bruner et al. (1956)** have suggested that people use **scanning** (a hypothesis is held until disproved, then another one is tried) or **focusing strategies** (focus on one feature and compare it with similar objects to see if features agree). In their experiment they gave subjects 81 cards, representing every combination of the available features (colour, kind of symbols, type of symbol and border). The subject had to work out the concept the experimenter was thinking by selecting cards which tested their hypothesis. Thus they could observe whether they were focusing or scanning. Focusing is similar to scientific procedures and more effective than scanning. The problem with this model is that subjects rarely hold to a single strategy.

REASONING OR LOGICAL THINKING

Reasoning is thinking according to logical rules or heuristics:

- *deductive* reasoning: moving from the general to the specific – starting from a theory and predicting examples;
- *inductive reasoning*: generalising, general principles inferred from specific cases.

However, human reasoning is not simple, logical processing of information, consider:

1 **Mindless behaviour**: Dewey's 'trouble' theory of thinking suggests that most of the time we function on automatic pilot but, if we encounter a discrepancy, we are forced to resolve the puzzle by thinking about it – the discrepancy calls for attention. **Langer et al. (1978)** demonstrated that people do function at a mindless level when complying (see 2.8 'Compliance').

2 **Formal operational thinking**: **Piaget** proposed this as the final stage of development. While everyone has the potential for it, it may not be achieved in practice. **Wason's (1966)** 4–card selection task is frequently given as an example of inductive reasoning and people's failure to achieve it (less than 10% in one study). The subject is presented with four cards (A, 4, D, 7) and a rule: 'If there is a vowel on one side of the card, then there is an even number on the other side'. What card or cards do you need to select to test whether the rule is true or false? The difficulty lies in the human tendency to look for cases which confirm rather than disconfirm the rule. Similarly we take longer to process negative rather than positive information even though the information is logically equivalent, e.g. 'A and not (not B)' is harder than 'A and B', or 'seven is not an even number' is harder than 'seven is an odd number'. Humans process the positive therefore a negative statement must be translated.

When the 4–card test is presented in thematic form subjects show a better grasp of logic. **Griggs and Cox (1982)** labelled four cards: drinking a beer, drinking a coke, 16 years of age, 22 years of age. On one side of a card is the person's age, on the other side what they are drinking. The rule is 'if a person is drinking beer, then the person must be over 19 years of age'. They found that still only 73% of undergraduates could cope with the operation.

3 **Probability judgements**: when predicting heads or tails, there is a tendency in humans to expect tails after a run of heads, though of course the probabilities are the same on every trial (called the *gambler's fallacy*). Humans reflect probabilties by matching. **Edwards (1961)** asked subjects to predict on 1000 trials whether a mark would appear on the right or left. As the probability of the left side was increased so the selection of left also increased. Animals are more likely to use a maximising strategy, to select the more common alternative most of the time thereby increasing their success. The human strategy is an artefact of our superior intelligence which, in this case, is maladaptive.

For gamblers there is a logical strategy (called a martingale). If you stick with your losing bet and double your stakes every time, you must eventually win and then cover your losses (providing you have sufficient funds).

4 **Methods of problem solving and decision making**: such as insight learning and availability heuristic indicate that human thinking doesn't always proceed along rationale, accessible lines (see 'Problem-solving and creativity' below).

Conclusion

Such lack of formal logic makes it hard to develop computer models of human thinking to cover all types of thinking. Not everyone thinks logically, and certainly even those who do, don't do it all of the time. Perhaps it is wrong to see logic as the top of the developmental chain. Creative and other thinking are equally important in extending human knowledge and are more appropriate for some situations.

PROBLEM-SOLVING AND CREATIVITY

Problem-solving embraces all thinking, though not all thinking is problem-solving. Concept formation and logic are the methods used in problem-solving. One of the key dimensions of problem-solving is convergent and divergent thinking. Neither is 'better' but each is more appropriate for different problems. People differ in their cognitive style and may need 'training' to use their less favoured method:

- **convergent** thinking is characterised by bringing information together – engaging previously encoded factual information;

- **divergent** thinking is that which involves generating many different answers to a single problem, 'correctness' depends on some subjective evaluation.

Howarth and Gillham (1981) have suggested a framework for all problem-solving:

1 *familiarisation*: identify the problem;

2 *incubation*: acquiring necessary skills;

3 *activity*: develop a solution.

Specifically describing the creative problem-solving process **Wallas (1926)** suggested four stages:

1 *preparation*: thinking about the problem;

2 *incubation*: sitting on it;

3 *illumination*: solution emerges;

4 *verification*: testing the solution.

The difference between the models (and types of problem-solving) lies in the time spent at any particular stage, the divergent involves more at the end whereas the convergent process requires more initial thought.

Examples of problem–solving

1. **Trial-and-error learning: Thorndike (1898)** looked at how cats learn to escape from a 'puzzle box' to reach the food placed outside. The solution was to pull a string dangling from the ceiling; a convergent problem.

2. **Insight learning**: a different approach is necessary for the problem set by **Kohler (1925)**, who dangled fruit outside a monkey's cage, providing a pole and some boxes as the 'solution'. Typically the monkey initially gave up and sat around, then would suddenly jump up and solve the problem. Called an 'Aha!' or Eureka experience (like Archimedes in the bath).

3. **Lateral thinking**: a term invented by **deBono (1970)** to describe the approach to a problem from a new angle, thus avoiding making typical assumptions (see 'Rigidity of thought' below). deBono claimed that people could be trained to identify presuppositions and thus overturn them.

4. **Brainstorming** is a group process whereby, in the initial phase, ideas are generated uncritically, then evaluated and finally elaborated, again uncritically. This may not be efficient in terms of 'person' hours but produces greater range of ideas (see 2.9).

5. **Computer models: Newell and Simon's (1963)** General Problem-solver used heuristic methods (ones which don't guarantee a solution) such as means–end analysis (see 1.2, 'Information processing approaches').

   Programs which play chess use a similar process of 'chunking' (setting subgoals), though they also use number crunching methods which examine all the available possibilities, a scanning strategy.

   Other computer strategies are bottom-up and top-down processing (see 1.2).

Rigidity of thought

Gestalt psychologists called it *Einstellung*. **Duncker (1945)** gave it the name *functional fixedness*; it is also termed *mental set*: a cognitive readiness, our tendency to view objects as serving only the function for which they are commonly used or to respond in a particular manner.

1. **Luchins (1942)** demonstrated such rigidity with the water jar problem (three jugs – *a*, *b*, *c* – can hold 8, 5 and 3 litres respectively: *a* is full, work out the necessary steps to leave 4 litres in *a* and 4 in *b*). Subjects were given a period of training and then presented with two more problems which could be solved using the same method as used in training or by another, easier method. Subjects demonstrated their 'set' by sticking with the original, long-winded method.

2. **Adamson (1952)** repeated an original experiment by Duncker, giving subjects two candles, a box of matches and a few drawing pins and asking them to mount the candles on the wall. Many subjects couldn't solve the problem, presumably because they were asked to use materials in unexpected ways.

3. Gestalt psychologists used the example of closure to illustrate innate mental sets. Given certain drawings people tend to fill in the gaps to create a unified picture, the perceptual system 'expects' completeness.

4. **Cognitive style**: individuals may prefer one kind of problem-solving over another. **Hudson (1966)** looked at school children studying arts and science and found that they differed in terms of cognitive style. Science-oriented pupils tended to be more logical and have a linear, focused style of reasoning, i.e. convergent thinking. Arts students were more divergent, intuitive or impulsive in their style of thought. Attempts to replicate Hudson's findings haven't been successful suggesting that this dichotomy is rather simplistic. Like all other types of thought, people use more than one strategy.

Tests of creativity

Hudson tested divergent thinking by asking subjects to think of unusual uses for everyday objects such as a brick. Look at 5.3 'Particular tests' for some other methods.

DECISION MAKING

Decision making is not a very well-developed field considering its potential importance. Decisions are based on evaluating probabilities of outcome of choice, an example is Stoner's Risky Shift dilemmas and group polarisation (see 2.9, 'Group dynamics'). Group effects have also been demonstrated in groupthink; decision making behaviour may be influenced by in-group pressures.

From the point of view of the individuals two particular strategies have been identified:

1 **Availability heuristic** (heuristics are rules which assist but do not guarantee solutions): we make decisions based on information which is more available, e.g. are there more words which start with k or have k as the third letter? Most choose the former, probably it is easier to access these, i.e. they are more available. **Tversky and Kahneman (1973)** gave subjects a list of 39 names of well-known people and, after reading it, they were asked whether there were more men than women. One list had 19 men and 20 women but the women were more famous than the men, another list reversed this. Subjects greatly overestimated the frequency of gender that was more famous, presumably because the famous names were more available.

2 **Representativeness heuristic**: when estimating probability a decision must be made about how representative a particular event is of the general population. **Kahneman and Tversky (1972)** asked subjects to identify a random distribution, they choose 4,4,5,4,3 rather than 4,4,4,4,4 seeing the latter as too orderly to be random.

3 **Biases in statistical judgement**: people make subjective and incorrect judgements of probabilties (see 'Probability judgements' on p.41).

IMAGINAL THOUGHT

How are thoughts represented? **Bruner** identified three modes of thinking: enactive, iconic and symbolic (which appear in this order during development). Iconic thinking or the use of images is another feature of individual differences, but is used to some extent by all people (1.1, 'Perception' and 1.5, 'Memory' include considerations of imagery).

1 **Cognitive maps**: this term originated with **Tolman** who suggested that even rats seem to have a 'mental picture' of where they are and where they want to get to when negotiating a maze (see 1.6). **Von Frisch (1967)** proposed that honey bees use imagery when communicating the location of pollen to other bees. **Saarinen (1987)** found that when college students were asked to draw a map of the world the majority enlarged the areas which they came from or which were important to them, one Australian drew the map upside down.

2 **Computational models**: the current focus of interest. For example **Kosslyn (1980)** described how visual images could be represented in a special, spatial medium. There would be two forms of data structures: image files (a skeletal outline and co-ordinates to position it) and propositional files (which contain information about components and their interrelations).

3 **Visual memory**: recognition of pictures is extremely high, supporting a visual mode of thinking. **Shepard (1967)** showed subjects 612 'memorable' pictures. He then showed them 68 pairs of pictures, one of which was new. Subjects were able to identify 99.7% of the original pictures after 2 hours and even 120 days later recognised just over 50%. **Eidetic thinking** or memory is a special ability possessed by some individuals. **Stroymeyer (1970)** tested one such eidetiker, 'E', with sets of computer–generated dots. She was first shown one set and later the other set. Taken together the dots produce a three-dimensional image, which E was able to see in her 'mind'.

LANGUAGE AND THOUGHT

(See Chapter 4, for a detailed look at language.)
There can be little doubt that language does affect our perceptions and thinking, but the key question is 'to what extent is this true?' **Miller and McNeill (1969)** suggest three predictions:

❶ language determines thinking (strong position),

❷ language affects perception (weak position),

❸ language affects memory (even weaker since memory is a symbolic process it *must* be affected by the codes we use to represent meaning).

(There is, of course the possibility, as early behaviourists suggested, that thought is no more than silent language.)

❶ **Strong position**: linguistic determinism is associated with **Whorf (1956)** and **Sapir (1958)** (Whorfian or Sapir–Whorf hypothesis). A person who does not have a particular word in their vocabulary cannot perceive that concept in the same way as someone who does have that word. Language 'cuts nature up'.

- **Carroll and Casangrande (1958)** compared Navaho and American children and found that Navaho children were better at form recognition, which was related to the fact that their language stressed the importance of form. However, these differences may be due to experience as much as language.

- **Ervin-Tripp (1964)** tested American–Japanese bilinguals on sentence-completion or word association tasks. When responding in Japanese their performance resembled that of Japanese monolinguals and the same was true for English responses, which suggests that language does restrict thinking.

- There is much evidence *against* the strong position. For example, **Heider (1972)** looked at colour perception in a tribe from New Guinea who only have two main colour terms, one for light and one for dark. Despite not having words for red and green (focal colours) they found these easier to recognise than non-focal colours. If language determined perception they should find all colours equally memorable.

❷ **Weak position**: while language may not *determine* conceptualisation it may alter it (linguistic relativity), a view also held by Whorf. **Brown (1986)** pointed out that this view is the reverse of the position that all languages are constrained to be similar because they are derived from the common thread of human cognitive processes and the physical world (see 'Nativist Language theory' in 4.1).

- Does the fact that some peoples in the Philippines have 92 words for varieties of rice (and similar can be said for the Eskimos and snow, and the Arabic and camels) mean that they perceive rice differently? Given *their* experience of rice, without the necessary vocabulary we might have the same ability to distinguish and, moreover, would probably set about 'inventing' the necessary vocabulary. In this sense *thinking drives language*.

- Work on 'leading questions' show how language can alter perception. For example **Loftus et al. (1978)** showed how the use of 'a' or 'the' in a question changes the way people answer a question, 'Did you see the broken headlight?' assumes that there was a broken headlight whereas 'Did you see a broken headlight?' is more open-ended.

  Bloom (1981) found that the linguistic differences between English and Chinese affect the way native speakers are able to process counterfactual sentences (e.g. 'It is not time to have lunch').

❸ **Weaker position**: this position is well supported by empirical evidence, for example:

- **Carmichael et al. (1932)** gave two groups of subjects different descriptions for the same set of drawings, e.g. a picture which looked like a thin crescent moon was described as a 'crescent moon' or 'the letter C'. The subjects' later drawings were positively influenced by the words they had been given.

- **Brown and Lenneberg (1954)** showed subjects four colours and later asked them to select them out of 120 colours. The more 'codeable' the initial four colours the better subjects were later able to identify them correctly. Codeability had been predetermined by finding how consistently a group of independent judges gave the colour the same name.

❹ **Is some thought independent of language?**

- **Berlin and Kay (1969)** found that native speakers of different languages selected the same colours from a selection of 300 as the best example of each of their 'focal colours', such agreement suggests that the perception of colour is independent of language.

- Studies of the deaf **(Furth, 1966)** have clearly established that many thought processes occur in the deaf without benefit of language.
- **Chomsky**'s suggestion (see 4.1) that the structures of language are innate again argue for the independence of language from thought, at least at a certain level.

5 **The developmental view**: which came first, the language or the thought?

- **Language depends on thought**: **Piaget** points out that intelligence begins developing at birth, well before language. First thinking is 'autistic thought'. Possible support comes from **Sinclair-de-Zwart (1969)** (see 3.2, 'Piaget – 'Effects of language').
- **Language and thinking are independent until the age of 2**: **Vygotsky** noted that babies have pre-linguistic thought and pre-intellectual language. Early thought consists of actions, perceptions and images, and early language (babbling, etc.) is devoid of any meaning or thought.
- **Thinking depends on language**: **Bruner** felt that the onset of symbolic functioning lead the way to language which in turn enabled qualitatively different thinking. **Bernstein (1961)** has argued that only elaborated codes articulate abstract meanings, and thus children who use restricted codes are also restricted in their thinking. **Labov (1970)** pointed out that there may be confusion between social and linguistic deprivation. This may be the case in the study by **Luria and Yudovich (1956)** which is often cited as evidence that thinking depends on language. The twins had little linguistic development and were also cognitively impaired, but this could be due to social deprivation. **Labov** also argues that 'restricted codes' can convey as much, if not more, complexity than elaborated codes.

Sexism and linguistic relativity

The following story has appeared in many different versions:

> A father and son are driving across a railway line when their car breaks down. Unfortunately they are struck by a train, the father dies on impact and the son is rushed to hospital and straight into the operating theatre. The surgeon arrives but immediately refuses to operate saying 'I can't, this is my son'.

Many people are at least initially confused because they have certain expectations (schema) which lead them to make assumptions about the gender of the surgeon, some even suspect the surgeon is the father's ghost. **Eakins and Eakins (1978)** told a similar story using a mayor, few people realised that the mayor was the boy's mother.

Another line of evidence was given by **Hartland (1991)** who claims that there are 200 English words applying to sexually promiscuous women but only 20 for men.

Language embodies our cultural expectations and experiences, as is the case with prejudice. Can changes in vocabulary alter stereotypes? There is evidence that attempts to 'liberate' an image do just this. For example the insistence on Ms rather than Miss or the word 'black' in place of other ethnic terms.

In conclusion, language and thought evolve together.

1.4 ATTENTION

Can I have your attention please? A broad definition of the term is 'the concentration of mental effort on sensory or mental events'. There is some question as to whether the term is too broad to be of value. For example D.A. Allport (1980) suggests that it is essentially used as a synonym for the wider concept of consciousness.

However there are two common and distinct uses of the term:

1 **Selective or focused attention**: a necessary feature of the cognitive system in order to cope with the mass of sensations which exist in the world. At any time a person must select which subset to attend, the others are tuned out to some extent. Example and models:

- *empirical investigation*: subjects asked to process and respond to one of two concurrent inputs (dichotic listening task and shadowing), tests selective effectiveness;
- *early filter models*: parallel inputs filtered because the system has a limited capacity and only processes a single channel at a time (serial processing), data driven;
- *late filter models*: some parallel processing may take place;
- *capacity models*: the capacity is flexible, parallel and top-down processing are possible.

2 **Divided attention or concentration**: several tasks performed in parallel, some which do not require conscious, focused attention, e.g. *automatic processes* or *absentminded* behaviour. Example and model:
- *empirical investigation*: subjects provided with at least two concurrent inputs and asked to process and respond to all, tests capacity;
- *parallel, multichannel processing* with variable capacity.

SELECTIVE ATTENTION: FILTER THEORIES

Broadbent (1958) first proposed the notion of filters – a structural bottleneck which is needed for a limited capacity system to select a single channel from the mass of parallel inputs. All later filter models are essentially modified versions of this not replacements, the difference lies in where the filter is placed.

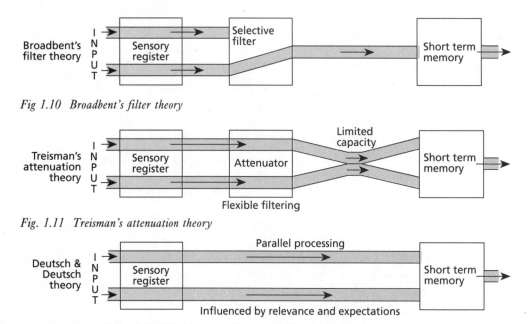

Fig 1.10 Broadbent's filter theory

Fig. 1.11 Treisman's attenuation theory

Fig. 1.12 Deutsch and Deutsch theory

1 The original **Filter Model: Broadbent (1958)**, Fig. 1.10:
- the filter is located at or just prior to perceptual analysis;
- messages are filtered on the basis of physical characteristics.

Evidence for
- The **cocktail party phenomenon,** where a person can follow one conversation when several people are talking at once, led **Cherry (1953)**, an electronics researcher, to conduct the first systematic research in selective attention. He presented two auditory messages and asked the subject to repeat (shadow) one of the messages and ignore the other (dichotic listening task). The task was easily done but he found a significant difference between the two messages: subjects were unaware of the content of the non-attended message (e.g. they didn't notice if it was in a foreign language) but did notice physical aspects of the non–attended message, such as sex of speaker. This led Broadbent to propose that messages are filtered on the basis of physical characteristics.

- **Broadbent (1958)** presented two sets of digits dichotically and concurrently (e.g. 493 to one ear, 852 to the other). He found that subjects usually recalled the digits ear by ear (493852) rather than in the sequence they were heard (489532). In this task they weren't instructed to attend to a particular ear. This suggests that single channel, serial processing is taking place.

Evidence against

- **Gray and Wedderburn (1960)** tested Broadbent's predictions with the 'Dear Aunt Jane' or 'What the Hell' task. If DEAR, 5, JANE is presented to the one ear, and 3, AUNT, 4 to the other, subjects recall by meaning rather than ear by ear (DEAR AUNT JANE rather than DEAR 5 JANE 3 AUNT 4) refuting Broadbent's finding.
- **Moray (1959)** found that information played to the 'deaf' ear was not remembered even if it was repeated 35 times. However, if the unattended message contained the person's name it was remembered one-third of the time. Therefore people are monitoring the unattended message for more than physical characteristics alone.

Evaluation

- far more processing takes place on the non-attended message than Broadbent's relatively rigid system allows,
- the filter acts not just on physical attributes but meaning as well.

2 Attenuation model: Treisman (1964), Fig. 1.11, proposed that, on the basis of the available evidence, some kind of analysis must take place before the filter. Specifically she suggested:

- the incoming signals become progressively *attenuated* (weakened) as they pass through successively more sophisticated filters,
- therefore the filters do not block information completely and if a weak signal triggers the subject's 'dictionary' of important words, the signal is enhanced,
- if there is insufficient capacity the more sophisticated filters are omitted,
- therefore the model is more flexible but is still essentially a single channel theory.

Evidence for

- **Gray and Wedderburn (1960)** and **Moray (1959)**,
- **Treisman (1964)** used bilingual subjects and a time delay between a speech given dichotically in French and in English. As the offset was reduced between the two messages, the subjects realised they were the same but in French and English, showing that they were attending to the meaning of both messages,
- **von Wright, Anderson and Stenman (1975)** paired certain shadowed words with an electric shock. Such conditioning can be later detected in the presence of a galvanic skin response (GSR), see 7.5, when the word is re-presented. This and other studies showed that if the word is later presented to the unattended ear the GSR is produced. This is also true if a synonym of the original word is presented, demonstrating that not only processing but also some semantic processing of the unattended message takes place.

Evaluation

- it is possible that subjects are switching attention between channels rather than truly parallel processing, i.e. they are multiprocessing,
- the attenuation process has not been precisely specified.

3 Late selection models: Deutsch and Deutsch (1963), Fig. 1.12, and **Norman (1968)**:

- all information is recognised before selection takes place,
- this recognition is done unconsciously,
- the recognition process is not a bottleneck but it does filter on the basis of relevance and/or importance,
- allows for the effects of, e.g. perceptual set,
- semantic *and* physical content, parallel processing.

Evidence for

- **McKay (1973)** gave subjects an ambiguous sentence to their shadowed side, e.g. containing the word 'bank'. Another word was played to the non-attended ear, in this case either 'river' or 'money'. They found that even though subjects had no recall of the words received in the non-attended ear, they affected the subject's interpretation of the word 'bank'.

Evidence against
- **Treisman and Riley (1969)** asked subjects to shadow one message for the presence of a target word. They should tap whenever the target was presented to either ear. Detection rates were much higher for the shadowed message. The late selection model would predict there should be no difference because both channels have complete perceptual analysis, whereas in Treisman's model the weakened non-attended signal would account for poorer performance.

Evaluation
- Treisman's model can account for the same evidence,
- a rather rigid and unnecessarily complicated system.

4 A flexible model: Johnston and Heinz (1978)
- selection occurs as early in processing as possible depending on the prevailing circumstances and task demands,
- semantic processing makes a greater demand on resources than physical messages and therefore makes early filtering necessary.

Evidence for
- **Johnston and Wilson (1980)** presented pairs of words dichotically; the task was to identify various target items. When subjects were told to attend to both ears all the words were processed for meaning. When subjects knew that the target words would arrive in the left ear words of a similar nature presented to the right side had no effect on target detection showing that semantic processing does not necessarily take place.

Conclusion

It is difficult to establish which is correct. **Eysenck and Keane (1990)** conclude that Broadbent's later model (1971) and Treisman (1964) account satisfactorily for most of the findings. It may be that a temporal model is inappropriate and one which is spatial (capacity) would better increase understanding.

Selective visual attention

The visual system seems to work like a spotlight with an adjustable beam, everything within the beam is attended to, whereas it is harder or impossible to see anything outside the beam. **LaBerge (1983)** presented 5-letter words. Subjects were asked in one condition to report the middle letter or, in another condition to categorise the whole word. At the same time they were watching for the presence of a probe presented in place of the word in the same space. When attending to the central position subjects were slower at responding to peripherally positioned probes.

Neisser *et al.* **(1963)** visual search task involved subjects searching through a list of letters for a target letter; subjects were faster searching for one letter than when searching for five letters. However, with practice people become almost as fast at both which is evidence of parallel processing.

SELECTIVE AND DIVIDED ATTENTION: CAPACITY THEORIES

The alternative approach is to look at attention in terms of the whole system, not just selective attention and ask how the resources (capacity) are allocated?

1 Central Capacity Theory: Kahneman (1973) and **Norman and Bobrow (1975)** and **Johnston and Heinz (1978)**: a central processor has the job of allocating one central pool of attention, the amount of capacity varies with circumstances:
- if you are wide awake you have more attentional capacity,
- different tasks require different mental effort, reducing capacity accordingly,
- automatic processes are economical on attention and capacity,
- attention is directed according to current needs, at any time the central processor can reallocate attention to that task, though failure to do so may result in absent-mindedness (see p.50),
- motivation increases capacity.

Evidence for

● The ability of people to perform certain tasks concurrently (see 'Automatic processing' below). For example, **Shaffer (1975)** found that typists could type and shadow. **Allport** *et al.* **(1972)** found that expert pianists could play from seen music and shadow.

Evidence against

● **Segal and Fusella (1970)** combined image construction (task A) with signal detection (task B), both in visual (C) and auditory (D) modes. According to central capacity theories tasks if A interferes with C more than B does we would expect the same to hold true for A, B and D. However, they found that the auditory image task interfered more than the visual one with auditory signals whereas the opposite was true for the visual signal task, in both cases due to task similarity. In other words similarity was more important than general capacity.

Evaluation

● addresses the overall issue of attention (selective and divided),
● it is a theory of resource allocation (multi- or parallel processing) rather than filtering (serial processing),
● both top-down and bottom-up processing.

②Modularity: Allport (1980) proposed a separate processor theory, which accounts for task interference on similar tasks; separate processors process dissimilar tasks and their capacities are independent.

Shiffrin and Schneider (1977) proposed a distinction between types of processing:

● controlled processes have limited capacity, require attention and can be used flexibly in changing circumstances. They involve serial processing and are best described by filter models;
● automatic processes have no capacity limitations, do not require attention and are difficult to modify once learned. They are examples of parallel processing.

③Synthesis of central and modular theories: Baddeley (1986): a hierarchical structure of processes, specific processing mechanisms function independently of each other and are co-ordinated by a central processor (this sounds very much like a computer system, see 'Information processing contributions', p.50).

EXAMPLES OF DIVIDED ATTENTION

Automatic processing

Posner and Snyder (1974) gave three characteristics of automatic processing:

● occurs without intention,
● concealed from consciousness,
● consumes few or no conscious resources.

Like attention generally, it is a way to use resources efficiently. With practice any activity becomes automatic, and then dual-processing is possible, for example, driving and talking, or touch-typing and reading, or walking and chewing gum.

Stroop (1935) investigated what is familiarly called the Stroop effect, when subjects are shown a list of colour words written in a different colour (e.g. the word RED is written in green) they take longer to name the colour of the ink than when the word and ink colour are the same (e.g. RED written in red). The explanation lies in the automatic tendency to read the words, which causes interference and slows down performance. In other studies it has been shown that the effect is strongest in children who are just learning to read. It has also been used to test brain damage (NFER publish a Stroop test for brain damage).

Logan and Zbrodoff (1979) adapted the task and showed how subjects could develop strategies for dividing attention. They placed the words ABOVE and BELOW above and below a line. The more often the word and position were in conflict the faster subjects were at identifying the position, which indicates that practice led to adopting more efficient strategies (similar to the results found by **Neisser** *et al.*'s visual search, see p.48).

Habituation

Like automatic processing, habituation is another means of economising on resources; the system becomes desensitised to any constant stimulus (a loudly ticking clock) but is re-aroused when that stimulus changes or stops. **Sokolov (1960)** proposed that the 'executive' monitors the congruency of incoming stimulus, when there is a discrepancy this 'calls for' attention (see also **Dewey**'s theory of thinking 1.3).

Absent-mindedness

Psychologists often refer to absent-mindedness as 'action slips'. **Reason (1979)** asked 35 people to keep diaries over a 2-week period. Of the 400 errors reported 40% were storage failures (intentions or actions were forgotten or recalled incorrectly), 20% were test failures (diversions from a planned activity), and 18% subroutine failures (small alterations of a well-used routine).

Reason noted that such errors are most common during highly-practised skills which seems strange since normally we expect mistakes during *learning*. He proposed that:

- during the process of learning, attention is required and a person is in a closed-loop or feedback mode of control;
- well-practised routines run largely without attentional control and in an open-loop mode of prearranged subroutines. Attentional control is only necessary when switching from one routine to another. Failure to attend to switching results in absent-mindedness, the wrong motor programme is activated or runs on.

These action slips are potentially very important. Many disasters are the result of such absent-mindedness. Tasks which require sustained attention or vigilance, such as driving or flight control, suffer from the process just described. As they are automatic they lose our attention. **Mackworth (1950)** found that when subjects had to monitor a pointer which changed every second and make a note when it moved two steps instead of one (simulating, e.g. a radar watching task) they were 85% correct in the first 30 minutes but this decreased to around 70% thereafter. In order to compensate it may be necessary to take a break and thoroughly re-arouse the system, which is the advice given to sleepy drivers.

OTHER CONSIDERATIONS

Neurocognition

Attention can be looked at in terms of **arousal**, a novel stimulus activates the RAS (reticular activating system, see 7.2), which alerts the sympathetic nervous system. This in turn activates internal organs for vigorous activity, including increased blood flow to the brain.

The RAS functions like a network, which accords with the idea of attention being a widespread modular system.

Attentional deficit hyperactivity disorder is characterised by an inability to concentrate for lengths of time, and being continually distracted. Sufferers, particularly children may be chronically over- or under-aroused. The over-arousal position is that they are easily aroused and therefore distracted; the under-arousal suggestion is that they can't maintain attention and therefore continually switch.

Posner (1992) reports that there appear to be anatomically separate systems of the brain which deal with attention and there are other systems (e.g. data processing) which attend to some inputs even when attention is directed elsewhere.

Information processing contributions

Throughout this section there has been a heavy emphasis on computer terminology: information processing; input and output; parallel, serial and multiprocessing and resource allocation.

The problems which face theorists attempting to present an adequate model of attention also face the designers of computer systems:

- parallel processing is advantageous but, in practice, systems use serial processing, often on a time-share basis (multiprocessing) see 1.2 for description of terms. Most tasks don't require the full attention of the central processor so the processor does little bits of each task repeatedly. In practice it is difficult to distinguish parallel from multiprocessing,

- there are times when a peripheral device needs to get the attention of the central processor, this is done by a system of interrupts. At any time the central processor has a set of flags (which are on or off) which it checks continually. One of these is the interrupt flag and, when this is on, the computer 'knows' that its attention is required in an area not currently being processed.

1.5 MEMORY

Memory research started out under the behaviourist influence and looked at the process only in terms of input and output. With the advent of the information processing approach, models were proposed for the activity taking place in between. Memory can be characterised as any one of the following:

- the mental function of retaining data, i.e. learning,
- the proposed storage system which holds the data,
- the data that is retained.

TYPES OF MEMORY

- **sensory:** sensory memory (SM), sensory-information store, or sensory registration. A form of memory which is a direct match to the stimulus (modality-specific), very short duration (less than one second), lost through process of decay. It is sometimes described as a buffer. Examples are: echoic memory (auditory) and iconic memory (visual).

- **semantic:** memory for meanings, and skills (how to do things), general knowledge.

- **episodic:** memory for personal experiences and episodes.

- **flashbulb:** a memory that surrounds a particular, significant event in one's life. Such as remembering what you were doing at the time of Kennedy's assassination (**Brown and Kulik (1977)**.

- **everyday:** as opposed to the recall or recognition of word lists common to empirical memory research, tends to be overlooked by research.

- **short-term:** (STM) information receives minimal processing, relatively limited in capacity (about seven items), rapid decay unless maintained through rehearsal. Also called primary or working memory (see below).

- **long-term:** (LTM) memory which has been processed in a relatively deep fashion and stored in some form of abstraction, potentially unlimited in terms of capacity or duration. Also called secondary or permanent memory.

- **working:** (WM) an alternative to STM, suggesting a more active, information processing role.

- **unconscious:** repressed memories.

- **rote:** memory through repetition, devoid of meaning.

- **genetic:** a metaphorical concept, that organisms have a genetically coded memories for behaviours which once served a purpose for their evolutionary ancestors. Also racial or biological memory.

- **memory span:** number of items which can be reproduced.

- **memory trace:** the neurological equivalent for any relatively permanent memory.

TECHNIQUES OF MEMORY RESEARCH

- **nonsense syllables:** Information devoid of meaning, such as trigrams (three letters, e.g. BDT) or CVCs (consonant-vowel-consonant trigrams, e.g. HIG).

- **paired associate learning:** Subjects given a pair of stimuli, such as a nonsense syllable and a digit. Recall tested by presenting the subject with one member of the pair and recording if its partner can be remembered.

- **recognition:** A list of possible stimuli are presented after learning, a better test than recall because it is independent of retrieval processes.

- **free recall:** Subjects allowed to recall items in any order they please. Semantic confusion is common in LTM therefore synonyms (such as big instead of large) are sometimes counted as correct.

- **serial reproduction:** Subjects must recall items in their order of presentation.

- **interpolated task:** A task, such as counting backwards in threes, to prevent rehearsal of information which would spuriously improve memory.

- **tachistoscope:** An instrument which presents visual stimuli for controlled, very short periods of time.

STAGES OF MEMORY

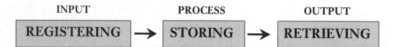

Each is a necessary but not sufficient condition for memory to have taken place. Memory can fail at any of these stages.

Input: registering/encoding information

Information is input in the form of various codes (encoded): visual (images), acoustic (phonological), articulatory (phonological plus muscle movements), motor (action), semantic (meanings), verbal (words). The physical stimulus is encoded into a form that memory accepts. These correspond with the various classes of information which must be stored. **Bower (1975)** outlined them as: spatial models, knowledge of things, beliefs about things, perceptual, motor and problem-solving skills.

Process: storage

In order for a memory to last it must be stored, the final resting place is called long-term memory. There is intermediate storage: short-term memory, which is limited in capacity and duration; information must be acted upon or it will disappear.

One demonstration of the difference between STM and LTM is found in the **serial position effect.** In free recall experiments it is found that both items at the beginning of the stimulus list **(primacy effect)** and items at the end of the list **(recency effect)** are better recalled than those in the middle. Primacy is due to the fact that the first items are more likely to have entered LTM. The recency effect is attributed to STM, since the final items in the list are often recalled first and were the most recent to enter STM.

Output: retrieval

Memories may be stored but are useless unless we can retrieve them. There are a variety of ways in which retrieval occurs:

- **recognition:** Information identified as familiar when seen or heard again, e.g. multiple choice tests.

- **recall:** Information directly retrieved from memory at will, e.g. examination essays. (Recognition is better than recall: remembering a face is recognition whereas remembering a name is recall.)

- **re-learning:** Information learned once takes less time to be re-learned, e.g. practice.

- **reconstruction:** Information organised into its original form, reconstruction rather than reproduction, influenced by expectations, e.g. Chinese whispers.

- **redintegration:** Similar to reconstruction, memory built up by going back to original events, e.g. eyewitness testimony and psychoanalysis.

- **confabulation:** When recall fails, you may manufacture something appropriate.

- **context/state-dependent memory:** Tied to the situation (internal or external) in which it was learned, such as a particular place, or drunken state. The memory returns when the context is the same.

- **imagery:** Visual image contains memorised material, used as a mnemonic device.

FEATURES AND TYPES OF MEMORY

Duration

1 **SM – Sperling's (1960)** experiment using cued-recall showed that the information immediately held in sensory memory is greater than that held in STM but disappears very rapidly. If subjects are shown the display on the right for 50 milliseconds, they typically remember four or five items. If the exposure is immediately followed by a tone signalling which row to report, they can recall three items in that row, an improvement from 25% to 75%. Limited capacity in STM may create a bottleneck so that not all the data from SM can be transferred.

```
R  T  K  M

H  L  B  F

S  J  W  D
```

2 **STM – Peterson and Peterson (1959)** presented trigrams and asked subjects to recall them after periods between 0 and 18 seconds. The subjects had to do an **interpolated task** between presentation and recall to prevent rehearsal. When delay was 3 seconds, subjects could recall 80%, after 18 seconds recall fell to 10%, giving a duration of generally less than 18 seconds. **Atkinson and Shiffrin (1971)** report a longer duration of 15–30 seconds. Explanations for such limitations include: lack of rehearsal, trace decay, displacement or interference (see 'Models of Forgetting' p.56).

3 **LTM** – Potentially unlimited, though explanations of forgetting are relevant.

Capacity

1 **SM** – restricted by duration rather than capacity. Capacity is equivalent to number of sense receptors.

2 **STM** – at one time the capacity of STM was used as a measure of intelligence. **Miller (1956)** presented the seminal notion that the capacity was a feature of the system itself, in fact it is '**the magical number 7±2**' chunks. The size of the chunks appears not to matter, which is a useful way to bypass the limits of STM.

3 **LTM** – again, supposedly unlimited.

Encoding

1 **SM** – encoding is directly related to the particular sensory modality, for example, a visual code is used in the iconic sensory store.

2 **STM** – encoding is primarily acoustic, even visual information is acoustically encoded as shown by **Conrad (1964)**; even when letters are presented visually, verbal recall shows mistakes based on sounds (B confused with P rather than F).

3 **LTM** – **Baddeley (1966)** presented subjects with lists of words which are acoustically or semantically similar. If they were asked to recall the words immediately (STM) they showed acoustic confusion, if there was a 20-minute delay (LTM) the confusion was greater for semantic similarities.

Effects of brain damage

1 **STM** – **Retrograde amnesia**, such as caused by an accident or electroconvulsive therapy (ECT), occurs when the events immediately prior to the trauma are permanently forgotten. This is ascribed to information having been lost from STM at the time of trauma.

2 **LTM** – **Anterograde amnesia** damages LTM while leaving STM intact. **Korsakoff's syndrome**, from severe alcohol poisoning, results in patients forgetting any information almost immediately. It would seem that there is a failure for material to be transferred from STM to LTM because they continue to have normal STM spans and to have LTM for events which preceded their illness.

Evidence for separate memory stores

William James (1890) first suggested a distinction between, as he termed them, primary and secondary memories. The evidence cited above still strongly supports two distinct stores (STM and LTM) plus a sensory input buffer (SM):

	SM	STM	LTM
duration	< 1 second	< 30 seconds	supposedly unlimited
capacity	all that is sensed	5–7 chunks	supposedly unlimited
coding	modality based	primarily acoustic	semantic and others
serial position effect		recency effect	primacy effect
brain damage: amnesia		retrograde	anterograde
explanations of forgetting (see below)	trace decay, displacement,	trace decay, displacement, interference	lack of accessibility rather than availability

MODELS OF MEMORY

The Two-process or Multistore model of memory

As described by **Atkinson and Shriffrin (1968)** and **Waugh and Norman (1965)**.

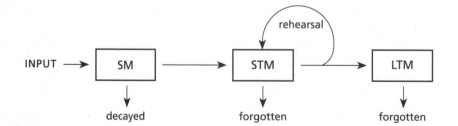

Evaluation

- There is some evidence to support two or three qualitatively different kinds of memory (see 'Features and types of memory', p.53).
- Alternative explanations can account for the empirical findings, e.g. the levels of processing model can explain differences in the amount of material recalled.

- The model is over-simplified, assuming that each store functions in a uniform fashion whereas evidence suggests that each has a number of different components.
- It is a useful conceptual tool but doesn't give an adequately detailed account.
- The concept of rehearsal may be unnecessary and too general.

Modifications of the Two-process model:

① **Working memory model** proposed by **Baddeley (1986)** was an attempt to provide more detail. He proposed that STM was not passive but actively involved in processing. It should be re-termed working memory (WM) and seen as:
- a modality-free central executive resembling attention,
- an articulatory loop holding information in phonological form,
- a visuospatial sketchpad.

Empirical evidence has come from studies where subjects have been shown to be able to perform two tasks which involve STM concurrently.

② **Single store model** proposed by **Wicklegren (1974)** on the basis that all information could be held in one store and differences in forgetting related to strength of and the number of competing items in storage.

③ **Semantic and episodic memories**: **Tulving (1972)** suggested that the differences observed in LTM may be due to different kinds of memory. Amnesiac patients lose their memory for personal events and people (episodic memory loss) while they retain their memory for language and other cognitive concepts and general knowledge (semantic memory). Tulving suggested that the material is organised differently in each of these and that they have different susceptibilities to forgetting; therefore each requires different explanations.

Episodic memory is lost rapidly, as new information arrives and interferes. It may be that, since semantic memory is constantly used, it is rehearsed. On the other hand, there is evidence for a kind of 'permastore' even for episodic memory – memories that are rarely used but retained for very long periods. For example, **Bahrick et al. (1975)** found that people, when shown their high school yearbook, could recall the names of classmates over 45 years later. **Bahrick (1984)** tested retention of Spanish in 773 people who had studied it in high school. Knowledge declined most over the first three years after leaving school and then reached a stable state even for people over 50. The success of hypnosis in revealing forgotten memories also suggests a permastore. An important aspect of this is that experimental evidence relates to episodic and not semantic memory.

Levels of processing model

Craik and Lockhart (1972) offered an alternative to the STM/LTM dichotomy, by suggesting that LTM is mainly determined by the processing that occurs at the time of learning. Primary memory (STM) involves continuous rehearsal; secondary memory (LTM) contains material which has been processed at a deeper level, which alone determines the duration of the memory.

The classic empirical test of this model was to present subjects with a list of questions to which they had to answer 'yes' or 'no'. The questions led subjects to unwittingly process the words at a physical (shallow), phonemic or semantic (deep) level. This was followed by an unexpected recognition test, those words that had been deeply processed were remembered best. Experiments showing how organisation of material unwittingly leads to good recall also demonstrate that processing and memory may well be equivalent. (See 'Memory as an Active Process', below).

Evaluation

- It is also over-simplified.
- The depths of processing model in some ways describes rather than explains what is happening.
- The notion of depth is an intuitive one and cannot be measured in any scientific sense.
- While depth is important in some situations, other features, such as relevance, can account for different results. **Morris et al. (1977)** showed that the test used for

retrieval affected the results. Where subjects were given a rhyming recognition test they remembered the words which had received shallow processing better than the more deeply processed ones.

Parallel distributed processing (PDP)

PDP models or connectionist networks, such as proposed by **McClelland (1981)**, are more recent attempts to formulate less simplified systems, stemming from an information processing approach. A chief distinction of this model is that it is assumes that information about a person, object or event, is stored in several interconnected units rather than a single place (hence, distributed), and that retrieval involves accessing one or more of these units.

Hebb (1949) felt that the apparent contradiction between the rapid yet permanent formation of memory called for two separate systems: STM for storing information quickly, and LTM for more durable storage. More recent developments in audio and computer technology show that media can be devised which do both simultaneously, e.g. tape cassettes and CDs. Similarly, computer programming has shown us that serial processing is inefficient; hierarchies and parallel processing are more effective.

Evaluation

- Offers a powerful conceptual framework.
- Such a model accounts for many features of memory, such as: reconstructive recall (known as default assignment in information processing circles), hierarchical organisation, spontaneous generalisations, and physiological descriptions of interconnected pathways.
- Can be tested by computer modelling techniques.
- The differences between this and earlier models are so great that comparison is difficult.

MODELS OF FORGETTING

The other side of remembering is forgetting. Consider the following:

- The distinction between **availability** and **accessibility**. The **tip of the tongue** phenomenon is an example of information that is available but not accessible. **Forgotten** information, on the other hand, is not available and therefore not accessible.
- Forgetting may be due to failure in SM, STM or LTM.
- Many psychologists, from Freud to Tulving, have taken the view that everything that is passed from STM to LTM remains there, it simply is not accessible. Alternatively, **Eysenck and Keane (1990)** claim there is little empirical support for this view that everything that has previously been learned is permanently retained.

Explanations of failure of availability

1. **Trace decay**: the physical form of memory disappears with time due to neural decay. This would explain the limited duration of SM and STM and the effect of rehearsal. Trace decay has been extended to LTM, to explain decay-through-disuse, though the childhood memories of the elderly and the experience of never forgetting to ride a bicycle, suggest that decay is not plausible in LTM.

2. **Displacement**: as STM appears to be limited in capacity, any excess would be displaced or overwritten. This cannot apply to LTM, which is unlimited in capacity.

3. **Interference**: one set of information competes with another. **Proactive inhibition (PI)** describes the situation where one set learned initially interferes with later learning. **Retroactive inhibition (RI)** is the reverse, interference works backwards rather than forwards:
   - the greater the similarity between the two sets, the greater the interference,
   - PI increases, while RI decreases, with time.

4. **Brain damage**: as through ageing, illness or injury, leads to physical alterations in LTM.

Empirical support

Jenkins and Dallenbach (1924): subjects who were allowed to sleep in the period between learning and recall of nonsense syllables remembered more than those who stayed awake. In both groups of subjects, memory declined with time (decay) but more so in the awake condition (displacement or interference).

Shallice (1967): by presenting digits faster forgetting was less marked (decay), however, speed was less important than number of subsequent items as a factor in subsequent recall (displacement).

McGeoch and McDonald (1931): subjects are given a list of words to learn, then another list of words, and then asked to recall the original list. If the interference task was a list of synonyms to the original list, recall was poor (12%), nonsense syllables interfered less (26% recall), numbers (37% recall) and finally jokes had the least effect (43%). Only interference can explain such findings.

The conclusion must be that no single explanation accounts for everything (see the essay on forgetting, at the end of the chapter).

Explanations of failure of accessibility

❶ **Prevention of consolidation**: even after information has entered LTM there is need for consolidation, otherwise it may not be permanently recorded.

❷ **Under-processing**: while much information is retained though seemingly inaccessible, some information may well disappear from LTM through disuse, such as facts learned for an exam. Relearning studies suggest that some trace may be left.

❸ **Retrieval cues**: **Tulving (1962)** presented subjects with a list of words followed by three successive recall trials. The specific words recalled each time differed though the response rate remained a fairly steady 50%. **Tulving and Pearlstone (1966)** found that performance was three times better when subjects were given appropriate retrieval cues. The information was clearly available but not accessible, presumably due to the use of different retrieval cues. **Abernethy (1940)** placed one group of subjects in the same room and seat for learning and subsequent recall; their performance was much better than those who were tested in different surroundings. **Godden and Baddeley (1975)** gave divers lists of words to learn on land or underwater, recall was better when the context was constant. State dependent recall also occurs. For example, **Goodwin et al. (1969)** report clinical evidence of drinkers who hide money when drunk and can't remember where when sober. However, they can recall when drunk again.

❹ **Repressed memories (motivated forgetting)**: **Freud** suggested that painful or disturbing memories are put beyond conscious recall. Patients under hypnosis may report things they had 'forgotten', though such 'memories' may be reconstructions and therefore unreliable.

MEMORY AS AN ACTIVE PROCESS

Memory, like perception, is a matter of active organisation rather than passive storage.

Organisation

Mandler (1967) demonstrated the effect of sorting (organisation) on memory by asking subjects to sort a pack of wordcards into their own categories. Later a test of recall showed no differences between subjects who had been prewarned to memorise the words. Additionally, their recall showed words clustered in categories.

Bower, Clark et al. (1969) gave subjects a list of 112 words arranged into conceptual hierarchies. When compared with subjects who were given the same words arranged randomly, performance was found to be twice as good.

The hierarchical network model of thought proposed by **Collins and Quillan (1969)** (see 1.3) also applies to memory. A hierarchy enables efficient searches of stored data, such as comprehending a simple sentence.

Language and memory

The relationship between language and thought is in part due to the effect of language on memory. Language is important at both input and output stages.

Carmichael *et al.* (1932) presented subjects with a set of ambiguous drawings accompanied by one of two word lists labelling each drawing. Later reproduction of the drawings was seen to be influenced by the words which had accompanied the drawings. **Brown and Lenneberg (1954)** demonstrated that recognition of a set of colours was related to the 'codability' (ease of naming) of the colour.

The manner in which a question is framed influences the answer given, as is shown in studies of leading questions (for example **Loftus** *et al.* **1978**). This is of particular importance in legal interviews.

Reconstructive memory

Bartlett's (1932) 'War of the Ghosts' is classically cited as evidence of how our concepts and expectations (schemas) affect recall in a similar way to language. People tended to alter the story in line with their own experience, such as leaving out the details of the spirits, and therefore the story made more personal sense.

PHYSIOLOGICAL BASIS FOR MEMORY

Physical location

1. **Lashley (1950)** found that memory deficit was proportional to the amount of **cerebral cortex** removed not damage to any specific area, suggesting that the cerebral cortex acted as a whole to store memories rather than individual localisation. However, more recent studies suggest that particular kinds of memory are in fact located in particular places.

2. **Penfield (1955)** electrically stimulated exposed portions of the cerebral cortex and found that specific episodic memories were recalled by the conscious patients. Lashley's results probably occurred because any memory relies on numerous connections, so that deletions of cortical material result in damage to connections and associated memories therefore apparently destroying the memory.

3. Contemporary views assume a network of interconnected nodes organised in a hierarchical fashion. One such formulation, by **Hebb (1949)**, is called the **cell assembly model,** a complicated system of neurons with interconnecting pathways forming as knowledge increases.

4. Different types of memory are located in different regions. The hippocampus, for example, appears to be of critical importance. Its removal, as in the classic case of **HM (Milner, 1959)**, or its destruction, as in the more recent case of Clive Wearing **(Blakemore, 1988)**, appears to result in being able to learn actions but not being able to verbalise the learning; knowing 'how' but not 'that'.

   Infant amnesia, the fact that people remember very little from their first few years, may be due to slow maturation of the hippocampus. **Tulving (1989)** used a radioactive tracer to track blood flow in the brain and found distinct patterns which could be related to episodic or semantic memory.

The biochemistry of memory

1. Alzheimer's disease has similar effects to anterograde amnesia, and is associated with degeneration of the neurons that release **acetylcholine,** a substance important to synaptic transmission.

2. **Protein molecules:** DNA and RNA are obvious candidates for storing a memory trace. They do record information (the basis of heredity) but could they be the basis of personal memory? **McConnell (1962)** classically conditioned planaria (flatworms) to avoid light. When he fed sections of these to other planaria they appeared to learn the response faster than normal, suggesting that they might have ingested some memory trace. **Oden** *et al.* **(1982)** trained a discriminative response in rats, extracted

RNA from their brains and injected this into untrained rats, who then showed a significant tendency to respond to the discriminative stimulus. However, the results of other studies were inconsistent and, in general the position is that such transfer is unlikely (**Kalat, 1988**), perhaps additional RNA simply speeds memory up rather than transfers it.

PRACTICAL APPLICATIONS

Eyewitness testimony

Wells *et al.* **(1979)** left a subject in a cubicle with a calculator, a confederate appears and pops it in her purse. When the experimenter asked the subject (witness) to identify the 'thief ' from six pictures, 58% were correct. In a follow–up mock trial, 80% of the witnesses were believed. Such unreliability and influence needs careful monitoring.

Loftus' research on leading questions (see 'Language and thought', 1.3) is also critical to court testimony.

Mnemonics

A mnemonic is a technique for improving one's memory. The research looked at here and on the preceding pages suggests many ways this can be done:

1 **Chunking**: the magic number 7 ± 2.

2 **Similar context (state-dependence)**: which is used in reconstructing crimes.

3 **Using cues or organisation: Tulving and Pearlstone (1966)** asked subjects to learn word lists, each with a category heading such as 'animals'. The subjects who were given the headings to help with recall did better than those who weren't.

4 **Use of imagery and acoustic links: Atkinson (1975)** pointed out that good learners have a 'bag of tricks' or 'mnemotechnics'. He found that introspective reports showed that such people used acoustic or imagery links in learning a foreign language. A keyword is one which sounds like the foreign word and an image to link the keyword to the English word. For example the Spanish for dog is 'perro', sounds like 'pear', therefore remember a dog with a pear in his mouth!

5 **Loci system**: objects to be remembered are 'placed' by forming strong visual images. The extraordinary mnemonist 'S' used such a technique. He could recall lengthy mathematical formula 15 years later by walking down a certain street 'in his mind' and 'seeing' the items he had placed along the way. For example: 'Neiman (N) came out and jabbed the ground with his cane... he looked up at a tall tree which resembled a square root sign ($\sqrt{d}$)...' (**Luria, 1969**).

6 **Meaning**: give meaning to an otherwise meaningless groups of letters or words, and meaning implies deeper levels of processing:
- **acronyms,** such as ROY G. BIV for the colours of the spectrum,
- **acrostics,** using the first letter of each word, such as 'Some old hippies can always have tankards of ale' for the trigonometry formula sine = opp/hyp, cos = adj/hyp, tan = opp/adj,
- **rhymes,** such as 'thirty days hath September...'.

7 **Flashbulb memories and context**: there are mental connections between events that occurred at the same time, so that by recalling one you can also recall the other, which may prove useful. For example, it is often possible to give the year of a hit record by recalling what you were doing at the time it was around.

1.6 LEARNING

Learning is:
- experience,
- a relatively permanent change in behaviour,

- evidenced in observable behavioural changes, and the acquisition of skills,
- it may result in unobservable changes in strategy and knowledge.

The topic of learning is not always located within cognitive psychology, some of the theories are distinctly non-cognitive and much of the research relates to animals. Reference to learning theories is a recurrent theme throughout the book as they are offered as explanations for most sorts of behaviour, e.g. social development, language and mental illnesses.

TYPES OF LEARNING

1 **Innate learning**:
- **imprinting** is a kind of restricted learning which takes place rapidly, within a relatively compressed time span and has a lasting effect (see 8.3).
- **maturation**: not all innate learning mechanisms are present at birth, some appear later as described by Piaget (see 3.2).
- in practice it is not always easy to disentangle acquired and innate behaviours. For example, smiling in an infant starts as an innate response but is affected by reinforcement; intelligence is an interaction between learning and innate factors (see 5.1).
- **Instinctive drift**: **Breland and Breland (1961)** found that when they tried to train a pig to put a token in a piggy bank, it would just repeatedly pick it up and drop it on the floor. Such refusal to be conditioned is taken as evidence that instinctive behaviour 'wins out' over learned whenever the two are in competition.

2 **Non-associative learning**:
- **habituation**: learning to stop responding as a result of repeated presentation of a stimulus without immediate consequences, not simply sensory adaptation or fatigue (see 1.4, 8.3); also sometimes called **desensitisation,** a term more commonly associated with a form of behaviour modification.
- **sensitisation**: becoming highly sensitive to a specific stimulus through experience.

3 **Associative learning**: the formation of causal links, as in classical and operant conditioning and social learning.

4 **Social learning**: which additionally involves observation, vicarious reinforcement and imitation as well as cognitive factors.

5 **Knowing** rather than learning, and knowing about knowing (metacognition).

THEORIES OF LEARNING: BEHAVIOURISM OR LEARNING THEORY

Watson (1913) coined the term 'behaviourism', taking the Pavlovian model of classical conditioning as the explanation for behaviour. His was a reaction against the prevalent fashion of his time for introspection which lacked scientific rigour. He replaced this with an eminently testable theory and view of human nature which had great appeal, man was a product of experience and therefore everyone had the potential to achieve anything.

Reinterpretations of his position realised that total environmental determination does not mean freedom, the reverse is true, you are controlled by your environment (see Jensen's view of intelligence, 5.1). **Skinner (1938 onwards)** maintained that autonomous man is a myth, as a species we exert control but not as individuals.

An outline of the behaviourist view

- the only appropriate matter for scientific study is that which is observable and quantifiable,
- animals don't talk and therefore there is no temptation to introspect,
- generalisations from animals to man are justifiable because the difference is only quantitative, according to the Darwinian evolutionary scale,
- the key components of behaviour are **stimulus** and **response**, therefore it is also called stimulus–response (S–R) theory,

- internal processes are epiphenomena, unnecessary concepts which play no part in behaviour and only confuse attempts to explain it, they can be represented by a **black box**,
- a **reflex** is an involuntary, unlearned, predictable response of importance for the protection and/or survival of the organism,
- through conditioning, S–R reflexes can be built up into complex behaviour,
- a **reinforcer** increases the probability of a making a certain response, through **positive** or **negative** reinforcement.

Classical conditioning

① **Pavlov (1927)** first demonstrated classical conditioning in a series of experiments where the sound of a metronome or bell was paired with the presentation of food. Salivation is a reflex response to the presentation of food, he soon found that the sound alone elicited salivation. The important terms are: neutral stimulus (NS), unconditioned stimulus (UCS) or response (UCR), conditioned stimulus (CS) or response (CR).

BEFORE: NS (bell)   elicits   no response

                                             UCS (food)   elicits   UCR (salivation)

DURING CONDITIONING: NS and UCS paired by concurrent timing

AFTER: CS (bell)   elicits   CR (salivation)

- conditioning occurs through association, in this case *temporal contiguity*,
- if the bell continues to be rung without food, the dog will eventually stop salivating, the CR is *extinguished*,
- if the dog is conditioned to salivate to a circle, then other shapes (ellipse, square, triangle) also will elicit the CR, the response is *generalised*,
- a *generalisation gradient* expresses the relationship between the new object to the original one, the more similar they are the stronger the response,
- if the circle continues to be paired with the food and the ellipse is shown without food, the dog learns to *discriminate* but only if the two shapes are significantly different.

② Many experiments have demonstrated the effect of classical conditioning on human involuntary reflexes:
- **Menzies (1937)**: asked subjects to put their hands in ice-cold water whenever a buzzer sounded, the cold temperature caused vasoconstriction (constriction of the blood vessels). Eventually the vasoconstriction occurred just in response to the sound of the buzzer.
- **Marquis (1931)**: showed classical conditioning in ten newborns. By associating a buzzer with the presence of a bottle, they began sucking or increased activity at the sound of the buzzer. Marquis therefore concluded that 'systematic training of the human infant can be started at birth'.
- **Watson and Rayner (1920)** conditioned **Little Albert** to fear white furry objects (see 7.6, 'Stress Responses').

③ **One–trial learning: Guthrie (1935)** thought that all learning takes place on a single trial. This is true in situations where learning is almost a basic emotional response. For example, one fearful incident in a person's childhood may lead to a lifelong fear of dogs. The reason it appears as if learning improves over trials is because a large number of simple components are being acquired.

Operant conditioning

① **Thorndike (1913)**: called this **instrumental learning**, because behaviours which are instrumental in obtaining a reward (or punishment) lead to learning. He proposed three laws of learning:
- **law of effect**: association does not explain all learning, learning is also dependent on consequences. Positive effects (rewards) lead to 'stamping in' behaviour whereas negative effects (punishments) do not produce unlearning ('stamping out') but rather suppression of the behaviour.

- **law of trial-and-error**: a method of problem solving. A cat placed in a puzzle box with food outside will inadvertently pull the string, which opens the door, in the course of trying to get out. Over a series of such trials the cat learns through trial-and-error. The food motivated the learning behaviour, which is rewarded.
- **law of readiness**: maturation and previous learning determine whether a particular stimulus is a reward or punishment. A reward is when you're ready to do something and are allowed to do it.

2 **Skinner (1938 onwards)**: distinguished between **respondent** behaviour (classical conditioning) and **operant** behaviour, his own term for behaviour which operates on the environment. The likelihood of its repetition depends on reinforcement:

- Skinner's classic experiment involved placing a pigeon in the Skinner box with a lighted button (the *discriminative stimulus*). Like Thorndike's cat the pigeon's random pecking (*emitted responses* or *operant*) results in accidentally pressing the button, a door opens and food is available for a time. In the end the pigeon learns to peck the button as soon as the door shuts so that it remains permanently open. Behaviour has been bought under *stimulus control*.
- However, it takes a long time for an organism to emit the right behaviour to receive a reward. This would make learning a time consuming process, which it isn't. Therefore Skinner proposed the notion of *shaping*, gradually building up operant behaviour by reinforcing successively closer behaviours to the final goal, thus simple behaviours are turned into more complex ones. This has been developed into *behaviour modification* and used successfully in therapy (see 6.4).
- If the reinforcer does not happen immediately after the UCS it can reinforce the wrong behaviour, which can be used to explain superstitious behaviour and has been seen in animals (**Skinner, 1948**).

3 **Reinforcement schedules**: in reality reinforcement is not consistent or continuous, how then does reinforcement work? Contrary to expectations it has been found that **partial reinforcement schedules** (fixed-interval, variable-interval, fixed-ratio, variable-ratio) are more effective. One might think that every time the reinforcer was absent the response would be decreased. Partially reinforced responses are more resistant to extinction, perhaps because under continuous reinforcement the organism 'expects' it on every trial and therefore 'notices' its absence more quickly. This is supported by the fact that variable schedules are even more effective than fixed partial reinforcement.

4 **Positive and negative reinforcement**:

- **rewards:** can be positive reinforcement but also the removal of an aversive stimulus is rewarding (negative);
- **punishment**: presence of an unpleasant stimulus or removal of a pleasant one (no pocket money) decreases probability of reoccurrence of a response.

However:

- **rewards versus punishment**: punishment may be useful in situations where an immediate effect is needed, such as a child putting its hand in the fire, but otherwise is often counterproductive (see 3.3 for discussion).
- **avoidance learning**: a type of operant conditioning where a response is learned as a means of avoiding an unpleasant (aversive) stimulus. However, the organism never has the chance to discover if the painful stimulus is still there, so it can't be extinguished.
- **learned helplessness**: is a learned generalised response to the experience of being unable to control an aversive stimulus, which results in a pathological state of helplessness and/or depression (see 7.6 'Stress responses').

5 **Secondary or conditioned reinforcement**: primary reinforcers are innate whereas secondary ones work because at some time they have been paired with a primary one, the classic example is money. They may arise through classical or operant conditioning, pairing with innate reinforcers or being instrumental in obtaining a reward:

- **Hull**'s drive reduction theory of reinforcement (see 7.4, 'Theories of Motivation') proposes that all motives are learned through the pleasure associated with drive reduction, first of primary drives but also secondary ones.

- **Wolfe (1936)** developed the token economy system, used in behaviour modification, from the principle of secondary reinforcement. Chimpanzees were given vending machines and learned that putting in tokens led to getting a grape. Even when the machine was not present the monkeys worked to get tokens (secondary reinforcers) to use later.

Classical versus operant conditioning

Classical	Operant
acts on innate reflexes, autonomic nervous system	acts on many kinds of behaviour, central nervous system
response (reflex) occurs naturally when UCS presented	shaping can only start when UCR occurs naturally
stimulus and response need to be temporally contiguous	response prior to reinforcement
both are susceptible to extinction, generalisation and discrimination	

Despite apparently clear theoretical distinctions, in practice both may occur at the same time and be hard to separate, consider the following arguments:

- In the classical conditioning experiment is food a UCS or a reward? The bell is a signal that the food is coming, salivating is an anticipatory response to food. If the bell comes immediately after the food it should still result in conditioning (backward conditioning) but such conditioning is rare, which suggests that the food is a reward and this paradigm is operant conditioning.

- It is not possible to set up an operant learning trial without also involving the conditions for classical conditioning, in which case it is possible that reinforcement is really not instrumental in forming learned responses.

Conclusion

Learning is just not as simple as behaviourism suggests:

- behaviour is more complex than a collection of S–R units,

- humans are qualitatively different from animals,

- much learning does not involve making any response (*behavioural silence*). Simply because we don't observe any change does not imply that no change has taken place. For example, when learning through observation or concluding that two events are unrelated. This means that cognitive processes must be involved,

- however, behaviourists produced well-controlled and productive experiments at a time when psychology was in need of a firm foundation,

- conditioning is a very powerful explanation and underlies a lot of human behaviour,

- behaviourism has made successful contributions to clinical and educational psychology: token economy systems, systematic desensitisation, behaviour modification, and programmed learning.

THEORIES OF LEARNING: SOCIAL LEARNING THEORY

Bandura extended classical and operant conditioning to include vicarious reinforcement through observation and imitation, which introduces the mediation of cognitive factors though the approach still emphasises external processes rather than internal control.

An outline of the social learning view

- social learning is the process of acquiring new behaviours and attitudes from others,

- its antecedents are learning theory and Freudian ideas of identification,

- *reciprocal determinism*: the environment determines behaviour through selective reinforcement, and we control these effects by choosing environments and behaviours,
- there are two steps: acquisition of behaviour (observation) and manifestation (imitation).

1 **Observation**: greatly increases the opportunities for learning:
  - *direct* as in **Bandura** *et al.*'s **(1961)** classic experiments with Bobo the doll (see 2.7) showed the effects of observing a model behaving aggressively with the doll,
  - *indirect* as on television or in a book (see 2.10).

2 **Imitation** may involve:
  - *modelling*: learning new responses through observing the behaviour of others; certain features of the model increase the likelihood, e.g. similarity and status,
  - *inhibitory–disinhibitory effect*: ceasing or starting deviant behaviour because model punished or rewarded (or not punished) for the same behaviour,
  - *eliciting effect*: imitating behaviour which is not novel,
  - imitation is probably learned through reinforcement, e.g. imitating gender-appropriate behaviour is rewarded,
  - it involves more than copying or identifying because the behaviours become internalised.

3 **Process**: Bandura described four stages:
  - *attention* is gained by models who are seen as attractive, successful, powerful or those whose behaviours are functional,
  - *retention*: we must remember how the model behaved, which involves cognitive skills,
  - *motor reproduction*: observer acts out and perfects,
  - *motivation*: is determined by external reinforcement, vicarious reinforcement or self-reinforcement (sense of pride or achievement). If the behaviour is successful it will motivate the person to repeat those actions.

4 **Uses of social learning explanations:**
  - social and moral development,
  - social behaviour generally, group processes, pro- and anti-social behaviour,
  - learning of language, particularly dialect and accent.

THEORIES OF LEARNING: COGNITIVE EXPLANATIONS

Cognitive approaches all address the processes inside the 'black box' rather than being concerned with stimulus, response or reinforcement, though they recognise that some learning can be explained in these terms.

An outline of the cognitive view

- mental processes are legitimate explanations,
- emphasis on knowing rather than learning, and knowing about knowing (metacognition),
- looks at learning from the point of view of problem-solving, encoding new information,
- uses information processing metaphors to explain activities, such as networks, concepts, schemata, categories, coding systems,
- intimately related to memory, as the enduring aspect of learning, theories of memory are therefore theories of learning.

1 **Insight learning**: **Köhler (1925)** set monkeys a problem solving task (see 1.3) and concluded that they used insight rather than trial-and-error learning, a cognitive not behavioural process. However:
  - **Harlow (1949)** showed how such behaviour might be the result of trial-and-error learning after all. He gave monkeys 'odd one out' problems such as two triangles and a square. Under the odd one would be a reward. He found they very quickly

learned to solve these problems and felt that they were generalising from one to another set of problems rather than using insight. The former is a simpler explanation.

- It is not always clear exactly how insight differs from ordinary learning. It may be a convenient label for behaviour for which we have no explanation and therefore presume some special ability.

②Latent learning: associative learning which involves a mental image but no immediate overt behaviour, learning without motivation. **Tolman** was a behaviourist who introduced cognitive explanations into his theory. **Tolman and Honzik (1930)** conducted a maze experiment with rats: group 1 were given reinforcement (food in the goal box) and over the test period made fewer and fewer errors in reaching the goal box, group 2 were allowed to freely explore the maze but there was no food present, they were removed from the maze when they reached the goal box. Their performance showed some improvement. After ten days some of group 2 (now group 3) were reinforced with food and immediately they began to perform as well as group 1, even slightly better. This led to the idea of **cognitive maps** to explain the immediate and superior learning shown by group 3. It is presumed that the group 2 rats had formed a mental image of the maze, which was useful later.

It is possible that the animal is following complex procedural rules rather than using a mental image but there is other evidence of spatial images (see 1.3).

③Discovery learning: **Piaget** emphasised the role of maturation and readiness in learning. Schemata (cognitive structures) are assimilated or adapted to a changing environment through the pressure of disequilibrium which results in accommodation (see 3.2).

Bruner used the terms attributes, categories, and coding systems. Thinking, learning, perceiving all involve categorising. Categorisation simplifies the environment and avoids relearning. Categories are related to each other hierarchically in coding systems. As memory is organised hierarchically a coding system is like a map of your mind. (see 1.3, 3.2).

A theory is a coding system, it allows the academic community to learn and to share their knowledge. It illustrates the power of the system in accounting for known facts and generating future predictions.

④Reception learning: **Ausubel (1963, 1977)** attempted to explain meaningful verbal learning (not rote learning). Meaning is given by the relationship between old and new cognitive material:

- material is learned (subsumed) either by relating it to existing material (derivative subsumption) or extending previous knowledge (correlative subsumption),
- this leads to hierarchical arrangement of knowledge,
- discovery learning is time-consuming and often impossible,
- expository teaching involves telling students the information, however, the use of **advance organisers** makes this knowledge meaningful,
- advance organisers are presented before a lesson to provide a stable cognitive structure into which the new material can be subsumed.

⑤Cognitive strategies: strategies for learning and metacognitive skills (knowing about obtaining and organising knowledge) are important concepts in current educational research. Aside from learning itself, we need to learn about how to learn. Young children lack metacognitive skills. **Moynahan (1973)** asked young children to select either a random or categorised list to learn, unlike older children they chose either equally.

- **Gagné's (1985)**: instructional theory outlined five major domains of learning: intellectual skills, verbal information, attitudes, motor skills and cognitive strategies. Each requires different instructional strategies. As a theory it provides a useful framework for understanding different kinds of learning.
- **Weinstein and Mayer (1986)**: suggested the following learning/thinking strategies:
  - **rehearsal**: transfer from STM to LTM,
  - **elaboration**: to make material more memorable (see 1.5),
  - **organisation**: chunking, arranging,
  - **comprehension monitoring**: metacognitive skills,
  - **affective–motivational**: maintaining interest, relaxation techniques.

COMPARISON OF APPROACHES

Behaviourism	Social learning	Cognitive
simple behaviours, skills, attitudes (metacognition)	scope increased because complex sequences can be imitated	knowing rather than just learning, and knowing about knowing
reinforcement	observation, vicarious reinforcement, imitation	structures for storing learning; e.g. cognitive maps, schemata, coding systems
all behaviour learned, reflexes are innate		some behaviour innate, evidenced by maturational factors (readiness)
assumes that humans and animals are equivalent	intercession of cognitive factors distinguishes man from animals	
cannot account for: complex behaviour, spontaneous production of new responses and behavioural silence	emphasises external rather than internal control	accounts for problem-solving
determinist	some free will, but environment exerts some control	allows for free will
All essentially based on laboratory research (see 8.4, for other views on learning)		

Chapter Roundup

All other chapters include related material:

- social psychology (Chapter 2): perception as applied to interpersonal understanding; cognition in the form of attribution and attitudes; learning of pro- and anti-social behaviours, and the media as a source of imitation;

- developmental psychology (Chapter 3) includes development of thought perception and learning in terms of cognitive, social and moral factors;

- communication (Chapter 4) covers language, in man and animals;

- intelligence (Chapter 5) is a product of learning and innate factors, and an aspect of thinking; psychometric techniques are also relevant;

- abnormal psychology (Chapter 6) includes learning disorders and the application of learning theory to treating mental illness;

- biological psychology (Chapter 7) gives neurological details; and offers coverage of motivation and affective processes which are current concerns of cognitive psychologists;

- animal behaviour (Chapter 8) contains more on learning and the work of ethologists;

- applied psychology (Chapter 9) provides further application of cognitive theories, e.g. learning theories in education;

- research and design (Chapter 10) evaluates methodologies.

Illustrative question

(a) Describe and evaluate **two** psychological explanations of forgetting from long term memory. (15 marks)

(b) What practical advice, based on either or **both** of these explanations, could you offer someone preparing for an examination? (10 marks)

(AEB, 'AS', 1993)

Tutorial note

The question has been specifically directed at a limited area to prevent preprepared answers being used. It is important to think about part (b) before deciding what particular explanations to use in part (a). They should be ones which will generate some answers for revision advice. For example, using repression in part (a) will severely limit your answer for part (b). The examiner's report for this question noted that many 'prepared' answers had little relevance to forgetting, a general lack of evaluation and a reluctance to support the answer with evidence.

Part (a) requires both description and evaluation, which can be in terms of alternative explanations and criticisms of methodologies. Part (b) is description only.

The answer given here is an attempt to provide an interesting argument, introducing material not used elsewhere in this chapter. In part (b) I've numbered the responses. It is not acceptable to answer a question in note form but a list need not be notes. The list should be tied to part (a) and include appropriate psychological evidence; an all-purpose list of exam hints would not receive many marks.

Suggested answer

(a) Forgetting is the reverse side of the coin to remembering. To enhance the later we try to prevent the former. This doesn't mean that the same evidence is relevant to both, though there is considerable overlap. 'Forgetting' assumes that something was once stored in long-term memory and now either it has disappeared (a failure of availability), or that it is there, somewhere, but you can't 'bring it to mind' (a failure of accessibility). Most psychologists believe that everything is permanently stored but sometimes particular items are unavailable (**Loftus and Loftus, 1980**), however **Eysenck and Keane (1990)** conclude that this is unlikely and certainly unfalsifiable. Therefore we require explanations of both unavailability and inaccessibility.

This essay will cover interference, an explanation in terms of lack of availability, and cue-dependent forgetting, which accounts for failures of accessibility.

Interference was a popular explanation in the first half of this century. It occurs when one set of information interferes with another and leads to a physical loss of a memory. This can apply to short-term and to long-term memory. Proactive interference is when an initially learned set interferes with later learning, retroactive interference is the reverse. Interference is typically tested by giving subjects two lists of word-pairs (A–B and A–C). List 1 might have BEM-lawn whereas list 2 would have BEM-aisle (i.e. the same nonsense syllable paired with a word). Retroactive inhibition is shown by learning A–B, then A–C and testing A–B; proactive interference is tested by learning A–C, then A–B and recalling A–B. In both cases performance on A–B is decreased, though retroactive inhibition is stronger. In such experiments memory loss can only be due to interference. This was further demonstrated in a classic experiment by **McGeoch and McDonald (1931)** who showed that the more similar B and C items were the less the subject was able to remember.

However, there are aspects of interference which suggest a more complex explanation. **Underwood (1957)** noted that if subjects in the standard experiment are retested after 24 hours, recall of list 2 (A–C) diminishes but list 1 (A–B) remains stable. He explains this as proactive inhibition following the spontaneous recovery of items from list 1 acting proactively on list 2. But if interference led to a physical loss of memory, there could be no improvement.

Ceraso (1967) found that recognition, as opposed to recall, is almost immune to interference. He tested recognition by giving subjects list 1 and 2, then presenting them with a list of the nonsense syllables and a jumbled list of the other words. To test recall, he asked subjects to list any of the words and scored this without regard to order. In both conditions, there were significant losses of memory. However, after 24 hours, recognition (accessibility) showed considerable spontaneous recovery, whereas availability remained stable.

Tulving and Psotka (1971) gave subjects lists of 24 words belonging to one of six categories. When subjects were asked to recall the lists, their performance was negatively related to the number of lists they were given, presumably due to retroactive interference. However, when the subjects were given category names as cues, their performance stayed the same regardless of the number of subsequent lists. It might be that the presence of cues makes the task more like recognition than recall, and that it is not interference that causes forgetting, but changes in retrieval information.

This interpretation is further supported by **Tulving (1968)**, who asked subjects to recall a list of words on several occasions, the words recalled each time were not the same. Like Underwood's results, this suggests that there is more in memory than is accessible at any particular time. Therefore an explanation is needed in terms of accessibility rather than interference leading to a disappearing memory trace.

Tulving (1974) first suggested cue-dependent forgetting; that 'forgetting' is due to a lack of good enough cues at the time of recall (in recognition tasks no cue is necessary). The reason for interference effects might be explained in terms of slower retrieval speeds, where cues overlap, or because of 'crowding'.

An example of interference slowing the speed of retrieval has been given by **Anderson (1983)**. Subjects were given sentences to learn, three were about a banker and two about a lawyer. Recalling information about the banker was slower, presumably because the cue (banker) accessed a larger bank of data. Related to this is the notion of 'crowding' proposed by **Ceraso (1967)**; a second learning task 'crowds' original learning and subsequent retention. One group of subjects were 'maximally crowded'; they had the standard ten trials to learn list 2. The other group had ten different list 2s, each exposed for one trial only. Therefore learning should be weak and lead to 'minimal crowding'. Immediate testing showed little difference between the groups, but after 24 hours the minimally crowded group showed considerable spontaneous recovery. Crowding actually affects the amount that is available not simply accessible. (This can also help to explain Tulving and Psotka's results.)

Therefore, we can conclude that interference effects are a combination of crowding, which actually prevents availability, or slows down retrieval. Some interference effects disappear over time due to some spontaneous recovery, which then leads to proactive interference.

Interference, as an explanation of forgetting, applies in a rather limited set of circumstances – when the two sets of data are very similar. Since this is relatively rare in everyday life, interference probably has limited application, whereas the opposite is true for cue-dependent forgetting. It can also be said that interference probably has little to do with semantic rather than episodic memory. **Tulving (1972)** outlined these two differently organised memories. Semantic memory (memory of words, concepts, rules and abstract ideas) suffers from little forgetting, is well organised and doesn't disappear in cases of amnesia. Episodic memory is more similar to that tested in empirical work, though it also accounts for much of everyday memory; it is unstructured, and rapidly lost, particularly as new information arrives and interferes. Theories of loss of availability can't account for the behaviour of semantic memory.

What makes for a good cue? **Morris, Bransford and Franks (1977)** asked subjects to recall the contents of a number of sentences. If they were given recall cues which closely resembled the original item their recall was 4.7, with inappropriate cues it fell to 1.6. **Tulving (1979)** proposed the encoding specificity principle: the more similar a cue is to the target item, the better it will aid recall. **Thomson and Tulving (1970)** demonstrated this by showing that cues which are strongly associated (white paired with black) lead to better recall than weak associations (train–black).

Tulving also claimed that cues should only be useful if they are encoded at the time of learning. However, **Jones (1982)** gave subjects unrelated word pairs to learn (e.g. regal paired with beer). When their recall was tested, one group ('informed') were told that the cue, if reversed, gave a clue to its partner (e.g. regal=lager). The informed subjects performed twice as well as uninformed subjects, despite the fact that initially the cue (regal) was ineffective yet it was none the less there to be used if it later proved effective.

Solso (1974) criticises the encoding specificity principle generally on the grounds that it is a circular argument, and one that is not falsifiable: an effective cue is one that was encoded, if it is not effective then it is not encoded.

Cues do not have to be a significant word, they may also be the context or state in which something was learned. **Baddeley (1982)** distinguished intrinsic context, the meaning of a word (jam in connection with strawberry or traffic), and extrinsic context, such as the room where learning takes place. **Abernethy (1940)** demonstrated that subjects who learned and were retested in the same room did better than those who weren't. **Godden and Baddeley (1980)** found that recognition is not affected by extrinsic context whereas recall is. This can be explained in terms of cues: recognition doesn't require cues whereas recall does. Police reconstructions of crimes are based on context-dependence. When a person revisits the scene of the crime their memory is jogged. A more common example is the smell of something like the sea may jog your memory for a particular incident at the seaside.

There are alternative explanations for loss of accessibility, such as repressed forgetting, but cue-dependent forgetting undoubtedly explains most instances of recall failures.

(b) A common criticism of memory research is that it has little bearing on everyday memory, or forgetting. Some of the familiar methods for exam revising can be tied to avoiding interference or cue-dependent forgetting:

Interference

1 It is often suggested that revision notes should be made in a structured manner. Semantic memory differs from episodic (easily forgotten) memory essentially in being organised. Semantic memory seems largely unaffected by interference and loss of availability. Amnesiacs rarely lose their general knowledge. This suggests that an organised memory is more resistant to forgetting.

2 Interference effects appear to be caused in part by crowding, as time passes the effects of crowding become greater and may lead to proactive interference. Therefore you should work for short spells with adequate breaks. A more common term for this is cramming. Don't try to cram too much of the same thing in at once.

3 The same thing applies to the last 24 hours before the exam, though you may think you've remembered an important chunk, the evidence above suggests that spontaneous recovery may led to proactive interference so that the last part learned is forgotten.

Cue-dependent forgetting

1 The superiority of recognition to recall shows that, while you might have the distinct impression that much of what you learned has been forgotten, in fact it is there if you had the right cues. It is a common sensation to know that you know the answer but you can't quite recall it.

2 Cues should be embedded in the material as you are learning it. For example, the keyword method of inventing acoustic or imagery links to remember otherwise meaningless associations **(Atkinson, 1975)**. The use of acronyms, acrostics or rhymes are examples of acoustic links. In these cases you store the keyword 'alongside' the data to be recalled. The loci system works by forming strong visual links with everyday items; you 'place' the items to be remembered in, for example, a well-known street and later 'walk' down the street recalling them.

3 Extrinsic context may also act as a cue. If you can imagine the page the item was on in a book or the day that you revised the material, this may serve to jog your memory. In a sense this is a problem-solving approach to recall, since the cues are unavailable but you try to locate them by various strategies.

4 Organising notes is a means of establishing cues. For example, creating category headings (as), numbered lists or maintaining a personal glossary.

Question bank

Allow 45 minutes for each question.

1 Critically discuss explanations of visual constancies and illusions.

(AEB, 'A', 1990)

Points: tends to elicit superficial answers limited to descriptions of visual illusions; the matter of constancy is equally important as is an evaluation of both constancy and illusions.

2 Describe how sound is processed and consider attempts to explain the perception of **either** the pitch **or** the location of the sound.

(AEB, 'AS', 1990)

Points: a straightforward question. The evaluative aspect is achieved by offering more than one explanation of how pitch or location are perceived which are related to frequency.

3 (a) Using evidence from experimental studies, describe what psychologists have discovered about the development, in human infants, of:
  (i) pattern perception. (6 marks)
  (ii) depth perception. (6 marks)
(b) Discuss **two** difficulties of investigating the development of perception in human infants. (8 marks)

(NEAB, 1991)

Points: in part (a) there are two strands, a description of development and the support of empirical evidence, simply stating the evidence is not enough.

4 'Whatever else a brain may be, it is most certainly not a digital computer' (Miller, 1976). Critically consider the usefulness of computer models in helping us to understand human cognitive activities.

(AEB, 'AS', 1990)

Points: not a popular area of the syllabus. It is reasonable to present arguments for and against, rather than taking an extreme position.

5 Many cognitive psychologists interpret attention as information processing. Use experimental evidence to consider this approach.

(AEB, 'A', 1989)

Points: the 'information processing' part of the question should not be ignored, nor should answers be limited to selective attention only. This is a popular area of the syllabus, answers are usually competent though lacking in evaluative skills.

6 Critically consider the role of divergent (as opposed to convergent) styles of thinking in problem solving.

(AEB ,'AS', 1991)

Points: the link between style of thinking and problem solving is important.

7 It has sometimes been asserted that the study of science encourages logical thinking.
(a) Devise a study to test this hypothesis. Give details of the procedures and measures that you would use and your reasons for choosing them. (14 marks)
(b) Discuss **one** strength and **one** weakness of the study you have devised. (6 marks)

(NEAB, 'A', 1992)

Points: two points are made in the examiner's report: any variables used in an experiment should be operationalised, and comparing arts and science students misses the point of the question.

8 Discuss models of memory in relation to duration of storage and mode of representation.

(AEB, A, 1990)

Points: such an unambiguous question attracts simple descriptive answers containing everything a student knows. For good marks the answer should be selective and critical.

9 Discuss psychological insights relating to the organisation of information in memory. (25 marks)

(AEB , 'A', 1993)

Points: Include models of memory as well as research specifically related to active organisation. A good answer should describe the appropriate models in terms of the way they explain organisation. Evaluation should be in terms of methodological difficulties, alternative explanations and applications.

10 (a) Outline the main aspects of Social Learning Theory, mentioning supporting empirical evidence. (10 marks)
(b) Briefly discuss **one** way in which Social Learning Theory differs from Operant Conditioning. (4 marks)
(c) Account for one aspect of social development from Social Learning perspective. (6 marks)

(NEAB, 'A', 1991)

Points: A nicely differentiated question. Note that part (b) is one point only, which should be described and evaluated. Part (c) refers to material from Chapter 3.

11 Describe what you consider to be key features of operant conditioning and discuss some practical applications of operant conditioning techniques in educational settings.

(AEB, 'AS', 1990)

Points: 'educational settings' can be interpreted very broadly to include anywhere that learning is taking place.

12 (a) Describe briefly what is meant by 'levels of processing' in the study of learning. (5 marks)
(b) Describe **one** experiment which was carried out to examine levels of processing. (5 marks)
(c) Discuss the major differences between levels of processing and interference as alternative explanations of forgetting. (10 marks)

(NEAB, 'A', 1991)

Points: The word 'learning' in part (a) may be misleading, as the question is essentially on memory, which of course underlies learning. Part (c) focuses on forgetting rather than remembering. Answers related to memory generally are not relevant. Interference should be discussed in terms of proactive and retroactive types.

SOCIAL PSYCHOLOGY

Units in this chapter:

Chapter overview

Social psychology is concerned with those aspects of human behaviour which involve people and their relationships with other people, groups, institutions and society as a whole. It is distinct from sociology, which is less concerned with the individual as a separate entity and more with the structure and functioning of reference groups such as the family, social classes and cultures. The focus is on human rather than animal behaviour, which is considered a separate discipline. There is little in the whole area of psychology which is not relevant to social psychology, since humans (and most animals) tend to be highly social.

At the core of social psychology is a desire to find good in human nature. Many social processes which may appear negative can be viewed in terms of their necessary contribution to cognitive and group processes, such as conformity or aggression.

Historical perspective

The roots of Western social psychology stretch back to the Greek philosophers pondering on humanity's social and political nature. The first true social psychology experiment was **Triplett's (1897)** demonstration of how competition facilitates performance. However, early psychology centred around psychoanalysis and behaviourism, and it wasn't until the 1930s that social psychology was truly underway, with such classic work as that by Sherif and Asch. Social psychologists made useful contributions to international relations and to troop morale and organisation during the Second World War. More recently racial and sexual prejudice have been vital areas of applied study, as have advice on inner-city life, football violence, the influence of the media and the health of organisations.

2.1 SOCIAL PERCEPTION

Many of the processes involved in physical perception, are also involved in social perception. We receive sensory data and modify this input in line with our learned expectations. In social perception these expectations are almost entirely due to cultural and personal learning.

IMPRESSION FORMATION

Impression formation consists of co-ordinating various bits and pieces of information into an integrated whole. On the basis of very limited information, we have a need to create a view of a person. We may need to do this for formal purposes, such as an interview, or for informal ones, such as deciding whether we believe in someone or like them. We need to go beyond the immediate information, and must rely on previous experience to suggest likely interpretations.

Empirical findings

Typically evidence has come from three types of study:

1. **Lists of adjectives,** as in the classic studies by **Asch (1946)**. Subjects were asked to rate a person on a number of personality characteristics after being shown a list of adjectives describing that person. The fact that the ratings included new, and consistent traits, shows the process of prediction.

2. **Full descriptions** of a person called Jim were given by **Luchins (1957)**. In one version, the introvert paragraph, words like 'alone' and 'shade' were included; the other, more extrovert paragraph, contained descriptions of 'chatting with others' and of 'sunshine'. Again subjects provided descriptions of Jim's other characteristics and made some predictions about what he would do in certain situations. Interestingly, no one said, 'How am I to know?'

3. A confederate can be used to elicit a response. **Kelley (1950)** arranged for a substitute lecturer to talk to a group of students, and afterwards asked them to assess the lecturer's performance and personality. Prior to the speaker's arrival Kelley had provided students with a short description of the man, in some versions including the word 'warm', and in others the word 'cold'. Those who preconceived the lecturer as 'cold' rated him as 'self-centred, formal, unsociable, unpopular, humourless'.

Are such studies a true reflection of reality, or are the results simply due to the demand characteristics of the experimental situation? Many 'natural' situations are equally limited in information, such as interviews. Much of the information on which judgements are made come from non-verbal channels of communication, such as race, mode of dress and accent. These are equivalent to the adjectives provided in the stimuli above.

Explanations of the underlying processes

Exactly how might these 'bits and pieces' be integrated into a whole model?:

1. **The halo effect:** the possession of one attribute leads an observer to believe that the owner also possesses a wealth of other similar traits. **Rosenberg et al. (1968)** found two significant dimensions for the traits that people use: intellectual and social, and high and low. Mention any trait and the possessor is then assumed to have all the other traits in that quadrant.

2. **Attribution theory** (see 2.2) explains how we convert observed behaviours into traits possessed by the owner – an essential part of the impression formation process.

3. **Implicit personality theory,** as opposed to the explicit theories formulated by psychologists. 'Implicit' describes the intuitive nature of the process. 'Personality theory' refers to the aspect of coherence that we expect from the traits possessed by a person. On first meeting someone, the intuitive 'scientist' begins with a snap judgement, a model. Further acquaintance is a matter of continual testing, modifying

and filling in the model or theory. It may be, however, that personality isn't as consistent as we expect, as suggested by the situational approach (see 5.2).

④ **Self-fulfilling prophecy.** This can be used to explain how such initial judgements are self-reinforcing; the observer's perceptions lead to behaviours which may encourage or discourage the observed. **Snyder *et al.* (1977)** showed men a photograph of a woman to whom they were supposedly talking on the telephone. If they thought they were talking to an attractive woman they behaved differently, *and* the women responded by behaving 'more attractively' (see also **Word *et al.* (1974)** and **Guthrie (1938)** (3.4).

⑤ **Stereotypes** provide an instant picture from meagre data.

Basis for weighting of cues

Initial perceptions consist of a series of disconnected cues, which are then combined, and the gaps filled in, to add up to a whole predictive model. Are some cues more important than others?

① **Non-verbal** cues are given greater weight than verbal ones. **Argyle *et al.* (1972)** played a videotape of three messages spoken in three different styles (friendly, neutral and hostile). Subjects based their interpretations of the meaning more on the non-verbal than the verbal content. For example, a hostile message in a friendly style was seen as insincere or joking, whereas a friendly message in a hostile style sounds hypocritical or sarcastic.

② **Centrality. Asch (1946)**, like Kelley, showed that adjectives such as warm/cold, murderous, or intelligent have greater weight than others such as polite and blunt. Asch called these 'central traits'.

③ **Primacy/recency** (another parallel with cognitive psychology). In the **Luchins'** study some subjects were presented with both versions of the 'Jim' account but in different orders. There was a strong primacy effect, which accords with the intuitive view that first impressions count. However, if a time interval was allowed between reading the versions, a recency effect was shown ('you're only as good as your last book'). **Asch (1946)** also demonstrated the primacy effect, recognising that it only works when subsequent words in the list are susceptible to meaning change, such as calm, aggressive and strong.

④ **Inconsistent data.** This usually leads to attempts to make it consistent by, for example, ignoring some of the data. This drive towards consistency is a feature of human cognitive processes and is used to explain such things as implicit personality theories.

⑤ **Salience.** Information which is unexpected, prominent or striking, such as negative features, are given greater weight. Working on the principle of inconsistency, we might expect such information to be overlooked. However, some data is too significant, and therefore the opposite occurs it is given *more* weight.

⑥ **Individual differences** exist. Women tend to use different cues from men. Your own personality influences the way you perceive or weight the same or different characteristics in others.

SELF PERCEPTION: A SPECIAL CASE OF IMPRESSION FORMATION

How do you form an impression of yourself? This self-knowledge is built on the same basis as all social perception – we observe behaviours and attribute internal traits:

● The **self** is a cognitive structure which integrates our capacities, attitudes, attributes, behaviours into a coherent whole (the 'self' is dealt with in 3.4).

● Our self-concept serves to help us predict how we will behave in future situations. In the same way, perception of others is a useful tool.

● Self-esteem is the evaluation you make of your self-concept.

● One sign of mental illness is a lack of self-unity.

● An interesting aspect of self-perception is that of emotion, for a discussion see attribution (2.2) and emotion (7.5).

STEREOTYPES

- A stereotype is a social perception of an individual in terms of his/her group membership or physical attributes rather than his/her actual personal attributes.

- It is neither possible nor desirable to react to each person (thing or situation) as if it were a unique thing. Stereotypes are cognitive schema which summarise large amounts of information. Overgeneralising is an inevitable outcome of the process of summarising.

- Many stereotypes are derived from indirect contact (*apriori* knowledge). Television has been responsible for many poor images in the past. Conversely, it can be used as a powerful tool in creating new stereotypes for women and ethnic subgroups.

- Stereotypes are rarely accurate for an individual, and they may or may not be valid for the group as a whole.

- Stereotypes are not 'bad' *per se*, but it is important for us to be aware of when they are inaccurate, and to be aware of their evaluative dimension.

- Once formed, stereotypes are extremely resistant to change, possibly because:
  - we seek out information which confirms rather than refutes beliefs,
  - the self-fulfilling prophecy also contributes to their perpetuation,
  - they may contain a kernel of truth.

- Stereotypes form the basis of prejudices, but need not be the same.

Staats and Staats (1958) demonstrated the formation of stereotypes through verbal conditioning. They presented six nationality names (Dutch, Swedish, French, Italian, German and Greek) 18 times each, each time paired with another word. Subjects, who were American undergraduates, were told to learn the pairs. In one group, Dutch was always paired with a favourable word, and Swedish with an unfavourable word. This was reversed with the other group. At the end subjects were asked to rate the nationalities and, not surprisingly, this was in accord with their learned pairings.

Confirmatory bias is one of the mechanisms through which stereotypes are perpetuated. **Cohen (1981)** described a woman in a videotape as either a waitress or a librarian, and showed her doing a variety of things. When subjects were later asked a series of questions, such as 'What was she drinking?' they tended to remember those features consistent with their stereotypes about a waitress or librarian.

Race, gender and physical attractiveness are the three strongest sources of stereotype or prejudice, possibly because physical features stand out most in initial or superficial encounters. Ageism and stereotypes of the handicapped are relatively newer concerns.

1 **Physical attractiveness. Benson, Karabenick and Lerner (1976)** left job application forms in a busy telephone booth. Each form had a photograph attached and the name and address of the applicant. They varied the photographs in terms of race, gender and attractiveness and assessed the likelihood of the form being sent back to the applicant. Physical attractiveness was the strongest predictor.

    Bull (1983) showed children before-and-after photographs of patients who underwent cosmetic surgery, asking them to imagine that this was a new teacher. The more attractive version was seen as more likely to be helpful and less likely to be cross.

    Stewart (1980) found that attractive defendants received lighter sentences.

    Landy and Sigall (1974) gave male college students a set of essays, each with a photograph attached, to be rated in terms of quality. Essays thought to have been written by attractive women were rated more highly overall.

    Harari and McDavid (1973) compared the effects of attaching different first names to essays and found that 'attractive' ones (David, Michael, Karen and Lisa) did better than less favourable ones (Elmer, Hubert, Bertha and Albert).

    However, attractiveness may sometimes call up a less desirable stereotype. **Dermer and Thiel (1975)** found that very attractive women were judged as being egotistic, vain, materialistic, snobbish and likely to have unsuccessful marriages.

2 **Race. Katz and Braly (1933)** asked college students to characterise 12 ethnic groups from a list of traits. Their responses were dishearteningly similar. However, **Gilbert (1951)** found that students showed an increased awareness of the undesirability of such statements; some refused point blank to participate and others commented on the inaccurate nature of such statements, whilst they still produced stereotypical views. **Karlins *et al.* (1969)** concluded that the content had changed since 1933 but stereotypes were very much in existence.

③ **Gender**. The issue of gender stereotypes is important both from the point of view of our own gender identity and the judgements we make about others of the same or different genders. Stereotypes are important in both processes.

From very early on male and female babies are treated differently, on the basis of culturally held stereotypes. **Condry and Condry (1976)** showed films of a baby, labelled alternatively as a boy or girl, and asked subjects to rate emotional responses. They showed that presumed sex led to different interpretations of the same behaviour.

Fidell (1970) sent personnel profiles about Dr Patrick or Patricia Clavel, to over 200 psychology professors – people who might have been expected to know better. Their professional assignments favoured the man.

Mischel (1974) used the essay-assessment technique to show how gender affected rating of academic abilities, again favouring men (John was better than Joan).

Collins *et al.* (1984) found that the male/female stereotypes portrayed in children's books were changing to reflect moves towards greater sexual equality.

Of course men and women *are* different, but does that mean one is uniformly inferior? **Goldberg (1968)**, the originator of the essay-technique, found that not only were the 'male' essays judged better when the topic was in a traditionally female field (such as nursing) but also that women were just as prejudiced as men against women.

(See 3.4 for more on gender roles and 2.10 for media stereotyping.)

④ **Ageism**. Negative age bias applies to all age stereotypes – those of adolescents as well as persons in late adulthood. Such stereotypes may be held by people of all ages, including peers. Unlike other stereotypes, age is something we all grow through or into, so we are, at various times, the object of such prejudices. Most people think that chronological age is a good predictor of certain behaviours such as difficult behaviour or decline in mental capacity. This is not true (see 3.4) and has important consequences for employment.

IMPRESSION MANAGEMENT

Impression management describes the species-specific strategies used in social encounters to establish, maintain and refine the impression that others have of us.

Goffman (1959), a social anthropologist, was particularly influential and described social life as being like a series of theatrical performances. We play a particular role and we manage our own performances in line with our intuitive understanding of the processes of social perception, using verbal and non-verbal cues.

We can distinguish between **strategic** and **authentic presentations**. In some roles we need to communicate certain specific aspects of ourselves, such as in an interview. At other times, the 'real you' is more appropriate.

Disclosure is part of self-presentation. A person controls the degree to which information about themselves is revealed to another. Such levels of intimacy play an important role in the formation of **friendships** (see 2.4), the more you trust someone, the more you disclose or reveal. Disclosure is also important in studying **animal behaviour**, such as those non-verbal signals Desmond Morris has portrayed so successfully.

People show individual differences in the degree to which they monitor and then regulate their behaviours. Such **self-monitoring** is also a function of the situation. High self-monitors are flexible types who shrewdly tailor their social behaviour to fit the situation. **Snyder (1979)** has produced a self-monitoring scale, showing that high self-monitors are more attentive to social cues, remember more about new acquaintances, are quicker to form impressions and quicker to change social identity.

The self-control involved in self-presentation is intuitively recognised in making **attributions** about a person. We assume that a person has controlled the expression of the behaviours that we observe and therefore we assume that the impression we receive is the same as a person's attitudes.

Self-presentation has an important role in **psychology experiments**, because the impression that a subject chooses to display may not truly represent their attitudes.

Practical applications: the interview

Many situations require a professional approach to self-monitoring. It has been increasingly recognised that people need training in improving such skills, such as doctors in dealing with patients, and interviewers and interviewees in managing the interview (see social skills training 4.2, and 6.2, and interview techniques 5.3). The interview is a familiar social situation with established rules and conventions. It may be used for the purpose of selection or guidance.

- Dress and manner of both interviewer (I) and the candidate (C) should reflect the formality of the occasion.
- It is understood that the C is not at his/her most typical, I should help C relax.
- It has been found that Cs who have a higher level of smiling, looking, head movements, gestures, and who speak more fluently and expressively are more likely to get the job.
- Physical appearance matters too, attractiveness has been shown to be a plus, fatness a minus.
- Advice from others may be useful about your self-presentation; it is easy to make superficial adjustments to dress, hair, manner which may influence the outcome substantially.

(4.2 covers such non-verbal behaviours in more detail.)

2.2 ATTRIBUTION THEORY

We do not observe traits, we observe behavioural cues and *infer* the traits or attributes of that person, or ourselves. We make assumptions about what *caused* that particular behaviour. Thus:

attribution theory = social psychological explanation of our perceptions of causality.

THEORIES OF ATTRIBUTION

Theories of attribution are sometimes collectively called 'Inference Theories' because they explain the process of making inferences.

Loci of causality: Heider (1958)

The term 'attribution' originally came from Heider, who proposed two sources or loci of causality:

- The **person: internal** or **dispositional** attributions. A person's disposition, their beliefs, attitudes and personality are seen as the cause of a particular behaviour.
- The **situation: external** or **situational** attributions. An external force, such as money, threats, social norms or luck, is seen as the cause.

We prefer to make dispositional attributions; this is called the **fundamental attribution error.**

A classic study by **Heider and Simmel (1944)** involved subjects viewing an animated film of three objects (typically, a large and small triangle and a circle). When subjects were asked to describe the events in the film they did so anthropomorphically, that is, they attributed human characteristics to the objects. This is taken as evidence of our strong unconscious tendency to infer 'personalities' on the basis of observed actions even when no causation could possibly be involved.

The correspondent inference theory: Jones and Davis (1965)

We observe behaviour and *infer* a *corresponding* attitude, an internal attribution. For example, we often make the mistake of thinking that film stars have similar personalities to the roles they play.

Jones and Davis suggest that any ambiguities which exist in a person's characteristics are resolved according to certain features of their behaviour. They call the participants in their studies the observer (the one making attributions) and the actor (the one who is observed). The cause of an actor's behaviour will be seen as dispositional rather than situational if:

1. *Intentionality*: the actor performed the action deliberately.

2. *Consequences*: the actor was aware of the effect of their behaviour.

3. *Choice*: the actor had a free choice of how to behave.

4. *Uncommon effects*: the behaviour is unusual (distinctive).

5. *Social norms*: the behaviour is non-conformist.

6. *Social roles*: behaving against the stereotype for a role, be it mother or doctor.

7. *Hedonical relevance*: an action is to likely to affect the observer.

8. *Past experience*: if past behaviour suggests that this person (or their stereotype) is more likely to be in control.

Evidence for the strength of dispositional attributions against situational ones comes from a study by **Jones and Harris (1967)**. They asked subjects to rate the true opinion of the author of an essay written either for or against Fidel Castro, the Cuban dictator. Subjects were inevitably biased by the views put forward in the essay (the fundamental attribution error). The subjects judged the essay writer's opinion to be the same as purported in their essay even when the subjects knew that the essay was written under no-choice conditions (i.e. the author was told what position to take). Only when they were told that the essay had been copied was the bias overcome.

However, when other information is available, the outcome is not so simple, as was shown later by **Jones and Nisbett (1971)**, again using the essay writing technique. This time the topic was pro- or anti-marijuana, and additional information about the author's political persuasions was provided. A moderate essay was seen as conforming to the author's opinion under the free-choice condition, however, the same essay was seen as moderately *unfavourable* if the author was supposedly asked to write a strongly favourable essay. It was then seen as 'foot-dragging', an interpretation based on the knowledge that people leave cues to show that what they are saying is not what they mean.

Covariation rule or cube theory: Kelley (1967)

Covariation is the tendency for two things to occur at the same time, such as drinking and hangovers, or sunshine and warmth. Attributions are based on our observation of correlations or covariations. Covariance is determined by three **axes** of covariation (a cube):

1. **consistency**: covariation over time,

2. **distinctiveness**: co-occurrence of two things *and* co-absence leads us to suppose that one causes the other,

3. **consensus**: if our observations are shared by others.

The theory predicts that external attributions will be made when there is sufficient evidence of all three. Internal attributions occur when distinctiveness and consensus are low and consistency is high.

McArthur (1972) gave subjects 12 event-depicting sentences which contained information (high or low) about consistency, distinctiveness and consensus, for example: 'John laughs at almost all comedians' (low distinctiveness) or 'Almost everyone who hears the comedian laughs' (high consensus). Subjects attributed external or internal causes as the model predicted.

Causal schemata: Kelley (1971)

Kelley's original model, when tested empirically, was found to be unsatisfactory:

● the three axes were not used to the same extent,

● people did use other sources of information,

● Kelley overestimated people's ability to assess co-variation.

Therefore, Kelley proposed an alternative model which describes what happens when information about consistency, distinctiveness and consensus is lacking. In that case we must rely on **causal schemata**, which are general ideas about the way causes interact to produce specific behaviours, a kind of 'causal shorthand' to provide rapid interpretation of often ambiguous, incomplete and complex social perceptions. The two main kinds of causal schemata are:

1. *multiple necessary causes* – the presence of a group of behaviours are jointly necessary for a particular cause to be attributed,

2. *multiple sufficient causes* – any one of several behaviours is sufficient to arouse an attribution.

The **discounting principle** is an example of the second kind of cause. We reject the more common, dispositional explanation for a behaviour when the situational explanation is more reasonable. A good example is the film star advertising a brand of soap powder. It is more likely that they are doing it because of a large fee (external) than because they really do think it's good (internal).

Three-dimensional model: Weiner (1980) and Abrahamson, Seligman and Teasdale (1978)

Weiner's three-dimensions of attribution are:

1. **Locus**   External   or   Internal
2. **Stability**   Stable   or   Unstable
3. **Controllability** Controllable   or   Uncontrollable

From this we can generate a series of attributions about being late:

L	S	C	Examples
E	S	C	It always takes me a long time to walk to school.
E	S	U	There is always a lot of traffic on the way to school.
E	U	C	There was something interesting on the breakfast news.
E	U	U	I was unlucky today, sometimes I slip in without being noticed.
I	S	C	I always forget to set the alarm clock.
I	S	U	I'm just a born latecomer.
I	U	C	If I feel hungry I have breakfast.
I	U	U	I was in a dream on the way to school and forgot the time.

Seligman's model of attributional style in the case of depressives puts global/specific in place of Weiner's third dimension. Seligman developed a useful questionnaire to assess attributional style.

Brown (1986) refers to such models as a 'causal calculus', a similar idea to Kelley's 'causal shorthand'. A calculus is a systematic method of reasoning, the causal calculus is intuitive in social perception, and Brown's model is drawn from all the theorists mentioned here. In its most reduced form it looks like this:

Type of attribution	Consensus	Distinctiveness	Consistency
Actor–stable	Low	Low	High
Situation–stable	High	High	High
Actor–unstable	Low	Low	Low
Situation–unstable	High	High	Low

Self perception theory: D.J. Bem (1972)

We use the same processes to infer our own motives.

Intrinsic and extrinsic motivation describe behaviour done for its own sake and behaviour motivated by some external reward or gain. Bem explains that we often assume that external factors are the primary force behind our actions. **Greene and Lepper (1974)**

gave some nursery pupils a reward for doing a nice drawing with felt-tip pens; some of the pupils had been told they would be rewarded, others received the reward unexpectedly. When observed later, it was noted that the pupils who had expected the reward were using the pens less than prior to the experiment, indicating that their former intrinsic motivations had been overtaken by extrinsic ones, in other words, the play had become work.

Locus of control: Rotter (1966)

Running through all the theories is the internal/external dimension of causality and the notion of control. The two themes can be integrated using a model of individual differences. Some people believe that behaviour, both theirs and others, is largely under external control, whereas others see themselves as 'in control'. For example, **Phares and Wilson (1972)** found that 'internals' saw the driver of a car as more responsible for an accident than 'externals'did. This aspect of control has many practical applications, and is discussed further in applications of attribution theory.

ATTRIBUTIONAL BIAS

A bias is a prejudice, a systematic factor which produces mistakes. When making attributions, people have certain biases in common:

1. **Self-serving bias.** We tend to take credit for our successes and disassociate with our failures, blaming external factors. The saying 'a bad workman blames his tools' encapsulates this idea. What does it achieve?:
   - protects self-esteem,
   - protects peer-group esteem, helps maintain respect of others,
   - gives us a sense of our own predictability and control over our actions.

   Jones et al. (1968) arranged for subjects to teach arithmetic to two pupils, followed by a test where pupil 1 reportedly did well and pupil 2, poorly. After further instruction and another test, subjects were told that pupil 2 had either done badly again or improved. When asked to account for this, subjects attributed performance to themselves in the case of improvement, but attributed it to the pupil if the pupil had continued to do poorly.

2. **Ingroup bias.** Attributions tend to enhance the status of the ingroup as a part of in- and outgroup processes. **Duncan (1976)** showed white subjects a video of a white or black person violently pushing another in the course of a heated conversation. When asked to explain the behaviour, they made internal attributions ('violent personality') when the pusher was black and external ones for the white aggressor ('he was provoked').

3. **Fundamental attribution error.** The overemphasis on dispositional rather than situational factors. **Ross et al. (1977)** gave subjects the role of questioner or answerer. The questioner had to make up some general knowledge questions. Another group of subjects rated the general knowledge of the first pair. They rated the questioner as being superior, ignoring the situational factors, which had given more power to the questioner.

4. **Actor/observer divergence.** There is a tendency for the actor to attribute cause to situational factors, whereas observers tend to attribute the same actions to disposition. This can be related to self-serving bias and the fundamental attribution error. **Nisbett et al. (1973)** asked subjects to explain, for themselves and a friend, the reasons for selecting a particular course of study. Their self-attributions included factors such as what the course has to offer (situational), whereas attributions about others was related to personality factors (disposition). They also asked subjects to predict future behaviour of a subject on the basis of an observed response to help with a social services task. In others, they made predictions which implied cross-situational consistency, whereas for themselves they made no such assumptions.

5. **Defensive attribution.** The greater the consequences of an action, the more attributions will be dispositional rather than situational. **Walster (1966)** described a car accident and asked subjects to assess the responsibility of the car's owner, Lennie. The more serious the consequences of the accident, the more responsibility Lennie was assigned.

The term 'defensive' refers to our inherent fear that 'it could happen to me' and therefore we must have some rational explanation as to why it won't. **Lerner's (1980) 'just-world-hypothesis'** explains our initial reaction to a disaster as a means of reducing our own anxieties, the greater the disaster, the greater our anxiety and therefore the more we want to find a scapegoat. In the tragic case of James Bulger (the toddler who was taken from a shopping centre and murdered) many people blamed his mother for carelessness, but this may be a mechanism to make us feel safer.

6 **Perceptual salience.** We tend to be selective about what we perceive, along the lines of our expectations. This has been used to explain the outcome of some of the studies mentioned above. For example, the reason subjects failed to attribute success 'correctly' in **Ross et al.'s** experiment could be because they had overlooked the advantage enjoyed by the questioners. If situational factors are made more salient (prominent), does the fundamental attribution error occur? **Quattrone (1982)** produced 'free-choice' essays, which were for or against nuclear power. Subjects were given ratings of the authors' attitudes and asked to assess how much the authors might have been influenced by the situation. The answer should have been 'not at all' because they were given free-choice. However, subjects had been given a document about experimenter bias to read before the experiment, and therefore might have thought that the experimenter had unwittingly influenced the position taken by the essay's author. The outcome was that the fundamental attribution bias was *reversed*, subjects preferred the situational explanation because the situation had been made more salient. Quattrone pointed out that we normally see people rather than situations as more salient, and that is why we appear to prefer dispositional explanations; he called this a *'fundamental delusion'*.

APPLICATIONS OF ATTRIBUTION THEORY

Attribution theory has found a wealth of practical applications derived from empirical studies showing how learning to make more appropriate attributions can overcome problems such as poor health, failure at a task, insomnia, depression and addiction. Such a process has been termed **'attribution retraining'** and places emphasis on developing an attributional style involving internal control.

1 **Health.** The ethos of self-help groups is to take control. **Wallston and Wallston (1978)** found that patients who believe that they, rather than doctors or other health professionals, are in control, tend to cope better with chronic illnesses such as diabetes.

2 **Failure. Diener and Dweck (1980)** categorised children as helpless or mastery-oriented, and gave them eight solvable puzzles (success) followed by four insoluble ones (failure). Helpless children attributed failure to themselves and saw it as unsurmountable, they saw success as unrelated to ability. **Dweck (1975)** retrained 12 children who showed extreme difficulty with failure to attribute it to lack of effort rather than lack of ability. Over a period of a month one group were told they were taking too long and should have tried harder, while a second group were given only reports of success (positive feedback). At the end of the month the first group showed greater persistence and attributed any failures to lack of effort, the second group were more likely to give up.

3 **Insomnia. Storms and Nisbett (1970)** retrained insomniacs who often misattribute sleep problems to feeling aroused (awake) – the more you can't sleep the more aroused you feel. They gave them a pill (placebo), telling group 1 it would relax them, and group 2 that it would arouse them. Group 1 continued to have difficulty sleeping, presumably because they expected to feel relaxed and therefore still attributed arousal to insomnia. The other group were able to attribute arousal to the pill and therefore disbelieved their insomnia and slept better.

4 **Depression. Seligman** reformulated his theory of learned helplessness to incorporate attribution theory. (**Abrahamson, Seligman and Teasdale, 1978**). Learned helplessness is a response to failure or stress. When an individual experiences lack of control over the stressor, they learn to respond to the stressor with apathy and inaction. Seligman proposed that the key factor in learned helplessness and depression was the person attributing failure to themselves (internal) rather than to external factors, and seeing these attributions as unchanging (stable) and global rather than specific.

5. **Addiction.** Addicts typically see their behaviour as being governed by physical craving and beyond their voluntary control. Psychologists have described addiction either in terms of a chemical dependency (but psychopharmacologists have yet to explain exactly why alcohol and nicotine are addictive) or in terms of conditioning. A more cognitive approach has been to point to the success that some people have in giving up drugs, even without professional help. A good example comes from **Robins *et al.* (1974)** of American servicemen returning from Vietnam, where opium was commonly used – a year later only 7% were still addicted. It is possible that their addiction was associated with environmental cues (external attributions) and, having left these behind, they were able to give up. Studies which show high relapse rates for alcoholics and smokers treated in clinics would support such a view.

6. **Paranormal phenomenon.** Some people prefer to attribute coincidental events to a paranormal cause rather than accepting chance as the explanation. This distinguishes between believers and non-believers.

2.3 ATTITUDES AND ATTITUDE CHANGE

An attitude is a 'posture or position'. There are a number of specialist meanings. For painters and sculptors it is a pose which reveals certain human emotions, in a mathematical sense it is 'an angle made relative to horizontal plane' and in a medical sense it is used to describe body posture and limb position.

Psychologists extended the use of the word to take on an explanatory rather than a simply descriptive meaning, which incorporates the following aspects:

- generally or entirely learned,
- relatively permanent,
- concerned with affect or feeling,
- governed by consistency,
- determines behaviour.

Importance

Allport (1935) felt the concept of attitude was 'the most distinctive and indispensable concept in social psychology'. Its importance lies in the degree to which it can predict or explain behaviour, particularly for the processes of impression formation and attribution of cause. It has many practical applications in opinion polls, advertising, market research and the reduction of prejudice.

The structural approach

Attitudes are generally held to have three components:

1. an **affective** aspect of liking/disliking, based on
2. beliefs (**cognitions**) about an object, which
3. leads to a readiness to **behave** in a certain way (the **conative** component).

The functional approach

Attitudes are essential for the well-being of an individual and serve four functions:

1. **Adaptive.** Helps us avoid unpleasant things and seek out favourable ones, also important in identifying with people or groups,

❷ **Knowledge**. Part of our knowledge of the social world, and an integral component of the stereotypes which help us simplify our social perceptions.

❸ **Self-expressive**. A means of expressing our emotions.

❹ **Ego-defensive**. Protect the ego by promoting a positive self-image through positive self-attitudes. Also by projecting feelings of threat or conflict onto others, as in the case of prejudice.

Descriptions of attitude change should incorporate the function that the attitude serves. For example, new information may alter an attitude serving a knowledge function but not one that is ego-defensive.

DEVELOPMENT OF ATTITUDES

❶ **Indirect or direct**. We learn what we *should* like or dislike, and/or we learn what we *do* like or dislike.

❷ **Instinctive**. The nature/nurture question is fairly clear. Attitudes are almost entirely learned but it is possible that some attitudes, such as fear of snakes, are innate. Also, in the sense that some aspects of our personalities, such as optimism or neuroticism, are genetically determined, we do inherit certain inclinations or attitudes.

❸ **Familiarity**. The evidence suggests that if people encounter an object frequently enough they generally form a positive attitude towards it. Politicians and advertisers put this to good use. **Zajonc (1968)** repeated nonsense words such as 'iktitaf' 5, 10 or 25 times. The more frequently a subject heard a word, the more positive their later response. **Cross *et al.* (1967)** played Mozart to rats when they were young. The rats later showed a preference for Mozart over Schonberg. **Mita *et al.* (1977)** showed subjects two self-portraits. The preferred photograph was the mirror image, presumably because it's the view of ourselves we most often see.

❹ **Classical conditioning**. A social or physical object (conditioned stimulus, CS) becomes associated with pleasant or unpleasant feelings (unconditioned response, UR). Advertisers typically pair attractive people (unconditioned stimulus) with their product (CS) to produce a positive response (UR) to the product. **Staats and Staats (1958)** demonstrated this by pairing nonsense words ('yof' or 'wuh') with positive words (gift, sacred, happy) or negative words (bitter, ugly, failure) and testing subjects' evaluative reactions.

❺ **Operant conditioning**. When a reward immediately follows a behaviour, that behaviour tends to occur more frequently in the future. **Insko (1965)** telephoned students and asked them a series of questions about Aloha week at the University of Hawaii. Half of the subjects were reinforced with 'good' every time they said anything favourable about the week. When tested a week later in a different context they showed more positive attitudes than those who had been negatively reinforced. It may be that such reinforcement is only effective with clearly existing attitudes and that operant conditioning serves to strengthen those attitudes.

❻ **Socialisation**. Attitudes are learned from significant others, in the same way that we learn social norms, language and cultural values. This may involve **explicit instruction** from teachers or parents about what things are good or bad. Or it may come through **social learning**, when we observe and imitate attitudes expressed by social models. There are similarities with conditioning, but reinforcement is vicarious. We imitate those behaviours which are seen to have positive consequences. A study by **Bandura and McDonald (1953)** suggests that imitation is more powerful than reinforcement. Children were told pairs of stories, one where a selfish act caused minimal damage and another where an unselfish act ended in considerable damage, and asked to say which was naughtier. Later those children who observed adults expressing contrary attitudes were seen to shift their stance, whereas others who were reinforced for expressing different attitudes didn't change as much.

Television presents people or ethnic groups in stereotyped ways which influences our attitudes, particularly where we have little personal experience of such people. In the past this may have had negative effects, more recently there have been deliberate attempts to show minority groups in strong and professional roles.

7 **Intergroup attitudes**. In the case of prejudice, certain attitudes are formed between groups as a means of defining oneself and one's group. They are also an ego-defence for the social group as a whole, to counteract the threats posed to the status quo.

8 **Personal reflection and decision**. Some attitudes, particularly 'higher' ones, result from reasoned thinking and empirical discoveries.

ATTITUDES AND BEHAVIOUR

'Without guiding attitudes the individual is confused and baffled' (G. Allport). However, there is evidence that behaviour cannot be so simply predicted from attitudes, which questions the usefulness of the concept of attitudes (see moral inconsistency 3.3).

The first suggestion that attitudes may not correspond with behaviour was presented by **LaPiere (1934)**. He travelled around the States for two years with a Chinese couple and noted that only once were they refused service by hoteliers. However, 92% of the same hoteliers claimed in response to a postal questionnaire that they did not serve Chinese. Critics have suggested that the fact that LaPiere was white and the Chinese couple were 'Americanised' may have affected the hoteliers' reactions.

DeFleur and Westie (1958) asked white students to be photographed with black colleagues. Thirty per cent of the students behaved differently from their previously expressed views (either they were prejudiced and agreed to be photographed or were unprejudiced but refused to be photographed).

What factors might lead to such a discrepancy?

1 **Availability**. If someone orders a meal that sounds good, you temporarily 'forget' your own favourite. Or it may be that there is a conflict of priorities. At any time your behaviour is a selection between possible courses of actions, and one attitude may take precedence over another. For example, a person may favour nuclear power but object to a nuclear power station being cited within view of their house.

2 **Relevance**. 'Funny, she doesn't look Jewish' (from the film *Cabaret*). Our image of a prejudiced group may be different from the reality. In LaPiere's study, the Chinese couple spoke and dressed like Americans and were with an American, therefore they may not have been perceived as Chinese. **Weigel** *et al.* **(1974)** assessed people's attitudes towards the Sierra Club, an organisation in America dedicated to environmental protection. When the same people were later asked to assist the Club, the highest predictor of saying yes was their attitude to the Club, not simply being pro-environment. **Fishbein and Ajzen (1975)** call this 'correspondence', the degree to which an attitude and action focus on identical objects in the same context at the same time. Their **theory of reasoned action** describes how specific and general attitudes differ and contribute separately to behaviour. (This is again discussed in 9.4.)

3 **Situation**. If our personal attitudes run contrary to prevalent social norms we may well follow the crowd. **Minard (1952)** studied prejudiced whites in a West Virginian mining town. In a general survey only 20% admitted to having black friends. However, at the mines, where black and white worked together, 80% expressed friendship towards blacks. This can also be taken as an example of correspondence or relevance.

4 **Personality variables**. Some people may be more or less consistent than others. **Snyder (1979)** found that low self-monitors behaved in consistent ways while high self-monitors are more influenced by the situation, and behaved in ways appropriate to the situation rather than their attitudes. Similarly, **Mischel (1968)** has suggested that personality is a product of the situation rather than internal variables.

5 **Research bias**. Methods of data collection, in particular attitude scales, are influenced by social desirability and response biases, so we can't be certain that the attitudes expressed are the person's real attitudes.

6 **Does behaviour affect attitudes?** We expect to predict behaviour *from* attitudes, but is it also the case that behaviour leads to an attitude? In observing our own behaviour we learn what our attitudes are (see self-perception, 2.1).

ATTITUDE CHANGE

- Attitudes are resistant to change, but they do change.
- Change occurs as a result of internal and external forces.
- Methods of attitude change are of interest commercially (e.g. advertising) and in implementing new social policies (e.g. reduction of prejudice).
- Attitudes can be changed through learning, persuasion or brainwashing.
- Attitudes are organised and changed according to principles of consistency.
- Different attitudes perform different functions, their relative resistance to change may be related to the importance of their function (see 'The functional approach' p.82).
- Consider also social influence (conformity, obedience and compliance) as means of attitude change.

Learning

One force that can change attitudes is learning, as described in the 'Development of Attitudes' on p.83.

Persuasion

Persuasive communications aim to induce a person to adopt a particular set of values. **Hovland, Janis and Kelley (1953)** identified four basic variables in all persuasion situations. Many other studies have contributed features to the original model, as summarised below:

	Source (who)	Message (what)	Receiver (to whom)	Context (where)
Independent variable	credibility expertise intentions motives similarity attractiveness likeability status race religion	fast speech rate confidence rhetorical summary explicit conclusions one-sided messages order of arguments appeals to fear	intelligence personality gender initial attitude persuadability self-esteem	formal vs. informal commitment laboratory vs. real life
Internal effect	attention	comprehension	acceptance	
Attitude change	opinions	perceptions	behaviour	

The illustrative question at the end of the chapter presents specific evidence and arguments.

Socio-cognitive models: predicting compliance

A more recent approach is to describe attitude change in terms of socio–cognitive factors. The **theory of reasoned action** (see p.84) is one example. The **health belief model** is another (see 9.4). Its central concern is to predict whether a person will take advice about preventive health behaviours, e.g. breast self-examination or decreasing HIV risks. The important factors which determine behaviour are: personal variables, perceived benefits (of preventive measures) and perceived threats (of a disease).

Reactance

People have a considerable ability to resist persuasion. One element in this is reactance: attempts to restrict or control personal decisions may lead to a move in the opposite direction. This principle may explain:

- The failure of hard-sell approaches – strong threats may result in negative reactions.
- The availability of a particular opportunity or object is inversely related to its attractiveness. The more someone tries to stop you doing something, the more you want to do it.

Venkatesan (1966) studied conformity and consumer behaviour. Groups of college students were asked to select one of three identical suits. In fact the group consisted of confederates except one member, the true subject, who was the last to register his opinion. In one condition half of the subjects conformed with the majority choice. In another group, each confederate made statements strongly suggesting that suit B was the right choice. In this case subjects did not conform, suggesting that consumers who are forced to conform may react by asserting their independence.

Brainwashing

The term is derived from the Chinese 'hsi nao', to cleanse the mind. It is a systematic attempt to alter a person's ideas and attitudes, a coercive type of persuasion which is usually not permanent, particularly when the source of coercion is removed. Familiar examples include prisoners of war, Patty Hearst, the Moonies and other cult groups. **Schein (1956)** studied Korean POWs, summarising the process as three basic phases:

1. **Unfreeze** or disrupt person's current attitudes and beliefs, through physical deprivation, social isolation and disorientation.

2. **Replace** with new attitudes, using direct and indirect instruction, and by forcing certain behaviours (forced compliance), which starts as outward conformity but leads to corresponding changes in privately held attitudes.

3. **Refreeze** new attitudes by giving rewards, asking for public statements of belief, initiation rites and awarding group membership. The person now identifies with the group.

PRINCIPLES OF CONSISTENCY

The principle of consistency is a basic human drive and can be seen in the process of homeostasis, such as temperature or thirst regulation, and as a means of lending coherence to cognitive structures in personality theory and for attitudes.

Congruity Model – Osgood and Tannenbaum (1955)

Objects (people, countries, ideologies) are placed on a scale, and affective bonds, which express attitudes, are formed between the objects. If two objects become joined by an **associative bond** (Tom likes Mary) they move closer together on the scale, **disassociative bonds** (Mary doesn't like football) cause the objects to move apart. The strongest held attitude changes the least.

Congruence, which is the change in an attitude in the direction of an already held attitude, is maintained by the changing positions of the objects.

Evaluation
Positive:
+ specifically concerned with how attitudes change in response to persuasive communications,
+ makes some useful predictions,
+ has some empirical support.
Negative:
− the model can't cope with multiple bonds,
− a simplistic formulation, imprecise and producing ambiguous predictions.

Balance Model – Heider (1958)

Elements are the objects of attitudes, each is given a sign: +, − or 0. There is equilibrium as long as elements of identical sign are linked by positive (p) or null (0) relations (+p+, −p−, +0+, −0−), or elements of the opposite sign are linked by negative (n) or null relations ($+n-$, $+0-$). The model is very similar to the congruity model except that no numbers are involved, and it extends to three entities: the person (P), another person (O), an object/third person (X). This leads to eight possible states, expressed as triads:

If a state of imbalance occurs:

1 It may lead to changing one or more signs of the elements or the relations between the elements, change taking place according to the principle of **minimum effort.**

2 It can restore balance by **differentiating** between different occurrences of the same element, such as lies and little white lies.

3 Simply don't think about it!

Evaluation

+ gains in flexibility against a loss in precision and power,

− the model doesn't predict which method of resolution will occur in any particular case of disequilibrium,

− doesn't account for degrees of positive or negative feelings,

− doesn't accommodate the eternal triangle, $P + O + X − P$,

− deals only with a maximum of three relations.

Cognitive Dissonance – Festinger (1957)

Dissonance theory is really in a different league from the others, offering a general theory of human social motivation and generating some intriguing predictions and research. **Dissonance** is 'a negative drive state which occurs whenever an individual holds two cognitions (ideas, beliefs, attitudes) which are psychologically inconsistent' **(Festinger, 1957)**. Aside from dissonance, attitudes can be **consonant** or simply **irrelevant** to each other. Situations leading to dissonance include:

1 **Forced-compliance or counter-attitudinal behaviour.** The classic cognitive dissonance experiment, conducted by **Festinger and Carlsmith (1959)**, involved students performing a very boring task (turning pegs in a board). They were then asked to tell another subject who was waiting to do the task that the task was very interesting. Some of the subjects were paid $20 others $1. When finally asked to rate the task the more highly paid subjects rated the task as boring whereas the low paid said it was enjoyable. The high paid have a reason for lying so they experience no dissonance, whereas the low paid have to overcome their dissonance by adjusting their assessment of the task.

2 **Post-decisional dissonance.** The feelings of unease which arise after a person has made a decision. Such dissonance is reduced by enhancing the attractiveness of the elected choice. **Brehm (1956)** asked women to rate various household items in terms of their preferability, and then gave them one of their top two. When the women were asked to rate the items again, the rating for the one they now owned went up and the other went down. This is related to confirmatory bias (as described in 2.1, 'Stereotypes'). People selectively choose information which confirms their attitudes and behaviour. In a survey, **Ehrlich et al. (1957)** found that people actively seek information which supports their behaviour, such as smokers finding evidence favouring smoking or a purchaser seeking more evidence from advertisements to support their choice.

3 **Effort**. Why are initiation rites so common and significant? Dissonance theory predicts that the amount of effort which is put into a task determines the strength of our attitude towards it. **Aronson and Mills (1959)** recruited women to join a discussion group about sex, prior to which they had to be screened. Group A had to read obscene and explicit material to men (severe initiation), group B had a milder passage and C had none at all. The ensuing discussion was deliberately made dull and boring. As predicted group A rated the discussion as most interesting.

④ **Social support.** Another classic study by **Festinger** *et al.* **(1956)** involved infiltrating a group whose leader, Mrs Marion Keech, received messages from outer space predicting the end of the world on a certain date. What would happen to the believers when the world didn't end? Mrs Keech told the assembled followers that their impressive faith had saved the world. The members who were together became even more fervent in their belief, whilst those on their own lapsed, demonstrating the role of social support in resolving dissonance.

The **magnitude of dissonance** depends on:

① The importance of the dissonant element.

② The number of dissonant and consonant elements, the higher the ratio of dissonance to consonance, the greater the dissonance felt.

③ The amount of cognitive overlap. Two events with little in common cause greater dissonance, for example choosing between fishing and the cinema is more dissonant than the cinema and the theatre.

④ The amount of commitment. A publicly announced decision is more likely to arouse dissonance than a private one. Issues of no importance don't arouse dissonance.

⑤ The degree of choice. If an action is forced, the amount of dissonance may be minimised (in the case of forced-compliance studies, the subject is not free to comply).

⑥ Your personality. Anxious people experience greater dissonance and have lower tolerance for it.

Evaluation

+ broad application,
+ novel and counter-intuitive predictions,
+ a great deal of interesting research,
− dissonance can't be measured,
− it is difficult to identify the existence of a psychological state of tension as suggested by dissonance,
− in some experiments subject dropout favoured dissonance,
− the empirical findings can be explained in terms other than dissonance.

Alternative explanations for dissonance experiments

① **D.J.Bem,** in his **self-perception theory,** claimed that dissonance is neither a sufficient (observed behaviour does not imply corresponding privately held attitudes) nor necessary explanation (attribution theory offers situational versus dispositional accounts).

② **Tedeschi** *et al.* **(1971)** argue that people are more concerned with *appearing* consistent than necessarily *being* consistent – the **impression-management hypothesis.**

③ **Self-generated attitude change. Tesser (1978)** describes occasions where a person changes their attitudes through thinking about them, which may occur through exposure to pro- or anti-arguments and experiences.

④ **The Reinforcement or Incentive Theory (Janis** *et al.,* **1965)** holds that the greater the incentive or reward, the greater the attitude change. There are times when this seems to be a better predictor of behaviour than dissonance.

MEASUREMENT OF ATTITUDES

Physiological observations

Hess (1965) found that dilated pupils indicated a positive attitude. The **lie detector** or polygraph uses changes in GSR (galvanic skin response) as a means of measuring stress; it can also serve as a deterrent to lying as demonstrated by the **bogus pipeline technique (Jones and Sigall, 1971).** If subjects are connected to a machine that they *think* is a pipeline to their innermost thoughts and feelings, they tend to make certain that their public statements do correspond to their private attitudes. However, not all studies have found this method to be effective.

Observed behaviour

For example, attitudes towards religion could be measured in terms of number of people who attend church.

The **wrong number technique** is an interesting way of randomly and indirectly assessing attitudes. For example, **Gaertner and Bickman (1971)** tested attitudes to race by making a phone call, ostensibly to a garage and then saying they had got a wrong number but could the speaker call the garage for them. They communicated race through accent and waited to see how many people rang the garage.

Using **stooges** (or confederates) to test attitudes, as in LaPiere's study, is common. For example, a study investigating racial prejudice in Bristol involved two men, one black and one white, trying to get accommodation.

The study by **Fidell (1970)**, see 2.1, tested attitudes to women using false job applications. **Stanton and Litwak (1955)** found that evaluating the attitudes of future foster parents through role play was more successful than interview techniques.

Opinion polls

A poll is a survey of opinions, usually involving a small number of questions. One of the chief concerns for pollsters is sampling techniques (see 10.2) since the attitudes of a large number of people are inferred from a highly selected sample.

Attitude scales

1. **Likert Scale (1932).** This is probably the most widely used attitude scale, typically a set of about 30 statements are prepared about a topic, representing both pro and anti views. The subject rates each statement on a 5- or 7-point scale:

strongly agree	agree	undecided	disagree	strongly disagree
1	2	3	4	5

The attitude is scored by summing the scores from each statement.

2. **Thurstone Scale (1931).** A list of statements is prepared and rated by judges in terms of how favourable or unfavourable they are with respect to the chosen topic. Each statement is then assigned a mean value to reflect its status and a selection of statements chosen which represent pro- and anti- positions. Subjects then indicate which statements they agree with and a score is calculated from the value assigned to their selected statements (see 10.1 for construction of a Thurstone scale).

3. **Semantic Differential Technique (Osgood, Suci and Tannenbaum, 1957).** A measure of the affective component can be obtained by rating the connotative meaning of words. A list of at least nine bi-polar adjectives are selected to include words representative of each of the three factors or dimensions of the attitude object. For example, rating the connotative meaning of the word 'pornography':

FACTORS		BI-POLAR ADJECTIVES							
evaluative:	good	+3	+2	+1	0	−1	−2	−3	bad
potency:	strong	+3	+2	+1	0	−1	−2	−3	weak
activity:	active	+3	+2	+1	0	−1	−2	−3	passive

Subjects are asked to indicate which value represents for them the meaning of the word in terms of the adjectives presented. The final score is a total of these values.

4. **Social Distance Scale (Bogardus, 1925).** Attitudes are inferred from the intentions or actions of the subject. The subject indicates the degree of intimacy which would be acceptable with the target person. For example: 'Would you marry one?' 'Would you live next door to one?' Each question has a numerical value assigned and the sum of these will indicate the attitude.

5. **Sociometry (Moreno, 1953).** This is used to express the feelings of liking which exist within a group of people. Members are asked questions like 'Who would you like to sit next to?' or 'Who would you like to go on holiday with?' The results are plotted to show reciprocal or one-way preferences and illustrate the popular and peripheral members of the group.

⑥ **Projective techniques,** such as the Rorschach or Thematic Apperception Tests can be used to express attitudes as well as their more common application in personality measurement.

Advantages and disadvantages

Direct measures (physical and behavioural observations)
+ not influenced by social desirability (response) bias,
+ attitudes are inferred which could provide a better indication of 'true' attitudes,
+ attitudes may be situation-specific so are best tested in particular situations,
+ subject is not aware of being 'measured' and therefore not affected by experimental biases,
− attitudes are inferred, based on the assumption that behaviour and attitudes are consistent,
− observed behaviours could be due to extraneous variables,
− such measures are not as reliable,
− can't assign a numerical value to an attitude.

Likert and Thurstone scales
+ provide a numerical value for an attitude,
+ measure cognitive component of attitudes,
+ ordinal rather than interval scales,
− subjects with the same score could have selected a different set of statements and therefore actually have quite different attitudes,
− Likert is simpler to create,
− for the Thurstone scale, it is unlikely that judges can be truly objective in their initial ratings,
− both are subject to response bias and lying.

Semantic Differential Technique
+ measure of affective component,
+ easy to construct and use,
− very subjective,
− prone to response bias, a subject may have a preference for the extremes.

Social Distance Scale
+ a measure of the behavioural component,
+ a simple tool,
− limited in application, used mainly for studies of prejudice,
− questions often negatively perceived by subjects.

2.4 INTERPERSONAL ATTRACTION

We interact with people all the time, some become friends, some friendships deepen to love. At whatever level, interpersonal contacts are amongst the most important things in our lives. Can psychology offer any insights?

AFFILIATION

To affiliate is to become closely connected to, to associate, co-operate, offer companionship or love. Affiliation serves many functions:

① **A basic human need.** The 'herd' instinct is biologically necessary for reproduction (see 8.4). This is not true for all animals, but humans are gregarious by nature. The effects of physical deprivation were shown in a study by **Bexton *et al.* (1954).**

Subjects were placed in a carpeted room with no furniture or window, they wore frosted glasses, ear muffs and mittens. Most lasted less than 24 hours, the maximum was 3 days. They experienced hallucinations, confusion of thought and transient psychosis. The nervous system requires stimulation, without it, it makes up its own. **Schachter (1959)** found quite similar effects when subjects were deprived of social stimulation alone, they were given plenty to do and their senses were not limited. Nevertheless most subjects lasted less than 2 days and were withdrawn, apathetic and showed some schizophrenic reactions; they reported that they thought and dreamt about other people. **Newcomb (1990)** suggested that this basic human need arises in early attachment in infancy.

2 **Social comparison.** Affiliation with similar others increases our confidence and self-esteem, it confirms the correctness of our personal constructs (see 'Development of the self', 3.4). Such social interactions also provide feedback about one's competence and worth.

3 **Uncertainty and fear. Schachter (1959)** told subjects that the electric shocks they were about to receive would either be painful or would merely tickle. They were given the choice of waiting on their own or with others, the group expecting a painful shock chose to affiliate more than those not in a fear situation. **Kamarck et al. (1990)** found lower cardiovascular response to a psychologically stressful task when subjects were with a friend.

4 **Individual differences.** In a variation of the Schachter (see 7.5) experiment **Sarnoff and Zimbardo (1961)** found that highly anxious people preferred to wait alone. Another personality variable is shyness. Shy people lack the social skills necessary to cope with social interaction and become anxious, but this doesn't mean they lack the desire to affiliate. We are all familiar with 'joiners' – people who like to belong. These people have a high need to affiliate, often abbreviated as *n*Affiliation. Many studies have looked at aspects of these need, finding that those high in *n*Affiliation also:

- watch other people more closely,
- are better liked,
- have high levels of anxiety in social settings,
- avoid making offensive comments,
- fear rejection,
- are concerned with establishing and maintaining friendships,
- they also probably study Psychology!

INITIAL ATTRACTION: FORMATION OF RELATIONSHIPS

Why do some people and not others become friends, and more? The factors suggested below may do little more than account for *initial* attraction. **Kerckhoff and Davis (1962)** used the term 'filter' to describe how superficial characteristics are used initially in selecting friends, other factors assume greater importance later. Though liking, like all attitudes, is resistant to change.

1 **Physical attractiveness.** There are some culturally agreed ideals of beauty but interpersonal attraction may be determined by the **matching hypothesis**. We perceive attractiveness in terms of its correspondence with our own. Possible explanations could be:

- consistency – matching attractiveness maintains a balance,
- it may simply be fear of rejection – 'someone that attractive won't like me'.

Murstein (1972) asked dating couples to rate themselves in terms of attractiveness, and asked independent judges to rate the pairs, and also to rate random pairings. He found that real pairs were more similar than random pairs. **Silverman (1971)**, in a field study, observed couples and rated their attractiveness. He confirmed Murstein's findings and noting that, the greater the degree of physical attractiveness, the more physical intimacy was displayed.

The matching hypothesis was not supported by the classic study by **Walster et al. (1966)**, who arranged a computer dance for 376 male and female students. Prior to the dance they were all asked to fill in a personality questionnaire, ostensibly for use in pairing, in fact the pairing was done randomly and the questionnaire used to provide data about similarity. Independent judges assessed attractiveness. Later subjects were asked to rate their date. Physical attractiveness proved to be the most important factor in liking, above such qualities as intelligence and personality. It was also the best predictor of the likelihood that they would see each other again.

The alternative position – that we choose friends and lovers who *are* physically attractive – is supported by studies of the effects of physical attraction (see 2.1). The **halo effect** may mean that physically attractive people are seen to possess a wealth of other positive characteristics making them more appealing.

2 **Proximity**. Closeness can be determined by actual physical distance (propinquity) or functional distance. **Festinger *et al.* (1950)** looked at residents' position in a U-shaped housing block as a determinant of the number of friendships they had, people living facing inwards had on average twice as many friends as those living on the outward side. **Clarke (1952)** found that 50% of the people living in Columbus, Ohio married people who lived within walking distance of their house. **Segal's (1974)** study of police cadets seated alphabetically, found that surname (because of the alphabetical seating) was a better predictor of friendship than religion, age, education or hobbies.

In the section on attitudes we saw evidence that familiarity (functional distance) can increase liking, physical proximity leads to increased familiarity and we tend to prefer things we know. **Saegart *et al.* (1973)** gave subjects the task of rating the tastes of various drinks, during which they came into contact with a stooge 1, 2, 5 or 10 times. At the end their rating of the person was related to the frequency of meeting (see also **Zajonc, 1968** in 2.3).

3 **Reciprocity**. Knowing that someone likes you enables you to reciprocate such feeling. **Backman and Secord (1959)** arranged group discussions, informing subjects beforehand that certain group members would like them very much. During initial meetings this was a good predictor of liking, after six meetings subjects preferred those subjects who expressed reciprocal feelings. This may be an example of initial 'filtering'.

Reciprocal liking may depend on a third dimension – esteem – though the relationship is a complex one. **Deutsch and Solomon (1959)** found that female telephone operators rated a colleague more favourably when that person's rating (esteem) of their performance was most similar to their own. **Hewitt (1972)** found that we like those who evaluate us positively, but only if it is deserved; otherwise it is seen as unfounded flattery (the **ingratiation effect**) and results in decreased liking. The opposite (the **extra credit effect**) occurs when we receive deserved criticism. We admire the honesty and our liking increases. A similar effect was produced by **Aronson and Linder (1965)** exposing subjects to a confederate who made either all favourable or unfavourable comments or varied them. Subjects expressed greater liking for the confederate who started out critically and became nicer.

4 **Similarity and/or capability**. **Byrne and Nelson (1965)** found a significant linear relationship between attraction and similar attitudes when subjects rated people on the basis of seeing their responses to an attitude questionnaire. **Catell and Nesselrode (1967)** found that stable marriages were likely to be between people with similar personalities. **Kandel (1978)** surveyed 2000 teenagers and found that best friends tended to be similar in terms of age, ethnic group and class at school. This result could also be interpreted as evidence for proximity. There are certain aspects of similarity to consider:
- the *kind* of similarity is more predictive than the *amount* (**Duck, 1973**),
- social comparison is based on similarities, as described above,
- evidence suggests that similarity may be more important initially, whereas complementarity is more significant later.

5 **Complementarity**. Do opposites attract each other? Some people seek a partner who fills in the gaps in their own personality or complements their personality, as in the case of dominant and submissive partners. This may be useful in avoiding stormy relationships.

6 **Perceived competence**. People who are capable, intelligent and knowledgeable appear more attractive. This may be due to the operation of a **halo effect,** they are endowed with other favourable characteristics as well. **Aronson *et al.* (1966)** coined the term **'pratfall effect'** to describe the outcome of their 'College Bowl' quiz.

Subjects were asked to rate the attractiveness of contestants, the most attractive was the intelligent but clumsy one.

7️⃣ **Skill at communicating.** All of the above depends on individual abilities to code and decode non-verbal messages, something children and the mentally ill are not very good at. **Duck (1992)** points out that people who have difficulty making friends and relationships often have difficulties communicating, particularly the basic skill of striking up a conversation.

MAINTENANCE OF RELATIONSHIPS

Once initial selection has taken place, what determines the likelihood of a relationship continuing or deepening? Some of the factors are the same, many of them involve the notion of balance or equal rewards.

1️⃣ **Balance Theory. Newcomb (1971)** reformulated Heider's attitude change theory (see 2.3) to apply to interpersonal attraction. Balance is achieved by liking those who are similar or compatible. We avoid imbalance, which occurs when we like someone who is dissimilar or dislike someone who is similar. **Newcomb (1961)** offered 17 male students rent-free housing. Fifty eight per cent of those who were paired with a similar room-mate formed friendships as opposed to friendships between 25% of those with dissimilar room-mates. **Hill, Rubin and Peplau (1976)** studied 231 couples who dated over a 2-year period. Those who stayed together (55% of them) tended to be more alike in terms of age, intelligence, education and other career plans; those who separated often explained this in terms of attitude differences.

2️⃣ **Equity Theory. Hatfield and Traupmann (1981)**; and **Walster et al. (1978)**, suggest that people are selfish and act to achieve the maximum reward from another at a minimum cost to themselves. Both partners should be rewarded in equal measure. A stable or equitable relationship is one where each partner feels that he/she is getting what they deserve. The matching hypothesis is an example of this. Empirical studies have yielded mixed support at best. It may be that physical attractiveness is not matched but that balance is maintained by other positive aspects of a person's character, such as money or status.

3️⃣ **Social Exchange Theory.** Really a special case of the more general Equity Theory. **Thibaut and Kelley (1959); Huesmann and Levinger (1976)** described relationships as an exchange of costs and rewards. You can predict the satisfaction felt (profit) in a relationship by looking at:
- how much reward a person gains,
- at how much cost,
- the ratio between actual rewards and expected rewards (the **comparison level**),
- the alternative – a relationship will end or diminish if a better alternative exists.

  The theory is an interesting if mechanistic attempt to quantify attraction, but in reality it is difficult to define rewards or costs precisely for any individual. In addition, it is clear that attraction is determined by more than personal satisfaction, social norms for example can be important.

4️⃣ **Theory of Complementary Needs. Winch (1958)** looked at long-term relationships and found many where a complementary relationship existed. It seems to be more important in long-term relationships than as an initial factor.

5️⃣ **Byrne–Clore Reinforcement–Affect Model (1970).** We learn to associate positive feelings (affect) with people or situations which reward us (reinforcement). Therefore our liking for someone may be due not to their personal attributes but to the fact that we associate them with positive feelings. Similarity also reinforces and confirms our own attitudes, and thus reduces uncertainty. **Veitch and Griffith (1976)** placed subjects in a waiting room where they listened to either good or bad news with a stranger present. When they were asked to rate the stranger the degree of liking they expressed was related to the kind of news they had been listening to. **Walster (1965)** found the same effect when subjects were given false feedback on test performance. Good results lead to positive rating of the stranger. **Rabbie and Horwitz (1960)** found that strangers expressed greater liking for each other when they were successful in a game-like task than when they were unsuccessful. **Duck**

(1992) criticises these bogus stranger methods for being laboratory based, though notes that Byrne also found evidence for similarity and liking in the real world. For example, bank managers giving loans to people with similar attitudes, jurors being more lenient with defendants with similar attitudes.

6 **Self-Disclosure.** Mutual self-disclosure is the very stuff of which relationships are made, by sharing information about yourself you are showing someone that you trust them and are prepared to risk such exposure. Friendships acquire depth through progressively sharing more intimate secrets, unless the friend 'matches' such behaviour the disclosure will stop. Women are more likely to disclose than men.

Certain characteristics distinguish between casual acquaintances and friends, such as enjoyment, trust, mutual assistance, respect, understanding and intimacy. **Argyle and Henderson (1984)** gathered 43 friendship rules from their subjects. They concluded that there are 'general rules' to distinguish friendship from other relationships and 'quality rules' to distinguish between ordinary and high-quality friendship.

7 **Relationships as daily routines: Duck (1992)** suggests that many of the above theories make a wrong assumption about conscious or even unconscious levels of rewards or reinforcement. Instead, he suggests that relationships are buried in daily routines, and offer comfortable predictability; the disruptive nature of the breakdown of a relationship is due to the key role it plays in daily routine. Other relationships are of a perpetual but dormant kind; once the bond is established they run with little maintenance, such as distant friends or parent-child relationships which continue with only occasional contact.

Duck and Pond (sic) (1989) noted that the key factor about such routines is the way that the partners talk to one another in and about their interactions; relationships are not a string of routines but the cognitions which surround them.

BREAKDOWN OF RELATIONSHIPS

Why do relationships break down?

1 Unstable relationships. Couples who are young, from lower socio-economic backgrounds, or from broken homes.

2 Dissonant relationships, e.g. different religious backgrounds or race.

3 Lack of social skills – partners misreading non-verbal messages.

4 Rule-breaking. Initial expectations of the relationship are embodied in 'rules', which may later be disregarded, particularly the rules related to intimacy and support.

5 Inequity. The balance of costs and rewards changes, negative feelings outweigh positive ones.

6 Deception. The betrayal of trust.

7 Boredom. A relationship that is not going anywhere or has run out of mutual interest. Passionate love may have cooled off.

8 Relocation. One partner moves away, so reversing the initial factors of proximity and exposure.

9 Conflict. Too much disagreement or disrespect, though some pairs are locked into a love–hate relationship as in *Who's Afraid of Virginia Woolf?*

10 Change. Partners' interests or attitudes change. Situations change, a better alternative presents itself.

How do relationships break down?

Duck (1982, 1992) has put forward a model of relational dissolution:

1 **Breakdown.** Dissatisfaction with a relationship leads to the point where 'I can't stand this any more'.

2 **Intra-psychic phase.** Brooding focus on the relationship, but this is not openly discussed. The end of the phase is marked by starting to discuss the matter with confidants preparatory to facing your partner. In some cases people leave relationships without facing the partner explicitly, though this is not always possible.

③ **Dyadic phase.** Talk with partner and sort out the future, whether to break up or repair the relationship.

④ **Social phase.** Include others in the debate, enlist support for your 'side'.

⑤ **Grave dressing phase.** Post-mortem on past events for public consumption and private re-adjustment.

In a similar vein, **Baxter (1984)** suggested six phases of (almost military) disengagement: onset of problem, decision to exit, initiation of unilateral disengagement action, initial reaction to the other party, ambivalence and repair scenarios, initiation of bilateral disengagement.

Repair

Duck (1984) also put forward a model of relational repair, allied to the phases of dissolution. At each phase a different strategy of repair is appropriate:

① Correct own behavioural faults or non-verbal behaviour.

② Re-establish liking for partner.

③ Express conflict, clear the air and reformulate rules for a future relationship.

④ Outsiders may help patch things up or encourage separation.

⑤ Decide on a mutually acceptable version of events, and/or attempt to salvage friendship out of the break up.

Duck (1992) identifies the dissolution and repair of relationships as a major aim of future research, for example in relation to the changing of a person's attitudes.

LOVE

How can liking and love be compared?

- Loving, more than liking, offers unconditional positive regard which nurtures the self-esteem.
- 'Mother' love in early life is critical for psychological health (**Bowlby**).
- Adult styles of loving may represent processes similar to attachments formed in infancy (**Hazan and Shaver 1987**).
- Loving is qualitatively more than intense liking (**Rubin**).
- Its importance is shown in the deep physical and psychological pain people experience when such bonds break down through death or separation.
- It offers an escape from the pressures of reality, for adults it is a kind of fantasy world.
- It comes in many different forms: companionate, passionate, romantic, sexual, physical and platonic, and is formed with different people: friends, family and partners.

Lee (1973) suggests there are six kinds of love, which may mix in various ways and may be different forms of the four attachment styles given by Bartholomew overleaf:

① Eros – romantic love.

② Ludus – game-playing love.

③ Storge – friendship love.

④ Pragma – logical, shopping-list love.

⑤ Mania – possessive, dependent love.

⑥ Agape – all-giving, selfless love.

Love, both companionate and passionate

Rubin (1973) suggests that the components are:

① **Attachment,** need for the other's physical presence and emotional support, a non-sexual form of passionate love.

② **Caring,** concern and responsibility for the other, an altruistic form of companionate love.

3 **Intimacy**, self-disclosure and companionship.

Freud saw the origins in the two first love objects: yourself and your prime caregiver (usually mother). Later in life we search for a mother-substitute to give **dependency** love, and look for a reflection of ourselves in others for **narcissistic** love. Men are more likely to seek the former, women the later.

Bartholomew (1990) (following the ideas of Hazan and Shaver, and Ainsworth) produced a scheme of styles of loving, based on the strange situation (see 3.1):

1 Secure attachment – sense of confidence and security.

2 Anxious/ambivalent attachment – lacking confidence and dependent on others.

3 Avoidant – fearful attachment – feel undeserving of love.

4 Avoidant – dismissive attachment – feel no need for the love and support of others, possibly as a defensive response to earlier experience.

The development of a style may be due to the individual's initial attachment experiences or may represent similar processes at work later in life.

What makes passionate love different?

Rubin claimed that passionate love does not necessarily involve physiological arousal. In today's society we find that the borders between sexual and physical affection are blurred. How do you know when a friend of the opposite sex means more than just friendship when he hugs you? When does parental caressing become abuse?

Attribution theory and the **Two-factor theory** or **Theory of the Self-perception of Emotions** predict that passionate love is a label we learn to place on arousal in appropriate situations. **White** *et al.* **(1981)** asked men to run on the spot for either 15 seconds (low arousal) or 120 seconds (high arousal), then showed them a video of a woman they would later be meeting. Where the video was an attractive woman the aroused men expressed stronger feelings than the less aroused, and weaker feelings if the video was of unattractively presented woman. **Dutton and Aron (1974)** interviewed men on a high suspension bridge (high arousal) and found that they showed greater feelings of attraction to the female interviewer than men interviewed in a low arousal situation.

It may be that arousal serves as an initial factor in relationships, like physical attractiveness, but needs other components to become a lasting form of love. Another arousal explanation was proposed by **Kenrick amd Cialdini (1977)** who believe that the reduction of arousal in a passionate relationship leads to positive **reinforcement**.

2.5 PREJUDICE

Prejudice is literally the act of pre-judgement, an attitude held prior to direct experience. The following points are worth consideration:

- Prejudices are generally regarded as negative or hostile, but there are positive prejudices, such as in-group favouritism.
- Prejudices are thought to be unfair, and often are, as they involve a failure to react to a person as an individual, instead seeing them as part of a group.
- They are rarely accurate for an individual, nor for the group as a whole.
- They are typically inflexible and extremely resistant to change, such resistance indicates their importance psychologically.
- They are not wholly rational, though they often contain a kernel of truth, both of which contribute to their resistance to change.
- They can be held about things (e.g. computers), people or groups.
- They are related to stereotypes (see 2.1), and, like stereotypes, are part of the natural processes of categorising, generalising and overgeneralising; stereotypes are less extreme and more likely to be positive, they form a ready basis for prejudices.

- They are simplistic attitudes, in part because they serve an important function as cognitive schemata which simplify our social world.

- As examples of attitudes, albeit an extreme kind, they have cognitive, affective and behavioural components. The behavioural component may not be expressed, it can range from ethnic jokes to genocide, and is called discrimination.

- Discrimination is a further aspect of prejudice. This is the unequal treatment of individuals or groups based on arbitrary characteristics such as race, sex, ethnicity.

- A minority group may not be one that is smaller in terms of the number of individuals in the group; 'minority' is a psychological concept related to power.

- Prejudices are an integral part of intergroup behaviour, as a means of distinguishing in- and out-groups.

- They are an aspect of kin selection (see 8.2).

ORIGINS OF PREJUDICE

Empirical evidence

The following three studies are given as examples of how prejudices may form:

1 **Robbers Cave Experiment (Sherif *et al.*, 1961)** is the classic study of the effects of in- and out-group behaviour. Twenty two white, well-adjusted, middle class, 11-year-old boys were selected to go on a summer camp at Robbers Cave (a place where Jesse James hid away) for three weeks. Parents were informed that the aim of the study was to observe co-operative behaviour.

In **stage 1** the in-group was developed. The boys were divided into two groups of eleven and did not know of the other's existence. They participated in lots of co-operative activities. Each group chose a name – the Rattlers and the Eagles, and were given caps and T-shirts with the name. Each group adopted some set behaviours, for example the Eagles went swimming nude and banished any mention of homesickness.

In **stage 2** an element of competition was introduced. The groups became aware of each other and showed signs of territoriality. This competition was brought out in the open with a grand tournament. After the Rattlers won the first contest the Eagles tore down their flag and burned it. The Eagles won the next match because, they thought, they had prayed for victory. There were constant skirmishes following every match. When the Eagles finally won, the Rattlers stole their medals.

Stage 3 attempted to resolve the conflict through co-operative activity, which, most importantly, involved superordinate goals – goals that could only be achieved if everyone participated. Examples are repairing a failed water supply and pushing the camp bus. By the time they went home all traces of in- and out-group favour and disfavour had disappeared.

The suggestion is that three factors led to the prejudiced behaviour: ethnocentrism, competition and stereotypes.

2 **The minimal group experiment (Tajfel *et al.*, 1971).** Could in-group behaviour be created with no competition? **Task 1** consisted of estimating the number of dots shown on a screen for a fraction of a second. The subjects were schoolboys. They were given false feedback about whether they were over- or under-estimators. It was emphasised that neither was preferable. In **Task 2** the boys were divided into two groups according to their initial performance, which was randomly assigned. Each boy had to sit alone and assess the performance of the others on a task, they were only told whether the boy was an over- or under-estimator. They found that such minimal group membership had been sufficient to create in-group favouritism.

3 **Blue or brown eyes are better (Aronson and Osherow, 1980).** Pupils were told by their class teacher that those with brown eyes were 'better' and more intelligent. The teacher backed this up by treating this group of pupils more favourably, for example seating them at the front and giving them extra privileges. In a short time, the blue-eyed children were performing less well, became depressed and had lowered self-esteems. The brown-eyed children's behaviour also changed. They made derogatory statements about the other group and ordered them about. When the teacher said she had lied, that in fact the opposite was true, the behaviour quickly reversed itself.

Explanations

1 **Ethnocentrism** is favouritism of the in-group and out-group disfavour. In-group favouritism is part of a **self-serving bias**, in order to enhance a positive self-image one needs to favour one's own group and disfavour outsiders.

2 The formation of **group identity**, part of our social and personal identity, relies on clearly distinguishing in-and out-group members through language, dress and frequently focusing on common 'enemies'.

3 The simple fact of having **stereotypes** leads to the formation of prejudices, but this would only account for different treatment, not the hatred that is found with prejudiced behaviour.

4 **Competition** for unequally distributed goods or resources, as in the Sherif experiment. However this appears to be a sufficient but not a necessary condition. **Tajfel** found that prejudice could be created without it. A study by **Tyerman and Spencer (1983)**, observing an annual scout camp with conditions fairly similar to the Sherif study, concluded that the presence of competition did not lead to intergroup conflict and hostility.

5 It may be that the empirical evidence is due to **demand characteristics,** in the absence of any other information in-group favouritism had to be produced. Later experiments by **Tajfel** involved telling the subjects that group membership was determined randomly, and even then subjects showed in-group favouritism. But the same may be true of real-life, we often have little other basis for determining our behaviour.

6 It is an example of uncritical conformity, a norm of behaviour in some societies. **Pettigrew (1959)** studied people in the northern and southern United States and attributed the greater incidence of prejudice in the south to the prevalent culture which found it acceptable. **Rogers and Frantz (1962)** found white immigrants to former Rhodesia became more racially prejudiced the longer they stayed there. They were progressively conforming to the dominant cultural norms.

7 It is commonly attributed to various **economic and political factors**. When resources are limited, jobs are scarce or there are conflicts over, for example, territory, prejudice tends to flourish and often the out-group blamed. The Marxist **Exploitation Theory** suggests that the ruling class uses prejudice as a means of maintaining its position and continuing to exploit the under-class.

8 **Frustration** arises from many situations, including economic ones or overcrowding. This in turn may lead to aggression (the frustration–aggression hypothesis, see 2.7) which may be projected onto other, less powerful, people or objects rather than blame ourselves. This scapegoat (and thus, **Scapegoat Theory**) is usually a socially approved group. **Weatherly (1961)** insulted subjects while they completed a questionnaire, and later asked them to describe a series of pictures some of which contained Jewish cues. Those who had shown strong anti-semitic tendencies in a prior questionnaire now showed exaggerated prejudices. Similarly **Miller and Bugelski (1948)** recorded subjects' attitudes towards ethnic minorities, subjected some of them to a mildly frustrating task and re-tested attitudes. Those who had watched a film (no frustration) did not show increases in prejudice unlike the other subjects. **Freud** explained this in terms of 'displacement' – when direct action against a frustrator is not possible, it is redirected through the out-group.

9 Prejudice may be an aspect of personality, as suggested by **Adorno's (1950)** book **The Authoritarian Personality** discussed below.

THE PREJUDICED PERSONALITY

The research conducted by **Adorno** *et al.* **(1950)** grew out of the anti-Semitism of the 1930s and 1940s in Germany and America, and was funded by the American Jewish Society. Adorno developed several scales, the potentiality for Fascism (F) scale being the most important. There was also an anti-Semitism (A-S), ethnocentrism (E), and Political and Economic Conservative (PEC) scale.

It became apparent that certain characteristics **covaried** with a prejudiced-type personality, typically such people:

- Had more favourable impressions of themselves.
- Extended this view to their parents.
- Found ambiguity harder to cope with, had a fixed cognitive style and closed minds.
- Favoured law and order, and traditional morals and customs.
- Were more concerned with status and success than with solidarity and intimacy.
- Were not given to insight or reflection, understanding or psychological interpretations, thus avoiding repressed feelings.
- Will change opinions on say-so of an authority figure rather than rationalising the arguments.

Part of the research involved questions about the person's upbringing and analyses of their personalities, leading to ideas about the conditions which foster such personality development:

- Upbringing – *conditional* love and severe discipline create an insecure adult who respects authority and power.
- One defence against psychological insecurity is to promote the in-group and disfavour the out-group.
- People who find ambiguity hard to cope with search for simplistic interpretations of reality and deny negative feelings in order to maintain consistency.
- A lack of insight or psychological interest is associated with repressed feelings, which in turn are projected onto minority groups.

Evaluation

- + Generally empirical findings have supported the authoritarian-prejudiced type. For example, **Christie and Cook (1958)** reviewed 230 related articles and found general support for the definition of the Authoritarian personality.
- – There have been criticisms of the methodology:
  - the sample comprised white, middle-class, native-born, non-Jewish Americans,
  - much of the data concerning upbringing came from retrospective questioning,
  - the F-scale is worded so that yes answers lead to authoritarian-type answers, i.e. a response set.
- – The study was correlational and therefore causal inferences are unjustified. Other factors, such as little education and low social class, could be more plausible explanations.
- – Personality might account for differences within a population but differences between groups are better accounted for in terms of social norms. These would explain why whole groups of people (such as Nazis or Afrikaners) hold certain prejudices and how these prejudices rise and fall in their popularity.
- – Authoritarianism of the right but not the left was indicated, which suggests bias on the part of the research. Theoretically a dogmatic person could appear at both ends of the political spectrum. **Eysenck (1954)** proposed the radical/conservative and the tough/tender minded dimensions to accommodate the extremes.

MAINTENANCE OF PREJUDICE

1 **Confirmatory bias**. We prefer evidence which confirms rather than disconfirms our beliefs, as shown by **Cohen** (see 2.1 and 2.3).

2 **Self-fulfilling prophecy.** The predictions generated by our prejudices come true because our expectations determine the behaviour of others. This was demonstrated in the study about physical attractiveness by **Snyder** *et al.* (see 2.1) and also in a study of racial prejudice by **Word** *et al.* **(1974)**. White college students interviewed black and white adolescents who had been trained to give the same answers. When interviewing a black candidate the interviewer was more negative, sat further away, displayed signs of nervousness and finished the interview sooner. Later, when interviewers enacted the same behaviours with white untrained adolescents, independent judges assessed the adolescent as less competent, less confident and less

desirable for employees suggesting that the interviewee will live up to, or down to, the interviewer's stereotypic beliefs, thus perpetuating them.

③ **Anchorage in personality.** Any change of attitudes involves some change in your self-image which threatens the coherence/consistency of your personality. Once learned they are maintained by the personal needs that they serve.

④ One response to being prejudiced against is to **promote one's own group identity**. We see this all the time in the behaviour of minority groups – they put greater emphasis on their language (promoting Welsh or Gaelic) or physical characteristics (black is beautiful). Any group member may choose to disassociate from such movements and does so by reducing the display of such characteristics. This does serve to redress the balance. The paradox of group behaviour is seen in the behaviour of minority groups, such as feminists, who form in-groups who denigrate the out-group, although it was such behaviour that had led to the formation of the particular in-group in the first place. The same is true in racial conflict.

REDUCTION OF PREJUDICE

① **Enforced contact.** A well-known study by **Deutsch and Collins (1951)** looked at two multiracial housing projects. On one project or estate where black residents lived in separate buildings, white residents maintained and possibly increased their prejudice. On another estate residents were allocated housing irrespective of race, and attitude surveys showed decreases in racial prejudice. **Bagley and Verma (1979)**, on the other hand, found that contact may in itself be unrelated to prejudice. They showed that levels of prejudice in Holland are lower than in Britain despite the same overall proportions of black and white residents.

② **Legislated desegregation.** The turning point in US segregation came in 1954 when the Supreme Court declared segregation unconstitutional in a case 'Brown *vs.* the Board of Education of Topeka'. Amongst those who testified were a number of social psychologists who argued that equal status would be necessary to eliminate false stereotypes. In theory, direct experience should provide the opportunity for prejudices to be re-evaluated, in practice it did little to change attitudes and in some cases aggravated racial tension.

③ **Co-operation.** Social psychologists also pointed to the effect of co-operation in, for example, Sherif's study. The Texan education authorities asked **Aronson *et al.* (1978)** to investigate methods for decreasing prejudice in schools. The **jigsaw method** which he developed aimed to develop mutual interdependence. A class was divided, irrespective of ethnic origins, into groups who were given a project. Each member of the group had a piece of the 'puzzle' to research and then teach to the other group members for an end-of-project test. The study found enhanced self-esteem, improved academic performance, increased liking of peers and improved ethnic perceptions, but the changes were small. Time spent in the classroom is limited compared with home and cultural influences.

④ **Persuasion.** Advertising has been used to change behaviour such as smoking. In America there have been campaigns to change social attitudes, for example, posters of a hospital nursery with the caption 'We shouldn't infect children with poisonous stereotypes'. More extreme measures were employed by the suffragettes in order to change public opinion about rights for women.

⑤ **Social modelling** is a form of indirect influence. However, there is a chicken and egg problem: attitudes are based on reality, reality is, at least in part, determined by our attitudes. Employers want thin attractive receptionists because we expect a successful firm to have one. **Legislation** was used in America to force all advertisements to represent ethnic majorities and minorities equally. **Television** programmes have recruited women, ethnic and other minority groups to play atypical and prestigious roles in an effort to subtly alter our stereotypes. Reality has changed as well, and led to changing expectations.

⑥ Direct instruction or **education** from parents and school can counter negative attitudes. For example, the **inoculation** approach suggested by **McGuire (1964)** as a defence against persuasion. Children need to be provided with counter-arguments to protect or 'inoculate' them against attitudes and behaviours they may meet later in life. He found this was more effective than just telling them why they shouldn't do something, like smoking. **Bem (1983)** suggested that sexism can be counteracted in children by teaching them that gender is a biological fact and not determined by clothes or toys. She told her son to counter any playground teasing about the slides in his hair with a demonstration of his masculinity, the fact that he had a penis. (One schoolfriend responded by saying 'everybody has a penis, only girls wear slides'.)

7 **Psychotherapeutic techniques** might be used, for example, by bringing repressed feelings to the fore or teaching people to cope better with inconsistency.

8 **Humour** is often seen as a means of perpetuating offensive stereotypes. However, **Saper (1991)** suggests that, in the case of jokes about Jewish American Princesses, such humour may act as a means of defusing antagonisms and frustrations.

Why have such attempts failed?

1 Some aspects of prejudice are probably **impossible to eradicate**, such as lack of equal status, continuing job shortages, fulfilling social and psychological needs. Some of these are basic to human behaviour and therefore immutable, others require massive social changes, which are at best slow. Stereotypes are **resistant to change** often because they contain a **kernel of truth** and form an integral part of one's personal and social identity.

2 Learning about the **particular** does not appear to **generalise** to the group as a whole. **Stouffer et al. (1949)** found that racial prejudice amongst soldiers diminished in battle but did not extend to relations back at base. The survey conducted by **Minard** (see 2.3) had similar findings.

3 **Forced desegregation** may even have an effect **opposite** to that intended. Prejudice may be founded in lack of direct experience, however, this is rarely a sufficient cause for hostile feelings. First-hand knowledge may even increase aggression through resentment. For the minority group, integration may lead to lowered self-esteem because it emphasises their inferior position, thus creating stronger hostilities.

4 It's a **slow process**, and requires attacks at all sources of prejudice.

5 For reasons of history, economics, politics and the roots of prejudice; i.e. the reasons for prejudices in the first place.

ETHNOCENTRISM IN PSYCHOLOGY

Consider the following:

- The psychology we study is inextricably linked with Western ideas and ideals. Our view of behaviour is inevitably blinkered by our historical and cultural vantage point.

- **Nobles (1976)** equates the domination of Western psychology with nineteenth century colonialism. Western conceptions have become the standard by which all peoples are understood and thus psychology is a tool of oppression and domination. He uses one example, the self-concept. The Western world view emphasises individuality, uniqueness, independence, survival of the fittest and control over nature; whereas Africans value commonality, co-operation, similarity, survival of the tribe and one with nature. This latter view leads to an 'extended' sense of self, one which is not limited to the individual but instead is defined in terms of 'we'. Another, more familiar, example is the investigation of black intelligence.

- Not only is psychology limited to a European view, the band of subjects studied is often drawn from a distinct group: white, middle-class and educated, drawn from college populations – either students or, in the case of developmental research, children of college staff.

- Important social policies are often based on psychological research. There are two opposing forces in today's society. On the one hand international fusion: (the multicultural nature of all societies), and on the other, cultural distinctiveness: (the wish for individualistic treatment for persons and groups, for example, nationalists in Wales or Northern Ireland).

2.6 PROSOCIAL BEHAVIOUR

Psychologists are often asked to advise over antisocial behaviour. However, *lack* of prosocial behaviour is equally responsible for some of the problems of today's society. Why do people help in some situations and not others?

- **Altruism** is acting selflessly, with the sole motive of someone else's good, not your own personal satisfaction, and sometimes at considerable personal cost. Common examples might be saving a drowning person or giving a considerable amount to charity.

- **Helping behaviour** is a psychological concept to describe the more commonplace behaviour which requires little or no 'cost' with some 'reward', even if it's only feeling good.

- **Co-operation** is doing something for someone for mutual benefits.

- **Routine courtesies,** such as telling someone they've left their lights on, are also prosocial behaviours.

In 1964 the tragic death of **Kitty Genovese** in New York horrified all Americans and led social psychologists to question bystander apathy. At least 38 people heard her screams, why did they fail to prevent her death? The attack started at 3.15 a.m., the lights went on in nearby apartments, someone shouted, the attacker fled, silence returned and so did the attacker, he stabbed her again and fled. A third time he returned and finally raped and killed her. At 3.50 the police received the first call for help and arrived two minutes later. More recently we have the case of James Bulger, where bystanders observed the young boy being roughly treated yet decided it was not appropriate to interfere.

There is evidence of another sort: the involvement of ordinary people in the French resistance or the Civil Rights movement in America at considerable risk to themselves. Or the anonymous bystander who jumped into the icy waters of the Potomac to help survivors of a plane crash. He drowned after helping many to safety. This reminds us that people can also be extraordinarily altruistic.

CHARACTERISTICS OF THE SITUATION

The bystander effect: empirical data

Latané and Darley (1970) wondered whether the large number of bystanders in the Kitty Genovese case had acted inversely on motivation to help. They performed an experiment where subjects were filling out a bogus questionnaire when the room filled with white smoke. If the subject was alone 75% reported the emergency within 6 minutes. If two other subjects were present this dropped to 12%; subjects persisted with the questionnaire despite rubbing their eyes and choking on the smoke.

A second experiment looked specifically at helping behaviour. The experiment was ostensibly to listen to students discussing their problems over an intercom, without the experimenter listening in. One 'student' admits he is prone to seizures and later complains of feeling unwell and begs for help. Eighty five per cent of subjects who thought they were alone helped before the subject lapsed into silence, compared with 31% who thought they were in a group of listeners. Replications of this study have produced average levels of 75% and 53% respectively.

Help may be more forthcoming when a situation is relatively unambiguous, **Piliavin, Rodin and Piliavin (1969)** conducted the classic field study of helping behaviour on the New York subway. One experimenter would stagger and collapse as the train pulled out of the station. When he carried a cane 95% of passengers offered help with 10 seconds, if he appeared drunk help came in 50% of the trials. The more passengers in the immediate vicinity of the victim, the more likely help would be given. This reversal of the 'diffusion of responsibility' may be because the costs of helping were low and not helping were high; it was also clearly an emergency and less easy to ignore.

Clark and Word (1972) also demonstrated the importance of ambiguity. Subjects were filling out a questionnaire in a lab. A maintenance worker walks through the room with a ladder; next door he can be heard working, then sounds of a crash. Regardless of whether the subject was alone or in a group, 100% helped when the crash was followed by 'Oh my back, I can't move', whereas only 30% helped in the ambiguous situation when nothing was heard after the crash.

Why?

1. **Diffusion of responsibility.** Everyone thinks that someone else in the group may be in a better or more qualified position to help. The psychology of the crowd assists each member in avoiding a sense of responsibility and encourages deindividuation. It is not unknown for a crowd to encourage a suicidal person to jump, rather than offering help. **Mann (1981)** examined such behaviour and found that large crowds of over 300 made this particularly likely. **Latané and Nida (1981)** reviewed 56 studies conducted before the Genovese incident and concluded that it was the presence of others which most commonly inhibited helping. However, even when a subject is alone there is not a 100% rate of helping.

2. **Informational influence.** In ambiguous or novel situations we look to others to tell us what to do. Each non-responding bystander sends the same message to the others, 'It's OK, no action needs to be taken', sometimes called **pluralistic ignorance**.

3. **An emergency situation** requires a person to take immediate, unplanned action. Given time to reflect, other moral and social factors might force certain behaviour, such as the altruistic acts mentioned at the beginning. Emergencies also often begin ambiguously, by the time this is resolved other factors have come into play.

4. **Evaluation apprehension.** The bystander fears that he or she may do something inappropriate or actually wrong, and wants to avoid looking foolish. The larger the audience the more inhibited we feel and the more spontaneity is suppressed.

5. **Confusion of responsibility.** If you help, other bystanders may mistake your involvement for actually being responsible for the victim's suffering or that you are with the victim.

6. **Costs of intervening.** Exchange Theory (see 2.4) predicts that our behaviour will be determined by relative costs and rewards. There may be real costs in terms of physical danger, or long-term matters, such as court appearances, which make people feel that they don't want to get involved.

7. **Being aware** of the emergency. **Darley and Batson (1973)** arranged a lecture on the Good Samaritan, the students had to pass a man lying in a doorway, moaning, as they went to the appropriate room. Some students thought they had to rush because they were late, 45% of them helped compared with 63% of those who had plenty of time. When asked why, some of the 'late' students said they hadn't noticed the man, others thought he might have been drunk and therefore were disinclined to help.

8. **Location.** Urban situations are more impersonal and therefore people are less likely to intervene than in rural ones. The **lost-letter method** was used by **Korte and Kerr (1975)**. They found that 70% of the stamped postcards dropped in small towns around Boston were posted as compared with 61% of those dropped in Boston itself.

CHARACTERISTICS OF THE PARTICIPANTS

1. **Victim's appearance.** Many instances of helping require immediate assessment and therefore it is not surprising that we use superficial clues to enable us to decide on appropriate action. **Piliavin** showed that varying the race (black or white) of the victim, or his attractiveness (presence of an ugly facial birthmark) would alter the likelihood of helping. **Bickman (1974)** left a dime in a telephone box. If the experimenter was dressed in a suit he got the dime back 77% of the time, if he was wearing unkempt work clothes there was a 38% return rate. A study by **Benson** *et al.* **(1976)** has already been mentioned as evidence of how physical attractiveness contributes, even more than race or gender, to the likelihood of helping (see 2.1).

2. **Victim's behaviour.** We may **misattribute** what we observe, for example thinking that the victim is only drunk or that the couple struggling are having an argument.

③ **Bystander's gender.** Piliavin *et al.* **(1969)** found that men are more likely to help than women, but this is probably because women feel more open to attack and also have less confidence in their ability to help where, for example, a car has broken down.

④ **Bystander's race.** Piliavin *et al.* also found more helping between members of the same race.

⑤ **Bystander's personality.** Is there such a thing as a 'helpful person'. **Hartshorne and May's (1928)** classic survey of children indicated that helping behaviour is situationally determined. They found a correlation of only 0.23 between various types of helping. However, some psychologists think there is a trait of altruism, otherwise why doesn't everyone become involved in some voluntary activity for the social good? There are certain characteristics which covary with a tendency to help, for example: empathy, those deeply committed to personal moral standards, self-confidence, those less concerned with their personal safety. Alternatively, altruism may occur in certain groups which have strong prosocial norms.

How to get people to help

Are people more likely to intervene if they know about the psychology of helping behaviour? **Beaman** *et al.* **(1978)** showed a group of students a film about such studies. Two weeks later each was observed in an apparent emergency, 43% offered to help compared with 25% of those who had not seen the film.

Similarly a prompt or model may encourage helping behaviour. **Bryan and Test (1967)** noted how many drivers stopped to help a stranded woman motorist. Fifty eight out of 4000 (1.45%) did when, a short time before, they had witnessed a man changing a wheel while a woman watched; only 35 (0.09%) did when there was no prior model.

The victim can also help. **Cialdini (1985)** remembered his thoughts as he lay by the roadside after a car accident, '"Oh no, it's happening just like the research says. They're all passing by!" I considered it fortunate that, as a social psychologist, I knew exactly what to do. Pulling myself up so I could be seen clearly, I pointed to the driver of one car, "Call the police". To a second and third driver, pointing directly each time, "Pull over, we need help". The results were instantaneous.' His advice was that you must de-victimise yourself.

CO-OPERATION

When a fire breaks out in a cinema, everyone would get out if their behaviour remained orderly. If there is a suggestion that a bank might collapse people do not behave co-operatively, they rush to get their money out, and so it does collapse.

Mintz (1951) sought to demonstrate such panic behaviour in an experimental situation. Subjects were paid to retrieve metal cones from a glass bottle with a narrow neck, the cones were attached to pieces of string, and only one could be pulled out at a time. Panic was created by filling the bottle slowly with water, subjects had to pay a fine if their cone got wet. Even with prior discussion and agreement, cone jams inevitably occurred. In panic we become selfish.

The **Trucking Game**, developed by Deutsch and Krauss (1960) is a game of co-operation and conflict. Players must co-operate over use of a one-way road and gates to avoid deadlock and mutual loss. The **Prisoner's Dilemma (Luce and Raffia, 1957)** has been more thoroughly researched. Two men are arrested by the police, the prosecuting attorney knows that there is not enough evidence to convict the men unless one of them confesses, so he applies psychology and, interviewing each man separately, offers: one year in prison if neither confesses, a severe sentence of 8 years if they both confess but a minimal sentence of 6 months if one confesses and the other doesn't (the other one who doesn't would then get the maximum penalty of 20 years).

Co-operation can be as low as 30%, though certain factors may increase this:

❶ The other player's strategy. One player reflects the strategy of his opponent.

❷ The nature of the rewards. **McClintock and McNeel (1966)** found that higher financial stakes made players more co-operative,

❸ The opportunity to communicate, which can be improved by helping one person see the other's situation. This has practical application in conciliation work.

ALTRUISM

Biological altruism

Sociobiologists have suggested that Darwinian strategies of natural selection which ensure the survival of the species operate at the level of altruism; they apply equally to humans as well as other animals (sociobiology is discussed in Chapter 8).

1 **Kin selection.** People are more altruistic with their kin than non-kin, and even with their race as a whole. At one time it was thought that some altruistic animal behaviour, such as a bird pretending to have a broken wing to attract a predator away from its nest, would lessen survival chances. It may do for the individual, but not for the species as a whole. **Dawkins (1976)** classic book *The Selfish Gene* argued that each individual and its offspring could be seen as a set of genes. Apparent altruism is selflessness for the greater good, an act of selfishness on behalf of your gene pool.

2 **Delayed reciprocal altruism** occurs between members of the same species who are not kin. For example grooming behaviour entails caring for those parts the individual cannot reach themselves. The 'groomer' appears to sustain costs but in fact indirectly contributes to his own survival and reproductive success because others return the favour eventually (reciprocal and delayed). A human example would be trust.

3 **Equity altruism.** Rules which govern the distribution of, for example, food. Such rules are enshrined in dominance order and territoriality.

Psychological altruism

Reinforcement theory is analogous to natural selection, therefore psychological altruism is 'an act that positively reinforces (or rewards) an individual other than the one performing the act at some cost (negative reinforcement) to the individual acting' **(Brown, 1986)**. The best example are the interactions found in intimate relationships. Altruism may also be determined by prevalent social norms and/or a developed sense of morals.

2.7 ANTISOCIAL BEHAVIOUR

Defining aggression causes more problems than one might expect. What is it?
- a first act of hostility or injury,
- **action** is implied, not just thinking about being aggressive,
- **intention** is implied, which is theoretically sound but in practice is not always possible to assess. Often a problem for courts to decide – accidental harm is not aggression, and hostile self-defence is also questionable in law,
- **outcome** is damaging, again not always practical.

Other factors to consider:
- **anger** is not aggression, it is a state of emotional and physiological arousal. Aggression is more destructive, they need not occur together.
- **hostility** is the cognitive component of aggression,
- **violence** is unrestrained, excessive or unjustified force,
- **self-assertiveness** is a form of aggression in pursuit of an objective,
- **instrumental** aggression has an underlying motive, such as fighting for a cause,
- **stages** of aggression are: autonomic arousal, cognitive appraisal, emotional expression,
- aggression can be verbal or physical; criminal, domestic or collective.

NATURE OR NURTURE?

Nature

1 **Psychodynamic perspective. Freud (1920)** argued that aggression is an innate, unconscious drive, a potential for destruction expressed by such behaviours as

rejection and hatred. He called it **Thanatos**, after the Greek God of Death, or the death-wish. In Freud's early work he took the view that aggression was a frustration-induced drive, but the senseless destruction of the First World War led him to shift to a more pessimistic, deterministic view. Like Lorenz, he felt that aggression builds up and then needs to be discharged (called the **'hydraulic' model**), either through destruction or through more socially acceptable forms, such as sport. However, if this was true, it should be possible to find physiological differences before and after aggression. Freud's views on aggression have never had a great impact.

2 **Ethological perspective. Lorenz** based his account on observations of animals in their natural environment, but felt it was equally applicable to man who is governed by the same laws of natural selection. Essentially his view is that aggression is innate and triggered by environmental signals. His conclusions were:

- **Animals are programmed to be aggressive.** Male sticklebacks act aggressively towards other males. If a piece of wood has a spot of red on its underbelly, the marking of a male, the stickleback will attack it. The red spot is an innate trigger, which releases an aggressive response.
- **Aggression is a highly adaptive response.** The strongest, most aggressive animal controls the food, territory and mating, thereby ensuring its own survival. Sociobiologists add that the survival of the gene pool is the paramount test.
- **Aggression is not harmful behaviour.** Otherwise it would disappear through natural selection, but it is necessary to have a form of natural regulation, a trigger to switch it off. In animals the 'loser' signals submission and the aggression stops.
- **The role of ritual.** Actions which are highly stylised, relatively rigid and stereotyped are used to express aggression and, importantly, appeasement. It is possible that violent people are less sensitive to such signals.

Criticisms
- The belief that animals have effective signals to turn aggression off has been challenged by a number of studies. For example **Goodall (1978)** noted that appeasement gestures did not stop fighting amongst a troop of chimpanzees – their behaviour was on a par with murder in humans.
- Parallels between man and animals may be oversimplified, social and learning processes are more prevalent in human behaviour and must be included in any explanation.

3 **Physiological perspective (brain differences).** Most work on the physiological basis of aggression has been done on animals and therefore needs cautious interpretation. Emotion generally is centred on the **limbic system**, which includes the hypothalamus and amygydala. **Bard (1934)** found that if parts of the cortex are removed, cats display 'sham rage', purring and hissing simultaneously, suggesting that the cortex normally inhibits the subcortical limbic system. If parts of the hypothalamus are also removed the sham rage disappears. In higher mammals such behaviours are controlled by the cortex, and therefore much more influenced by experience. Electrical stimulation of monkeys brains produces more socially-mediated aggressive responses such as attacking subordinate males but not females **(Delgado, 1969)**. In humans there is some evidence that limbic tumours are associated with aggressive behaviour. Lobotomies were performed to reduce aggression. However **Siann (1985)** concluded that no physiological system has been found to have an 'invariant' effect on aggressive behaviour (see also 7.5).

4 **Biological perspective (hormones and genes).** It is sometimes suggested that the reason males are more aggressive than females is because male hormones create aggression. However, **Floody (1968)** reviewed many studies of female behaviour and found significantly higher rates of irritability, hostility, child abuse, crime and other symptoms of aggression when women are in their premenstrual phase. The hormonal changes may promote a change in behaviour in readiness for parenthood; mothers need to be aggressive.

A **genetic link** was proposed by **Jacobs *et al.* (1965)**, who provoked great interest with the suggestion that men in prison had a higher incidence of XYY chromosomes, which would predispose them to behave violently. Later studies have not supported this.

Gender is largely determined by socialisation processes so sex differences to aggression are more likely to be due to environmental factors.

⑤ **The aggressive personality.** Personality is also largely a function of experience. There may be exceptional cases of criminal insanity which lead to inexplicable, random violence.

Nurture

① **Motivational perspective:** the **frustration–aggression hypothesis (Dollard** *et al.* **1939)**. This hypothesis states that frustration always leads to some form of aggression, and aggression is always the result of frustration. It has the properties of basic drives such as hunger, but is triggered by external, social factors rather than internal, biological ones. It is a learned drive.

Criticisms
● in cases of learned helplessness, frustration may lead to depression rather than aggression
● aggression may arise from sources other than frustration.
● frustration doesn't always lead to aggression.
● what about instrumental aggression (aggression directed at achieving a particular goal)?
● what about individual differences?

② **Environmental factors.** The fact that aggression occurs through other factors, such as noise or overcrowding, suggests a broader **arousal–aggression hypothesis**.
Miller (1941) suggested that frustration may make aggression likely but other factors must be present for aggression to be expressed.
Berkowitz (1962) has proposed several modifications using the concept of 'readiness'. Frustration leads to a predisposition to behave aggressively *if* an appropriate trigger is present. **Geen and Berkowitz (1967)** first frustrated their subjects and then showed a film of an aggressive or non-aggressive nature. Aggression was later assessed through the level of electric shocks the subjects administered to a learner who made a mistake. If the subject had watched a boxing film or there was an aggressive trigger present in the room, such as a gun, the number of shocks given was greater.
Zillman (1983) has used the term **excitation transfer** in the same context. Physical exercise, loud music, stimulating drugs and high temperatures are 'exciting' and increase the likelihood of aggression. Another source of excitation or arousal is getting angry.
Calhoun (1962) showed that **crowding** could produce aggressive behaviour in rats – despite plenty of food, some ate the young. In humans, excessive human contact creates **stress**, particularly if personal space is violated and there is forced eye contact, signalling aggression. Studies of human response have shown how overcrowded prisons, rooms or day nurseries can lead to more aggressive behaviours such as crime and competitiveness, as well as higher rates of illness and depression (see 9.2 on density and crowding).

③ **Psychological factors,** such as a sense of unfairness or damaged self-esteem lead to **aggression. Prejudice** is often expressed through aggression (see 2.5); **pain** is also a cause of aggression. **Berkowitz** *et al.* **(1979)** induced pain by placing subjects' hands in cold or warm water while they delivered rewards or punishments to a partner (not shocks). The cold water condition led them to cause greater harm to their partner.

④ **Social learning theory perspective.** Whatever causes aggression in the first place, if it is successful, it is **reinforced**. It isn't just our own behaviour that can be reinforced but, through watching others behave aggressively and achieving positive results, we are more likely to imitate those actions. This is called **social, vicarious** or **observational learning**.
Bandura, Ross and Ross (1961, 1963) conducted an experiment with the famous **Bobo-the-Clown doll**, an adult-sized inflatable doll. Children were placed in a room with a model who either behaved aggressively (punching the doll, shouting at it and hitting it with a hammer) or non-aggressively. Later the children were observed playing in a room full of aggressive and non-aggressive-type toys, including Bobo. The ones who had seen an aggressive model behaved more aggressively and also imitated specific actions. Other findings and later variations include:
● If the child identified with the model, e.g. was the same sex, imitation increased.
● If the model was either rewarded or punished, this led to respective increases or decreases in the likelihood of imitation.

- If the model was warm and friendly rather than cool and detached, the children imitated it more (**Bandura and Huston, 1961**).
- Seeing the model on a film or a cartoon lessened the effect.
- Models high in prestige or status were more likely to be imitated.
- People low in self-esteem were more prone to imitation.
- If the child, rather than the model, was rewarded, then even children who didn't see the model behaved aggressively.

This research has importance for media influence, see 2.10 for details.

Criticisms
- Oversimplified. It is not often that a behaviour is so clearly demonstrated and rewarded, in fact people are more often punished for aggressive behaviour.
- The unfamiliar social situation produces demand characteristics – children look for cues of what to do with Bobo, they were conforming to norms.

5 **Socialisation.** Whether learning is direct or indirect, the norms of a society influence levels of aggression with respect to both child rearing and adult conformity. In a large study of child-rearing practices, **Newson and Newson (1968)** found social class differences in parental attitudes to aggression, working-class parents actively encouraged their children to stand up for themselves, while middle-class ones objected to such behaviour. Working-class families also used more physical punishment. **Rothbart and Maccoby (1966)** observed that mothers tolerated aggression from sons more than daughters, thus abetting **gender** differences in aggression. If an aggressive **personality** exists, there is evidence that it is established in childhood and remains relatively stable thereafter (**Eron, 1987**).

6 **Normative influence.** We are aggressive or antisocial when it is acceptable. However, we should distinguish between antisocial behaviour and situations of mob rule, where no social norms govern behaviour.

7 **Deindividuation** masks individual identity. **Diener, Fraser, Beaman, and Kelem (1976)** left Halloween trick-or-treaters alone with bowl of candy, if they had given their names 20% helped themselves against 57% in the anonymous condition. The two studies by **Zimbardo** described in 2.8, showed how deindividuation led to more obedient and aggressive behaviour.

8 **Cross-cultural studies**. The fact that peaceful, non-aggressive societies do develop, such as the Amish or Quakers, can be taken as evidence that aggression is not universal. **Mead (1935)** observed the Arapesh tribe of New Guinea and thought that their child-rearing practices encouraged gentle and non-aggressive behaviour in both boys and girls.

Nature and nurture

The ethological arguments make sense. We undoubtedly are born with some necessary aggressive tendencies but, in man at least, social factors can modify these to the point of erasing them, and environment and learning determine when and how we express aggression.

CONTROLLING AGGRESSION

Solutions are related to cause. A biological cause requires aggression to be redirected or dissipated; an environmental or learned cause calls for relearning or social change.

1 **Catharsis.** Both Freud and Lorenz felt that aggression wouldn't simply disappear – it must be 'purged' or released somewhere else. We can learn to express our aggression verbally or channel it into other activity, such as sport. Verbal abuse has been found sometimes to increase rather than decrease arousal (and therefore aggression), leading sometimes to over-reaction. **Hokanson (1970)** found that blood pressure was lowered as a result of a displacing aggressive feelings by administering electric shocks or fantasising about harming the experimenter who had mildly irritated the subject. Other studies have not found catharsis effective.

2 **Undoing aggressive motives.** A tense situation might be diffused through **incompatible responses**, such as tickling someone who is angry. **Baron (1983)** annoyed subjects and then gave them a chance to vent their anger. Those subjects who had been shown a non-violent cartoon in the interim were less aggressive than those shown neutral pictures. In an earlier study **Baron (1974)** found that mild sexual arousal also reduced overt aggression. Alternatively, knowing **mitigating circumstances**, such as hearing that someone was late because their dog was run over, will reduce anger.

3 **Unlearning aggression.** As aggression is learned, it can be unlearned. For example, by watching non-aggressive or negatively reinforced (punished) models.

4 **Changing social norms.** Reduced violence in the media can change our perceptions of what is acceptable and typical.

5 **Ritualising aggression** can be a way of channelling it in a comparatively safe way. **Marsh** *et al.* **(1978)** suggest that football hooliganism can be seen as an example of rules of disorder which prevent violence escalating beyond a certain point (see aggression and rituals in animals, 8.4).

6 Encouraging **prosocial** behaviour reduces antisocial behaviour.

2.8 CONFORMITY, OBEDIENCE AND COMPLIANCE

The distinction between these three processes is not entirely clear. Some psychologists suggest that conformity and compliance are nearly the same thing, except conformity involves a change in private opinions as well as public behaviour. Others equate obedience and compliance, suggesting that compliance is a response to a direct request.

- **Conformity**
  - yielding to others,
  - typically group pressure rather than individuals,
  - a change in opinions *and* behaviour,
  - conformity is affected by example, obedience by direction **(Brown,1986)**.

- **Obedience**
  - 'acting so as to *conform* with rules or orders',
  - *doing* what you're told but not changing your *thinking*,
  - less likely to involve group pressure.

- **Compliance**
  - is it conformity or obedience?
  - responding to an *explicit* request,
  - *doing* it but not *believing* in what one is doing.,
  - only lasts as long as the situation does,
  - an initial stage prior to any internal change.

- **Conformity, obedience, and compliance** can apply to:
  - attitudes,
  - behaviour,
  - total personality (as in a conformist or obedient type of person).

- Are they **undesirable** characteristics?
  - not inherently, they lead to predictable behaviours which simplify social interactions, they are a part of cognitive balance, and an important aspect of the process of socialisation,
  - if conformity is bad then non-conformity should be good, and it is when associated with independent thought. Many important scientific discoveries are due to non-conformists, such as Galileo insisting that the earth moved round the sun,
  - non-conformity has little value when it is 'anti-conformity' – disobeying rules for the sake of it – or apparent non-conformity when conforming to alternative set of rules.

- **Leaders, power and norms** are important concepts in explaining the processes of conformity, obedience and compliance (see 2.9).

CONFORMITY

1 **F.H.Allport (1924)** found that subjects behaved differently in groups than when they were working alone. When he asked them to judge the pleasantness of odours, the individual judgements when in groups tended towards the mean of the group.

2 **Jenness (1932)** asked students to estimate the number of beans in a bottle, and then arranged for them to discuss their guesses with a group. When later asked again for their estimates, these had shifted towards the group's estimate.

3 **Sherif (1936)** used a visual illusion to test conformity and group pressure – the **autokinetic effect** (a point of light moves erratically when viewed in total darkness). Subjects were shown the light individually and asked to estimate how far and in which direction it moved. For each subject an average was calculated and subjects were grouped so that they were as different as possible. After a few exposures the judgements of the group tended to converge, even though they were not asked to arrive at group estimates, and these judgements persisted when the individuals were tested later.

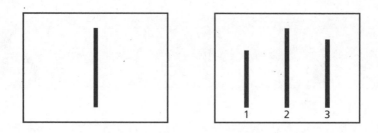

Fig. 2.1 Stimulus lines for Asch's conformity study

4 **Asch's (1951, 1952, 1956)** studies are regarded as the classic conformity experiments. Asch felt that Sherif's results had been caused by an ambiguous stimulus, and he therefore aimed to place subjects in a situation where there was clearly no doubt. He showed groups of seven subjects two cards, one with a 'standard' line, the other with three lines of varying length (Fig. 2.1). Which line was the same length as the standard? The comparison was repeated and each time the subjects gave their answers out loud. Unknown to the penultimate group member the rest were confederates, who gave the wrong answer on certain 'critical' trials. Approximately 75% of the subjects conformed at least once, 5% conformed all of the time and 25% never conformed; the average rate was 37%. Asch commented that 'people submit uncritically and painlessly to external manipulation by suggestion'. Later variations showed that:
- three subjects were sufficient to create the effect, larger numbers did not increase conformity,
- a second dissenter cut conformity rates by 25%, even when the dissenter disagreed with the subject,
- conformity increased if the group members were regarded as of high status,
- conformity decreased if the subjects were not face-to-face,
- **Venkatesan (1966)** found that mass conformity had the opposite effect, the last subject displayed reactance (see 2.3).

5 **Crutchfield (1955)** designed the **Crutchfield apparatus**, where a subject is seated in a cubicle with a series of switches to indicate their choice and lights to show what other subjects have selected; the other subjects did not in fact exist. This was a more efficient method than Asch's and some 600 subjects were studied. Crutchfield tested subjects with a set of obvious problems and also with attitudinal statements. Again, responses were affected by majority opinions, though to a slightly lesser degree than in Asch's study.

6 **Stoner's (1968)** classic study of the **risky shift** (described in 2.9) again showed the effects of group influence on an individual's private opinion, expressed at the end of the experiment. The shift was always in the direction of greater polarisation.

OBEDIENCE

1 One of the classic psychology experiments of all time was **Milgram's (1963)** behavioural study of obedience – classic because of its intriguing findings and also for the ethical questions it raises (see also 10.4). His starting point was the inhumane policies of the Nazis and the obedience of the German nation. Would ordinary Americans behave in the same way? In essence the experiment involved two subjects who drew lots for their roles, the 'learner' (in fact a confederate) was strapped in a chair in another room, the 'teacher' (the true subject) administers increasingly stronger electric shocks as punishment for mistakes. The experimenter uses special 'prods' or instructions to encourage the 'teacher' continue, despite hearing the 'learner's' yelps of pain. 65% of the subjects continued to the highest level of 450 volts, past the level marked 'danger, severe shock'. No one stopped below 300 volts (intense shock). Later variations included:

- proximity of learner; 30% of the teachers continued even when they were pushing the learner's hand down onto the shock machine,
- proximity of experimenter; when instructions were given over the phone the teacher often said they were giving the shocks when they weren't,
- perceived authority, when the experiment was conducted in a run-down setting obedience was decreased,
- individual differences, educated subjects were less obedient; military subjects were more so,
- social support; the presence of other teachers increased obedience, but if they dissented obedience fell,
- responsibility; if the learner had a heart condition obedience didn't change!

All the subjects were thoroughly debriefed afterwards but, none the less, many people have raised questions about the **ethics** of this experiment. Some subjects felt the study was justified because they had learned from the experiment; they were shocked by their own behaviour and wouldn't behave so mindlessly in future. Milgram reported 'the extraordinary tension and emotional strain generated by the procedure' but felt vindicated by the insights the study afforded into human nature – the ends justify the means. He also said that he had simply not foreseen the behaviour that would be produced, though he went on to test a further 1000 male subjects after the initial experiment.

2 **Zimbardo (1969)** performed a variation of the Milgram experiment, showing the effects of deindividuation. This time the learner was either introduced to the subject and wore a name tag, or alternatively was disguised in lab coat and hood. The 'deindividuated' confederate received more electric shocks.

3 **Hofling** *et al.* **(1966)** conducted a more realistic experiment where nurses were told to administer a drug to a patient. This instruction was contrary to their rules: nurses were not permitted to accept instructions over the telephone, nor from an unknown doctor, nor for a dose in excess of the safe amount. Nevertheless 21 out of 22 nurses obeyed the order. Nurses defended themselves by saying it often happens, a doctor would be annoyed if they refused. Were they conforming to expected role behaviour rather than being obedient?

COMPLIANCE

1 **Zimbardo (1975).** Like Milgram, Zimbardo was prompted to conduct some research because of disturbing real-life behaviour. In the US there had been much alleged brutality by prison guards, was such behaviour universal to all humans or specific to certain sections of the community? The **Stanford Prison Study** gave a remarkable demonstration of compliance (though it's often cited as evidence of conformity or obedience). He selected 24 healthy, intelligent, psychologically 'normal' male volunteers to serve as either prisoners or guards in a simulated prison set up in the basement of the psychology department at Stanford University. Roles were decided by the toss of a coin. The 'prisoners' were arrested, booked, searched, given ID numbers, issued with uniform and ankle chain; generally treated in a degrading manner. Guards had uniforms, clubs, whistles, handcuffs and reflective sunglasses (deindividuation).

Zimbardo intended to run the study for two weeks but had to stop after six days because the subjects became too involved in their roles. The guards became increasingly tyrannical and arbitrary, woke prisoners in the night, locked them in a closet and got them to clean the toilet with their bare hands. The prisoners also changed their behaviour, one went on a hunger strike, those who broke down asked to be paroled not simply to quit. On day 3 one prisoner was released because of 'acute emotional disturbance', the next day another prisoner broke down and cried hysterically. Finally the increasing malice of the guards and depression levels amongst the prisoners forced Zimbardo to abandon the study.

The study shows the pressure to comply with social norms and roles, but did subjects change internally? Probably not, though they may have experienced long-term effects. Like Milgram's work, this study raises ethical doubts, in not complying with many of the accepted ethical guidelines (see 10.4).

2 **Langer** *et al.* **(1978)** approached people who were using a photocopier. In condition 1 no excuse was offered, in condition 2 a reasonable explanation was offered, 'I'm in a rush', and for condition 3 a senseless excuse, 'I have to make some copies'. When the request was to make five copies there was no difference between conditions 2 and 3 (93% complied). This dropped considerably when the request was for 20 copies. There was now no difference between conditions 1 and 2 (24% complied in both). The conclusion is that people often obey 'mindlessly', most of the time we are 'on auto-pilot', running well-practised routines without attentional control.

3 **Freedman and Fraser (1966)** showed how initial compliance may turn into conformity, a change in opinion as well as behaviour by using the **foot-in-the-door** technique. A housewife was approached with a small request, in one case she was asked a few questions about household products. A few days later a team of five men visited the house asking if they could count and classify all the products in her home, 53% agreed to this compared with 22% of women who had only had the second request. A person's initial compliance affects their self-perception and they now see themselves as a person who is likely to do that sort of thing, thus internalising the behaviour.

4 **Cialdini** *et al.* **(1975)** demonstrated another sales technique – the **door-in-the-face**, which reverses the above by starting with a large request followed by something smaller, both methods are examples of 'getting X by asking for Y'. Students were first presented with a substantial request to do voluntary work for two years, later when they were asked to help out for a day they were more willing to offer help than a control group.

EXPLANATIONS OF CONFORMITY, OBEDIENCE AND COMPLIANCE

Experimental artefacts

1 Subjects want to **please the experimenter**. When **Crutchfield** asked his subjects for feedback after the experiment, many of them said they didn't want to spoil the results so they had gone along with the others. There were some who actually thought they had been wrong, these are the true conformists, the others were merely complying.

2 The psychology experiment as **a social situation**. Subjects don't want to be the odd one out, belonging to the group is more important than correctness particularly in **ambiguous** situations.

3 **Perceived responsibility. Milgram** suggested that we perceive it as a moral responsibility to be obedient to authority, thus conforming to social norms. It would be wrong to refuse to follow orders having agreed to participate. The subject abnegates responsibility to the experimenter, the subject is a tool not an independent agent.

4 The experiments largely used **paid volunteers**, thus the subjects had entered into a social contract.

5 As the experimenter is perceived as being in charge and bearing responsibility, the subject can behave **mindlessly. Tuddenham (1958)** found that some subjects would agree with some of the most absurd statements, demonstrating their lack of thoughtful behaviour.

6. Are the results a **'child of the times'**? **Perrin and Spencer (1980)** replicated Asch's study but did not obtain evidence of conformity. Could it be that today people have learned to be more self-reliant? On the other hand, **Doms and Avermaet (1981)** did obtain the original results and suggest that using science and engineering students, as Perrin and Spencer did to get naive subjects, could bias the results.

7. How much are social psychology experiments seen as **role-playing games?** One subject in the **Milgram** study said she knew the learner wasn't really getting the shocks.

8. In real life people sometimes have the option to simply **do nothing**, which may not be possible in an experiment.

9. Was the observed behaviour **a measure of private opinions**? For conformity both need to have changed.

10. Many of the above factors apply equally to real-life, they are not just experimental artefacts.

Factors which lead to conformity, obedience and compliance

1. **Normative social influence.** Group norms are necessary as a framework for interpersonal communication and a basis for a society. We drive on the left because it would be madness not to conform; we use agreed rules of spelling so that we can understand each other. **Kelman and Lawrence (1972)** conducted a national survey after the trial of William Calley for his part in the My Lai massacre. Fifty one per cent felt it was desirable to obey legitimate authority.

2. **Informational social influence.** In some situations, in experiments and real-life, there is no right answer or no answer known to you. Therefore you rely on norms for 'social reality', for example, what cutlery to use.

3. **Ingratiational social influence.** A person agrees in order to impress or gain acceptance.

4. **Mindlessness.** Most of the time we are on auto-pilot, because most behaviour is routine.

5. **Public statements** of opinions are more likely to lead to change.

6. **Gradual changes** mean that a person can almost be unaware of complying before it's too late, they've already committed themselves. This was shown by **Freedman and Fraser (1966)** as well as in the **Milgram** study, where the shocks increased by only 15 volts each time, what does one more step matter?

7. **Deindividuation.** Both **Zimbardo** studies show how anonymity shifts our sense of responsibility.

8. **Group composition and status.** The size of the majority and commitment of the members determines the likelihood of conforming, as do factors such as distribution of power and type of leadership. Conformity, obedience and compliance are part of **group processes** as an affirmation of group membership.

9. **Social pressure.** A dissenter makes everyone feel uneasy. **Schachter (1951)** demonstrated how a group puts pressure on an individual to stop being deviant and agree with the majority. Such conformist pressure is important in juries. This is different from fear of dissent.

10. **Fear of dissent.** People don't usually want to appear deviant, particularly amongst their peer group. Deviation itself is governed by a set of norms.

11. **Personality.** Some people are 'affiliators' and need social approval more than others. **Crutchfield** found that non-conformists tended to be self-reliant, expressive, unpretentious and lacked feelings of inferiority. Conformists respect authority, are submissive, inhibited, lack insight and are overly accepting. Generally however, the evidence favours a situational approach. There are situations in which we all conform rather than there being a conformist personality.

12. **Gender.** There has been evidence that women tend to be more conformist. **Eagly (1978)** suggests that women may be more oriented towards interpersonal goals and thus appear more conformist.

Are the results surprising?

Milgram (in **Tarvis, 1974**) conducted an experiment with his university students. They had to ask a stranger in an underground train if they could have their seat, offering no excuse. When Milgram tried it himself, he felt overcome with blind panic. He suggests that this reveals the enormous inhibitory anxiety that ordinarily prevents us from breaching social norms. Prior to his classic experiment, Milgram had asked psychiatrists, college students and ordinary people how they thought the subjects would behave. The average prediction was a level of 150 volts (a strong shock). They thought that at most only 3% of the subjects might go as far as 450 volts, whereas 65% did.

People often express surprise at Milgram's unexpected results – we don't think that people are so conforming or obedient. In fact the surprise is that we *are* surprised – we don't expect human behaviour to be what it clearly is. The important lesson from this work is 'that to man himself, not to the devil belongs the responsibility for, and the control of, his inhumane actions' (**Erikson, 1968**). Conformity, obedience and compliance are good in their place but we must all know when to accept responsibility and take control.

Ethics

These studies are often used as examples of ethics, dealt with fully in 10.4. Measured against any of the ethical criteria, these studies have at best made mild infringements of subjects' rights.

2.9 GROUP DYNAMICS

Group dynamics are intragroup processes such as cohesiveness, communication, power, roles, leadership, decision-making and social facilitation.

A *small* group is usually given as between three and ten members. The work looked at in this section applies mainly to small groups. Social facilitation is relevant to pairs; power and leadership should be considered in the context of large groups.

A group, rather than say a set of people queuing for a bus, implies:

- interaction over a sufficient period of time,
- perception of the group's existence and their membership of it,
- norm formation, an expectation that members will conform to group norms,
- roles, affective relations, shared goals.

GROUP EFFECTS

A group is more than a sum of its parts, its behaviour is different from that of the individuals working separately. Here is a summary of some of the effects mentioned previously and in this section caused by the presence of others:

- inhibits helping behaviour (bystander apathy, see 2.6),
- facilitates antisocial behaviour (deindividuation, see 2.7),
- defines in- and out-group, personal and social identity (see 2.5),
- generates more ideas but is inefficient in terms of time or quality (see 1.3),
- polarises the opinions of individual group members (group polarisation),
- influences opinions through conformity to group/social norms (see 2.8),
- facilitates performance where tasks are simple, well-learned or innate (social facilitation).

GROUP STRUCTURES

All aspects of group structure are important to the effectiveness of the group and the satisfaction felt by the members. The 'best' structure is a function of the group's task, or lack of one.

Affective structure

This can be studied with sociometry (see 2.3) – who likes whom. The **cohesiveness** of the group can be measured by how often the members use the term 'we', when it is high, group performance is usually good.

Communication structure

The study of types of network has proved fruitful. **Bavelas (1950)** introduced a neat method to show the development of communication networks. He placed subjects in individual booths with slots in the walls to pass messages to other group members. **Leavitt (1951)** used this to show that a centralised network based around a leader, such as a wheel, was faster and led to fewer errors in problem-solving tasks; individual satisfaction was highest in a decentralised, leaderless network. **Shaw (1954)** found, for complex tasks, that the 'all channel net' was best to ensure free exchange of information.

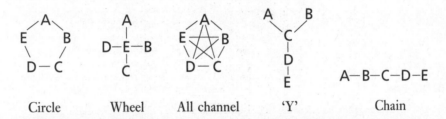

Circle   Wheel   All channel   'Y'   Chain

Communication networks can be seen in terms of status rather than centralisation. **Back, Festinger** *et al.* **(1950)** planted a rumour in a factory at five different status levels and waited to see who reported it to whom. The tendency was for people to tell someone of higher status, not to report it downwards or to people of the same status.

Power structure

Power is the capacity to produce intended and foreseen effects in others; it is important in the processes of compliance and obedience. **Collins and Raven (1969)** have suggested six sources or bases which explain why some people have greater influence over others:

1. *Reward* power: tangible or social rewards promised, such as money, approval, love, group membership.
2. *Coercive* power: threats, warnings, actual punishment, best when administered immediately, too much may have a reverse effect.
3. *Legitimate* power: such as an employer or parent, from sense of duty, loyalty or cultural norms.
4. *Referent* power: gained through being liked or respected, such models provide reference points for social comparison.
5. *Expert* power: when uncertain we follow the advice of experts, someone gains power by, for example, convincing you that they know the correct course of action.
6. *Informational* power: based upon information which is independent of the nature of the source, as in information to blackmail someone.

Role structure

A role is the behaviours expected of a person occupying a certain position in a group. Roles:

- only have meaning in relation to a group,
- can be expected, perceived and enacted,
- are normative – we expect people to behave in line with their role,
- have attached status,
- a person may have more than one role and thus role conflicts.
- a prime empirical example is **Zimbardo**'s prisoners and guards (see 2.8).

Interaction process analysis (Bales, 1950)

Bales produced the Interaction Process Analysis (IPA) as a result of observing the behaviour of small groups in a laboratory. It provides a powerful tool for measuring group dynamics and structure. Both verbal and non-verbal behaviours can be allocated to one of four main areas:

- socio-emotional behaviour: either positive or negative
- the task area: either questions or answers about it

Within each of these four areas are three specific categories of behaviour.

SOCIO-EMOTIONAL AREA	POSITIVE	1	shows solidarity, raises other's status, gives help, reward
		2	shows tension release, jokes, laughs, shows satisfaction
		3	agrees, shows passive acceptance, understands, complies
TASK AREA	ANSWERS	4	gives suggestion, direction, implying autonomy for other
		5	gives opinion, evaluation, analysis, expresses feeling, wish
		6	gives orientation, information, repeats, clarifies, confirms
CONCERNING THE TASK	QUESTIONS	7	asks for orientation, information, repetition
		8	asks for opinion, evaluation, analysis, expresses feeling, wish
		9	asks for suggestion, direction, possible ways of action
SOCIO-EMOTIONAL AREA	NEGATIVE	10	disagrees, shows passive rejection, formality, withholds help
		11	shows tension, asks for help, withdraws out of field
		12	shows antagonism, deflates other's status, defends/asserts self

LEADERSHIP

Leadership is any behaviour that moves a group closer to attaining its goals.

Emergence of a leader

1. **Personality.** The most obvious answer, and historically the first, is to suggest that leadership is something to do with personality – the **Great man (or woman) theory (Carlyle, 1841)** – a belief that 'leaders are born not made' because of natural factors. **Trait theory** suggests that certain personality attributes might be associated with leader success, e.g. height, weight, physical attractiveness, self-confidence, greater sensitivity, dominance and intelligence. It may be factors of a more general nature, such as the person who talks most, or who possesses good organisational skills. **Mann (1959)** reviewed the literature from 1900–57, and concluded that there was little evidence to differentiate leaders from non-leaders.

2. **Situation.** At the simplest level the seating position of a group may determine who becomes leader. Many leaders arise because they have been appointed. Even when this appointment is random, a group may perceive that person as a leader. **Bell and French (1950)** showed that acting petty officers who were selected randomly were nevertheless kept in that position and regarded as leaders by their subordinates. Similarly **Leavitt's (1951)** study found those who were given the leadership role through seating position became leaders.

   A situation may also be defined by circumstances, such as a crisis precipitating the need for a leader. **Hamblin (1958)** conducted a game-playing experiment where, for some of the subjects, the rules changed halfway creating a crisis situation. They found that such a crisis resulted in group members being more willing to be influenced than the non-crisis, i.e. selecting and obeying a leader. The size of the group influences the structure and the kinds of leadership. A group larger than ten tends to divide into subgroups, each with its own leader and an overall leadership hierarchy.

3. **Interaction.** A person who is a leader in a football team would not necessarily emerge as a leader in the classroom - there is an interaction between personality and situation.

Effectiveness of a leader

Riggio (1990) distinguished three groups of theories:

1 *Universalist theories:* the ones which describe leadership in terms of a central characteristic or cluster of characteristics, as in personality explanations (above), or McGregor (below).

2 *Behavioural theories:* which isolate particular behaviours or styles leading to success.

3 *Contingency theories:* where success depends on further factors such as situation (Fiedler's contingency theory and path–goal theory).

Theories of leadership effectiveness

1 **McGregor (1960)** describes the effectiveness of a leader in terms of two basic beliefs held by the leader: **theory X** is the traditional view that workers dislike work; **theory Y** is the reverse, that workers are self-motivated and committed. The orientation or personality of leaders (management) will influence the organisation.

2 **Skills.** An effective leader must have or develop certain leadership skills. **Morley and Hosking (1984)** suggest that a leader must be good at:
- processing information,
- bargaining and negotiation,
- knowing and representing the surrounding environment.

3 **Authoritarian, democratic and laissez-faire style. Lewin *et al.* (1939)** showed how leadership styles affect behaviour in a study involving groups of children making soap models:
- *authoritarian leader:* made all decisions, didn't give reasons, was remote,
- *democratic leader:* decisions made only after consultation, gave reasons for any criticism or praise, offered help if required and joined in with group,
- *laissez-faire leader:* played passive role, no attempt to direct or co-ordinate, no positive or negative evaluations.

The democratic group had the highest morale and co-operation, and kept working when alone. They made fewer models but these were of better quality than those made by the other group. The authoritarian group misbehaved when left alone. The laissez-faire group had the poorest performance, made the fewest models and misbehaved, but were friendly towards their leader. Subsequent research has not produced such clear findings.

Weiss and Friedrichs (1986) found that basketball coaches who engaged in more frequent rewarding, social support and adopted a democratic style, produced more satisfied athletes, and that such behaviours were related to successful team performance.

4 **Task versus relationship-oriented style. Bales (1950)** found that two types of leader emerged: a task leader and socio-emotional leader. In any group there may be more than one leader, one legitimate and task-oriented, the other socio-emotional. **Hersey and Blanchard's life-cycle approach (1976)** suggests that a leader should have both qualities adapted to fit the demands of the group life-cycle. Newly formed groups need a task-oriented leader to get them started, later a more relationship-oriented leadership and finally no leader at all.

Evaluation

The two dimensions (leader and relationship-orientation) represent two very different styles yet both are linked to effective leadership, which suggests that their effectiveness is contingent on certain situations.

5 **Interaction of situation and style.** Studies of communication structures have shown that certain structures are most effective for certain tasks, i.e. there is an interaction. **Fiedler's contingency theory (1971)** suggests that effectiveness of a particular *style* is contingent on the favourability of the *situation* for the leader. There is no such thing as a 'good leader' *per se* but some leaders are good in some situations.

Style is expressed in terms of a leader's least preferred co-worker (LPC). Fielder asked leaders to rate their LPC using the semantic differential technique.
- a high LPC score: a friendly, accepting, relationship-oriented style of leader would have a favourable attitude towards their LPC and therefore give the LPC a high score,
- a low LPC score would arise when a task-oriented leader who is aloof and demanding rated his LPC.

A *favourable situation* is one where the leader finds it easy to control and direct the group, has their loyalty and confidence, and the group has a clearly defined task structure. By looking at the high and low LPC scores and the 'favourability' of the situation we can see whether a leader would be effective or not in that situation:

	SITUATIONAL FACTORS		
STYLE	HIGHLY favourable	MODERATELY favourable	HIGHLY unfavourable
HIGH LPC	ineffective	effective	ineffective
LOW LPC	effective	ineffective	effective

When conditions are unfavourable, members are willing to overlook interpersonal conflicts in order to get on with the task, therefore a task-oriented leader is best. In favourable conditions there is little interpersonal conflict and therefore a task-oriented leader is again best – one who gets on with the job. In a moderately favourable situation, when conflict and tension within a group is highest, one needs a relationship-oriented leader.

The situation can further be defined by: (a) leader–follower relations; (b) task structure (high means well-defined); (c) power of leader (high is legitimate), and combined in eight ways or octants:

	1	2	3	4	5	6	7	8
relations	good	good	good	poor	poor	poor	poor	poor
task	high	high	low	low	high	high	low	low
power	strong	weak	strong	weak	strong	weak	strong	weak
OVERALL EFFECT	extra high	high	high	moderately high	moderately high	low	low	extra low

Fiedler tested this model with managerial boards, basketball teams and bomber crews and found support.

Evaluation

- has been used to train leaders to fit strategy to situation, for example the Leader Match programme (see **Fiedler, 1965** p.119),
- hundreds of studies have been mostly supportive,
- its complexity reflects the complex nature of leadership,
- can't be sure that style *causes* effectiveness,
- leadership may change with time, this is **not** reflected in this model,
- it ignores group members.

6 **Other contingency theories:**
- **Path–goal theory.** A leader's job is to help the work group attain its goals, to act as a facilitator (**House, 1971**). To this end the leader may be directive, achievement-oriented, supportive and/or participative, depending on the situation and characteristics of the workers. For example, a routine task with an experienced set of workers would benefit from supportive or participative rather than directive leadership.
- **Decision-making model (Vroom and Yetton, 1973).** Decision-making in a group should alternate between three styles: autocratic, consultative and group decisions, to encourage greater worker participation in appropriate situations. They provide a decision tree with questions such as 'is conflict among subordinates likely?' to aid choice of style (see also 'Job satisfaction', 9.1).

Application of leadership theories

1 Leadership training programmes:
- teach diagnostic skills so that leaders can adapt their behaviour to suit the situation,

- teach specific skills which the leader lacks, and allows practice of these,
- are very expensive and not always successful. Attempts to train personal characteristics are difficult, and newly acquired behaviours may not be accepted in the work place (a relationship-oriented police sergeant may be regarded as soft).

2 Redesigning the job to fit the leader:
- **Fiedler (1965)** claimed that the leader's orientations are inflexible, and therefore a better strategy is to change the job to fit the leader (Leader Match programme) or transfer the leader to a more appropriate situation,
- training schemes are ineffective; instead the Leader Match programme should be used to alter the work situation to fit the leader's predominant style,
- redesign is limited to those jobs where this is possible,
- job enrichment schemes may make the role of a leader superfluous (see 9.1).

DECISION-MAKING IN GROUPS

Group efficiency

Groups generate more ideas but individual group members can be inhibited. Groups can take a long time to reach a decision and rarely perform as well as the most able members. Groups are inefficient in terms of man hours.

Hall and Watson (1970) used a 'moon' problem to test the quality of group decisions. One way of studying such performance is in terms of cost–benefit analysis, but it is difficult to assess costs and benefits objectively. This study compared performance with expert opinion. The problem was to rank a set of 15 items in terms of their importance to a space crew who have crash landed and need to reach their mother ship. The group members did the task individually first and then reached consensus as a group. Their rankings were compared with those from NASA experts. The groups produced better quality decisions than the individuals, though the best individual was better than any of the groups. Groups who received instructions to facilitate decision-making in groups didn't do particularly better than the other groups.

Group polarisation

Common sense suggests that groups will make more cautious decisions than individuals. **Stoner (1968)** first introduced the idea that group decisions may in fact be more risky, and termed the trend the **risky shift**. He presented subjects with 12 dilemmas (choice dilemma questionnaire or CDQ) each describing a situation where a central character is forced to make a choice between two actions, one being more attractive than the other but less likely to succeed. Subjects were asked individually to indicate at what level of probability they would take the riskier choice. They then discussed and reached a decision with a group. Later they were asked to register their opinion privately again, 39% of the subjects increased the risk factor from the beginning to the end of the experiment

It wasn't always a shift to risk, though. Sometimes there was a consistent shift to caution. Hundreds of other studies have supported the finding that, whatever the person's and the group's initial position, group discussion serves not to average the opinions of individual members but to **polarise** them. **Myers and Bishop (1970)** found that when prejudiced persons discuss racial issues with similar others, their attitudes become more prejudiced; whereas if mildly biased people discuss such matters with like-minded people, they become less prejudiced.

Why?

- **Increased caution** is associated with a very large stake and the involvement of others in the eventual outcome.
- **Risk** is linked with a very large prize and a small stake.
- **Diffusion of responsibility.** More members means that risk can be spread amongst them, though this only explains the shift to risk. It is possible that caution could be regarded as being over-responsible and therefore the presence of others increases caution through shared responsibility.

- **Persuasive arguments.** Group members will collectively develop more and better arguments favouring their initial position, thus polarising it further.
- **Social comparison.** Members who previously saw themselves as either risky or cautious now find, in comparison with others, they aren't so extreme. Therefore they must take a more extreme position in order to maintain their self-image.
- **Dissonance theory** predicts a change of opinion after a public statement in order to maintain attitude balance.
- **Experimental artefact.** In real life, particularly where strangers are not involved, the effects may be averaging rather than polarising.

Groupthink

The term 'groupthink' describes how a group may be influenced by in-group pressures to conform and express solidarity rather than to objectively evaluate a decision. It is a disease which renders groups inefficient and unproductive. **Janis (1982)** coined the term after his teenage daughter insisted that he couldn't explain the Bay of Pigs disaster using social psychological factors. The Presidential advisors in 1961 should have known better, but collectively they made a series of mistaken decisions which led to the Bay of Pigs invasion of Cuba.

Possible causes:

- **cohesiveness**, an inherent quality of any group,
- **isolation**, working in secret,
- **biased leadership**, increases conformity, discourages dissension,
- **decisional stress**, which the group aims to reduce by reaching a decision quickly, with little argument and concentrating on minor issues,
- **polarisation**,
- **institutional factors**, which encourage conformity. People may be promoted for the wrong reasons, for example, a good soldier does not make a good commander. Or the **Peter principle** (people are promoted to the level of their least efficiency because a person is promoted as long as they are doing well).

Possible means of avoidance:

- **reduce isolation**,
- use **impartial leadership** which will encourage criticism,
- **reduce stress**, for example, have a second meeting to make the final decision.

SOCIAL FACILITATION

When two or more people work together, their performance is sometimes enhanced even by the mere presence of each other. This was one of the earliest areas of social psychology to be researched.

Triplett (1897) was intrigued by the fact that cyclists performed better when in a race than in practice. It was suggested that the answer might be physical, perhaps the other cyclists created a vacuum which helped pull each other along. Triplett thought that the presence of others is psychologically stimulating and enhances performance. He tested it in an experiment with 40 children and some fishing reels; those in pairs turned the reels faster.

The effect has been observed with puppies, chickens, mice, rats, armadillos, ants, opossums and even cockroaches. **Zajonc et al. (1969)** placed a bright light at the start of a maze, if cockroaches were in pairs they ran away faster. If the task was made more complex, by adding a right turn, the lone cockroaches did better. Performance was also increased when an audience of four cockroaches watched! Demonstrating, even for cockroaches, that there is an interaction between task difficulty and audience or co-actors.

Effects

1. **Audience effects**. A passive audience increases performance on simple tasks but depresses it on complex tasks. **Travis (1925)** trained subjects for several days on a

hand–eye co-ordination task until they reached a standard, 90% performed better in front of an audience than when alone. **Pessin (1933)** asked subjects to learn a set of nonsense syllables, those who did so in front of an audience took longer and made more errors than those who learnt alone. **Schmitt *et al.* (1986)** demonstrated that the mere presence of another speeds up completion of a simple task (a subject typing their name into a computer); but slows a more complex one (typing their name backwards). A confederate wore a blindfold and earphones in the 'mere presence' condition, in the other condition the confederate watched the subject, to create evaluation apprehension. However, **Cottrell *et al.* (1968)** found that an audience wearing a blindfold produced no effects at all.

2 **Co-action effects.** Co-acting means working side-by-side but independently. Co-action may improve quantity at a sacrifice to quality. **Allport (1924)** compared the performance of subjects doing a variety of tasks, such as multiplication problems, word associations, developing arguments. The quantity of the work was greatest when the subjects were co-acting, the quality improved when working alone.

3 **Interaction effects.** Group interaction is best for tasks involving creativity but has a counterproductive effect on physical tasks. As we have seen, when solving problems groups produce more varied ideas and identify errors more quickly, though in terms of man hours groups aren't better. **Shaw (1932)** set 'eureka'-type problems, such as the missionaries and the cannibals (the Tartaglia). Four-person groups were able to solve these faster than individuals. There have been interesting practical applications.

Brainstorming, which originated with **Osborn (1957)**, is a method of producing a rich assortment of ideas. First, everyone should suggest ideas in the absence of evaluation. Second, criticism is given after all ideas have been presented. Finally, all the ideas are elaborated again in the absence of criticism. It doesn't always work well because leaders are often unskilled and not enough time is allowed.

The **Ringlemann effect**, named after a German agricultural engineer who studied group performance in a tug-of-war situation. The pressure exerted on the rope did not increase in a simple linear fashion with the size of the group, some members pull less when their performance is not directly observable (social loafing) and there are losses due to difficulties co-ordinating action. Maximum efficiency is never reached because not everyone is pulling at the same moment. In a factory situation, maximum production can be achieved when people co-act and are also identifiable, which explains why some items have the assembler's or sewer's initials on them.

4 **Task effects.** Co-action increases performance on simple tasks but depresses it on complex tasks. Motor, well-learned and instinctive tasks fare better than conceptual, novel, complicated or untried tasks. **Zajonc (1965)** called these dominant and non-dominant responses, respectively. The **Schmitt *et al.* (1986)** study showed how simple and complex tasks were affected differently.

Explanations

For facilitation:

- **increased arousal** created by evaluation apprehension or competition,
- desire to present a **favourable image** to self and others increases motivation and effort,
- **competition** increases motivation.

For inhibition:

- **distraction and conflict** may depress performance because the audience reduces concentration and attention, which is important for non-dominant responses,
- **social loafing** reduces group productivity, knowing others will take up the slack, there are additional difficulties in co-ordinating action in some tasks.

Application to juries

Juries are a special and important example of a small group. Much of the above has obvious relevance to the behaviour of juries – Hall and Watson's findings about instructions not improving performance, the polarisation of group decisions and groupthink to name a few. In America, some states allow juries of six rather than twelve, a practice which has been challenged. The Supreme Court turned to evidence from social psychologists, in particular Asch's work on group size and conformity. The court concluded that juries of six took less time to deliberate, cost less money and were sufficiently representative of the population. A sample of less than six is likely to experience unjust pressures to conform when the jury is split because a minority of one could well be critical.

2.10 INFLUENCE OF THE MEDIA

Media are channels through which information is transmitted. The media includes: television, radio, films, videos, computers, books, and magazines. Research has been largely concerned with television and children, and particularly the effects of violence on television.

TELEVISION

When television first appeared it was predicted that it would lead children to lose interest in books and school, to become intellectually lazy, more isolated, passive or, alternatively, hyperactive; and families would talk less. But television also has the potential to educate and inform, and does, most obviously through school broadcasts and the Open University.

The viewing statistics cannot help but give cause for alarm – many children are doing little else but watching television. In a survey of 7–12 year olds **Cullingford (1984)**, found that 80% said they watched television the previous night and typically watched between three and six programmes. Many 9-year-olds and almost all older children, at sometime watched after midnight.

Middle-class children watch somewhat less television, young adolescents watch more than other children.

THE MEDIA AND VIOLENCE

One of the most often quoted statistics is that 80% of television programmes are estimated to contain violence, increasing to 93% at weekends. A child watching four hours a day may see 13 000 murders by the age of 16. But does this make them more aggressive?

Evidence

1. **Case history approach.** An 18-year-old student walked into a beautician's in Arizona and shot five people, he explained that the idea came from news stories about a man who shot eight nurses. A 9-year-old was raped by three older girls who had watched a similar crime in a film. In the case of a 15-year-old who shot his neighbour in the course of a burglary, the defence presented at his trial was that his addiction to television distorted his understanding of reality.

2. **Laboratory/experimental approach.** The study of children watching an adult acting violently towards Bobo-the-Clown (**Bandura** *et al.* **1961**, see 2.7) showed how violent acts are imitated, and aggression increases. **Steuer** *et al.* **(1971)** showed aggressive cartoons to a group of under 5-year-olds daily for 11 days. The children became more aggressive, in terms of kicking and pushing their classmates. **Ellis and Sekgra (1972)** found that children behaved more aggressively after watching an aggressive cartoon, such as Tom and Jerry, than a neutral one. **Comstock and Strasburger (1990)** concluded from a review of the literature that the evidence from this sort of study overwhelmingly indicates a link between TV violence and aggressive behaviour.

3. **Field/experimental approach. Friedrich and Stein (1973)** observed children in a nursery school for three weeks. Over the following four weeks the children watched either aggressive cartoons, prosocial or neutral films. During this period, and in the

final two weeks, behaviour was again observed. Children who initially were above average in aggression were affected by the violent cartoons. Those who were neutral did not react to either type of programme, indicating an interaction between personality and the effects of violent programmes. **Milgram (1974)** was approached by an American television company to test this possibility. Two versions of the same programme were broadcast simultaneously in different areas, one version showed someone breaking into a charity box and making an abusive phone call. A control version omitted these features. Six people made similar calls to the company after the programme compared with four who called in after the control version. **Turner et al. (1986)** reviewed a number of quasi-experimental studies about the effects of naturally occurring media violence and concluded that it produces long-term increases in boys' but not girls' aggressive behaviour.

④ Longitudinal approach. Most studies show that observing violence has some effect but are the effects lasting? **Williams (1985)** studied a town in British Columbia, before and after it was able to receive television. Two years after television arrived the children were observed as being more aggressive and holding more stereotypes. **Eron et al. (1972)** determined the extent of a 9-year-old's exposure to violence by asking their parents what their favourite television programmes were. They also asked their peers to rate them for aggressiveness. The two measures showed high correlation between aggression and violent television watching. Ten years later the same measures were taken and, for boys, violent television at age 9 correlated with peer-rated aggression at 19, but peer-rated aggression at age 9 was not correlated with watching violent television at 19, which suggests that watching violent television leads to aggression rather than vice versa. The findings for girls, if anything, went in the reverse direction, perhaps because there are fewer aggressive female role models. A Dutch study by **Wiegman et al. (1992)** followed over 400 secondary pupils for three years and found positive correlations between TV violence and aggressive behaviour. However, these disappeared when corrections were made for starting levels of aggression and intelligence. Therefore they concluded that there was no support for the view that TV violence leads to aggressive behaviour.

⑤ Physiological approach. Cline et al. (1973) showed that 5- to 12-year-olds who watched a lot of television violence showed less emotional response in terms of heart rate, blood pressure and pulse, when shown a film containing violence; thus supporting the view that violence desensitises the viewer.

⑥ Correlating the amount of TV violence with delinquency. The first issue is establishing how much violence appears on TV. **Cumberbatch et al. (1988)** reviewed studies which measured violence, noting that the amounts vary enormously. The most reliable estimate may be five or six violent acts per hour on prime time American TV. Rates on British TV are probably considerably lower. **Cumberbatch (1987)** noted that most people thought that violence on TV was increasing, but this was not supported by the evidence. **Messner (1986)** found that populations with high levels of exposure to violent TV exhibited *lower* rates of violent crime.

Explanations for and against

① People **copy** particular acts of violence, supported by **Bandura**'s original study and anecdotal evidence from case histories.

②ValueValue shaping. Television influences our norms and attitudes.

③ Much of the evidence is **correlational**. Notions about cause are based on theory and other branches of psychology.

④ Television violence may **directly cause** increased levels of aggression through copying or value shaping, as suggested above. As television characters are often seen as heroes who gain respect and other rewards through their actions, they are especially likely to be imitated. It may also act as a cue to aggressive behaviour.

⑤ Television violence may **indirectly cause** increased levels of aggression through **desensitisation, disinhibition or arousal.**

⑥ **Aggressive** people may simply choose to watch violent programmes more. **Friedrich and Stein (p.122)** found that aggression-prone children are likely to become even more aggressive after watching violent television.

⑦ **Discord at home** may result in children wanting to watch violent programmes and behaving aggressively. **Rutter (1981)** found such discord to be a high predictor of later aggressive behaviour.

⑧ The evidence suggested by empirical studies may in part be due to **experimenter bias.** The children might be trying to please the experimenter, especially as children are notoriously suggestible.

⑨ The studies are often of **artificially contrived** situations, which may not generalise to real life.

⑩ The effects produced were mainly from short term studies, do they **last over time**?

⑪ Watching television might be **cathartic,** providing fantasy outlets for aggressive drive. Folk tales provide a safe framework for experiencing frightening things; the same is probably true of violent films.

⑫ The effects of television are not as great as some claim, many scenes of violence are not taken seriously by children, such as James Bond, the A team or cartoons. **Bandura** *et al.* **(1963)** compared the effects of aggression seen live, on film and in cartoons and found progressively smaller effects, though there were some effects.

⑬ With regard to **anti-social behaviour**, it has been suggested that both television and computer games have led to a decline in the traditional social games played by children, and that childhood is now a more solitary (less social) experience.

Conclusion

The **USA Surgeon General's Report** concluded, after a massive amount of research, that TV violence is influential, as many as 25% of child viewers may be affected. On the other hand, **Howitt and Cumberbatch (1974)** concluded from their own study of over 2000 children and 300 other studies, that there was no direct effect of media violence, though there is considerable disagreement between different studies. **Selfe (1987)** concludes that violence can never be considered the sole cause of delinquent behaviour, it may reinforce or affect those already prone to such tendencies.

THE MEDIA AS A SOURCE OF SOCIAL STEREOTYPES

Media present a stereotyped picture of life, which may lead to undesirable prejudices (and, in turn, aggression). Children's programmes in particular tend to exaggerate stereotypes, presenting goodies and baddies, and children often have their only contact with some minority groups through the television. For adults, the confirmation of their stereotypes may make them feel more comfortable, programmes which try to present life against common perceptions may prove unpopular.

Content

It is still the case that women, ethnic groups, the disabled, certain professions such as social workers, the old and the physically unattractive are presented according to accepted stereotypes.

Durkin (1985) suggests that there are more men than women on television; that men are portrayed as more powerful, dominant, rational and intelligent; and women watch admiringly and passively as men perform. **Manstead and McCulloch (1981)** used the content analysis technique to look for sex stereotyping in British commercials, and found that men and women continue to be portrayed in traditional roles – males have expertise and authority, women are shown as consumers and unknowledgeable about the reasons for buying a particular product. **Russo** *et al.* **(1982)** found similar demeaning stereotypes for women in American ads.

Himmelweit *et al.* **(1958)** found that foreigners were more often portrayed as villains than heroes.

Children's books have tried to reflect the changing roles of mothers and fathers in terms of work and child care, and also to reflect today's multicultural society.

McRobbie (1978) performed a study of the girls' magazine *Jackie*, and found that it reinforced traditional gender stereotypes relating romantic love to attractiveness, and portraying love as the main motive for adolescents.

Effect

However, the question is whether such biases affect the viewer. **Greenfield (1984)** found that *Sesame Street*'s use of ethnic and disabled minorities has had positive affects on children, particularly those from the minority groups who feel greater cultural pride and self-confidence.

Hartmann and Husband (1981) argue that the media do not change or form racial attitudes, but do provide a framework for thinking. For example, the persistent portrayal of race issues in terms of conflict.

Not everyone will respond to stereotypes in the same way, and it is difficult to separate what we learn from the media from attitudes we already hold when they are consistent with each other. Where there are differences, people impose their existing stereotypes on what they watch and this moderates any influence they might have.

One such explanation is the *amplification of deviance*. Certain events are over-reported, such as violent or sex crimes, and this acts to alter public opinion. **Cohen (1965)** suggests that the media creates moral panics by widely reporting an initially minor event, which leads to further detailed reports, identification of causes or troublemakers ('folk devils'). One example he gives is the mods and rockers of the 1960s. It has also been suggested that female fears about rape are exaggerated by the over-reporting of such incidences.

POSITIVE INFLUENCE OF THE MEDIA

Television and prosocial behaviour

O'Connor (1969) found that 'loners' who watched a specially made film about children their age interacting with others with positive results, were then able to become more socially involved. **Stein and Friedrich (1975)** observed increases in prosocial types of play in children who watched programmes emphasising such behaviour.

Wilson *et al.* (1992) found that a TV movie on date rape had some prosocial value. For example, that older women in their sample of more than 1000 adults were less likely to attribute blame to women in date rape situations after viewing the film than a control group of non-viewers. **Brown and Cody (1991)** examined the effects of a soap opera *Hum Log*, designed to promote women's status in Indian society, but found that, despite the female viewers' emotional involvement, women had not changed their attitudes.

Counter-stereotyping

Attempts to produce counter-stereotypes could be equally effective, unless real experiences counteract these unusual roles. **Geis *et al.* (1984)** showed female undergraduates sex-role reversals in advertisements and demonstrated that this had a positive effect. But there is also evidence of resistance and individual differences to such attempts.

Interaction with the media

It should be remembered that we are not a passive audience, we can switch the television off and select what we read. Many writers suggest that parents should take an active role in monitoring what their children watch and watch it with them to encourage discussion.

THE ETHICS OF THE MEDIA

Is it ethical to manipulate social stereotypes, even if they are deemed positive?

Any attempt to censor, even if it's to reduce the amount of aggression or smoking, is problematic.

The control of the mass media is a question which concerns sociologists; it is the means by which particular groups of people wield power – the ruling class, the rich, the unions or even televangelists. Of particular concern is the amplification of deviance (see above) and the handling of the news and current affairs. **Lewis and Rowe (1994)** present two opposing arguments. Lewis claims that the news is currently biased in a negative direction. Rowe counter-argues that any attempt to correct this would present a misleading 'rosy' picture.

> ## Chapter roundup
>
> All other chapters include related material:
> - cognitive psychology (Chapter 1), perception;
> - developmental psychology (Chapter 3), early socialisation and social development;
> - language (Chapter 4), non-verbal communication and communication generally;
> - intelligence, personality and assessment (Chapter 5), explicit personality theories and techniques of measuring attitudes, opinions, and so on;
> - abnormal psychology (Chapter 6), antisocial and disturbed behaviour;
> - biological psychology (Chapter 7), includes emotion and aggression;
> - comparative psychology (Chapter 8), studies of social and antisocial behaviour in animals;
> - organisational psychology (Chapter 9), the social aspects of work, environmental influences on, for example, antisocial behaviour and attitudes towards health;
> - research and design (Chapter 10), details psychological methods and ethical matters.

Illustrative question

Discuss, using experimental evidence, some of the psychological factors which contribute to successful advertising.

Tutorial note

In this essay we should first aim to *describe* the available evidence on topics such as attitudes, attitude change, persuasion, conformity, compliance and so on, as well as *evaluating* this evidence in terms of its possible relevance to advertising.

For maximum marks this account should be coherent and not simply strung together, should be more than descriptive, should go further than the obvious material on persuasion and should give evidence which is accurate and well detailed.

Suggested answer

The advertising message has two components, first the content itself and second, the evaluative aspect of the message. **Petty and Cacioppo (1981)** call these the central and peripheral routes to persuasion. It is more often the aim of an ad to encourage a positive attitude towards their product rather than pass on particular information. **Love and Greenwald (1978)** found that people don't remember the content of a persuasive message as well as they remember their reactions.

Advertisers aim to create a positive 'image' (evaluation) for their products. Classical conditioning provides an explanation for how this process works. The product (conditioned stimulus) is paired with a positive image (unconditioned stimulus) such as an attractive person or idyllic country scene, and thus becomes associated with a pleasant feeling (unconditioned response).

Social Learning Theory and research has shown how people are operantly conditioned through seeing models being rewarded for certain behaviour, thus increasing the likelihood that we might copy them. A familiar television actor buys a product and shows how it saved them money or made them look younger. **Bandura, Ross and Ross (1961)** showed how children imitated the *specific* actions of a model acting violently towards Bobo-the-Clown, and also how this resulted in generally increased aggression.

Many advertisements use stereotypes. This serves many functions. First, a great deal of information can be communicated using a minimum number of cues. Second, because we like our expectations to be confirmed. This is called the confirmatory bias and has been demonstrated by showing that people remember things better if they are consistent with their existing attitudes. For example, **Cohen (1981)** showed subjects a film of a waitress or a librarian, later recall was better for those behaviours which were consistent with the role. Third, stereotypes are associated with group norms and a desire to conform to such norms is strong, particularly in situations where there is no right or wrong answer. **Sherif (1936)** demonstrated such situations are resolved through the 'social reality' created by a group.

Advertisers aim to make their product more familiar, either simply because exposure makes it recognisable when we see it in the supermarket or through increased liking due to familiarity. Psychologists have shown us that if people encounter things frequently enough they develop a positive attitude towards them. For example, **Zajonc (1968)** repeated nonsense words 5, 10 or 25 times, the more frequently subjects heard a word the more positive was their response.

A common technique in selling is 'getting x by asking for y', this may involve starting with an initial small request which prepares the way for a larger one because it leads to changes in the way a person sees themselves. **Freedman and Fraser (1966)** asked housewives if they could classify all the products in their home. This outrageous request was more successful when it had been preceded by a telephone survey about household products. Conversely a large request, turned down, can lead to an increased likelihood that a subsequent, smaller request will be complied with **(Cialdini *et al.*, 1975)**. Such techniques are frequently used by children to get what they want from parents.

All the evidence examined so far relates to the message itself, and in particular to its connote rather than denote – the peripheral route. **Hovland *et al.*, (1953)** suggested that three features influence the likelihood of persuasion: the source, the message, and the receiver. Later they added a fourth dimension: the context. This framework is useful for looking at a vast body of evidence.

Features of the source that will increase persuasion include such things as: power, expertise, credibility, motives, similarity, likeability and other personal attributes such as race and religion. If the speaker directs the message at the consumer this may detract from its value. **Walster and Festinger (1962)** found that a message which is overheard is more believable than one directed at the listener. A more attractive person is more likely to be imitated, but **Zimbardo (1960)** found that a disliked source can sometimes be more persuasive than an admired one.

The presentation of the message can help. For example, rhetorical questions, such as 'Isn't it clear that Daz is better than powder B?' are more persuasive, particularly in apathetic situations. **McGuire (1968)** found that explicit conclusions may help when listeners are not intelligent or motivated enough to draw their own conclusions. Similarly, one-sided messages, rather than two-sided arguments, work better with an uneducated audience **(Hovland *et al.*, 1949)**. The order of the arguments may be important. The primacy effect is strong especially where both arguments are presented by the same person and when the listener makes a public commitment after the first message **(Hovland, 1957)**.

People often don't listen to the exact content of a message. They remember the evaluative element better, as already discussed, or prefer to use other features of the message. One dimension is the number of arguments. **Petty and Cacioppo (1986)** found that people use a rule of thumb to determine 'truth', the more arguments there are the more persuasive the message.

Another dimension is repetition. It leads to familiarity and therefore increased liking, and to rehearsal and therefore better recall.

Advertisements which arouse fear can have either positive or negative effects. Where threats are made such as, 'smoking can kill' this may arouse a defensive response unless the viewer is given an effective means of avoiding the consequences. On the other hand, using shock tactics, as in some of the drink-drive advertisements, has been successful.

The third variable in the effectiveness of a persuasive communication is the receiver, the target audience. Advertising companies put a great deal of effort, understandably, into constructing consumer profiles – a cluster of personality characteristics of a particular type of person so that they can direct their advertising at the right sort of person. Someone who might buy cans of lager might like an advertisement with football and humour, whereas a housewife might like something homey and orderly.

Another aspect of the receiver that has been found to be important is intelligence. The more intelligent receiver is better able to remember the message, but also more likely to be more confident about already held attitudes and therefore more resistant to change.

Women are slightly more persuadable than men **(Eagly, 1978)**. A particularly useful concept is **Sherif and Hovland's (1961)** 'latitude of acceptance or rejection'; where the view presented differs too much from the listener's initial stance it is unlikely to be successful. This can also be explained in terms of dissonance. **Kleinhesselink and Edwards (1975)** found that people were more likely to switch off experimentally-created static (so that they could hear) when the message they were listening to supported their views. Where an advertisement creates too great a degree of dissonance people switch off, metaphorically or actually.

The final dimension is the context – whether the message is written, visual, spoken, audio-visual or face-to-face. It appears that more complex messages are best when written. It is thought that television reaches a vast audience but some research has shown that, though the television is on, often no one is watching it. It may be more appropriate to select other media for advertising, and this must be related to who you want to reach.

Having understood and designed the advertisement, how can its effect be assessed? One of the particular problems is the question of how long do such effects last? **Osgood and Suci**'s Semantic Differential Technique could be used to assess the evaluative component of people's attitudes towards a product. A more experimental approach might look at attitudes and behaviour before and after a particular advertising campaign, utilising Thurstone or Likert methods of attitude assessment.

The research into persuasion and related topics amounts to a vast collection of interesting phenomena but few general principles. There has been one attempt to offer a theoretical perspective – the Cognitive Response theory developed by **Petty and Cacioppo (1986)**. This asserts that it is the thoughts and emotions evoked by the communication, not the communication itself, which lead to attitude change. If the message generates a positive internal cognitive response the message will result in attitude formation or change – the person persuades themselves. If a negative response is generated this can cause a 'boomerang' effect.

Question bank

Allow 45 minutes for each question.

1 Discuss some of the problems faced by social psychologists in conducting laboratory and field investigations.

(AEB 'A', 1981)

Points: Refer to Chapter 10 for advantages and disadvantages of the research methods.

2 Describe and evaluate psychological research concerning the strategies of self presentation which people may use in social encounters.

(AEB 'A', 1991)

Points: Avoid 'lay' answers; may need to research the topic more widely.

3 Critically consider the role played by stereotypes in how we perceive other people.

(AEB 'AS', 1991)

Points: Unfortunately, the question lends itself to anecdotal answers. Empirical evidence from interpersonal perception will be relevant. Positive as well as negative stereotypes should be discussed.

4 (a) Discuss errors and biases which may occur in the attribution process. (15 marks)
    (b) Discuss one practical application based on research into attributions. (10 marks)

(AEB 'AS', 1992)

Points: Candidates often know a lot about one part and very little of the other. In this case, knowledge of applications is usually thin, but if you take time you can usually think of some using common sense. You should decribe them using your psychological knowledge.

5 (a) Define briefly the following three terms and give an example of each.
    (i)   stereotyping (3 marks),
    (ii) racism (3 marks),
    (iii) sexism (3 marks),
  (b) Discuss, making reference to empirical studies, the main social factors influencing the choice of friends that a young person makes. (11 marks)

(NEAB, 'A', 1991)

Points: Should include conformity as well as attraction. How does the phrase 'a young person' limit the question?

6 Discuss, with reference to ethological studies, the extent to which human aggression may be explained as a product of evolution.

(NEAB 'A', 1987)

Points: The question essentially asks whether violence is a matter of nature or nurture. Any material in this chapter can be used if relevant. Refer also to the section on ethology in Chapter 8.

7 Critically evaluate studies of conformity.

(AEB 'A', 1987)

Points: It is important to be clear about what constitutes conformity. Any studies can be used as long as their inclusion is justified.

8 Discuss psychological investigations of obedience in humans and consider the implications of this type of research.

(AEB, 'A', 1989)

Points: The question can be divided into two parts: description and evaluation of empirical studies, and a discussion of the ethical and social implications.

9 'Leaders are born not made'. Discuss.

(AEB, AS, 1990)

Points: Essentially a nature/nurture question, which should be discussed specifically in terms of leaders, rather than behaviour generally.

10 Discuss some of the ways in which the presence of others may affect the behaviour of an individual.

(AEB, 'A', 1981)

Points: A straightforward question, which may lead to an oversimple answer. A good answer needs to go further than listing the ways. Relevant evidence is necessary for each way given, plus a critical appreciation of any theory or research.

11 (a) Describe one study in which an attempt was made to assess the influence of television on social behaviour. (6 marks)
  (b) Name and discuss **one** weakness and **one** strength in the methodology of the study you have described. (6 marks)
  (c) Discuss two major problems which limit the extent to which clear-cut evidence can be found to show that television may influence social behaviour. (8 marks)

(NEAB, 'A', 1988)

Points: Television can have a pro- or antisocial influence on behaviour. The problem with much research in this area is its poor validity, a point addressed by part (c).

CHAPTER 3

DEVELOPMENTAL PSYCHOLOGY

Units in this chapter

Chapter overview

Development refers to the systematic changes that occur in an individual from conception to death, the lifelong process of change. At one time developmental psychology was almost entirely concerned with childhood but now extends to adolescence, adulthood and old age, though these aspects are sometimes specifically referred to as 'lifespan development'. This recent perspective emphasises the individual's prior development, current level of development and likely development in the future.

Historical development

Philosophers of the 17th and 18th centuries have had a significant influence over education, then and now, with their views about children. Locke described the mind at birth as a tabula rasa, a blank slate, thereby emphasising the role of experience and socialisation. On the other hand, Rousseau claimed that children are born with an innate sense of right and wrong – noble savages. His view was that education must enhance natural sensibilities and protect the child from the corrupting influence of civilisation.

The first steps towards a systematic study of child development were taken by diarists such as **Darwin (1877)**, who kept a day-to-day record of his own children, like a naturalist studying a strange animal.

G. Stanley Hall (1844–1924) is frequently regarded as the founder of developmental psychology. He set out to collect more objective data from larger samples 'discovering' and developing the questionnaire as a tool for psychological research. He was influenced by Darwin's ideas and thought that the stages of development recapitulated social evolution, concluding that the distinctive character of childhood must be respected. Going beyond childhood, he wrote books on adolescence and senescence.

Freud, at the same time, revolutionised thinking about children and childhood with his view that 'the child is psychologically the father of the man and the events of his first years are of paramount importance for his whole subsequent life'. In fact Hall was an early exponent of psychoanalysis, inviting Freud and Jung to speak in America in 1909.

3.1 EARLY DEVELOPMENT

The two main topics are:
- **sociability**: the active and reciprocal nature of infant interactions,
- **attachment**: the consequences of attachment, or its absence, deprivation.

Sociability is the willingness to interact with others, whereas attachment is a specific bond. Both sociability and attachment are innate mechanisms to ensure:
- social interaction,
- physical protection,
- the physical proximity and continuing involvement of a caretaker(s).

EARLY REPERTOIRES OF SOCIAL BEHAVIOUR

Innate behaviours of infants should be considered in the light of the following:
1 infants are born with important interpersonal reflexes,
2 some of these reflexes elicit specific attachments,
3 others engage general social interest of people,
4 it is a system of mutual demands – both participants are equally active and involved,
5 the emergence of some behaviours may await sufficient cognitive and/or physical maturity,
6 such initially innate behaviours go on to be shaped by experience.

The specific behaviours which are critical to socialisation and attachment include:

1 **Smiling**: invites the interactions of others:
- **Ahrens (1954)**. There is an inherited tendency to smile at anything which appears like a human face, such as two dots on an oval piece of card. As the child gets older the 'face' needs to resemble the real thing more closely in order to elicit a smile.
- **Gewirtz (1965)** found that smiling will tail off if it is not successful, e.g. in institutional care.

2 **Imitation**: important for learning but is also a non-verbal means of communicating liking, e.g. perceived similarity increases affiliation (see 2.4):
- **Meltzoff and Moore (1983)** found that babies 12–21 days old mainly imitated mouth opening and sticking out their tongue but this gradually developed to include more complex routines.

3 **Crying**: an obvious method of importance to survival, but also varied to communicate more than danger or hunger. It's no accident that adults find a baby's cries uncomfortable:
- Only in species where the infants are immobile do they cry, e.g. kittens but not foals.
- **Wolff (1969)** showed that inexperienced mothers responded differently to a tape of a 'pain' cry to one of 'hunger' or 'madness'.
- Do we learn to respond to the meaning of our own infants or is this innate behaviour? **Kaye (1984)** calls it an evolved fit, though the response time is learned.

4 **Cooing**: a sign of pleasure and the beginnings of vocalisations such as babbling and echolalia, leading eventually to language which enables the infant to enter fully into social interaction.

5 **Eye-contact**: a non-verbal means of signalling liking:
- **Robson (1967)** suggests that early mutual gaze may play a part in bonding.
- **Fraiberg (1974)** studied blind babies, who often turn their head away in order to hear better, and found mothers felt rejected and unhappy with the infant.

6 **Interactional synchrony**: an example of reciprocal interaction:
- **Jaffe et al. (1973)** noted the timing of the interactions between mother and baby and found that they were similar to normal adult conversation.

7 **Emotional sensitivity:**
- **Johnson *et al*. (1982)** noted that many mothers of 1-month-old babies could discern at least five distinct emotions: interest, surprise, joy, anger and fear.
- **Tronick (1989)** found that 3-month-olds became gleeful in response to a happy expression from their mother and distressed by their mother's anger or sadness. This 'social referencing' extends to strangers by 12 months.

Age in months	Social behaviour
1	reacts to voices, attentive to faces, asocial
2/3	social smile
4	reacts differently to familiar and unfamiliar people
7–9	specific attachments (related to ability to discriminate), followed by multiple attachments
9	stranger and separation anxiety, facial signs of anger and frustration
11/12	sadness to loss of an attachment figure
24	reduction of attachment behaviours, such as clinging and following, beginnings of exploration and independence

THEORETICAL APPROACHES TO EARLY DEVELOPMENT

1 **Psychoanalytic theory:** an infant is born with innate drives towards sensory pleasure. **Freud** described psychosexual stages, **Erikson**'s emphasis was on psychosocial stages. Fixations can be caused by over- or under-gratification and may lead to serious problems later. 'Love has its origins in attachment to the satisfied need for nourishment'. **Bowlby**'s origins were psychoanalytic, maternal deprivation may be a latter day equivalent of oral deprivation.

2 **Behaviourism – social learning approach:** behaviourists also believed that hunger, pain and thirst were the basic biological drives which motivated an infant. At a very early age babies show evidence of conditioning. An infant is attracted to those individuals who reinforce their social signals and who provide pleasant experiences. The caregiver is a conditioned reinforcer, an initially neutral stimulus which acquires reinforcement value by virtue of its repeated associations with other reinforcing stimuli.

3 **Structuralist/cognitive: Piaget** has described maturational stages in cognitive development, which can be related to the appearance of social behaviours, for example, before an attachment can occur the infant must be able to discriminate familiar persons from strangers, and must have reached Piaget's sensorimotor substage of object permanence.

4 **Ethology:** the work of **Lorenz** and **Tinbergen** emphasised the survival value of innate behaviours and introduced several important concepts, such as critical or sensitive periods and imprinting. **Bowlby**'s later work incorporated these ideas.

5 **Cross-cultural:** the fact that psychologically healthy individuals can be shown to emerge from all types of rearing styles shows that there is not a single route to optimal attachment. Even our culture has used different techniques in different generations ostensibly related to 'scientific' knowledge but also fitting in with prevailing attitudes, e.g. scheduled feeding and feeding on demand that was prevalent earlier this century.

KEY STUDIES

1 **Lorenz (1932 onwards)** demonstrated that goslings and other mobile newborns show a fairly indiscriminate attachment to moving objects, a person, a crude model duck or even a cardboard box. His chief observations were that:
- imprinting is automatic,
- it occurs within a narrow critical period,
- it is irreversible, once imprinted on a particular object they remain attached to it.

Lorenz saw imprinting as an adaptive response, the survival of the young is helped if they stay close to their mother for protection and food-gathering. It can easily be seen how animals without this innate response would never survive to reproduce (see also 8.3).

② Harry and Margaret Harlow (1958 onwards) have conducted extensive research with rhesus monkeys on the effects of maternal deprivation. Their main projects have been:

(a) Tending bottle-fed monkeys. They noted that the monkeys were distressed when the sanitation pad at the bottom of the cage was changed daily, like a child with a special blanket. This led them to investigate the relative importance of feeding and body contact.

(b) Providing solitary, caged infant monkeys with wire and cloth 'mothers'. In each case only one mother actually provided milk. However, regardless of which mother provided milk, all the infants spent more time with the cloth mother and, when frightened, went to that mother; the wire mother was ignored altogether. Later the monkeys were totally unsuccessful at mating (**Harlow and Zimmerman, 1959**).

(c) Raising monkeys in total isolation or partial isolation (monkeys could see and hear other monkeys but could not touch them). The experimental monkeys in both conditions, when released, showed complete social maladjustment and autistic behaviour, difficulty mating and became abusive mothers. If isolation stopped after the first three months the monkeys could recover.

(d) They wondered if isolation might not just be maternal deprivation but also peer deprivation, and raised four infants together. They spent most of their early months huddled together but later appeared to develop normally.

(e) Using two types of cloth mother, one who blasted the infants with a strong current of compressed air at random intervals, which Harlow suggested is equivalent to abusing them. The strongest attachments were shown by those who were abused (**Rosenblum and Harlow, 1963**).

(f) Raising infant monkeys in total isolation for one year and then introducing younger 'therapist' monkeys, who played and interacted with them. This led to a reversal of earlier privation (**Novak and Harlow, 1975**).

Summary of work:
- physical contact is more important than feeding in development of an emotional bond,
- early social deprivation permanently impairs reproductive success. Females who do become pregnant are inadequate mothers,
- peer bonds may provide effective substitutes for lack of maternal ones,
- deprivation can be overcome.

③ John Bowlby was asked by the World Health Organization to study the effects of maternal deprivation on children who were made homeless during the Second World War. Bowlby's training was as a psychoanalyst. His views have had a profound effect on social policy and psychological research:

(a) His book *Maternal care and mental health* emphasised the importance of an intimate, continuous relationship with the mother (or a permanent substitute) as being essential for mental health. 'Mother love in infancy and childhood is as important for mental health as are vitamins and proteins for physical health' (1953).

(b) *Attachment and Loss* published as three volumes revised his initial views in terms of an ethological/evolutionary perspective. The infant's need to stay close and form an attachment has survival value, ensuring the safety of the infant and the reproductive success of the parents. The process is related to imprinting and also has a critical period, probably up to 3 years.

(c) **Research:**
- **(1946).** Compared 44 juvenile thieves with 44 emotionally disturbed teenagers. Significantly more of those in the first group had been separated from their mothers for at least one week under the age of 5, and showed an inability to show or feel affection (affectionless psychopathy). However, the evidence is flawed in several respects: it is retrospective and correlational, and no good explanation is offered as to why all those who had been separated didn't experience problems.

- **(1956).** Retrospective study of 60 children who had spent up to 2 years in a TB sanatorium when they were younger than four. When compared with their 'normal' schoolmates there appeared to be some small but not significant differences.

Summary of work:
- instinctive nature of bonding and survival value,
- critical or sensitive period,
- attachment to one individual, not necessarily mother,
- also other attachments but of less importance,
- the importance of continuous care up to age five,
- effects of deprivation on later behaviour.

4 Mary Ainsworth (1967 onwards)
(a) **1967.** Studied Ganda tribe of Uganda: most infants cared for by several adults and formed multiple attachments.
(b) **1973.** Studied babies in Baltimore: noted that the mother is used as a secure base for exploration.
(c) **1978.** Developed the **Strange Situation**, a standardised means of assessing strength or quality of attachment. The procedure consists of seven 3-minute episodes:
- parent and infant enter,
- stranger joins parent and infant,
- parent leaves,
- parent returns, stranger leaves,
- parent leaves,
- stranger returns,
- parent returns, stranger leaves.

The key events are the parent's departure and return, and the child's behaviour in response, which has been classified as follows:

Type A   anxious–avoidant   no protest, ignore mother's return (10%)
Type B   securely attached   mild protest on departure, on return seeks mother and easily comforted (70%)
Type C   anxious–resistant   seriously distressed, alternatively clings and pushes mother away (20%)

The percentages vary somewhat between studies and, significantly, when tested in other cultures. For example, a German study found 40% of type A, and a Japanese study found 35% type C. However type B is the majority group, such children have been found to be more socially outgoing, independent, co-operative, compliant and curious, and better able to cope with stress.

Secure attachment is particularly related to responsiveness of the mother, this is called the **'caregiving hypothesis' (1979).**

5 Michael Rutter
(a) **1976.** Studied 9–12-year-old boys living in London and the Isle of Wight who had experienced maternal separation. Those who later showed maladjustment had been separated because of family discord rather than illness, housing problems or holidays.
(b) **'Maternal deprivation reassessed' (1981, 2nd edition).** Felt that a distinction should be made between deprivation and privation, the complete absence of attachment.
(c) Has produced many more books and focused attention on hospitalisation, education and autism.

Summary of work: Bowlby's original work on maternal deprivation is flawed in certain respects:
- recovery from maternal deprivation is possible,
- some cases of deprivation are due to privation,
- in other cases ill effects are due to other, covarying factors, such as family discord.

6 Schaffer and Emerson (1964) provided a large and useful body of data from naturalistic observation of 60 Scottish babies aged 0 to 18 months.

ATTACHMENT

Bonding

The affection and recognition between a mother and her child is established soon after birth. The bond is to form a relationship.

Attachment

The further development of such initial bonds, an affective tie between an infant and caregiver, which has several theoretical and practical functions:
- indicates degree of dependence or independence,
- evolutionary function,
- critical for healthy emotional development.

Behaviours which are associated with attachment are:
- a child's tendency to seek closeness to certain people and to feel secure when they are present,
- the target of the attachment is best able to placate infant,
- the infant is more likely to go to the target for play and consolation,
- the infant is less likely to feel afraid when the target is present.

Attachment is often measured by the Ainsworth Strange Situation (see p.134).

What factors may lead to attachment?

① **Feeding**: Freudian and Behaviourist theory predicts that the infant will be attracted to any person who provides oral satisfaction.
- **Lorenz (1953)**: attachment of goslings to mother-figure takes place through mere exposure regardless of feeding.

② Physical contact:
- Feeding is associated with close physical contact and social interaction, which may give the false impression that feeding is associated with attachment. See for example, the **Harlow and Zimmerman (1959)** experiment described on p.133.
- In the recent past, hospitals frequently separated mothers and infants, which may have had profound effects on early bonding. **Klaus and Kennell (1976)** arranged for one group of 14 mothers to have extra contact time with their newborn babies, one hour rather than 5 minutes after birth and an extra 5 hours daily. A month later and a year later there were some differences favouring the extra contact group.
- **Goldberg (1983)** has reviewed many studies and concludes that the effects of early contact are neither large nor long-lasting.

③ **Time and caregiving**: also predicted by Behaviourist theory.
- **Schaffer and Emerson (1964)** asked mothers to give details of their feeding practices, none of which predicted the character of the infant's attachment. In 39% of the cases the person who usually fed, bathed and changed the child was not the child's primary attachment object.
- **Fox (1977)** studied Israeli kibbutzim, and found evidence that children still formed strong attachments with their mothers despite spending shorter amounts of time with them than with the kibbutz nurses. This supports the notion of quality time.

④ Critical period:
- **Klaus and Kennell (1976)**, described above, felt that the first 6–12 hours were critical. It was not the contact itself but the timing of the contact, which may be directed by the presence of hormones at the time of delivery.
- **Bowlby** claimed the first three years were critical to later development.
- **Rutter** suggests that though there may be a sensitive period, recovery is still possible at any time (see p.138).
- **Maturational level**: It is no accident that attachment and object permanence appear at a similar time, around 8 months. **Lester et al. (1974)** showed that a child's level of object permanence was consistent with their separation anxiety, a measure of their attachment.

⑤Individual differences:
- **Schaffer and Emerson (1964)** found evidence that some babies like cuddling while others don't. These differences were evident very early on and not related to how mothers handled their infants.

⑥Sensitivity and responsiveness to child's signals: the currently favoured conception:
- **Ainsworth et al. (1974)** proposed that it is the quality not quantity of interaction that counts. Anxious attachment results from mothers who respond less readily to a child's needs. Secure attachment occurs when a mother is sensitive, sees things from an infant's viewpoint and is accepting.
- **Schaffer and Emerson (1964)** found that maternal responsiveness and total amount of stimulation were related to the infant's attachment.
- **Anisfeld et al. (1990)** showed that babies were more securely attached to their mothers when they had experienced close physical contact in the form of a pouch-like baby-carrier than if the mothers had used plastic infant seats. The two groups had been randomly assigned and the researchers felt that the effect was due to increased responsiveness as a result of the closer physical contact.

One or multiple attachments?

1 an infant needs mother love,
2 an infant needs one attachment, not necessarily the mother – 'monotropy',
3 a child needs and develops qualitatively different attachments.

❶Mother love: Mead (1949) is often quoted for her view that fathers are 'a biological necessity but a social accident'. We never talk of paternal deprivation or paternal instinct. Is this fair? Until recently there has been little opportunity to assess men in a mothering role:
- **Parke (1981)** found fathers' style of play to be more vigorous, physically stimulating, unusual and unpredictable. Mothers were more conventional and read stories.
- **Lamb (1981)** found each of the infant's attachment figures may serve different functions rather than being in a hierarchy. Mothers may be preferred if upset or frightened, fathers as playmates.

❷One major caregiver: attachments need not be just to a mother-figure, they can be to the father, a sibling, a grandparent or an adoptive/foster family (see evidence on deprivation):
- **Freud and Dann (1951)** studied six orphans from German concentration camps, who had no relationships with adults. Their emotional survival is attributed to the attachment bonds they formed and maintained with each other.

❸Multiple attachments: more than one kind of satisfaction can be derived from an attachment, it may be positively beneficial to have many rather than one attachment:
- **Schaffer and Emerson (1964)** noted that specific attachments started at about 8 months and, very shortly thereafter, the infants became attached to other people. By 18 months very few (13%) were attached to only one person; some had five or more attachments.
- **Ainsworth (1967)** found that the Ganda tribe relied on multiple attachments.

❹Stability
- **Vaughn et al. (1979)** studied single parent families and found that between 12 and 18 months, some children had changed from being securely attached to being anxious, or vice versa. This suggests that attachment is subject to changing circumstances.

DEPRIVATION

This is the other side of the coin – what happens when children are deprived of an attachment figure? There are two processes:

❶Syndrome of distress and separation anxiety, resulting from, for example, a short-stay in hospital. A distinct sequence of behaviour is observed:

- protesting but able to be comforted,
- despair and inconsolable,
- denial and detachment – denies any affection or response to mother on eventual reunion.

2 **Symptoms of deprivation** as a result of prolonged separation:
- psychosomatic reactions,
- increased aggressive behaviour towards mother,
- more clinging behaviour,
- detachment,
- fluctuation between clinging and detachment,
- school phobia.

Delayed bonding

When children are born prematurely or are ill, or if they are adopted, they miss important early contact which may disturb the attachment process:

- **Brackbill et al. (1985)** concluded from a review of nearly 60 studies that mothers who received large doses of medication during birth had babies who smiled infrequently, were inattentive and irritable, and were difficult to feed and comfort. This may be related to problems in bonding. Such babies continue to show deficits in physical and mental development for at least one year after birth.

Part-time separation: Child care

1 If, as Bowlby has suggested, a child needs its mother continually for the first five years, what effect does childcare arrangements have on development?:
- **Belsky (1988)** noted that half the mothers of 1-year-olds in the US were in employment. He analysed a number of recent studies and concluded that many of such infants were insecurely attached.
- **Mayall and Petrie (1977, 1983), Bryant et al. (1980)** found that British children were often insecure in the childminder's home.
- **Kagan et al. (1978)** studied 30 infants between 3 and 29 months. Half attended day-care facilities, the others were at home. Both groups were equivalent in terms of language development, quality of attachment to the mother and separation anxiety.
- For some children, day-care may be a positive advantage. **Burchinal et al. (1989)** tested the IQ of children entering kindergarten and found that disadvantaged children who had been in day-care usually did better than those who had been cared for by their mothers at home.

2 How does staying at home affect the mother?:
- She may feel frustrated and cannot provide suitable care.
- **Brown and Harris (1978)** looked at causes of depression in women. They found that being at home full-time with two or more children was one cause.
- **Hoffman (1989)** reviewed the relevant literature and concluded that working mothers often compensated for lack of quantity with quality time. Employment does not prevent secure attachment *per se* but may be correlated through other factors, such as low socio-economic grouping.

Short-term deprivation or separation

Deprivation occurs where attachments exist but the child is temporarily deprived of them, this might even include parents going on holiday alone (while leaving children well cared for):

1 **Affectionless psychopathy**. Bowlby suggested that early deprivation would result in a clinical condition characterised by poor social relationships and a lack of a social conscience:
- **Bowlby's (1946)** study of juvenile thieves produced evidence of affectionless apathy, though the results are questionable (see p.133).
- **Rutter (1976)** looked at similar data and concluded that maladjustment was due to concurrent family discord rather than disrupted attachments (see p.134).

❷ Hospitalisation:
- **Quinton and Rutter (1976)** conducted a large scale survey which showed a correlation between repeated hospital admissions under the age of five and later behaviour problems in adolescence. These of course may equally be due to family problems or continuing poor health.
- Bowlby *et al.* (1956). This study of children in a TB sanatorium suggested that separation may not have lasting consequences, but the retrospective nature of the data makes detailed conclusions difficult.

❸ **Factors which moderate the ill-effects of separation:**
- Age of the child. **Maccoby (1980)** found that children between 6 months and 3 years found separation most distressing, with a peak around 12–18 months just after attachments first formed.
- Past, good experiences of separation. **Stacey *et al.* (1970)** looked at 4-year-olds having their tonsils removed and found that those who coped well without their mothers were generally those who had, for example, stayed with grandparents.
- A stable secure attachment.
- Stable schemas. **Kagan (1972)** claimed that violations of 'familiar faces in familiar places' leads to anxiety. **Littenberg *et al.* (1971)** found that infants protested more when their mothers exited through an unfamiliar than a familiar doorway.
- Control. Infants who initiate separation experience less anxiety.
- See also 'Counteracting deprivation' p.140.

Long-term deprivation: privation

Where no attachments are formed, e.g. institutional care, **Bowlby (1951)** maintained that even a bad home is preferable to any institutional upbringing provided the maternal bond remains unbroken. One of the problems with assessing the effects of adoption is that adoptive parents tend to be more intelligent and more able than the average because they are specially screened for the task:

- **Goldfarb (1943)** matched two groups of 6-month-old babies for genetic factors, mothers' education and occupational status. Fifteen were raised in an institution while another 15 went to foster homes. The institutionalised group was largely socially isolated and, when tested at age three and later at 10–14 years, they were backward in cognitive and social development compared with the fostered group, though even the fostered group were below average in some respects. However, the babies were not randomly assigned to the groups, so the reasons they were selected for fostering may have affected the outcome.

- **Spitz and Wolf (1946)** visited poor orphanages in South America and observed that the infants received only irregular attention and were extremely apathetic and depressed.

- **Tizard and Rees (1975)** and **Tizard and Hodges (1978)** gave evidence against Bowlby's view – natural parents are not necessarily the best. They studied 65 children who were placed in care before the age of 4 months. By the age of four years, 24 were adopted and 15 had returned home, often to single parents. In terms of intellectual and social development the adopted children were doing best at the age of eight. The findings may be due to the higher social class of the adoptive families and to the poorer emotional adjustment of those children who were restored to their biological families. In any case, it indicates that mother is not always best and that attachment may take place after the age of four.

- **Rutter (1972)** describes cases of sexually and developmentally immature children who may have been subjected to physical abuse, but in some cases emotional deprivation alone leads to these extreme cases. The reason is that abnormal emotional states lead to disturbed hormonal functioning and impaired development. This condition is referred to as **deprivation dwarfism**.

Loss of attachment

When a child loses its initial primary caregiver, are substitutes equally effective?:

❶ Death:
- **Rutter** found a higher rate of loss of parent through death in a sample of young psychiatric patients, the 3–4-year-old period seemed to be the most critical.

❷ Adoption:
- **Singer et al. (1985)** found the incidence of secure attachment to be equally high in adoptive children as non-adoptive ones.

❸ Divorce:
- **Hetherington (1989)** concluded from a number of studies that, depending on circumstances, some children remain insecure, others recover and others positively benefit by developing special ways of coping and caring. Age and experience affect the child's response; a turbulent home may be more unsettling than a divorce.

LONG-TERM EFFECTS OF EARLY EXPERIENCE

❶ The long-term effects of deprivation and privation include:
- intellectual underfunctioning (**Goldfarb**),
- social maladjustment and problems with mating (**Harlow**),
- mental disorder (**Bowlby**),
- deprivation dwarfism (**Rutter**),
- child abuse (see p.140),
- little effect.

❷ Evidence from studies of deprived children:
- **Case studies**: a number of children have been rescued from deprived circumstances and studied by psychologists. These include: Anna (**Davis, 1947**), Isabelle (**Mason, 1942**), the Czechoslovakian twins P.M. and J.M. (**Koluchova 1972, 1976, 1991**), Genie (**Curtiss, 1977**) and a Japanese brother and sister (**Fujinaga et al. (1992)**. In general these children were discovered around the age of six in situations of extreme deprivation. The Czech twins had been locked in a cupboard, though they had had each other for social support. The Japanese siblings were in a shack with their dog.
- **Recovery**: all the children showed some recovery, in terms of physical maturation, socialisation, cognitive and linguistic development. But, critically, they were never able to recover full abilities. Genie was of particular interest because she was 13 years old when found, the 'critical age' after which linguistic recovery should not be possible (see Lenneberg, 4.1). The fact that she did learn to speak shows that some recovery is possible.
- **Cautious interpretation** is necessary with all these studies because:
  - there is no way of knowing whether the child was not brain damaged at birth, Genie was supposedly locked away *because* she was mentally retarded,
  - the histories of the children are not reliably known and some may have had significant interactions in their early years. **Fujinaga et al. (1990)** claim that Genie was initially brought up under good circumstances.
- **Larger samples:**
  - **Dennis (1960)** studied orphanages in Iran and found that those adopted after two years of age seemed capable of catching up, whereas this was not true for those under two who suffered developmental retardation.
  - **Koluchova (1991)** followed 90 severely deprived children entrusted to foster families and concluded that subsequent adjustment is possible where there is suitable care.

MATERNAL DEPRIVATION REASSESSED

❶ The effects attributed to attachment may be due to other factors:
- good and poor parenting generally. **Fishbein (1984)** suggested that those parents who form good early attachments continue to be good parents,
- general sensory deprivation. Harlow's monkeys, and children in orphanages, are deprived in many ways,
- cultural values. Evidence from kibbutzim show that, in other cultures, different methods of child-rearing can be perfectly healthy.

❷ **Flaws in the empirical data.** The topic is not one which can be experimentally manipulated, particularly with humans, the evidence is:
- retrospective and therefore open to distortion (e.g. Bowlby),
- based on small samples,
- drawn from research with animals (Harlow),
- correlational – children who suffer deprivation usually also experience many other difficulties and deprivations; those from 'good' homes tend to cope better with 'attachment problems',
- longitudinal studies involve complex interactions, e.g. studies of divorce have to accommodate remarriage or the presence of other attachment figures.

COUNTERACTING DEPRIVATION

Furman *et al.* **(1979)** have adapted the younger-peer therapy suggested by Novak and Harlow to help socially withdrawn preschool children. The children were given a series of play sessions with a partner who was either their age or 18 months younger. Both sets of children became more socially outgoing than a control group, and the ones playing with younger children did best of all.

Skeels and Dye (1939) attributed the large differences in intellectual functioning between one group who were moved from a state orphanage to a state school and the other group who stayed behind, to the individual care offered by older girls who were also resident in the state school. This is particularly noteworthy because the girls were considered educationally subnormal (IQ less than 70). Therefore it is likely that they provided social rather than intellectual stimulation.

The **Robertsons** produced a series of film studies of children experiencing short-term separations. Their work indicates the usefulness of a substitute attachment figure. Their first film study was of John (17 months) over nine days in a residential nursery, it was a graphic illustration of separation distress, and later his rejection of his mother. The Robertsons later fostered (and filmed) four children while their mothers were in hospital having babies. The children visited beforehand, brought their own things with them and their fathers were encouraged to visit daily, thus avoiding potentially harmful 'bond disruption'.

Conclusion

Children have reached healthy emotional adulthood throughout the centuries and in different cultures with many and varied forms of upbringing, multiple carers and extreme deprivations. The swing to child-centred thinking which began with **Dr** (not Mr.) **Spock** and **Dr Bowlby** should be regarded with due scientific scepticism.

However, important changes have resulted from Bowlby's work:
- children in hospital are often accompanied by a parent, for both their sakes,
- institutions place equal emphasis on emotional as well as physical care,
- state intervention in problem families must weigh up the potential physical danger against the emotional trauma of removing a child from home,
- childcare provision for working mothers, or the decision of some mothers to remain at home with their children.

CHILD ABUSE

The field of child abuse has grown rapidly since the 1960s, there have been a number of well-publicised tragedies which represent the tip of an indeterminate iceberg. **Jones** *et al.* **(1987)** report that there are no agreed definitions nor agreed estimates of the incidence of child abuse.

Definition

Gross child abuse is easy to define and identify, but the boundary between inadequate parenting and minor abuse is problematic. General definitions might be given as 'any maltreatment of children which prevents attainment of the child's full potential' or 'misuse of parental power'. However, such wide definitions are impractical, not least because they may lead to too many cases being dealt with ineffectively.

Jones *et al.* (1987) suggest that there is general agreement about types of abuse and their order of importance: sexual abuse, physical injury, inadequate supervision/leaving alone, failure-to-provide, encouraging delinquency, emotional mistreatment, educational neglect, moral danger because of parental sexual mores and parental drug/alcohol abuse.

There are analogies with mental illness, whose diagnosis is open to personal interpretation, political or religious views and social control (e.g. the Orkney child abuse case which involved alleged cult practices).

Studies of 'normal' children are one means of assessing what constitutes abuse, e.g. **Newson and Newson (1976)** found that about 33% of 7-year-olds are smacked once a week, and 8% at least once a day. Our society makes greater use of corporal punishment than Europe generally.

Incidence

NSPCC (Creighton, 1984) estimated, for the year of 1982 in England and Wales, that approximately 6400 children under the age of 15 were injured, including 650 who were killed or seriously harmed; this is 0.63 per 1000 or about 0.06% of the total population. The NSPCC studies have shown an increase in the number of notified cases but a decrease in those involving serious or fatal injuries. In 1990 about 46,000 children were on the Child Protection Register.

Negative attitudes towards child abuse first appeared in the mid-19th century, possibly in relation to dropping infant mortality and changes in the occupations of those under 15. In 1874, the neighbours of a child, Mary Ellen, in New York decided to seek protection against her parents who had neglected and beaten her and insisted that they could do as they liked. At the time there were only laws protecting animals, so they argued that she was a member of the animal kingdom. In Britain the first child protection legislation was in 1889.

Characterising abusive parents

Characteristics of abusive parents may help identify those families at risk but are not predictive because many families or individuals with the same characteristics are not abusive. The factors themselves tend to be correlated regardless of child abuse, and therefore are not likely to be causal.

1. **Socio-economic factors:** abusive parents tend to be young, unemployed, with a criminal record, with a history of marital discord and violence, have large families, are highly mobile and have a low socio-economic status. The same childcare difficulties occur at higher levels but probably are hidden behind by, for example, a front of respectability, better use of health services, and money for alternative care.

2. **Personality characteristics:**
   - Impulsive behaviours, rigid approaches to discipline, distorted perceptions of the child's behaviour, ignorance of normal child development, and physical or mental handicap. The material circumstances are usually reasonable, and prognosis of response to assistance is good.
   - Mental illness, such as a sociopath who erupts during a minor incident, or puerperal psychosis – a mother has a distorted sense of what is best for the child. Such cases have a poor prognosis and are often behind fatalities. The failure-to-protect parent is often present in association with the sociopath.
   - Maternal/paternal deprivation in the parents' own childhood.
   - Mother/infant attachment. **Crittenden (1988)** interviewed 124 mothers in the US and found that abusing mothers tended to represent relationships in terms of power struggles, were controlling and hostile, with anxiously attached children, and had angry, unstable adult relationships. Other abusing mothers were emotionally empty, were unresponsive to their children and had stable but affectionless relationships. There is a danger of stereotyping abusive situations and families. For example, **Lynch and Roberts (1982)** found that lack of attachment between mother and child was a key feature of abusive interactions. Other correlated factors include: separation of mother and baby in the neonatal period, young maternal age, a history of parental psychiatric illness, the parents themselves being abused as children, and multiple social problems.

3. **Environmental triggers:** a build-up of problems may lead to abuse.
   - **Egeland *et al.* (1988)** found that high-risk parents were only likely to become abusive if they were suffering other kinds of social or environmental stress.

4 Parent/child mismatch:
- Primary rejection. In rare cases, parents may feel a lack of affection or dislike for a particular child,
- Self-righteous overdiscipline. Perfectionist parents dealing with a marginally disturbed child create an ever-worsening cycle of punishment and alienation, culminating in abuse.

Characterising the victims of abuse

1 At birth: premature/low birth weight, illegitimacy.

2 Temperament: it has been suggested that some children 'invite' abusive interactions:
- Boys are more at risk than girls, except in adolescence when the reverse is true. The youngest children are the most likely to be abused (**Jones** *et al.* **1987**).
- **Belsky (1984)** suggested three main influences on parental functioning: the personal psychological resources of the parent, the contextual sources of support and the characteristics of the child, i.e. whether they have a particularly easy or difficult temperament.
- **Egeland and Sroufe (1981)** found that emotionally unresponsive, hyperactive or ill infants are more likely to be abused than ones who are easy to care for.

3 Attachment: a failure to develop a relationship with the child may increase the likelihood of abuse:
- **Browne (1989)** found that 70% of maltreated infants have insecure attachments, compared with 26% for children with no history of maltreatment.

Managing child abuse

1 Prevention:
- identify high-risk families,
- provide early intervention programmes, **Schinke** *et al.* **(1986)** worked with single teenage mothers and created higher levels of confidence and competence through the teaching of relaxation and problem-solving techniques.
- provide help in maternity units for high-risk mothers in bonding with their newborns.
- develop parental skills in mother and baby units or special day centres.

2 Support:
- improve the family's social circumstances,
- therapy with parents and children, promoting emotional development and childcare skills,
- family social worker to monitor and provide support. **Hill (1980)** found that over 75% of families had at least one change of social worker in the first year, this makes it hard for a therapeutic relationship to develop,
- provision of 'hotline' support, such as Childline,
- self-help groups, such as Parents Anonymous, to offer help to parents who feel in danger of injuring their children.

3 Control:
- media campaigns,
- removing the child permanently from its home,
- prosecuting adults for abuse.

3.2 THEORIES OF COGNITIVE DEVELOPMENT

Cognitive development includes language, which is dealt with separately in Chapter 4. The two main theoretical formulations are from **Piaget** and **Bruner**; **Vygotsky** is also discussed briefly. The theories have had an important impact on education.

PIAGET

Jean Piaget (1897–1980) is undoubtedly the most influential developmental psychologist this century. He trained as a zoologist; became interested in psychoanalysis when working in a psychiatric clinic, and went to Paris to study clinical psychology. He was employed in a laboratory run by **Binet** who developed the first IQ tests in Paris around 1900. Piaget became interested in the kind of mistakes that children made and in epistemology (knowledge). He combined his interests to found 'genetic epistemology'.

The essence of Piaget's theory (1928 onwards)

● a *biological* approach: cognitive development is mainly a consequence of maturation (stages) and of innate structures,

● a *structural* approach: intelligence is a matter of innate structures for acquiring and storing knowledge,

● a *dynamic* approach: we are in a constant process of reconstructing knowledge,

● a child's thinking is not merely a less informed version of an adult's but has *qualitative* differences,

● thought shapes language far more than language shapes thought.

The structure of the intellect

1 **Schema**: an internal representation of some specific mental or physical action. The child is born with innate schema, which are equivalent to reflex responses, e.g. grasping or sucking schema. During development, these schema integrate with each other, becoming more elaborate and leading to the formation of entirely new ones in response to the environment.

2 **Operations**: a higher order mental structure which appears in middle childhood. They involve physical or symbolic manipulations.

3 **Adaptation**: cognitive structures (schema and operations) are adapted to meet the demands of the environment through the processes of assimilation, accommodation and equilibrium. These processes are present throughout life.

4 **Assimilation**: a new object or idea is understood in terms of schema, which the person already possesses. The new experience may extend the range of the pre-existing schema but not challenge the conception.

5 **Accommodation**: the complementary process to assimilation, to modify schema in order to fit new situations, objects or information.

6 **Equilibrium**: the driving force. In a new situation the person uses existing schema (assimilation). If these are inadequate a state of disequilibrium occurs, 'driving' the person to accommodate the schema instead, thus ensuring cognitive development.

7 **Variant cognitive structures**: those structures that change as a child gets older, e.g. schema and operations.

8 **Invariant cognitive structures**: the fundamental processes involved in adaptation, and the desire for homeostasis or equilibrium.

9 **Horizontal decalage**: uneven cognitive performance probably due to different learning experiences, an inability to solve certain problems despite being able to solve similar problems requiring the same mental operations, e.g. the ability to conserve number and volume doesn't occur simultaneously.

Developmental stages

Piaget's theory can be understood in terms of an 'ages and stages' framework. A concise version of this is given in the table overleaf. However, it is important to go beyond mere description and understand the evidence for and against the notion of maturational stages. Such arguments follow the table.

	Stages	Years	Characteristic behaviours
1	Sensorimotor	0–2	focused on sensory and motor experiences, reflex activity, e.g. sucking, circular (repetitive) reactions, e.g. kicking
			internal representations, emergence of symbolic thought, language
2	Pre-operational		
	(i) pre-conceptual	2–4	animism, unsystematic (syncretic) nature of thought, egocentric thought, centration
	(ii) intuitive	4–7	inability to conserve
3	Concrete operations	7–11	centration now possible, can classify and order, class inclusion but not with abstract ideas, understanding numbers, reversibility, random thinking and problem-solving
4	Formal operations	11 on	hypothetical thinking, systematic and organised deduction/induction, strong idealism

Typical empirical evidence

Piaget's methods involved naturalistic observation and interviews, using a small sample, and often his own children:

1 Object permanence (e.g. 'If I can't see it, it doesn't exist'):
- Show all infants a bright, attractive object, then hide it. At 4–5 months they will immediately forget it, by 10–12 months they will look for it (see **Bower (1981)** p.145, for criticism).
- The emergence of attachments at 7–8 months is thought to relate to object permanence, though person permanence may occur earlier (horizontal decalage).

2 Unsystematic nature of thought:
- **Transductive reasoning.** If A has four legs and B has four legs, A must be B; a child may call all dogs Spot.
- **Appearance/reality distinction.** DeVries (1969) showed 3–6-year-olds a cat called Maynard, she then hid the cat's head behind a screen while she strapped on a dog's head. The 3-year-olds found it hard to see it as anything but a dog, even though they saw the transformation, while the 6-year-olds were able to distinguish appearances from reality (see **Frank (1966)**, p.146, for criticism).

3 Egocentrism: a young child finds it hard to see the perspective of another:
- Three mountains experiment: **Piaget and Inhelder (1956)** asked children between four and twelve to say how a doll, placed in various positions, would view a model of a mountain range. The children were given various ways of demonstrating this: through selecting a correct picture, placing the doll themselves according to a picture, or arranging the cardboard mountains. The youngest children could only work from their own perspective, by age nine they were sure of the doll's perspective (see **Hughes (1975)**, p.145, for criticism).

4 Centration: focusing on the central part of a problem (inability to **decentre**).
- **Class-inclusion tasks:** a pre-operational child cannot focus on the whole and the parts at once. If given 18 brown beads and 2 white beads (all of which are wooden), and asked 'are there more brown beads than wooden beads?', the reply is typically that there are more brown beads (see **Donaldson (1978)**, p.146, for criticism).
- **Conservation:** requires decentration and the development of compensation, reversibility and identity (see **Rose and Blank (1974)**, p.146, for criticism):
  - **number conservation:** the experimenter shows the child two rows of counters, each row has the same number of counters. The experimenter then makes one row longer by moving the counters further apart. The child thinks that there are more counters in the longer row.
  - **conservation of mass:** the experimenter shows the child two equal-sized balls of clay. One ball is then rolled so that it is longer than the other. The child thinks that the longer ball contains the most clay.

- **conservation of volume:** the child is shown a squat-shaped jar containing water. The water is then poured into a tall, thin container. The child says that there is more water in the tall container than there was in the shorter container.

5 Formal operational thinking:
- **Seriation:** making transitive inferences, e.g. if A > B and B > C, then A must be > C. 'Edith is fairer than Susan. Edith is darker than Lily. Who is the darkest?' (from the Stanford–Binet Test). Children find this impossible during the concrete operations stage, unless it is presented in a concrete form, such as using dolls (see **Bryant and Trabasso (1971)**, p. 146, for criticism).
- **Deductive reasoning**, as in a scientific inquiry, e.g. the pendulum task: a person is given some string and a set of weights, and asked to discover what determines the swing of the pendulum, the length, weight, height of release or force of push? (see **Shayer and Wylam (1978)** below for criticism).
- **Piaget and Inhelder (1956)** tested the beaker problem. Children are given four beakers of colourless, odourless liquid. Which liquid or combination of liquids will turn yellow when a few drops are added from a bottle of the same? They found that concrete thinkers try to solve the problem randomly whereas formal thinkers are systematic.

6 Influence of thought on language: if linguistic development is related to age rather than exposure to a native language then this supports Piaget's view of prior cognitive maturity.
- **deVilliers and deVilliers (1979)** studied the use of 'hypotheticals'. In English these require complex forms (e.g. 'What would we do if it were raining?'), in Russian they have a simpler form. Nevertheless they appear at the same time in children's speech, suggesting cognitive maturity as the key factor rather than linguistic sophistication.

Evaluation

The counter-evidence suggests that children can do more and earlier than Piaget suggested.

1 Age:
- Object permanence may occur earlier. **Bower (1981)** showed that infants 5–6 months old showed surprise when an object that had been hidden behind a screen was no longer there when the screen was lifted. He also demonstrated that babies of 8 weeks tracked an object as it moved behind a screen by showing with their eyes where it should emerge.
- Formal operations may occur later or not at all. **Shayer and Wylam (1978)** found that only 30% of 15- and 16-year-olds had achieved formal operations. **Piaget (1972)** took the view that while all adults are capable of formal reasoning, experience and interest limit the development of such an ability. There may also be higher stages of intellectual development.

2 Appropriateness of the task:
- **Bower and Wishart (1972)** suggested that it was the way an object is made to disappear which influences the baby's response. If a baby is watched after the lights have been turned out (using infra-red cameras) they found that the baby continues to look for the object.
- **Hughes (1975)** asked 3-year-olds to hide a doll from a toy policeman. Hughes claimed that understanding of another's perspective is needed for this task and the fact that young children were able to cope is because it made sense to them.
- **Borke (1975)** gave 3- and 4-year-olds practice in a perspective task, using the character Grover from *Sesame Street*. In the actual experiment the children were asked to adjust their display so that it looked the same as the one Grover could see as he drove along in his fire engine. One of the displays was the three mountains, which proved much more difficult than the other two displays used and may be an unusually difficult task. In general the children were able to decentre more than Piaget suggested.

3 Form of questioning: children use contextual cues in deciding how to respond. Like any experimental subject they aim to please and so they respond to demand characteristics and/or experimenter bias. The younger the children, the more suggestive they are:

- Children interpret the conservation experiment as one of change, why else would the experimenter repeat the question? **McGarrigle and Donaldson (1974)** used 'naughty teddy' to muddle the experimental displays 'accidentally', many more 4–6-year-olds were then able to demonstrate conservation abilities, presumably because the question now made sense.
- Asking a second question implies a second answer. **Rose and Blank (1974)** and **Samuel and Bryant (1984)** found that asking the question only once, after the transformation had a significant effect, though there were still age differences.
- **Bruner and Kenney (1966)** suggest that the question 'more' may confuse the child.
- The class-inclusion questions don't make sense. **Donaldson (1978)** reports a study where children were asked 'Are there more black cows or more sleeping cows?' rather than 'Are there more black cows or more cows?' The percentage who answered correctly moved from 25 to 48%.

④ **Failure wrongly attributed:**
- **Bryant and Trabasso (1971)** claim that difficulty with transitive inferences is caused by memory failures rather than lack of ability. They trained children until they could perform a transitive task successfully, and found that they could then perform a more lengthy series of comparisons.

⑤ **Practice:** children may lack skills simply because of experience not because of maturational deficits:
- **Borke (1975)** and **Bryant and Trabasso (1971)** showed that practice improved abilities.
- **Danner and Day (1977)** coached students aged 10, 13 and 17 in three formal operational tasks. The effects were limited with the younger subjects but very marked at 17 years, showing that training was only possible in conjunction with cognitive maturation.
- **Sonstroem (1966,** cited in **Gross, 1991)** gave 6–7-year-olds who failed a standard conservation task the opportunity to manipulate and/or describe the ball of clay. When re-tested the effect of doing both led to improved performances, suggesting that by employing all three of Bruner's modes of thinking (see p.147) the physical appearance ceased to dominate.
- **Tait (1990)** compared the performance of blind and sighted children on tasks of conservation and found the blind children performed less well, emphasising the role of experience.

⑥ **Effects of language:**
- **Frank (1966)** claimed that language can help overcome concrete thinking. He tested 4–6-year-olds on the volume conservation task with a screen in front of the beakers so the level was not visible. Almost all the older children coped, and half the 4-year-olds. When tested without the screen performance was improved over a pre-test experiment, which was attributed to the children's speech having been activated and thus overcoming domination by the iconic mode. They were also able to distinguish between appearance and reality.
- **Sinclair-de-Zwart (1969)** taught children appropriate vocabularies for dealing with conservation tasks, but did not find that this helped their performance. In another experiment he found that understanding of key terms such as 'more' and 'bigger' was positively related to success at the conservation task.
- **Ochiai and Mizuno (1979)** found a correlation between the ability to conserve and linguistic capacity in Japanese 5–6-year-olds. When they gave non-conservers training they found that operational rather than language techniques were more successful, and that operational methods did not improve language performance; suggesting that language and conservation are distinct skills.
- See also **Liublinskaya (1957)**, 1.3, 'Language and thought'.

Conclusion

Criticisms of Piaget's theory:
- *underestimation* of children's early logical abilities,

- *overestimation* of the later stages. Piaget (1972) conceded this possibility,
- *it emphasises a child's failures* rather than successes, and often the reason for failure is wrongly deduced,
- *language* is largely overlooked and is taken to reflect cognitive structures, which have already developed (see 1.3, Language and thought),
- *emotion* is excluded,
- *Piaget's evidence often lacks scientific rigour.* The samples were small and open to experimenter bias; longitudinal data could have been used for greater insight,
- *it is more a description than a theory*, because it lacks explanatory power.

Support:
- *it is the most detailed and comprehensive account* of cognitive growth that is available,
- *it changed the traditional view* of the child as passive,
- *it stimulated research*,
- *it had a large impact on education*, particularly in primary schools,
- *critics tend to take the model too rigidly*, and supporters suggest it should be viewed as a metaphor. The stages are not fact but a useful structure for understanding behaviour and generating research.

BRUNER

Jerome Bruner (born 1915) is foremost a cognitive rather than a developmental psychologist. He made a key contribution to founding that branch of psychology in the 1950s. Later he turned his attention to education, including the development of Vygotsky's ideas (see p.150).

The essence of Bruner's theory

- *thought* requires ways of representing the environment, which we do through action, image and word (modes of thinking),
- *modes of thinking* are 'recurrent themes', which develop sequentially and remain throughout adult life,
- *language* shapes and enables the development of thought,
- *social framework* and *experience* influence cognitive development,
- it is a *biological* approach, the tendency to organise is innate,
- it is an *information processing approach*, concentrating on how strategies for organising information change with age.

Structure of the intellect

1. **Enactive mode:** thinking is based entirely on physical actions, we learn by doing not through internal representation and use of language. This mode of thinking is present in infants and later in many physical activities.
2. **Iconic mode:** the use of mental images (icons), which may be visual, auditory, olfactory or tactile.
3. **Symbolic mode:** representation of the world through language, and other symbolic systems such as number and music.
4. **Thinking** consists of:
   - **Categories** (= concepts): our interactions with the world involve forming categories in order to reduce its complexity, to recognise and relate objects, and to direct activity. A category is an abstraction of commonalties among events and experiences.
   - **Hierarchies:** categories are interrelated and organised into a framework (coding system) with the more general (generic) at the top. Through such hierarchies we can explain remembering, discovering and learning; the coding system can be referred to and/or adapted/expanded to incorporate new experiences.
   - **Knowledge** is a complex arrangement of categories and coding systems.

Developmental stages

Each mode of thinking appears in a sequence developmentally, they are all present in mature thinking.

Mode	Age in years (approximately)
Enactive	0–1
Iconic	1–7
Symbolic	7 onwards

Evidence

1 **Transition from iconic to symbolic:** this mirrors the move from concrete to systematic, abstract thinking in Piaget's theory:
- **Bruner and Kenney (1966)** arranged nine glasses on a 3 × 3 grid, according to height and diameter. Subjects were given a variety of tasks, e.g. reproduction (the glasses are scrambled and the child is asked to replace them), or transposition (the bottom row was replaced but in a transposed manner, left swapped with right), the child must work the rest out. The percentage of successes were:

	5 years (%)	6 years (%)	7 years (%)
Reproduction task	60	72	80
Transposition task	0	27	79

- **Mosher (1962)** looked at the strategies used by children aged 6 to 12 in the game of twenty questions, to ascertain why a car went off the road. Older children used constraint-locating questions ('was it night-time?') whereas younger children asked direct hypothesis-testing questions ('did a bird hit the window?').

2 **Effects of language,** see **Frank (1966)** and **Sinclair-de-Zwart (1969)** p.146, and 1.3.

3 **Use of categories and hierarchies,** available through symbolic thought:
- **Mandler (1967)** and **Bower** *et al.* **(1969)** showed how the provision of conceptual hierarchies can improve memory (see 1.5).
- **Bruner, Goodnow and Austin (1956)** demonstrated how concepts are formed by focusing or scanning attributes. They observed the behaviour of subjects when trying to establish the 'concept' selected by the experimenter, such as a 'green cross', from all the possible arrangements of colour, symbols and border shown on 81 cards (see 1.3).

4 **The role of tutoring.** Bruner followed Vygotsky in suggesting that expert instruction was important in stretching a child's capabilities:
- **Wood, Bruner and Ross (1976)** showed how 3-, 4- and 5-year-olds could be cajoled and coached into completing a task. In each group showing them how to do it was more effective than telling them. They called this instruction 'scaffolding'.

Evaluation

- offers an alternative to *Piaget*,
- includes *language* and the influence of the *social environment*,
- important *educational* implications.

EDUCATIONAL IMPLICATIONS

Piaget: child-centred, active learning

- what is appropriate for adult learning is not appropriate for children,
- he introduced the notion of *readiness*,
- the teacher should set tasks which are appropriate for pupils and intrinsically motivating,

- the teacher's role is not to impart knowledge but to ask *questions* or create situations which ask questions,
- the teacher should be concerned with *process* rather than the end product,
- it involves *individualised learning* plus discussion and exposure to others' attempts,
- *Nuffield Science* is an example.

Bruner: discovery learning

- you should present pupils with specifics and let them actively *organise* these,
- the *spiral curriculum* – the same principles are encountered at increasingly sophisticated levels. The same topics are redeveloped at later grades,
- learning is not a matter of *mastering* facts but inventing the *structure* for the facts,
- *language* and *social interaction* are important,
- the teacher guides and supports the pupils' discovery – *'scaffolding'*.

A COMPARISON

	Piaget	Bruner
Language	reflects cognitive structures which have already developed	shapes cognitive development
Qualitative changes	stages of development	modes of thinking
	there are similarities in the age boundaries: around 2 and 7	
	child's thinking qualitatively different from adult	by age 7 child's thinking is qualitatively the same as adult thinking
Biological basis	invariant structures: assimilation, adaptation, accommodation	hierarchical structure of categories
Experience	level of maturation determines cognitive abilities	appropriate instruction can extend capabilities (Vygotsky's Zone of Proximal Growth)
Education	teacher sets appropriate tasks for level of maturation (stage)	teacher sets tasks to stretch and instruct the pupil, curriculum repeatedly encounters the same principles (spiral)

OTHER VIEWS

Understanding two views of cognitive development is quite sufficient, for the purposes of examinations at least. There are many others, though there is rather less to say about them. Below is a summary, plus some details of **Vygotsky**'s contribution:

1. **Learning theory**: cognitive processes develop as a result of their consequences (whether they are rewarded or not).

2. **Ausubel's theory of learning**: limited to meaningful verbal learning. A new object/experience only has meaning if it can be related to something already present in the learner's cognitive structure. This theory has had important educational consequences, including expository teaching and 'reception learning' using advance organisers. It recommends maximum intervention as a teaching strategy.

3. **Information-processing approach**: concentrates on specific abilities such as attention, memory and perception, and how the strategies for organising information change with age. It may be possible to explain all developmental changes in terms of improved memory capacity and to 'measure' development by, for example, the number of items that can be recalled.

4. **Social cognition**: focuses on the role which social factors play on how a person interprets information and is a new approach.

VYGOTSKY

Lev Vygotsky (1896–1934) died at 38 from TB. He worked at same time as Piaget, but they never met, and Piaget only learned of Vygotsky's work when it was translated into English in the 1960s.

The essence of Vygotsky's theory

A complex and far-reaching theory, with three themes:

1. **The influence of culture** (social settings): leads to the development of higher mental functions from the elementary ones that are unlearned. Social processes shape language, and language makes thought possible. However, language and thought start independently, only influencing each other later (see 1.3). Unlike language, thought is biologically determined.
2. **Language:** language is critical to thought and also regulates behaviour.
3. **Zone of Proximal Growth (ZPD):** the distance between actual and potential capabilities, development depends on the guidance of more expert peers or adults (expert intervention). Therefore, Vygotsky takes the position that learning precedes development.

Developmental stages

Speech stage	Age	Function
Social	0–3	controls the behaviour of others, expresses simple thoughts and emotions
Egocentric	3–7	controls own behaviour but spoken out loud, a bridge between other two
Inner	7 on	self-talk, directs behaviour and thinking, involved in all higher mental functioning, like stream of consciousness

Evidence

- **Vygotsky (1987)** demonstrated the value of instruction in increasing the capability of 7- and 9-year-olds in understanding scientific and everyday concepts. He assumed that the former would be more developed because they would be shaped through direct instruction. The procedure was to give the children sentences ending in 'because…' or 'although…' and see if they could finish them appropriately.

Educational implications

- the fundamental role of education is *cultural transmission*, through the intervention of others in learning,
- children learn from those who are more knowledgeable – peers or adults, *experts*,
- it is important to pay special attention to *language* as a means of developing cognitive processes,
- tasks set should always be sufficiently hard to present a challenge (at the upper edge of a pupil's *zone of proximal development*).

3.3 THEORIES OF MORAL AND SOCIAL DEVELOPMENT

Social = any situation involving two or more members of the same species.

Moral = pertaining to notions of right and wrong conduct, within a particular moral code or society. Morals guide behaviour, in particular prosocial and antisocial ones (see Chapter 2 and 3.4 on socialisation).

LEARNING THEORIES

Behaviourist theory

Based on classical and operant conditioning, reward and punishment (see also 1.4).

Evidence

A great body of evidence exists to show how behaviour can be increased through a system of reward and punishment. A few examples are:

1 **Effectiveness of conditioning:**
  - **Eysenck** believes that the conscience is a conditioned response (conditioned emotional response, see 7.6),
  - **Aronfreed (1963)** punished a group of young boys verbally for touching attractive toys either in the act of reaching (group 1) or a few moments after (group 2). When later left alone with the toys, group 1 held out longer, suggesting a stronger conscience.

2 **Counter-effectiveness of punishment:**
  - punishment may produce hostility and a desire to rebel, **Glueck and Glueck (1950)** found that severe punishment was associated with delinquency in boys,
  - habituation to punishment means that punishment has to be increased continually,
  - humiliation in front of others may lead to more aggressive behaviour, **O'Leary et al. (1974)** found that the use of quiet rather than public reprimands in class was more effective with disruptive children,
  - punishment may have an inverse effect, increased attention albeit negative, turns out to be a reward.

3 **Counter-effectiveness of rewards:**
  - extrinsic rewards may destroy intrinsic motivation. **Lepper et al. (1973)** selected a group of nursery children who enjoyed working with felt tip pens. Group 1 were told they could win a 'good player award' if they did a good drawing, group 2 were given a reward but not prewarned, group 3 had no reward mentioned or given. Two weeks later the children were observed working with felt tip pens. Group 1 showed less interest than pre-test (extrinsic motivation destroyed intrinsic value), whereas the other groups remained the same.

Social learning theory

Extends the principles of behavioural theory to include observational learning and cognitive factors. We do things because of reinforced consequences, but this behaviour is not 'blind' – we also anticipate the outcomes of our behaviour and exert cognitive control over our responses (see 1.4 for a fuller discussion of principles and evidence, and 2.7).

Evidence

1 **Studies of imitation:**
  - **Bandura et al. (1961)** found evidence that antisocial behaviour is learned through imitation (see 2.7),
  - **Bryan and Test (1967)** gave evidence that prosocial behaviour can also be learned through modelling (see 2.6),
  - Who is likely to be imitated? Factors which are important include the child identifying with the model (gender, age, occupation, similarity, relevance) or the child perceiving the model as being advantaged (status, rewards),
  - Television is an important route for learning moral behaviour.

2 **Inconsistency of moral behaviour:**
  - Evidence presented below suggests that moral behaviour is not consistent. Learning theory can explain how moral behaviour is situation-specific rather than guided by principles.
  - On the other hand, there must be some consistency in the system of rewards and the behaviour of models, otherwise no learning would take place.

Evaluation

Behaviourism:

- extrapolating results from animal experiments to human behaviour,
- a system of reward and punishment does not have straightforward effects.
- omits the effects of how a person thinks about the situation.

Social Learning Theory:

- based on laboratory settings where social situation is unreal.

Concerning both theories:

- how does naturally occurring behaviour continue to be exhibited without continual reinforcement?
- biological factors and their part in development are not mentioned,
- it accounts for inconsistency of behaviour,
- there is some explanatory power but not the whole story. It is inadequate for explaining all the complexities of human behaviour,
- stimulated good amount of research,
- bears some resemblance to psychodynamic theory.

PSYCHODYNAMIC THEORIES

Freud

Freud's view of child development grew out of his psychoanalytic theory (see 5.2 and 6.4 for fuller discussion of principles and evidence).

Arguments and evidence:

1. Moral behaviour is controlled by the **superego**, which is divided into:
   - **Conscience**, which punishes us when we do something wrong. It is the source of 'guilt feelings', represents the 'punishing' parent and is composed of prohibitions imposed on us by our parents.
   - **Ego-ideal**, which rewards us when we behave in accordance with moral values. It is the source of feelings of pride and self-satisfaction and represents the 'rewarding' parent.
   - The **superego** develops during the phallic stage. Satisfactory resolution of the Oedipus Complex comes through identification with same sex parent. In identifying, you take on their attitudes, in particular, their moral views.

2. **The conscience.** Freud saw this as an internal judge of whether our behaviour conforms with our moral code, it appears at the age of five or six. Freud predicted that a child raised leniently should have a strong conscience and vice versa.
   - **MacKinnon (1938)** gave nearly 100 subjects a test, they were left alone with the answer book. Of those who cheated (about 50%) fewer said they felt guilt about it, which would confirm the inverse relationship between guilt and wrongdoing.

3. **Inconsistency of moral behaviour:**
   - Freudian theory explains this by positing a split between rational and irrational behaviour,
   - on the other hand, the existence of the conscience suggests consistency.

Evaluation of Freud's psychodynamic theory:

- its emphasis on early childhood made an immense impact,
- the notion of the unconscious, irrational self has proved useful,
- it can account for moral inconsistency,
- it lacks evidence,
- it is open to variable interpretation,
- Freud's formulation of the 'conscience' causes problems, limits moral learning to the family, which may have been true in Freud's time,
- there are similarities with learning theory, drawing on rewards and punishment,

- it suggests a largely unconscious, biologically driven control system which can't account for all the complexities of moral behaviour.

Erikson: a theory of social development

Whereas Freud's theory is psychosexual, Erikson's is psychosocial and extends to cover the whole lifespan – the 'eight stages of man'. Erikson's approach is sometimes called 'ego psychology' since he de-emphasised the unconscious and emphasised the social world.

The theory:
Each stage of life is marked by a crisis, which must be confronted and resolved. The stages are universal. Both parents influence the development of moral behaviour, which is a product of the superego (determining what is acceptable or not) and the ego (inhibiting undesirable impulses of the id). Since the ego is the rational component of the personality, morality must be related to cognitive development generally.

Age	Life crisis	Activity	Outcome favourable	Outcome unfavourable	Important relationship
1	TRUST VS. MISTRUST	consistent stable care	trust	suspicion, insecurity	maternal figure
2–3	AUTONOMY VS. SHAME	independence from parents	sense of autonomy & self-esteem	shame and self-doubt	parents
4–5	INITIATIVE VS. GUILT	exploration of environment	initiate activities	fear of punishment, guilt about feelings	basic family
6–11	INDUSTRY VS. INFERIORITY	acquisition of knowledge	sense of competence and achievement, self-confidence	feelings of inadequacy and inferiority	family, neighbours, teachers
12–18	*Adolescence* IDENTITY VS. ROLE CONFUSION	seeks coherent personality and vocation	strong personal identity	confusion	peers, in-groups, out-groups
20–40	*Young adulthood* INTIMACY VS. ISOLATION	deep and lasting relationships	ability to experience love and commitment	isolation	friends, lovers
40–64	*Middle adulthood* GENERATIVITY VS. STAGNATION	being productive and creative for society	wider outlook	lack of growth, boredom and self-involvement	spouse, children
65+	*Late adulthood* INTEGRITY VS. DESPAIR	review and evaluate life	sense of satisfaction, acceptance of death	regrets, fear of death	spouse, children, grandchildren

Evidence: see 3.5 for studies which support this view of life changes.

Evaluation:

- it provides a useful framework for appreciating lifespan changes,
- it moves away from sexual emphasis of Freudian theory,
- it is descriptive, as it is vague about the causes of social development,
- it is based on Erikson's own observations rather than any large scale research.

COGNITIVE DEVELOPMENTAL THEORIES

All cognitive developmental theories are characterised by:

- invariant progression through stages at particular ages,
- links between cognitive and maturational changes,
- the consistent and predictable way that morals develop which suggests a biological and universal basis.

Piaget (1932)

The theory:

	Children under 5 years	Children between 5 and 10 years	Children over 10 years
Moral Stage:	*premoral judgement*	*moral realism* heteronomous morals	*moral subjectivism* autonomous morals
Use of rules:	rules not understood	rules from higher authority and and unchangeable	rules mutually agreed and can be changed by mutual consent
Means of evaluating right and wrong:		evaluate actions by outcomes	evaluate actions by intentions
Chosen punishment:		expiatory punishment (to make atonement)	punishment to fit the crime, principle of reciprocity.

Evidence:

1. **Realism vs. relativism:** *Game of marbles:* Piaget played the game with a group of children and asked questions about the rules, 'who made them?', 'can we change them?':
   - Heteronomous child thought they were inviolable and same from semi-mystical authority,
   - Autonomous child understood that people invented them, they could be changed but only if all players agreed.
   - **Linaza (1984)** found the same sequence of development in Spanish children, supporting the universal nature of such stages

2. **Intentions vs. consequences:** *Moral stories:* Piaget presented pairs of stories to children who were asked 'are these children equally guilty?' 'which of the two is naughtiest?':
   (a) Albertine had a little friend who kept a bird in a cage. Albertine thought the bird was very unhappy, and she was always asking to let him out. But her friend wouldn't. So one day when her friend wasn't there, Albertine went and stole the bird. She let it fly away and hid the cage in her attic so the bird should never be shut up again.
   (b) Juliet stole some sweeties from her mother one day when her mother was not there, and she hid and ate them up.
   - In each pair of stories one has a greater consequence but the intentions are good, the other has smaller consequences but bad intentions.
   - Heteronomous children could distinguish between intentional and unintentional actions but based their judgement on the severity of outcome, thus showing objective or external responsibility.
   - Autonomous children used the motive/intention as the means for judgement, thus showing internal responsibility.
   - **Armsby (1971)** manipulated the stories so that there was a small amount of deliberate damage or a large amount of accidental damage, and showed that children can distinguish intentionality but have difficulty weighing up the relative importance of value and intention (don't we all – can you say whether animal liberationists are right or wrong?).

Evaluation of Piaget's cognitive development theory:

● children's understanding of intentions is more complex than Piaget thought,

● it does not explain moral inconsistency,

● the moral stories were poorly designed, they demand inferences.

Kohlberg

Elaborated Piaget's theory and extended the scope right through to middle age. His theory has been influential in education and criminology.

Kohlberg's theory

	Level	Age	Stage	
I	pre-conventional	6–13	1	heteronomous, avoid punishment
			2	individualism, one's own interests, egocentric
II	conventional	13–16	3	interpersonal conformity, 'good boy/girl'
			4	'law and order', conscience, unquestioning acceptance of authority
III	post-conventional or principled	16–20	5	social contract, individual rights, questioning the law and authority
			6	universal, ethical principles (this stage was later dropped because rarely, if ever exhibited)

Evidence:

➊ Moral stories: **Kohlberg (1969, 1978)** collected a wealth of evidence. He was not interested in the actual choices people made so much as why they made them, i.e. more in *how* people think rather than *what* they think:

● the stories were based on ten moral issues/values: punishment, property, law, roles and concerns of affection, authority, life, liberty, distributive justice, truth and sex,

● e.g. 'John is seven and has recently been beaten up by an older boy who attends his brother, Alan's, school. Alan is a very protective older brother and they are every close. Alan decides to avenge John's victimisation and to beat up the older boy. But his parents strongly disapprove of physical aggression and he could get into serious trouble with them (as well as with the school authorities). One day after school, Alan waited for the boy and gave him a thorough beating. Should he have done that? Why?'

➋ **Research supporting stages:**

● **Colby *et al.* (1983)** followed 58 US males over 20 years and found that they progressed systematically through the stages as Kohlberg predicted.

● **Snarey (1985)** lists 27 different cultural areas in which Kohlberg's stages have been confirmed; stages 5 and 6 are most doubtful.

● **Fodor (1972)** found that delinquents operate at a much lower level on the Kohlberg scales than non-delinquents.

➌ **Research against:**

● **Colby and Kohlberg (1987)** performed a more careful analysis of the original data and found that only 15% of people reached stage 5, and there was no evidence whatsoever of stage 6 judgements.

● **Holstein (1976)** found that many subjects skipped stages, and reverted apparently randomly to earlier stages.

● **Gilligan (1982)** argues that men are oriented towards justice while women are oriented towards responsibility, therefore morals are not universal.

Evaluation:

● The research method of intuitively written dilemmas is not objective.

● Some dilemmas are inappropriate (e.g. 'What would you do if you were in the war?') This is particularly inappropriate for children.

● It is directed more towards 'male' rather than 'female' morality, and is partly because the original data comes from male subjects.

● It is culturally biased. Kohlberg found that American children were 'more' morally developed than other nationalities.

- It is a theory of moral reasoning rather than behaviour. It does not explain moral inconsistency nor the distinction between thinking and behaviour.
- The stages may not be sequential.
- It omits the effects of emotions (moral affects).
- There is an overemphasis on justice.
- The last two stages may be best omitted.
- Nevertheless it probably is the best available approach.

Two other alternatives

Damon (1977) developed a more practically based system of morals, founded on sharing, fairness and distributive justice. In brief, the stages are:

        0-A: fairness is what the self wants,
        0-B: the self is still dominant but also other characteristics are also used to justify choice,
        1-A: equality of treatment is primary,
        1-B: 'deservingness' – one is paid back for merit,
        2-A: special needs (poor or weak) are recognised in a reward structure,
        2-B: a fair solution is sought.

  Gilligan (1982) proposes horizontal rather than vertical stages to describe the processes involved reaching a (female) moral decision:

1 selfish concerns – what is right for me,
2 recognising responsibility for others – objective moralising about right and wrong,
3 reaching a decision based on the best for everyone – taking sole responsibility.

EDUCATIONAL IMPLICATIONS

- teaching strategies should be adapted to suit the particular stages of moral development,
- the attitudes necessary for behaviour at each level can't be taught but await appropriate cognitive maturity,
- 'caring', rather than morality, *can* be taught,
- discussion may enable moral conflicts to be resolved,
- role-playing may help with younger, and even older children,
- modelling is a further means of promoting morals.

A COMPARISON

	Behavioural: Learning theory	Affective: Psychodynamic	Cognitive: Stage theories
Active or passive	passive, influenced by environment	passive, influenced by inner drives	active
Direction of development	quantitative changes	directional, qualitative changes from child to adulthood	
Cause of development	learned through reward/punishment and experience	both maturation and experience	subject to maturation
Biological influences	environment only	development influenced by biological changes	
Peer vs. adult influences	interactions with adults, particularly parents		peer influences
Guilt and emotion	painful anxiety states associated with wrongdoing (conditioning)		not mentioned
Practical vs. theoretical	practical basis	theoretical	theoretical
Moral inconsistency	predicted by situational conditioning	split between rational/ irrational behaviour	a problem for stage theories
Theoretical status	explanatory	Freud: explanatory Erikson: descriptive	explains development in terms of maturation, and processes

MORAL INCONSISTENCY

People tend to assume there is a connection between moral judgements and social actions, but the truth is that the connection is not a simple one; the issue is similar to the question of attitudes and behaviour (see 2.3).

Evidence for inconsistency

Hartshorne and May's (1928) classic study of moral and helping behaviour looked at 12,000 11–14-year-olds and found little consistency. A child who cheated in one situation didn't in another; a child who shared money with classmates but didn't volunteer to help raise money for charity. They also found that immoral behaviour was governed more by the probability of being caught than by any principles of morality, such as religious training or conscience.

Gerson and Damon (1978) asked children to distribute a reward amongst themselves for making bracelets. The reward was ten candy bars, to be shared among four children. Initially the children were asked to share pretend rewards (cardboard cut-outs) after a hypothetical bracelet-making session, and to explain their reasoning. Were rewards given for the most bracelets, the nicest bracelets, the biggest boy/girl? They found neither consistency or inconsistency from the pretend to the real situation, but both. There was an interaction between the context and the stage of moral reasoning a child had reached: it was not context alone, as the situationists would have it, nor was it simply the stage of moral reasoning, as the moral theorists would suggest.

Fishkin *et al.* (1973) found a lack of consistency among responses given by the same subject for different Kohlberg dilemmas.

Gilligan (1982) described a study where she interviewed 29 women attending an abortion and pregnancy counselling service. Faced with a very real moral dilemma she found that the women focused less on the 'justice' dimension as suggested by Kohlberg and more on 'responsibility'.

Piaget and Kohlberg's dilemmas offer the suggestion that different situations have different moral judgements.

Evidence for consistency

Walker *et al.* (1987) asked 240 people of all ages to resolve three Kohlberg dilemmas plus one real-life dilemma that the subject had faced, they found 62% were consistent in the way they reasoned.

Burton (1976) reanalysed Hartshorne and May's data using more sophisticated behavioural techniques, and found support for consistency as long as the contexts were sufficiently similar.

Conclusion

(See also 2.3 and 5.2.)

- moral judgements are based on a complex interaction between intentions, previous experiences, and social, material and personal consequences,
- there are probably different types of moral behaviour. Some are rational and context-dependent, and others more abstract and principled,
- this difference may reflect two different moralities – 'female' and 'male' (people before principles or vice versa),
- such evidence poses a particular problem for cognitive theorists, who need to incorporate situation and individual differences into their theories.

3.4 SOCIALISATION

Socialisation is the process of transmitting a culture to children and teaching them behaviours appropriate to their sex and other social circumstances (see also 8.1). The processes and effects of socialisation can be observed in:

- emotional development (see the illustrative question at the end of the chapter),
- self-concept and self-esteem,
- gender roles and sex differences,
- play,
- sources of influence.

SELF-CONCEPTS

We hold a number of attitudes and concepts about ourselves:

- *self-concept*: one's conception of oneself, self-image (id + ego),
- *self-esteem*: one's evaluation of oneself,
- *ideal self:* loosely, the super-ego,
- *self-efficacy:* one's own perceived competence,
- *self-actualisation* (Maslow): the motive to realise one's full potential,
- *self perception:* is a special case of person perception (see 2.1), we only know ourselves through observation.

One of the classic dualisms is the knower and the known; the self as an entity or as a process. **James (1890)** suggested that the self has two components: me and I. 'Me' is the sum total of all a person can call their own (abilities, personality characteristics, material possessions); 'I' is the self as knower, self-reflective. The 'I' might be regarded as nature and the 'me', as nurture.

The self-concept

Argyle (1978) suggests four major factors which influence the development of the self-concept:

1. **The reactions of others.** We are reflected in the reactions of others, therefore it is through social interaction that we gain knowledge of ourselves:
   - **Cooley (1902)** called this the *looking-glass self*, the product of seeing ourselves through the image held by others.
   - The *self-fulfilling prophecy:* a child's parents tells them that they are clever and this influences the child's self-perceptions. **Guthrie (1938)** described a trick played on an unattractive girl by her classmates. They pretended that she was the most desirable girl in the college and took turns asking her out. By the sixth date the general opinion was that she had actually become more attractive, presumably because her self-image changed and this led her to behave differently.

2. **Comparisons with others.** Many self-concepts are comparative terms, such as tall or clever, and therefore require the standards set by others. It has been suggested (see 2.4) that one of the reasons to seek the company of others is in order to make such comparisons.

3. **Roles played.** When **Kuhn (1960)** asked the question 'Who am I?' people listed their various roles (see p.159, the categorical self).

4. **Identification with models.** Both social learning and psychoanalytic theory suggests the role of models as a means of developing a self-image.

Developmental milestones

Allport (1961) described four stages of self:

- Ages 0 to 3: a sense of bodily self, a sense of continuing self-identity and self-esteem,
- Ages 4 to 6: the extension of self and a self-image,
- Ages 6 to 12: self-awareness of your own ability to deal with problems through reason and thought,
- Adolescence: forming intentions, and distant goals.

A similar scheme is given by the empirical evidence:

1. Self-recognition: knowing that you are:
   - The core or physical self: the infant hearing its own cry, or matching the action of their hand with the sensation (10 weeks).

- Distinguishing the self from others. This is shown when a child responds to the emotions of others (social referencing, 12 months).
- **Lewis and Brooks-Gunn (1979)** adapted **Gallup's (1977)** technique for testing self-recognition. They coloured infants' noses with rouge. A child who responds by touching their own nose shows self-recognition. At 9–12 months, few children touched their noses, by 20 months 75% did. By 18 months most children can point to a photograph of themselves.
- Chimps raised in isolation fail to react to their mirror images, which supports Cooley's view that social interaction is essential for the development of a self-concept. **(Gallup, 1979).**

2 **The categorical self:** a person's classification of the self in terms of categories. In early childhood the self-concept is physically based, gender is particularly important:
- **Kuhn (1960)** asked children to give answers to 'Who am I?'. In answers given by 7-year-olds, 25% related to social roles. This increased to 50% when 24-year-olds were asked.
- Ethnic awareness of self and others appears around the age of four or five.

3 **The psychological or private self:**
- **Flavell (1977).** By 4 years a child can distinguish bodily self from inner thinking self.
- **Harter (1983).** It is not until the age of 10 that children have a sense of self-esteem, the under 7s do not fully understand the concept.

4 **The adolescent identity crisis:** The self-concept is under constant revision, but nowhere more critically than during adolescence:
- **Erikson's (1963)** adolescent 'identity crisis' is a critical period for self-concept, trying out new roles to find a coherent sense of who and what one is. Body image is an important part of this.

5 **Coherent sense of self:**
- The *fragmented self* is an attribute of some mental illnesses.
- Theories of personality use the notion of self to explain behaviour, e.g. **Rogers' self theory**.
- However, **Mischel (1968)** has suggested that there is no such thing as a coherent self or personality. The self is a cognitive structure useful for organising the information you have about yourself; implicit personality theory (see 2.1) does this for the information you hold about understanding others.

Self-esteem

1 **Self-fulfilling prophecy:** self-esteem is commonly related to performance and other factors:
- **Coopersmith (1968)** related differences in self-esteem to differences in behaviour in boys aged 10 to early adult. He found that high self-esteem boys were confident, active, academically and socially successful; medium were less confident, more in need of social acceptance; and low were self-conscious, isolated, reluctant to join in activities and constantly underrated themselves.

2 **Is it a cause of success/failure?** High self-esteem is commonly given as a reason for success, low self-esteem for failure; in fact it is probably second only to low intelligence as a reason for failure:
- **Lawrence (1971)** gave backward readers counselling to improve their self-esteem as a means of breaking the cycle of failure, he had some degree of success.
- **Seligman (1978)** (see 2.2) attributed the cycle of failure to a misplaced sense of control; people with low self-esteem tend to attribute success to external factors (luck) and failure to internal factors (lack of skill) and therefore abnegate their control.

3 **Is it an effect of success/failure?** What determines self-esteem in the first place?
- *Early experiences*, chiefly parental influence (or that of significant others). **Coopersmith (1968)** found that those high in self-esteem had parents with high self-esteem and who were more affectionate, used consistent methods of reward and punishment, and showed greater interest/respect than low self-esteem parents who were either very punitive or over-permissive.

- · **Rogers** felt that self-esteem was determined by the distance between the self-concept and ideal self; successful people have high self-esteem because their ideal self and self-concept are close and high.
- *School performance,* **Lawrence (1978)** found a correlation between poor reading and low self-esteem, however, it may be that some readers are quite accepting of their failure and therefore failure has little effect on their self-esteem.
- *Social comparison* with peers provides a means of establishing competence.

④ **A cause and an effect**: low self-esteem produces a downward spiral; whatever starts it, it is self-perpetuating. **Kernis *et al.* (1989)** gave evidence that people low in self-esteem tend to overgeneralise their failure, thus perpetuating it. College students with low self-esteem were more affected by low test results than those with high self-esteem. In particular they were less motivated to do well in later tests, which therefore would lead to poorer performance and confirmation of their low ability.

On the other hand, positive self-esteem is maintained through positive feedback even if such self-conceptions are unrealistic; it is better to be optimistic.

⑤ **Do all abilities matter?** No one is successful at everything:
- Esteem remains high as long as you fulfil the expectations of your ideal self.
- *Self-serving bias,* people ignore those things which don't maintain self-esteem, though 'depressives' seem to do the opposite thereby maintaining low self-esteem (see 2.2).

⑥ **Evaluation:**
- Self-esteem is hard to measure since it relies on self-report, you are very likely to collect only socially acceptable answers in a questionaire.
- Almost all the evidence is correlational and therefore cause and effect are inevitably muddled up.

Self-efficacy

Efficacy is the capacity to produce desired results with the minimum use of resources – capability, effectiveness and efficiency. Self-efficacy is the belief in one's abilities, as distinct from the abilities themselves. Such beliefs generate expectancies, which in turn affect behaviour positively or negatively (self-fulfilling prophecy). **Bandura (1977)** first introduced the concept and claims it is one of the most important features of self-perception. It has gained a wide application, to some extent replacing self-esteem as an explanation for success or failure. For example:

- *Health psychology,* where it is used as a predictor of whether a patient will engage in health behaviour. **Kaplan *et al.* (1984)** found that patients high in self-efficacy were more likely to adhere to a prescribed regime of exercise.
- *Cognitive therapy* stresses the importance of cognitive processes in mediating therapeutic change. Low self-efficacy is related to depression and a sense of helplessness, coping is better when efficacy is high.

Bandura (1989) outlined the four processes involved:

- *cognitive:* such beliefs are cognitive and they lead to expectations which are also cognitive,
- *motivational:* self-efficacy affects how much an individual will persist at a task,
- *affective:* it is related to sense of anxiety,
- *selection:* people select tasks which provide enough of a challenge, based on their sense of their own competence.

① **Effect of high self-efficacy on achievement:**
- **Collins (1982)** compared children who had a high or low sense of self-efficacy in terms of their performance on mathematical tasks. They found that, regardless of ability, those children with high self-efficacy solved more problems and, moreover, had better strategies for dealing with errors. Their beliefs were related to the amount of effort they made.
- **Sylva (1992)** claims that the evidence about the effects of pre-school education suggests that early positive self-efficacy is crucial to success.

② **Effect of positive achievement on self-efficacy:**
- **Weinberg** *et al.* **(1979)** raised or lowered subjects' self-efficacy by giving them false feedback on physical endurance tasks – raised self-efficacy led to better performance.
- This was put into practice in the USSR where athletes were shown edited films of their performance to make it look better, this presumably created high self-efficacy that led to a good performance **(Baron and Byrne, 1991)**.

③ **Self-efficacy and personal control:** a sense of control is related to high self-efficacy, whereas learned helplessness is associated with low self-efficacy:
- **Diener and Dweck (1980)** (see 2.2) found that cognitive style was related to task persistence and success. Those children who were helpless gave up more easily than those who were mastery oriented.

④ **Physiological basis:** high self-efficacy may make it easier to cope with stress and thus mean that performance is not impaired:
- **Litt (1988)** used the cold pressor task to test subjects' ability to tolerate pain, those high in self-efficacy did best.
- **Bandura** *et al.* **(1988)** suggested that Litt's findings are the result of self-efficacy or a sense of confidence enabling the production of endorphins, which block pain sensations, whereas tension leads to a decrease in their release.

GENDER ROLE AND SEX DIFFERENCES

Gender is a fundamental part of the self-concept, and of one's interactions with others.

Terms

- *sex:* male/female, usually associated with biological difference,
- *sex typing:* differential treatment of children according to sex,
- *gender:* psychological/social aspects of maleness/femaleness,
- *gender role:* masculine/feminine – the behaviour expected from an individual on the basis of their (perceived) biological sex.

Evidence for how gender is determined

The debate is essentially one of nature versus nurture, clearly biological and social factors are involved, but how?

① **Straightforward biological determination:** Nature's impulse is to create a female. Initially male and female embryos have the same genital 'precursors'. In males the release of certain hormones causes the female parts to be absorbed and the male parts to develop. Without the hormone the embryo remains externally female.

Sexing at birth is generally straightforward, but in the case of ambiguous individuals (hermaphrodites and pseudohermaphrodites) the practice is generally to go with external appearance; since such individuals are infertile, what they actually look like matters most.

	Male	Female
chromosomal sex	XY	XX
gonadal sex	testes	ovaries
hormonal sex	androgens, mainly testosterone	oestrogen, progesterone
internal organs	prostate gland, sperm ducts, seminal vesicles, testes	womb, fallopian tubes, vagina, ovaries
external genitalia	penis and scrotum	outer lips of vagina (labia majora)

② **Socio-biological conflicts:** This evidence suggests that biological sex and gender identity need not concur.
- **Hermaphroditism:** true cases are extremely rare, like Hermaphrodite, the mythical Greek god/goddess, they must have both sex organs. **Mr. Blackwell**

(Goldwyn, 1979) was the 303rd hermaphrodite ever to be recorded. He was an 18-year-old Bantu 'boy' who developed breasts at puberty, which led to the discovery that 'he' had an active ovary on one side and an active testes on the other. He elected to have the female parts removed, remaining with his original gender identity. If his tubes had been connected differently he might have been able to fertilise himself, in fact a Filipino hermaphrodite did become pregnant (*Sunday Times*, June 1992).

- **Testicular Feminising Syndrome** (pseudohermaphrodites) is a rarely occurring disorder where a normal XY fetus is insensitive to testosterone and therefore fails to develop testes in early development. The infant appears to be female but is internally male. **Goldwyn (1979)** described the case of **Daphne Went**, who sought help because she could not become pregnant. She was married and went on to adopt two children and live happily as a woman.

- **Androgenital Syndrome** is the reverse. A normal chromosomal female receives an excess of male hormones during embryonic development. This may occur if the mother is prescribed certain hormone treatments, e.g. to avoid miscarriage. The result is that the female infant has external male genitalia but is internally female. **Money and Ehrhardt (1972)** studied 25 such girls, all of whom chose to be 'women' after corrective surgery.

- **The Batistas (Imperato-McGinley** *et al.*, **1974)** had ten children, four of whom were born with normal female genitalia and grew up as girls. At puberty their vaginas healed over, testicles descended and they grew full-sized penises. The same thing had happened to other families in their remote village in the Caribbean. They all had a common ancestor, who had carried a mutant gene which meant that the hormone necessary for the female genitalia to be absorbed wasn't produced during embryonic development. This meant that some chromosomal males had an external female appearance, though the male organs were present internally. The massive amounts of testosterone produced during puberty finally triggered the process.

- **Identical Twins. Diamond (1982)** has documented the case of a pair of male monozygotic twins who were circumcised at 7 months. The physician accidentally used too high an electric current to cut the tissue and more or less burned off one penis. The decision was finally taken 10 months later to raise the child as a female. 'She' was given oestrogen and had a vagina constructed. The later evidence is not altogether clear, she was more feminine than her brother but had some social difficulties and found it difficult to accept her female role. (Apparently penis amputation isn't unknown but is rarely documented.)

③ **Cross-cultural evidence:** Other cultures allow a greater variety of gender expression:

- The case of the **Batistas** suggests that, in another culture, gender reversal need not be a major issue.

- **Mead (1935)** took the view that gender is completely unrelated to biological sex. She found evidence of very different male/female roles in different societies. Chiefly, she reported on three tribes from New Guinea. The Mundugumour tribe were all aggressive (masculine quality) regardless of sex; the Arapesh were all warm, emotional and non-aggressive (feminine qualities); and the Tchambuli exhibited a reversal of our own gender roles. However, **Mead (1949)** changed her views from cultural determinism to relativism – gender roles are not universal but related to cultural practices.

- **Crow Indians:** a 'beardache' is a biological male who chooses not to follow the ideal role of warrior and instead became the 'wife' of a warrior, e.g. Little Horse in the film *Little Big Man*.

- The **Sakalavas** of Madagascar raise 'pretty' boys as girls. Such boys seem happy to adopt a female role.

④ **Sex differences – Biological cause?**

- **Role differences,** such as child-bearing and hunter/gatherer would lead one to expect that innate differences might have evolved, and may show themselves in different male/female orientations. For example, women are more oriented towards interpersonal goals whereas men function on a level of principles (see 3.3).

- Men have been found to be more **aggressive**. As this seems to be related to hormones, it suggests a biological difference.
- **Spatial ability** may have a genetic component and be sex-linked, favouring boys (**Lambert, 1978**), this may be related to boys' superior mathematics skills.

5 Sex differences – Social cause?
- **Differential perception**: if we perceive men and women as being different this can only lead to the self-fulfilling prophecy. **Goldberg (1968)** showed that affixing male or female names to essays led to different assessments, men were seen as better (see 2.1). **Fidell (1970)** showed that this might lead to a man being selected for a job rather than a woman.
- **Differential treatment**: masculinity/feminity may result from such behaviours being reinforced. **Smith and Lloyd (1978)** showed that mothers selected sex-appropriate toys according to the perceived sex of babies 5–10 months old. They thought a baby was a girl or boy according to the clothes it wore. However, **Fagot (1985)** also found evidence that teachers tend to reinforce 'feminine' behaviours in boys *and* girls such as quiet, sedentary activities, suggesting that children are exposed to a multiplicity of stereotypes and reinforcements. **Weinberg *et al.* (1979)** found that performance sex differences disappeared if female subjects were given raised expectations and male subjects' expectations were lowered on a physical endurance tasks. This suggests that, where differences are observed, they are the result of initial differential expectations as a result of socialisation.
- The existence of persistent **stereotypes** (a typical male is assertive, independent, good at maths and science; a typical female is dependent, relatively passive, good at verbal tasks) supports the claim that such beliefs are self-perpetuating.

Theoretical accounts of gender development

1 **The Biological Approach**: behaviour differences are suited to the roles that have to be played, and cross-cultural similarities are much greater than differences such as male aggressiveness and female interest in babies. This suggests a dominance of biological influences:
- this is undoubtedly part of the story,
- however, cases like the Batistas, Mrs Went and Mr Blackwell, demonstrate that gender need not correspond to biological sex,
- there is cross-cultural evidence for different, as well as similar, male/female roles.

2 **Biosocial Theory**: it is the interaction between biological and social factors which is important rather than biology directly. There is probably a critical or sensitive period, after which gender identity is fixed. **Money and Ehrhardt (1972)** took the view that 'anatomy is destiny'. The key factor in gender identity is what sex you're told you are. They found that when pseudohermaphrodites were wrongly sexed at birth they rarely sought re-assignment and it was generally successful only if done before the age of two.
- this theory gives a fuller account,
- however, in the case of the Batistas, gender role did not remain consistent with sex of rearing,
- the behaviour of the Batistas does not accord with the notion of a sensitive period.

3 **Psychoanalytic**: sex-appropriate attitudes become internalised from identifying with the same sex parent. **Freud** presented a complex description of how gender identity is learned (see 5.2 and 6.4 for fuller details). Satisfactory resolution of same and opposite sex parental conflicts during the phallic stage (Oedipus complex and Electra complex) leads to identification with same sex parent:
- what about one-parent or homosexual families? The evidence suggests that children follow typical psychosexual development in such families (e.g. **Hoeffer, 1981**),
- Freud said that women are sexually inferior, they have to make do with babies as a poor substitute for a penis. **Horney (1924)** suggested that the envy is not of the penis but of status, the penis is a symbol of men's superior status,

- Freud was probably correct in identifying the age of four as a time of gender awareness,
- Freud was also right in drawing attention to the child's sexual awareness of their parents. Children do have to cope with sexual feelings towards their parents.

④ **Social Learning Theory**: gender role identity is learned through reinforcement and modelling – (e.g. **Bandura**) – a child is rewarded for sex-appropriate behaviour and punished for inappropriate behaviour. Behaviour is also learned indirectly through modelling: parents, stereotypes and media:
  - even the earliest sex differences can be explained by parental reinforcement (see **Smith and Lloyd** p.163),
  - like Freud, the Social Learning Theory draws on identification (modelling),
  - however, reinforcements are not sufficiently consistent to explain observed differences.

⑤ **Cognitive–Developmental Theory**: gender identity is a combination of social learning mediated by maturational and cognitive factors – the child actively organises its own identity, e.g. **Kohlberg (1966)**:
  - basic gender identity between two and five accords with cognitive development,
  - other factors must mediate the exposure to stereotypes and reinforcement. (see **Fagot, 1985**, p.163).

⑥ **Cultural Relativism**: you can only evaluate gender with reference to the culture from which it arises, e.g. **Mead**. **Historical relativism** points to the fact that gender roles are also related to the time in which they occur.

Conclusion

The different approaches are by no means mutually exclusive, they each emphasise a different aspect of gender development:

- hormones and other biological factors *predispose* children to a particular gender identity,
- sex typing may override biological sex, but is usually the same as biological sex,
- stereotyping occurs at a very early age, therefore it is impossible to separate biologically-perceived sex from socially determined gender,
- learning accounts for most gender-appropriate behaviour.

Bem (1974) has claimed that the bipolar approach to masculine versus feminine is false, in reality it is a continuum, and many people possess characteristics of both (androgynous).

Deaux (1984) has pointed out that what differences do exist between men and women are small when compared to the wider variance within each sex, and the extent of the overlap. The question of difference remains popular despite the fact that sex is a very poor predictor of an individual's performance.

PLAY

One dictionary gives 55 meanings for the word 'play', which indicates the difficulty in developing a theory of play. The 'lay' view is that it is not an earnest activity; while it may not be earnest it is an important activity.

Garvey (1977) lists the following characteristics of play:
- it is pleasurable and enjoyable,
- it has no extrinsic goals,
- it is spontaneous and voluntary,
- it involves some active engagement.

The functions it serves are:
- practising physical and cognitive skills (**Vygotsky**),
- exploring new ideas (**Bruner; Hutt** called this 'exploratory play'),
- rehearsing social routines (role play),
- establishing autonomy (**Erikson**),
- resolving emotional problems – cathartic (**Freud**),

- social contact, the need for affiliation,
- a means of resting from mental exertion,
- not limited to childhood (**Erikson**),
- a safe escape from reality, as in 'I was only playing'; or a safe harbour to 'overhaul' the ego (**Erikson**).

Developmental sequence

This was first outlined by **Parten (1932)**:

0–2 years	*Solitary activity.*
2–4	*Parallel activity:* children enjoy playing together. They watch and imitate but do not truly interact. Play is in short bursts. By the age of three they use toys as an active agent rather than themselves.
4 on	*Social activity: associative or co-operative:* children interact: taking turns and co-operating with each other.
6–7	The peak of social pretend play. Sex segregation becomes apparent.
10–11	Boys' and girls' games differ. Boys: play in larger groups; they play competitive team games with more complex rules, which involve co-operation and leadership. Girls: place more emphasis on intimacy and exclusiveness (**Berndt, 1982**).

Theories of play

1 **Freud** (psychodynamic): play is a means of **catharsis**. We relive and relieve pent-up emotions in fantasy play (regression or projection), playing with dolls (displacement) or playing with water instead of excrement (sublimation of innate desires). Different kinds of play are associated with different psychosexual phases, for example, in the oral phase play is centred around the mouth (see 5.2 for description of Freudian phases).

Freud's ideas have been applied in **play therapy** (e.g. **Axline, 1947**) as a means of helping disturbed children by allowing them to express problems through regression, sublimation, etc. It also can be used in the diagnostic phase of child therapy.

2 **Erikson** (social): play is often a means of resolving psychosocial crises in children and adults. Play is an important behaviour throughout one's life to provide a means of mastering reality through experiment. It is a safe way of escaping the boundaries of reality for self-teaching and self-healing. There are differences in the ways that boys and girls play. Specifically, girls focus inwards (reflecting their anatomical differences) while boys construct elaborate external protrusions. (**See Smith** *et al.*, p.166).

3 **Piaget** (cognitive): used the following scheme to describe the different kinds of play:
- *mastery play*: (0–2 years) practice and control of movements, exploration, repetition gives pleasure,
- *symbolic play*: (2–7 years) fantasy and make-believe, allows the child to control the world and reduce interpersonal conflicts,
- *play with rules*: (7 plus) more logical, uses rules which are progressively less egocentric (each of these can be related to Piaget's stages of cognitive development, see 3.2).

4 **Sylva, Bruner and Vygotsky** (social/cognitive) emphasised the learning potential of play. Exploratory and manipulatory characteristics of play contribute to problem-solving abilities. **Vygotsky (1967)** claimed that when a child is confronted with a new problem, it is incorporated into play as a means of working through the problem. Play extends the current level of capability.

Empirical studies of play

1 **Naturalistic observation: Sylva** *et al.* (1980) developed their work under Bruner's guidance to test the role of play in cognitive development, using nursery schools in Oxfordshire. They identified different kinds of activity:
- *high yield activities*: the most challenging, stimulates complex, goal-directed, self-reinforcing activity, e.g. building, drawing, doing puzzles,

- *medium yield activities*: somewhat more 'playful', e.g. pretending, playing with toys, sand or dough,
- *low yield activities*: informal games, gross motor play, unstructured social play,
- the *conclusion* was that *high yield or elaborated play* is of greater cognitive value than the more unstructured types.

② **Experimental observation: Hutt (1966)** observed the effect of a novel object on the behaviour of 3–5-year-olds. Initial behaviour involved exploring the object, this later led on to playing with it. Hutt concluded that there are two distinct behaviours involved in children's activities:

- *exploration*, which is fairly serious and focused, 'what does this object do?'
- *play*, which is relaxed and diverse, 'what can I do with this object?'.

③ **Experiment: Smith *et al*. (1981)** gave one class of 4-year-olds extra 'play tutoring' and another class extra 'skills tutoring'. The amount of verbal interaction was the same for both groups. When the children were tested 10 weeks later, they found that play tutoring had fostered social participation and fantasy play. However, the results were less pronounced than expected. Earlier findings might have been due to verbal interaction rather than 'play tutoring' *per se*.

Sylva (1977) gave subjects either a play opportunity or training experience prior to a problem-solving task involving sticks and clamps. Those who had played were faster at solving the problem than the others.

④ **Correlation: Johnson *et al*. (1982)** found that constructive play, but not sociodramatic play, was positively correlated with intelligence scores. **Hutt and Bhavnani (1972)** traced subjects from Hutt's original studies and found that, four years later, those children who used the toys most imaginatively scored higher on tests of creativity. Perhaps imaginative play fosters creativity, or does creativity lead to imaginative play?

SOURCES OF INFLUENCE

① **Parents:** the first and probably most profound and enduring influence. Research concentrates on parental styles:

- *Authoritarian parental styles* are associated with prejudice (see 2.5).
- The *'induction method'* was associated with fostering moral emotions, moral reasoning and moral behaviour in a study by **Hoffman (1970)**, which compared three major approaches to discipline: (1) *love withdrawal* – creating anxiety over loss of love; (2) *power assertion* – techniques that may generate fear, anger or resentment; (3) *induction* – explaining why a behaviour is wrong, its effects and how it might be undone.
- **Siegal and Cowen (1984)** asked 100 children aged 4 to 18 to indicate their most preferred disciplinary strategy. They selected induction, followed by physical punishment as the most effective.
- **Coopersmith (1968)** found that parents *high in self-esteem* had children who were the same (see details in 3.4).

② **School:**

- introduces competition,
- peer comparisons,
- learn aggression at school,
- learn failure – learned helplessness.

③ **The media:** see section 2.10 for a discussion of the effects of the media on behaviour.

④ **Friendships/peers:** are critical in social and emotional development. Through friendships children learn to understand the feelings of others, and modify each other's behaviour through rewards and punishments:

- **Freud and Dann's** study (see 3.1) showed how peers can offer vital emotional support,
- *Stages*: **Damon (1977)** interviewed children about their best friend and developed a stage 'theory' for friendship:

Level	Age (approx.)	Description
1	5–7	No real feelings of liking or disliking, no understanding of another's feelings, in line with the egocentric child. Friendship easily started and finished, based on proximity and sharing things.
2	8–11	Mutual interests, responding to other's needs, tend to form cliques.
3	12 plus	Deeper, more enduring friendships, sharing thoughts, feelings and secrets. Friends give comfort and support, confidants and therapists.

- *Categories:*
  - *intense, intimate relationships*, which enhance self-esteem, social skills,
  - *cliques*, which provide opportunity for close relationships as a replacement for the family,
  - *crowds*, for social interests (more at adolescent stage).
  - see also 6.1 and 2.4.

3.5 ADOLESCENCE, ADULTHOOD AND AGEING

The fact that age does not have the same meaning in all cultures or eras demonstrates the importance of social influences in determining age-linked behaviours and responses to critical life events. For example, childhood is considered to be a phenomenon of the 20th century, and Western culture; adolescence is a different experience in different cultures.

Adolescence is most commonly associated with being a period of transition, but middle and late adulthood are equally transitional. Therefore all three require psychological adjustment to physical, mental and social changes. It should be remembered that all terms are comparative rather than absolute. Although ageing is essentially a biological process, many aspects of development are socially determined.

ADOLESCENCE

From the Latin 'adolescere' to grow into maturity, adolescence is essentially an 'invention' of **G. Stanley Hall (1904)**. In some societies there is no adolescence, there is a moment of change from boy to man marked by a rite of passage.

Adolescence starts around the age of ten, with the beginnings of puberty (sexual maturity), and ends with entry to adulthood (see p.170) traditionally celebrated at 21 but lowering the age of majority to 18 makes this a more appropriate watershed.

It is a period of several transitions in a relatively short period of time (sexual maturity, career and life choices, leaving home, self-definition).

Changes and adjustments

1. **Physical changes:** sexual dimorphism (the difference between the sexes) is greatly enhanced:
   - The *hypothalamus* stimulates the pituitary to produce female or male hormones, it is not known what triggers this.
   - *Primary* sexual changes (menstruation, enlargement of penis and ejaculation).
   - *Secondary* sexual changes (pubic hair, body shape, growth spurt, facial hair).
   - The *timing of onset* of puberty seems to be decreasing at a rate of 0.3 years per decade, the reason is probably improved diet and health standards.
2. **Psychological responses to physical changes**
   - *Menstruation*: **Ruble and Brooks-Gunn (1982)** found that in early maturers this might lead to negative feelings, but generally girls did not find it a traumatic experience.

- *Body image*: **Arnhoff and Damianopoulos (1962)** presented 20- and 40-year-olds with a set of six photos, with faces blacked out, one photo in each case was of the person themselves. The younger subjects were better at recognising themselves which suggests that their body image looms relatively large in their minds. A distorted body image is associated with anorexia (see 6.1).
- *Early maturation*: **Jones and Bayley (1950)** found that those who reached puberty earlier were seen as more attractive, self-confident, popular, and less attention-seeking and dependent by peers and adults. The effect was still apparent at age 17, and possibly even later. **Clausen (1975)** suggests that some advantages are because of size (for sports) and confidence with the opposite sex. **Weatherly (1964)** found that average maturers were the same as early ones, concluding that maturation doesn't confer an advantage but late maturation has a disadvantage. **Douglas and Ross (1964)** looked at the mental ability of all adolescents born in one week in 1946 and found early maturers had higher performance. They thought that this may be due to greater physical maturity leading to earlier cognitive development.
- *Gender differences*: early maturation is more important in boys than girls, perhaps because it is more obvious and girls can manipulate their appearance more (e.g. with make-up).

③ Psychological factors
- *Cognitive changes*: quantitative (become quicker, more efficient) and qualitative (Piaget's move from concrete to formal operations: thought more reflective, analytical, introspective, developing complex strategies for social and academic problems, able to intellectualise and over-intellectualise). Such changes enable: moral development, tackling complex academic subjects, becoming critical of existing social, political and philosophical systems, defining new identity.
- *Establishing a sense of identity:* **Erikson** sees this as the major developmental task of the adolescent, to develop an enduring and unified concept of self. **Marcia (1980)** extended some of Erikson's ideas into four non-sequential stages/outcomes: *identity diffusion* (confusion, possible rebellion), *identity foreclosure* (uncertainties avoided by committing self to safe, conventional goals without exploring alternatives, potentials not realised), *identity moratorium* (decisions about identity put on hold), *identity achievement* (emerges with firm goals, ideology, commitments).
- *Self-esteem*: this is often lowered during adolescence, perhaps because of the adolescent's perception of physical appearance but also because of identity confusion.
- See also 6.1.

④ Social factors:
- Effects of *unemployment* (see p.175).
- *Friendships*: **Hartup (1983)** found that the popular stereotype of adolescents as being highly conforming to group peer pressures is not supported by research. See 3.4 for more discussion of friendship.
- *Parental influence*: certain parental styles may lead to greater difficulties in adolescence. **Baumrind (1971)** found that authoritative parents, as opposed to authoritarian or permissive ones, are more likely to have independent and relatively content adolescents. **Elder (1980)** suggested that authoritarian parents expect unquestioning obedience, which leads to less confident or independent children. Democratic but authoritarian parents tend to have adolescents with high self-esteem and independence. Such parents respect the adolescent's right to make decisions but expect disciplined behaviour.

A time of storm and stress?

This phrase was introduced into psychology by G. Stanley Hall who, influenced by evolutionary theory, felt that the adolescent had to experience the volatile history of the human race before reaching maturity. Many have agreed with his view that adolescence is a troubled time, a time of teenage rebellion, drug use, delinquency, disenchantment and confusion.

1 **Evidence of stress and confusion:**
- **Erikson**'s picture was of adolescence as a time of confusion.
- **Masterson (1967)** found that 65% of 12–18-year-olds showed evidence of anxiety.
- **Rutter** *et al.* **(1976)** looked at behavioural or psychiatric disorder in their survey of 14–15-year-olds on the Isle of Wight, and concluded that there was evidence of 'turmoil' but felt it should not be over-exaggerated. Many of the problems experienced were mainly ongoing from childhood.
- **The National Children's Bureau study (Fogelman, 1976)**, which looked at a cohort of 11,000 16-year-olds, found that adolescence was a difficult time, particularly for parents who saw their children as solitary, irritable, and fussy.

2 **The alternative view**, i.e. reasons other than adolescence *per se* which lead to stress in some individuals:
- *Cultural relativism*: **Mead (1928)** in her book *Coming of age in Samoa*, suggested that turmoil may be due to growing up in an industrialised society. She observed that, in Samoa, sexuality is dealt with in an open, casual manner and therefore children are spared the guilt, anxiety and confusion which we experience. Growing up in Samoa is easier because life is easier, competitiveness and ambition are non-existent. Mead concluded that it is the range of opportunities in Western society which creates stress, not adolescence *per se*, and recommends *not* that we should remove these pressures but prepare adolescents better. **Freeman (1983)** has criticised Mead's methods, but, even if they were wrong, her conclusions offer a useful insight.
- *Historical relativism*: when the 'generation gap' is at its greatest, adolescence may be a greater time of stress. In the 1960s the gulf between parental expectations and teenage realities may have been greater than it is now in terms of, for example, sexual activity, drugs and employment.
- *Pre-existing problems*: **Coleman (1961)** felt that adolescence is normally tension-free, where problems exist they are due to other factors such as a history of disturbance before adolescence. **Rutter** *et al.* **(1976)** support this view.
- *Multiplicity of pressures*: more decisions are left to the adolescent, and more choices are available. The pressures are increased through advertising. Teenagers are seen as a major consumer group and therefore targeted by advertisers who create desires and expectations.
- *Stressful time for parents not their children*: perhaps the observed stress in adolescents is due to their parents' stress at this time of change. Coping with a physically and psychologically different person and the conflict of wanting them to stay at home but valuing independence.
- *Person–environment fit*: **Eccles** *et al.* **(1993)** suggest that the reason many adolescents experience stress is due to the mismatch between their developing needs and the opportunities afforded to them by their social environments.

Theories of adolescence

1 **Freudian:** the balance of the personality becomes disturbed again during the genital stage (see 5.2 for description of stages). New ego defence mechanisms appear to deal with the upsurge of instincts: asceticism (to deprive self of pleasurable experiences, particularly sexual) and intellectualisation (to deal with anxiety-provoking subjects by discussing at great length).

2 **Neo-Freudian/Cognitive, Erikson:** (see 3.3 for details) combines biological, social and psychological factors in a revision of the Freudian approach.

3 **Cultural relativism (e.g. Mead):** a reaction against the psychoanalytic views. Claims that problems are due to social factors, though there are also universal changes, such as having to unlearn certain behaviours and move from dependence to independence.

4 **Coleman's Focal Theory (1980):** disagrees with the traditional views of: (1) storm and stress; (2) identity crisis; (3) generation gap, and claims that none of them is by any means universal. Coleman studied 800 11- to 17-year-olds and found that the process of adaptation is spread over the years. The adolescent solves one crisis before tackling the next. He suggested that problems only occur when issues accumulate, e.g. from late maturation. This is supported by the work of **Holmes and Rahe** (see p.173).

⑤ **Biological**: there are major hormonal and physical changes requiring adjustments to self-image and equilibrium.

⑥ **Ethological**: an analogy is drawn between the fledgling being kicked out of the nest by the parents at the appropriate time, and innate pressures on human parents to sever the parent–child ties.

Conclusion

● The difficulties experienced during adolescence may be due to a variety of other factors, not transition *per se*.

● Adolescents may benefit by being offered more explicit help in making the transition. Other societies have rites of passage, which elevate the transition rather than creating the expectation that it is a difficult time.

● The differences in theoretical formulation may be related to whether it is based on abnormal data (e.g. Freud) or normal studies (e.g. Coleman).

ADULTHOOD

Development does not end with reaching physical maturity. Behavioural adaptation is made necessary by continuing physical changes and critical life events. What is an adult? Theoretically, a person who has achieved:

● formal operational thought (Piaget),

● Kohlberg's moral stage 6,

● a developed sense of personal identity (Erikson),

● the ability to engage in a truly intimate relationship (Erikson),

● employment (Erikson),

● it starts at the end of adolescence and ends with 'old age', at about 65, a time of retirement and death.

Neugarten (1968) has suggested that adults have a 'social clock' which advises them about the best time to reach social milestones, e.g. getting married and having children. We are affected by these age-related norms and stereotypes, and tend to conform. However, the problem for any 'theory' of adulthood is that such social norms are different for different social groups and generations.

Theories of adulthood

① **Erikson** (see 3.3): young adulthood (intimacy versus isolation, focusing on relationships) and middle adulthood (generativity versus stagnation, focus on wider productivity), the change occurring around the age of 40.

② **Alternatives to the 'stage' theory:**
  ● Levison *et al.* (1978) used the term 'seasons' because it doesn't imply progression as much as simply change,
  ● Hopson and Scally (1980) talked of 'themes',
  ● White (1975) described five growth trends.

③ **Life event theory**: rather than use an 'ages and stages' approach, it may be better to consider the events which occur and how people cope (see p.173). The fact that it is harder to generalise about certain events happening at a particular age (such as having your first child) means that event theory may be more appropriate.

Mid-life crisis

Traditionally the age of 40 is a time of mid-life crisis, not dissimilar to the adolescent time of transition. People become conscious of and depressed about life changes, such as children leaving home. They are aware of the physical and psychological effects of ageing. There may be occupational changes. Like adolescence, there may be significant hormonal and sexual changes for women, the menopause signals the end of reproductive life and creates physical difficulties for some. It may also be more difficult for women who have been at home looking after children.

On the other hand, for some people it is a time of becoming more accepting of themselves, and being ready to approach life with renewed vigour. The change of life may not be all bad, when children leave home the parents may find themselves better off and able to pursue their own interests. The evidence available suggests, that for most people, it is not a traumatic time of life.

LATE ADULTHOOD: AGEING

Late adulthood has been defined as 'over 65', however, the key factors are not so much age itself as common physical and life changes. Gerontology, the scientific study of the elderly, has become an increasingly important subject because of the continually increasing population over 65. In 1900 the average life expectancy was 49, in 1976 it was 73 and by the year 2030 20% of the population will be over 65.

Beware of the danger of being swayed by stereotypes – either the picture that all the elderly are senile or that they are sages.

Erikson characterised the ageing years as a time of **integrity versus despair**. The individual reviews and evaluates their life, which results in either feeling satisfied and accepting the inevitability of death, or feeling regret and fearing death.

Physical changes

As a person gets older, their body and abilities become smaller, slower, weaker, lesser, and fewer. For example, the bones become more brittle, brain cells are reduced (after the age of 30 neurons die at a rate of 30 per minute), reflexes and reaction times are slower, tissue renewal is slower (**Bromley, 1988**).

Apart from these basic features, more changes may not be related to ageing specifically but happen only in relation to specific conditions. **Williams (1993)** reports that, when healthy older subjects are tested, 50% show signs of previously undetected heart disease. The remaining 50% are essentially no different from subjects in their 20s. The same is true for other physical tests, such as brain glucose metabolism and kidney disease.

Mental capacity

1 **Does mental capacity decline?**
  - **Wechsler** found that intelligence reaches a peak around the age of 30 when he was compiling the normative data for WAIS, the test of adult intelligence that he devised.
  - **Burns (1966)** reported a longitudinal study where a set of people were tested at age 22 and again when they were 56, on average their IQs were *higher*.
  - **Talland (1968)** found that subjects aged 77 to 89 remembered less than half the number of items that a 20–25-year-old age group can recall on a short-term memory task, and also forget more in the initial 90 seconds after presentation of a 3-letter word.
  - **Crossman and Szafran (1956)** established that older subjects took longer on tasks involving discrimination when the number of alternatives increased.
  - **Rabbitt (1965)** found that older people find it hard to ignore irrelevant stimuli.
  - **Warren and Warren (1970)** found older subjects used different strategies to compensate for poorer short-term memories (see 1.1, auditory illusions).

2 **What is it that declines, or increases?**
  - IQ: **Schultz *et al.* (1980)** found declines in fluid intelligence and spontaneous flexibility with age, but they found that some older subjects were the best of all. **Horn and Donaldson (1980)** suggest that the consistency of crystallised intelligence is due to cumulative effects of experience. **Birren *et al.* (1963)** found subjects over 65 scored better on tests of verbal intelligence than younger subjects.

- *Memory*: **Welford (1958)** found deficits in short-term memory. Long-term memory, particularly of a semantic nature may remain relatively unaffected (see **Bahrick, 1984**, 1.5). **Kimmel (1990)** also argues that the changes are complex, there may be dramatic declines shown in laboratory memory experiments and some everyday memory skills, but older people show highly competent memory skills in other areas, such as long-term recall or expert memory skills. Motivation is probably an important factor in whether memory improves or not.
- *Psychomotor skills*: tests of performance, such as reaction time, show a decline. These can be related to physical damage to components of the nervous system.
- *Wisdom*: in other cultures the old are revered for their wisdom. Conversely this kind of knowledge may be seen as old-fashioned or inflexible. **Kimmel (1990)** distinguishes between practical wisdom (in personally relevant situations) and philosophical wisdom (the meaning of life); both are means of coping with the uncertain matters of life and not simply abstract ones. **Arlin (1977)** has suggested a fifth stage of cognitive development: divergent thinking or problem-finding (rather than solving).

3 **Possible explanations:**

- *Health*: where any measurements are drawn from a *'mixed' population*, some have decreased ability due to the effects of strokes and other progressive illnesses. **Birren *et al.* (1963)** separated a sample of men aged 65–91 into two groups: one who were in optimal health in every way, the other had no obvious symptoms of disease but, on close medical examination, had certain mild diseases. The first group performed better on 21 out of 23 tests of intellectual performance.
- *Social deprivation*: intellectual stimulation and physical activity are important to maintain mental ability; institutionalised elderly people may suffer similar ill-effects to children in orphanages. **Rubin (1973)** compared elderly people living in homes or on their own on Piagetian tasks. The matched subjects who lived independently did better on conservation tasks and were less egocentric.
- *Cohort and selective dropout effect*: much of the evidence is from cross-sectional studies which, for example, compare the 20-year-olds of 1940 with those of today. Since diet and education have improved we would expect the former to have lower intelligence levels, so comparisons are spurious. People today are smarter. **Schaie (1983)** has reported, from a longitudinal study in Seattle, that cohort effects equal or exceed age differences.
- *Competence versus performance*: findings may be due to slower physical responses or 'peripheral' mental abilities rather than a decline in intelligence.
- *Everyday skills versus performance under pressure*: **Welford (1958)** found significant differences but suggested that this was because individuals were tested to their limits. In general people function within their limits and older individuals suffered no particular problems. In addition they can compensate for some of the more obvious declines, such as failing eyesight or loss of mental and physical agility.

The management of old age

1 **Social Disengagement Theory (Cumming and Henry, 1961)**: psychological well-being is promoted by a gradual withdrawal from personal contacts and world affairs.

2 **Activity**: continued or new interests and involvements maintain psychological health. For example, **Havighurst *et al.* (1968)** felt it was important for the elderly to maintain 'role count', the number of social roles they have to play. **Rubin's** (see above) research demonstrates how deprivation can lead to mental deterioration.

3 **Social Exchange Theory (Dowd, 1975)**: suggests that an individual 'agrees' to give up certain things (being a financially active member of society) in exchange for their increased leisure time and pension. This informal 'contract' contains expectations about how an old person will behave (see also exchange theory, 2.4).

4 **Individual differences (Bromley, 1988)**: argued that some people have no desire to disengage. However, some factors (social, physical or economic) may dictate the amount of activity which is possible. Prescriptive theories, such as activity or disengagement, suggest what old people should be doing to promote well-being, whereas in fact there are the same individual differences as at any stage of life.

⑤ We need to develop **innovative ideas** about how to cope with the growing elderly population. One solution in America is retirement villages, though not everyone wants to spend their old age surrounded by the elderly. The trend for children to live at some distance from their parents means that many elderly people miss out on the opportunity for grandparenting. One novel idea, which seems obvious, has worked successfully in a nursing home in Washington State. They combine looking after disabled elderly residents with running a day centre for pre-school children, the residents feel the children provide the 'best therapy' (*People* magazine, April 1993).

Training older workers

Belbin and Belbin (1972) have been engaged in long-term research into the problems of the older worker. They have reported that older people learn new tasks less well, but this may not be due to their inability to learn but to the unsuitability of the training methods. Older workers have difficulty translating verbal instructions into action, understanding long, complex instructions and unlearning incorrect habits. Therefore, they suggest, instruction should match the learner.

Stammers and Patrick (1975) report a number of other research outcomes:

- Decline in mental capacity, as described in the previous section. Also problems transferring learning from training to the task itself.
- Decline in certain performance skills, e.g. difficulty with paced activities, slower reaction times.
- Preference for accuracy rather than speed.
- Possession of strategies for learning to learn, which may be helpful or, if they are rigid, will make training difficult.
- A tendency to be cautious in decision making.
- May be over-anxious in retraining and over-sensitive to any suggestion of failure.

(See also 1.4 and 9.1).

Conclusion

There is an *average* decline in functioning with age but, for some individuals there may be no decline or even an improvement on some measures. Older people also learn to compensate by adopting suitable strategies. Therefore chronological age may not be a good predictor of behaviour. It is wrong to discuss the elderly as if they were a homogenous group.

CRITICAL LIFE EVENTS

There are life changes which occur throughout the lifespan. Rather than describing development in terms of age, it can be approached by looking at the effects of certain critical events on behaviour.

Holmes and Rahe (1967) developed a 'Social Readjustment Rating Scale'. They examined 5000 patient records and made a list of 43 life events which seemed to appear in the months preceeding the onset of illness. Each life event has a stress 'score'. The scale has generated much research and, in general, studies have found a modest but significant relationship between life events and illness episodes. **Coleman**'s Focal Theory (see p.169) also predicts that it is the accumulation of problems that leads to stress (see also 7.6 for an explanation of how stress may lead to physical problems).

Most critical life events have associated **'rites of passage'**, which often are founded in religion. Our society is generally lacking in such 'celebrations' and this absence may contribute to the difficulties experienced.

All the life events discussed below are subject to major changes in our continually developing society. People marry less and have children in non-traditional circumstances, divorce and unemployment are increasing, retirement ages are changing, there are more people who are living past retirement age, and the experience of death is changed by improvements in medicine and attitudes.

Marriage

1 **Psychological factors:**

- *Stress*: scores 50 (7th) on the Holmes and Rahe Scale.
- **Erikson**'s life crisis for young adulthood is 'intimacy versus isolation', the task of 20- and 30-year-olds is to form a deep and lasting relationship. The experience of love and commitment is essential for psychological wellbeing, the alternative is isolation.
- *Interpersonal attraction*: the formation and maintenance of relationships is discussed in 2.4.
- *Health and happiness*: **Burman and Margolin (1989)** found that the quality of marriage was linked to health problems but concluded that the effect is probably indirect and non-specific. **Chiriboga and Thurnher (1980)** found that having separate interests and hobbies was associated with greater happiness.

2 **Variables:** the decision to marry depends on individual, social and cultural differences:

- The arranged marriage: **Yelsma and Athappilly (1988)** compared happiness in arranged Indian marriages with both Indian and American love matches, and found satisfaction higher in the former. However this may be because of specific personality characteristics in those Indians who continue to accept arranged marriages.
- Individual needs: **Duberman (1973)** described three types of marriage, which need not be mutually exclusive: *traditional*, where the husband is the main decision-maker though the wife may have authority over childcare and domestic matters; *companionship*, which is more a partnership and *colleague*, which has a stronger emphasis on sharing and lack of distinct male/female roles.
- Changing norms: **Chellin (1985)** found a 40% increase in the numbers of partners who cohabit between 1977 and 1979 in the USA.

1 **Psychological factors:**

- Pregnancy scores 40 (12th) on the Holmes and Rahe Scale, a new family member 39 (14th) and a child leaving home scores 29 (23rd).
- **Erikson**'s notion of generativity can include the production of children, though he put this stage at 40 plus.
- *Socialisation*: parents socialise and are socialised by their children, many people comment how rearing a young child has enabled them to see the world differently. The advent of children also inevitably changes the parents' circle of friends and, mainly for women, changes their work or at least de-emphasises their career.
- *Stressful*: causes marital problems, possibly because people sometimes have children as a way of patching up their difficulties and also through conflicts over child-rearing practices and jealousy.
- *Self-image*: this can be altered in the light of the new role. Becoming a parent also leads to a reassessment of your own parents.

2 **Variables:**

- Childcare: some women receive much help from mothers and their extended family; well-off families can afford nursery facilities. Otherwise much of the burden is usually placed on mothers.
- *Expectations*: **LeMasters (1957)** found that new parents who experienced a major crisis tended to be the ones who had a 'romanticised' view of parenthood.

3 **The empty nest:** another side of parenthood is when it ends, often associated with mid-life crisis but it may also be a time of increased wealth and freedom. Most parents look forward to extending their parenting into grandparenthood.

Divorce or breakdown of lasting relationships

The how and why of relationship breakdown is discussed in 2.4. The statistics are that one in three marriages end in divorce, mainly in the first seven years.

1 **Effects on the partners:**

- *Stress*: divorce scores 73 (2nd) on the Holmes and Rahe Scale, separation 65 (3rd) and reconciliation 45 (9th). **Kiecolt-Glaser and Glaser (1986)** found poorer immune functions where persons were suffering marital disruption. **Segraves**

(1985) points out that since marriage serves a health function, divorce will lead to ill-health, even when the stresses involved are excluded.

- *Loss*: **Clulow (1990)** argues that divorce is similar to death, both for the couple and their children. It involves grief, sorrow and anger.
- *Variables*: reactions vary depending on the marriage itself and who ended it, though it is always distressing for both partners.
- *Identity crisis*: involves reorganisation of routines and social circles.
- *Legal*: equitable distribution of possessions, including children.

2 **Effects on the children**: the effects of divorce or disharmony are complex, for example:

- *Psychiatric problems*: **Wallerstein and Kelly (1985)** claim that, in the USA, more than 80% of the children appearing in psychiatric clinics come from broken homes.
- *Difficulties assessing the effects*: prior to the break-up the family may have been having problems. **Cherlin et al. (1991)** found that the effects of divorce were considerably decreased when they took behaviour problems prior to divorce into account. Control groups from non-divorced families may equally hide family strains.
- *Broken versus unhappy home*: **Illsley and Thompson (1975)** argue that disturbed relations between parents will inevitably lead to disturbed relations between parents and children. Generally a stable one-parent family is better than an unhappy home.

Unemployment

Some of the same factors which apply to retirement will be involved in unemployment.

1 **Psychological factors:**

- *Stress*: fired at work scores 47 (8th) on the Holmes and Rahe Scale, change in financial state 38 (16th), and there are at least ten other associated changes on the scale.
- *Health and happiness*: **Warr (1978)** found that the unemployed had more psychological problems and poorer health than before they lost their jobs.
- *Vocational identity*: part of general identity definition. **Erikson** suggests that lack of employment in adolescence may result in unsatisfactory role resolution, continued life at home, extended period of adolescence and retarded adulthood.
- *Loss*: of economic status, social contacts, sense of purpose and self-esteem.
- *Increased*: depression, alcoholism and suicide. **Platt (1986)** found attempted suicides eight times more common among the unemployed, and most likely in the first month of unemployment.

2 **Variables**: unemployment need not cause distress, for some it is actively sought:

- **Argyle (1989)** suggests five major causes of distress: length of unemployment, commitment to work, social support from the family, level of activity, and perceived causes of unemployment.
- *Age and prospects of re-employment*: the older you are the more likely you are to remain unemployed and to have heavy family and financial responsibilities. **Bromhall and Winefield (1990)** found that men over 40 experienced poorer mental health and less life satisfaction than those unemployed for a similar length of time who were under 30.
- Other interests and money help.

3 **Phases of unemployment**: **Argyle (1989)** reports that most studies suggest a series of regular reactions to unemployment: *shock*, anger and incomprehension, followed by a holiday period of *optimistic* job searching. When the job search is unsuccessful, *pessimism* about money and the future sets in. Finally there is *fatalism*, apathy and no further job-seeking. (This could be related to learned helplessness.)

Retirement

The problems associated with retirement are also covered in the section on ageing, though that only relates to old age retirement. Some of the difficulties are also similar to those for unemployment, though retirement is generally a happier prospect involving a smaller decline in income.

❶ Psychological factors:
- *Stress*: scores 45 (10th) on the Holmes and Rahe Scale.
- *Health*: retirement is often accompanied by a *decline* in psychological and physical well-being. However, some people are forced to retire through ill health, which leads to a biased picture of health in retirement.
- *Losses*: identity, sense of purpose, habitual daily routines, familiar surroundings (some retired people move at this time), social circle. Leads to a sense of mourning, uselessness, insecurity.
- *Adjustments*: increased time with spouse, possibly moving house, loss of friends.
- *Self-image*: new role, loss of income and status, change from active, economically-productive member of society. Retirement may trigger the start of **Erikson**'s last phase of development, completing the work phase gives impetus to reviewing one's life.
- *Pluses*: more time for sleep, relaxation, family, friends.

❷ Variables:
- **Argyle (1989)** suggests that adjustment is dependent on: health, finance, purpose in life, number of strong interests, education and social class, whether the retirement is planned or not, and gender.
- *Individual differences*: some people look forward with anticipation and relief, others don't feel ready; for some, work had little to do with their self-identity. **Reichard *et al*. (1962)** suggested that certain personality types are associated with good adjustment (e.g. mature or passive) whereas others (angry or self-haters) coped less well.
- *Type of retirement and age*: voluntary or involuntary; early or at normal time; continued freelance or voluntary work; leisure interests.
- *Previous job*: for some manual labourers, retirement may lead to improved health.

❸ Ways of coping:
- **Turner and Helms (1989)** suggest that adjustment is helped by developing a lifestyle which has continuity with the past and meets long-term needs.
- Entering new social groups, people to share activities with.

❹ Phases of retirement: **Atchley (1985)** describes six phases: remote, honeymoon, disenchantment, reorientation, stability, and terminal when the person becomes ill or seeks re-employment.

Bereavement

❶ Psychological factors:
- *Stress*: death of spouse scores 100 (1st) on the **Holmes and Rahe** Scale; the death of a close family member 63 (5th), and of a close friend 37 (17th). **Hinton (1967)** found a higher incidence of death in recent widows than a sample of married women of the same age. **Parkes (1987)** found that 75% of widows sought medical advice within six months. However such findings are not universal (see 7.6). **Mor *et al*. (1986)** suggest that illness may have been ignored in the period leading up to a spouse's death.
- *'Normal' grief*: without it, it is unlikely that the person will recover. It usually lasts between one and two years, which is reflected in the historical practice of wearing black for a year. **Clayton *et al*. (1971)** interviewed widows, whose symptoms were crying, lack of concentration, sleeping and poor memory.
- *Abnormal grief*: as a response to extreme circumstances, this may be unhelpful. **Lindemann (1944)** described extreme reactions after the Coconut Grove night-club fire: somatic distress, guilt, hostility, sense of unreality and preoccupation with the deceased.
- *Ostracism*: some people avoid the bereaved because they don't know how to cope and it may arouse their own fears.
- *Self-control*: social pressure to control one's emotions may inhibit grief behaviours, and may also exaggerate fears of not being able to overcome the problems.
- *Loss of control*: the bereaved is often treated as a sick person, (see sick role, 6.5), e.g. others take over decision-making and they are given time off work.
- *Reorganisation of self*: change in relationships and resocialisation, new feelings of grief may change the view of self.

- *Expectations*: **Caserta and Lund (1992)** followed subjects for two years after the death of a spouse. Stress levels were lower and the ability to cope was higher than those expressed by a control group. This suggests that people's expectations differ from the actual experience.

2 **Variables**: the experience of bereavement can be related to:
- *Individual differences*: may vary with person's own feelings about death, and their emotional type.
- *Type of death*: accidental deaths lead to extreme bereavement reactions (see above).
- *Age of deceased*: harder to cope with the death of a younger person.
- *Relationship with the deceased*: closeness, dependency, duration. Where interpersonal problems were unresolved the grieving is much harder.

3 **Ways of coping**:
- *Cultural practices*: e.g. funeral service, period of mourning.
- *Social supports*: e.g. making immediate plans. Family members and friends are particularly important when the initial caring tails off.
- *Psychotherapy or reading books*: helps to review the relationship and understand one's feelings.
- **Weisman and Kastenbaum (1968)** suggest a *psychological autopsy*, to analyse the ways in which a person's death might have been handled better psychologically. This may be helpful in the same way that understanding of the cause of death is important for bereavement.

4 **The bereavement process**: models are useful as a means of assisting the bereaved, as well as understanding them. There are parallels with the dying process. **Bowlby (1980)** distinguished five phases of grief and mourning:
1 initial shock, denial, concentration on the deceased,
2 anger,
3 appeals for help,
4 despair, withdrawal, disorganisation,
5 resolution, reorganisation and new focus.

Death

1 **Acceptance of death**:
- The taboo of death: death is a frequently avoided topic and is discussed in euphemisms such as 'passed away' or 'no longer with us'. This suggests poor acceptance and lack of understanding, which may not help coping.
- The timing of **Erikson's** last stage – integrity versus despair – is related to a person feeling that death may happen soon. Successful resolution involves a positive life review. **Butler (1963)** also suggests the importance of the life review process, involving reminiscence and 'mirror gazing'.
- **Bengston et al. (1977)** found that 25% of the older persons he interviewed felt fear of death compared with about 50% of those who were middle-aged.

2 **Timing of death**: psychological indicators may serve as a better predictor of the nearness of death than physical factors alone:
- **Botwinick et al. (1978)** tested over 700 elderly persons. They found that those who died within the subsequent five years differed on a number of psychological measures to those who remained alive.
- It is not clear whether psychological or physical factors are primary. Undetectable physical deterioration may start off psychological deterioration; on the other hand, the relationship between stress and health suggests that psychological factors may come first.
- Modern medicine means that we have more and more control over when someone dies ('switching off the machine'). The patient themselves may indicate their wishes by refusing surgery or by writing a 'living will'.

3 **Ways of dying**: the quality of death stems from emotional and clinical sources, which often are antagonistic:
- *Natural death*, equating with natural birth. Your family support you in your own environment.
- The *hospice* movement, providing emotional as well as clinical support, particularly for pain.

● The anxiety associated with death can be reduced through understanding, thus alleviating some of the pain (see 7.7).

4 The dying process: **Kübler-Ross (1969)** interviewed over 200 dying patients and distilled five processes which characteristically occurred. She called them stages but there is probably no rigid progression or timing. The aim is to provide a framework for helping people through the dying process:

1 *Denial*: there's been an error. This is a healthy way of dealing with the initial shock.

2 *Anger*: 'why me?' Denial is difficult to sustain, the dying person is angry at the healthy.

3 *Bargaining*: make promises to church, charity, etc. in the hope of an extension of the period of life.

4 *Depression*: crying, deep sense of loss, need to express emotions.

5 *Acceptance*: if there's sufficient time to work through the previous feelings, the person often becomes emotionless and detached, welcoming quiet companionship.

Critics object to the notion of stages, to the simplistic approach, and to the image of one process of dying regardless of individual differences such as sex, age, attitude towards death or type of death.

Chapter roundup

Other related chapters are:

● cognitive psychology (Chapter 1), includes perceptual development and learning (imprinting), and is generally related to cognitive development;

● social psychology (Chapter 2) is linked to social development and includes effects of the socialisation process on the self, gender, parental styles and the influence of the media;

● communication (Chapter 4) covers language development;

● intelligence, personality and assessment (Chapter 5), outlines Freudian and other theories of personality development;

● abnormal psychology (Chapter 6) details atypical development and behaviour problems;

● biological psychology (Chapter 7) contains details of emotional behaviour and stress, which is relevant to the effects of critical life events;

● animal psychology (Chapter 8) examines the work of ethologists and the importance of genetic factors;

● applied psychology (Chapter 9) offers further consideration of the effects of work and vocation;

● research and design (Chapter 10) evaluates methodologies.

Illustrative question

From your knowledge of the development of social behaviour, what advice would you give someone wanting to set up a day-care centre? Refer to relevant theory and research to justify your answer.

(NEAB, 'A', 1990)

Tutorial note

This question is a haven for misdirected answers. First, it is important to recognise that cognitive aspects of development are irrelevant except insofar as they 'allow' certain other behaviours to develop. The question is about social behaviour. Second, it is also irrelevant, though tempting, to use evidence which demonstrates the general effect of day-care. The question is not *whether* there is an effect but *how* the positive aspects can be enhanced and negative consequences avoided. Finally, the question lends itself to a 'common sense' approach but explicitly requires 'relevant theory and research'.

Critical evaluation skills should be demonstrated by the candidate's ability to adapt their knowledge to a novel situation, often an application of psychological research to a commonplace situation.

Suggested answer

The two main issues are attachment and social stimulation. A psychologist would be concerned that a child would suffer from disruption of the primary attachment bond with its mother and not find suitable replacements, and would lack the stimulation necessary for cognitive and social development. On the other, hand the nursery environment may be able to offer better care than at home, certainly in terms of quantity of interaction and, for some children, quality of personal attachments and stimulation. (Note: throughout the essay I've used the word 'mother' to indicate the primary caregiver).

Before the age of one, an infant is still forming primary attachments, and therefore it may be best to take children over this age. However, evidence from kibbutzim, where children are cared for all day from a very early age, suggests that quality rather than quantity of time matters most for successful attachments. **Fox (1977)** found that the children still formed stronger attachments to their mothers than to the metapelet (nurse) with whom they spent more time. It is possible that the adjustment to multiple caring in kibbutzim may be helped by the fact that all the carers hold the same value system and ideas concerning child-rearing.

Bowlby held the view that children need the continued care of their mothers until the age of five. More recent evidence has indicated that not only can multiple attachment figures be acceptable (for example, **Schaffer and Emerson, 1964)**, they can be positively beneficial in offering different kinds of satisfaction. Therefore the staff of the day-care centre should be aware of how best to fulfil this role. Sensitivity and responsiveness to a child's signals are the most important factors in forming a good attachment. **Ainsworth (1974)** found that secure attachments occurred when mothers were sensitive and accepting and saw things from the child's point of view. Another aspect of good attachment is stability, it is important that there is a low staff turnover to ensure that children do not feel insecure in their attachments **(Howes, 1990)**.

Another aspect of attachment to consider is the disruption which is caused when separating mother and child – separation anxiety. Securely attached children should cope reasonably well, but other children may become very upset and anxious. **Ainsworth's Strange Situation** could be adapted to test children's reaction to their mother's departure by observing the mother and child playing on their own and then with an unfamiliar adult. The mother should leave the child with the stranger for a short period (three minutes). The child's behaviour when the mother leaves and when she returns gives an indication of attachment. A securely attached child will protest mildly when she leaves and, when she returns, go to her and be easily comforted. The other behaviours which would occur are either a child who makes no protest and ignores mother's return (anxious avoidant) and one who is seriously distressed and ambivalent about the mother's return (anxious resistant).

Obviously the best way to overcome these problems is, for all children, to extend the periods of separation from mother slowly so that the child is reassured that when she goes she always comes back. Anxious children should be given especial help through this transition period. In this way the nursery may provide assistance in actually improving the bond between mother and child.

If anxiety persists for more than two weeks this may indicate a particular problem, perhaps there have been some traumatic events at home such as the death of a relative or the birth of a baby. The child may show physical symptoms at nursery such as stomach upsets, or may be difficult at home and have nightmares. It seems that the only way to help this is to persist with gradual and sensitive separation, a system akin to systematic desensitisation **(Rosenhan and Seligman, 1989)**. Such problems may manifest themselves later in school phobia.

Play therapy is a recognised method of treating childhood psychological difficulties, and might be used effectively at nursery. **Axline (1947)** used play as a means of increasing a child's sense of self-worth and self-confidence by using the techniques which underline counselling; non-directive, unconditional, positive regard and interaction. Since the preschool child cannot converse effectively, communication can be made through play.

Another form of therapy has been suggested by the experiments of **Novak and Harlow (1975)** who showed that socially deprived monkeys could recover with the help of younger 'therapist' monkeys. **Furman et al. (1979)** tested this with socially withdrawn preschool children, they found that those who were given extra play sessions with children 18 months younger than themselves benefited in becoming more socially outgoing.

The second issue identified at the beginning of the essay was stimulation. The great worry in placing children in any 'institutional' care is that their personal contact time is decreased and therefore they receive insufficient stimulation for normal social and cognitive development. As long as the adult:child ratio is good (1:4 for infants, 4:7 for preschoolers) the quality of care should not suffer **(Shaffer, 1993)**.

Melhuish (1990) studied children cared for by relatives, with childminder or nursery care, and found that language development was correlated with the adult:child ratio and was slowest in the nursery group. However, this covariance may be due to other factors, such as the socio-economic status of the mother who has to use nursery care because it is cheaper. In fact, in the case of disadvantaged children, day-care may improve developmental rates. **O'Connell and Farran (1982)** looked at infants identified as high risk in terms of developmental problems, and found that those who were in day-care had more advanced language development by the age of 20 months than those who remained at home.

Language development is very important for social interaction. For all children the increased social contact of a nursery may lead to increased exposure to language and promote its development. **Bernstein (1971)** suggested that some children use 'restricted' linguistic 'codes', which will limit their cognitive development, indicating the importance of language development. The milestones in linguistic development are: the production of single words (20 words by 18 months), two–word combinations (around 18 months), ungrammatical longer utterances (2 to 3 years), largely intelligible conversation (3 to 4 years).

Play is an important element of social development. As we have seen, it can help emotional development and also fosters moral development, self-definition, co-operation and sharing, and the beginnings of friendships. Day-care and the presence of other children obviously provides increased opportunities for play, though it is important that the curriculum of games and activities are age-appropriate.

Psychologists typically expect children under two to engage in solitary play, moving on to parallel activity when children may watch and imitate each other but not truly interact. By the age of four years, play becomes increasingly social; children can understand rules, interact and co-operate. **Piaget** has suggested that the under twos are concerned with 'mastery', practising and repeating skills; and that the over twos move on to symbolic and fantasy play. **Garvey (1977)** underlined the fact that play should be enjoyable, have no extrinsic goals and be spontaneous and voluntary.

The early fears that a child may suffer emotional and social deprivation from placement in day-care can be seen as erroneous. With careful consideration such care can be an asset to a developing child.

Question bank

Allow 45 minutes for each question.

1 Do babies need mothers? Illustrate your answer with reference to relevant studies.

(NEAB 'A', 1985)

Points: The question might cover the issue of mothers versus fathers, parents as opposed to any significant other, and finally any significant other as opposed to no primary caregiver.

2 'The evidence is now such that it leaves no doubt regarding the general proposition, that prolonged deprivation of the young child of maternal care may have grave and far-reaching effects on the whole of his future life' (Bowlby, 1951). Discuss.

(AEB ,'AS', 1989)

Points: This is a fairly obvious question about deprivation and long-term consequences. If the quotation is answered specifically it might be worth considering that, in 1951, the evidence was different from what we know now.

3 A test situation, consisting of eight episodes, was used to observe infants (aged between 10 and 15 months) with their caregivers in an unfamiliar playroom. The episodes were:
   (i) caregiver and infant brought into the room by the observer,
   (ii) caregiver and infant play together for several minutes,
   (iii) caregiver and infant play with an unfamiliar adult,
   (iv) caregiver leaves the infant with the stranger for maximum of three minutes,
   (v) the stranger leaves the room and the caregiver returns,
   (vi) the caregiver leaves the infant alone,
   (vii) the stranger returns without the caregiver,
   (viii) the stranger leaves and the caregiver is reunited with the infant.

   (a) Outline the findings you would expect from this test. (4 marks)
   (b) Discuss how findings from this test help us to understand the relationship between infant and caregiver. (10 marks)
   (c) Drawing on your answers to (a) and (b), discuss ways in which children might behave when they start at a play-group or nursery school. (6 marks)

(NEAB, 'A', 1992)

Points: The description is of the Ainsworth Strange Situation.

4 Outline **two** theories of cognitive development and evaluate these theories in terms of empirical evidence.

(AEB ,'A', 1992)

Points: A recurring question, which is often very well prepared by candidates. In order to answer in the allowed time you must be selective in *outlining* the theories. The question specifically asks for evaluation in terms of empirical evidence.

5 Compare and contrast pre-operational thinking with concrete operational thinking, referring to relevant empirical studies.

(NEAB, 'A', 1986)

Points: The NEAB questions tend to focus on specific aspects of Piaget's theory rather than the general outline. It is important to restrict your answer to the specific stages in the question, and not merely describe them but specifically contrast them.

6 (a) Outline Piaget's ideas of 'accommodation' and 'assimilation' to describe a child's cognitive strategies for coping with new information. (10 marks)
   (b) Discuss what is known about the manner in which a child learns a general concept such as 'toy' or 'food'. (10 marks)

(NEAB, 'A', 1993)

Points: Part (a) requires that you can distinguish the two concepts and relate them to some other key concepts, which might include schema, equilibrium/disequilibrium, mastery learning, imitation and play. Part (b) can draw upon other theorists, e.g. the role of reinforcement, hypothesis testing (see 1.3 as well as object permanence and over-generalisation).

7 To what extent is it appropriate to see moral development as progressing through a series of separate stages?

(AEB , 'AS', 1989)

Points: What are the alternatives to a stage theory of moral development? Why might this be a more, or less, appropriate way to describe behaviour?

8 (a) Outline what is meant by the term 'instinct'. (5 marks)
(b) Choose one aspect of human social behaviour. Evaluate evidence which suggests that this behaviour is instinctive. (15 marks)

(NEAB, 'A', 1989)

Points: A look at the nature–nurture problem in relation to social behaviour, though 'instinct' is a particular kind of biologically determined behaviour, and reference should be made to ethological concepts such as kin selection.

9 'The self that is most important is a reflection, largely from the minds of others' (Cooley, 1902). Discuss.

(AEB ,'AS', 1991)

Points: The quotation provides an opportunity to discuss social versus non-social determinants of self. A good answer should focus on the quotation rather than producing a standard prepared answer.

10 (a) Briefly outline **two** possible functions of play. (6 marks)
(b) Describe **one** empirical study in which play has been investigated. (6 marks)
(c) Evaluate how this study contributes to our understanding of play in young children. (8 marks)

(NEAB, 'A', 1992)

Points: A popular *NEAB* question, but generally not answered well as candidates seem to have a very limited conception of play and their descriptions of empirical work lack detail.

11 To what extent does the age of a person affect his/her ability to learn? Illustrate your answer by reference to appropriate studies.

(NEAB, 'A', 1986)

Points: This question is not about old age but ageing generally. Therefore cognitive maturation is relevant of the young and the old.

12 In the light of psychological theory and research, discuss the view that adolescence is inevitably a period of 'storm and stress'.

(AEB, 'AS', 1990)

Points: A question which attracts anecdotal answers. When it appeared in an examination it was rarely answered, which is strange considering the relevance it has to many candidates.

13 'One of the many myths of old age is that work is central to an individual's self-concept and that retirement is a sign of declining self-worth'. (Schaie and Willis, 1986). Discuss this statement in relation to psychological research into the process of adjusting to retirement.

(AEB, 'AS', 1992)

Points: Probably the least popular area of the syllabus, but an important area of applied psychology and will undoubtedly become the focus of more questions.

COMMUNICATION

Units in this Chapter

Chapter overview

Communication systems may use any of the senses and serve social and cognitive purposes. At its most basic level communication is necessary for mating and therefore survival. The more social a species, the more communication is elaborated for the management of interactions. At the other extreme, language is used to manipulate abstract ideas. Attempts are made to distinguish non-verbal communication from verbal (linguistic) behaviour, and to ask whether man alone has language.

4.1   LANGUAGE

Language is:

- *symbolic*: a number of arbitrary, conventional units,
- *a rule system*: can generate an infinite number of expressions,
- *communication*: over time and space,
- *social*: a shared system, a means of group or cultural identity,
- intimately related to thought (and memory) see 1.4 for discussion of 'Language and Thought'.

It should be compared and contrasted with:

- *animal communication*, which is a finite system consisting of various combinations of set patterns (see 4.3),
- *vocal but not linguistic behaviour*, such as accent and paralinguistic behaviours such as cries or laughter,
- *non-verbal human communication* (see 4.2), some of which is vocal and some of which *is* linguistic, e.g. gestures have a grammar (see language acquisition).

Psycholinguistics is the study of any and all behaviours that are linguistic. Sociolinguistics is a subsidiary study which views language in its social context and is concerned with the language, paralanguage and non-verbal behaviours which communicate social information.

There are four main aspects of language:

1. *Phonology*: a **phoneme** is the basic sound. English has 45 phonemes, some languages have as few as 15, some as many as 85.

② *Syntax:* the rules for combining words – grammar.

③ *Semantics*: meanings. **Morphemes** are phonemes combined into meaningful units, e.g. PINS has two morphemes (PIN + S). Some morphemes are 'bound', like 's', which has no independent meaning, others are 'free'. The words that a person knows are stored in a **lexicon**, each word has **denotation** (the agreed meaning of a word) and **connotation** (what the word means to you, including its affective component).

④ *Pragmatics*: knowledge about how language is used in different contexts.

THEORIES OF LANGUAGE

Learning theory: e.g. Skinner

In 1957 Skinner published *Verbal Behaviour*, his account of how operant conditioning can explain language acquisition. Language is learned through the same processes as all other behaviour: selective reinforcement, shaping and imitation:

Key elements:

- a **mand**: a random sound, e.g. dada, which is attributed meaning by an adult and reinforced,
- a **tact**: the response made when a child utters the correct word for an object and is rewarded with approval,
- **echoic responses**: a child imitates the sounds made by others and is positively reinforced,
- **positive reinforcement** comes from a child getting what he wants, e.g. 'cup water' or, **Staats and Staats (1963)** noted, when parents provide reinforcement through touching, feeding and being excited when children vocalise.

Evidence for:

- **Clarke-Stewart (1973)** found that children whose mothers talk to them a lot have larger vocabularies, which indicates the importance of the learning environment as well as social interaction.
- **Gelman and Shatz (1977)** suggest that adults use a 'baby talk register' (BTR) when talking to children. This is spoken in a high pitch, short sentences and with an emphasis on key words. The length and complexity of the sentences is adjusted to the ability of the child. Studies of mean length of utterance (MLU) have failed to show whether this can have a positive effect on children's development.

Evidence against:

- **Brown, Cazden and Bellugi (1969)** found that mothers responded to the *content* of what their children said rather than the *grammatical structure*, therefore they were not shaping performance.
- There seems little relation between correct grammar and positive reinforcement. **Nelson (1973)** found that children who were corrected developed more slowly. **Slobin (1977)** noted that adults reinforce incorrect grammar. **Brown *et al.* (1969)** felt that adults reinforce meaning rather than grammatical correctness. In fact, adults often reinforce incorrect grammar and words (**Slobin, 1979**).
- Babbling increases despite the fact that adults don't imitate it.
- Deaf children learn language without speaking and being reinforced.

Evaluation: learning theory can't explain:

- the remarkable rate of acquisition,
- why so many different responses are made to the same verbal stimuli,
- the occurrence of creative and novel utterances, e.g. overgeneralisations,
- the universal sequences of acquisition, in all languages,
- how children understand the meaning of sentences which are often not equivalent to the sum of their component words,
- how ungrammatical adult speech leads to learning correct speech.

However:

- this is a theory of production rather than competence,
- it does explain certain aspects of linguistic acquisition, such as word meaning and accent.

Nativist theory: Chomsky

Chomsky (1959) criticised Skinner's account along the lines given above, and proposed an alternative view **(Chomsky, 1957, 1965)** that we are born with an ability to formulate and understand language:

Key elements:

- **Language acquisition device** or **system (LAD or LAS)** is an innate hypothetical brain mechanism which is pre-programmed with the underlying rules of a universal grammar. This acts upon the linguistic input to form the representative grammar. Some see it as a physical reality.
- **Surface structure** is the grammatical structure actually used, the words and phrases.
- **Deep structure** is a 'translation' of the surface structure, which more or less corresponds to the meaning of the sentence. The same surface structure can have different deep structures, e.g. 'the peasants are revolting' has two different deep structures whereas 'the cat chased the dog' or 'the dog is chased by the cat' differs in surface but not deep structure.
- **Linguistic universals** are those elements which are common to all languages, such as phonology (vowels, syllables) and syntax (nouns, verbs). These exist at deep structural levels, the differences between languages are surface.
- **Transformational grammar**, enables meaning to be transformed to speech and vice versa; it is an innate structure or predisposition which gives language its generative power.

Evidence for innate capacity comes from:

- brain specialisation,
- the existence of linguistic universals, e.g. nouns, verbs, plurals and tense,
- the speed at which language is acquired,
- the generative nature of language systems, i.e. the ability of a finite set of rules (grammar) and words (morphemes) to produce an almost infinite set of utterances,
- language is species-specific (see 4.3 for evidence on animal 'language').
- **Lenneberg (1967)** put forward the *critical period hypothesis*, which suggests that unless language is learned at an early age, its development will be permanently affected. **Labov (1970)** reported that adults find learning a language difficult while this is not true for adolescents. **Curtiss's (1977)** documentation of Genie (see 3.1), who never developed normal language but was able to produce novel sentences, can be taken as evidence for or against critical periods.
- Virtually all children acquire language at about the same age and in the same sequence. Even congenitally deaf children or those whose parents are deaf mutes create some kind of mainly non-verbal language. **Brown and Fraser (1963)** concluded that telegraphic speech is perfectly grammatical, supporting the view of an innate readiness for grammar. **Lenneberg (1967)** studied normal and Down's syndrome children and found significant correlations between motor milestones such as sitting and standing, and language milestones, which indicates the role of maturation in language development. **Brown (1973)** found that his three intensively studied subjects all acquired 14 main grammatical morphemes in the same order.

Evidence against:

- plainly learning is part of the process, e.g. how else would 'goed' become 'went'?
- the model only concerns competence. Explanations of performance involve memory, attention, the nervous system, etc,
- feral children don't develop language,

- it can't explain single word utterances which have no grammar,
- adults are still able to learn a second language,
- a sensitive rather than critical period may be more accurate,
- it overstated the automatic and independent nature of acquisition,
- as a theory, it lacks falsifiability.

Cognitive or interactionist theory: e.g. Piaget

Piaget stressed the role of maturational factors in both cognitive development and, as language depends on cognitive readiness, this too is related to maturation:

Key elements:
- Rather than an innate specialised processor, a nervous system which matures slowly and predisposes children to develop similarly.
- Development depends on *interaction* with the environment. The child prompts conversations in order to shape their use of language. Children are actively involved.
- Acquisition can be explained through information-processing strategies or operating principles.

Evidence:
- **Slobin (1979)** described innate information-processing strategies, such as 'pay attention to the ends of words or the order'. In Turkish they say 'pot stove on' rather than 'pot on stove', which may explain why they appear to learn prepositions earlier than English counterparts and this suggests an 'end of sentence' strategy.
- See 1.3 'Language and Thought'.

Evaluation:
- An extension of the Nativist position, stressing maturational aspects of language and thought and their interdependence.

Social theory: e.g. Bruner

Social approaches are a reaction against the emphasis by linguists on grammar which obscures the main function of language – as a means of social interaction. It is an extension of the interactionist position and is often included with such approaches.

Early pre-speech interactions are important precursors to linguistic development, such as games of peek-a-boo. **Bruner (1983)** suggests a Language Acquisition Support System (LASS) which predisposes children to such interactions:

Key elements:
- Language develops through social not just 'environmental' interaction, the beginnings of speech are social (see 3.1).
- Language continues to have an important social role, for example as a means of group identity in dialect and grammar.
- All other theories assume that exposure is sufficient for acquisition, however motivation is important e.g. in learning a second language.

Evidence for:
- **Sachs *et al.* (1981)** studied 'Jim' and his sister, whose parents were both deaf and dumb. Jim heard language from TV and briefly at nursery school, but his speech was below age level and structurally idiosyncratic. By the age of five his speech was normal with the help of specialist training. This suggests that mere exposure to language is insufficient, the social stimulus needs to be present as well.
- **Brown (1973)** studied an autistic boy, John. He noted the connection between the idiosyncratic forms of communication in autistics and their lack of social interaction, suggesting that the latter might cause the former.

Evaluation:
- not contrary to any of the other positions but an addition to them.

Conclusion

All positions are true to some extent – language is due to learning, to cognitive and linguistic maturation and to social interaction.

The evidence from **Curtiss (1977)** and **Fujinaga** *et al.* **(1990)** (see 3.1) suggests that, once a sensitive period is passed, language will still develop but not perfectly.

LANGUAGE ACQUISITION

Speech landmarks

As we have seen, there seems to be a universal timetable, regardless of culture, cognitive ability or training, in the acquisition and sequence of language. Both maturation and experience have a role to play.

1 **Pre-linguistic**: 0–1 year (approximately), cooing and crying. Until around six months the nervous system and oral cavity are not sufficiently developed to form or distinguish different sounds. This is not strictly language, Vygotsky called it 'pre-intellectual' language:

- **turn-taking** by two months **(Trevarthen, 1974)**,
- **babbling** (6–9 months): phonemes (ma, pa), the same whatever the linguistic environment, even in deaf children. By nine months, deaf children have stopped and phonemes are restricted to those in the native tongue,
- **echolalia** (11–12 months) the baby echoes itself, phoneme expansion (mama),
- **gestures**: a kind of pre-language which uses a grammar. **Bates** *et al.* **(1979)** found that 10-month-olds used gestures to say 'What's that?' or 'Look at that'. These are part of the pragmatics of language.
- **accent**: match babble to the qualities of language they hear. **Bates** *et al.* **(1987)** say that they are 'learning the tune before the words'.

2 **One-word utterances** (12–18 months) the word 'infant' comes from the Latin 'infas', meaning without speech. 'Officially' the onset of speech is the end of infancy:

- **'jargon'**: overlap of babbling and non-word sounds,
- **first words** are often invented. A word is a 'systematic matching of form and meaning', so a baby's first word is the first occurrence of the same sound being consistently matched with a meaning,
- **holophrases** are words which convey complex messages, e.g. 'milk' may mean 'I want more milk' or 'I spilled my milk', competent speakers often amplify the meaning for the child,
- **understanding** is always more advanced than production,
- **productive lexicon** is typically ten words by 15 months, four months later it is 50 words and 200 words by the age of two.

3 **Early sentences: Bee and Mitchel (1980)** distinguished two stages, from the beginning production is not imitation, children create their own:

Stage 1 grammar (18–30 months): **two-word utterances**:

- **'pivot grammar'** was suggested by **Braine (1963)**. Key or pivot words appear repeatedly and always in the same position, e.g. 'see' always first and 'it' last. The words combined with pivot words are called 'x' or 'open' words,
- **telegraphic speech** is an alternative description by **Brown (1970)**. Key words are combined with a grammar to preserve meaning, a 'semantic grammar'.

Stage 2 grammar:

- **overgeneralising or overregularising**: natural evidence of acquiring grammar is in the application of a rule across the board ('goed' instead of 'goes') shows that the child isn't imitating but understanding and applying a rule. **Herriot (1970)** called these 'virtuous errors'. They can be investigated by teaching children new words and observing how they apply grammar, e.g. **Berko (1958)** showed children a picture of a 'wug', 'if there are two what are they called?',
- **overextension**: use 'daddy' as a word for all men,
- **underextension**: **Clark and Clark (1977)** observed that limiting the use of a word to a specific context gives meaning, e.g. 'car' means a moving car otherwise say 'parked car',

- 'Wh-' questions and interest in rhymes and song. **Weir (1962)** noted how her own son, aged 30 months, talked himself to sleep, practising social exchanges and making up songs,
- **pragmatics**: by the age of two, children are proficient at using many non-verbal signals, such as raising the head to signal the start of conversation.

4 **Later speech**: typical difficulties and examples of more advanced forms:
- **pronunciation**: until the age of five, most children usually have trouble with at least one phoneme,
- **overmarking and redundancy**: e.g. 'the girl pushed the dog and then the boy he repushed the boy once more',
- **pragmatics**, e.g. **Shatz and Gelman (1973)** found that 4-year-olds used longer and more complex grammatical constructions when they spoke to adults than they did when speaking to 2-year-olds.
- **metalinguistics**, e.g. playing with words: **Chukovsky (1963)** reports examples of 3- and 4-year-olds creating rhyming poems. **McGhee (1979)** asked riddles such as 'Why did the man tiptoe past the medicine cabinet?' Younger children select a serious answer whereas 7-year-olds choose 'because he didn't want to wake the sleeping pills'.

Methods of study

Some examples of the various techniques which have been used:
- Longitudinal observational case studies:
  - **Brown (1973)** conducted naturalistic observation of Adam, Eve and Sarah in their own homes over a 10-year period. A transcript of the recordings was made available to many other researchers. Such rich data suffers from the omission of paralinguistic behaviours.
  - **Nelson (1973)** studied 18 children aged between one and two, using direct observation and diaries kept by their mothers. She classified the first 50 words acquired according to type, they tended to be specific and general nominals.
- Observation: **Trevarthen (1974)** noted that very young babies 'take turns' in non-verbal conversations.
- Investigation: **Shatz and Gelman (1973)** compared children talking to younger children or adults and noted the differences in speech as cited above.
- Correlation: **Clarke-Stewart (1973)** compared young children's vocabularies with the mother's speech patterns, finding evidence to support Skinner.
- Experiment: **Berko (1958)** tested children on wugs, as described on p.187.

PRODUCTION AND COMPREHENSION

Language, like reading (see 9.3), is a process which lends itself to an information-processing analysis; it involves concurrent bottom-up and top-down processing.

Production

Dell (1986) proposed the **spreading-activation theory** – a series of processing stages:
- semantic level: the meaning is worked out,
- syntactic level: the outline of the utterance is produced, including the grammar,
- morphological level: 'flesh' out; the root is decided on (such as 'jump' plus appropriate inflection, e.g. 'ed'),
- phonological level: phonemes selected.

Processing takes place concurrently at all levels, though higher levels are always working slightly in advance of lower levels. The model should also account for feedback. In the middle of a sentence a person may make alterations on the basis of self-monitoring. A look at common errors is one means of testing the model: Spoonerisms, or other phoneme/morpheme exchange errors, are an example of failure at the phonological level, and the 'tip of the tongue' phenomenon is evidence of successful processing at the semantic level but failure at a lower level.

Comprehension

The process of comprehension involves word recognition and semantic interpretation. It typically occurs very rapidly, and acts on parts of sentences rather than waiting for the whole. We have to make inferences because sentences are often fragmentary, the auditory signal is usually somewhat unclear and even ambiguous, due to pronunciation differences and interference. Two of the strategies for dealing with these problems are top-down generation of expectations and lip-reading:

- **Warren and Warren (1970)** played sentences which had one sound missing '*eel'; subjects heard 'wheel', 'heel', 'meal' or 'peel' depending on the rest of the sentence (see auditory illusions, 1.1).

- The significance of lip reading was shown by **McGurk and MacDonald (1976)**, who played subjects a videotape of someone saying 'ba' repeatedly. However the tape was dubbed with the sound 'ga'. Subjects thought they heard 'da', mixing the lip reading with the sound they heard.

There are a number of theoretical approaches:

1 **Schema and scripts**, as described in 1.3. It is fairly obvious that our organised knowledge of the world is used in a systematic way for comprehension. In fact, comprehension is probably more affected by schema than recall (as in Bartlett's study). Comprehension involves extracting meaning, going beneath the surface level. When subjects realise it is the literal meaning which is required they can perform much better, for example:

- **Gauld and Stephenson (1967)** stressed the need for accurate recall on a task like Bartlett's and found almost half as many errors.

- **Bransford and Johnson (1972)** presented subjects with a passage which made little sense, unless you were told the title was 'Washing Clothes'. Analysis of subjects' strategies to remember it and their later recall showed how much memory relies on initial comprehension.

- **Ausubel's** advance organisers (see 1.6) can be explained in these terms. They enable meaningless material to be comprehended and thus stored effectively.

2 **Bottom-up and top-down processing:**

- **Cohort model: Marslen-Wilson and Tyler (1980):** a 'word-initial cohort' is the set of words which are consistent with the initial auditory stimulus. Gradually words from this cohort are eliminated in line with subsequent sounds or meaning. In an experiment subjects had to identify a target word lodged in context or in a set of unrelated words. They were faster in the former situation, as predicted by the theory.

- **Propositions: Kintsch and van Dijk (1983):** proposed their own model:
  - starts from the top with 'goal schema', which decide what material is relevant,
  - works bottom-up from the text, generating *propositions* – the smallest unit of information that is meaningful (e.g. 'John is tall'),
  - a working buffer of limited capacity (like working memory) holds a few of these propositions at a time, they can then be linked together in a coherent fashion,
  - the strength of this model is that it makes very precise predictions. For example, **Kintsch and Keenan (1973)** showed how sentences with the same number of words can take different amounts of time to process depending on the number of propositions, e.g. 'Romulus, the legendary founder of Rome, took the women of Sabine by force' has four propositions whereas 'Cleopatra's downfall lay in her foolish trust of the fickle political figures of the Roman world', has eight, and takes about four seconds longer to process.

3 **Artificial intelligence:** attempts to write computer programs capable of discourse comprehension require a working model of comprehension. A major problem is understanding non-literal language, such as metaphors. Scripts and schema have been used in text comprehension, for example **Schank (1975)** developed a program called MARGIE which is based on three modules:

- a semantic parser, which produces conceptual dependency diagrams,
- an inference mechanism, which elaborates these diagrams using knowledge about the world,
- a response generator, which uses the elaborated diagrams to produce paraphrases and answer questions.

PHYSIOLOGICAL PROCESSES AND LOCATION

Language is one of the best examples of brain lateralisation. In most people the left cerebral hemisphere contains the language centres, though this may be reversed in left-handed people. There is also some plasticity. Brain damage to these areas before the age of ten can usually be recovered by non-damaged parts of the brain taking over, i.e. the right side. Such localisation of function and existence of a critical period is further evidence for the innate nature of language.

There appears to even greater specialisation within the language centre:

1 **Broca's area** (named after Broca who discovered it in the 1860s) is located in the anterior frontal lobe of left cerebral cortex language area, has sensory–motor connections and is associated with speaking and understanding grammatical connections. Damage to Broca's area alone results in mild, temporary speech impairment. When normal people speak, there is increased blood flow to Broca's area, the motor cortex, the left thalamus and basal ganglia. These areas show damage when a patient is permanently unable to speak. **Broca's aphasia** results in difficulty with language production (slow and poorly articulated, difficulties writing), telegraphic speech, some difficulties with comprehension. In fact, it is fairly similar to children's speech.

2 **Wernicke's area** (named after Wernicke who discovered it in 1874) is located in the posterior left temporal area, has visual and auditory connections and is related to speech production and comprehension. **Wernicke's aphasia** is shown by poor language comprehension and difficulty finding the right word, yet there is no difficulty with articulation; speech is grammatical but makes little sense.

Damage to the connection between Broca's and Wernicke's areas is called **conduction aphasia**, patients can't repeat what others say, and can't name objects.

4.2 NON-VERBAL COMMUNICATION IN HUMANS

Human communications consist of linguistic and non-linguistic (non-verbal) behaviours. Some linguistic behaviours are non-vocal (gestures), some non-linguistic behaviours are vocal (cries). The field of non-verbal communication (NVC) is a rapidly expanding one. **Argyle (1988)** notes that more work was done between 1975 and 1988 than had been done before 1975. It is also an area of charm and interest, as shown by **Desmond Morris'** popular books (e.g. 1967, 1969, 1977).

Significant considerations about NVC:

● such behaviours are subtle and often unconscious,

● they are an essential part of social competence and are often lacking in mental patients,

● many non-verbal behaviours are the same in all animals, including humans,

● human NVC is more complex, it either interacts with language or is independent of it,

● NVC can have a grammar (e.g. gestures or music)

● NVC is described in terms of signals (e.g. a smile) or channels (e.g. gaze).

CHANNELS AND SIGNALS

These channels and signals are culturally bound, but based on innate principles.

1 **Facial expression:**
  ● **Birdwhistell (1970)** described 32 kinemes or basic facial expressions,
  ● The origins of **smiling** are variously suggested as an appeasement behaviour, or an aggressive signal (as animals baring their teeth), or as the 'playface', found in animals as an invitation to play.

2 **Gaze:**
- *Threat signal*: in animals. The natural response is aggression or submission.
- *Affiliative signal*: as a means of controlling conversation or a sign of interest (staring into your lover's eyes).
- *A game*: peek-a-boo.
- **Pupil dilation**: communicates liking, for example **Hess (1972)** found that men preferred photographs of women who had more dilated eyes. **Stass and Willis (1967)** conducted a more realistic study, where pupil dilation was controlled using a drug. Subjects chose partners who looked at them more, though dilation also had some effect.

3 **Gestures and other body movements:**
- *Greeting rituals*.
- Some gestures are universal such as: head-nod, clap, beckon, wave, shrug, point, outline female body, indicate child's height with flat hand, pat on back, halt sign. The reason for this may be that some are innate while others are just obvious and therefore adopted by everyone, e.g. beckoning.

4 **Posture**: communicates a variety of behaviour: threat, sex, grooming, defecation, and sleeping:
- A *rich source* of communication. Simply showing matchstick figures or schematic drawings, as **Rosenberg and Langer (1965)** did (Fig. 4.1), communicates clear meaning of emotional state.

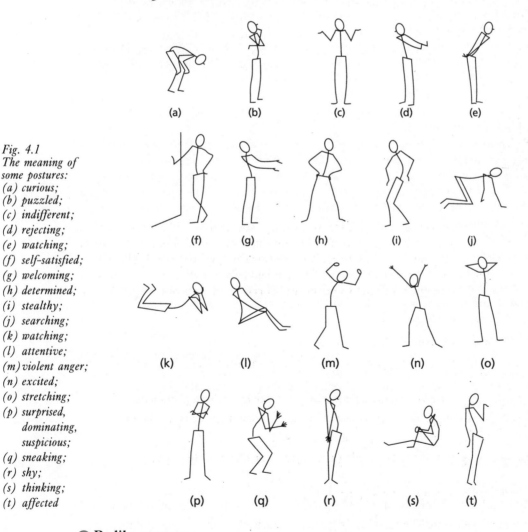

Fig. 4.1
The meaning of
some postures:
(a) curious;
(b) puzzled;
(c) indifferent;
(d) rejecting;
(e) watching;
(f) self-satisfied;
(g) welcoming;
(h) determined;
(i) stealthy;
(j) searching;
(k) watching;
(l) attentive;
(m) violent anger;
(n) excited;
(o) stretching;
(p) surprised,
    dominating,
    suspicious;
(q) sneaking;
(r) shy;
(s) thinking;
(t) affected

5 **Bodily contact:**
- *Aggression*: as in hitting, related to loss of personal space.
- *Affiliation*: **touch** is an interpersonal bond with possible sexual overtones, e.g. shaking hands, pat on the back. Its effects are unconscious and more powerful than people realise. For example, **Kleinke (1977)** left a coin in the telephone box

and then asked the next person who used it if they found the coin. When the request is accompanied by touch 96% returned the coin compared with 63% when they were not touched. Kissing may come from mouth-to-mouth feeding (**Goodall, 1968**).

- *Comfort*: e.g. teddy bears, see also bonding (see 3.1),
- *Cultural and situational*: in our culture there is a fine line between contact and sexual intimacy, e.g. body contact is permitted between men on the football pitch, or between adults and children up to a certain age.

6 **Body space:**
- *Personal*: closer than 1.5 feet tends to be uncomfortable, any closer and vision isn't very good.
- *Social distances*: tend to be 4–12 feet.
- *Public distances*: are over 12 feet, though this varies with standing or sitting.
- It is a means of signalling *interaction*.
- Related to *territory*, body space extends to one's house, car, or favourite table in a pub.
- *Overcrowding*, leads to increased galvanic skin response (GSR) because of increased autonomic arousal, feelings of stress and longer term illness (see 2.7). In other situations such as a party or co-operative tasks this is not true (see 9.2).

7 **Appearance**, e.g. clothes, tattooing, adornment:
- Most aspects of appearance are under *voluntary control* but, for example, face or body type often leads to stereotyped judgements about personality (see **Goffman** on self-presentation, 2.1).
- *Profound effect* on social interactions, e.g. helping behaviour (see 2.6) and conformity: *uniform* is a means of imposing group identity and norms on individuals, e.g. school uniform. Other uniforms have important effects on the receiver, e.g. the white coat a doctor wears.

8 **Smell** is less well-developed in humans than animals. What does exist often makes people uncomfortable:
- **Pheromones** are chemical substances which carry messages from one animal to another, like hormones do within the body. **Russell *et al.* (1980)** collected samples of women's underarm sweat, mixed it with alcohol and applied this to the upper lip of their female subjects three times a week. The menstrual cycles of the subjects began to synchronise with those of the odour donor, demonstrating a potent, unconscious effect of smell.
- *Body odour* is not universally taken as unpleasant, **Eibl-Eibesfeldt (1970)** reports a courtship dance where the man places a handkerchief in his armpit and then waves this in front of the woman of his choice, the smell is intended to arouse her. *Perfume* is used by women as a means of attraction as a substitute for body odour. Strangely, it is often derived from musk, a secretion from deer which is used in *their* sexual attraction.

9 **Non-verbal vocalisations:**
- Linked to speech: prosodic (timing, pitch, emphasis), synchronising (turn-taking), speech disturbances (stutters or 'um').
- Independent of speech: emotional noises, paralinguistic signals showing interpersonal attitudes, personal voice quality and accent.

10 **Paintings** and **music** also convey meaning without words.

FUNCTION

1 **Emotions**, mainly using face, body and voice:
- Some aspects of emotion are involuntary, such as sweating or pupil dilation; others are learned behaviours.
- *Liking*: dilated pupils, close proximity, touch, direct orientation (posture), mutual gaze, smiling, lively head movements, open arms, touch, higher pitch.
- *Infant–caregiver interactions* are mainly emotional and non-verbal.
- **Non-verbal leakage**: some of the voluntary aspects of emotional expression are easier to control than others, namely the face rather than the voice or the body from the neck down. These are called *leaky areas*. **Ekman and Friesen (1969)**

were the first to observe this when showing a video tape of a patient's behaviour, those who saw her head rated her as sensitive and friendly whereas those who saw the body thought she was tense and fearful. Other examples of leakage are *speech errors*, such as 'Freudian slips', stuttering and repetition. **Kasl and Mahl (1965)** found 'um' and 'ah' increase the more uncertain a person is. *Deception* is indicated by pupil dilation, slower speech, raised pitch, fewer head movements.

2 **Interpersonal attitudes**, proximity, tone of voice, touch, gaze, facial expression:
- *Dominance*: standing tall with hands on hip, asymmetrical arm and/or leg positions, sideways lean, hand relaxation, backwards lean.
- *Sexual signals*: touch, body contact and signals of liking.

3 **Paralinguistic**, head-nods, glances, non-verbal vocalisations:
- *Conversation*: changing emphasis to indicate the end of a sentence, head movements to indicate a question, eye contact and forward posture to show you are listening, gestures and facial expression to amplify meaning. Your disagreement may be signalled by the reverse behaviour, as well as facial expression and accent divergence (to emphasise your differences). Some people find talking on the telephone very difficult because such signals are lacking.

4 **Self-presentation**, hair, clothes, adornment, accent:
- *Body type* has been equated with personality (see **Sheldon, 5.2**).
- A person's *face* may lead to judgements about their personality. **Secord *et al.* (1959)** found that people judged an older face with thickish lips as meek and studious, whereas thinner lips were regarded as distinguished and refined.
- *Voice* appears to be correlated with extroversion, competence and assertiveness (**Argyle, 1988**).
- *Accent* has a profound effect on stereotypes. **Giles and Powesland (1975)** asked subjects to judge tape recordings of actors imitating a range of accents. Received pronunciation (RP; BBC English) was judged as a sign of intelligence, self-confidence, industriousness. Subjects judged speech which was similar to their own accent as more good-natured and good-humoured than RP.

5 **Rituals**, such as greeting behaviour or ceremonial performances. Ritual behaviour is highly stylised, relatively rigid and stereotyped.

Relationship between language and nvc

Words are often an awkward way to express things, particularly emotions. Non-verbal behaviour is like a picture (worth a thousand words). NVC is a means of regulating the flow of speech and controlling interpersonal exchanges. It can replace language altogether as in the case of the deaf or in a noisy environment. It has a much smaller vocabulary, and many of the representations are iconic rather than symbolic. The close co-ordination of both speech and NVC has been called a *gestural dance*, and starts in infancy (see 3.1).

Power of the message

Non-verbal communication is more powerful than language because much of it is unconscious and not manipulated by the sender, and is therefore more likely to express the person's true feelings. When non-verbal and linguistic messages are in conflict it is the NVC which carries greater strength, an experiment by **Argyle *et al.* (1972)** showed this (see 2.1). Additionally, such dual messages may combine in a special way, e.g. head down but eyes raised indicates a challenging submission, possibly a flirtatious message.

Meaning of NVC

Meaning is a function of the sender, the context and the receiver. There are several combinations from sender (A) to receiver (B), based on **Argyle (1988)**:
- B decodes incorrectly because A was a poor sender or B a poor receiver,
- A sends a deceptive message, B may or may not see through this,
- A sends an unconscious signal, B may or may not interpret it correctly,
- A sends and B receives the intended or unconscious meaning.

Some people are more sensitive than others at both sending and receiving. Women are apparently better than men at decoding.

Foa (1961) found that the main dimensions of NVC are friendly versus hostile and dominant versus submissive, using factor analysis.

NATURE VERSUS NURTURE

Which aspects of NVC are innate and which are culture-specific?

1. **Facial expressions** are related to emotion and seem to be largely innate. **Ekman and Friesen (1971)** worked with groups from places such as New Guinea who had no contact with Western society. The subjects were shown photographs of Europeans and asked to select an appropriate facial expression to match the emotion conveyed in a story. They had a high success rate in recognising the intended emotions, better than 80% for happiness, sadness, anger and disgust. **Tronick (1989)** found emotional responses in 3-month-olds to their mother's facial expressions, again suggesting an innate mechanism (see 3.1). **Andrew (1965)** pointed out that humans share many of their basic emotional expressions with animals, e.g. snarling or expressions of pain; supporting the biological importance of emotional expressions as warnings (e.g. aggression) or communications related to survival (e.g. pain).

2. **Gestures.** Some are universal, as described earlier, though the meaning is usually culturally-determined. In Greece 'no' is signalled by a backward jerk of the head.

3. **Clothes and appearance** are highly associated with cultures and subcultures, they function as an important means of group identity and ritual performance.

4. **Display rules** are social (learned) norms about which behaviours are acceptable in particular situations. Children use them from an early age (see 3.4). In this way innate responses, such as crying, are modified.

5. **Training**: people can be trained to be better senders or to be more aware of signals (see 'Practical Applications' p.195). Actors become very conscious of non-verbal ways of communication. **Lanzetta et al. (1976)** found that subjects who were told to inhibit their reactions to shocks showed lower galvanic skin response (a measure of emotional arousal) and reported less pain than those who were told to exaggerate their expressions of pain.

THEORETICAL APPROACHES

The study of body language is a union between social psychology and **ethology**. Many non-verbal behaviours are similar in man and primates, which suggests an evolutionary theme. NVC has a crucial role in behaviours related to kinship selection such as mating and aggression.

In humans, other factors have a greater role than in animals: cognitive and learned (social) ones have more effect on behaviour. In addition language interacts significantly with NVC.

Social psychology emphasises a different approach, placing NVC within the context of social interaction. For example **Goffman's** self-presentation model explained social life as a series of theatrical performances. We learn to manage our own performances chiefly through manipulation of non-verbal signals. We also apply the same rules to understanding others.

MEASURING NVC

Techniques have included:

- one-way mirrors and videotapes, which allow people to be watched when they are not self-conscious,
- judges may rate behaviours as shown in videotapes, pictures, schematic drawings or matchstick men, or be asked to assess stooges, particularly trained actors,
- observations may be made of seating (personal space), helping behaviour (e.g. touch and appearance), conversation, role play,
- scoring techniques are developed, such as **Ekman et al.**'s (1971) Facial Affect Scoring Technique (FAST) dividing the face into three areas: eight positions of eyebrows, 17 for eyes and 45 for lower face,
- gaze can be studied by tracking eye movements.

PRACTICAL APPLICATIONS

1 **Social skills training**:
- For *mental patients* or others, focuses on self-expression using mirrors or videotapes, useful for outpatient neurotics, adolescents and depressives.
- *Interpersonal problems*, such as marital therapy, aims to increase mutual rewards.
- *Professional*: teachers (assessing pupils' understanding), doctors and nurses (for eliciting information and communicate caring), air hostesses (control of emotional expression), politicians (advice from public relations companies). **Leathers (1986)** was called in to advise President Carter's support team when Carter 'lost' the first television debate he had with Ford. Up until the debate Ford was thought to have a serious credibility problem, however he used skilful visual cues to convey dominance. For example, he stood with his feet wide apart, used karate-type gestures and fixed his opponent with an unremitting stare. On the other hand, Carter's eyes were downcast, he used few gestures and held a rigid pose. Leathers' advice changed Carter's style and he went on to win the second debate and, ultimately, the election.

2 **International relations**: the fact that different cultures use subtle non-verbal signals has the potential for misunderstandings, either a matter of awkwardness or serious interracial conflict. For example, Arabs tend to have less personal space and interpret our distance as a sign of dislike. The thumbs up sign for hitchhiking is interpreted in some Mediterranean countries as an insult. Japanese 'inscrutability' seems like a lack of interest to Europeans. Black people may have a limp stance and lowered head when speaking to someone in authority, but this is not a sign of submission, it indicates lack of interest.

3 **Ergonomics**: when designing with humans in mind, many aspects of non-verbal behaviour need to be taken into account, for example feelings about personal space influence the way seating on a train is planned (see 9.2).

4.3 ANIMAL COMMUNICATION

Animal communication is entirely non-verbal, therefore much of the previous section applies equally to animals as to man. How does animals' communication differ from language? The question is important for two main reasons:

- language is often taken as the particular thing which makes humans different from animals,
- if animals can use language then the nativist position is in question. Nativists claim that language is an innate tendency, i.e. that only humans have a brain which has specially evolved to decode the complex rules of grammar. If animals can be taught to speak, then learning rather than innate potential is at least equally important.

DO ANIMALS USE LANGUAGE?

Defining language

The first problem is to define language in such a way that doesn't *a priori* exclude animals (definitions often start with 'language is human speech'). Second, there has been a tendency to refine the definition to keep one step ahead of current achievements in training primates to speak.

Any definition revolves around a group of sufficient but not necessary conditions, in order to include, for example, deaf signing as language. Is Esperanto a language? What about computer 'languages'? On what basis can we exclude animal communication?

Hockett (1958) proposed that there are qualitative not just quantitative differences between human and animal communication (the *discontinuity theory of language*), the sixteen 'design features' of language that he identified were:

1 vocal–auditory,
2 broadcast transmission and directional reception,
3 rapid fading (transitoriness),
4 total feedback (you hear what you are saying),
5 interchangeability (a sender is also a receiver),
6 specialisation (precision of communication),
7 semanticity (meaning rather than reference),
8 arbitrariness (use of neutral symbols),
9 traditional transmission (handed down not inherited),
10 learnability,
11 discreteness (meaning is communicated by order, grammar),
12 duality (order is important at the level of phonemes and morphemes),
13 displacement in time and space (e.g. 'My Granny broke her leg in Bolton last Thursday),
14 openness/productivity (novel utterances),
15 prevarication (to lie or talk about impossible things),
16 reflexiveness (metalanguage).

Observations of animal communications

Some of the above are clearly true for some animal communications, e.g. numbers 1 to 5. The following are also true of some animal communications:

1 **Arbitrariness**: the waggle dance in honey bees uses the sun as an arbitrary reference point in communicating the position of food.

2 **Traditional transmission**: chaffinches learn their local dialect from other chaffinches at a critical time in development. Birds reared in isolation are never able to function normally.

3 **Displacement in time and space**: dogs leave their scent, whales communicate over long distances. Honey bees perform their dance taking the movement of the sun into account.

4 **Learnability**: circus and farm animals are trained to understand commands.

Attempts to train language

1 **Speech** (vocal–auditory): **Hayes and Hayes (1952)** used operant conditioning to train *Viki*, a chimpanzee. After prolonged training she could manage mama, papa, cup and up.

2 **Understanding**: **Kellogg and Kellogg (1933)** raised a chimpanzee called *Gua*, who learned to recognise about 95 words and phrases, but was unable to speak.

3 **Sign language**: chimps may not have suitable apparatus for speaking but they do have nimble fingers, so it might be more successful to teach them signing. **Gardner and Gardner (1969)** used American Sign Language (ASL or Ameslan), much of which is iconic, but some is arbitrary and includes tense and grammar in its gestures. They trained a female chimp, *Washoe*, from the age of one using operant techniques. She was treated like a child and all conversation was held in ASL. By the age of five she had 133 signs and her development mirrored that of children, she was able to generalise, also overgeneralise, and had spontaneously combined signs into strings of 2–5 words. The Gardners raised another four chimpanzees, including *Tatu* and *Dar*. **Fouts (1973)** later worked with *Washoe* (see below).

    Patterson and Linden (1979) taught *Koko* (a gorilla) ASL. After seven years he knew almost all 700 signs and could understand many spoken equivalents. He had syntax, produced some novel sentences (his own form of swearing, 'you big dirty toilet') and invented his own combinations of signs, such as 'runny nose'.

    Terrace (1979) worked with a chimp called *Nim Chimpsky* (after Noam Chomsky), producing a very thorough record in the form of videotapes which others have been able to analyse. Terrace also notes that there are significant differences between chimp acquisition of ASL and a baby's acquisition of spoken language, a criticism of claims for animal linguistic competence. *Nim* never reached *Washoe's* standard, which the **Gardners (1980)** suggest is because he was deprived of close relationships.

4 **Reading: Premack (1971)** taught *Sarah* (a chimpanzee) a language based on small, plastic, arbitrary symbols to exclude any restrictions due to memory. She was able to interpret messages left for her on a magnetic board and to respond by placing the appropriate shapes on the board. **Rumbaugh *et al.* (1973)** used lexigrams to teach *Lana* to operate a computer with 50 keys, each key was a pattern representing a word in 'Yerkish'. The computer was able to recognise correct grammatical usage and reward her, it could also converse with her. She learned to correct mistaken displays (reading), conversed with the screen, initiated conversation and, when shown a new object, created a word for it.

5 **Conversation: Fouts (1973)** continued work with *Washoe* and her adopted son, *Loulis*. Would *Loulis* learn sign language without human intervention? The researchers never signed directly to Loulis but, by the time he was five years old, he had learned 51 signs.

    Savage-Rumbaugh (1978, 1991) has perhaps made the greatest progress with two chimpanzees, *Kanzi* and *Panbanisha*. She aimed to teach them language in the same way that children are taught: they are exposed to it in the course of everyday life, use it to talk about future plans and they are encultured by it. She conversed using lexigrams while roaming around a natural environment, the large forest surrounding her home. Another chimpanzee, *Tamuli* was raised solely by her mother, and had no comprehension of English. The difference lies in the fact that Kanzi and Panbanisha entered the human culture. The results were a rich use of language: 90% accuracy in being able to identify pictures, novel combinations of words and introduction of new rules.

6 **The language of children: Greenfield (1993)** filmed her own children to record how their language behaviour was nothing like that described by linguists. They were not combining rules using words but instead combining words with non-verbal elements such as gestures or things. Greenfield felt that this same process could be seen in the Gardners' films. *Kanzi*'s skills were compared, on film, to the progress of a 2½ girl, they both showed correct comprehension about 75% of the time. An important point is that we assess a child's competence in terms of their comprehension rather than just performance

7 **Parrot talk: Pepperberg (1983)** has taught her parrot *Alex* to name 40 objects. He can answer questions such as 'What colour or shape?' suggesting an understanding of abstract categories. More recently, **Pepperberg (1990)** has developed a technique for giving *Alex*'s novel utterances meaning, effectively demonstrating linguistic innovation.

8 **Marine mammals**: may have intellects superior to that of primates and have complex communications systems of their own. There is evidence of understanding from **Herman**'s work with dolphins and **Schusterman**'s with sea-lions. **Schusterman and Gisiner (1988)** taught sea-lions and dolphins a series of commands and tested their comprehension with novel presentations. They concluded that both sea-lions and dolphins can be taught to comprehend sentence-like constructions. **Herman *et al.* (1990)** have conducted a number of experiments involving auditory and visual communication with dolphins.

Do these attempts amount to language?

The work with primates has demonstrated the remaining of Hockett's design features:

1 **Specialisation: Fouts (1973)** and **Savage-Rumbaugh *et al.* (1978)** demonstrated chimpanzees use language to perform precise tasks.

2 **Semanticity: McFarland (1993)** suggests that understanding meaning can be shown in the ability to name things spontaneously. *Nim* did this when shown a picture of a dog or if he heard one bark.

3 **Discreteness**: *Lana* apparently was able to distinguish 'Lana groom Tim' from 'Tim groom Lana'.

4 **Duality**: *Koko* combined symbols to make new meanings.

5 **Openness/productivity**: *Koko* and *Washoe* produced novel utterances, most notably their 'swearing'.

6 Displacement: *Kanzi* was able to talk on the telephone about a future picnic.

7 Prevarication: *Koko* was asked to say something funny and pointed to a green toy and said, 'That red'. (The same question is asked in order to test the ability of machines to think, see 1.2). *Tatu* teased her carers by asking the colour of a picture, which was black, her favourite. She knew the colour but wanted to talk about it.

8 Reflexiveness: *Koko* responded to another gorilla's signs by saying 'good sign Michael'.

Objections

1 Experimenter bias: are the animals responding to inadvertent cues from their trainers? The **Gardners (1978)** tested *Washoe* with questions to which they didn't know the answer, she was correct 72% of the time. *Dar* was tested under double-blind conditions with two independent observers assessing his signs. *Kanzi* was tested with **Savage-Rumbaugh** behind him and performed well. Two previous chimpanzees trained by **Savage-Rumbaugh**, could only respond when face-to-face, which suggests they were responding to some subtle cues. **Terrace**, on the other hand, observed from a film that *Nim* was actually imitating his teachers rather than making sentences. Terrace claimed that *Washoe* was doing the same with the Gardners.

2 Subjective interpretations: there is considerable disagreement as to whether primates have actually demonstrated the important design features, evaluation is often subjective. For example:
- The *spontaneous* production of language: **McFarland (1993)** reports that *Washoe* never asked for an object unless she could see it. *Nim* seldom signed on his own initiative.
- *Novel utterances* tend to be relatively few and may have occurred by chance. *Nim*'s utterances were novel 12% of the time, far below that of children.
- On the other hand, **Greenfield (1993)** reports strong evidence of creative combinations of symbols by *Kanzi* and *Panbanisha*, original both in the words and the rules used. This has important implications for the evolution of language (see 8.1).
- *Grammar*: the ability to structure two or more words is not always consistent and sometimes made no sense unlike the two-word utterances of children. **Petito and Seidenberg (1979)** concluded that primate language is typified by repetitive, inconsistent strings.
- *Naming objects* appears to some (**Seidenberg and Petito, 1987**) as evidence of 'manding' as described by Skinner. However, **Nelson (1987)** argues that, in the same way, such behaviour forms the basis of language acquisition in apes and children.

3 A limited system: **Terrace (1979)** concluded that although it was possible for primates to reach a certain standard, their abilities reached a plateau. The **Gardners** suggested that *Washoe*'s development was that of a 2-year-old. This may be due to intellectual restrictions rather than linguistic competence *per se*. To what extent is language related to thought? (see 1.3) Are primates only capable of **Vygotsky's** pre-intellectual language?

Conclusion

1 Quantitative: it appears to be a question of degree, animals can use language but to a limited extent. Language is not an all-or-nothing affair.

2 Qualitative: there are some unique features of human language:
- the grammatical nature of human language is not clearly apparent in animal communication, and is probably tied to intelligence,
- the fact that animals do not acquire language spontaneously and humans do so with great speed and ease suggests an innate qualitative difference,
- animals may lack the necessary cognitive development to advance any further.

3 Emotional: the issue of whether there is a dividing line between apes and humans raises strong emotions about our own identity and about the ethics of how we treat apes, and animals generally.

Of course 'speaking' to animals isn't just about proving a point. **Dworksky (1981)** noted that communication with a gorilla gives a glimpse into another world. Also, being able to communicate with animals, whether it is language or not, changes our relationship with them. **Fouts** had to tell *Washoe* that one of her babies was dead. She thought he was returning with her baby and signed 'baby' enthusiastically. He signed back 'He's dead, he's finished'. *Washoe* dropped her head, moved to a corner and stopped signing.

EXAMPLES AND FUNCTIONS OF ANIMAL COMMUNICATION

All social behaviour is mediated and organised by communication, therefore reference should be made to Chapter 8 for further examination of animal social behaviour.

Anything which is a potential source of information is a channel of communication, such as the red spot on a gull's beak. More precisely, communication, or a signal, is when the behaviour of another animal is changed, through sensory perception rather than physical force. The notion of intention is hard to establish, two behaviours may be correlated but this does not mean that one caused the other.

Sensory modalities

1 **Visual**:
- The *dance* of the honey bees to communicate where to find food.
- *Threat and dominance displays*: facial expression (bared teeth, staring eyes), posture (head lowered, swaying), movement (slow approach), vocalisation (barking). Responses may be submissive or aggressive.
- *Deceit and mimicry*: the cuckoo imitates and exaggerates the appearance of another bird's eggs in order to deceive the host. Spots on caterpillars give the appearance of a larger animal and communicate danger to potential predators.
- *Appearance*: markings are also important for identifying your own species, and also to recognise individual members.
- *Sexual* displays communicate readiness, e.g. a peacock's fan or a female primate's genitalia, which are blue and swollen in oestrus.

2 **Auditory**:
- *Bird song* is mainly to do with mating and mainly by males. It either acts to defend territory or attract and stimulate females. **Krebs and Dawkins (1984)** removed pairs of great tits and replaced them either by loudspeakers or nothing. Where loudspeakers played a full repertoire of their bird song it took longer for new pairs to occupy the territory. **Kroodsma and Miller (1982)** found that female canaries built their nests more slowly when played reduced repertoires.
- *Alarm call*: **Marler (1959)** noticed that the calls of different species sound fairly similar, they tend to make it hard to locate the source.
- *Aggression*: e.g. barking and growling.
- '*Vocabularies*': **Marler (1976)** found about 13 categories of sound in chimpanzees, which communicated particular messages, such as greeting or food.

3 **Olfactory**:
- *Pheromones*: many animals are particularly sensitive to odours, which can communicate effectively over time and space. The female silk moth produces bombykol, which can be detected by a male over a distance of a mile. Their taxic response is simply to fly upwind, if they lose the scent they zigzag. (A taxic response is an innate response to a specific stimulus.) Smell is the main method of communication in ants. If an ant finds food it hurries back to nest, leaving a trail of pheromones which is followed by the others using their antennae. Ants also have colony odours to detect enemies.
- *Marking territory*, e.g. urination in dogs, defecation in hippopotami.

4 **Kinaesthetic**:
- *Grooming* is partly functional but is also an important social signal, for bonding and the establishment and maintenance of dominance hierarchies. Gorillas don't groom as much as baboons, who have a much greater number of dominance conflicts.

- *Huddling* as a response to fear.
- *Mother–infant signals*, bonding is related to touch (see 3.1).
- *Affiliative behaviour*: greeting may involve touching, smelling, mounting, or mouth-to-mouth contact based on feeding.

The origins of communication and rituals

Necessary acts become ritualised and inevitably take on a communicative function. **Darwin (1872)** noted that certain facial expressions which protect the sense organs when the animal is in danger, such as flattening the ears, become signals of fear or danger. Such behaviours are modified, sometimes into elaborate, precise and stereotyped rituals which make the signal less ambiguous and therefore more likely to be successful. Any successful communication is one that is ultimately for the good of the species.

Behaviours which become ritualised into signals:

1. **Intention movements**, such as the first moves in an act of aggression becoming a signal for hostility (see 8.4),

2. **Antithesis**: a signal acquires its meaning by being the opposite of another one, for example gaze aversion to communicate submission.

3. **Displacement activities**: when an animal experiences conflicting motivations (approach/avoidance) they may yawn or groom themselves, thus communicating conflict. When a cat does something awkward they frequently start grooming, communicating embarrassment.

4. **Autonomic displays** (emotion): such as bristling hair or panting, which communicate arousal or exertion. Urination is another example which evolved into territorial marking.

5. **Sexual displays** (see 8.4): evolve as a by-product of competition between prospective mates as a means of communicating their 'fitness'.

Theoretical approaches

Communication may be intra- or interspecies. In both cases such signals become **ritualised**. The original functional behaviours evolve into elaborate, exaggerated signals. Why? There are two answers, appropriate to different situations:

1. **Honest signals**: the process acts to make signals less and less ambiguous to improve communication effectiveness. Therefore the ritualised form becomes *more exaggerated* than the functional one, though it may be briefer. The same, less exaggerated behaviours may still serve the original, functional purpose.

2. **Dishonest signals**: the **manipulation hypothesis (Dawkins and Krebs, 1978)** proposes that animals give signals to manipulate the behaviour of other animals into doing things for the benefit of the signaller. The signaller's fitness is increased at the expense of the receiver. When instances of dishonest signals outnumber honest versions, the signal becomes devalued and will no longer be effective. Therefore it progressively evolves into more and more *extravagant* forms. Examples include mimicry by cuckoo eggs, by poisonous prey, the behaviour of the young cuckoo, and displays of aggression.

Chapter roundup

Other related chapters are:
- cognitive psychology (Chapter 1) includes a section on language, thought and reading;
- social psychology (Chapter 2) is intimately related to communication, especially non-verbal behaviours, communication networks and group processes;
- developmental psychology (Chapter 3) examines the role of language in cognitive and social development;

- abnormal psychology (Chapter 6) contains details of the interplay of non-verbal behaviour and maladjustment;
- biological psychology (Chapter 7) further explains the neurological background of language;
- animal behaviour (Chapter 8) expands on animal communication in terms of social behaviour, and looks further at the evolution of language and communication;
- applied psychology (Chapter 9) offers more on social skills training;
- research and design (Chapter 10) includes ethical and methodological considerations.

Illustrative questions

Below are three short pieces of dialogue (i, ii and iii) each involving a small child.

(i) Susie: This is my fis.
     Adult: This is your fis?
     Susie: No, my fis.
     Adult: Oh, your fish?
     Susie: Yes, my fis.

(ii) Adult (pointing to child's foot): What's that?
     Derek: A footsie.
     Adult (pointing to both child's feet): What are these?
     Derek: Two footsies...no, two feetsies, I mean.

(iii)Adult: Where is mummy?
     Nathan: Mummy goed out.

(a) (i) What does this tell you about Susie's ability to deal with speech sounds? (3 marks)
   (ii) What does this tell you about Derek's understanding of speech plurals? (3 marks)
   (iii) What does this tell you about Nathan's understanding of tense? (3 marks)

(b) What general conclusion might be drawn from these extracts about the way children's language develops? (3 marks)

(c) Discuss two main purposes of language in young children. Give examples of children's speech in your discussion. (8 marks)

(NEAB 'A', 1992)

Tutorial note

There is a trend to structure examination questions more explicitly. The intention is that candidates should find it easier to identify what is required of them and be less likely to waffle.

The question given here is a popular one from NEAB, in the sense that it is both often asked and often answered. A good question should give all candidates something to tackle, but must also distinguish the better candidates from the less able or less prepared. Part (a) offers everyone a chance to get full marks as it is purely descriptive. Part (b) becomes more difficult. In the examiner's report it was noted that candidates did not always relate their answers to the dialogue extracts as directed. Part (c) asks for a discussion, suggesting both description and evaluation. The examiner commented that there tended to be an overemphasis on communication at a cost to cognitive functions. He also criticised the tendency to merely elaborate stages of development and to give too few examples of children's speech.

Suggested answer

(a) (i) Speech sounds: Susie appears to have difficulty with the 'sh' phoneme. To start with, the adult checks that the word is not an invented one, however Susie knows what she *intended* to say and therefore insists 'no, my fis'. Susie thinks she is saying 'fish'.

(ii) Speech plurals: the grammatical rule for indicating plurals is to add the morpheme 's', however, there are many exceptions such as foot and feet. Derek first shows understanding of the general rule, saying 'footsies' but then recalls the irregularity 'feet' and attempts to incorporate this new understanding using both the exception and the rule imposed on his own idiosyncratic form of foot/feet 'feetsies'.

(iii) Tense: again the general rule is to add 'ed' to show the past tense, however again there are exceptions, 'went' rather than 'goed'. Nathan overgeneralises the morpheme 'ed' to the irregular verb 'go'.

(b) These extracts show how children's language develops through discovering the general rules (the grammar or syntax) and using them. This is demonstrated in cases where a child makes logical errors such as 'goed' rather than 'went'. The child can't be imitating this and therefore must be spontaneously generating speech according to grammatical rules.

Gradually a child is able to incorporate all the irregularities, though there is some overlap, as in 'feetsies', where both the rule and the irregularity have been used.

Another aspect of linguistic development is the progression from phoneme acquisition ('sh') to morphemes and words, which are often invented or idiosyncratic at first (such as footsie), and finally to sentences.

(c) The two main purposes of language are for social interaction and for thought; communicating with others and with yourself.

Nelson (1973) found that a large percentage of the first words used by children were for the names of things which can move, make noise or be acted upon, such as trucks, buses, shoes, balls. This reflects the child's first use of language to talk about things which can change rather than those features which are simply 'there', such as the oven or plates.

Language enables a child to get what it wants. This is of key importance to learning theorists as the means by which language production is positively reinforced. By saying 'milk' a child gets a drink of milk rather than, say, squash, and this is reinforcing.

A further aspect of social interaction is in terms of emotional needs. From birth a child has non-verbal means of expressing emotion, but language enables a more specific formulation of such feelings and a means of feedback.

Language may be used to communicate no specific content but simply social pleasantries, such as a child learning to say 'bye-bye'. This is a means of entry into the world of relationships outside the immediate family. Some social concepts are encoded in linguistic forms, such as terms of address (first or last names) or formality ('hi' or 'good morning').

Many games played with children involve language, such as nursery rhymes which develop a child's ability to distinguish phonemes, a necessary pre-reading skill. **Bryant and Bradley (1985)** found that early ability to discriminate between sounds was related to later advances in reading ability. Games are an example of metalanguage, using language to talk about language. Other examples are playfulness with language. **Chukovsky (1963)** recorded 3- to 4- year-olds' rhyming poems such as 'I'm a flamingo, look at my wingo'. Phrases like 'good song' or jokes based on word play (throwing the clock out of the window to see time fly) are other examples of metalinguistics.

Play between children as well as with adults relies on language. Traditional children's games involving singing songs or games of make-believe all rely on linguistic communication.

Many later developments seem to depend on prior linguistic abilities, the question is whether language is a prerequisite or whether neural maturation is the cause; the views of **Bruner** and **Piaget** respectively. **Vygotsky** described three stages of linguistic development. It is first social, for controlling the behaviour of others. Next, between the ages of three and seven, it is egocentric; controlling one's own behaviour but spoken out loud, a bridge between the other two forms. Finally, inner speech or self-talk is for directing your own behaviour and thoughts. Inner speech is necessary for all higher cognitive functioning.

The ability to use certain language forms is related to performance on some Piagetian tasks, for example **Sinclair-de-Zwart (1969)** found that the ability to use words like 'bigger' was positively related to success in conservation tasks; though there is the question of which comes first. **Liublinskaya (1957)** gave children the task of matching drawings of butterfly wings with examples on display. Those children who were taught words to describe the various patterns could perform the task more accurately than a control group.

These studies are related to the question of language and thought generally. At the very least language shapes memory, since it is based on symbolic forms of representation. **Carmichael, Hogan and Walter (1932)** showed how providing different words for the same set of pictures led subjects to recall the pictures differently.

Learning is profoundly affected by language, though for young children imitation is probably the strongest influence on learning as their linguistic skills are still rudimentary.

Question bank

Allow 45 minutes for each question

1 (a) What do psychologists mean by 'language'? (3 marks)
    (b) Describe **two** models or theories of language. (10 marks)
    (c) Critically consider the psychological evidence for *and* against **one** of these models or theories. (12 marks)

(AEB 'A', 1992)

Points: Many students lack an understanding of what a 'theory of language' is and again write about 'Language and Thought' generally, which is only partly appropriate and needs to be explicitly connected to the question. Part (c) asks for evidence for *and* against your chosen theory, often candidates only present one kind of argument in a question of this kind.

2 (a) Describe **two** different methods that have been used to study the language development of children between the ages of two and five years. (8 marks)
    (b) Evaluate **one** study that has used either of the above methods. Discuss how the findings contribute to our understanding of children's language development. (12 marks)

(NEAB 'A', 1991)

Points: Evaluation should include strengths and weaknesses.

3 What do **each** of the following examples of young children's speech tell us about their language skills?
    (a) Child "Tractor go floor" (3 marks)
    (b) Child 'What doing Daddy?' (5 marks)
    (c) Child 'Nobody can do painting' (5 marks)
    (d) Child 'My shoes on polish', Mother 'The polish is on your shoes', Child 'Polish on my shoes. My shoes on a brown polish'. (7 marks)

(NEAB 'A', 1986)

Points: A similar question to the illustrative one. The extracts are provided as a stimulus for discussion of acquisition of language skills.

4 What are the main features that psychologists have found out about the development of communication in the first year of a child's life?

(NEAB 'A', 1990)

Points: The question is on communication, not just language and should be concerned with social interaction and development as well.

5 (a) What is meant by the term *prelinguistic communicative behaviour*? (5 marks)
   (b) Explain how this type of behaviour may help children's language development. Use empirical evidence to support your explanation. (15 marks)

(NEAB, 'A', 1985)

Points: Reference should be made to 9.3 on the acquisition of reading and pre-reading skills.

6 Using empirical evidence, discuss the role that non-verbal communication may play in classroom interactions.

(NEAB, 'A', 1992)

Points: Social skills are again relevant, therefore Chapter 2 contains much useful material. The question attracts common-sense answers but should be backed up with psychological theory and evidence.

7 (a) Explain what psychologists understand by the term 'non-verbal communication'. (5 marks)
   (b) Critically consider the role of non-verbal communication in human social interaction. (20 marks)

(AEB, 'AS', 1993)

Points: This question appears in the AS section on social behaviour and therefore incorporates material from Chapter 2 as well. It is important to use psychological evidence rather than make common sense answers.

8 Explain systems of communication between non-human animals, including those of audition and olfaction.

(AEB, 'A', 1990)

Points: Another question which appeals to anecdotal knowledge, drawing on nature programmes on the TV. This may be acceptable if you can impose a psychological framework on it, such as social function or inter- and intraspecies communication.

9 Critically consider the view that only humans possess language.

(AEB, 'AS', 1989)

Points: A useful starting point is a working definition of language. The question is not specifically about animals, and could include views on machines and language (see 1.3).

10 Discuss the evolutionary development and significance of communication in non-human animals.

(AEB, 'A', 1992)

Points: This question elicits a descriptive approach, listing non-verbal behaviours. Evaluation should be in terms of their significance, particularly in evolutionary terms.

CHAPTER 5

INTELLIGENCE, PERSONALITY AND ASSESSMENT

Units in this chapter

Chapter overview

Intelligence and personality are studies of *individual differences*, they focus on the dimensions along which people differ rather analysing general tendencies (the ways in which people are similar). Assessment and testing are some of the most visible areas of psychology and are concerned with the ways people differ. They are used in education, job selection, the diagnosis of mental illness and psychological research. They draw on the theories of individual difference.

Historical perspective

Both intelligence and personality were amongst the first areas to occupy early psychologists.

Sir Francis Galton (1822–1911), scientist, explorer, anthropologist and inventor, turned his interest to human intelligence. In the wake of the new theory of evolution, described by his cousin, Charles Darwin, Galton applied the same principles to mental abilities, thus founding the science of eugenics. Human intelligence could be improved in the same way that we produce better cattle, through selective breeding. He maintained that mental and physical characteristics are both inherited and closely related. If you measured features such as the size of a person's skull, reaction time, breathing capacity and visual acuity, this would give you an index of their mental ability. To this end he took over 9000 measurements at the London Exposition of 1884 (and charged subjects 3d. for the privilege) but was disappointed to find that no correlations existed, though in processing his data he did invent the correlation coefficient and many other psychological techniques. He saw his ideas as being for the betterment of mankind; history has shown eugenics in a different light.

Sigmund Freud (1856–1939) was an original thinker who radically altered the prevailing views of human nature. His notions about sexuality and the unconscious shocked Victorian society as much as Darwin's theory of evolution. Freud's theories had sensational and intuitive appeal, though they were founded on a very limited sample of human behaviour. Despite the fact that his theories are more a matter of faith than proof, Freud has had a greater influence than any other single psychologist over psychology and psychiatry, as well as in the arts, education and politics. The reasons for this are suggested in 5.2.

5.1 THE CONCEPT OF INTELLIGENCE

Definitions

Intelligence is perhaps the most important concept in psychology, it is also one of the most 'slippery'. At the core of most attempts to define it are the following aspects:

- it is an **ability**, it enables certain activities but is not the activities themselves,
- the ability to learn,
- the ability to apply what has been learned to *new* situations,
- the ability to respond appropriately,
- the ability to think rationally and solve problems,
- the ability to think abstractly,
- to use these abilities in an effective way and thus master the environment.

It is important to distinguish intelligence from:

- **thought**: a conscious activity, the study of which belongs to cognitive psychology. The study of intelligence focuses on the ways that people are different in terms of their mental ability, cognitive psychology examines the generalisations that can be made,
- **related abilities**: such as memory, knowledge, self-awareness. The relationship between intelligence and other abilities is a one-way process. Intelligence is the underlying ability which is expressed in all these other abilities, the reverse is not true. If it were, we would not need all these separate words, and we could dispense with the concept of 'intelligence' altogether. There have been attempts to do this,
- **intelligence tests**: 'intelligence is what intelligence tests measure'. A definition of intelligence is necessary for constructing tests, though it is necessary to distinguish theoretical from practical (workable) definitions. One of the problems of this approach is *circularity*.

Some questions:

- Is intelligence one **common thread** underlying everything or are there different factors or even 'intelligences'?
- Can intelligence be **taught**, or is it mainly influenced by inherited factors?
- Non-human animals are intellectually **inferior**, can some races of people be considered intellectually inferior?
- How can we explain the abilities of **idiot savants** – people with extremely low IQs but extraordinary abilities?

MODELS OF INTELLIGENCE

The factorial approach

Factor analysis is a statistical procedure to reduce data to a number of dimensions or clusters. The theoretician identifies various hypothetical entities, such as reasoning or verbal ability. All these variables are correlated individually with each other, yielding a vast number of correlation coefficients. Those that are highly correlated are identified as a single factor. Any so-called 'factor' has been labelled by the theoretician and should not be confused with reality:

1. **Spearman's two-factor model (1904):** proposed a general *(g)* as well as specific *(s)* factors. (The *g* in fact stands for *neogenesis*, the ability to 'draw out' relations, a common feature of test items.) The differences between individuals is largely due to the *g* factor, but the *s* factor explains why people are not uniformly better at all tasks.

② **Burt (1949)** and **Vernon's (1950) Hierarchical model:** they felt the two-factor model was too simple and constructed a hierarchy: *g* factors divide into major group factors: verbal–educational and spatial–mechanical abilities, which divide into minor group factors, which finally lead to *s* factors.

③ **Thurstone's Primary Mental Abilities (1938):** found seven distinct factors in his testing, called Primary Mental Abilities (PMAs): spatial, perceptual speed, numerical reasoning, verbal meaning, word fluency, memory, inductive reasoning. Later, Thurstone conceded that there was a *g* factor running through the factors.

④ **Guilford's 'Structure of Intellect' Model (1967):** totally rejects the *g* factor. The model is based on three dimensions: content (task-related), operations, and product (answer). Within each there are different groups which, multiplied together, provide 120 distinct mental abilities. Tests designed to measure these abilities suggest that there aren't anything like as many as this. Guilford's inclusion of 'operations' can be related to more recent, information processing approaches.

Evaluation of the factorial approach:

● the factor analysis method of measuring intelligence has difficulties because the results depend on the particular method of factor analysis, the subjects, and the tests used,

● factor naming is arbitrary and leads to reification – confusing the name with reality itself,

● it turns out that an apparently objective approach is really very subjective,

● these approaches are founded on an inherited view of intelligence.

Potential versus acquired intelligence

① **Cattell's (1963)** version has the *g* factor subdivided into **fluid** intelligence (g_f) – the ability to solve abstract relational problems, which is biological and therefore free of cultural influences – and **crystallised** intelligence (g_c), encompassing problem-solving and knowledge which comes from experience. Such a view reconciles the four models described above.

② **Hebb (1949):** suggested two types of intelligence *A*, our genetic potential; and intelligence *B*, the intelligence that develops as a result of experience interacting with potential. This view eliminates the nature *versus* nurture dilemma because they are never separated. **Vernon (1950)** has also suggested intelligence *C* which is that sample of intelligent behaviour which an intelligence test measures.

③ **Piaget's (1950)** model of intelligence is biological and qualitative. His concern is less for the differences between people and more for the process of intelligence. Intelligence is the ability to adapt to environmental change. It is not acquired all at once but developed in stages, which are invariate and innate. We are born with cognitive structures (schemas and operations), which enable us to meet the demands of the environment through the processes of adaptation, assimilation and accommodation. New experiences often create disequilibrium amongst existing concepts, which must be altered to recreate cognitive balance. **Bruner (1966)** took a similar position to Piaget, though he felt the environment played a greater role in shaping intelligence and that modes of thinking (iconic, enactive, symbolic) were more appropriate than Piagetian stages (see 3.2).

These developmental approaches are more qualitative (cognitive) than the quantitative (individual difference), though the notion of stages or modes does lend itself to testing.

Processes

① **Guilford** (see above) identified five processes.

② **The Information Processing Approach:** in the 1960s there was a move away from 'factors', instead it was felt that we should look at how greater intelligence might be associated with: greater speed of processing, greater familiarity with the steps in problem-solving, how information is internally represented, the strategies that people use, and so on.

For example, **Sternberg (1985)** proposed a componential model of intelligence. Mental processes are components which must be organised to solve problems. Such processes would be: metacomponents (control), performance, acquisition, retention and transfer components (see 1.2).

❸**Physiological Processes**: this is a strange throwback to **Galton**, who originally suggested that intelligence could be related to physical measurements. Correlating intelligence to physiological processes is an attempt to bypass intelligence as a concept altogether, and is more of a practical approach. We can still validate the measurements in terms of selected criteria such as scholastic success.

Different kinds of intelligence

❶**Gardner (1983)** suggested a range of separate intelligences: linguistic, logical–mathematical, spatial, musical, bodily–kinaesthetic and personal. This is a broader conception than usual, including the personal amongst other abilities. However, it may be nothing more than different names for different processes. It may also turn out that there still is a common thread running through all.

❷The case of **idiot savants** might be taken as evidence that what we see as one thing in fact consists of quite separate abilities. **Scheerer et al. (1945)** studied L., who could give the day for any date between 1880 and 1950, perform addition and spelling feats, play and sing difficult musical scores, and yet scored 50 on an IQ test (but had no signs of brain damage).

NATURE OR NURTURE?

By 'nature' we mean the genotype of an individual, synonyms include: heredity, innate, inherited, biological, inborn, genetic. 'Environment' is everything around you, including even your diet *in utero*, or exposure to X-rays, which may cause genetic mutation. The 'phenotype' is the actual behaviours or abilities exhibited.

Evidence – biological links

❶**Twin studies.** 'If I had any desire to live a life of indolent ease, I would wish to be an identical twin, separated at birth from my brother and raised in a different social class. We could hire ourselves out to social scientists and practically name our fee.' (**Gould, 1981**, p.234).

Theoretically, if intelligence was entirely inherited, the IQ scores of identical (monozygotic, MZ) twins reared apart should have 100% correlation. Since correlations are much lower than this, environmentalists argue that this shows that environment must play a role. However, the fact that siblings or non-identical (dizygotic, DZ) twins have lower correlations than MZ twins when reared together indicates the importance of heredity. **Newman et al. (1928)** found correlations for MZ twins of 0.67 reared apart and 0.91 when raised together; whereas ordinary siblings reared together were 0.64. This upholds both genetic and environmental positions. **Hermann and Hogben (1932)** found correlations between MZ twins reared apart of 0.84, whereas DZ twins were 0.53, supporting the genetic view. **Shields (1962)** advertised for MZ twins reared apart through the BBC, and found that whether reared apart or together they had correlations of about 0.75, supporting the genetic view. **Burt (1955)** found even higher correlations for those reared together (0.94) but this is ignored because some of the data were probably fabricated (see discussion of this in 10.4).

Evaluation:
- all of the early studies are based on small samples,
- as they are correlations we cannot be sure of the cause, and there are arguments that genetically similar people 'create' similar environments around them,
- in reality, the twins that were used in such studies had often spent a substantial amount of time together, the first eight years in one case, thus the assumption of different environmental influences was unjustified,

- adoption agencies try to match the background of the adopted families to their natural parents, thus suggesting again that the environmental influences were similar,
- in the Shields study there have been suggestions of experimenter bias, since he tested all twins,
- volunteer bias leads to an overestimation of heritability (**Lykken** *et al.* **1978**),
- in the early studies determination of MZ or DZ was based on the subjects' word and may have been wrong,
- the assumption that MZ twins are identical is wrong. **Allen** *et al.* **(1976)** found constitutional differences based on different birth and intrauterine experiences, and found that these could be related to different parental perceptions and expectations of the twins.

❷ Other close genetic links: Erlenmeyer-Kimling and Jarvik (1963) and Bouchard and McGue (1981) surveyed over 100 studies looking at familial correlations of IQ, they found a positive correlation: the more close the genetic link, the greater the correlation between IQ.

Evaluation:
- this would seem to support the genetic position, but it could be taken equally as evidence for environment, as genetically related people usually also live in the same environment,
- comparisons from one study to another involve grouping together many different tests,
- the Erlenmeyer-Kimling and Jarvik study is often cited but is based on a weak sample of studies, which included some of Burt's work.

❸ Foster children: if you correlate the IQ of a child and its foster parents (environmental link), and a child and its natural parents (heredity link), which is higher? Genetic support comes from **Skodak and Skeels (1949)** who found that the IQs of adopted children were closer to their natural rather than their adoptive parents. Environmental evidence was produced by **Schiff** *et al.* **(1978)** looking at children born to low socio-economic status parents who were subsequently adopted by high socio-economic families. Their average IQ was 111, compared with an average of 95 for siblings who had remained at home.

Alternatively, you can compare an adopted parent and their own child with the same parent and an adopted child. **Scarr and Weinberg (1983)** looked at adoptions where a black child was brought up in a white family. The correlations between the mother and her biological child were not significantly different from the correlations between the mother and the adopted and racially different child.

Evaluation:
- the evidence is equivocal,
- like the twin studies, adoptions are made to similar environments.

❹ Sex differences: at one time women scored better in verbal ability than men (biological influence). This difference has become less pronounced and it has been suggested that this is due to changes in socialisation (environment). **Age differences**, if they exist, would also suggest a biological basis for at least some of the processes involved in intelligence (see 3.5).

❺ Physical disorders: clearly in some incidences, intelligence is affected by a genetically determined condition, for example Down's syndrome.

Evidence – effects of experience

❶ Effects of diet: Harrell *et al.* **(1955)** gave low income, expectant mothers supplementary diets. When their children were tested at three years they had higher IQs than those whose mothers had been given placebos. **Benton and Cook (1991)** supported their previous findings, showing that IQ scores increased by 7.6 points when children were given vitamin supplements rather than a placebo.

❷ Parental attention: birth order has been found to be positively correlated with intelligence, according to **Zajonc and Markus (1975)** who analysed the results of a Dutch study involving 40,000 19-year-olds. First-borns are treated differently from subsequent siblings in terms of factors such as greater parental time. **Yarrow (1963)** found a correlation of 0.65 between IQ at six months and the amount of time the mother spent in social interaction with her child. In Israel the differences in IQ scores between children of European and Arabic origins mirror those of black and white Americans, when such children are brought up together in kibbutzim these differences disappear.

❸ **Deprivation studies** (a favourite of examination candidates): the classic studies of deprivation, such as **Koluchova (1972, 1976, 1991)** and **Dennis (1960)** are mentioned in 3.1. They show that IQ is depressed by lack of stimulation in early life. Another approach to deprivation is to look at the effects of early total deafness, which on average lowers IQ by 20 points.

❹ **Education: Vernon (1958)** measured children's IQ before and after their 11-plus examination and found that children who went to grammar school showed average increases of 5 points compared with average decreases of 1.9 points in those who went to secondary modern schools. **Rosenthal and Jacobsen's (1968)** classic study showed how teacher expectations of success can influence IQ scores significantly.

❺ **Enrichment: Operation Headstart**, an American project, which began in 1965 in an effort to give disadvantaged children social and cognitive stimulation, has had mixed reviews. The first studies suggested any gains were short-lived but a 'sleeper' effect was detected, for several years later there were marked social changes. **Lazar and Darlington (1982)** have suggested that the Headstart programme was too directed at middle-class values and therefore missed some of the problems entirely. Other enrichment programmes have focused on particular aspects, such as language development or parental involvement and been more successful.

For some children, intervention day-care has been shown to improve IQ levels. **Burchinal et al. (1989)** found that mainly black preschool children of low socio-economic status benefited in terms of cognitive development from day-care.

The benefits of such intervention programmes may be due to the fact that they raise parental expectations, which has a positive effect on the child's performance. This is a mutual reinforcement process (**Lazar and Darlington, 1982**).

Bernstein's work on restricted language explains why children from low social-economic status groups fare poorly in tests of verbal intelligence and may have had less opportunity to develop their intelligence because of lack of stimulation.

General empirical evaluation

❶ Almost all of the evidence is **correlational**, other factors may be the cause. For example **Benton and Cook (1991)** found a correlation between the amount of sugar in a child's diet and improved intelligence.

❷ Are IQ tests valid and reliable? They are based on the assumption that intelligence is inherited and there is good evidence that they are culturally biased.

❸ The fact that researchers tend to produce results consistent with their expectations leads one to suspect some experimenter bias.

Arguments

❶ **Polygenetic inheritance:** some characteristics, such as eye colour, are determined by one set of genes. Intelligence is the result of many genes interacting – thus polygenetic. Therefore it will not possible to make clear predictions from the actual genes to observable behaviour even if intelligence was *entirely* due to heredity.

❷ **Trying to separate nature and nurture** is not possible in practice. How can we distinguish the effects of a mother's diet on the fetus *in utero* from the infant's genetically determined abilities. In the case of phenylketonuria, a genetic disorder, mental retardation will result unless phenylalanine is eliminated from the diet. Manipulation of the environment prevents the genes being expressed.

❸ **Transgenerational link;** the poor diet of a women when she herself was *in utero* may effect the development of her children a generation later. In this case what appear to be genetic influences are in fact environmental.

④ **A meaningless question, Hebb (1949)** said it's like asking how much of the area of a rectangle is due to width and how much to length?

⑤ **Notion of potential range:** height is a good example of a characteristic which is distinctly inherited but influenced by environment. We are born with a potential height range, our experiences including diet affect the extent to which that range is fulfilled.

⑥ **Estimates of heritability** are generally agreed to be about 80%, on the basis of evidence from MZ studies. This figure means that 80% of the variability in intelligence can be traced to genetic factors. Hereditarians support the view that such a measurement has meaning, whereas counter-arguments suggest that any such 'measurement' is flawed and therefore valueless. Flaws include experimental shortcomings (see evaluation of twin studies) and **Bodmer**'s (see below) argument about the difference between within- and between-group measures.

⑦ **Eugenics:** even if intelligence is entirely inherited, some take the view that the position this advocates is inhumane. Selective breeding or the notion of a super race may sound reasonable in some descriptions but is it possible in practice? The question of nature or nurture is essentially a political one.

⑧ **Race and intelligence: Jensen (1969)** sparked off an emotional and political controversy when he found that black people in America test about 15 IQ points (one standard deviation) lower than whites. The question is not whether this is correct but how we interpret it. Jensen claimed that this showed that 'Negroes' were genetically inferior, but:

- **Bodmer (1972)**, from a genetic standpoint, argued that average differences between racial groups must be due to environment, whereas the differences between individuals from the same genetic pool are due to innate factors.
- The **tests** themselves are **culturally biased** so we would expect members of other cultures to do worse (see 'Black IQ tests', 5.4).
- **Tyler (1965)** found that blacks from the northern states did better than those from the southern states, which must be due to environment.
- **Scarr and Weinberg** (see p.209) showed that black children adopted into white homes are equivalent to white children.
- **Experimenter bias:** testers are usually white and may have different expectations for white and black subjects, which may affect the IQ performance of testees.
- **Different doesn't mean better**, different genders, ethnic groups or cultures undoubtedly have different potentials and acquired abilities, the notion of 'better' is inherently biased.

5.2 THEORIES OF PERSONALITY

Personality comes from the Latin 'persona', meaning an actor's mask. It is at the core of psychology, both historically and in terms of present-day applications. Personality is probably of greater consequence, and is even more ill-defined, than intelligence.

What is a personality?

- a characteristic pattern of behaviours, attitudes, interests, capabilities,
- this pattern is integrated,
- it is unique, (a means of differentiating between individuals),
- it is relatively stable (though there is some disagreement about this),
- it forms a basis for predicting future behaviour.

The study of personality is:

- a systematic account of the ways that people differ,
- and a logical framework for predictions,

- we need it to make sense of ourselves and others, and, professionally, to assess certain groups of people, such as parolees,
- a personality theory should describe a *structure* and describe the *dynamics* of how behaviour is produced.

Idiographic versus nomothetic approaches

Idiographic is an approach based on individuals, it emphasises uniqueness and concreteness. Nomothetic is abstract, universal and general. Nomothetic approaches attempt to summarise differences between people through generalisations, and therefore use statistical techniques to accumulate large amounts of data.

APPROACHES

Theories of personality do not fit neatly into a scheme of classification, many theories are listed under more than one approach. However, imperfect as it is, the common classification provides a useful framework.

1 The **trait approach**: expresses individual differences in terms of quantities of selected traits. Traits are selected adjectives subjected to **factor analysis**, they are attributed on the basis of observed behaviour.

Theories: Cattell, Eysenck, Allport, Kelly, Freud.

Evaluation:
- it reflects a natural tendency to categorise people as, for example, talkative or shy,
- it is not very sophisticated, little more than a list of adjectives,
- see the comparison with the type approach.

2 The **type approach**: each person fits into a broad, temperamental category, each type being qualitatively different from other types.

Theories: Eysenck, Hippocrates, Sheldon, Friedman and Rosenman (Type A), Freud, Jung.

Evaluation:
- it offers powerful concepts, as shown by the frequency of their usage in common parlance (introvert, extrovert, sanguine, endomorph, egocentric),
- it is an oversimplified view, blurs the unique nature of personality.

Trait and type:
- the type approach is sometimes given as an example of trait theory as it is based on clusters of traits. These are often called multi-trait as opposed to narrow-trait approaches, such as Type A,
- conversely, a trait matrix or profile can be produced for an individual, people who have similar profiles are similar *types*,
- psychometric approaches lend themselves to testing,
- clear and unambiguous empirical (testable) definitions,
- based on factor analysis and locating clusters,
- labels are artefacts and may misrepresent reality (reification),
- naming is not explaining,
- have natural validity, operate along the same lines as implicit personality theories and the halo effect,

Trait versus type:
- the trait approach emphasises the differences between people whereas types suggest the similarities,
- quantity versus quality.

3 The **psychoanalytic (psychodynamic) approach**: theories derived from Freud's work, which concern themselves with the child as father of the man (or woman), deep meanings and unconscious motives.

Theories: Freud, Jung, Adler, Horney, Fromm, Bowlby (attachment).

Evaluation:
- it represents the complexity of human nature, the idiographic approach,

- it is centred on maladaptive behaviour, in terms of empirical observations and its major influence,
- it has intuitive appeal, sensational, sensual and dreamlike,
- it is not a scientific theory because it is not falsifiable or easily testable, it is ambiguous and overly complex,
- it claims to be universal but may be cultural.

4 The **individual approach**: emphasises the person here and now, focuses on higher human motives and views personality as an experience rather than an object of study. The total is greater than the sum of the parts, if you split personality into its constituent parts you lose the essence.

Theories: phenomenological, existentialist or humanist; Kelly, Rogers, Maslow (Hierarchy of Needs, see 7.4), Allport, Murray (Personology), Laing.

Evaluation:
- an idiographic approach,
- stresses free-will and potential for change.

5 The **cognitive approach**: the study of mental representations of events: processes of interpreting and evaluating the environment; beliefs, thoughts and expectations.

Theories: Kelly, Bandura (Attribution Theory).

Evaluation:
- it has produced some successful therapies, such as those developed from Attribution Theory (see 6.2), cognitive restructuring therapies such as rational–emotive therapy (Ellis), and some forms of behaviour therapy.

6 The **learning or behaviourist approach**: man is a bundle of conditioned reflexes, the behaviourist sees psychology as the study of observable behaviour only, the causes are irrelevant. The lawfulness of behaviour reduces to the same dimensions as the laws that determine what will happen when a snooker ball hits the cushion. Behaviour is learned through selective reinforcement.

Theories: Skinner, Bandura, Dollard and Miller (Reinforcement Theory).

Evaluation:
- Skinner questioned the relevance of theories and suggested simply organising behavioural data into a framework of laws with no explanatory 'fictions',
- it is an objective, empirical 'theory',
- it offers a fragmented explanation of human behaviour,
- it is derived largely from the study of animals, therefore it may be inappropriate to extrapolate it to man,
- it is difficult to see how all behaviours can have been reinforced,
- it offers a simplistic view of human behaviour but the therapy (behaviour therapies) has been useful.

7 The **situational approach**: a startling deviation from all others in suggesting that personality is not consistent. If behaviour *is* consistent then that is because the situation is the same. Is a shy person always shy? We learn to behave in ways appropriate to situations through selective reinforcement.

Theories: Mischel.

Evaluation:
- it accounts for differences in the way the same person behaves at different times,
- it has presented a major challenge to other theories,
- it has major implications for testing, if personality is situationally determined tests cannot accurately predict behaviour,
- it is a deterministic view,
- it is regarded as an extreme position.

8 The **interactional approach**: a compromise between situational and trait approaches; consistency itself may be a trait. There are a variety of ways that situation and person variables may interact:
- cross-over interaction: one person may be anxious in lifts but not in planes, another person may experience the opposite,
- scalar interaction: two people may not be anxious in lifts, one may be anxious on planes.

Evaluation:

- it is difficult to separate situation and person, therefore interaction should be the solution. A physicist studying the properties of molten metal doesn't ask 'is it the quality of the heat (situation) or the substance that is being melted which is more important?'. It is the interaction which is measured. Nevertheless, it is possible to describe the properties of metals regardless of the source of heat (situation).
- it allows for free-will and self-determination,
- it has yet to be developed into an adequate theory.

MAJOR THEORIES IN DETAIL

Cattell (1965): a trait theory

Cattell started with a list of all the adjectives or trait names, removed any synonyms, rated a group of subjects and factor analysed the data. He produced 16 'source' traits and, later, 'surface' traits, such as exvia (like extroversion), anxiety, depression, arousal and fatigue, which are produced through combinations of source traits:

reserved	outgoing
less intelligent	more intelligent
affected by feelings	emotionally stable
submissive	dominant
serious	happy-go-lucky
expedient	conscientious
shy	venturesome
tough-minded	tender-minded
trusting	suspicious
practical	imaginative
forthright	shrewd
self-assured	apprehensive
conservative	experimenting
group-dependent	self-sufficient
undisciplined self-conflict	controlled
relaxed	tense

Tests: Cattell's 16 Personality Factor (16PF) Questionnaire, Eight State Questionnaire.

Evaluation:

- it provided the basis for a popular personality test,
- Cattell provides profiles of trait clusters, leading to a type theory,
- it lacks validation of source traits; the surface traits agree broadly with Eysenck (see p.215),
- see also evaluations of trait theories (p.212).

Allport (1937): an idiographic trait theory

Allport viewed traits as neuropsychological entities. He thought that they existed somewhere in the brain. His approach was idiographic. The uniqueness of each individual is primary, and the study of personality should focus on this. He started with a list of 18,000 words for personal characteristics and reduced these to two basic kinds:

1 *Common traits:* which are possessed by all individuals from a particular cultural or ethnic background.

2 *Individual traits:* a set of selected traits which each person has. These cannot be measured by standardised tests but observed through detailed study of an individual. For example, Allport (1965) and his students used a collection of 301 letters written over a period of 12 years from 'Jenny'. They were interested to identify the persistent traits which recurred through the letters. Individual traits can be further divided into:

- cardinal traits: one or two traits which pervade the whole personality, not everyone has them,

- central traits: a small set of characteristic traits,
- secondary traits: less consistent.

Allport also used the concepts of:

1 The *proprium*: a sense of self, for example, which embodies the developing personality. It is not a separate entity.

2 *Functional autonomy:* the dynamics of behaviour. Any particular activity may become an end or a goal in itself. **Hall and Lindzey (1970)** provide the following example: a hunter may hunt even when not hungry, not to fulfil some aggressive drive but simply because he likes hunting.

Evaluation:

- **Allport**'s emphasis on idiographic methods was influential,
- this concept of uniqueness of the individual has been criticised widely, particularly because it does not facilitate measurement and direct comparisons between people, and therefore lacks usefulness,
- related to this is the failure to generate testable propositions or to be falsifiable,
- his theory has been particularly popular with psychiatrists, a study by **Schafer** *et al.* **(1951)** found Allport as the second most influential theorist, after Freud, to be listed by clinical psychologists.

Eysenck (1947 onwards): dimensions of personality – a type theory

Eysenck drew on Jung's introvert and extrovert types. He has factor analysed data using numerous groups of people. Initially he proposed two dimensions (neuroticism–stability and extroversion–introversion, see Fig. 5.1), and later added a third (psychoticism–intelligence, see table overleaf). Each dimension or type is composed of a cluster of traits, an individual high on one such trait will tend to be high on other traits in the cluster.

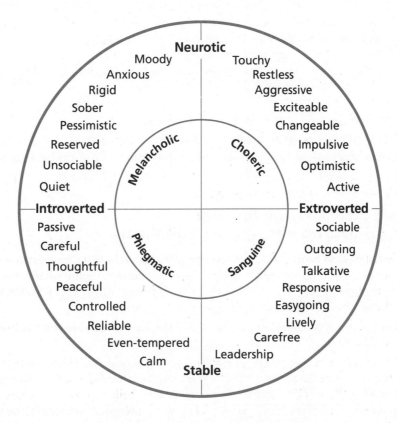

Fig. 5.1 Eysenk's dimensions of personality (the inner circle shows the Hippocrates body types related to Eysenk's dimensions)

Dimension	Associated traits
neuroticism–stability	neuroticism is: anxiety and depression proneness, guilt feelings, low self-esteem, tension, moodiness, emotionality
extroversion–introversion	extroversion is: sociability, liveliness, assertiveness, sensation-seeking, carefreeness, dominance
psychoticism–intelligence	psychoticism is: aggressiveness, coldness, lack of empathy, a divergent kind of creativity

Key features of the theory:

● The dimensions are continuous. The first two are normally distributed and the last is skewed away from psychoticism, i.e. most people score average on extroversion and neuroticism and low on psychoticism.

● *Biological basis:* extroverts have lower *cortical arousal* than introverts, this leads to various empirically testable predictions:
  ● introverts are more easily conditioned, more socially conforming, higher in task 'vigilance' (readiness to respond), have lower sensory thresholds and therefore feel pain more acutely,
  ● Extroverts are 'stimulus hungry' They seek greater excitement and dangerous pastimes.

● *A hierarchical view:* type level is highest (e.g. introversion), then trait (e.g. shyness) then habitual response level (responses likely to be repeated) and finally, specific response level.

Tests: Eysenck Personality Questionnaire (EPQ) and Inventory (EPI).

Evaluation:

● the theory has precision, detail and breadth,

● it has generated much research and tests are familiar to most students,

● *factor analysis* is a subjective method, relying on labels assigned and interpreted by the theorist, can produce different results from using the same data but different analysis,

● one means of assessing *validity* is to compare with results of factor analysis. Cattell used different data and a different method of factor analysis yet found two surface traits – anxiety and exvia – which correspond closely to Eysenck's original two. Using abnormal subjects he found a third surface factor, which resembles psychoticism,

● the theory is based on use of *questionnaires*, which are affected by the mood of the respondent, it may not be a valid sample of personality,

● while Eysenck's theory is essentially a type theory, a case can also be argued for it as a trait theory, because it identifies individual differences in terms of selected traits.

● see also the evaluation of trait and type theories (p.212).

Temperament: personality types

Hippocrates (400 BC) claimed that a preponderance of one body fluid (or humour) led to personality type. His theory has had a lasting effect on our language.

Fluid	Latin or Greek	Personality type	Description
blood	sanguis	sanguine	optimistic, hopeful
black bile	melan coln	melancholic	sad, depressed
bile	coln	choleric	irritable
phlegm	flegma	phlegmatic	apathetic

Sheldon *et al.* (1940, 1954) focused on body types:

Type	Body shape	Personality
endomorph	short, plump person	sociable, relaxed, even-tempered
mesomorph	heavy-set, muscular	noisy, callous, fond of physical activity
ectomorph	tall, thin person	restrained, self-conscious, fond of solitude

He photographed thousands of naked men to identify the types and tried to establish correlations between somatotype and temperament. A somatotype was the score a person had, out of seven on each of the three types. People are undoubtedly judged in terms of their outward appearance **Hall and Lindzey (1970)** conclude that there is some support for a relationship between physique and personality. It may be that the perceptions of others influence self-expectations (the looking-glass self, see 3.4).

Friedman and Rosenman (1959) found much evidence to support the view that certain personality types were more prone to stress-related illnesses. This is an extension of studies which link illness to personality (see 7.6).

		Associated with
type A	competitive, ambitious, impatient, restless, subjective sense of time, pressurised	heart disease, cancer, risk-taking pastimes
type B	lacks the above	

Freud: (1890–1939): Psychoanalytic theory

Key features of the theory:

- It offers a *dynamic* view of personality. The ego must maintain a balance between three sources of demand – id, superego and reality – concerned with the forces that drive behaviour.
- It focuses on the *unconscious*, particularly in motivation, and the *pre-conscious*.
- There is a reliance on *biological* factors, especially sexual and aggressive ones.
- It looks for deep meanings.
- The individual differences in adult personalities can be traced back to the specific manner in which the *conflicts* aroused during the first five years of life were handled, conflicts between base desires and higher intellectual functioning.
- It describes personality *types*, therefore it is a type theory.

❶ **The structure of personality:**
   - *id:* the primitive, instinctive, libidinous and unconscious. It demands immediate satisfaction and is governed by the pleasure principle,
   - *ego:* the conscious and intellectual part. It regulates the id and mediates between the id and superego. It is governed by the reality principle and the need to behave in acceptable ways,
   - *superego:* the ethical and moral component, learned from others, particularly parents. It gives rise to guilt feelings.

❷ **The unconscious is revealed through:**
   - *ego defence mechanisms*, e.g. sublimation, repression, denial, displacement, projection,
   - *neurotic symptoms*, which appear when wishes have become repressed,
   - *parapraxes*, or Freudian slips, i.e. everyday forgetfulness, such as slips of the tongue, forgotten names or appointments.

❸ **Psychosexual stages** (sexual means physically pleasurable):
   - *oral stages:* in the first year the id is dominant, tension is reduced through satisfying basic needs, pleasure is gained through sucking and body stimulation. Any disturbance of this may result in a permanent *fixation* on the oral channel for gratification, e.g. smoking, overeating, thumb-sucking, pencil chewing; also personality: impatience, passivity, greediness, dependence, preoccupation with issues of giving and taking,
   - *anal stage:* at the age of about two, the anus becomes the favoured *erotogenic* zone, pleasure is derived from expelling and withholding faeces. Fixations may be caused by either exceptionally strict toilet training or intense pleasure associated with taboos such as smearing faeces on the wall. The anal/obsessive character has a wish to make a terrible mess and therefore must build defences against this, e.g. orderliness, rigidity, hatred of waste. They are also obstinate, stingy, punctual, possessive. The opposite would be untidy, hot-tempered, destructive.
   - *phallic stage:* around the age of three children's sexual interest focuses on their genitalia and their opposite-sex parent. In boys this is the Oedipus conflict. A boy

wants his mother and therefore is jealous of his father and wants to remove him. The fear that his father will discover the son's feelings are expressed in terms of fear of castration, but is finally resolved through identifying with the father. For girls, the Electra complex describes the events leading up to gender resolution (Electra urged her brother to kill their mother). The young girl has 'penis envy' and resents the mother for not providing her with one. The conflicts may result in homosexuality, authority problems, and rejection of appropriate gender roles if not resolved, .

- *latency period:* up to adolescence,
- *genital stage:* the final stage of personality development, the development of independence. If too much libidinal energy is taken up in first three stages, the individual cannot reach maturity, cannot shift the focus from their own body, their own parents and their immediate needs to larger responsibilities involving others.

Therapy: psychoanalysis

Evaluation:

- quite a remarkable theory for his time. It introduced novel concepts such as the unconscious and sexuality, and had a wide impact,
- the validity of the theory is suggested by the fact that it continues to have a strong influence. Freud's enduring appeal, say **Hall and Lindzey (1970)** is due to a fine literary style, exciting subject matter, challenging ideas and a conception of man which is broad and deep and combines the world of reality with make-believe.
- the theory lacks scientific veracity,
- it offers a deterministic, biological view,
- it ignores social values,
- it is based on poor data:
  - the subjects were a small and highly selected group of middle-class Viennese women,
  - many of the patients were disturbed,
  - the theory uses retrospective (recalled) data,
  - it revolves around case studies, where generalising on the basis of one or two detailed analyses is possible,
  - Freud's interpretations were subjective, this may lead to experimenter bias,
- see also evaluation of psychoanalytic approaches in general.

The Neo-Freudians

Those who followed the psychoanalytic traditions have tended to include social influences and played down the role of biology, specifically sex. For example, the following theorists have introduced some idiosyncrasies of their own to the psychoanalytic theory:

- **Jung:** introduced several lasting concepts: the collective unconscious which is universal ideas and images; and personality types: introvert and extrovert,
- **Adler:** the main struggle is to overcome physical, psychological or social feelings of inferiority. Adler originated the term 'Individual Psychology' and is also considered to be a humanist,
- **Horney:** focused on the effects of anxiety particularly in childhood,
- **Fromm:** concentrated on the structure and dynamics of a particular society and how they shape its members,
- **Erikson:** translated the Freudian notion of stages into psychosocial stages (see 3.3). Each stage represents a potential conflict, there is development throughout life.

Rogers (1959): the self-theory

Rogers founded non-directive therapy, and his views of personality are derived from the therapeutic context rather than being an explicit theory of personality.

Key features of the theory:

- The conflict between *the self and the ideal self* leads to anxiety, which then leads to maladaptive behaviour.

- *Self-acceptance* is crucial to mature, adjusted behaviour. It develops through the positive unconditional regard of significant others.
- *Self-actualisation* is the desire to be congruent, it is innate and drives the organism to resolve self/ideal conflicts.
- *Neurotic behaviour* develops through parents giving love conditionally. Individuals therefore seek approval from others and neglect their own self-actualisation. The ideal-self and the self concept are mismatched, the individual is striving to attain the impossible.

Test: Q-sort technique, compare self and ideal-self.

Therapy: non-directive, client-centred, counselling.

Evaluation:

- its contributions to therapy (counselling and encounter groups) have had an enormous impact,
- it encompasses the concept of self, free-will, man's complexity and the potential for change,
- it ignores the unconscious,
- it doesn't account for the normal development of individual differences.

Kelly's (1955): personal construct theory

Key features of the theory:

- Each person is a *personal scientist*. They hold theories about the world, form hypotheses (expectations) from these, test them, and then modify, retain or reject them as a result.
- The personality consists of constructs – *bipolar categorisations* such as loving–unloving, open-minded–dogmatic. These are organised into hierarchies of broader constructs such as good–bad. The broader constructs work somewhat like personality types.
- The *constructs are personal*. The implications of a particular trait vary from person to person in terms of their meaning.
- By detecting one construct in a person you hypothesise that they might possess all the other constructs within this hierarchy; this works like the halo effect and implicit personality theories, see 2.1).

Test: Repertory grid.

Therapy: Personal construct therapy.

Evaluation:

- one of the most systematic and clearly formulated theories. More than a theory of personality, it covers learning, cognition, motivation, emotion and psychophysiology. Its abstract terms are an attempt to divorce it from cultural ties,
- it ignores many factors, such as genetic or physiological ones,
- it doesn't suggest how constructs are developed initially or how they relate to behaviour,
- it allows for changes in behaviour according to role.

Bandura (1977): Cognitive social learning theory

Key features of the theory:

- It emphasises the role of *vicarious reinforcement* – behaviour is learned through modelling and observation.
- It includes the role of *cognitive mediation* in learning, thus differing from traditional learning theory.
- A *reciprocal determinism* can be reinforced by one of three factors: past experience, the environment and the person. Thus there is an element of self-determination.

Therapy: behaviour therapy.

Evaluation:

- it incorporates many approaches: learning, cognitive and situational,
- it allows for self-determination (self-efficacy),
- it accounts for the influence of television on personality,
- it is currently one of the most favoured therapeutic approaches (see 6.2),
- it lacks clarity, e.g. the operation of cognitive factors not specified,
- it lacks the cohesiveness of a theory, it is currently a collection of diverse ideas,
- see also the evaluation of learning approaches.

Mischel (1968): situational theory

Mischel and Peake (1982) used family, friends and unknown observers to rate 63 students in several situations involving conscientiousness. They found almost no correlation (0.08). This supports the classic study by **Hartshorne and May (1928)** who found little consistency between moral behaviour and attitudes (see 2.3).

Key features of the theory:

- People are not, for example, 'honest', they merely tell the truth in some situations.
- Any *regularity* of behaviour is due to the fact that we tend to find ourselves in similar situations.
- The attribution of 'traits' is a useful tool in *organising our perceptions* (implicit personality theory) but traits are not the same as reality.
- We all deceive ourselves by ignoring our inconsistencies (self-confirming bias) in an effort to maintain a sense of coherence. We have a similar need to see others consistently.
- The utilisation of a particular behaviour is related to the outcome we have learned it will generate, and how desirable that outcome is, e.g. you learn when it is appropriate to make a joke after a misdemeanour. Sometimes it will diffuse the situation, other times it will backfire.

Testing: work sample tests.

Therapy: learn to control the situations in which a behaviour is likely to occur.

Evaluation:

- the empirical evidence has been criticised, e.g. where children are used as subjects we would expect them to be less consistent than adults,
- see also the evaluation of the situational approach, p.213.

HOW TO COMPARE AND CONTRAST THE THEORIES

Value as a theory?	Practical use?	Position on key issues?
• is it comprehensive?	• for testing?	• learned versus biological factors?
• is the structure of personality explicit?	• for therapy?	• the self-concept and self-determination (free will)?
• does it explain the dynamics of behaviour?		• the role of the unconscious?
• is it falsifiable, testable?		• idiographic versus nomothetic approach?
• is it valid?		• relation to other personality approaches?
• how much thought has it stimulated?		
• how much research has it generated?		
• what empirical support is there?		

5.3 PSYCHOMETRIC TECHNIQUES

'Psychometric' refers to the mental testing of any facet of psychology. The field of assessment is somewhat wider, encompassing attitude scales (see 2.3); projective and other personality techniques (see 5.5); physiological measures (see 7.5 and 7.6); observation, surveys and questionnaires (see 10.1); interviews and educational evaluation (p.233).

A psychological test is an objective and standardised measure of a small but carefully chosen, *sample* of behaviour. They are used in psychological research, job placement (see 9.1), educational selection or assessment (see 9.3) and clinical diagnosis (see 6.3).

A 'GOOD TEST'

A good test must have the following:

1 *Discriminatory power:* a good test should produce a wide distribution of scores. If everyone does well (ceiling effect) the test is not providing useful information in distinguishing between candidates. Conversely, if the measuring device does not go low enough (floor effect) everyone may do poorly.

2 *Standardisation:*
(a) **norm referencing**: the establishment of norms, testing a large representative sample of the population for whom the test is designed and establishing normal ranges for any age, gender, class, ethnic or geographical group,
(b) **criterion referencing**: rather than compare performances between particular children, targets or criteria are selected objectively and assessment is measured using these as standards,
(c) to enable **comparisons** to be made between tests, it is necessary to know the mean and standard deviation,
(d) **standardised instructions** prevent experimenter/tester bias. They also mean that different tests can be compared.

3 *Reliability:* a test result should be consistent and reproducible, both internally (all test items should measure the same thing) and externally (the test should produce the same score when repeated). A well constructed test usually has a reliability coefficient of 0.90 or more, which allows for some chance errors. Tests can be made reliable using the following techniques:
(a) **split-half technique**: to assess internal consistency. The original test items are split into two halves either randomly or placing odd and even items in different halves,
(b) **test–retest**: same test is given to the same people on different occasions, but this may suffer from a **practice effect**, (see 10.2),
(c) **equivalent, alternate or parallel forms** can be used to overcome practice effects, these can be constructed using the split-half technique.

4 *Validity:* does the test measure what it claims to measure? The test's validity is expressed as high or low, and sometimes given a correlation coefficient. The type of validity used depends on the particular test:
(a) **reliability**: an unreliable test can't be valid,
(b) **face (internal) validity**: on the face of it, does it look 'valid'? Are the questions appropriate?
(c) **content (internal) validity**: a systematic examination of test content to see if it covers a representative sample of the behaviour it is intended to cover – a subjective process,
(d) **criterion (external) validity**: demonstrating validity by showing a high correlation between test scores and some independent, non-test criterion,
  - **concurrent validity**: where this correlation between the test and the non-test criterion is demonstrated immediately, such as looking at a teacher's ratings or using the test on a group of people known to be proficient and see how they score,

- **predictive validity:** the extent to which test scores are predictive of future performance, therefore check the scores at a later date against performance.

⑤ *Item selection:* these considerations are important for both assessing and designing written tests. The test items:
  - must be within the **repertoire** of target population, e.g. children or the illiterate,
  - should be **interesting**, to ensure high and sustained motivation,
  - should be **brief** and **unambiguous**,
  - should not have cultural or gender **bias**,
  - should **discriminate** – if one item can be answered correctly by everyone then it should be dropped, (except when used as a gentle introduction to the whole test),
  - should correlate with the test as a whole. If one item is answered by weaker but not better candidates it should be dropped because it is obviously not measuring the right quality,
  - the content should be chosen while bearing in mind:
    - **theoretical keying:** select items that seem appropriate and prove this by showing that all the items correlate,
    - **criterion keying:** use items that discriminate the target population, e.g. if testing neuroticism, use items that a known group of neurotics score highly on; it doesn't matter why.

⑥ *Factors which affect test performance:*
  - **anxiety:** start the test with easy items to reduce test anxiety,
  - **response sets:** subjects may prefer certain responses such as 'yes' – a stylistic consistency. Therefore correct responses should be evenly distributed over the whole range,
  - **social desirability bias:** subjects try to appear in the best light and may not be truthful, consciously or unconsciously; use:
    - **lie scale:** set of questions, randomly placed through the test which assess the degree to which the subject is answering in the direction of social desirability, for example, 'Do you ever lie?'
    - **forced-choice technique:** subject has to choose between two equally desirable statements: Which is more like you?
      'I like to talk about myself to others'
      'I like to work towards some goal that I have set for myself',
  - **lying:** conscious untruths are difficult to avoid except by increasing the subjects' motivations or by deluding them, e.g. the **bogus pipeline technique** – a subject is connected to a machine which they are told will register lying, though it doesn't in fact do anything,
  - **conditions:** lighting, temperature, noise.

IMPORTANT CONSIDERATIONS FOR TESTING

❶ **Theoretical basis:** all tests are designed from some theoretical vantage point in terms of the form they are presented in, their content and the criteria for their validation. This is especially true for intelligence and personality.

❷ **The effects of learning:** it is impossible to divorce potential from the ways we have learned to use it. **Practice effects** demonstrate how subjects can learn to answer any tasks set, and make interpretations of results difficult.

❸ **The effects of culture:** if we are testing learned skills then the test must be culture-biased. This is not a problem *unless* 'better' or 'genetically superior' judgements are made, and preferential treatment is accorded to some subjects.

❹ **The illusion of reality:** a numerical value has a profound effect, giving the illusion that we are measuring something real like foot size. The score has no absolute meaning or 'reality'. It is valid only insofar as the designer has validated it with their chosen criteria.

❺ **Labelling:** once tested, forever marked? If what we are measuring is potential then the result should be unchanging, being labelled 'below average' or 'neurotic' is forever. This may significantly affect a person's future (see the illustrative question at the end of this chapter for evidence that intelligence results are not fixed).

6 **Quantity rather than quality**: the psychometric approach tends to reduce 'humanity'.

7 **A political tool**: testing is part of the social process of discrimination. It legitimises classification and maintains the status quo while masquerading as being objective and scientific.

8 **Ethics**: should people have a right to know their results? Should their results be available to a third party? Should a subject know the nature of the test (which may then influence their performance)?

9 **Misuse**: the importance of standardised instructions, experimenter effects and validity mean that only qualified testers should be allowed to administer and interpret test results.

10 **Diagnostic tools**: many tests do provide more than a single number and are perhaps the only way of assessing people in order to provide them with appropriate remedial or therapeutic help.

INTERVIEWS

Interviews are appropriate for certain situations but generally they have low reliability and validity. They can be highly structured or little more than an informal 'chat' (see also 6.3).

Validity and reliability

Anstey (1977) compared the results of Civil Service board interviews with the rank held 30 years later, and found a validity coefficient of 0.35. This is relatively high compared to other studies of interviews. **Arvey and Campion (1982)** concluded a review of research concerning the employment interview with the judgement that interviews have low validity and reliability, and are susceptible to bias and distortion. They suggest various reasons why interviews persist despite these glaring shortcomings, such as the interview provides some useful information and may be valid in terms of limited criteria.

Advantages:

1 An interview allows direct observation of a rather limited sample of behaviour.

2 Rich data, especially for speech and manner, can be obtained.

3 A skilled interviewer may be able to elicit information not otherwise obtainable.

4 Interviews may be held for practical considerations, such as saving the time and money necessary for more elaborate measures (**Arvey and Campion, 1982**).

Disadvantages:

1 Untrained and inexperienced interviewers, often do much of the talking.

2 Even with training, interviewers' performance doesn't always improve:
   - **Stevenson et al, (1992)** found no improvement in simulated interviewing after a 10-day course on techniques for interviewing children in sexual abuse cases.
   - **Taylor et al. (1988)** found better quality 'talk time' from teachers and head teachers after training in interpersonal skills.

3 Interviews not comparable because different interviewers ask different questions.

4 Subjective judgements by interviewers with inevitable biases (halo effects, confirmatory bias, attribution errors, too lenient/severe, racial/sexual/ageist prejudices).

5 The interviewer's expectations may influence the interviewee's performance, an example of the self-fulfilling prophecy:
   - **Word et al. (1974)** (see 2.5) demonstrated how the behaviour of interviewers led subjects to behave with less competence and confidence.

6 The interviewee's behaviour (see 2.1) may influence the interviewer. Success is often related to the skills in self-presentation and/or intelligence rather than possession of job-related skills:

- **Dipboye and Wiley (1978)** controlled for content but nevertheless found that interviewers rated subjects who had a passive rather than aggressive self-presentation style less favourably and as more emotionally unstable,
- **Kacmar** *et al.* **(1992)** found that self-focused-type self-presentation skills were more effective than other tactics.

Improvements

- structure the interview,
- use a method of scoring/rating the applicant,
- ask questions which are job-related,
- train the interviewers,
- use a panel of interviewers, who discuss judgements.

EDUCATIONAL ASSESSMENT

Macintosh and Hale (1976) suggest the following reasons for assessment in schools: diagnosis, evaluation, guidance, prediction, selection and grading.

① *Essay questions:* the different varieties are: timed, question selections, open book, continuous assessment:
  (a) test a variety of skills: organising, expression, evaluating ideas,
  (b) assessment is subjective,
  (c) continuous assessment may be less anxiety provoking and more effective for learning than traditional timed exams, it is also more susceptible to fraud.

② *Objective tests:* these have one 'correct' answer and include: recall (simple recall, sentence completion, unlabelled diagram), recognition (true/false, multiple choice, matching items and rearrangement in order of magnitude or chronology) and case study (e.g. in a medical exam):
  (a) objective marking, using scorer's key or computer,
  (b) setting the questions is difficult, badly constructed tests can become subjective,
  (c) many more questions can be set in given time,
  (d) candidates spend less time writing (more time for thinking?),
  (e) can test a greater ability range by having graded difficulty of questions,
  (f) susceptible to practice effects, though the same could be said of essays,
  (g) guessing is possible,
  (h) student's depth of understanding may not be tested.

5.4 INTELLIGENCE TESTS

Intelligence tests are the most widely used of all psychological tests. Psychometric techniques and testing generally are considered in 5.3.

CONCEPTS

① **Defining intelligence and testing it:**
  (a) Any intelligence test is founded on a particular definition of intelligence, the questions in the test are designed to reflect the theoretician's view of intelligence.
  (b) The test is validated by showing that it correlates highly with the criteria that the theoretician regards as evidence of intelligence, such as scholastic success.
  (c) When testing intelligence we are actually testing abilities through which intelligence is expressed, not intelligence itself.

② **IQ (intelligence quotient):** the statistic used to express intelligence. As mental ability increases with age, we must adjust the test score which indicates mental age (MA), using chronological age (CA); $IQ = MA/CA$ multiplied by 100. Over the age of 18 mental ability ceases to develop, and therefore MA is sufficient.

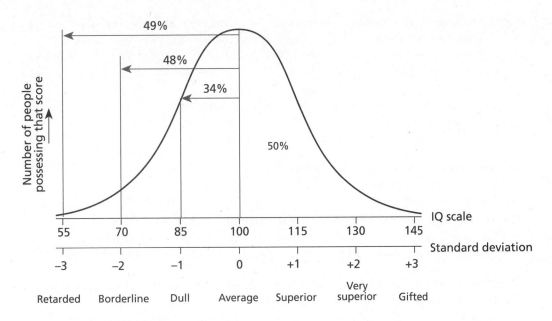

Fig. 5.2 Standard normal distribution for IQ, showing that approximately 68% of the population should have an IQ in the range 85 to 115, and only 16% should have an IQ higher than this. The mean is 100, and standard deviation is 15.

3 **Distribution:** is theoretically normal, though certain populations, such as a grammar school, would be skewed. According to normal distribution we expect that roughly 68% of the population will have a score within one standard deviation of the mean, and that 5% should have a score which is greater than two standard deviations (Fig. 5.2).

PARTICULAR TESTS

Typical test items

1 Testing relations between abstract items – non-verbal and 'culture-fair' (Fig. 5.3):

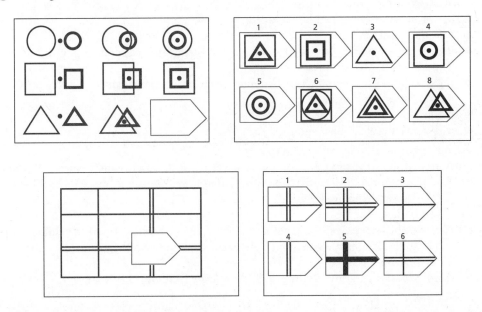

Fig. 5.3 Examples of the easier and more difficult items from Raven's Progressive Matrices. Select missing item on left from choices given on right.

2 Testing relations using learned skills. 'Fairness' is assumed on the basis that all testees are equivalent because these are all common concepts:
'Fish is to swim as bird is to: man, fly, walk, aeroplane, sparrow'
'Here are three figures: 3 2 5. Add the largest two figures together and divide the total by the smallest figure.' (from AH5 see p.226).

③ Testing verbal ability, such as measuring the extent of a subject's vocabulary: '*Choose the word which is opposite in meaning to the word in capital letters: PARTISAN: A, commoner; B, neutral; C, unifier; D, ascetic; E, pacifier.*' (from the Scholastic Aptitude Test).

④ Testing divergent or creative thinking:
   (a) unusual uses for objects, such as a toothpick, brick or paper clip,
   (b) using a circle, draw as many pictures as possible,
   (c) think of common problems, e.g. when making a cup of tea,
   (d) consequences, what happens if national laws were to be abolished?
   (e) suggest improvements for common articles (toys, toasters),
   (f) remote associations (find a fourth word to go with 'rat, blue, cottage'),
   (g) word association, write as many meanings for duck as you can.

⑤ Performance, testing the deaf (pictures), children or other non-literates, for example:
   (a) picture completion: the subject must say what part of picture is missing,
   (b) block design: subject must reproduce a pattern using blocks with red, white or red/white sides,
   (c) picture arrangement, in correct order to tell a story,
   (d) object assembly,
   (e) mazes.
   (taken from the Wechsler Performance Scales).

Tests

❶ *Individual tests:* the best known examples are:
   (a) **Stanford–Binet:** started out as the **Simon–Binet test (1905)**, developed by two researchers commissioned by the French government to identify children of inferior intelligence. **Terman and Merrill** at Stanford University in America revised the test in 1916, producing two equivalent forms (L and M). It is continually revised.
   (b) **The Wechsler Scales:** Adult Intelligence **(WAIS)**, Intelligence Scale for Children **(WISC)** and Preschool Primary Scale of Intelligence **(WPPSI)** first appeared in 1939.

   Evaluation of individual tests:
   ● performance subtests can be included,
   ● it is time consuming,
   ● it depends on the experimenter's 'rapport' with the subject, and so is prone to 'experimenter' (tester) bias,
   ● the procedures are non-standard, standardised instructions can't eradicate individual differences,
   ● marking is subjective,
   ● it is generally used for diagnostic purposes.

❷ *Group tests*, some common examples are:
   (a) **Army alpha and beta** (verbal and non-verbal) tests: used widely during World War I for military placement. The first attempt to produce a scientific tool for psychology and the model for all subsequent testing,
   (b) The **11-plus**,
   (c) **British ability scales:** designed at Manchester University (1976) for children up to 17. With 12 subscales including divergent thinking and Piagetian developmental tasks,
   (d) **AH4/5/6:** designed by **Heim (1970)** for selected, intelligent groups.

   Evaluation of group tests:
   ● 'pencil-and-paper' and more like other written examinations,
   ● usually timed, can determine score in terms of percentage correct or the most difficult task successfully completed,
   ● more objective, typically only one correct answer,
   ● marking is simple, by a computer or with a special marking key.

❸ *Attainment and aptitude tests:* Intelligence tests are aptitude tests. However, there are also tests for specific aptitudes on their own, or as subtests of an intelligence tests, for example: verbal, spatial–perceptual, motor, talent (musical or artistic), occupational (clerical, mechanical, arithmetic), creativity. Achievement and aptitude represent opposite ends of the same spectrum, you might want to test someone's mathematical ability to see if they could do a particular course (aptitude) or at the end of the course to assess how well they've done (achievement). Most achievement tests are aimed more at specifically learned skills (see also 9.3).

4 *Other tests of mental abilities* are directed at special populations, for example tests for dyslexia, the elderly and neuropsychological tests for brain damage.

5 *Psychophysiological approaches:* one way to avoid culture-bias is to test the physiological and psychological processes, as discussed in 5.1. Can measurements of brain activity distinguish different abilities? Attempts have been made to use electro-encephalogram (EEG) or reaction times with moderate success in terms of concurrent validity with IQ tests.

6 *Culture-fair tests*, using non-verbal, performance or physiological methods. However, it is almost impossible to be equally fair to more than one culture. Examples include:

(a) **Raven's Progressive Matrices**, which is one of the most widely used,

(b) **Cattell's Culture Fair Intelligence Test,**

(c) **Dove (1968)** devised the **Dove Counterbalance General Intelligence Test** ('Chitling Test'), this was not culture-fair, but a parody of white middle-class tests highlighting culture 'unfairness'.

(d) **Williams (1973)** produced the BITCH test (Black Intelligence Test of Cultural Homogeneity), which is written in a dialect in which black children are proficient, rather than in standard English. **Genshaft and Hirt (1974)** found that white children did very poorly when tested using the black dialect. **Matarazzo and Wiens (1977)** tested black and white police applicants and found that no whites did better on the BITCH test, the opposite was true on the WAIS test. Correlational analyses revealed no relation between scores on the two tests, raising questions of concurrent validity and the viability of cultural tests.

Difficulties with IQ testing

See 'A Good Test' for general points about testing, in 5.3.

1 Intelligence tests are mainly validated in terms of educational achievement.

2 The assumption behind most tests is that intelligence is a fixed quantity and genetically determined. (This is largely, but not entirely, true. **Binet**, for example, believed that intelligence could be enhanced.)

3 Intelligence is too complex an activity to be reduced to a single number.

4 While tests are reasonably good at assessing a person's ability to learn or reason abstractly, they almost entirely ignore other aspects of intelligence, such as divergent thinking, adaptability or motivation. Computers offer a new media through which wider skills might be measured rather than the traditional pencil-and-paper methods.

5 IQ tests assume that intelligence of a particular sort is better, that people with this quality are superior.

5.5 PERSONALITY TESTS

For the purposes of testing, 'personality' refers to the measurement of motivational, emotional, interpersonal and attitudinal characteristics, as distinguished from abilities.

1 **Self-report personality inventories:** pencil-and-paper tests suitable for group use. These tests comprise a list of questions or statements, produced with factor analytic techniques. They are generally for adults aged 16 upwards, though there are some designed for children:

- *Cattell's 16 Personality factor, Eight State Questionnaire* measures short-term mood factors. It has profiles of personality scores which relate to various diagnostic and occupational groups.

- *Eysenck's* Personality Inventory and Questionnaire (EPI, EPQ), Junior Eysenck Personality Inventory (JEPI).
- *Minnesota Multiphasic Personality Inventory* (MMPI): the most widely used test with 558 statements measuring ten clinically-oriented scales: hypocondria, depression, hysteria, psychopathic deviancy, masculinity/feminity, paranoia, psychaesthenia, schizophrenia, hypomania, social introversion, plus a lie scale. Subject answers 'true', 'false' or 'cannot say' to each affirmative statement.

2 Measures of interest:

- *Kuder Vocational Preference Record:* this uses forced-choice triads, e.g. 'Which would you most and least like to do: visit an art gallery, browse in a library, visit a museum?'. Used in occupational counselling.

3 Measures of opinions and attitudes:

- see 2.3.

4 Phenomenological techniques:

- *Repertory grid:* subjects are asked to name important figures in their life. They are then given three of them and asked to say in what way two are alike and the third is different. This is continues with different triads, each time their answer produces a bipolar personal construct, such as 'funny–serious'. At the end all the names are arranged along the top of a grid and the constructs (no more than 25) are put down the side. Ticks and crosses represent relations between elements (people or almost anything) and constructs. The grid allows a subject to show reality as they see it.
- *Q-sort:* subject 'self-sorts' a pile of about 100 cards with statements such as 'I am quite an anxious person'. They can use nine piles ranging from 'like me' at one extreme to 'unlike me' at the other. The distribution should be approximately normal. They can do this for their ideal self and, using numbers on the back of the cards, the self and ideal-self statements can be correlated. It is a time-consuming procedure.
- *Coopersmith's Self-Esteem Inventory:* a self-report method indicating 'like me' and 'unlike me'. The statements are similar to Q-sort.
- *Semantic Differential Technique* (see 2.3): subjects indicate their feelings about significant others such as mother and father.

5 Projective techniques: these rely on a subject's interpretations of a stimulus. The subject 'project' their personality into the interpretation. These techniques are not developed in the same systematic way as tests, and it is not possible to score objectively. They are prone to 'tester' influence:

- *Rorschach:* standardised ink blots. The interpretation of the ink blots involves questions such as, does the subject use the whole blot, include unusual detail or the white space? What is the content of their interpretation: people, parts of people, animals, plants, inanimate objects, sexual objects, symbols?
- *Thematic Apperception Test* (TAT): a series of pictures is presented and the subject is asked to make them into a story.

6 Work sample tests: individuals are asked to perform a set of tasks directly relevant to the job they are being selected for. This is costly in time and effort but valid from the point of view of situationalism:

- e.g. a *committee exercise*, a group of candidates must function as a committee and take turns chairing.

7 Interviews: see 5.3.

8 Physiological:

- *Polygraph* (lie-detector): the galvanic skin response (GSR) is an emotional response. Emotion leads to arousal of the autonomic nervous system, one feature of this is sweating, which increases the electrical conductivity of the skin. It is not wholly reliable in detecting liars but is used in psychological research to evaluate emotional response (e.g. McGinnies' research on emotion and perceptual defence).

9 Others:

- Peer ratings,
- Argyle's Test of Happiness (1987),

- IPAT Humor Test of Personality: 104 pairs of jokes are presented and the subject is asked to indicate which is funnier, e.g. 'Epitaph to waiter: by and by, God caught his eye' or 'One prehistoric man to another: 'Now that we've learned to communicate with each other – shut up!'. Also, 130 jokes or cartoons to rate as funny or dull,
- IPAT Music Preference Test of Personality: listen to 100 short piano pieces to rate as like, dislike or indifferent. This is correlated with Cattell's 16PF and certain psychiatric syndromes,
- famous sayings: subject indicates agreement/disagreement with 130 proverbs. This gives an indication of hostility, fear of failure and social mores,
- graphology (handwriting),
- astrology.

Chapter roundup

Related material in other chapters:
- cognitive psychology (Chapter 1), covers topics, particularly learning, memory, thought and artificial intelligence, which are integral to intelligence;
- social psychology (Chapter 2) covers implicit personality theories and the consistency of attitudes and behaviour, attribution and other topics related to personality;
- developmental psychology (Chapter 3) includes cognitive development, and the effects of age on intelligence, and social development which is important in the development of personality;
- abnormal psychology (Chapter 6), looks at the applications of personality theory and testing;
- applied psychology (Chapter 9) also applies assessment techniques;
- research and design (Chapter 10) considers material related to test design.

Illustrative question

'If the impression takes root that (IQ) tests really measure intelligence, that they constitute a sort of last judgement on the child's capacity, that they reveal scientifically his/her predestined ability, then it would be a thousand times better if all the intelligence testers and their questionnaires were sunk without warning' (Lippmann, 1922).

Discuss the above view in the light of the controversy surrounding the use of IQ tests.

(AEB , 'A', 1992).

Tutorial note

There are two parts to the answer, first to address the quotation and second to discuss controversies (these can be done separately or concurrently). If only description or evaluation is attempted the maximum is 16 out of 25. A 'limited' answer (maximum of 12 marks) would discuss one issue only, such as cultural bias.

The quotation is complex, and **one** method of approaching it is to first make it clear for your own sake and for the examiner's. An essay is more 'readable' if the structure is explicit. It is worthwhile writing an introduction for this purpose but not if it's just 'waffle'.

The answer given below contains evidence not mentioned elsewhere in this chapter and tries to avoid repeating material already presented which would be equally relevant and more obvious.

Suggested answer

Lippmann has made a number of statements about intelligence. If they are true, he says, we should stop using tests immediately. His propositions about IQ tests are that they:

1 really measure intelligence,
2 provide a fixed 'label',
3 are seen as scientific,
4 reveal innate potential (predestined).

Do IQ tests really measure intelligence? This is a question about their *validity* and also about what intelligence is. A fairly cynical definition says that intelligence is what intelligence tests measure. Alternatively, intelligence is the 'ability to profit from experience', which suggests the importance of potential, learning and the effective use of such learning.

If we agree on a definition and design a test which we think examines that capacity, how do we prove that the test is what we say it is? Most validation is done by correlating test performance with some measure of success particularly academic success. When we test intelligence we are testing educational potential, not some universal ability.

When using a test we may be measuring other things besides intelligence and learned abilities. Other variables, such as motivation, attitude, test anxiety, examiner and situational factors will affect performance.

The second point raised by Lippmann is the notion of 'labelling', which implies that the quantity being measured is fixed. However, performance increases as a child gets older, and IQ is adjusted to account for that by dividing mental age by chronological age. There is evidence to show that maturation is not the only cause of change. **Anastasi (1968)** cites studies which found variations of up to 50 points between the ages of 6 and 18, and noted that the differences were consistently up or downwards and probably due to environment. **Rosenthal and Jacobsen's (1966)** classic study of 'Pygmalion in the Classroom' showed that IQ results could change.

Labelling is a particular problem with 'lay' users, such as employers or even teachers, who are frequently unaware of the limitations of the measurement. For this reason it is important that only suitably qualified people administer such tests. Equally the results should be highly confidential.

The third question about tests and their viability is whether they are 'scientific'. The use of this term implies that the tool we are using is objective, standardised, reliable and valid, as we would expect from say a metre ruler. All tests are founded on the theoretical and philosophical view of their authors and are therefore subjective at least to that extent. Problems such as influence of the tester and scoring also detract from objectivity.

In order to make sense of the score that a person gets we need to know how people normally score. These norms are established through standardisation procedures when the test is used on a representative sample. In fact it is very difficult to obtain such a thing as a representative sample and therefore 'norms' are an ideal rather than a reality. Often there have been glaring omissions, for example, the Stanford–Binet 1960 revision used only white children.

The question of reliability is usually demonstrated using test–retest techniques. If the time between two testing sessions is too long, any change in the test score may be due to changes in ability. If the time is too short, practice effects may influence the score. **Dearborn and Rothney (1941)** analysed test data from 3500 children and found that their IQ scores rose 11 points when re-tested in successive years with an equivalent form, but remained the same when a different test was substituted, thus showing practice effects occurred even over long periods of time. Practice effects also indicate that the ability we are measuring is learned and not innate.

Which brings us to the final question about whether tests reveal innate potential? Evidence for the inherited view comes from studies of genetically similar or even identical persons who have not shared the same environment. However, the truth is that it is virtually impossible to find cases where nature and nurture have been so clearly separated. The environmental position is supported by studies which show how such things as diet, education and enrichment (or deprivation) can increase (or decrease) a person's IQ. However, the view is no longer seriously seen as one or the other, but how much of each? **Eysenck (1973)**, who supports an innate view, puts the 'heritability estimate' at 80%. **Kamin (1977)** maintains that nothing more than zero would be correct, though this is an extreme position. However, there are philosophical and social arguments, given below, which suggest that the nature–nurture question has an inevitably dangerous outcome.

A critical point to remember is that the psychometric approach is based on assumptions of inherited ability, otherwise what we are measuring, to a greater or lesser degree, is experience. And experience is related to culture.

Tests have a long history of association with demonstrating racial inferiority. **Galton (1883)** first proposed eugenics as a method of increasing the intelligence of man through selective breeding. The authors **(Yerkes and Terman)** of the Army Alpha and Beta tests were convinced that Americans would soon be a 'nation of morons' if 'Negroes' and immigrants from Europe polluted the gene pool **(Gould, 1982).** Their work had a profound effect on US immigration policy of the 1920s. **Jensen (1969)** reopened the debate, citing evidence that 'Negroes' were typically 15 IQ points below whites on IQ tests, and claiming that this demonstrates genetic inferiority.

It seems that it is impossible to divorce test results from the racial issue. The true question is not whether such results are valid but what do we do with such knowledge? Galton felt that his ideas about eugenics were for the betterment of mankind, so did Hitler. Is any form of social or educational engineering ethical? Enrichment programmes presume that there are universal standards. Educational engineering occurs when tests are used more for diagnostic purposes, which why intelligence tests were first developed by **Binet**.

It is a nice thought that tests could be 'sunk without warning' but the reality is, like Pandora's box, they cannot be so simply put away. Therefore it is important for people to appreciate their shortcomings.

Question bank

Allow 45 minutes for each question.

1 (a) Outline **two** problems in defining intelligence. (6 marks)
  (b) Relate the problems you have outlined in (a) to any **one** intelligence test. (8 marks)
  (c) Discuss problems involved in the construction of intelligence tests with very young children (approximately three to five years old). (6 marks)

(NEAB, 'A', 1991)

Points: Part (b) often proves difficult for candidates to relate problems to a particular intelligence test, which might reflect the fact that many are unfamiliar with specific tests. Part (c) is a straightforward discussion of reliability and validity.

2 Discuss the evidence that IQ scores can be modified by environmental factors. (20 marks)

(NEAB, 'A', 1992)

Points: Beware of the obvious question: do not overlook the word 'evidence' and present both sides of the argument. The examiner's report for this question notes that candidates tend to present several pieces of evidence for the same point, thus becoming repetitious. Marks are awarded for breadth rather than repetition.

3 Many children from economically disadvantaged minority groups obtain lower IQ scores and perform less well in school than does the average child in the same country. Why might this be so?

(NEAB, 'A', 1986)

Points: This is not simply a question about race and intelligence.

4 Compare and contrast the objectives and uses of a standardised intelligence test with those of school examinations. (20 marks)

(NEAB, 'A', 1990)

Points: You should be able to list the objectives and uses of intelligence tests. The taxing part of the question is to work out the similarities and differences with school examinations and to base your comments on psychological knowledge.

5 (a) In the context of intelligence testing, describe briefly what is meant by **each** of the following:
   (i) standardisation (3 marks)
  (ii) reliability (3 marks)
 (iii) validity (4 marks)
(b) 'Measuring intelligence at the lower and upper ends of the normal distribution is notoriously unreliable.' How useful are intelligence tests in establishing levels of retardation and giftedness? (4 marks)

(NEAB, 'A', 1989)

Points: Part (b) is intended to stretch the candidate's ability to apply knowledge from various areas and requires some thought.

6 Give an account of the ways in which intelligence tests differ and explain the reasons for such differences.

(NEAB, 'A', 1988)

Points: The differences can be taken in terms of theoretical origins, specific subject matter (e.g. verbal or non-verbal, specific or general, etc.) or the form of the test (e.g. group or individual).

7 Compare the usefulness of interviews and tests as techniques for personnel selection. (25 marks)

(AEB, 'AS', 1989)

Points: There is relevant material in Chapter 2 (self-presentation, 2.1) and Chapter 9 (selecting employees, 9.1),

8 Critically discuss individual and situational approaches to personality.

(AEB , 'A', 1990)

Points: For 'critically discuss' read 'describe and evaluate'. A sound description and evaluation of two suitable theories will suffice, but some attempt to explain the terms and to contrast the approaches would be found in a good answer.

9 Critically discuss trait **and** type approaches to personality.

(AEB, 'A', 1989)

Points: Similarly prescriptive to the previous question.

10 'Behaviour is more a manifestation of social role than of personality'. Discuss.

(AEB, 'A', 1981)

Points: You can draw on situational theories as well as evidence from social psychology, in particular work on self-presentation (see 2.1).

11 (a) Outline Freud's theory of psychosexual development. (6 marks)
(b) Discuss **one** problem psychologists encounter in empirically investigating Freud's claims about development. (6 marks)
(c) Discuss **one** way, using examples, in which Erikson's theory differs from that of Freud. (8 marks)

(NEAB, 'A', 1992)

Points: The length of answer for each section should reflect the available marks. For 6 marks you should write a good summary of Freud but nothing too detailed (15 minutes-worth), and you must focus specifically on psychosexual development. The rest of the question is much more taxing. Part (b) is *not* related to Freud's methodology and part (c) requires a thorough discussion for the 8 available marks.

ABNORMAL PSYCHOLOGY

Units in this chapter

Chapter overview

'Abnormal psychology' is a polite euphemism for mental disorders and disabilities. The intention is to suggest that such problems are simply 'not normal'. Physical handicaps have been included in this chapter, despite the fact that they are often classified separately, presumably to avoid the stigma associated with mental illness. The term 'psychopathology' refers to the scientific study of mental disorders distinguished from the actual practice of treating them.

A historical view

Possession: through history people have attributed mental disturbance to various factors. It seems likely, from the evidence of skulls found with holes in them, that Palaeolithic cave dwellers believed in possession by evil spirits. The practice of trepanning (boring a small hole in the skull) continued to be practised by many cultures. In the 16th century the 'stone of folly' was removed, from patients possessed with madness; this may well have been a brain tumour.

A belief in witchcraft is another example of explanations of possession. One of the most notable incidents was the Salem witch trials in Massachusetts, 1692. The unstable behaviour of some adolescent girls was attributed to bewitching and led to a local hysteria. The 'guilty' were put to death.

Physical causes: The Greeks diagnosed various illnesses and attributed them to the disruption of various humors (body fluids) or physical abnormalities. For example, a wandering uterus was thought to cause hysterical behaviour in women (the Greek for uterus is *hysteron*, thus 'hysterical').

Loss of reason: the asylums of the 18th century segregated the insane and reserved their most inhumane treatments for them, on the basis that, having lost their reason, they were no different from animals. They were chained, beaten and kept in cellars in the hope that they would learn to behave better. One of the more notorious institutions was St Mary's of Bethlehem in London (Bedlam) where many eminent people were incarcerated. The poet John Clare is an example. He wrote of his loneliness and despair, a testament to his predicament:

> I am: yet what I am none cares or knows,
> My friends forsake me like a memory lost;
> I am the self-consumer of my woes,

They rise and vanish in oblivious host,
Like shades in love and death's oblivion lost;
And yet I am, and live in shadows lost.

(an extract from *I am*). **(Reeves, 1956)**

6.1 THE CONCEPT OF ABNORMALITY

It is clear that there is behaviour which is not only abnormal but which is also detrimental to the individual and/or society. This is a necessary social and legal judgement. The problem lies in defining *mental* abnormality:

1. **Statistical frequency:** 'normality' can be defined by statistical norms – that which is most frequent, typical, usual or average. Psychometric testing employs this definition in establishing the normal range of performance. For example, mental retardation is taken as being more than two standard deviations from the mean IQ test score. Using the normal curve, this encompasses less than 5% of the population.

    As a means of defining abnormal behaviour, rather than performance, this approach is unsatisfactory because:
    - many unusual behaviours, such as genius, are statistically uncommon but not aberrant, in fact they may be highly desirable,
    - some aberrant or undesirable behaviours or disorders, such as anxiety, divorce or depression, are sufficiently common that they can be considered statistically normal,
    - what is common at a certain age or in a certain context, is not universally applicable – there are different developmental and cultural norms.

2. **Social deviation:** abnormality is defined in terms of certain standards of social behaviour. Examples through history have been witchcraft, homosexuality, unmarried mothers and delinquency. The problem with this approach is that it varies according to prevailing social and moral perspectives and allows serious abuse of individual rights. Some countries, e.g. the former USSR, have hospitalised people for political dissent.

3. **Mental healthiness:** in the same way that the concept of physical health provides a yardstick for what constitutes ill-health, we can attempt to define psychological well-being in order to recognise mental illness. **Jahoda (1958)** suggested the following list:
    - self-acceptance,
    - potential for growth and development,
    - autonomy,
    - accurate perception of reality,
    - environmental competence,
    - positive interpersonal relations.

    Rogers also defined abnormality in terms of the characteristics of a mentally healthy person, namely a sense of self and self-acceptance. However:
    - such approaches are still open to culturally prevailing attitudes,
    - these are ideals and perhaps too vague for the purpose of diagnosis.

4. **The medical model:** asserts that psychological symptoms are manifestations of an underlying disease, which may or may not have a known cause. This approach involves diagnosis followed by treatment to eradicate or subdue the symptoms:
    - **Szasz (1960)** wrote the classic text, *The Myth of Mental Illness*, in which he suggested that the medical model is a 'worthless and misleading definition', which is 'scientifically crippling' because it prevents us investigating the true problems, it undermines personal responsibility, and it ignores socially expressed symptoms which are better viewed as problems in living. He claimed that it is a modern day

version of demonology and serves the same political purposes, namely social control by those invested with undisputed authority – the medical profession.

- **Clare (1980)** has defended the medical model by pointing out that physical illness itself is not a simple matter of body alone. *All* illness has a physical and mental component and is defined in terms of current views and knowledge. In particular, stress has a significant effect on susceptibility and recovery of all illness.

- **Heather (1976)** focused on the distinction commonly accepted between organic and functional psychoses, which suggests that at least some mental illnesses do *not* have an organic or medical basis. Organic psychiatrists believe that, eventually, an organic cause will be found for all psychoses, but Heather argues that the same claim has never been made for neuroses (though this situation is changing as new discoveries about the genes and biochemistry are made). And therefore at least some mental illnesses must be non-medically based.

- **Goffman's (1968)** *Asylums* describes how the institution sets its own rules, to which the mental patient must learn to conform, as well as learning how to perform 'well behaviour'. The patient's 'career' in hospital involves a change in their status and view of themselves. Essentially this destroys the person's previous identity. Like Szasz, this view is of mental institutions as a force for social control.

⑤ **Psychological model:** certain behaviours are dysfunctional for the individual. For example, they disrupt the ability to work and to conduct satisfying relations with people. This concept of **maladaptiveness** appears in both behaviourist and humanist approaches, as a superficial symptom or an underlying condition (lack of a sense of self) respectively.

⑥ **Existential model: Laing (1965)** identified insanity as a normal response to an abnormal world, either to a disturbed family or society generally. It is typically the observer, not the patient, who is disturbed by abnormal behaviour. Laing focused particularly on schizophrenia, describing the patient as a voyager on a journey of enlightenment, self-exploration and growth. His views appealed to the anti-establishment mood of the 1960s and were an important step in the direction away from somatic treatments.

⑦ **A combined approach:** drawing on a social and psychological notion of well-being, **Rosenhan and Seligman (1989)** suggest that there are certain elements or properties which together determine abnormality. While none are necessary or sufficient, where several exist they are symptomatic of abnormality:
- suffering,
- maladaptiveness: personally and socially,
- irrationality and incomprehensibility,
- unpredictability and loss of control,
- vividness and unconventionality,
- observer discomfort,
- violation of moral and ideal standards.

6.2 MODELS AND TREATMENT OF ABNORMALITY

The previous analysis looked at ways of *defining* abnormality. In this section ways of *explaining* abnormality are examined: different but similar! The models discussed below vary in the degree to which:
- the therapist or client is seen as the expert,
- they are focused on the here and now,
- they are based on psychological theory,
- they use drugs, communication or training.

THE BIOMEDICAL APPROACH

The move away from inhumane treatment of the insane and the beginnings of psychiatry were medically oriented. Rather than blaming the patient for his illness, the psychiatrist 'blamed' an illness. One of the early breakthroughs was the discovery that general paresis, the most common mental illness of its day, was caused by syphilis (**Krafft-Ebing, 1931**).

Underlying assumptions

Mental disorders, like physical illnesses, are caused by biochemical or physiological dysfunctions of the brain or body which may be inherited. They therefore need to be diagnosed accurately, leading to appropriate treatment.

Therapy: somatic treatments

Somatic means pertaining to the body.

1 **ECT (electroconvulsive therapy)** was a popular treatment prior to the advent of drug therapies and gained a bad reputation for its indiscriminate use and lack of refinement in application. Today it involves little discomfort, as the patient is given an anaesthetic and muscle relaxant. An electric shock is applied to the non-dominant cerebral hemisphere to produce a seizure. The individual awakens soon after and remembers nothing of the treatment, which is desirable, but they may also suffer long-term memory loss. A course of treatment usually involves six sessions.

The origins of ECT lie in the observation that epilepsy and schizophrenia appear to be negatively correlated (**Trimble and Thomson, 1986**). In the 1930s insulin shock was used to induce a seizure but later **Cerletti and Bini (1938)** introduced the use of electric shock rather than insulin.

ECT is now rarely used for schizophrenia, however there appears to be grounds for using it in cases of severe depression. **Janicak et al. (1985)** found that 80% of all severely depressed patients respond well to ECT, compared with 64% given drug therapy. **Fink (1985)** concluded, from a review of studies on ECT using measures such as suicide rates, that it is effective in over 60% of psychotic-depressive patients.

Current understanding suggests three possible explanations for its effectiveness:

- ECT acts as a form of punishment, therefore extinguishing undesirable behaviours,
- memory loss allows restructuring of disordered thinking,
- the shock activates noradrenalin transmission, reduces serotonin re-uptake and increases sensitivity of dopamine receptors, all of which may help alleviate depression.

2 **Psychosurgery** has an understandably poor reputation, for similar reasons to ECT. **Moniz (1937)** introduced the practice of lobotomy as a means of reducing antisocial behaviour. The operation involved removing large portions of the frontal cerebral cortex to induce personality changes and make a patient more controllable. Moniz received a Nobel prize for his work, which was not always successful. In fact one patient was so aggrieved that he shot and paralysed Moniz.

Today, it is used only rarely, in cases of severe depression, obsessive-compulsive disorder or pain where all other treatment has failed (**Griest, 1992**). The technique is much refined; electric probes destroy specific nerve fibres and cause minimal intellectual damage.

3 **Drug therapy:** the advent of drug therapies in the 1950s changed the face of mental treatment. It meant that many of the crippling symptoms of mental illness could be relieved, enabling sufferers to lead more normal lives outside mental institutions. However, the problem of addiction and a range of side-effects means that it should not be a permanent solution. The fact that effectiveness varies considerably between individuals also detracts from its power as a therapy. The classes of drugs used are:

- *anti-anxiety*, tranquillisers such as Valium are associated with major problems of overuse and addiction,
- *anti-psychotic*, sometimes called the major tranquillisers, such as chlorpromazine, which is used to treat schizophrenia,
- *anti-depressant* drugs, such as lithium, act to energise and to increase neurotransmitter levels.

Evaluation of the biomedical approach

- Current research has shown that at least some disorders have a biological basis (see 6.4). However, an exclusive emphasis on biological bases may mean that other factors are overlooked.

- It overlooks the fact that mental disturbance is defined in terms of social difficulties and therefore the application of medical principles is inappropriate (**Szasz**, see 6.1).

- Control is taken away from the patient, who relies on expert guidance.

- The approach purports to be value-free and scientific, but is just as subject to prevailing attitudes as other models.

- The use of drug therapies has offered significant relief to many sufferers and has changed the face of psychiatry for good and bad.

- In 1955 there were 560,000 patients in American psychiatric institutions, by 1977 this had declined to 160,000 (about one-quarter of the previous figure) with a comparable increase in outpatient care. This is because drugs have enabled the release of patients. However, it does not tell us anything about their quality of life (see 6.6 'Institutionalisation').

- Drugs are not cures, they are short-term remedies which inevitably become long-term with attendant ill-effects. They are long-term in the sense that they can prevent relapse.

- Drugs treat symptoms not causes. The revolving-door phenomenon – where patients are discharged and readmitted – should be considered.

- Drugs are not a universal solution, there are individual differences in their effectiveness (see 7.1).

- Drugs can be particularly effective when used in conjunction with psychotherapy, they can relieve some of the disabling symptoms and allow the contributing psychological factors to be dealt with.

PSYCHOTHERAPY: THE PSYCHODYNAMIC APPROACH

This approach is essentially Freudian, though there have been many adaptations of his theory and treatment. They all focus on explanations of conflict leading to anxiety which, in turn, is dealt with by ego defences. The existence of unconscious and unresolved problems is expressed in disordered behaviour. Recovery depends on insight and working through past problems. (See 5.2 for details of Freud's personality theory.)

Underlying assumptions

- Instinctual drives are satisfied during the stages of childhood (oral, anal and phallic), any disturbance results in a fixation and anxiety.

- Defence mechanisms, such as the repression of unpleasant memories, serve to protect the ego.

- Neurotic symptoms are the result of conflicts between repressed or unfulfilled desires and attempts to control or resolve them.

- Socialisation is the process of learning which desires should be repressed, when and where.

Therapy: psychoanalysis

Treatment relies on the therapist's ability to make the unconscious conscious and guide the patient in resolving the conflicts. Diagnosis occurs alongside treatment:

- *free association:* therapist introduces a topic and client talks about anything that comes into their mind,

- *rich interpretation:* the therapist uses their knowledge of the dynamics of personality development to explain causes,

- *analysis of dreams*: the expression of the innermost workings of the mind, particularly repressed 'wishes',
- *transference:* the patient transfers their feelings about others onto the therapist. During the course of therapy these may move from negative to positive and may have to be dealt with as an additional 'problem'.

Evaluation

- The emphasis on early experience means that present conflicts may be overlooked.
- It has somewhat limited applicability: for intelligent and verbally able patients and, since appointments are usually several times a week over a period of years, the wealthy with time on their hands.
- It has been adapted for children in the form of play therapy.
- It is not scientifically rigorous, the method is based on research with a limited sample, but it is supported by extensive theory and practice.
- The fact that it is a particularly well known method is due to its intuitive appeal and evocative ideas.

PSYCHOTHERAPY: THE HUMANIST APPROACH

These approaches emphasise the uniqueness of each person, the human potential for growth and self-actualisation and the importance of approaching the problem from the client's point of view. They are based on phenomenological theories of personality, though in most cases the theory of personality grew out of clinical practice, as with psychoanalytic theory.

The most notable approach is self theory and counselling, which was developed by **Rogers** (e.g. **1951**) (see 5.2 for a description of the theory).

Underlying assumptions

The concept of self is all-important:

- self-unity or a sense of self is critical in promoting development and well-being,
- self-acceptance, the evaluative aspect of the self, is lowered by experiences of failure or troubled relationships. In order for recovery to be possible, self-esteem must be raised,
- unconditional positive regard is the basis of all good relationships, only under such conditions is a person able to assimilate contradictory emotions and thereby accept themselves.

Therapy: counselling

Counselling has been a very successful approach, ranging from its application as an individual psychotherapy to self-help co-counselling groups. The emphasis is non-directive, client-centred, empathetic and accepting:

- therapy is *an enabling process*: the therapist enables the client to reveal their problems to themselves,
- the therapist's role is *non-judgemental*: to listen, reflect and accept the client's feelings by showing unconditional positive regard,
- the approach is *person-centred*: it is the problem as experienced by the client which is important, the client is in control,
- the *emphasis is on the present:* though the past may be important,
- the *aim* is for the client to become self-accepting and self-directing.

Similar techniques are used in groups with or without an expert leader, in play therapy or family therapy. In family therapy one member of the family may be experiencing problems, but this may be only the 'tip of the iceberg' and for treatment to be effective the whole family should be treated.

The importance of self-esteem has been shown experimentally. For example, **Coopersmith (1968)** found that young boys who were higher in self-esteem tended to be higher in competence (see 3.4).

Evaluation

- This is an approach of our age. Rogers commented that he had 'expressed an idea whose time had come'.

- It is a widely applicable approach for non-serious disturbances: addiction, depression, and family conciliation services. It can be used with a minimum of training, for example the Samaritans or marriage guidance.

- The fact that it has such wide application is an advantage, but is also a disadvantage because it means that in many situations counselling has become a substitute for good interpersonal relationships.

- Like psychoanalysis, it relies on good communication skills, though it can be used as a form of play therapy.

- It may be that the approach generally is little more than a good relationship rather than a specialist psychotherapy.

- It lacks rigour and is not readily susceptible to scientific analysis.

- It is rather class- and culture-specific.

PSYCHOTHERAPY: THE COGNITIVE APPROACH

A slightly more recent approach, which grew out of the behavioural approach, has taken the view that disordered cognitions cause disordered behaviour. The therapy aims to restructure these cognitions, either short-term expectations or long-term beliefs. The psychotherapy is client-centred – only the client knows their own cognitions. Some examples are:

- **Kelly's (1955) Personal Construct Therapy**: the therapist establishes the client's 'constructs' using the rep test (see 5.2 and 5.5) and aims to loosen them so they can be redefined.

- **Ellis' (1962) Rational Emotive Therapy**: irrational and illogical beliefs underlie maladaptive behaviour. The therapist's role is to actively and aggressively point out the patient's inconsistencies and help find better cognitions.

- **Attribution retraining**: focuses on transferring control to the patient, as recommended by, for example, **Seligman's (1978)** model of learned helplessness for depression (see 2.2). Seligman suggested that depressives make internal attributions of failure, which maintain their low self-esteem. If they can be trained to make specific rather than global attributions, to use external rather than internal attributions where appropriate, and to take control for their own actions, they can overcome depression. This approach has also been used for panic attacks and drug addiction. It is related to social skills training (see 6.4).

THE BEHAVIOURAL APPROACH

Advocates of behaviourism developed a distinctively different form of therapy. They suggested that the cause of the illness was immaterial, in fact the concept of illness is unnecessary. You need look no further than matching symptoms to effective treatments, which are based on classical or operant conditioning techniques (see p.240).

Underlying assumptions

- Psychological problems are seen as maladaptive behaviour patterns which have arisen through traumatic or inappropriate learning.

- What was learned can be re- or unlearned.

- Only behaviours which are currently observable are important, the patient's history doesn't matter.

Therapy: behaviour therapy using classical conditioning

❶ Aversion therapy: e.g. alcoholics are injected with a drug which makes them vomit when drinking, eventually the nausea becomes a conditioned response to the presentation of alcohol (conditioned stimulus). The bell and pad method for treating bedwetting is another example.

2 **Systematic desensitisation:** used to treat phobias, such as fear of the outdoors or fear of flying. The patient extinguishes the pairing of anxiety and the feared thing, and replaces this with relaxation as the conditioned response to the thing. **Wolpe (1958)** described the following steps:
- patient learns deep muscle relaxation,
- patient constructs a hierarchy of increasingly threatening situations,
- the patient is asked to imagine each scene while deeply relaxed.

There is evidence that relaxation is not a necessary component and that using real life situations is more effective. This technique can be explained in terms of cognitive restructuring rather than classic learning theory; the patient learns to reappraise themselves.

3 **Implosive therapy or flooding:** presents the patient with maximum exposure to the feared stimulus, which continues until their fear subsides, thus extinguishing the conditioned response. This can be done in one's imagination but real life exposure is more effective. The classic example is throwing someone in at the deep end of a swimming pool to overcome their fear of water.

Therapy: behaviour modification using operant conditioning

1 **Modelling:** the patient first watches the therapist experiencing the phobic situation calmly, then the patient does the same. This is based on social learning theory (see 1.6).

2 **Token economy (Allyon and Azrin, 1968):** patients are given tokens as 'secondary' reinforcers when they engage in correct/socially desirable behaviours. The tokens can then be exchanged for 'primary' reinforcers – food or privileges. This mirrors the system of rewards used by parents. The drawback to this therapy is that it often fails to transfer to life outside the institution though **Woods et al. (1984)** found that short-term changes did lead on to more fundamental long-term ones. This can be explained in terms of the newly acquired behaviours being 'trapped' by social reinforcers. The effectiveness of tokens may be due to other factors, such as being positively reinforcing for the nursing staff, who feel they are making positive gains and therefore are stimulated to persist.

3 **Social skills training**, for example:
- **Lovaas et al. (1967)** trained autistic children in language skills using shaping and positive reinforcement.
- **Azrin et al. (1974)** were successful in treating children with enuresis (bed wetting) by waking the child hourly and taking them to the toilet in order to give them practice in doing this for themselves. Any accident was dealt with by the child and any hour with no accident was praised.
- 'Time out' is a technique used to train hyperactive children. When they behave uncontrollably they receive attention which, despite being negative, is positively reinforcing. In order to break this cycle, unacceptable behaviour is treated with time in temporary isolation until they calm down. To be effective this should be accompanied by child-centred attention for good behaviour.
- **Goddard and Cross (1987)** described a course developed for disruptive pupils which included skills such as: listening, apologising, dealing with teasing and bullying, and gaining feedback from video recordings.
- In all cases long-term benefits were gained by training the parents so that they could continue the training programmes at home.

Evaluation

- The therapies are successful for the target range of disorders, e.g. phobias, obsessive–compulsive and developmental disorders. In fact for some disorders it is the only viable option, e.g. the brain injured.
- The firm scientific basis and operationalised procedures makes the therapies easy to research.

● As only symptoms are treated, the underlying problems remain, though behaviourists argue that the symptoms are all that matters.

● The success of behaviour therapy may be quite unrelated to learning theory, but this is true of all approaches.

EVALUATING AND COMPARING EFFECTIVENESS

Attempts to evaluate and compare therapies are fraught with difficulties:

1 What constitutes a cure or improvement?

● Improvements in therapy may not carry over into real life or be long-lasting.

● The concept of 'cure' varies from one approach to another. For example, a psychoanalyst would not regard simply removing the symptoms as evidence that underlying problems had been cured, whereas this would be acceptable to behaviourists.

2 What measures are valid for assessing effectiveness?

● The client's self-report may suffer from the **hello–goodbye effect**. People tend to exaggerate their unhappiness at the beginning of therapy to convince the therapist that they are in genuine need. At the end of therapy the reverse is true, in order to express thanks to therapist they exaggerate their well-being.

● The therapist is not likely to be an objective judge.

● Psychometric tests may be unreliable.

● Changes in target behaviour: such as counting the time an agoraphobic spends away from home or successful toilet training. In the long term it is difficult to reliably obtain such information.

3 How do we know what caused the change?

● Spontaneous remission is a possibility. In the case of depression particularly, time alone may affect an improvement. **Smith** *et al.* reviewed 475 studies which compared patients who underwent therapy with an untreated control group and concluded that the average patient showed greater improvement on such measures as self-esteem, anxiety and achievement than 80% of the untreated patients.

● Expectations of success might explain the improvement associated with therapy – a self-fulfilling prophecy.

● All methods involve an increase of attention for the patient, this alone may account for any change.

● When methods are the subject of a study, the health workers and patients may benefit from the Hawthorne effect. The improvement may be due to increased attention, or from increased staffing levels.

● Even when a therapy is shown to be effective, it may be for reasons other than the underlying assumptions or supporting theory.

4 Ethical considerations

● Withholding therapy from some patients is the only possible way of obtaining a control group. This can be done if a waiting list exists and patients are not selected except in order of arrival, though this is still ethically unsound.

● Random allocation to therapy would be unethical, any other method introduces bias into research.

● The information required may be considered confidential.

● Therapies such as ECT and psychosurgery are considered unethical by some authorities, such as MIND.

5 Are they comparable?

● Each therapy works best with a particular set of problems therefore it is inappropriate to try to compare them.

● Treatments in reality usually use a mixture of approaches such as drugs and psychotherapy or cognitive restructuring with social skills training. CCRT (core conflicting relationship theme) combines cognitive, behavioural and psychodynamic approaches.

● All therapies have certain features in common: they all offer time, attention, support and sharing. Such underlying factors may explain the effectiveness of all therapies.

- **Hock (1992)** reports that 40% of all therapists claim to be eclectic, which vastly outnumbers any other single approach. An eclectic approach means selecting the technique which seems most appropriate for a particular patient.
- It may be most appropriate to compare factors across therapeutic methods, rather than contrasting specific methods.

6.3 DIAGNOSIS AND CLASSIFICATION

Diagnosis is the identification of a disease by its symptoms, a formal determining description using a scheme of classification.

The Greeks made certain diagnoses which are still common today, such as alcoholism, mania and depression. The first comprehensive system of classification was started by **Kraepelin (1896)** who believed that mental illnesses, like physical ones, could be diagnosed from a cluster of symptoms. There were a number of other systems but Kraepelin's has remained influential, though the most recent revision of the DSM has finally moved away from it.

Psychoses and neuroses

At one time the major distinction made between mental illnesses was to group them as psychoses (the schizophrenias, manic depression, organic psychoses) or neuroses (phobias, depression, anxiety disorders, hysteria). Differentiation can be made in terms of whether:

- the whole personality is affected (yes for psychoses, no for neuroses),
- contact with reality is maintained (no/yes),
- the patient has insight into their condition (no/yes),
- behaviour is qualitatively/quantitatively different (respectively),
- no precipitating cause/often a response to a stressor (respectively),
- related to the person's pre-morbid personality (no/yes),
- treated mainly by physical/psychological methods (respectively),

However, in reality, such distinctions are not clear or particularly helpful, and the dualism has been dropped though the terms continue to be used.

DSM-IV and ICD-10

In 1993 the American DSM-IV (Diagnostic and Statistical Manual of Mental Disorders) and, the system used in the UK, ICD-10 (International Classification of Disease) were presented as revisions of previous classification systems (DSM-III-R and ICD-9).

Changes to DSM over the years have aimed to improve reliability and decrease ambiguity. To this end symptoms have been operationalised and diagnosis is made along different axes. The main innovation of the DSM-IV is that it is more soundly based on empirical data than previously. The DSM-IV and ICD-10 should be much more alike than their previous versions.

Kendell (1991) states that DSM-IV should not be revised again without compelling scientific reasons. However, **Fabrega (1992)** advocates a more culturally sensitive DSM, so that cultural, social and linguistic factors are considered. Possibilities include: a special category for atypical or cultural specific entities, to incorporate all diagnostically relevant cultural–ethnic factors, and the creation of an additional axis incorporating cultural factors. **Carson (1991)** argues that DSM-IV remains inadequate because, for example, it continues to use traditional categories and is overconcerned with interdiagnostician agreement.

DSM-IV

Axis	Description
I	clinical syndromes (see below)
II	disorders which often accompany axis I disorders: • developmental disorders: mental retardation, autism, specific learning disabilities • personality disorders: Cluster A: paranoid/schizoid Cluster B: antisocial/histrionic/narcissistic Cluster C: avoidant/dependent/obsessive–compulsive
III	physical disorders/conditions which may affect psychological functioning and treatment
IV	severity of psychosocial stressors
V	assessment of current potential to function adaptively

The clinical syndromes:

Category	Examples
Other developmental disorders	see 6.5
Organic mental disorders	Alzheimer's, senile dementia, presenile dementia (e.g. Korsakoff's)
Substance abuse disorders	alcohol, amphetamine, cannabis, cocaine, hallucinogen, inhalant, nicotine, opioid, PCP, sedative
Schizophrenia	catatonic, disorganised, paranoid, undifferentiated, residual
Paranoid disorder	paranoia
Psychotic disorders not elsewhere classified	brief reactive psychosis, induced psychotic disorder, schizophreniform
Mood disorders	depression, manic-depression
Anxiety disorders	panic disorder, phobia, obsessive–compulsive
Somatoform disorders	conversion disorder, hypochondriasis, pain disorder
Dissociative disorders	hysterical neuroses, multiple personality, fugue, amnesia
Sexual disorders	exhibitionism, fetishism, paedophilia, voyeurism, sexual dysfunctions
Sleep disorders	insomnia, sleepwalking, night terror
Factitious disorder	Munchhausen syndrome
Impulse control not elsewhere classified	intermittent explosive disorder, kleptomania, pathological gambling, pyromania
Adjustment disorder	impairment due to identifiable life stresses

Tools for diagnosis: psychological assessment

1 **The clinical interview** (see also 5.3): information is obtained through what is said and how it is said, the interviewer must be non-threatening, supportive and encouraging:
  - the unstructured interview is not random but influenced by the clinician's orientation to a theoretical view,
  - the structured interview enables standardised judgements to be made and can be scored by a computer, e.g. SADS (Schedule of Affective Disorders and Schizophrenia).

2 **Testing** (see 5.4 and 5.5) intelligence tests, or personality tests (inventories, Q-sort, rep test, projective tests).

3 **Behavioural assessment**: a functional analysis, a record of the behaviours and thoughts that the patient wishes to change.

4 **Classification scheme**: DSM and ICD for classifying.

EFFECTIVENESS OF DIAGNOSIS AND CLASSIFICATION

Advantages

Diagnosis and classification:
- is a form of communication shorthand,
- may indicate a cause,
- may lead to an appropriate treatment and eventual prognosis,
- is useful in assessing any later improvement or deterioration,
- is helpful for empirical research.

Limitations

1 Orientation: the notion of a classification scheme is linked to the medical model. Behaviourists prefer to focus on feeling or behaviour rather than a syndrome. Psychotherapeutic approaches see psychopathology as a continuum rather than discrete disease entities.

2 Illusion: the use of diagnostic techniques gives the impression of being a medical diagnosis, despite the fact that many symptoms are inferred or social rather than physical.

3 Labelling: the act of putting a label on a set of behaviours can lead to:
- reification,
- the impression that a cure has taken place,
- viewing a complex problem as a simple one,
- causal assumptions which may or may not be justified,
- 'stickiness', once assigned it is hard to remove the stigma and morally questionable,
- a diagnosis of mental illness, such as schizophrenia. This tends to result in the whole person becoming a schizophrenic; unlike most labels for physical illness.

4 Reliability: in order for any measurement to be useful, different assessors should generally arrive at the same diagnosis of a patient. The Kappa statistic is used to correct for chance agreement between interviewers:
- The DSM-III showed fair but not satisfactory reliability.
- Other methods used in assessment, such as interviews and psychological tests have variable reliability,
- **Beck *et al.* (1962)** found that the agreement amongst diagnosticians was at about the level of chance. However **Heather (1976)** claims that there is only a 50% correlation between a diagnosis and the treatment which is used suggesting that diagnosis is not always necessary for treatment.

5 Validity: (see 5.3 for general discussion)
- Predictive validity: in the sense that diagnoses lead to suitable treatments which in turn effect a 'cure', the diagnosis is valid.
- **Heather's (1976)** claim that the same diagnosis had a 50:50 chance of leading to the same or a different treatment, raises doubts about validity.
- Descriptive validity: to what extent does a diagnosis differentiate one category of patients from another? **Zigler and Phillips (1961)** found that the symptom of depression was just as likely to be found in someone diagnosed as manic–depressive as in someone labelled 'neurotic', and in 25% of those termed schizophrenic. This suggests that a diagnosis conveys little information about a patient.

6 Bias: the fact that psychiatrists have expectations can have profound consequences:
- **Rosenhan's (1973)** classic study engineered a situation where eight 'normal' students, were presented to admitting doctors in psychiatric hospitals. They were instructed to behave normally except for reporting that they heard a voice. All except one were admitted as schizophrenic, and later released (between 2 and 52 days later) as schizophrenics in remission (a rare diagnosis which might suggest a recognition of unusual circumstances). It would seem that the context mattered more than the symptoms. Though it might be a case of a type II error, psychiatrists preferred to call a healthy person sick rather than a sick person healthy, which would certainly be preferable for physical illness.

- What would happen if the hospital knew some new patients were stooges? **Rosenhan** arranged that a hospital expected one or more pseudopatients over a period of three months. In that time 193 patients were admitted and all staff were asked to rate the likelihood of whether they were 'real'. In fact all patients were genuine but more than 20% were judged as pseudopatients by one member of staff and 10% were judged so by two members of staff.
- **Langer and Abelson (1974)** showed a videotape to mental health professionals of a younger man telling an older man about his experiences in various jobs. If the viewers were told the speaker was a job applicant, they judged him attractive and conventional looking. If they were told that he was a 'patient', he was described as tight, defensive, dependent and frightened of his own aggressive impulses.
- The *prestige effect*: psychiatrists influence each other's diagnoses, particularly where one is held in esteem.

Conclusion

The fact that diagnosis is so prone to counterproductive outcomes and is unreliable would suggest it should not be used. However, the same is at least partly true of medical diagnosis generally, yet we wouldn't suggest abandoning that. Diagnosis and assessment are fundamental to treatment and necessary for scientific advancement. Methods of classification are changing quite rapidly, and advances in aetiology promise greater reliability in the future.

6.4 DESCRIPTION AND AETIOLOGY

Aetiology is the science or philosophy of causation – the inquiry into origin or cause of anything but especially diseases.

In this section the aetiology of some major disorders will be discussed.

SCHIZOPHRENIA

Schizophrenia means literally 'split-mind' but is wrongly confused with split or multiple personality. It is more correctly a group of psychoses which have some similarities, rather than a distinct disorder. Much of the research and thinking on the aetiology of mental illness has centred on schizophrenia because it is so common and debilitating.

Symptoms

The symptoms of schizophrenia are:
- lasting for more than six months,
- onset before the age of 45. It was once called 'dementia praecox' (early senility) to distinguish it from disordered thinking caused by age-related illness,
- gross impairment of reality testing,
- type I: disturbances of thought such as delusions, hallucinations and bizarre thoughts; often hearing voices or being controlled by aliens,
- type II: withdrawal, blunted affect and reduced motivation; such sufferers have a much poorer prognosis (both types may co-occur but they are independent),
- autism is often regarded as a childhood form of schizophrenia.

Causes: genetic evidence

1 *Twins:* **Kendler (1983)** found that concordance rates for schizophrenia in dizygotic (DT) twins is about 15% whereas it rises to 50% in monozygotic (MZ) twins, indicating some environmental influence but a larger genetic component.

② *Adoption studies:* **Wender *et al.* (1974)** found that a child of a schizophrenic parent who is adopted is more likely to become schizophrenic than a child of normal parents adopted into a family where one parent is schizophrenic. **Heston (1966)** found that adopted children whose natural mothers were schizophrenic were five times more likely to be diagnosed schizophrenic than those of normal natural mothers.

③ *Viral:* **Crow (1984)** has proposed that a retrovirus, which becomes incorporated into DNA, causes schizophrenia and is passed on to offspring. This is consistent with a number of facts, including gradual brain damage and the appearance of schizophrenia in families where it never occurred before.

④ *Chromosome evidence:* **Sherrington *et al.* (1988)** found evidence for a specific cluster of genes on chromosome 5, which might make an individual *susceptible*. This has not been confirmed.

Causes: biological evidence

① **Neurochemical:** an excess of dopamine activity is clearly related to type I schizophrenic symptoms. It may be a cause (supporting a genetic link) or an effect:
- *drugs* used to alleviate schizophrenic symptoms (neuroleptics) block dopamine synapses and the release of dopamine,
- *psychotic states*, which resemble the behaviour of schizophrenics, can be induced by large doses of amphetamines, cocaine, LSD, and L-dopa (used to treat Parkinson's disease). All of these drugs stimulate the dopamine synapses. Conversely, if L-dopa is given to schizophrenics it aggravates their symptoms,
- *post-mortem* examinations show abnormally high levels of dopamine.

② **Neuroanatomy:** it has been suggested that type II symptoms are related to structural changes rather than dopamine levels:
- *post-mortem* examinations of the brains of type II schizophrenics show that their brains are 6% lighter and have fewer neurons in the cerebral cortex,
- *PET and CAT* scans show that schizophrenics have larger ventricles, meaning that less space is occupied by neurons and smaller than normal frontal cortex.

③ **Known organic disorders**, such as brain tumours, which lead to psychotic states suggest an organic basis for schizophrenia.

Causes: environmental factors

① **A learned response: Bateson *et al.* (1956)** first proposed the *double-bind theory*. Schizophrenia is a response to mutually-exclusive demands being made on a child, neither of which can be avoided or satisfied. It is a learned response to impossible demands.

Laing (1959) also regarded schizophrenia as a sane response to a disordered environment. The *'divided self'* is a split between the person's internal and external worlds. Like Szasz, he claimed it was not an illness but a tendency that some people have which is exacerbated by certain 'pathological' families.

② **Triggers:**
- *faulty communication* within the pathological family,
- *stress* may aggravate a tendency towards schizophrenia. However, **Rabkin (1980)** found that schizophrenics do not report significantly more stressful episodes during the months preceding the initial onset of the disorder.

③ **Social drift or social causation:** schizophrenia affects the poor more than the rich. Is this because the illness has caused persons to sink to low socio-economic status (social drift) or because the socio-economic disadvantages of the lower classes cause schizophrenia? A survey of the entire state of New York by **Turner and Wagenfeld (1967)** confirmed the relationship between social class and schizophrenia, and found evidence for both social drift and social causation by looking at the schizophrenic's father's socio-economic status.

Treatments

The treatments for schizophrenia are:

- *biomedical:* drugs (neuroleptics) have lead to increasing de-hospitalisation,
- *psychotherapy:* it may be possible for patients to gain insight, particularly where symptoms have been alleviated with drugs,
- *family therapy:* for the 'schizophrenic family',
- *therapeutic communities:* these stress the positive aspects of the mental outlook and adapt the schizophrenic for social living,
- *outpatient treatment:* the increasing number of de-institutionalised schizophrenics need supervision to ensure they continue taking their medication, if for nothing else.

MOOD DISORDERS

Depression is the most common mental disorder, it may exist on its own or is often just one symptom of a more involved disorder.

Unipolar depression

Symptoms are similar but more intense than 'normal' depression:
- *emotional:* sadness, melancholy, self-involvement,
- *motivational:* passivity,
- *cognitive:* hopelessness, pessimism, lack of self-esteem,
- *somatic:* loss of appetite, weight and sleep disturbance.

On average chronically depressed patients recover spontaneously after about three months. About 10% of patients remain depressed.

Possible causes:
- *Genetic* causes seem unlikely. **Allen (1976)** found that MZ twins showed concordance for unipolar depression only 40% of the time. For bipolar depression the figure is a much higher 72%.
- *Viral:* **Amsterdam et al. (1985)** found that, when several hundred people were tested for Borna disease, a viral infection which causes, usually fatal, inflammation of the brain in horses and sheep, 12 tested positive and *all* of them were suffering from uni- or bipolar depressive disorders, suggesting that the virus caused the depression.
- *Neurochemical:* there is a possibility of depletion of noradrenaline leading to a loss of motivation. The fact that antidepressant drugs affect the availability of noradrenaline supports this finding. However, the activity is complex and not fully understood.
- *Brain anatomy:* there is evidence that depressed people have a relatively inactive left frontal cortex.
- *Triggers:* some forms of depression, such as post-partum depression, pre-menstrual syndrome and seasonal affective disorder, have been clearly linked with *hormonal* changes in someone who is predisposed to be depressive.
- *Environmental:* the 'learned helplessness' syndrome (see 7.6) has been used to explain how depression is learned. It is also invariably true that environmental stressors trigger episodes of depression, despite the fact that the person does not feel depressed about a particular thing (unlike 'normal' depression).

Treatment:
- *biomedical:* drugs, ECT,
- *psychotherapy:* counselling,
- *cognitive:* learning to take control.

Bipolar depression: manic depression

Symptoms:

The two phases (mania/elation and depression) may occur separately or oscillate over weeks and months with normal spells in between. Depression may be suicidal; elation is euphoric, hyperactive, sleepless; the person behaves in socially unacceptable ways and makes grandiose and unrealistic plans.

The syndrome is associated with creativity and its attendant grandiosity may lead to great achievements. Many successful and famous people (e.g. Winston Churchill and Abraham Lincoln) were sufferers; many top writers and artists experience serious mood swings. However, for most sufferers it is a crippling disorder which ruins their lives.

Possible causes:

- *Genetic:* **Gershon (1983)** looked at adopted persons with manic depression. Two per cent of their adoptive parents had the disorder whereas 30% of their biological parents had it. **Allen (1976)** found that MZ twins were more likely than DZ twins to both have manic depression (a 28% discordance rather than 60%).

- *Genetic and neurochemical:* the Amish, an American religious sect, were studied by **Egeland** *et al.* **(1987)**. They were able to identify part of chromosome 11 which was present in 63% of those with the disorder. Such a defect might lead to a lack of certain neurotransmitters (see 7.1). The gene responsible for production of adrenaline is also on chromosome 11.

- *Homeostatic trigger:* **Wehr** *et al.* **(1987)** have suggested that alterations of sleep phases (see 7.3) may set off an imbalance of homeostatic control between depression and mania, each swing wildly overshooting its mark.

- *Environmental:* the evidence indicates a genetic element, but this predisposition must be triggered by some other factors. **Allen's (1976)** study indicates that environmental factors are involved.

Treatment:

- *Biomedical:* sufferers are usually treated with Lithium for both mania and depression, though about 20% do not respond to this. It has serious side-effects.

ANXIETY DISORDERS

Phobias

Symptoms:

Extreme, persistent, irrational fear with lack of control, which is strongly out of proportion with the danger. Three categories are distinguished by DSM-IV:

- *Agoraphobia:* fear of going out and open spaces, often associated with panic attacks – the most common phobia.

- *Social phobias:* such as talking or eating in public, an exaggeration of fears we all have of being anxious in social situations.

- *Specific phobias:* such as zoophobias (animals) or nosophobias (fear of becoming ill). It is only a phobia when it interferes with normal functioning.

Possible causes:

- *Ego defence:* 'Little Hans' **(Freud, 1909a)** was one of Freud's classic studies of a little boy whose fear of horses stopped him leaving the house. Freud's interpretation of phobias was that anxieties are displaced onto the phobic object which symbolises the initial conflict, if the conflict is resolved the phobia will disappear. Hans had probably developed his fear through classical conditioning and it would have disappeared without Freud's intervention.

- *Classical conditioning:* 'Little Albert' was deliberately conditioned to fear furry objects (see 7.6, **Watson and Rayner, 1920**) as an evidence of the ability to condition emotional responses (CERs) or the learning of anxiety. It is likely that most phobias are learned through the association of trauma with some neutral stimulus.

- It may be that some fears, like zoophobias, arise through faulty learning, whereas more generalised fears, such as agoraphobia or nosophobia, reflect a more complex cause (see also panic disorders, p.249).

Treatments:

- *biomedical:* drugs to reduce anxiety,

- *psychotherapy:* insight into feelings and causes of anxiety,

- *cognitive:* reinterpretation of events,

- *behavioural:* unlearning the learned responses: systematic desensitisation, flooding, modelling, social skills training. These are the most commonly used methods with phobics.

Obsessive–compulsive disorder

Symptoms:

These are uncontrolled feelings, associated with seemingly senseless ritual as an attempt to control the feelings. Such behaviours are not dissimilar to the classic childhood game of avoiding the cracks in the pavement.

Possible causes:

Obsessions are a symbol of underlying, unresolved conflicts which provoke anxiety; the compulsion is a way of dissipating the anxiety. They are learned in a similar way to superstitions. **Freud (1909b)** described the 'Rat Man', who had obsessive thoughts about rats chewing at his intestines among other things. His real desire was to kill the grandmother of his girlfriend, whose ill-health meant the girlfriend left him. He displaced the rage onto himself, a more acceptable outlet.

Treatments:

- *psychotherapy:* to gain insight into impulses,
- *behavioural:* social skills training.

Panic disorder

Symptoms:

Anxiety is experienced but there is no specific feared object. Instead, there is unfocused 'free-floating' anxiety. An individual experiences intense apprehension and physical symptoms such as racing heart, shortness of breath, dizziness (acute emergency reaction).

Possible causes:

- *Genetic:* **Torgersen (1983)** found that 31% of MZ twins show concordance, whereas there is none for DZ twins.
- *Neurochemical:* panic attacks can be induced using sodium lactate. Drugs are effective in treating panic attacks. The spontaneous emergency reactions experienced by sufferers may be a neurochemical abnormality.
- *Cognitive:* these physical symptoms may be mislabelled as panic.

Treatments:

- *biomedical:* anti-anxiety and anti-depressant drugs,
- *cognitive:* **Beck (1988)** has pioneered a new therapy where patients are taught to see these symptoms for what they are, physical sensations and not panic.

Other panic disorders include:

- **Post-traumatic stress disorder:** a fear disorder set off by a specific event such as abuse or a major catastrophe, treated with psychotherapeutic methods.
- **Stuttering** (speech anxiety): **Olson and Ross (1988)** taught stutterers to attribute successful performances to a placebo treatment. They were told that a subliminal noise would relax them and improve their performance, and were thus able to restructure their cognitions and reduce stuttering.

DISASSOCIATIVE DISORDERS

In disassociative disorders some part of memory is disassociated from the rest.

Multiple personality

Symptoms:

In this condition more than one integrated personality exists in one person. Each personality separately takes control of functioning at different times and may not be aware of the existence of others. It is sometimes confused with schizophrenia, which may entail divisions within one personality but not separate personalities. It now seems that it may be more common than was once thought, and has been detailed in a number of books and films such as *The Three Faces of Eve* and *Sybil*.

Possible cause:

Its origins seem to lie in the experience of some emotional trauma around the age of five (about 97% of sufferers have suffered child abuse), the subject is usually highly susceptible to self-hypnosis and creates different trance states to cope with life's pressures. Having experienced relief from painful emotions once, this method is used again as a coping strategy so that some sufferers have developed as many as 17 personalities.

Treatment:

This is slow and difficult. The psychotherapist must come to some agreement between the existing personalities about who will survive. In some cases there is no resolution.

PERSONALITY DISORDERS

Personality disorders are essentially trait disorders. They are based on the assumption that people respond consistently in different situations (see 5.2, 'Situational theories of personality'). The ability to diagnose personality disorders has very low reliability and is relatively meaningless, with the exception of the Antisocial Personality Disorder, once called psychopaths or sociopaths.

Antisocial Personality Disorder

Unlike other illnesses, which are largely a matter of personal suffering or danger, the sociopath is perfectly self-content but a danger to society. The condition is associated with criminal behaviour. It is only diagnosed in those over 18 though one of the symptoms is antisocial childhood behaviours.

Symptoms:

- emotional flatness, lack of understanding for others,
- absence of conscience, childlike moral reasoning,
- inadequately motivated antisocial behaviour, i.e. senseless crime,
- originates in childhood as truancy, lying, theft and vandalism. These continue and become more serious in adulthood.

Possible causes:

- *Genetic:* **Christiansen (1977)** looked at over 400 pairs of twins and found concordance in 69% of the MZ ones compared with only 33% of the DZ twins. However concordance for opposite-sex DZ twins is 16%, which suggests a strong role for environmental gender-related factors.

- *Neurochemical:* **Lykken (1957)** used a 'mental maze', where subjects learn to press a correct sequence of levers, receiving shocks when the wrong one is selected. He found that sociopaths made more errors leading to shocks than 'normals', suggesting that their's was an inability to learn from painful experiences. **Schachter and Latané (1964)** found that, if all subjects were injected with adrenaline, sociopaths performed in the same way as normal subjects. In the placebo condition they made more errors leading to shocks. This supports the hypothesis that they are *under-aroused*.

- *Neuroanatomical:* this underarousal may be due to a dysfunction of the limbic system (involved in emotion) and to cortical immaturity. **Robins (1966)** found that sociopaths showed marked improvement later in life, possibly because their cortex finally matures.

- *Environment, learning:* the condition may result from an inability to learn from punishment, because of their underarousal.

- *Environmental deprivation:* sociopaths tend to grow up in emotionally tense low socio-economic status households.

Treatments:

- *imprisonment:* is ineffective because it only increases their contact with other criminals,
- *behavioural:* physical punishment is particularly ineffective with sociopaths; moderate, de-institutionalised punishment is most effective,
- *psychotherapy:* sociopaths usually lack the emotional maturity and sensitivity necessary for insight.

CONCLUSION REGARDING ALL MENTAL ILLNESSES

The kinds of evidence presented for the aetiology of mental disorder can be summarised in the following table:

Cause	Kind of evidence	Argument
GENETIC	twins:	concordance rates compared between MZ and DZ twins; since both share the same environment this supports a genetic link. However, it should be remembered that the environment is also more similar for MZ twins.
	adoption studies:	comparisons between adopted and natural parents, and the children.
	viruses:	viruses may alter DNA.
BIOLOGICAL	neurochemical	• effectiveness of drugs • presence/absence of neurochemical substances • hormones as a trigger.
	neuroanatomical:	anatomical brain differences.
	diseases:	of known organic origin, implying cause of similar mental disorder.
ENVIRONMENTAL	learned responses:	to neutral stimuli paired with trauma or negative reinforcement.
	deprivation:	socio-economic or emotional.
	stress:	acting as a trigger.

The last conclusion must be that mental illness appears to be the result of inherited and biological factors, which predispose certain people to become dysfunctional when exposed to particular life circumstances. However, the evidence is almost entirely correlational and only causal by analogy. It should be remembered that most mental disorders, in terms of overall frequency of occurrence, are non-serious and non-pathological.

One current approach to studying the aetiology of mental disorder is 'at risk' studies. **Hartmann *et al.* (1984)** did such a study with 1000 teenage boys, who were interviewed extensively. Over 20 years later they re-examined the same sample to see which of them had become schizophrenic. They were able to identify certain personality factors which were specific to those who became disturbed.

6.5 ATYPICAL DEVELOPMENT

In this section the whole range of developmental disorders associated with childhood will be examined, this includes physical as well as emotional and mental handicaps. Any discussion of childhood disorders is complicated by the fact that 'normal' development proceeds at different rates. What is normal at one age becomes abnormal later, for example bed-wetting or echolalia. Emotional disorders are a matter of degree rather than being qualitatively different. The same can be said of physical handicaps, which are not all-or-nothing states but continue from mild to severe disabilities.

Including atypical behaviour in a chapter on abnormal behaviour is perhaps questionable, but there are similarities between what is atypical and abnormal, such as: associated stigma, lack of statistical frequency, interference with normal functioning, similarity with normal behaviour and physical causation.

THE PSYCHOLOGY OF HANDICAP

Disabilities arouse strong stereotypes. The term 'invalid' represents a once dominant approach to the disabled as 'non-people' (not valid). It is an important area for applied psychology, yet not a popular examination topic, which is perhaps an indication of how people prefer to avoid it.

The World Health Organization defines:

- *disability* as 'the loss of physical or intellectual impairment as a consequence of...the loss or reduction of certain anatomical or physiological properties of an individual',

- *handicap* as 'the social and environmental disadvantage experienced by an individual as the result of a disability.' In addition, being a woman or a homosexual is handicapping in the wider sense of the word.

Severity of handicap

The relationship between physical disability and degree of handicap is not straightforward, a disability may become a handicap to a greater or lesser extent depending on many factors:

1. **A continuum of handicap:** disabilities represent one end of a continuum, from normal through mild to severe disability, only in the most extreme case is a person unable to function 'normally'. **Mild handicaps** often go unnoticed. A child with mild cerebral palsy or with high frequency hearing loss may simply be regarded as below average intellectually.

2. **Multiple handicaps:**
   - **Rutter *et al.*'s (1970)** Isle of Wight study found that 25% of the children with intellectual, educational, psychiatric or physical handicaps had more than one.
   - It is *difficult to diagnose* multiple handicap, e.g. someone with cerebral palsy may have a hearing loss which is difficult to detect. Lack of attention, poor performance, etc. may be attributed to the main handicap.
   - Handicaps can be *over-diagnosed*, e.g. a blind child may be labelled as mentally retarded because of slow cognitive development. The term 'dumb' was first applied to deaf children in this way.
   - Multiple handicaps *do not form a simple addition* of problems. Someone who is suffering from cerebral palsy may be able to cope reasonably, but the addition of a deprived home background may result in an individual who requires residential assistance.
   - *Secondary handicaps* develop as a direct or indirect result of the primary handicap, such as slow cognitive development. These are not to be confused with multiple handicaps.

3. **Individual differences** influence the psychological ability to cope:
   - **motivation:** some people view their handicap as a challenge,
   - **age and stage** of life,
   - **sex differences:** boys are more likely to be considered handicapped than girls (**Shakespeare, 1982**).

4. **The influence of the family and society (environment):**
   - *overprotection:* particularly by the family, encouragement of the 'sick role' (see p.253),
   - the *expectations of family, employers and educators* are influenced by social norms. Such expectations will influence individual performance (self-fulfilling prophecy) and decisions about future treatment (e.g. residential or self-care). Expectations may be too low or too high. **Ringness (1961)** found that the expectations of 40 mentally retarded children showed greater disparity with reality than groups of average and high intelligence children, probably because they are given an accepting and encouraging educational environment. Such unrealistic attitudes may eventually cause difficulties.

- *political and financial resources:* the amount of help which is made available.
- see also *loss of privacy*, below.

Psychological effects of handicap

1 Development of self-image:
- In the same way that the self-concept develops through interactions with others and as a consequence of their attitudes, the handicapped learn negative self-attitudes (see 3.4).
- The handicapped have far less access to role models with whom they can identify.
- For some it is not clear whether they belong to the 'handicapped' or the 'normal' population. Those in no-man's land may have difficulty with their identity. **Cowen and Bobrove (1966)** found that the totally disabled were better adjusted than those who had partial disabilities, because their group identity was clearer.

2 Communication: many handicapped persons have communication difficulties – verbal or non-verbal. The effect these have on social skills is crucial.

3 Person–environment fit:
- In terms of the community: in fast-moving, industrial, competitive settings a disability is more of an obvious disadvantage than in a rural community.
- In the home: a sport-oriented family would find it more difficult to adjust to a child with physical disabilities.

4 Prejudices:
- The negative attitudes of others play a major role, e.g. in employers' attitudes to hiring handicapped people, and in affecting the handicapped person's self-image (see above).
- **Sinson and Stainton (1990)** suggest that media images of handicapped persons which elicit pity tend to reinforce outdated stereotypes.
- Attitudes are changing, though still negative: from 1949 to 1964 the number of people believing that epilepsy was a form of insanity decreased from 65% to 26%. Studies generally report that half of those interviewed have negative attitudes towards the physically disabled **(Shakespeare, 1982)**.

5 Sense of control: many handicapped persons assume 'the sick role': expecting to be looked after, being absolved of responsibility, learned helplessness, relinquishing control for major decisions. If handicapped persons are given and take greater control, this may lead to improvements.

6 Loss of privacy: invasion of personal space may lead to stress and exacerbate ill health (see 4.2).

7 Labelling: there is some question about the extent to which labelling helps individuals. While they may receive more appropriate education and greater understanding they may also suffer some stigma and have their own self-image shaped by the labelling (self-fulfilling prophecy).

Ways of reducing the problem

Reducing the problem is of general interest because then the handicapped will become less of a financial and psychological burden to society. The sign of a civilised society is the care that it offers to all its members. There are a number of strategies:

- Give people the experience of being handicapped, e.g. blindfolded for a day.
- Provide information: **Cumming and Cumming (1957)** spent six months holding group discussions and films for the residents of a Canadian town, but found that change was resisted when a strongly-held view was challenged. See also **Sinson and Stainton (1990)** above.
- Personal contact: this may lead to increased negativity. If it arouses disturbed feelings it may produce a desire to avoid such situations in future; therefore it is important to ensure that any contact is a positive experience.
- See attitude change generally (2.3).

Personal and social problems in dealing with handicap

Both the sufferer and their immediate family must experience a series of adjustments, not dissimilar to bereavement. The degree of difficulty experienced is associated with coping skills, personality, social support available, the nature of the disability and the amount of impact it has on daily life.

Shontz (1975) described a sequence of reactions following the diagnosis of a serious illness:

1. *Shock*: being stunned, behaving in an automatic fashion and having a sense of detachment.

2. *Encounter reaction:* disorganised thinking, feelings of grief, loss, helplessness and despair.

3. *Retreat:* responding to loss with denial. However, the problems don't go away and reality demands coping strategies, although some avoidance may be useful in the early stages.

One difficulty for all disabled people is coping with the responses of others. People are frightened, for example, by epileptics, and often ostracise such people. Many jobs are closed to people with certain disabilities. They may be barred from acquiring some major skills, such as driving, which reduces their independence.

Strategies for coping with handicap

These are:

- *avoidance:* minimising the seriousness – prevents a person from being overwhelmed by the various implications,
- *seek information* about the problem and ways of treating it,
- learning to *take control,* e.g. the diabetic learning to give injections,
- setting *concrete, achievable goals* gives the patient things to look forward to,
- *recruit help* and emotional support,
- *talking* through the future and preparing for unexpected difficulties,
- finding *long-term meaning* for the experience. This may be provided by religion.

Examples of common disabilities

These can be categorised as:

- *birth defects:* due to genetic or uterine environmental influences, e.g. spina bifida, cerebral palsy, thalidomide, deafness from rubella,
- *chronic problems with onset during childhood:* e.g. epilepsy, asthma, diabetes, kidney disease,
- *accidental injuries and childhood illnesses:* e.g. head or spinal injury, polio, meningitis, cancers (leukaemia).

The details of four of these common disabilities are:

1. **Cerebral palsy:** a motor disability in which the individual has difficulty controlling the muscles of their arms, legs and/or head. It is caused by lack of oxygen (anoxia) often at birth, leading to brain damage, which particularly affects the motor cortex but also may affect other functions. Mild anoxia may have no long term consequences. The renowned Peto Institute in Hungary has had some success in helping impaired children to gain some motor control through a regime of rigorous training.

2. **Diabetes:** the pancreas stops producing sufficient insulin, which results in too much glucose in the blood. If untreated this leads to death. Treatment involves rigid eating patterns, dietary restrictions, daily glucose monitoring and, for some people, injections of insulin. This involves major changes to lifestyle and considerable psychological readjustment which may lead to anger, mourning, guilt, and feelings of flawed identity.

3. **Asthma:** a respiratory disorder often caused by an allergic reaction to, for example, pollen, dust and foods. Attacks may be aggravated by infections, weather, exercise or psychosocial factors such as stress. The symptoms include difficulty breathing, which

can be very frightening. In the US 4000 asthmatics die every year. Treatment often involves behavioural and counselling techniques, as well as the use of inhalers, which dilate the bronchial airways and help breathing.

4 **Epilepsy:** recurrent sudden seizures from electrical discharges in the cerebral cortex. The two most common forms of attack are: **grand mal**, which involves loss of consciousness and severe muscle contortions; and **petit mal**, which may simply be a person staring blankly and possibly some twitching. It is treated with anticonvulsant drugs, which are not totally effective. They may cause drowsiness and possibly long-term cognitive impairments. The split brain operation has been used with severe epileptics.

SENSORY DISABILITIES

Hearing impairment and deafness

Approximately one to two children in 1000 children have some hearing impairment, which increases with age. Ninety nine per cent of the hearing impaired have some degree of hearing. There are different causes, which may occur together:

- *Nerve deafness* (inner ear): damage to cochlea, hair cells or auditory nerve. This results in loss of a particular range of frequencies, usually the high ones. Hearing aids can compensate for loss. This type of deafness may be inherited; acquired in pregnancy from rubella; be a side-effect some diseases, such as multiple sclerosis; or may result from prolonged exposure to loud noise.

- *Conductive deafness* (middle ear): the bones of the middle ear don't transmit noise properly. This type of deafness is usually caused by infections. Some hearing remains because the cochlea is still functional and sound is transmitted through the skull. In some cases surgery may correct it.

- *'Glue' or sticky ear* (secretory otitis media): catarrh collects in middle ear of young children. This would drain naturally as the tubes get larger, but because it may have a negative effect on their cognitive development, it is therefore treated with surgically implanted grommets.

Other problems:

- *Language:* prelingual hearing impairment obviously affects language and leads to significant lag in verbal–educational skills. Early diagnosis is of great importance, as is provision of compensatory education and hearing aids.

  Non-verbal IQ scores for prelinguistically deaf children are consistently one standard deviation or more below normal (**Phelps and Branyan, 1990**).

- *Behaviour and emotional problems* arise as a secondary effect of attainment and adjustment problems.

- *Sign language:* this is a language in its own right but lacks some of the structures of English, which may affect thought processes (see Language and Thought, 1.3 and 4.1).

- **Covariance with many other handicaps is frequent:** visual, mental or learning disorders, for example. Any difficulties may not, therefore, simply be due to a hearing deficit.

Blindness

There is no internationally agreed definition for blindness. In the UK and US the statutory regulations specify limits for acuity and width of visual field. Considerations:

- *Age of onset:* some experience of sight makes learning very much easier. Congenital blindness may be due to cataracts. If these are surgically removed later in life patients are not able to 'see' immediately but have to learn the association between known words and their visual manifestations (see 1.1).

- *Developmental implications:* in the first year of life smiling is important for attachment and eye gaze is a part of pre-speech. Later blindness restricts learning opportunities leading to a developmental lag in motor, perceptual and cognitive capacities, e.g. conservation skills (see 3.2).

- *Social implications:* consequences for sociability stemming from problems with attachment and eye gaze. Parents must learn their blind baby's behavioural repertoire.

- *Braille* is a poor substitute for reading, which uses a wider visual field, and makes less demand on short-term memory. Scanning is faster and easier to learn. Tactually-presented information is slower to process, which obviously disadvantages blind pupils.

PSYCHOLOGICAL DISORDERS

The major clusters of childhood disorders are:

Developmental disorders	mental retardation, learning disorders, autistic disorder
Disruptive behaviour disorders	attention-deficit hyperactivity disorder, conduct disorder, oppositional defiant disorder (see 9.3)
Emotional disorders	separation anxiety disorder, avoidant disorder (shyness), overanxious disorder, childhood depression, phobias (see 6.3)
Habit and eating disorders	elimination disorders (e.g. bed-wetting), speech disorders (e.g. stuttering), anorexia nervosa, bulimia nervosa
Gender identity disorders	gender identity disorders, transsexualism

(from Rosenhan and Seligman, 1989, based on DSM–IV)

Mental retardation

This is a problem which affects 3% of children, more boys than girls. It is a lifelong economic burden and there is a high emotional cost to family and society. In part the difficulties are due to stereotypes. The American Association on Mental Deficiency list the defining criteria as:

- subaverage general intellectual functioning: two standard deviations below the mean on an IQ test (under 70),
- deficits in adaptive behaviour: lack of personal independence and social responsibility appropriate for age and cultural group,
- manifestation during the period from birth to age 18,
- sub-divisions: mild (55–69 IQ), moderate (40–54), severe (25–39), profound (below 25).

Possible causes:

- *Pathological condition:* due to genetic factors or disease, most commonly Down's syndrome and a number of metabolic disorders, such as phenylketonuria (PKU).
- *Cultural-famial retardation:* the most common cause, in conjunction with genetic and environmental influence.
- *Perinatal lack of oxygen* due to difficulties during birth.

Treatment:

- Language training.
- Remedial help in school. There is a continuing argument over whether these children are better served in separate schools or within the mainstream. For humanistic reasons children who can function in a normal classroom probably should. It helps them adjust to normal life, helps 'normal' children to better understand the problems of subnormality and reduces stereotyping.
- Genetic counselling: amniocentesis is used to detect the chromosomal abnormality to allow parents to choose whether to continue with certain pregnancies.

Details of specific causes are:

1 **Down's syndrome:** children have distinctive facial features (almond-shaped eyes, round face, superficially 'mongoloid') and often other physical defects, such as heart or gastrointestinal problems. They are usually very friendly and co-operative. Twenty five per cent do not live beyond their first few years. The cause is an extra chromosome, but the expression of this varies enormously so that cognitive impairment may be moderate to severe. The incidence increases with maternal, and possibly paternal, age. (1:1500 for women in their twenties, 1:40 over the age of 40).

② **PKU** (phenylketonuria): these babies are born with an inability to metabolise phenylalanine, an essential component of proteins. Levels of phenylalanine build up in the body and affect the central nervous system causing irreversible brain damage. It is caused by recessive genes. All babies are tested for PKU at birth. If the defect is found early enough, babies can be kept on a diet which controls the levels of phenylalanine and suffer no brain damage.

③ **Cultural–famial retardation:** when there is no clear injury or disease, retardation it is assumed to be a result of inherited low intelligence combined with environmental deficit (see 5.1). Various factors associated with low socio-economic status may cause or exacerbate the problem, such as fetal alcohol syndrome, smoking in pregnancy, low birth weight, malnourishment, poor health and lack of mental stimulation.

Specific learning disabilities

Educational tardiness is viewed as a psychological problem when age, IQ and background indicate that the child should be functioning at the expected level. A delay of more than two years is significant and the child needs help before secondary problems (such as behaviour disorders) compound the tardiness, though it is usually correlated with a host of other psychological symptoms.

The value of such a diagnosis has been questioned. Does labelling help or hinder a child?:

- While it may be possible to provide some remedial education scheme these are not always successful as many of the problems are outside the educational setting.

- The label of 'disabled' may set the child apart and remain with them for life.

- Many people feel that diagnosis is the same as cure, which is not always the case. The label 'dyslexia' explains that a person's failure to read is not due to stupidity but to some specific learning problem (see 9.3 on Dyslexia).

- Labels may be self-fulfilling. The sufferer is essentially told to accept their failure as a recognised disability. The intention is to make them feel better, the effect may be to remove any sense of control.

Autistic children

Literally 'self-orientation' – a term coined by Bleuler for schizophrenia. It is also used to denote a range of normal inwardly directed activities, such as autistic thought. *Infantile autism* is a pathological condition first recognised as a distinct syndrome by **Kanner (1943)**. It occurs in about three children per 10,000, boys outnumber girls 3:1, and is more common in high socio-economic status children (which may be because it goes unrecognised elsewhere or is labelled differently).

Characteristic behaviours:

- The primary diagnostic symptom is the lack of *social responsiveness*. Eye contact is avoided, there is an aversion to physical contact and there are communication deficits.

- *Withdrawn state:* the child shuts out, disregards and ignores anything from outside. There is a failure to develop normal *attachments*.

- *Linguistic impairments:* the child is mute or uses words in idiosyncratic ways, such as echolalia (to repeat and echo words) or pronominal reversals (to reverse the use of 'you' and 'I').

- *Stereotyped, bizarre ways of behaving:* including a fascination with and intense attachment for inanimate objects. Mechanical and repetitive behaviour, more interested in pattern than functional or imaginative play.

- *Poor response to change* in their routines or environment, e.g. temper tantrums if furniture is moved, insistence on taking the same route to school.

- *Abnormal response to sensory stimuli,* insensitivity some of the time to pain. Variation between excessive sensitivity to stimuli and no reaction.

- *Specific, limited intellectual abnormalities:* 'islands' of intelligence, generally perform poorly on verbal intelligence but often above average for spatial or rote memory, may be talented in music and drawing.

- The term may mistakenly be used to describe several different conditions. The symptoms vary widely, recovery rates differ and the evidence from experimental work is contradictory.

Possible causes:

- *Emotional refrigeration:* an early belief was that the parents are introverted, distant, intellectual and meticulous, which leads certain children to respond in an autistic way. **Bettleheim (1967)** suggested their behaviour was similar to children in concentration camps; in this case they were withdrawing from maternal hostility. However, it is unlikely that parents are the primary cause; to some extent their behaviour may be a reaction to a difficult child.

- *Emotional lack of response:* **Hobson (1986)** found that autistic children were far less able to match pictures of facial expressions to an emotion, and concluded that they have difficulty right from the start in distinguishing people from objects and attributing emotional states to other people. This would explain their lack of pretend play, and other deficits.

- *Cognitive view:* **Leslie and Firth (1990)** take performance on a false belief task as evidence that autistics lack metarepresentational (second order representation, representing something which is already a representation) ability. While a person is out of the room an item is moved from that person's basket to another basket. The autistic child sees this happen. The question is where will the person, now returned, look for the item? Autistic children find it hard to understand that one person can hold a different belief (metarepresentation) than themselves, and therefore say that the other person will look in the place where the object is hidden. **Baron-Cohen (1990)** uses the phrase *'mind-blindness'* to describe this inability to attribute mental states, both to other people and to themselves. He concludes from a review of other studies that a specific cognitive disorder may underlie the social and communicative disorder.

- *Neurological approach:* 30% of autistics develop epileptic seizures during adolescence. A similar number show abnormal levels of serotonin (a neurotransmitter involved in perception and memory). There is evidence of abnormal brain waves and some anomaly of endorphins and lowered sensitivity to pain. All this suggests a neurological basis to autism. The patchy intelligence and linguistic deficits would accord with some brain damage.

Treatments:

- *Behaviour therapy*: focuses on specific deficits, e.g. operant conditioning of vocalisations. **Lovaas (1987)** found that 47% of autistic children receiving intensive training achieved normal functioning by age seven compared with 2% of a control group receiving minimal institutional care.

- *Structured education:* eliminates many of the distractions used to 'entertain' normal children, such as words written in different colours.

- *Play therapy:* as used by, for example, **Axline (1947)**. This focuses on the emotional aspects of behaviour and aims to increase responsiveness through unconditional positive regard.

Enuresis (bed-wetting)

Some bed-wetting continues to be normal through childhood. However, it is a problem if it occurs more often than once a month. The cause may be physical but it is more usually related to anxiety. It tends to run in families, suggesting an inherited predisposition. It is also about twice as common in boys.

Treatment:

- *Bell and pad:* behaviour modification: the wet pad causes a bell to ring. This seems effective in about 90% of cases, though there is a relapse rate of 35%.

- *Dry bed procedure:* over the period of a few nights the child is roused hourly and taken to the toilet to establish the habit of waking and going to toilet. It is a more effective method than the bell and pad, though more involved.

Stuttering

This is another problem which is more common in boys (four times as common). Sufferers are often teased by peers, and teachers avoid calling on them. The social problems and continuing stutter lead to increased tension, which only exacerbates the problem.

Treatment:

- *Distraction:* the stutterer focuses on something else while speaking, e.g. syllable-timed speech using a metronome. Delayed auditory feedback distracts the speaker from monitoring the current speech.

Anorexia nervosa

This is literally 'nervous lack of appetite', and is associated with the deliberate restriction of calorie intake and considerable weight loss:

- It is largely a problem of middle-class, adolescent girls. It affects about 1% of all 12–18 year olds, 95% of those affected are women.
- Anorexics usually continue to see themselves as overweight and to resist food. **Crisp et al. (1992)** estimate around 10% mortality arising from complications and suicide.
- It is sometimes seen as a modern problem, however **Tolstrup (1990)** documents cases prior to 1600, when the condition was described in connection with religious life.

Possible causes:

- *pressure to conform* to body type, feminine stereotypes in the media and emphasis on dieting,
- *rejection of womanhood:* a means of warding off maturity and stopping periods,
- *autonomy:* sufferers may experience a general lack of control, therefore by becoming anorexic they are exerting control over their body. This may be related to parental expectations,
- *vulnerable to life events:* anorexics tend to be somewhat obsessive personalities, with low self-esteem and desire, and fear of own autonomy,
- *parental pressures:* such as private school, professional fathers, intelligence, career and academic pressures,
- disorder of hormonal system.

Treatment:

- *hospitalisation:* many continue to insist they have no problem and have to be forced to eat,
- *behaviour management,*
- *therapy:* to increase sense of control and acceptance of self.

Bulimia nervosa

A more common problem and probably more related to dieting. It is characterised by periods of bingeing followed by forced vomiting. It is estimated to affect 1–5% of the female population over 20:

- sufferers are unable to control their food intake and therefore purge as means of dieting,
- associated with depression,
- secondary problems arise from the persistent vomiting, e.g. tooth decay from the acid of the vomit.

Treatment:

- *counselling:* helping the bulimic to identify the situations and feelings which precipitate the desire to binge and teaching other techniques for coping with negative moods.

Obesity

A problem which often starts during childhood, though it is not strictly speaking a psychological disorder. It is a combination of a genetic tendency and a formation of habit.

Treatment:

- Short-term treatments have had reasonable success but over the long-term the best methods have de-emphasised weight loss as the main goal and focused on self-control more generally.
- Parental involvement is important.

6.6 SOCIAL AND ETHICAL ISSUES

The need to identify mental illness

We need to identify some people as mentally ill for:

- *Their protection:* where people are not capable of looking after themselves a caring society should provide care for them, in institutions, sheltered housing or other communities.
- *The protection of others:* some of the mentally ill are a danger to others, which gives society the right to enforce some kind of treatment on them, possibly incarceration.

The difficulties encountered in labelling a person 'mentally ill' are:

1. *Reliable diagnosis:* we will never have a totally objective and accurate system of diagnosis.
2. *Rights of the 'mentally ill':* once a person is labelled, they may be stigmatised for life.
3. *Rights of the public:* if someone has been diagnosed mentally disturbed do 'we', as a prospective employer or as a neighbour, have a right to know this? When a person applies to work with young children, should that person (or the 'authorities') be required to disclose any history of mental disturbance? Teachers are banned if they have a criminal record.
4. *A natural reaction:* the avoidance of those who are ill or deviant has important survival benefits, such as avoiding contagion in the case of illness and possibly the same is true for deviance.

Legal considerations

1. **Criminal insanity:** does it matter whether we 'excuse' some criminals on the grounds of insanity or 'diminished responsibility'? In British law the question of insanity is determined by whether the defendant was partially or wholly irrational at the time of the crime:
   - If the person is found to be insane they may serve an indefinite sentence in a mental institution. A plea of insanity may act against the defendant's interests. **Szasz (1974)** used the case of Joe Skulski to demonstrate the injustice of this. He was imprisoned indefinitely, for a relatively minor crime, because the district attorney declared him unfit to stand trial. He served a much longer sentence than he would have done if he had been considered sane. For this reason defendants are reluctant to enter a plea of insanity.
   - It could be argued that the reason why a patently insane person, such as Peter Sutcliffe, the Yorkshire Ripper, is not judged to be insane is that people need to blame someone. A verdict of insanity removes this satisfaction.
   - In the US a new solution has been increasingly adopted by individual states, the *GBMI verdict* (guilty but mentally ill), in which case the person is sent to a mental institution rather than a prison, but the question of whether the person has or has not any responsibility is side-stepped.
2. **Involuntary commitment and treatment:** it is possible for a person to be committed to a mental institution against their will, if they are judged to be a danger to themselves or others.

- A caring society tries to ensure the well-being of all its members. This includes occasions when that person may want to harm themselves.
- Equally, society wants to protect its members from those who are potentially dangerous.
- The fear is that this power to commit can be, and occasionally is, abused.
- In Britain, initial committal (called 'sectioning' because of the use of sections of the Mental Health Act) involves two professional people, usually the person's own GP and a social worker, and only lasts for a maximum of six months. The Mental Health Review Tribunal can be appealed to.
- Any sectioned patient can be given medication for three months and/or ECT if they give informed consent or a second independent medical opinion is obtained. Psychosurgery or hormone treatment requires the patient's consent. The use of hormones might arise in the practice of birth control.

Mad or bad?

There is an unexpected twist to the question of where to lay responsibility:

- If you label the illness as 'mad' and suggest that the person is suffering an illness, you remove responsibility and place the patient in the care of others, creating a potential victim. This approach works, at least to some extent, *if* there is a known cause and cure, though even then (as with genetic and neurochemical causes) the patient is an unequal partner.
- If you use the idea of 'bad' (or preferably maladapted) you hold the person responsible for their ills and make them responsible for resolving them (you got yourself into this mess, you get yourself out).
- The judgement 'bad' can also be applied to those who do the locking up. In the right hands locking up can be humane, not bad. But there is a potential for abuse and this gives it a bad name.
- Are some treatments bad? One reason given for the effectiveness of ECT and psychosurgery is that the patient sees it as a punishment. Are such treatments unethical because we don't understand how they work?

The problems of institutionalisation

1 The problems of institutionalisation:
- Many key legal trials have involved the patient's lack of right to appeal against indefinite incarceration.
- A person who has been cared for in an institution for a prolonged period becomes incapable of life in the real world.

2 The problems of de-institutionalisation:
- The theory of releasing mental patients into the care of the community (de-institutionalisation) is seen as enlightened social policy. It may work *if* there is adequate community care and it *depends* upon the continuing use of drugs.
- The practice of such a social policy has led to an increase in homeless persons.
- A similar issue exists in the educational world – should children with special needs be educated in separate institutions or integrated into normal schools?

Chapter roundup

Related material in other chapters:
- cognitive psychology (Chapter 1), includes learning theory, which underlies behavioural approaches;
- social psychology (Chapter 2) introduces attribution theory and practice, antisocial behaviour and the effects of the media;
- developmental psychology (Chapter 3) examines 'typical' development, maternal deprivation, the self and self-esteem;

- intelligence, personality and assessment (Chapter 5) describes theories and psychometric tests of intelligence and personality;
- biological psychology (Chapter 7) covers the effect of drugs on the nervous system, biological rhythms, homeostasis, emotion, anxiety and stress;
- animal behaviour psychology (Chapter 8) looks at evolution and ethological approaches to understanding normal behaviour;
- applied psychology (Chapter 9) examines some environmental influences on behaviour;
- research and design (Chapter 10) includes a discussion of ethics in relation to psychological practice.

Illustrative question

Jane is a fifteen-year old female with Down's syndrome. She is a pupil at a local school at which she enjoys using computers, playing hockey, singing and the company of boys.

Jane's condition was obvious at birth, but her parents never considered treating her differently from their other children. She was the first pupil with Down's syndrome to attend the school and now there are three other such pupils younger than her at school.

Jane has learned to read and write, she takes regular classes as well as some special education classes. Her parents report that she has a positive self-image, and is aware that she is different from most other children. Her classmates accept her most of the time though she does get teased and called names. Jane would like to find work when she leaves school, be independent and perhaps have children of her own.

(a) Describe problems Jane's peers and teachers might have had integrating Jane into school. (6 marks)

(b) Describe problems Jane might encounter in trying to realise her ambitions as an adult. (6 marks)

(c) Discuss, citing empirical evidence, how the cognitive development of a person who is mentally retarded may be affected by their self-image. (8 marks)

(NEAB, 'A', 1992)

Tutorial note

This question, like many from this area of the syllabus, tends to attract common-sense answers, particular where candidates have personal knowledge of Down's syndrome children. In order to score high marks answers must draw specifically on psychological theory and empirical research. This question is an example of one that draws on knowledge that you have but don't realise you have from many other areas of pscyhology, and therefore makes extra demands in an examination situation.

This question covers important issues: the attitudes and prejudices which we all hold about the mentally and/or physically disabled and how society might help change this.

Suggested answer

(a) There has been a move in this country to integrate those with special educational requirements into the mainstream. **The Warnock Report (1978)** suggested that decisions should be made based on each individual's needs. Some very seriously disabled children require special schools but others would benefit from integration into ordinary education. The **Education Reform Act (1988)** states that the **national curriculum** should be broad enough to cover most of the ability range. However, current pressures on the accountability of schools may mean that in practice teachers may not be able to devote sufficient time to this end of the spectrum.

From the point of view of the teachers, the incorporation of Down's syndrome children like Jane may stimulate them to develop more creative and flexible teaching methods. It will be necessary to enlist the help of specialist teachers for support and surveillance.

The presence of a child like Jane gives both teachers and the other pupils the chance to develop positive attitudes towards her disability based on understanding rather than prejudice.

For Jane, and children like her, who have some retardation, there are many benefits. An ordinary school offers better facilities to develop their potential, such as sports or library amenities, and a full range of school subjects. Perhaps even more importantly there is the opportunity to mix with ordinary children and learn the social skills necessary for survival in adult life. Since Down's syndrome children are particularly responsive to social stimuli they will be able to make good use of the human interactions.

However, there are many problems. Even given time, teachers may lack the specialist skills necessary to adapt the lessons to special needs. It is possible that resentment from other children may arise from the extra time spent on the Down's syndrome child and this could exacerbate their feelings of being stigmatised, undoing any positive effects of integration. Any initial problems would only serve to confirm the stereotypes held by the teachers and other children. A continuing self-fulfilling cycle would not benefit anyone.

(b) Most Down's syndrome sufferers spend their adult years in an institution because they are not able to be economically self-sufficient, particularly as such people are most often born to older parents who will eventually not be able to care for them. Jane's competence in reading and writing suggests that she might be able to find some work but might have to live in some form of institution.

It is unlikely that she would have children. This is because her children might inherit her disorder, but also because her inability to care for herself would lead carers to ensure that she didn't become pregnant. This is an important ethical question relevant to all mentally retarded adults in institutions.

From the point of view of health, 25% of Down's syndrome children don't survive beyond their first few years, largely because of associated congenital heart defects. Those who do survive may still have a number of other linked problems, such as disorders of the digestive system or cancers, particularly leukaemia.

Most Down's syndrome sufferers who survive until middle age almost invariably suffer from Alzheimer's disease, which, like Down's syndrome, is controlled by chromosome 21.

(c) The development of all people is affected by their self-image, in particular their self-esteem. The self-fulfilling prophecy is one way of explaining how a positive self-image can lead to successful performance. **Coopersmith (1968)** found that boys with high self-esteem were more confident and academically successful.

The social environment is important in developing a person's self-concept and self-esteem. **Cooley (1902)** suggested that our self-understanding (the looking-glass self) is developed through our perception of how others see us. This is supported by **Tizard and Hodges (1978)**, who found that Down's syndrome children reared in a residential setting scored lower on measures of play maturity than those at home, who have more social contact and toys. The importance of play for learning is supported by many psychologists, such as **Bruner** and **Vygotsky**. **Thompson et al. (1985)** found that Down's syndrome children did best when parents and others were persistent in their efforts to stimulate them and provide emotional support.

An important way of raising self-esteem is to place the mentally retarded in mainstream education, to increase their social and contact and raise their self-image by seeing themselves as more 'normal'. However, rubbing shoulders with ordinary children may also exacerbate the differences, because the disabled children may become more aware of their problems and may also be subject to teasing. This may serve to lower their self-esteem.

Question bank

Allow 45 minutes for each question.

1 How do definitions and classifications of abnormality influence society's response to abnormal behaviour?

(AEB, 'A', 1987)

Points: A thoughtful question, which combines a straightforward essay on abnormality with the effects this has on the way that people behaviour towards the mentally ill.

2 'Abnormal behaviour is not an illness but merely that which society regards as unusual or dangerous'. Discuss this statement in relation to criticisms which have been made of the medical model of abnormality.

(AEB, 'AS', 1992)

Points: The question is specifically aimed at the medical model, which should not be presented as all bad – it has made many positive contributions.

3 Discuss the practical and ethical implications of defining and classifying behaviour as abnormal.

(AEB, 'AS', 1991)

Points: A very obvious and frequently occurring question. Note that both practical *and* ethical implications are required. There is a danger of giving a pre-prepared answer, which may not always be entirely relevant.

4 Consider the following cases:
   (i) Dan is viewed by those who know him as a quiet, well-mannered man. However, one day, gripped by a sudden seizure in the temporal lobe of the brain, he throws a fellow worker out of a seventh floor window and kills him.
   (ii) Jane, a teenage girl, eats nothing at all for several days then gorges herself sick on chocolates, cakes and ice-cream for two hours, is violently sick then eats nothing for the next three days.
   (iii) Alison's religious principles forbid her from wearing make-up, eating meat or taking drinks which contain stimulants. Her school friends do all these things.
   (iv) Peter hears voices in his head, these voices are constantly criticising him and make him feel guilty. Peter believes people are out to kill him; he thinks that the television set controls his behaviour.
Discuss problems of defining normal and abnormal behaviour using the cases given above.

(NEAB, 'A', 1991)

Points: The cases are provided as an aid to discussion, but this should become a more wide-ranging look at the issue, not neglecting legal considerations.

5 Discuss some of the therapeutic approaches which may help in the treatment of phobic patients.

(AEB, 'A', 1987)

Points: Evaluation is implicit in the comparison of the various approaches.

6 (a) Outline what is meant by 'schizophrenia'. (6 marks)
   (b) Discuss **two** possible causes of schizophrenia suggested by psychologists and evaluate evidence supporting **each**. (14 marks)

(NEAB, 'A', 1991)

Points: A straightforward essay, which should include evaluation rather than just description.

7 Describe how different types of therapy may be applied to one type of problem behaviour. How might their effectiveness be determined?

(AEB, 'AS', 1989)

Points: The first part of the question is descriptive only; you should select a problem behaviour where many different kinds of treatment are used. The second part is a straightforward discussion of effectiveness but it must relate to the treatment you originally described.

8 Compare and contrast the psychoanalytic and somatic approaches used in the treatment of abnormal behaviour.

(AEB, 'A', 1990)

Points: Strangely, candidates sometimes misunderstand 'somatic', thinking it refers to behavioural rather than biomedical treatments. The 'contrast' aspect of the question is important for more than half marks and should include ethical considerations.

9 Describe and evaluate behavioural approaches used in the therapeutic treatment of abnormal behaviour.

(AEB, 'A', 1989)

Points: Again the evaluative component is essential and might draw on other approaches as a means of doing so.

10 Examine some of the controversies involved in diagnosing and explaining psychosis as a mental disorder.

(AEB, 'A', 1989)

Points: Psychosis is an old-fashioned umbrella term, but one which should be familiar to all candidates. The question is broad but must address the issue of controversy rather than diagnoses and explanation generally.

11 To what extent has research shown that handicap involves coping with a double disadvantage: the handicap itself and also societal responses that accompany it?

(AEB, 'AS', 1991)

Points: A difficult question, which attracts anecdotal answers. Look for psychological evidence to support the issues.

12 (a) A person born with the loss of a major sense is bound to be affected to a considerable extent. What, in your view, are the most serious adverse consequences for a person with the loss of a major sense? Choose **either** blindness or deafness to answer this question and justify your answer using empirical evidence. (12 marks)

(b) With reference to **either** blindness or deafness, examine evidence for 'compensation' of one sense by another. (8 marks)

(NEAB, 'A', 1991)

Points: Yet another question which attracts anecdotal answers. A good candidate can bring a whole range of psychological reasoning and evidence to bear on this question, others should avoid it.

13 (a) Outline the main features of:
(i) anorexia nervosa; (5 marks)
(ii) bulimia nervosa. (5 marks)

(b) Discuss the effectiveness of **two** different treatments for **one** of the above disorders. Make reference to empirical studies in your answer. (10 marks)

(NEAB, 'A', 1992)

Points: The question does not ask for theories of anorexia or bulimia, but only descriptions and treatments. Anecdotal descriptions of counselling should be avoided.

14 In 'A Code of Conduct for Psychologists' (1985), the British Psychological Society says that 'In all their work, psychologists shall seek to establish the highest ethical standards'.

Identify the major ethical constraints on the work of practising psychologists. Discuss the difficulties faced by psychologists involved in the treatment of abnormal behaviours in staying within these guidelines.

(AEB, 'AS', 1990)

Points: Reference should be made to the ethical guidelines in Chapter 10.

BIOLOGICAL PSYCHOLOGY

Units in this chapter:

Chapter overview

Biological psychology forms the bridge between psychological, physiological and genetic processes. The genetic elements will be discussed in Chapter 8. A strictly reductionist, materialist or behaviourist approach would take the view that all behaviour can be reduced to neurological and biochemical processes. Very few would claim that the physical is an illusion. The question is *how much* insight can be gained into behaviour and experience through a study of physiology? A recent development is the combined approach – the *biopsychosocial* perspective.

Philosophical background

In thinking about physical processes we have to make some reconciliation with our own sense of experience. Such dilemmas have plagued philosophy and psychology for centuries and are considered major philosophical issues.

1 **The mind and mental processes:** some psychologists dispense with these 'mental' concepts altogether (epiphenomenalists and materialists). Others are almost afraid of their connections with introspection as used by early psychologists; they threaten psychology as an objective science. However, the mind is something we all experience and a concept we all use. Therefore, it is important for psychologists to incorporate 'the mind' in their theories:
   - the processes carried out by the brain (see 7.1),
   - consciousness, and unconsciousness, (see 7.2),
   - the sense of being in the world (see humanist psychology, 5.2 and 6.2).

2 **Monism:** only *one* reality exists:
   - materialism: only the physical has reality, the mind is ultimately a function of the brain,
   - subjective idealism: only the mental realm has the reality, the physical world is an illusion,
   - phenomenalism: only ideas and sense impressions exist.

③ **Dualism, the mind–body problem**: in general, dualism is the position that two spheres have no bearing on the understanding of each other, many dualisms exist such as good–evil or subject–object. If the mind and the body exist, how are they connected?:

- interactive dualism (Descartes): the mind and body are separate but interacting. The nature–nurture dualism is usually formulated in terms of interaction,
- parallelism (Leibniz): mind and body travel on separate but parallel paths which are correlated. For every mental event there is a corresponding physical event, and vice versa. A familiar example is the Cannon–Bard theory of emotion,
- epiphenomenalism (Skinner): both exist but the only true causes are physical, the mind is a by-product. Because mental and physical events occur at the same time it is easy to be confused and think that mental events have been the cause.

④ **Determinism**: behaviour is predetermined by an internal or external force other than free will, as in the biological determinism of Bowlby or Freud, or the environmental determinism of the behaviourists.

⑤ **Reductionism**: a behaviour is *reduced* to its simplest elements. The opposite view is suggested by the Gestalt approach, which holds that the whole is greater than the sum of its parts, and that if you reduce things too much the units become meaningless.

Reductions can be rendered down to psychological constituents, as in Freudian theory, or to physical units, such as neurons, or computer analogies.

⑥ **Structuralism**: is the study of the relations among phenomena rather than the nature of the phenomena themselves, and the systems formed by these relations. This can lead to reductionism, as in the case of Wundt, who held that all mental experience could be viewed as blends of simple processes, in this case revealed through introspection.

Structuralism need not be reductionist. Piaget suggested a system based on mental structures (stages). Freud's personality theory is based on structures such as the ego and id. (Structuralism and functionalism are important perspectives in sociology, along with interactionalism, Weberian, and Marxian explanations.)

⑦ **Functionalism**: stresses the analysis of behaviour and mind in terms of uses rather than their contents. It is not a physical solution, for example, artificial intelligence puts explanations in terms of functions rather than proposing a physical basis. Evolutionary explanations are functional.

⑧ **Gestalt school of psychology**: emphasis on the whole rather than the parts (see 1.1).

7.1 THE NERVOUS SYSTEM AND BEHAVIOUR

The nervous system comprises of all the structures and tissues of the body made from neural tissue. It contains about 12 billion nerve cells (neurons). About ten times as many glia cells perform a variety of supporting functions including nutrition, waste removal and filling the spaces of dead neurons. The neurons are bathed in cerebrospinal fluid, which is filtered from the blood and collects in the cavities of the skull and spine.

Nervous impulses (messages) are relayed by electrical potentials in the case of the neurons themselves, but chemical substances (neurotransmitters) relay the signal across the gaps (synapses) between neurons. Hormones are another form of chemical messenger; they are transported in the blood.

THE STRUCTURE OF THE NERVOUS SYSTEM

The Central Nervous System (CNS)

① Forebrain: the forebrain comprises:
- *thalamus:* great relay station of the brain, receives sensory data, performs some processing before passing on to the cerebral cortex,
- *hypothalamus:* integrates the activity of the **autonomic nervous system** (ANS) (see below), motivation, homeostasis and stress,
- *pituitary gland:* controls hormonal secretions and other ANS glands,
- *pineal gland:* an endocrine gland which controls bodily rhythms,
- *cerebral cortex:* responsible for higher order thinking. It is not very important in lower animals but in man it accounts for 50% of the nervous system. It is divided into two halves (hemispheres) joined by fibres (the corpus callosum); each half has four lobes:
  - *frontal cortex:* controls fine movements,
  - *parietal cortex:* touch information,
  - *temporal cortex:* hearing, and other functions,
  - *occipital cortex:* primarily responsible for vision,
- *limbic system:* a collection of structures important in emotion and motivation, incorporates parts of the cortex and hypothalamus. It also includes the hippocampus and amygdala, which are involved in certain aspects of memory.

② Midbrain: a small area connecting the forebrain to the hindbrain:
- *reticular activating system (RAS):* sleep, arousal and attention. The ascending system (ARAS) sends signals to the cortex; the descending system (DRAS) sends signals down the spinal column.

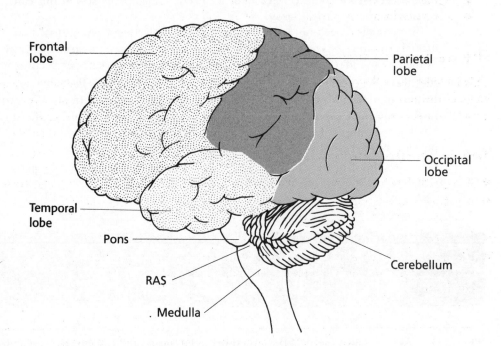

Fig 7.1 A lateral (side) view of the brain

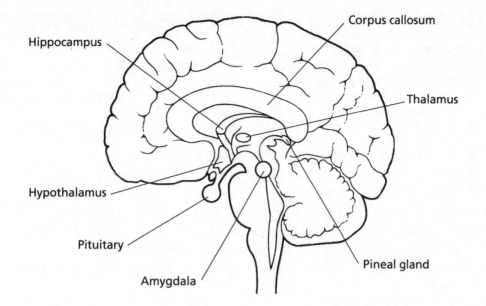

Fig 7.2 A simplified cross-section of the brain, showing important subcortical areas

3 Hindbrain:
- *medulla* (brain stem): the 'vital centre' controlling heartbeat, breathing and blood pressure. It connects the spinal column to the higher brain,
- *cerebellum:* controls movement,
- *pons:* possibly related to sleep.

4 Spinal cord:
- conducts messages to and from the brain,
- integrates many complex reflexes without the mediation of the brain.

The peripheral nervous system

This includes the ANS (below) and the **somatic nervous system** (soma = body), which includes the nerves from the sense organs and those to the voluntary muscles. Involuntary muscles, such as the stomach and heart, are controlled by the ANS.

The autonomic nervous system (ANS)

- it is called 'autonomic' because many of its functions are *self-regulating* or *autonomous*,
- it produces effects through direct neural stimulation or stimulating the release of *hormones* from endocrine glands (see below),
- it is largely controlled by the *hypothalamus*,
- it consists of two divisions: the **sympathetic** and the **parasympathetic** nervous systems, which work in a correlated but antagonistic fashion to maintain internal equilibrium:

Effect on:	Sympathetic	Parasympathetic
	(activates internal organs for vigorous activities and emergencies, 'fight or flight')	(conserves/stores resources, monitors the relaxed state: digestion and metabolism)
digestive processes	inhibits	promotes
liver	sugar is released	sugar is stored
pupils	dilates	constricts
saliva	inhibits (mouth feels dry)	stimulates
heart beat	accelerates	slows

Effect on:	Sympathetic	Parasympathetic
respiration	increases	slows
temperature	cools (activates sweat)	returns to normal
bladder	relaxed (some loss of control)	contracted

- it generally governs motivational and emotional behaviour.

The endocrine system and hormones

- a collection of ductless glands, controlled by the ANS, which secrete **hormones** directly into the blood,
- hormones are chemicals which profoundly affect behaviour and development,
- hormones are present in very small doses and the individual molecules have a very short life, so their effects quickly disappear if not secreted continuously,
- their action is rapid but slower than the nervous system because they are transported by the blood.

The main endocrine glands:

- The *pituitary gland* in the forebrain. Controls much of the endocrine system by producing hormones itself. Growth hormone, prolactin (responsible for milk production), oxytocin (which acts on the uterus), vasopressin (which acts on the kidneys and controls blood pressure) and trophic hormones (which target the adrenal gland, thyroid and gonads), are all produced by the pituitary gland.
- *pineal gland:* in the brain. Secretes melatonin, which regulates sleep,
- *adrenal gland:* located just above the kidneys. Consists of:
  - the *adrenal cortex:* secretes glucosteroids, mineralocorticoids, and sex steroids. It is important in homeostasis, appetite, water and sugar balance,
  - the *adrenal medulla:* produces epinephrine (also called adrenalin) and norepinephrine (noradrenalin), which are associated with arousal of the ANS and also act as neurotransmitters,
- *thyroid gland:* controls metabolism and growth,
- *parathyroid:* responsible for calcium deposits,
- *pancreas:* produces insulin,
- *gonads* (ovaries or testes): promote and maintain secondary sexual characteristics. Control menstrual cycle and pregnancy,
- (The *exocrine* system comprises glands with ducts which empty into, for example, the digestive system or sweat glands.)

NEURAL AND SYNAPTIC ACTIVITY

1 Neurons:
  - *sensory or receptor cells* (temperature, touch, taste, hearing, light): must convert environmental stimuli into the electrochemical activity of the neurons (sensory transduction),
  - *motor or effector cells:* muscles or glands, which secrete chemicals (neurotransmitters or hormones) to stimulate or relax the muscles,
  - *neurons:* generally connect receptors to effectors, may be several metres long,
  - each neuron ends in numerous *dendrites*, so that each neuron has a multiplicity of connections,
  - *electrical activity:* is created by changes in the concentration of sodium and potassium ions across the membrane of the axon,
  - *a nerve:* is a bundle of neurons.

2 Synapses:
  - Synapses are the junctions between nerve cells – a 200 angstrom gap.
  - **Neurotransmitters** are released from presynaptic vesicles when these are stimulated by an electrical signal. The receptor site of the adjoining dendrite is excited or inhibited by the action of the chemical.

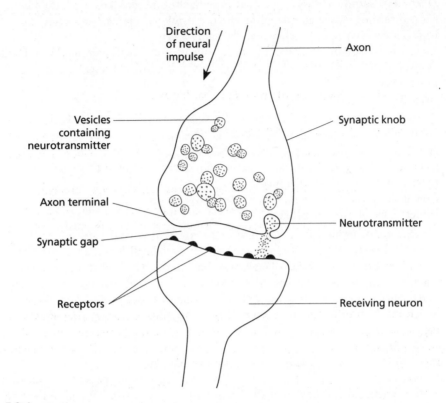

Fig 7.3 A synapse

- A single release of neurotransmitter is usually insufficient for a response *(subthreshold)*. To achieve sufficient stimulation to trigger a nervous impulse (the *threshold*) there needs to be a release of neurotransmitter from:
    - more than one dendrite *(spatial summation)*, and
    - within a certain time frame *(temporal summation)*.

3 Neurotransmitters:
- each cell produces and responds to more than one type of neurotransmitter. It used to be thought that they were specific to only one transmitter, but recent research has indicated a more complex picture **(Julien, 1992),**
- each neurotransmitter has a variety of effects, depending where it is injected, e.g. acetycholine variously induces drinking, aggression or tremor,
- the main transmitter substances (there are more than 40) are:
    - *acetycholine:* among its actions is the stimulation of parasympathetic muscles,
    - *dopamine:* also released by the hypothalamus as a hormone,
    - *serotonin:* involved in sleep,
    - *epinephrine* and *norepinephrine:* hormones of the sympathetic ANS as well as neurotransmitters,
    - *GABA* (gamma aminobutyric acid): has an inhibitory action that seems to decrease anxiety among other things,
    - *endorphins* and *enkephalins:* neuromodulators that relieve pain by inhibiting neurons which produce substance P.
    - *catecholamines:* a term referring collectively to epinephrine, norepinephrine and dopamine, which are chemically related.

METHODS USED TO INVESTIGATE THE BRAIN AND ITS INFLUENCE ON BEHAVIOUR

1 Methods involving deliberate damage:
- *Ablation:* removal of a section of the brain, e.g. removing the reticular activating system (RAS) from cats which would cause them to sink into a deep coma and not wake up. See **Lashley (1950)** (1.5), who removed large sections of the cortex from cats.
- *Lesions:* cutting and therefore functionally destroying a section of the brain.

- *Drugs:* **Grossman (1964)** found that norepinephrine injected into a rat's brain elicited feeding, while acetylcholine elicited drinking. He demonstrated that transmitters have specific effects at the same location.
- *Implanting electrodes:* to detect the behaviour of individual neurons. **Hubel and Wiesel (1962)** demonstrated (with cats) that individual neurons had specific functions (see 1.1).

Problems:

- Cannot be certain that the primary cause has been located. If you sever a person's vocal chords they cannot speak. However, this does not mean that the vocal chords are central to the process of speaking.
- Cannot be sure that the damage caused in surgery is limited to specific parts, there may be other minor injury.
- Conclusions drawn from animals may not always generalise to humans.
- Ethical controls are important.

❷ Observations of behavioural change resulting from brain injury or illness:

- *Accidental damage:* one of the inspirations for prefrontal lobotomy came from the case of an American, Phineas Gage, who had a crowbar fired through his skull when working with explosives. Miraculously he survived, but underwent major personality change. Another example is damage to Broca's and Wernicke's areas which result in different language problems, arguing for localisation of function (see 4.1).
- *Brain operations:*
  - *prefrontal lobotomy:* used to relieve intolerable pain.
  - *split-brain* (see details below): observations of split-brain patients demonstrates the functional asymmetry of the brain with respect to verbal and non-verbal tasks.
- *Brain illnesses:* X-ray scanning techniques can examine the brains of stroke patients and associate inactive areas with deficits.
- *Post-mortem examinations* of the brain of persons suffering from known disorders. For example, the brains of schizophrenics have been found to be about 6% lighter than the brains of other mental patients. The particular problem with this evidence is it is not clear whether the damage was a cause or effect.

Problems:

- It is difficult to know the exact nature and extent of an injury.
- It is not usually possible to make before-and-after comparisons of patient, therefore there is no control for individual differences.
- Again, cannot be certain whether primary or peripheral cause identified.

❸ Effects of chemicals:

- *Drugs:* for treating mental illnesses. For example, schizophrenics are helped by drugs which block dopamine. On the other hand, drugs which stimulate dopamine production can cause temporary psychoses. Both observations suggest a chemical basis for schizophrenia (see also section on drugs below).
- *Diet:* if a person eats high or low concentrations of certain things which are precursors of neurotransmitters, this will effect neurotransmitter production. For example, acetycholine is synthesised from choline. Eating foods rich in choline (cauliflower, peanut butter, liver, egg yolks) leads to a brief increase in acetycholine levels in the brain.

Problems:

- It is difficult to prove the precise effect of any drug, particularly as it is never exactly the same from one person to the next.
- Most drugs have more than one effect.

❹ Techniques with no side effects:

- *Temporary lesions:* sodium amytal, an anaesthetic, can be used to deactivate a hemisphere for short periods in a fully conscious patient.
- *Electrical stimulation:* **Penfield (1955)** produced recollections of specific memories (see 1.5).
- *EEG* (electro-encephalogram): electrodes attached to the scalp detect general electrical activity. This is relevant to states of awareness.

- *Tomography:* tissues are radioactively labelled. The neurons functioning in the brain at any one time take up more radioactively labelled matter than the neurons that are not functioning. It is therefore possible to detect tumours, or simply more active parts of the brain. Used with computer assisted tomography (CAT) and postitron emission tomography (PET) scanning techniques.
- *X-ray photographs:* CAT and PET scans are taken from various angles to build up a 3D structure. These reveal, for example, that schizophrenics have larger than normal ventricles. A more unusual application is to study the development of the human brain, e.g. frontal lobes do not show much activity until 7 months. X-ray photography is also used in nuclear magnetic resonance imaging (NMR).
- *Neurospinal fluid, blood and urine:* these are checked for traces of chemicals. For example, large amounts of cortisol in urine indicate stress.

LOCALISATION OF FUNCTION

Phrenologists claimed that there was a clear relationship between specific brain areas and particular mental functions, and that if a particular function was well developed so too would be the functional area, and that this could be 'read' on the skull. Such practices are now discredited as are phrenologists' maps.

The opposite position, of almost no localisation of function, assumes that almost any area can take over a function if necessary (**equipotentiality**).

1. **Memory: Lashley (1950)** thought that memory deficit was related to the amount of cortex removed, not to the areas removed (*laws of mass action* and *equipotentiality*). However, **Penfield (1955)** showed by electrical stimulation that memory had specific locations. However, these localisations are formed with experience rather than being predetermined areas.

   Tulving (1989) recorded the case of K.C., who suffered brain damage to specific areas, which led to a loss of semantic but not episodic memory (see 1.5).

2. **Language:** in general the left and right hemispheres take on specific functions related to language (see Lateralisation of function, below). However, this is by no means fixed and, even in adults, can change (see 4.1).

3. **Vision: Holmes (1939)** noted that First World War servicemen who had shrapnel injuries to the back of the head suffered from blindness in parts of their visual field, which demonstrated the functional localisation of visual interpretation.

4. **Plasticity:** is the ability for the nervous system to regenerate or reorganise beyond the normal developmental (critical) period after injury or environmental change. Children show less dominance by one or other side of the brain, and certain areas of the brain are capable of generating new neurons even after maturity. Dendritic branches can grow or retract, thus forming new connections. In healthy, alert older people there is increased growth of dendrite branches to compensate for the loss of neurons, whereas senile people have shrunken dendrites (found from post-mortem examination).

   Levy *et al.* (1992) detail the case of a 3-year-old with a massive left hemisphere lesion who nevertheless appears to be developing normal linguistic function, supporting the plasticity model.

   The **Kennard principle (Kennard, 1938)** states that it is easier to recover from brain damage earlier rather than later in life. In fact, recovery depends on location, type and extent of damage, as much as on age. For example, young children suffer more than adults when infection, inadequate oxygen or diet disrupts the organisation of developing neurons (**Kalat, 1988**).

LATERALISATION OF FUNCTION

1. **Cerebral dominance:** each hemisphere controls the opposite side of the body. In a right-handed person the left hemisphere is dominant.

2. **Non-lateralised functions:** sensory, motor and perceptual functions are represented equally in both hemispheres. Sight and hearing are both lateralised (e.g. the right eye has connections to the same side, the right visual cortex) and crossed-over (e.g. the right eye also has connections to the opposite side, the left visual cortex, and the same is true for the left eye).

③ **Language specialisation**: language is generally located in the left hemisphere, whereas the right side is dominant for non-verbal activities related to imagery or artistic expression, and for spatial skills. However, for left-handed people this may be reversed.

④ **Split-brain studies**: if the fibres connecting the two cerebral hemispheres (the corpus callosum) and the optic connection are cut, it creates two functionally independent brains. This procedure is used in patients suffering from severe epileptic seizures. **Sperry and Gazzaniga (1967)** typically placed such a subject behind a screen with their hands free to handle objects unseen. If a word was flashed to left side of the screen it was 'seen' by the right hemisphere only. This is because the left visual fields of both eyes are processed by the right visual cortex (see 1.1). If the subject was asked to pick up the object they could only do this with their left hand (controlled by the right hemisphere), and could not say what the object was, thus demonstrating that their language centres were on the left side of the brain.

NEUROTRANSMITTERS, DRUGS AND BEHAVIOUR

① **Evidence from behaviour abnormalities:**

Disorder	Neurotransmitter or neural location	Effect	Symptoms
Parkinson's disease	dopamine	degeneration of neurons producing it	tremor and rigidity of the limbs
Huntington's chorea	acetycholine and GABA	degeneration of neurons producing it	abnormal involuntary movements and cognitive deterioration
Alzheimer's disease	acetycholine	degeneration of neurons producing it	senile dementia
Korsakoff's syndrome	thalamus	neurons destroyed through thiamine deficiency	memory deficiencies
Schizophrenia	dopamine	receptors are over-sensitive	see 6.4
Gilles de la Tourette's syndrome	dopamine	receptors are over-sensitive and over-respond to dopamine	symptoms ranging from facial tics to uttering obscene words uncontrollably

② **Evidence from the effect of drugs:**
- drugs modify ongoing processes,
- all neurotransmitters, and therefore drugs, have multiple effects. For example, movement, arousal, alertness. Therefore any drug will have a range of side-effects.
- drugs have different effects at low and high doses,
- people react differently to drugs and therefore there are no certainties.

Julien (1992) lists the following classes of drugs, given with some examples:

Class	Drug e.g.	Neurotransmitter or neural location	Effect	Effect on behaviour
Non-selective CNS depressants	barbiturates and injected general anaesthetics	RAS and neuron thresholds	depressed	reduces nervous activity and lowers cortical arousal
	centrally-acting, inhaled general anaesthetics	RAS and nerve membranes (lipids)	depresses and blocks nervous transmission	loss of consciousness, overdose results in respiratory failure
	alcohol	inhibitory synapses	depresses	elation, long-term shrinkage of dendrites leading to memory loss
Anti-anxiety (minor tranquillisers)	benzodiazepines, Valium	GABA	promotes release	relieves anxiety

Class	Drug e.g.	Neurotransmitter or neural location	Effect	Effect on behaviour
Psychostimulants	caffeine	dopamine and serotonin	affects release	arousing at cellular level
Anti-depressants	tricyclics	acetylcholine	blocks receptors	increases arousal, creating generally pleasant feeling, followed by rebound effect (see below)
Mood stabilisers	lithium	norepinephrine and serotonin	decreases release	does not affect normal persons
Narcotic agents	heroin, morphine, codeine	endorphins	mimic natural processes	relieves pain
	placebos	endorphins	mimic natural processes	see 7.7 on pain
Anti-psychotic agents (major tranquillisers)	chlorpromazine	dopamine	blocks receptor sites	strong side effects, e.g. Parkinsonism
Hallucinogens	cannabis	norepinephrine	releases	moods or emotions
	LSD, angel dust, PCP	serotonin	blocks receptor sites	inhibits thought processes and emotions
Neurological drugs	non-narcotic, peripherally-acting analgesics, e.g. aspirin	endorphins	block pain receptors	relieves pain (see also placebos)
	local anaesthetics, e.g. procaine	sodium ions	paralyses electric potential in region where administered	affects sensory and motor neurons, no pain and muscle paralysis

Many of the psycho–active drugs listed above achieve their effects by modifying **neural transmission**, either inside or outside the CNS. **Kalat (1988)** classifies drugs according to the ways they affect synapses, some examples are given below:

Effect of drug on synapse	Example	Some effects
Mimics the effect of a neuro-transmitter by stimulating the receptor of a *post-synaptic* cell	nicotine stimulates one kind of acetycholine receptor	increases heart rate, arouses cerebral cortex
Stimulates the release of a transmitter from its storage in the *pre-synaptic* neuron	amphetamine increases the release of norepinephrine	*rebound effect*: the brain is unable to resynthesise new transmitter fast enough, so after a few hours the opposite effect is felt. In the case of amphetamine, depression often occurs after the initial euphoria
Slows the presynaptic neurons' reuptake of the transmitters it released	cocaine blocks the reuptake of norepinephrine and dopamine	prolongs the effect of the transmitter on the post-synaptic cell
Interferes with an enzyme which usually deactivates transmitters after they have stimulated the post-synaptic receptor	nerve gas destroys the enzyme which breaks acetycholine down	prolongs the effect of the transmitter
Inhibits the reactions necessary for the production of a particular transmitter	AMPT (alpha-methyl-paratyrosine) inhibits conversion of tyrosine to L-DOPA	decreases production of norepinephrine and dopamine
Blocks the receptors for a particular transmitter	curare blocks acetycholine receptor sites	paralysis as long as drug is present; if breathing maintained artifically the person can recover
	ergot (a fungus) blocks serotonin receptor sites	may have been cause of Salem witchcraft episode because the girls had eaten mushrooms containing ergot

Effect of drug on synapse	Example	Some effects
Attaches to a receptor and modifies the sensitivity of a neighbouring receptor	benzodiazepine attaches to receptors adjacent to GABA receptors	increases sensitivity of GABA receptors

7.2 STATES OF CONSCIOUSNESS

'Consciousness' in psychology has had a chequered history. It is a matter for subjective rather than objective observation (introspection) and was therefore popular with early psychologists and philosophers. However, it was rejected as an unnecessary concept by the behaviourists ('epiphenomenal flotsam of bodily activity'). Many psychology textbooks still ignore it, yet human behaviour cannot be fully explained without some reference to it.

What is consciousness?:

- a subjective thing, it is the sense of 'I' that each of us experiences,
- covers a wide range of qualities from awareness of a sound to awareness of philosophical issues. The more recent use of the term 'states of' is an attempt to compensate for this lack of differentiation,
- related concepts are the mind, awareness, soul, self,
- it is a fundamental distinction between man and other animals. Animals may have self-awareness or even self-recognition. Although these are necessary, they are not sufficient conditions for consciousness.

Consciousness has three levels:

1 Conscious: the individual is capable of:
- *self-awareness:* monitoring themselves and their environment, having sensations, responses, thoughts and emotions,
- *self-control:* which implies free will and moral 'consciousness' (conscience).

2 Preconscious: information at the edge of consciousness which can be made conscious if desired. For example, the cocktail party phenomenon (see 1.4) which shows that processing occurs outside consciousness, and automatic skills (see 1.4) such as driving or the Stroop effect. The **subconscious** is a less precise term for a similar thing, and tends to have more Freudian connotations.

3 Unconscious, lacking in awareness either:
- *loss of:* is a coma-like state, as in 'he lost consciousness',
- *not conscious:* as in 'I was not conscious of it', in a sense which is not even pre-conscious. A person speaks grammatically but may well not be 'conscious of the rules',
- **psychoanalytical:** refers to repressed thoughts and memories. Unconscious awareness is essentially a contradiction.

Measuring states of consciousness

The **electro-encephalogram (EEG)** measures general activity of the brain and shows different patterns in relation to different levels of consciousness. Each individual has a unique pattern, and there are differences related to age and some neurological conditions. The subject has about six electrodes fixed with glue to the scalp. The recording which is produced shows certain characteristic **waves**, whose frequencies are expressed in cycles per second (hertz):

- alpha: calm and relaxed,
- beta: alert and aroused,

- delta: sleep, infants, adults with tumours,
- theta: children under five, psychopaths and possibly associated with memory storage processes and frustration.

SLEEP

Sleep is not unconsciousness, it is an altered state of consciousness such that there is a decreased responsiveness to the external environment. It is a bodily rhythm, it occurs daily (circadian; see 7.3) and has distinct stages (ultradian see 7.3).

Why?

There are two theories of sleep; which need not be mutually exclusive:

1 **The repair and restoration theory**: during sleep various physiological and/or psychological states are recovered. During slow wave sleep (see p.279) the body makes repairs, such as removing waste products and replenishing the supply of synaptic transmitters. During rapid eye movement (REM) sleep (see p.279), it may be that, for example, memory is consolidated and dreams serve to sift through personal experiences.

   If this was the only function of sleep we would expect to observe:
- Detrimental effects of sleep deprivation (see p.279).
- Increased sleep following great physical exertion. **Shapiro** *et al.* **(1981)** found that marathon runners did require extra sleep, whereas **Horne and Minard (1985)** tried to exhaust their subjects with numerous activities and found that they went to sleep faster but not for longer.
- Metabolic processes increasing at night. There is increased production of growth hormone and increased protein synthesis, particularly in REM sleep.

2 **The evolutionary theory**: explains sleep as an **adaptive** response to environmental and internal demands, akin to hibernation. Animals have evolved an innate programme to:
- protect them at times of danger (such as darkness or daylight),
- protect them from excessive wear and tear,
- conserve energy by limiting metabolic requirements.

If this was the only function of sleep we would expect:
- An inverse relationship between the time needed to search for food and the time needed for sleep. This is true for cows which graze all the time and sleep little; cats eat rapidly and sleep a lot.
- That animals likely to be attacked will sleep little and lightly. This is also largely true except that, taken to its logical conclusion, some animals shouldn't sleep at all to ensure their safety. The fact that all animals sleep means that that there must be another purpose for sleep. (Beware of evolutionary arguments which sound as if the animal has made some deliberate choice about behaviour, the 'choice' is made through natural selection of the fittest.)

Empirical and other data about sleep

1 Stages and cycles of sleep and wakefulness:

Stage	EEG recording		Behaviour
Relaxed, awake	alpha waves, 8-12 hertz, synchronised		
REM sleep	theta activity		associated with dreams
1	desynchronised		transition to deeper state
2	sleep spindles, k-complexes	slow wave sleep, synchronised	progressively harder to awaken though personal sounds (baby crying) still heard
3	delta waves, 1–2 hertz		
4	more than 50% delta waves		

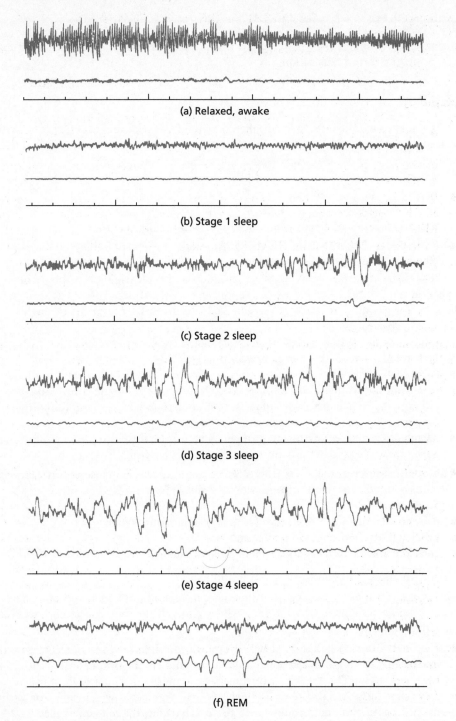

(a) Relaxed, awake

(b) Stage 1 sleep

(c) Stage 2 sleep

(d) Stage 3 sleep

(e) Stage 4 sleep

(f) REM

Fig 7.4 EEG recording showing brain activity (top lines) and eye movements (bottom lines) associated with the five stages of sleep

These stages alternate through a typical 8-hour sleep, starting with a very rapid descent into deep sleep (stage 4). Through the night deep sleep occurs less and REM periods become longer.

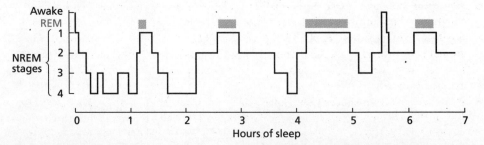

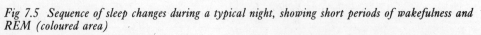

Fig 7.5 Sequence of sleep changes during a typical night, showing short periods of wakefulness and REM (coloured area)

② **Non-rapid eye movement (NREM) or slow wave sleep (SWS):**
- relaxed mental state, lack of brain activity,
- **Herman** *et al.* **(1978)** reviewed the literature relating to dreams and sleep. The occurrence of dreams in NREM sleep ranged from 0 to 75%, and for REM sleep from 74% to 100%. NREM dreams tend to be less emotionally charged.

③ **Rapid eye movement (REM):**
- **Jouvet** called this **paradoxical sleep** because of the contradictions:
  - the person is very active. There are increases in the heart and breathing rates, and in blood pressure,
  - the body is most relaxed. There is loss of muscle tone and sensory input,
  - they are hardest to wake, yet 'lightest' asleep,
- It is associated with **dreams**, though dreams also occur in NREM sleep and not all REM sleep has dreams. **Dement and Kleitman (1957)** woke subjects during REM episodes, 80–90% of the time they reported dreaming.
- Evolutionary argument for REM. REM occurs in mammals, but it is not clear whether it extends to fish and reptiles, because even when awake the eyes of these animals do not move much.

④ **Dreams**

Dreams are images and fantasies temporarily confused with reality; what one researcher counts as a series of thoughts, another may see as a dream. 'Dreamlike' qualities include: fragmentation, the association of apparently disconnected memories and a sense of premonition. What function do dreams serve? The following explanations are not mutually exclusive:
- *Activation–synthesis model:* suggests that dreams are a response to spontaneous neural activity during sleep; either external stimuli (a dripping tap) or internal stimuli (memories) activate the brain. Dreams are an attempt to impose coherence on 'nonsensical' stimuli **(Hobson and McCarley, 1977** and **Crick and Mitchison, 1983)**.
- *Consolidation of memory:* **Ornstein (1986)** suggests that schemas are reorganised to accommodate new information, which would explain why newborns need more REM sleep.
- There is a need for *periodic arousal* of the brain to maintain minimum levels of CNS activity. **Vertes (1986)** suggests that failure to do this could be connected with sleep-associated disorders, such as sudden infant death syndrome (SIDS). However, if arousal is a counterbalance to low CNS activity (slow wave sleep; SWS), REM periods should always follow periods of SWS. **Carskadon and Dement (1975)** woke subjects repeatedly after 30 minutes of sleep. This did not stop REM sleep, which sometimes occurred immediately with onset of sleep, and not always after a period of SWS.
- *Cognitive restoration:* **Evans (1984)** uses **computer analogy** to liken dreams to updating memory files, discarding redundant data, rehearsing and checking routines.
- *Emotional catharsis:* **Freud's (1900)** traditional view was that dreams are 'the royal road' to the unconscious enabling repressed desires or memories to become known. This approach cannot explain why animals dream, and why we forget most of our dreams.
- *Problem-solving:* emotional or cognitive.

⑤ **Deprivation studies:** in trying to understand the need for sleep or dreams, psychologists have looked at the effects of deprivation without much success:
- *Flowerpot technique:* place an animal on a platform just large enough to hold it. Surround the platform with water. During slow wave sleep the animal snoozes, but loss of muscle tone in REM sleep causes them to slip off the platform. The animal soon learns to awaken when its head begins to nod. **Jouvet (1967)** found that cats deprived of REM sleep in this way experienced hypersexuality and eventually death.
- *REM rebound phenomenon:* **Dement (1960)** woke eight volunteers every time they had an REM; on the first night this was typically 12 times, by the 7th night they were woken 26 times. The main effect of losing REM sleep was to need more, otherwise only mild temporary behavioural changes were reported. Dement

originally claimed that his subjects exhibited psychiatric symptoms, but subsequently he recognised that these were the result of experimenter expectations. Despite this, the misconception remains that lack of REM is associated with temporary insanity **(Empson, 1989)**.

- *Stage 4 rebound phenomenon:* observed by **Agnew et al. (1964)** as well as some physical lethargy, depression and increased sensitivity to pain.
- *Total sleep deprivation:* **Webb (1985)**: found that sleep-loss over 48 hours had little effect on precision and cognitive processing tasks, whereas subjective and attention measures suffered. Performance may be more due to motivational factors than cognitive components.
- *Case studies:* such as the disc jockey, **Peter Tripp**, who stayed awake for 200 hours as a publicity stunt. He developed severe paranoid psychosis with the delusion that he was being poisoned **(Dement, 1972)**. **Gulevich et al. (1966)** reported another case, of a 17-year-old who stayed awake for 264 hours, who suffered no ill-effects and only slept for 15 hours at the end of it.

  Oswald and Adam (1980) observed a man in their laboratory who claimed not to sleep at all as the result of an accident. After three nights without sleep his speech was slurred, he made visual misinterpretations and appeared very sleepy, in fact he slept that night.
- *Pathological disorder:* **Lugaresi et al. (1986)** reported the case of a man who gradually began to sleep less and less; he suffered from waking dreams, disorientation, inability to concentrate and lack of intelligibility. When he died, he was found to have an inherited condition that caused his thalamus to degenerate.
- In general, the evidence suggests that effects of sleep deprivation are not great. Animals may learn tasks more slowly, humans feel more sleepy and find it easier to go to sleep.

  However, **Empson (1989)** concludes that nobody has ever demonstrated that they can maintain any semblance of normal health without sleep.

6 Neural mechanisms of sleep:

- *Pineal gland:* generally controls bodily rhythms. Secretes melatonin, which affects serotonin levels and the raphe nucleus.
- *Suprachiasmatic nucleus:* (in the hypothalamus) responds to light (or lack of it) and tunes the sleeping pattern to the amount of daylight.
- *RAS (reticular activating system):* normally receives inputs from 'lower' centres in the CNS but can generate activity on its own, and thus control wakefulness through the ascending RAS (ARAS). Stimulation of the RAS awakens a sleeping individual or increases alertness. Damage or lesions to the RAS lead to prolonged sleep or inactivity. Any strong stimulation activates the ARAS, which then activates the entire cortex. Equally, lack of stimulation decreases arousal of RAS and sleep occurs.
- The *raphe system:* located in the hindbrain and extending into the midbrain, the raphe system promotes sleep. Damage to the system leads to persistent wakefulness. The animal may eventually sleep, though never as much as before.
- Activity in the *pons* may trigger REM sleep, but research is inconclusive.
- *Factor S:* a biochemical substance that has been found in the blood of sleeping animals and can induce sleep when injected into other animals. However, the fact that Siamese twins who share the same blood supply do not have the same sleep cycles suggests that a chemical foundation cannot be a critical factor. There may be chemicals in the brain which do not cross the blood–brain barrier.
- *Serotonin*: is the predominant transmitter of the cells of the raphe system. Tryptophan leads to the production of serotonin and has been tried as a kind of sleeping pill, with some effectiveness, though not universal.

7 Sleep and age:

- Newborns spend half their sleep in REM sleep; this drops to 25% by the age of five. Research may be mistaken as it's hard to distinguish a sleeping infant from a waking one with its eyes closed.
- By the age of five, the adult sleep pattern has usually been established, due to both environmental and maturational factors.
- Older people have less stage 3 and 4 sleep; it may disappear altogether.

OTHER STATES OF CONSCIOUSNESS

Hypnosis, relaxation, meditation and biofeedback may all be aspects of the same process: relaxation. This leads to a reduced state of physiological arousal, triggering the parasympathetic branch of the ANS and decreasing heart rate, blood pressure, oxygen consumption and so on. Relaxation, like placebos, may also lead the ANS to release endorphins thus lowering sensitivity to pain.

Hypnosis

- 'A social interaction in which one person responds to suggestions offered by another' **(Kihlstrom, 1985)**.

- The first known mention of the use of hypnosis was the Cult of Aesculapius in 400 BC. In the 18th century Mesmer popularised it with claims of medical cures. This led to its use in surgery and treating mental disorders.

- A hypnotised person ceases to initiate activity and becomes narrowed in terms of attention. Their reality testing is reduced and they become receptive to suggestion and analgesia. There can be age regression, posthypnotic amnesia, sensory changes like blindness, increased physical strength, and so on.

- It can be induced either through relaxation or, less commonly, a hyperalert trance can be achieved, as in 'whirling dervishes', a sect who induce trances.

- Self-hypnosis is also possible. Meditation is probably a kind of self-hypnosis.

- 5–10% of the population cannot be hypnotised.

Is it qualitatively different from other states?

- The brain patterns are those of relaxation, not deep sleep.

- When normal memory fails, such as after an accident, hypnosis can reach otherwise inaccessible memories, though it is not admissible in court as evidence because suggestion is involved.

- Some behaviour is hard to explain, for example a subject touched with a pencil that they think is a red hot poker will get blisters.

Explanations:

- *Psychoanalytic orientation:* hypnosis is a unique and altered state of consciousness.

- *Neo-dissociation theory:* the consciousness is split into several streams somewhat independent of each other (see p.282).

- *Social factors:* it is not a distinctive state but a consequence of role-playing and/or the influence of a number of social or experimental variables. **Barber (1969)** suggests that the concept of hypnosis is superfluous, the phenomena can be explained more easily in other terms such as demand characteristics.

- *A variant of the placebo effect:* there are parallels between hypnosis and placebos, they both rely on 'suggestion' and 'belief'.

Self-hypnosis, relaxation, meditation and biofeedback

Self-hypnosis, relaxation and meditation may be achieved through rituals and exercises such as controlling and regulating breathing, assuming positions and isolating oneself from the environment using, for example, a mantra.

Is biofeedback any more than this? It is described as the *conscious* control of the ANS. A person learns to control involuntary systems through being given objective evidence of their activity such as hearing their heart rate.

Experiments by **Dicara and Miller (1968)** first indicated the possibility of biofeedback, though it has long been attributed to yogis and other meditators. They conditioned involuntary responses in rats and rabbits. For example, the animals could learn to increase or decrease the contractions of their intestines. However, there has been little success in replicating these experiments, and it seems that what may be learned is short-lived and is more an ability to control certain voluntary muscles than ANS control. **Anand et al. (1961)** looked at yogis who claimed to be able to stop their hearts and found that what they had learned was to shut off the return of blood to the heart, thus stopping the sound of the heart beat so that it appeared as if the heart had stopped.

Phillips (1991) concludes that biofeedback is an effective technique for a group of narrowly defined disorders, including some types of pain and cardiac and neuromuscular disorders where patients are trained to self-regulate physiological states. He cites programmes where patients with cerebral palsy use head or foot position monitors to learn to better control their movements. Stroke patients who use feedback of muscular activity can regain control over muscles and cardiac patients can use feedback to control their heart rate.

Others argue that biofeedback is little more than relaxation, which nonetheless has useful applications in medicine and the control of stress.

MULTIPLE CONSCIOUSNESS

Some of the observations made about different states of consciousness may be alternatively explained in terms of more than one consciousness.

1. **Neo-dissociation and the 'hidden observer'**: it appears that there can be a self which is hypnotised and a second consciousness which is not hypnotised and aware of the self that is. **Hilgard (1977)** instructed a hypnotised subject that he would not hear anything, but then, out of curiosity, told the subject that, if there was some part of him which could hear, he should raise a finger. The finger was raised. When the subject was later asked if he had heard anything, he said that he hadn't but that he was aware of the finger being raised, through his 'daydreaming', although not the reason why.

2. **Multiple personality**: there are a number of detailed descriptions of such psychopathologies, perhaps the best known being **Thigpen and Cleckley's (1957)** *Three faces of Eve* (see 6.2). The patient's consciousness becomes pathologically disassociated as a way of coping with emotional problems. The different personalities show different voices, postures and even dress. It may start as a form of self-hypnosis, an extension of 'normal' childhood fantasy play. It was thought to be very rare but this may not be true because it can easily remain undetected. Except through hypnosis, one personality is often only dimly aware of the existence of the others.

Such dissociation or multiple consciousness may explain:

● preconscious activity, such as automatic processing,

● fantasy play and daydreaming,

● automatic writing.

PARANORMAL (PSI) PHENOMENA

Paranormal phenomena hold irresistible interest for students of psychology. Examples are psychokinesis and extrasensory perceptions (ESP) such as telepathy, clairvoyance and precognition. These are called PSI phenomena after the Greek letter psi (ψ) used as an abbreviation for psychology.

One experimental approach is the **ganzfeld** (German for 'total field') studies which test telepathic communication. The receiver is placed in isolation, with ping-pong ball halves taped over their eyes, white noise played through headphones, and so on. The sender is also isolated and shown a randomly selected picture, which they concentrate on. The receiver tries to describe or identify the image they are receiving. Such studies have had some success, achieving greater than chance results, though **Hyman and Honorton (1986)** found such results in less than half of the 28 studies they analysed.

How can we explain such phenomena?

1. They are **real** and represent a special state of consciousness, therefore science must uncover the 'forces' responsible.

2. **Experimenter bias**: can explain the experimental results. **Ayerhoff and Abelson (1976)** found that people who believe in the paranormal (sheep) are more likely to experience PSI than non-believers (goats). It is difficult to say which might come first, belief or experience, but in either case the self-fulfilling prophecy would predict this cycle will be self-perpetuating.

③ A form of **cognitive illusion**: in the same way that visual illusions show us features of the visual system, PSI illustrate some cognitive processes. Psychic events create the expectation of an explanation, an illusion of causality. Depending on your cognitive style you will either seek an explanation or happily attribute the 'psychic' event to chance. **Blackmore (1992)** found that there are differences in the way people do explain chance events, and that these can be related to their belief in PSI (sheep or goats). The chance events were such things as trying to produce random generation of numbers.

④ PSI phenomena may occur at a **preconscious** or **unconscious level**.

7.3 BIOLOGICAL RHYTHMS (OR CHRONOBIOLOGY)

A rhythm is a periodically repeated feature. All biological systems exhibit such periodicity. Alternative terms are 'biorhythms' or 'bodily rhythms', though the former is associated with the pseudoscientific technique of using certain rhythms to predict a person's behaviour on a given day. Biological rhythms are usually classed according to their duration:

- **circadian**: a cycle that lasts about 24 hours, such as sleep/waking,
- **ultradian**: shorter than a day; such as sleep stages, heart beat, breathing,
- **infradian**: the most common rhythms. Those last longer than a day, such as the menstrual cycle, seasonal mating, migration or hibernation,
- also: **circalunar** (the moon), **circannual** (year), **diurnal** (daily), **nocturnal** (night-time).

Rhythms are set off or triggered by:

- **External** stimuli: rhythmic or other factors in the environment. Day length is the dominant **zeitgeber** (German for 'time-giver'), also important are the seasons, weather, temperature, phases of the moon, tides (in aquatic animals), availability of food, pheromones and social stimuli.
- **Internal, clock-driven**: the fact that rhythms persist even in the absence of external physical stimuli suggests some form of internal or biological clock, and probably more than one.

EMPIRICAL EVIDENCE

① **A 90 minute cycle:** **Kleitman (1969)** suggested a basic rest activity cycle (BRAC) through the day and night. This can be related to regular REM rhythms, which show periodicity regardless of whether subjects are woken (see **Carskadom and Dement (1975)**, 7.2). **Klein and Armitage (1979)** tested subjects' performance on verbal and spatial tasks through the day and found a 96 minute cycle.

② **A 24.9 hour cycle:** a blind person who receives no light input still experiences circadian rhythms according to **Miles, Raynal and Wilson (1977)**. It appears from this and other studies that the 'free-running' cycle is slightly closer to 25 hours, which indicates the working of an internal clock, and means that we have to adjust our clocks each day.

③ **Cycles of more or less than 24 hours:** a number of studies have placed subjects in caves where circadian cycles can be controlled with artificial lights and clocks. **Kleitman (1963)** studied two volunteers living on a 28-hour day; neither subject was fully able to adjust to this cycle. **Folkard et al. (1985)** controlled for bias by not telling subjects that their clock was fast. The group of 12 started coping alright when the clock was reduced to a 23-hour cycle, but by the time it had worked down to 22 hours their bodies reverted to a natural cycle.

④ Two clocks?: What happens if people are allowed to choose when to wake and sleep but are still isolated from daylight? **Aschoff and Wever (1976)** observed that some maintain 24–25 hour cycles whereas others develop idiosyncrasies such as 29 hours awake and 21 hours asleep. All other circadian rhythms follow the sleep–waking pattern except temperature, which stayed at a 24–hour cycle, suggesting that there are two clocks at work. The study by **Hawkins and Armstrong-Esther (1978)** of nurses on shift duty, described below, also found that temperature cycles did not change.

⑤ Body temperature: covaries with heart rate, urine secretion, plasma content or any measure which indicates metabolic rate. It reaches a peak at 4 p.m. and a trough at 4 a.m. The cycle remains the same even if you sleep during the day and are awake at night. **Colquhuon (1970)** reports that a variety of cognitive functions have been positively correlated with the rise, though there is usually a post-lunch dip. This is a factor in general work patterns not just shift work.

⑥ Influence of smell: **McClintock (1971)** found that women who spent a large amount of time together had synchronised menstrual cycles, and that women who spent time in the company of men tended to have shorter cycles. **Russell *et al.* (1980)** collected daily samples of women's underarm sweat, mixed it with alcohol and applied this to the upper lip of their female subjects. The subjects' menstrual cycles began to synchronise with the odour donor, thus suggesting that **pheromones** may be involved. Pheromones are chemical substances which carry messages from one animal to another; they affect the receiver through the ANS, which is under the influence of hormones.

⑦ Migration: **Gwinner (1986)** kept wild birds in cages for three years, exposing them to 12 hours of light and 12 hours of darkness daily. Despite a lack of external stimuli they still showed signs of migratory restlessness. Indeed birds fly south because of changes in light but why do they fly north again? The countries where they migrate have little change in daylight.

⑧ Other rhythms: flowers open and close in response to daylight; annual plant rhythms are directed by temperature and day length; marine animals such as crabs respond to tidal rhythms even when kept in constant conditions, suggesting an endogenous lunar clock (**Palmer, 1989**).

PRACTICAL APPLICATIONS

① Shift work: the effects are not large and there are extensive individual differences, on average it takes about three days to adjust to a 12 hour shift in time (which applies to jet lag as well). The most difficult pattern to cope with is one week on nights and the next week on days; just when the body acclimatises the change leads to considerable strain.

The dangers are that workers are not sufficiently alert and/or they fall asleep, leading to poor performance and accidents. **Novak *et al.* (1990)** found higher injury rates for shift workers in a chemical plant. **Gold *et al.* (1992)** recorded sleepiness and errors in nurses on rotating shift work. There were twice the number of such incidents in nurses on rotating shifts compared with those on permanent day or night shift.

Hawkins and Armstrong-Esther (1978) studied 11 nurses during the first 7 nights of their duty. Performance was significantly impaired on the first night but improved through the week, though temperature was still not adjusted by the last night. However, individual differences were large.

Considerable research focuses on ways of improving shift work performance. For example, **Dawson and Campbell (1991)** exposed subjects to a 4-hour pulse of bright light on their first night and found that this helped their subsequent adjustment as measured by body temperature.

② Jet lag leads to tiredness, headaches and minor adjustment problems; such side effects may be due to internal desynchronisation of circadian rhythms.

Wegmann *et al.* (1983) concluded that resynchronisation is essentially independent of the number of time zones crossed. **Webb and Agnew (1971)** interviewed regular travellers and found that sticking to a rigid schedule of meals and exercise helps adjustment and efficient operation, even if this means eating out of phase with everyone else.

Redfern (1989) suggested the use of benzodiazepines to induce phase shifts and melatonin for resynchronisation as pharmacological means of alleviating the symptoms of jet lag. Non-pharmacological approaches include a regimen of timing meals, scheduled exposure to light and outdoor activity. Winfree (1986) proposed that the effects of benzodiazepines might lead to a pill for jet lag.

③ Premenstrual tension (PMT): Floody (1968) reviewed a large body of research indicating that PMT or PMS (premenstrual syndrome) was positively associated with child abuse, irritability, hostility, crime and aggression generally. Such findings have led to its use as a criminal defence. One possible explanation is that female hormones lead to increased aggression in readiness for parenthood.

④ Seasonal affective disorder: some people become seriously depressed at the onset of winter and sometimes slightly manic in summer. It is the darkness not the cold which creates the effect, which can be relieved by using bright lights.

⑤ Medical diagnosis: it is important to take the time of day into account when checking blood or urine samples, or taking a patient's temperature.

PHYSIOLOGICAL BASIS OF BIOLOGICAL CLOCK

The evidence above clearly indicates the existence of at least one, and probably two, internal mechanisms for controlling biological rhythms. The **suprachiasmatic nucleus (SCN)** of the hypothalamus has been identified as the most likely central control or main biological clock:

- it receives information about light directly from the retina,
- brain tumours of the SCN produce sleep/waking disorders in terms of onset but not the amount of sleep,
- the SCN forms numerous connections with other parts of the brain,
- it is hardly disturbed by things such as brain damage, lack of oxygen, inactivity or activity, ECT, alcohol, anaesthesia,
- some drugs such as caffeine and barbituates can reset it,
- when the SCN is damaged in animals the temperature control remains intact, though it may temporarily be altered.

It is likely that:

- the SCN can generate rhythms itself and is 'fine tuned' by light or other stimuli,
- the SCN co-ordinates the activities of other biological clocks by secreting neuromodulators,
- the 'tick' of this clock is a result of protein synthesis, which is remarkably immune to interference.

7.4 MOTIVATION

The following section represents yet another way of approaching the eternal question, what causes behaviour? Motives are what makes the organism 'go'. Motivation is:

- a *cause* of energising, goal-directed, purposeful behaviour,
- a state of *arousal* that impels or drives an organism to action,
- there can be *primary/basic/innate* motives which are:
  - necessary in order to ensure survival and proper functioning,
  - not under voluntary control,
- or *secondary/acquired/learned* ones:
  - may be outside conscious awareness, i.e. preconscious,
  - or used as rationalisation for behaviour,
- intertwined with *emotion,* emotional states create motivations and the energising component of a drive has a strong emotional tone.

Motives, needs, drives and incentives

- **Need:** a state which ensures the well-being of an organism, as in **tissue needs**. There are needs without drives: there is a need for oxygen but the drive is to reduce carbon dioxide.
- **Drive:** a motivational state produced either by deprivation of something one needs (food, drug) or presence of noxious stimuli (noise, cold). A drive, unlike a need, implies a motivational state.
- **Incentive:** things which co-occur with drives and act as enablers; water has incentive value for a thirsty person, weight loss is an incentive for a dieter.

Internal or external?

Extrinsic motivation is behaviour motivated by external rewards or punishments, usually the question of inner satisfaction is considered secondary. Getting good grades is a form of extrinsic motivation. **Intrinsic motivation** arises from feelings of satisfaction and fulfilment, such as altruism.

Extrinsic rewards can destroy intrinsic motivation. The following folk tale illustrates how intrinsic motives (in this case, pleasure seeking) are extinguished by extrinsic motives (money), so that when the extrinsic motive is removed, the original motive has disappeared:

> Each day the children harassed the old woman. After school they would play outside her window; if she asked them to be quiet, they only called her obscene names and shouted more loudly.
>
> One day as the children approached, she called to them, "I have grown fond of listening to you play, but my hearing isn't what it used to be. If you will play in front of my window, I will pay each of you fifty cents."
>
> The children laughed at the woman's foolish request, but agreed. For a week they collected their payment and raised a tremendous din.
>
> The next week, however, the woman greeted them with a frown. "Times are hard. I can only pay you 25 cents this week." The children complained, but agreed to her offer. Three days later, the woman met them again. "Times are hard. I can only pay you ten cents," she told them.
>
> "Ten cents? That's not enough," they said. And they left her in peace.
>
> (From Forsyth, 1987, page 158)

(see also the experiment by **Lepper** *et al.* **(1973)** in 3.3).

Homeostasis

Homeostasis is a state of dynamic equilibrium. Continuous small changes ensure that uniform conditions prevail. Homeostasis is important for survival and is one of the most important concepts in biology. Mechanical devices, such as a thermostat, operate on the same principle as biological ones, usually employing negative feedback; any departure from the pre-set level is detected and processes set in action to return to the 'normal' state. In animals such mechanisms are largely located in the ANS and control temperature, bodily fluids, metabolism and blood pressure, though none of them is exactly homeostatic because the set point varies from time to time. Homeostatic principles also operate in the control of fine motor movement and many cognitive states, such as attitudes, which are explained in terms of balance.

THEORIES OF MOTIVATION

Theories or explanations fall into three broad categories:

1 *Physiological:* describes motivation in terms of organic needs, concerned with only the primary drives and based on homeostatic principles – hunger, thirst, avoidance of pain and so on.

2 *Behavioural:* drive and learning theories using principles of reinforcement.

3 *Psychosocial:* oriented towards complex, higher-order behaviours (secondary drives) such as need for achievement and self-actualisation. Found in psychoanalytic, humanist and cognitive approaches.

The theories are by no means mutually exclusive. They differ in the level at which they approach motivation and generally distinguish in some way between basic and other motives. All involve some notion of homeostasis.

❶ Physiological: Homeostatic Drive Theory, Cannon (1929): proposes that behaviour is driven by states of imbalance which occur when basic needs are not fulfilled; the organism is motivated to return to a state of balance. Cannon coined the term 'homeostasis' to describe this. He thought that hunger arises from the contractions of an empty stomach and thirst from dryness in the mouth. He cited, as proof, an experiment by **Cannon and Washburn (1912)**, where Washburn swallowed a balloon so his stomach contractions could be measured. They found a high correlation between hunger and contraction. However there is much evidence against this and the theory in general.

Evaluation:
- the experimental evidence doesn't prove that one *causes* the other,
- people with no stomachs still get hungry,
- other evidence (see physiological descriptions below) demonstrates that the stomach is peripheral to, though involved in, hunger,
- more generally, there are many things we need for which we have no drives, such as vitamins,
- the principle of homeostasis is valid,
- it ignores higher-order needs, such as self-actualisation, which do not operate on homeostatic principles.

❷ Behavioural: Drive-Reduction Theory, Hull (1943): primarily a theory of learning, though drives are physiological states. The fundamental point of the theory was to incorporate reinforcement: physiological deprivation leads to a homeostatic need and results in a drive; this unpleasant state increases arousal and activity which eventually brings the animal in contact which something which will satisfy the need, such as finding food; eating reduces the drive (hunger) thus reducing the unpleasant stimulus and reinforcing the behaviour which brought about food. Therefore, next time that behaviour is more likely to occur. Hull believed that all human behaviour is a result of satisfying primary needs.

Evaluation:
- offers a useful distinction between needs and drives: a need is physiological and objectively definable; drives are psychological, hypothetical constructs which can be operationalised,
- produces testable equations,
- no doubt that it explains *some* behaviour,
- but **Tolman and Honzik (1930)** demonstrated that learning can take place without reinforcement (see 1.6),
- as with Cannon's theory, drive-reduction theory was limited to biological, homeostatic mechanisms, but the principle of reinforcement can be adapted to cope with secondary motives; for example **Mowrer (1950)** incorporated anxiety,
- see also Arousal theory.

❸ Behavioural: Hydraulic model: produced by ethologists. This suggests that a fixed action pattern (FAP) or behaviour is initiated by a trigger or innate releasing mechanism which produces action-specific energy (ASE) to 'power' the behaviour (see 8.2).

❹ Psychosocial: Need hierarchy, Maslow (1954): a psychosocial framework. All human motives can be organised into a hierarchy, where the more fundamental needs are **prepotent** (more powerful when unfulfilled) to intermediate and meta needs.

Level		Need	Examples
fundamental needs	1	physiological	food, water
intermediate or deficiency needs	2	safety	freedom from threat, security
	3	belongingness	love, affiliation, acceptance
	4	esteem	achievement, status, prestige
meta needs	5	cognitive	knowledge, understanding, curiosity
	6	aesthetic	order, beauty, structure, art
	7	self-actualisation	self-fulfilment, realisation of potential

Many of the non-homeostatic concepts included have been developed by others, for example:

- **self-actualisation:** is a central tenet of **Rogers' (1959)** personality theory (see 5.2),
- **competence** is seen as the 'master reinforcer' by **White (1959)**. Our capacity to deal effectively with and to control our environment is intrinsically rewarding and underpins all activity,
- curiosity is discussed below,
- **Murray (1938)** described 20 different human motives or needs, particularly the need for achievement (**nAch**) and the need for affiliation (**nAff**); nAch is discussed later in terms of performance, nAff is considered in 2.4.
- **nPower** has also been suggested and measured (**Winter, 1973**).

Evaluation:

- accounts for social environment, individual differences and long-term goals,
- reflects the complexity and wholeness of human behaviour,
- somewhat vague and lacks scientific status,
- **Alderfer's (1972)** ERG (Existence Relatedness Growth needs) theory is similar to Maslow's except that he suggests that people also move downwards, using lower level needs as a substitute when frustrated at a higher level.

⑤ **Psychosocial: Psychoanalytic theory, Freud:** emphasises internal determinants and is homeostatic in principle. In the infant the libido starts as an undifferentiated amount of psychic energy; the forces of pleasure (life or Eros) and death (Thanatos) act through this to shape the id, which is the reservoir of instinctual impulses. The ego and superego regulate the expression of instinctual drives and needs, and provide higher order motives learned from society.

Evaluation:

- wide scope and holistic approach,
- does not account for free will and learning because of emphasis on unconscious, innate forces,
- lacks scientific rigour.

⑥ **Arousal theory** was first proposed in the 1950s and can incorporate all of the above:

Physiological level:

- **Physiological deprivation:** increases arousal levels and therefore the organism is motivated to reduce them to an acceptable or optimum point. In a way this is similar to drive reduction but now seen as arousal reduction.
- **Sensory deprivation studies:** (see **Bexton** *et al.* **(1954)**, 2.4) one explanation offered for the profound effects is that the sensory system requires stimulation/arousal to function, making sensory deprivation equivalent to tissue needs.

Psychological level:

- **Exploring the unfamiliar** increases arousal. If arousal gets too high we become anxious; too low and we're bored. We have a drive for the optimum level, which may not be the same every time, depending on other factors.
- **Yerke–Dodson Law (1908)**, states the same – when arousal is too low or too high performance is depressed. **Davis and Harvey (1992)** found that major league baseball players performed less well in the closing stages of the game if the pressure was great.
- **Dominant responses** are enhanced by arousal, as shown in studies of social facilitation (see 2.9).
- **Excessive stimulation** ('sensory overload') such as too much noise is debilitating. **Ludwig (1975)** suggests that this could be responsible for disorders in our highly urbanised society.
- **Curiosity** is related to arousal: an interesting example comes from the disturbed behaviour of animals in zoos. In the wild most of their time is occupied searching for food but when this is provided they have little else to do but look forward to the next feeding time. It seems that boredom can have profound psychological consequences. The function of play and games may provide necessary arousal for children and adults.
- **Increased sensitivity:** when **Gilchrist and Nesburg (1952)** showed hungry subjects pictures of food, the hungrier the subjects, the brighter the pictures were judged.

- See also **frustration–aggression hypothesis** and **emotion**, all linked with arousal.

Evaluation:

- has not been specifically formulated to encompass all the above,
- a reductionist approach, reducing behaviour to physiological processes.

MECHANISMS OF HOMEOSTASIS

The hypothalamus is the obvious candidate for homeostatic control in the brain:

- it has the richest blood supply,
- is known to contain osmoreceptors (detect water),
- it is well-connected to other relevant structures such as the cortex and pituitary,
- damage to the area results in alterations in appropriate behaviours.

However, much more than the hypothalamus is involved.

Temperature

Constant temperature enables an animal to evolve chemical reactions that are precisely co-ordinated, and to be independent of the environment in terms of activity and resistance.

Behavioural mechanisms: e.g. moving into the shade when hot, or putting on more or less clothing.

Physiological mechanisms: temperature is monitored by the **preoptic area** (in front of the hypothalamus), which leads to various ANS functions such as sweating, shivering and vasodilation. Fever is caused by the release of prostaglandin E from the body's defence mechanisms (leucocytes). Prostaglandin E stimulates cells in the preoptic area to raise the temperature. A moderate fever helps combat infection.

Thirst

Behavioural mechanisms: feeling thirsty if the water deficit is too great for the physiological mechanisms alone to cope.

Physiological mechanisms:

1. **Intracellular fluid loss** (inside body cells) raises levels of salt in the blood, which is detected by osmoreceptors in the hypothalamus, which become shrivelled. This changed cell shape is detected by a comparator in the anterior hypothalamus, which in turn alerts the pituitary to secrete ADH, which results in the kidneys secreting more concentrated urine.

2. **Extracellular fluid loss:** loss of blood or water from the blood (sweating) leads to decreased pressure, which is detected by receptors in the heart and kidneys. The kidneys secrete renin causing vasoconstriction, preventing further blood loss.

3. **Satiety centres:** in the mouth and intestines detect the influx of fluid so that you stop drinking before the deficit is made up, otherwise you would drink too much. Learning is important for judging this.

Hunger

Behavioural mechanisms: hunger pangs are felt in the stomach, leading to a search for food and eating. This can lead to behaviour such as that observed by **Postman and Crutchfield (1952)**, who showed subjects lists of skeleton words such as pick – – (picket or pickle). Hungry subjects selected food-related words, showing a behavioural set which might help satisfy their need, in the same way that seeking shade controls temperature. Cessation of eating is also behaviourally controlled in terms of sight, taste, smell, texture and experience of consequences. **Jordan (1969)** fed subjects through a tube. They reported a desire to taste or chew something despite physiologically being satiated.

Physiological mechanisms:

1. **The stomach:** the most obvious answer, however:

CHAPTER 7 BIOLOGICAL PSYCHOLOGY

- people with no stomach still feel hungry,
- involved with satiation. **Deutsch, Young and Kalogeris (1978)** showed that an animal stops eating even when food goes no further than the stomach,
- stretch receptors stop eating for protective reasons.

② **The duodenum** produces cholectystokinin (CCK) as a response to the presence of food; this may act as a neurotransmitter in the brain.

③ **The liver:** produces glucose in response to CCK and signals the brain via the vagus nerve. **Russeck (1971)** found that his dog subjects stopped eating only when glucose was injected into their liver rather than into their blood supply. If the nerve from the liver to the brain is blocked, the effect is removed, therefore suggesting that the liver assesses satiation and signals the brain.

④ **Neuroanatomical explanations:** it is clear that the brain mediates in some way, comparing the amount of glucose in arteries and veins as a means of assessing how much is being used. It also monitors amino acids and fats. It may initiate an involuntary, hormonal response or stimulate a behavioural response (a feeling of hunger):

(a) **The lateral (LH) and ventromedial (VMH) hypothalamus:** at one time these were thought to be the hunger and satiety centres of the brain:
- LH: damage leads to undereating, electrical stimulation leads to eating. For example, **Quaade (1971)** used extreme measures on obese patients, lesioning their LH. If this was electrically stimulated they reported feeling hungry.
- VMH: damage leads to overeating (aphagia) and excessive thirst (adipsia). **Reeves and Plum (1969)** performed a post-mortem examination of a patient who had doubled her body weight in two years. They found a tumour in the VMH.
- However, **Teitelbaum and Stellar (1954)** showed that rats with LH lesions could recover normal appetites. **Zeigler and Karten (1974)** damaged nerves of the trigeminal system (nerves involved in chewing, swallowing and facial sensations) and produced the same pattern as LH lesions.

(b) Damage to **nerve bundles** which pass through the hypothalamus, such as the nigrostriatal bundle (NSB), may account for the effects observed for the LH and VMH.

(c) **Arousal:** may further explain feeding behaviour. **Antelman et al. (1976)** found that pinching a rat's tail after LH lesions will lead to immediate feeding, the sensations from the tail are carried to the brain via the NSB.

⑤ **Neurochemical sources:**

(a) **Insulin:** the LH increases the release of insulin; damage to the LH decreases insulin levels, which triggers the conversion of stored fats into glucose; the increase of glucose depresses hunger. Conversely, damage to the VMH raises insulin levels, resulting in no glucose in the blood because it is all stored away. Thus the animal feels permanently hungry and in fact must eat or it will starve.

(b) **Glucose:** there is some evidence that hunger is cognitively mediated rather than instigated by falling levels of glucose. **Pollack et al. (1989)** isolated subjects from all temporal cues and monitored glucose levels. They did not find that these declined in the period before a meal request.

(c) **Neurotransmitters:** dopamine is a transmitter in the NSB. Injections of dopamine and epinephrine inhibit eating. Amphetamines, which stimulate the production of dopamine and epinephrine, are known to be associated with weight loss.

Sex

Sexual and parental behaviours are a special class of basic need, and largely not homeostatic. They do not affect the daily survival of the organism but are vital in terms of the species. Desire, gender-appropriate behaviour and changes related to pregnancy are hormonally controlled. The hypothalamus oversees the pituitary, which releases sex-related hormones and stimulates other endocrine glands.

The section on gender roles in 3.4 contains a full discussion of physiological versus psychological factors.

Pleasure

Hedonists, and **Freud,** suggested that we are motivated by a desire to seek pleasure and avoid pain.

Olds and Milner (1954) found that rats would increase their lever-pressing if certain 'pleasure centres' located in the hypothalamus were subject to ESB (electrical stimulation of the brain). This was confirmed by **Campbell (1973),** who implanted electrodes in the hypothalamus of patients suffering from severe pain as a possible means of pain relief. The patients could press a button which electrically stimulated parts of the brain, which they did so for the maximum permitted time.

This offers a principle second only to homeostasis in driving motivation. In fact it can explain homeostasis itself, as imbalance creates tension, and restoring balance leads to tension-relief (pleasure). It can also explain reinforcement, drive reduction and cognitive dissonance.

7.5 EMOTION

Emotion comes from the Latin 'to move, excite, stir up or agitate'. The *Penguin Dictionary of Psychology* comments that 'probably no other term shares its non-definability with its frequency of use'.

The experience of emotion involves several elements:

- *instigating stimuli:* external or internal (thoughts and images),
- *physiological correlates:* CNS (cortical activity, limbic system) and ANS (arousal). Little conscious control but awareness of sensations,
- *cognitive appraisal:* the subjective experience dictated by personal significance and external cues. **Buck (1984)** describes the subjective experience as a 'read-out' of the physiological state. **Emotional expression** is similarly a 'read-out' for the benefit of others,
- *behaviour:* emotion has motivational properties. It drives emotional expression, such as crying or shouting.

A few aspects to consider:

- there are clearly learned and culturally determined elements. For example, sadness has a great range of expression (and therefore sensations),
- many affective disorders of personality are characterised by inappropriate chronic experience of emotional states,
- to some extent it is evolutionarily determined and has species-specific survival value, for example aggression,
- animals experience emotion, though it lacks most, if not all, of the cognitive, conscious elements,
- emotion has an important effect on many other behaviours, such as:
  - perception, as in perceptual defence (see 1.1, McGinnies),
  - memory, as in repressed memories (Freud) and pathological amnesia,
  - performance; arousal can improve performance (see 7.4).

THEORETICAL FORMULATIONS

1 **The James–Lange Theory: James (1884)** and **Lange** independently suggested that emotion is the reverse of the common sense view. You are frightened when you see a bear *because* you run, not the reverse – that you run because you are frightened. 'We feel sorry because we cry, angry because we strike, afraid because we tremble'. Bodily changes come first and it is the perception (label) of these which is the emotion.

Evaluation:
- the theory predicts that:

- the more intense the arousal the greater the emotion
  (see **White** *et al.*, **1981**),
- that many different physiological states must exist
  (see **Ekman** *et al.*, **1983**),
- one physiological state leads to different emotions
  (see **Schachter and Singer, 1962**),
- but the theory has no room for learning or cognitive control.

2 **The Cannon–Bard Theory: Cannon (1927)** criticised the James–Lange view and
put forward his own, which was later modified by Bard. Cannon and Bard's
objections were:

- each emotion would need a corresponding physiological state, yet there are very
  few of these and very many emotions,
- physiological changes do not necessarily produce emotional states,
- emotional states may occur without any physiological changes,
- emotional experiences occur quite rapidly, yet the ANS is slow to react.
- Cannon and Bard's view was that changes of emotional state and changes in the
  ANS occur *simultaneously*, both caused by the arrival of the same sensory input.

Evaluation:
- the criticisms are all only partly true,
- the theory predicts that you can have emotion with no arousal (see **Valins, 1966**).

3 **The Cognitive Labelling Theory:** associated with the work of **Schachter**. A
general state of physiological arousal is given an appropriate 'label' according to the
individual's cognitive appraisal of the situation. This incorporates elements from the
previous two theories. Like the James–Lange theory it suggests that physiology
precedes experience but, like the Cannon–Bard theory, it sees the cognitive element
as critical in determining the mental experience. Unlike Cannon–Bard, the two
processes are seen as connected rather than independent.

It is also known as the **two-factor theory** of emotion, because two factors need to
be present: arousal and situational cues. It can also be explained in terms of **attribution** or **misattribution**. Arousal which is caused by one factor, such as fear, is
mistattributed to another, such as attraction.

Evaluation:
- predicts that one physiological state may produce different emotions (see
  Schachter and Singer, 1962),
- it fits with most of the facts given below,
- it incorporates learning, as the label is determined by previous experience of
  emotion in a similar situation.

4 **Cognitive Appraisal Theory:** an extension of Cognitive Labelling Theory. This
theory offers a kind of calculus for predicting the emotion that will be felt when
arousal is experienced. There have been a number of formulations: one example is
Smith and Ellsworth (1987), who describe emotions in terms of the different
cognitive expectations:

- the desirability of the situation (pleasant or unpleasant),
- the effort one anticipates spending,
- certainty of the situation,
- the attention one wants to devote to the situation,
- the control one feels,
- the control one attributes to other forces.

For example, an unpleasant situation may lead variously to anger (if caused
by another), or guilt (if brought about by self), or sadness (when controlled by
circumstances).

EMPIRICAL EVIDENCE

The evidence can be organised into the following framework:

1 *Is physiological arousal sufficient?*
  (a) If this is true there would have to have *distinct physiological state* for each
      emotion. For a long time this was held to be wrong. Recently a few studies have

found evidence for at least some differentiation, though the cognitive component is not negated. For example, **Ekman** *et al.* **(1983)** asked subjects (mainly actors) to show surprise, anger, disgust, sadness, fear and happiness using the facial muscles which they watched in a mirror. They measured heart rate, skin temperature and other measures of autonomic arousal and found that each emotion did have a different 'signature'. **Ax (1953)** also found distinctly different physiological reactions related to fight (anger) or flight (fear) emotions. The experiment was ostensibly studying hypertension, so subjects were wired up to a device which measured galvanic skin response (GSR) while they listened to music. During this they received an 'inadvertent' light electric shock to finger (fear) and were subjected to an annoying and rude technician (anger).

(b) Evidence that arousal alone doesn't reliably lead to emotion is given by **Maranon (1924)**, who injected his patients with epinephrine and asked them to report what they experienced. Seventy one per cent reported physical sensations with no emotional overtones, the rest used phrases like 'it's *as if* I was afraid'. Considering the antiquity of the study, its location in a foreign journal (so no one checks its veracity) and its reliance on introspection, it is remarkable that it is reported so often.

(c) The **Schachter and Singer** experiment, reported below, also gives evidence that arousal is sufficient and leads a person to find an appropriate label.

❷ *Is physiological arousal necessary? Can there be emotional experiences without arousal?*

(a) **Valins (1966)** showed slides of semi-nude women to male college students. The slides were accompanied by false feedback about their heart rate, to suggest arousal. The slides viewed when the subject was supposedly aroused were rated as more attractive and the subjects were more likely to ask to keep these pictures. This so-called 'Valins Effect' supports the view of emotion without arousal.

(b) **Hohmann (1966)** interviewed patients with spinal cord injuries which severely limited the information the brain received from the ANS. The patients said they still felt emotions but not to same extent as before. They reported 'as if' experience when in presence of appropriate cognitive stimulus.

(c) **Laird (1974)** told subjects that he was measuring activity of facial muscles using electrodes and instructed them to relax and contract muscles, eliciting smiles and frowns presumably without their conscious awareness. Cartoons viewed when 'smiling' were seen as funnier. Subjects were amused because they were smiling, not smiling because they were amused.

(d) **Sherrington (1900)** severed the spinal cord and vagus nerves of dogs, which then showed apparently normal emotional reactions.

❸ *Does arousal come first and is it then labelled appropriately?*

(a) **Schachter and Singer (1962)** conducted one of the classic experiments in psychology to demonstrate the effect of cognitive labelling. They asked subjects to help test a new vitamin, Suproxin, thought to affect visual skills. The injection was in fact epinephrine, which is produced naturally at moments of intense emotion. Subjects were either:

- correctly informed: told of the side-effects,
- misinformed: told that the vitamin would cause numbness of the feet,
- uninformed: given no extra information,
- given a placebo and no extra information.

After the injection, the subjects were placed in a room with a stooge who acted in a euphoric manner or as if he was angry. Results:

- those correctly informed were least affected by the stooge's behaviour. They could unconsciously 'explain' their emotional sensations in terms of the epinephrine,
- the misinformed and uninformed mimicked the emotional behaviour of the stooge; they had the physiological sensations but the only available explanation was that they were feeling that emotion,
- some placebo subjects also mimicked the stooge's behaviour; perhaps they had experienced some arousal through anxiety.

Therefore, they concluded, one physiological state (ANS arousal) can lead to varying emotional states depending on the contextual cues.

Evaluation:
- data from a number of subjects was excluded because they either seemed to know what was going on or they felt no arousal from the epinephrine,
- in any case, epinephrine will not affect everyone in the same way,
- and additionally, placebos have been shown to affect the ANS (see 7.1),
- can you compare arousal states created by drugs with real-life emotions?
- several studies have failed to replicate these findings (for example, **Marshall and Zimbardo, 1979**).

(b) Further evidence for arousal being attributed, or in this case misattributed, to situational cues comes from a clever study by **Dutton and Aron (1974)**. An attractive woman approached men on a high suspension bridge and asked them to complete a questionnaire about scenic attractions. One question involved describing a picture which was later analysed for sexual content, thus giving a measure of the amount of attraction that the man felt. It was expected that the state of arousal created by fear of heights would be misattributed to feeling sexual attraction given the situational cues. Men on the suspension bridge showed greater attraction than those interviewed on a low bridge or when the interviewer was male.

4 *Does labelling come first and cause arousal?*
(a) **Darley and Katz (1973)** set a task for a group of young subjects. If they were told it was a test their heart rate increased, if they were told it was a game their heart rate decreased. This suggested that cognitive appraisal may lead to different states of arousal.
(b) **Speisman *et al.* (1964)** showed a film, *Subincision in Arunta* about aboriginal puberty rites where a boys' penis is cut with a jagged knife. The sound track was manipulated so that:
- group 1: trauma, the pain, jaggedness of knife, etc. was emphasised,
- group 2: denial, the boys' eagerness about entering manhood was stressed,
- group 3: intellectualisation, the traditions of the tribe were stressed,
- group 4: silent condition.

Highest arousal (measured by GSR) was in group 1, followed by groups 4, 2, and 3. Again this supports the view that arousal is affected by the situation.

5 *Does arousal affect the strength of emotion and cognition affect the subjective experience?*
(a) **White *et al.* (1981)** asked male college students to run on the spot and then showed videos of some women they would meet later. Those that ran for 120 seconds found videos of attractive women more attractive than those who ran for only 15 seconds. The opposite was true if the woman was unattractive, suggesting that arousal *polarises* or enhances feelings.
(b) **Hohmann's (1966)** subjects experienced less emotion in the absence of arousal. Was this a question of less intensity because there was no physiological component?
(c) **Aggression and stress** are also related to arousal.

6 *What about emotional responses with no cognitive awareness?*
(a) **McGinnies (1949)** coined the term 'perceptual defence', showing that perceptions below the level of conscious awareness could still lead to an emotional response. She measured subjects' reactions to taboo words using GSR. This behaviour can be linked with Freud's notions of repression.
(b) **Lazarus and McCleary (1951)** supported this by classically conditioning subjects, pairing random words with electric shocks. When the words were subsequently presented subliminally the subjects still showed a strong GSR response.

A conclusion

1 Both factors – arousal and cognitive – are sufficient but not necessary conditions.
2 There are different kinds of emotional experience, some more physiological, some more cognitive which explains the above contradictions. For example:
- A jet screams over your head, you duck and experience a tightness in your chest. Past experience and individual differences will determine the emotion you might report feeling – fear, surprise, elation.

- You hear that you have passed A-level psychology and feel ecstatic, which may lead to physiological sensations.

PHYSIOLOGICAL BASIS

❶ Detecting changes in the ANS:
- autonomic arousal can be measured in terms of increased heart rate, blood pressure, respiration, etc.,
- the galvanic skin response (GSR) is also a measure of ANS arousal. It detects changes in the electrical conductivity of the skin, due to sweating. This is the basis of the polygraph (lie detector), which assumes that lying leads to stress and increased ANS activity,
- emotion increases activity of sympathetic branch, removal of stimulus activates the parasympathetic branch as a rebound effect.

❷ Locating centres in the brain (a neurobiological approach):
(a) **The limbic system:**
- **Maclean (1970)** distinguished three circuits and their behavioural effects:
  - amygdala and hippocampus: self-preservation, such as aggression,
  - cingulate gyrus, septum and other structures: pleasure, sex,
  - hypothalamus and thalamus: co-operative social behaviour, certain aspects of sexuality and motivation.
- *Amygdala:* species-related aggressive behaviour: **Aronson and Cooper (1979)** studied male cats with lesions of the amygdala and found that they mounted anything. It is not simply that they became hypersexual, but that they became indiscriminate about partners. Therefore the lesions did not simply cause or prevent a behaviour, but seemed to *change how animals interpret information.* Other studies have found that electrical stimulation leads sometimes to vigorous attacks, or sometimes to inhibition of such an attack.
- *Sociopaths* have positive spikes in their brain waves, which appear to reflect a dysfunction of the limbic system. Sociopaths may be physiologically unable to experience fear, which prevents them learning through punishment **(Rosenhan and Seligman, 1989).**
- *Sham rage:* **Bard (1929)** ablated the cerebral cortex in cats, which led to 'cool' aggression – emotion without arousal. If the hypothalamus was also removed the rage stopped, suggesting that the cortex ordinarily inhibits, directs and organises attacks, whereas the hypothalamus and related areas are necessary for expression of rage.
(b) **The temporal cortex:**
- **Kluver and Bucy (1939)** found that bilateral removal of the temporal cortical lobe resulted in profound changes in affective and social behaviour in monkeys (the **Kluver–Bucy syndrome**).
- *Prefrontal* (includes temporal lobes) *lobotomies* are associated with dramatic affective changes. These were first observed in monkeys, which led Moniz to develop psychosurgery.
- *Rabies* leads to violent behaviour, associated with infection of temporal lobes and amygdala.
- Some cases of temporal lobe *epilepsy* have affective overtones. For example Dostoyevskian epilepsy (named after the novelist), where sufferers experience feelings of extreme happiness, including a sense of oneness with the universe and the Creator.
- *Lateralisation:* the right hemisphere is involved with recognition of emotion and negative affect, while the left hemisphere is involved with positive affects. **Gainotti (1972)** found that patients with damage to the left cortical hemisphere could perceive the emotional tone of a statement even though they couldn't understand the words. The opposite was true of people with right hemisphere damage.

❸ Neurotransmitters:
- **Serotonin** is associated with increase in aggressive behaviour. The evidence is correlational rather than causal. **Valzelli (1973)** found that four weeks of social

isolation leads some strains of mice to become aggressive, it also decreases the turnover of serotonin. **Amphetamine** lowers serotonin turnover and increases violent behaviour.

- Epinephrine is both a hormone and a neurotransmitter. Increased ANS activity leads to increased production of epinephrine.

7.6 ANXIETY AND STRESS

Stress is a state of psychological tension produced by certain pressures or forces – physical or psychological. In engineering terms, stress is any force which causes some significant modification of form, usually a distortion, to a system:

- it is important to distinguish between stressors and stress responses,
- it is important to distinguish between short and long term stress,
- stress is an emotional response with important cognitive components,
- stress is a state of arousal related to the innate fight-or-flight response,
- stress is considered to be an important factor in modern-day ailments,

Anxiety is a vague, unpleasant, emotional state of tension (stress):

- it is a subclass of stress in general – a stressor,
- it is distinct from fear, which is situation-specific and short term,
- it is often accompanied by physical symptoms of ANS arousal,
- it is an innate response: it is an appropriate response to danger at optimum levels, otherwise it leads to impaired performance,
- it is a learned response: it may become paired with an unconditioned stimulus in early experience (Little Albert; see p.298),
- it is a focus of clinical psychology as a symptom and cause of some illnesses,
- it is an important concept in learning theory: the reduction of anxiety by the conditioned response is reinforcing.

STRESSORS

Sources of stress

- **environmental:** noise, temperature, pollution, architecture, overcrowding, the urban environment generally (see 9.2),
- **occupational:** job demands and controllability,
- **life events:** e.g. marriage, divorce, death of spouse,
- *psychological or physical injury*/illness leading to pain or shock,
- *emotions:* anxiety, fear, aggression (see 2.7), frustration, conflict (contradictory motives/goals),
- *disruption of circadian rhythms* (see 7.3)

Cox (1975) simplified these as three different models of stress:

❶ the *engineering* model: concentrates on the causes of stress,

❷ the *physiological* model: focuses on the internal processes which accompany stress,

❸ the *transactional* model: is concerned with the mismatch between the person and the environment, and with ways of coping.

Empirical work

Most of the studies not only provide evidence for stressors but stress responses as well.

① **Work-related stress:** a classic experiment was **Brady's (1958) 'Ulcers in Executive Monkeys'**, which showed that stress from emotional strain, rather than physical distress, had profound effects. The work began as an investigation of ulcers. One monkey was strapped in a chair and given shocks every 20 seconds unless it pressed a lever in the same period. Two discoveries were made: hormone levels in the blood were raised and many of the monkeys died. Post-mortem examination revealed that ulcers had developed. Restraint could not be the cause as monkeys had been strapped-in for up to six months in previous studies with no ulcers, therefore it must have been the conditioning procedures.

To test this they used a yoked control. Another monkey also received the shocks but had no control over the lever, only the 'executive' monkey received the psychological stress of having to press the lever. After 23 days of a six-hours-on, six-hours-off schedule, the executive monkey died due to a perforated ulcer.

② **Rest-related stress:** Brady thought that stress might be related to the reinforcement schedule. If it was 18 hours on and six hours off, or 30 minutes on, 30 minutes off, very few ill effects were noted. Therefore he concluded that it was the relationship between stress and rest time. It is now understood that stress leads to sympathetic arousal; when this stops the parasympathetic system rebounds and this is when excessive digestive juices are released.

One criticism made of the study in general is that the monkeys were not randomly selected, the 'executive' was chosen because it was faster at learning an avoidance response. This may of course have parallels with the human world.

While **Brady**'s experiment is regarded as a classic, its relevance to human work stress is questionable. Aspects of human stress at work are discussed in 9.1. **Argyle (1972)** lists lack of control as one of the fundamental sources of stress, in opposition to Brady's finding.

③ **Noise:** leads to depressed performance on some cognitive and mathematical tasks, but such effects are soon overcome. **Glass *et al.* (1969)** showed that unpredictable noise can't be blocked out so successfully and continues to act as stressor (measured by GSR). Further, they found that stress was reduced if the subject thought he could control the noise.

Unpredictable noise may cause stress because:
- habituation: we can 'tune out' constant stimuli while still attending at preconscious level (cocktail party effect) but non-constant stimuli require vigilance,
- noise and/or attention decreases the amount of psychic energy and therefore less is available to deal with stress.

Perceived control avoids a sense of helplessness and anxiety, which would exacerbate stress (see also 'Crowding', 9.2).

④ **Temperature: Baron and Ransberger (1978)** looked up past weather records and found that the incidence of riot and civil disturbance was greatest when the temperature was moderately hot, rather than extremely hot. **Baron and Bell (1976)** found that subjects delivered fewer shocks when the laboratory temperature was in the mid-ninety degrees Fahrenheit than in the low seventies. However, it may be that the hottest subjects had the greater desire to complete the experiment, which overcame their increased aggression (see also 9.2).

⑤ **Life events: Holmes and Rahe (1967)** devised a scale to measure stress in terms of life events. Correlations between the scale and a wide range of symptoms are small but significant. For example, **Rahe and Arthur (1977)** found an increase of various psychological illnesses, athletic injuries, physical illness and even traffic accidents. One explanation offered, as for the unpredictable noise, is that psychic energy is being spent in adapting to changes therefore lowering resistance and attention.

The work has been criticised:
- there may be many other factors intervening, e.g. a stressed person may be drinking more, or not sleeping,
- there are large individual differences as to impact of any life event, e.g. stress from a marriage break-up depends on who left whom.

(see also 3.5.)

6 Daily events: daily frustrations and hassles create stress, probably more than life events. **DeLongis** *et al.* **(1982)** devised a **hassles and uplifts scale** and found correlations between hassles and health. But there were significant individual differences; some subjects thrived on stress.

7 Shock: the body's defence against sudden trauma – physical or psychological – is the state of shock. All energy is concentrated on maintaining the vital systems. **Post-traumatic stress disorder** is a long-term response to psychological shock. It involves numbness, repeated reliving of the trauma, anxiety and guilt about surviving. It has previously been called shell shock or combat fatigue. Lack of control may be one of the key factors; such traumas disorder our orderly world.

8 Frustration: Coon (1983) defines this as the negative emotional state arising when we are prevented from reaching a goal. **Gross (1992)** offers three conflict situations: approach–approach, avoidance–avoidance or approach–avoidance, which describe having to choose between equally attractive, equally unattractive or equally attractive and unattractive choices.

9 Disruption of circadian rhythms: shift work, jet lag, etc. are stressful (see 7.3 for empirical studies).

10 RSI (repetitive strain injury): in the 19th century Morse key operators suffered telegraphists' wrist – pain from repetitive movements was associated with distinct physical abnormalities such as joint inflammation. In recent years the diagnosis of RSI has been given to persons who are suffering pain severe enough to stop movement altogether, but without any physical signs. It appears to be a complex condition with elements of psychosomaticism.

11 Person–environment fit: a recent trend has tried to describe stress in terms of mismatch between stress and personality variables. Some people function better at high levels of stress and some jobs require an optimum level of stress. **Furnham and Walsh (1991)** failed to find much support for a relationship between measures of 'fit' (such as consistency) and absenteeism or stress. The problem may lie in difficulty measuring 'fit'.

12 Individual differences: different people have different responses to stress. For example, **Gannon** *et al.* **(1987)** created laboratory conditions of stress using arithmetic problems and found that 67% of subjects who were chronic migraine sufferers experienced headaches when stressed compared with 25% of subjects who were occasional headache sufferers; i.e. some, but not all, people respond to stress with a headache. **Chesney and Rosenman (1980)** found that Type A (see p.300) managers experienced anxiety most when they were not in control, whereas the opposite was true of Type Bs.

STRESS RESPONSES

Learned responses

1 Classical conditioning of anxiety: stress results from pleasant and unpleasant emotions. Maladaptive emotional responses are learned (conditioned emotional responses, CERs) and explain phobias; this understanding has lead to a successful form of behaviour therapy (see 6.2).

The classic experiment demonstrating CERs was conducted by **Watson and Rayner (1920)**, using **Little Albert** – a boy of 11 months, who was the son of one of the nurses working in Watson's hospital. A white rat was put in front of the baby, and as he reached out to touch it, the experimenter made a loud noise with a steel bar; the boy showed a strong fear response. This classical conditioning procedure was repeated six times, at which point the boy reacted to the sight of a rat by crying. Later this was shown to extend to other objects such as a fur coat, a rabbit and white cotton wool. A year later the conditioned emotional response was still evident. Unfortunately the experimenters never had the opportunity to extinguish the CERs because the boy's mother removed him.

2 Operant conditioning – learned helplessness: a negative reinforcer, such as produced by stress, should reduce the likelihood of a behaviour. When an individual experiences lack of control the learned response is no response or apathy to the stressor.

Seligman (1975) gave animals unavoidable shocks for a prolonged period; not surprisingly the animals ceased to respond. If the animal was then placed in a situation where the shocks can be avoided (controlled) it nevertheless continued its response of doing nothing. When the same principles were applied to humans, the picture wasn't quite as clear and therefore the process was restated in terms of attribution theory (see 2.3). Some people attribute failure to themselves rather than, when appropriate, to external factors. These attributions are mistakenly taken as global and unchangeable.

Physiological responses

The **hypothalamus** is regarded as the stress centre:

- It arouses the **pituitary**, which secretes adrenocorticotrophic hormone **(ACTH)**, which stimulates growth of the **adrenal gland** and the production of adrenal hormones.
- The adrenal gland secretes **adrenaline** (epinephrine) which stimulates the sympathetic ANS and releases sugar.
- ACTH may also act as a neuromodulator to reduce anxiety by blocking GABA receptors, in the same way that enkephalins block pain.

Stress can be **measured**:

- By the size of the adrenal gland, which becomes enlarged under prolonged stress.
- From the amount of cortisol in the urine, a hormone produced by the adrenal gland.
- With GSR, a measure of activity in the ANS.

How have these mechanisms been linked with stress?

1. **Selye (1956) described the general adaptation syndrome (GAS)**: prolonged stress will produce a distinct physiological reaction. Stress from any source will trigger off the sequence of events below:
   - *alarm reaction:* release of ACTH and epinephrine in readiness for fight or flight,
   - *resistance:* hormone production maintained at lower level as body habituates to stressor,
   - *collapse:* eventual depletion of body's resources and adrenal cortex not functioning properly leaves individual unable to fight infection.

2. **Reduced immune response: Jemmott *et al.* (1985)** found lower levels of certain antibodies in students during examination periods.

3. **Production of hormones: Brady (1958)** showed that the increased metabolism caused by release of epinephrine can lead to ulceration and other somatic disorders. **Jenner *et al.* (1980)** found that non-manual workers in senior positions demanding greater mental effort had higher levels of epinephrine in their urine. **McCaul et al. (1992)** tested the hormone levels of winners and losers in a game of chance and found higher testosterone levels in the winners. Levels of cortisol were the same for both groups.

4. **Arousal:** is a general factor in most stressors and associated with activity of the ANS. The innate fight-or-flight response explains the evolutionary value of stress. Arousal serves useful purposes, though too much arousal is counterproductive (Yerkes–Dodson effect), and long-term arousal is maladaptive.

   Arousal may have positive as well as useful consequences, as shown by the Yerkes–Dodson effect (see 7.4). **Selye** uses 'eustress' to signify pleasant stress associated with fulfilment.

   Arousal can also come from pleasurable activity, such as emotional highs or loud music, which presumably can lead to the same unpleasant side-effects as other forms of stress but different cognitive appraisal.

5. **Parasympathetic rebound: Cannon (1942)** documented a series of voodoo deaths and observed that in some way the terror and feeling of hopelessness led to death. **Richter (1957)** showed that rats who normally can swim for prolonged periods will

die when their whiskers are cut off and they are placed in water. It seems that they don't drown but their heart stops (and therefore they sink) because the two traumas (loss of whiskers and sudden immersion) lead to high activation of parasympathetic system and heart failure.

Psychological responses

Most of the psychological responses have been mentioned already:

1. Anger, apathy and anxiety are the most common responses. In excessive amounts these become states of psychological disorder, such as post-traumatic stress disorder, free-floating anxiety, rages, and so on.

2. The relationship between stress and, for example, depression or schizophrenia, may be more in terms of it acting as an aggravation to a pre-existing problem.

3. **Individual differences**: as responses such as anxiety and apathy are learned (see Little Albert and learned helplessness) there will be differences in individuals related to experience. **Friedman and Rosenman (1974)** found a link between stress, personality type (A and B) and heart disease. Type A personalities are competitive, restless, hyperalert and tense, whereas type B may work as hard but are more relaxed, can delegate and switch off when resting. **Eysenck (1963)** related arousal to individual differences.

REDUCING STRESS - COPING

There is a choice: either reduce the problem or reduce the stress. In some cases there is no choice, for example with exam nerves the problem is immovable but the stress itself can be reduced. Short-term stress should also be distinguished from long-term stress.

1. **Direct action**: deal directly with the problem.

2. **Control**: reducing the problem: if a person can feel in control stress is considerably reduced (**Glass et al., 1969**). If an individual lacks a sense of control they respond with 'learned helplessness'. The process can be reversed by training a person to attribute control internally (see **Rotter (1966)** and **Dweck (1975)** in 2.2). (On the reverse side of the coin, **Brady**'s monkeys expressed stress because they were in control.)

3. **Relaxation**: reducing the stress: meditation, self-hypnosis and biofeedback techniques are all forms of relaxation which decrease activity of ANS so decreasing stress.

4. **Rest periods**: reducing the stress: **Brady (1958)** found that the rest periods are the time when physiological damage takes place, therefore the advice is not to stop suddenly: taper off with gentle exercise or a meal to absorb the digestive juices.

5. **Physical exercise**: the evidence is largely correlational. For example, **Goldwater and Collis (1985)** found that exercise was positively related to decreased anxiety.

6. **Ego defence mechanisms**: reducing the stress and the problem: repression, denial, projection and displacement are all unconscious means of reducing stress. Intellectualisation and rationalisation are ways of consciously and cognitively reshaping the problem.

7. **Emotional discharge**: expressing tension through crying, anger or humour. A catharsis. Related to this is using alcohol or drugs.

8. **Cognitive redefinition**: using cognitive strategies to reappraise the situation, such as noting that things could be worse.

9. **Social support**: seeking help or comfort from close friends and family. Therapy offers a kind of social support.

10. **Re-adjust stressors**: match one's activity and one's stressors to our perceived ability to cope with them. Only when the calculation is in error do we experience stress (environment–person fit). Therefore, the advice is to reduce the stressors.

7.7 PAIN

Pain is intimately linked with stress and emotion. It is a sensation with strong motivational properties. It has an obvious survival function in alerting a person to injury but prolonged or chronic pain ceases to be informative. It is probably the most common symptom in medical practice and musculoskeletal pain accounts for 25% of all sick leave. The interest in the topic lies in its frequent and chronic occurrence, and the challenge of understanding the physical and psychological processes involved.

Physiological basis

- a stimulus (mechanical, chemical or thermal) causes the release of *algogenic substances,*
- *nociceptors* (nerve endings) are activated by these biochemicals,
- there are two types of nerve fibres:
  - *A-delta fibres* carry impulses for immediate or sharp pain,
  - *C fibres* (unmyelinated) communicate slow, diffuse, burning or aching pain,
- the nerve fibres have synapses in the dorsal horns of the spinal cord, where *substance P* is released,
- second-order neurons send information on to the thalamus and brain stem,
- the presence of *endorphins* (natural opiates) reduces the sensation of pain by inhibiting the neurons which produce substance P.

Sensation and perception of pain

The *experience* of pain varies from person to person, and situation to situation:

1. **Damage with no pain:** a common example is an injured athlete who only feels pain when the contest is over. Many techniques used to relive pain, such as yoga, show that pain can be reduced by psychological methods.

2. **Pain with no damage:** as in phantom limb pain; some amputees report severe pain in the area of the amputated limb even years later (**Melzack, 1973**).

3. **Referred pain:** pain originating from internal organs is perceived as coming from elsewhere because the internal organs share the same neural pathways with other body parts; the brain attributes the source. For example, the pain felt in a heart attack is often felt in the shoulders or arms; appendicitis is felt in the upper-middle abdomen, whereas the appendix is on the lower right.

4. **Variability:**
   - some people (masochists) like pain,
   - high self-efficacy appears to be negatively associated with pain perception (see 3.4),
   - the effect of emotion on pain: tension acts like a volume control on pain, the greater then tension the greater the pain,
   - **Beecher (1956)** found that only 33% of soldiers in battle in the Second World War required morphine, whereas civilians with similar wounds required much higher doses,
   - **Block et al. (1980)** found that chronic patients who knew they were being watched by a 'solicitous' spouse during an interview about their chronic pain showed higher levels of pain than those watched by less supportive spouses and when they were watched by their employer. This suggests a cognitive influence over pain perception.

5. **Placebo effect:** the drug *naloxone* blocks the production of endorphins and therefore is useful in their investigation. **Levine et al. (1978)** gave volunteers receiving dental surgery a placebo injection either two hours before or two hours after an injection of naloxone. Pain increased when subjects received naloxone suggesting that, prior to injection, there were endorphins present which were responsible for pain relief. Not all patients reacted as strongly to the placebo, but those who did showed the greatest naloxone effect, demonstrating that the endorphins were produced by the placebo.

Theories of pain

Pain is clearly a combination of the sensory component and the emotional–motivational aspect, which accounts for the lack of correspondence between pain sensation and stimulation.

1 **Linear models:** concerned with stimulus and responses:
- **Sternbach (1968)** identified three components: the personal sensation, the harmful stimulus, and the response to avoid it. This describes the straightforward relationship between tissue damage and pain, but not the psychological influences.
- **Pattern theory:** clearly somatic nerves respond to excessive stimulation, but how are pain, touch, tickle or temperature distinguished? Presumably each has a different 'code' arising from stimulating different patterns in terms of time and space (**Crue and Carregal, 1975**).

2 **Gate-control theory of pain: Melzack and Wall (1965, 1982)** proposed the most influential theory based on endorphin action, which is likened to a gate. The gate is located at the neuronal synapse in the spinal cord. When the gate is open signals are relayed to the brain; in this case no endorphins are present to block transmission. The more 'closed' the gate, the more signals are inhibited. In other words the gate, or endorphin action, acts to modulate pain signals. The factors which 'close the gate' are: the amount of activity in the pain fibres (amount of activity in peripheral fibres may decrease pain), and messages that descend from the brain (emotional conditions may open or close the gate).

Evaluation:
- **Dyck** *et al.* **(1976)** have produced clinical evidence that inhibition doesn't occur,
- it doesn't account for the fact that people don't always avoid pain situations,
- it is a useful conceptual framework and a clear physiological account.

3 **Cognitive models:** these models particularly try to explain the behaviour of chronic pain sufferers: how does a person become trapped in this non-adaptive behaviour?
- **'Fear of pain' model: Lethem** *et al.* **(1983)** suggested that individual differences in coping strategies are critical in determining future behaviour. People are either avoidant or confrontational in response to pain. Avoidant responses lead to an avoidance spiral: the more you don't do something the greater the avoidance response. A person who injures their leg and finds exercise difficult may give up exercise, in which case the next time they try to exercise the pain will be worse and their inactivity will be reinforced. Another person might be determined to persist and therefore their pain will decrease, positively reinforcing their actions.
- **Beliefs about pain: Philips and Jahanshahi (1986)** emphasise the role of an individual's beliefs about the likelihood of pain in certain situations. Beliefs rather than actual pain experienced can best predict an individual's future behaviour. **Kent (1985)** found that anxious dental patients estimated pain as more severe three months after treatment than they had immediately after treatment, supporting the notion that expectations are more important than actual experience.

Measuring and investigating pain

1 **Self report:**
- interview, patient's diary,
- rating scales, e.g. *McGill Pain Questionnaire* (MPQ), which contains words to describe pain,
- questionnaires: means of indicating amount of pain, e.g. *Pain Behaviour Checklist* (PBC) relates situations to likelihood of avoidance.

2 **Behavioural assessment:** e.g. verbal complaints, non-verbal indications (moans, face or body posture, tone of voice), displays of functional limitation (e.g. lying down), or frequency of medication. Such data can be gathered through direct observation while subjects are engaged in set tasks or through self-report.

3 **Physiological measures:** objective means of assessment which do not wholly reflect the experience, e.g. electromyograph, which measures tension in the muscles; polygraph or heart rate to measure autonomic activity.

④ Experimental techniques for inducing pain:
- the cold-pressor procedure: placing arm in ice water for a few minutes, e.g. **Girodo and Wood (1979)**, below,
- muscle ischaemia: reducing blood supply with a cuff like used for checking blood pressure, causes pain but no damage, e.g. **Cogan et al. (1987)**, below.

Controlling pain

A test of any model is its ability to develop procedures for managing pain, which is an important focus for medicine particularly where chronic sufferers are concerned, but any medical intervention is improved by lessening pain.

❶ Chemicals: tablets or injections. Peripherally acting analgesics (e.g. aspirin), centrally acting analgesics (e.g. morphine), local anaesthetics (e.g. novocaine) and depressants (e.g. sedatives). Such methods are used extensively but they are not useful for chronic pain because of addiction problems and side-effects.

❷ Cognitive methods: (see 6.2) generally aim to alter the way the person views the pain in terms of cognitions (e.g. beliefs, expectations):
- Increasing sense of control: **Wernick (1983)** worked with severe burn patients and found that enhancing their sense of control led to their spontaneous decision to reduce medication. **Girodo and Wood (1979)** trained subjects to cope by making positive self-statements ('I can cope'). One group of subjects additionally were given explanations as to why this method works (enhancing their sense of personal control) and experienced less pain, presumably as a result.
- Attention diversion for brief episodes: looking at a nice picture or singing a song. This non-pain imagery is similar to relaxation.
- Pain redefinition: at a simple level 'it hurts but it's good for you'.

❸ Insight therapies: aims to change how the *whole* person feels as well as thinks. A chronic pain sufferer often becomes depressed, embedded in the sick role or 'game-playing'. Counselling or group therapy may help.

❹ Behaviour therapy: setting goals and operant conditioning to reverse the initial, non-adaptive learning between pain and aversive stimulus, e.g. helping a child to overcome fear of injections:
- Works best when pain behaviours are ignored, otherwise attention only serves to reinforce these. Instead reward health behaviour.
- **Cogan et al. (1987)** found that subjects tolerated 50% more pain when in a laughter group (listening to a recording of Lily Tomlin) or relaxation group than in a narrative condition (a educational lecture) or control group.
- Biofeedback involves learning new associations (see 7.2).

❺ Hypnosis: related to relaxation and endorphin blocking (see 7.2).

❻ Physical therapy:
- Decrease tension which exaggerates pain, e.g. relaxation, massage.
- Increase suppleness, e.g. exercise or hot compress. Chronic sufferers do less and less and therefore movement becomes more painful.
- Counterstimulation, e.g. TENS (transcutaneous electrical nerve stimulation). Leads to release of endorphins. **Goldstein (1980)** suggests that listening to exciting music can reduce pain in this way.
- Acupuncture.
- Surgery.

❼ Pain clinics: offer a multicomponent approach to help chronic sufferers cope with psychological problems which worsen the pain and to avoid reliance on drugs. **Philips (1987)** found considerable improvements in subjects compared with an equivalent group left on a waiting list for a pain clinic. They had an increased sense of control and self-efficacy, and decreased depression, avoidance response and feelings of pain. One year later such changes persisted.

Chapter roundup

Many topics covered in this chapter are also explored elsewhere but from a more behavioural stance.

- cognitive psychology (Chapter 1), includes some physiological details of perception, learning and memory; attention is related to arousal;
- social psychology (Chapter 2), aggression – an important emotion – is discussed as an antisocial behaviour;
- developmental psychology (Chapter 3) examines emotion in terms of its development, and gender in terms of biological or social determination;
- communication (Chapter 4) covers the physiology of language;
- abnormal psychology (Chapter 6) explores the relationship between mental illness and physiological factors. Anxiety and stress are important concepts in this chapter;
- animal behaviour (Chapter 8) examines further physiological research and introduces evolutionary arguments; also a discussion of the ethics of using animals in research;
- applied psychology (Chapter 9) offers alternative explanations of behaviour in terms of the environment, and explores stress factors and strategies for coping;
- research and design (Chapter 10) includes a discussion of methodology and ethics.

Illustrative question

Critically consider the extent to which behaviours can be explained in terms of activity of the nervous system.

(AEB, 'A', 1992)

Tutorial note

When this question appeared in an exam the answers were very poor according to the examiner's report, yet it is the underlying purpose of the section of the syllabus covered in this chapter. It is also a question that most people can actually answer quite well drawing on their knowledge of all areas of psychology, however they don't realise they can.

Such a broad question can be answered in a variety of ways; the approach below will sacrifice detail for breadth, to demonstrate the wealth of material which could be included.

The AEB mark scheme looks for description *and* evaluation. This question lends itself to description; the evaluative element can be tackled by comparing explanations in terms of the nervous system with other explanations. A more detailed approach might have selected only one or two behaviours and criticised the empirical evidence raised.

Suggested answer

What is 'the nervous system'? The central nervous system consists of the brain, spinal cord and neurons. The peripheral nervous system includes the nerves of the body (somatic nervous system) and the autonomic nervous system, which is associated with hormone production. Activity in the nervous systems is electrical and chemical: nervous impulses, neurotransmitters and hormones.

Just about any behaviour you could think of has been given some explanation in terms of nervous system activity, but to *what extent* are such explanations sufficient?

One might expect there to be relatively simple correlation between a *drug*, the nervous system and behaviour. However, just about every drug has multiple effects. Some effects, the primary ones, are fairly predictable and can be shown in terms of the effect on synaptic transmission. The secondary effects vary from person to person, which explains why it is impossible to predict the exact behavioural corollaries of a drug. For example, of the women who took *thalidomide* during the critical period of pregnancy, only about

20% gave birth to deformed babies. *Drug addiction* is an example of the interaction between pharmacological properties and personality variables. Not everyone is equally susceptible to becoming an addict which indicates that the experience of addiction is not simply physiological. The process of giving up can be achieved through attribution retraining, again demonstrating the importance of other factors in what is sometimes viewed as a simple physiological process.

Sight is another example of interaction. It can be explained in terms of the properties of rods and cones, and the specialised nature of the cells in the visual cortex which respond to very specific stimuli. However, *perception* is more than this: what we 'see' is a combination of sensory data and organisation of this data on the basis of past experience.

The process of *motivation* has been explained at various levels. The most basic needs such as body temperature and thirst are controlled by autonomic homeostatic mechanisms. Other, higher order behaviours or 'meta' needs, such as curiosity and self-actualisation, are psychological concepts requiring psychological explanations. Even basic needs are sometimes mediated by cognitive factors, for example we often feel hungry not because of real hunger but because the food looks good.

Arousal has been used to explain motivated behaviour at various levels, physiological and behavioural. Too much or too little arousal leads to poor performance, as described, for example by the Yerkes–Dodson model. The state of physiological *arousal* is critical to many other behaviours, such as emotion and sleep.

Attempts to explain the processes involved in an *emotional experience* involve strands from both physiology and psychology. It is clear that in some cases arousal alone can account for a person's emotional state; for example **Schachter and Singer's (1962)** classic experiment demonstrated that injected epinephrine can lead to an emotional experience. However, the tone of the experience, in this case, depended on cognitive factors.

Much work on *sleep* has focused on nervous activity. It is an example of arousal, or the lack of it, mediated by areas of the brain, such as the reticular activating system. One explanation for the need for sleep is as a time for the nervous system to be 'restored'. **Crick and Mitchison (1986)** suggest that dreams may also serve a restorative function; they are the subjective experience of random neural firing needed for the daily debugging and fine tuning of the neural network.

However, the evidence for sleep as a necessary physiological need is equivocal. Deprivation studies have failed to find consistent ill effects. Alternative explanations suggest that sleep is a form of protection. For example, **Meddis (1979)** has suggested that the long sleep periods of babies have evolved in order to help their mothers to cope.

In recent years, *mental illnesses* have been more clearly linked with nervous activity. One example comes from studies of the Amish, which have provided evidence that a chromosome defect predisposes a person to *manic-depression* **(Rosenhan and Seligman, 1984)**. This genetic defect has been associated with a lack of certain neurotransmitters (catecholamines) which in turn affects brain activity. One important practical consequence is the link with suitable drug therapies. However, not everyone with the defect becomes mentally ill, the defect only 'predisposes'. All this is also true for physical illnesses, and this can be used to explain the efficacy of non-drug therapies for mental and physical illnesses.

The preceding examples are all ones where physiological explanations are usual, but in each case such explanations are clearly not sufficient. What about behaviours which have been viewed as psychological, but have turned out to have a physical, neurological basis? Can we explain *insomnia* and *jet lag* in terms of the nervous system? The biological clock, the suprachiasmatic nucleus located in the hypothalamus, appears to be set to a cycle of just under 25 hours. **Weitzman et al. (1981)** investigated delayed sleep phase disorder. In some individuals, staying up late a few nights in a row or travelling eastwards resets their biological clock and they then maintain a pattern of staying up late and waking late. The researchers recommend that the only way to reset the clock is to take some time off work and stay up a few hours *later* each night until a suitable bedtime is reached. The reason for staying up later rather than going to bed earlier is the 25-hour cycle.

Some of the effects of *hypnosis, relaxation, biofeedback* and *placebos,* in particular for pain relief, may be due to the production of endorphins – neuromodulators which block pain. There is emerging evidence that endorphins may have other effects as well, such as the control of blood pressure and thermoregulation. Such processes are under the control of the autonomic nervous system, and relaxation is generally associated with the parasympathetic activity of the ANS.

It may be possible to explain *personality* in terms of the nervous system. **Shields (1983)** reviewed research on autonomic responsiveness and concluded that there were consistent individual differences: those with high sympathetic responsivity tended to show more emotion, more gregariousness, more overall activity, less patience, and responded more quickly though sometimes less accurately. **Eysenck (1963)** has suggested that extroversion is related to cortical arousal, which may, if true, not only explain some individual differences but offer us a means of objective personality assessment.

The original question as to the 'extent' that behaviour can be 'explained in terms of nervous system activity' is a reductionist one: can we reduce all behaviour to such units? The current failure to do so completely may simply be because we do not know sufficient detail, but theoretically it will one day be possible. Alternatively, Gestalt, or humanist, psychologists take the view that such data is illuminating, but will never explain the complexity of human behaviour. Such an approach is not even relevant to some aspects of behaviour. For example, *language,* which has long been identified with specific areas of the brain and, being closely associated with memory, clearly has a biochemical basis. However, other aspects of language, such as dialect, are explained in terms of in-group processes. Nervous activity may underlie such behaviour but as an explanation it makes no sense.

This leads us finally to the philosophical issue of the mind–body dualism. The three main resolutions are: interactive, parallel or epiphenomenal. Interactive explanations are by far the most common, such as the effect of drugs, the process of perception and the occurrence of mental and physical illness. The parallelist position is illustrated by some emotional experiences which involve the two processes of cognition and arousal, unconnected but correlated. An example of epiphenomenalism is shown by one interpretation of dreams as the epiphenomena which incidentally accompany the biochemical and neurological events which occur during sleep.

In summary, the answer is that nervous activity can explain behaviour but only in conjunction with other phenomena.

Question bank

Allow 45 minutes for each question.

1 Discuss the role played by neural processes in any one type of behaviour found in humans.

(AEB, 'AS', 1991)

Points: Note the word 'humans'; evidence regarding animals is irrelevant. Only one behaviour is called for, no credit would be given for other behaviours.

2 (a) Explain the processes of synaptic transmission. (10 marks)
(b) Discuss the way in which behaviour might be explained in terms of these processes. (15 marks)

(AEB, 'AS', 1992)

Points: Candidates who are familiar with such material are rare but it's a wonderfully straightforward and rich topic.

3 Discuss the function of the endocrine system and its interaction with the central and autonomic nervous systems.

(AEB, 'A', 1989)

Points: A very straightforward question if you know the material.

4 Discuss some of the findings of research into localisation of function in the human cerebral cortex.

(AEB, 'AS ' 1993)

Points: Consider perception, learning, memory, aggression, language, as well as the functions mentioned in this chapter. Describing the necessary material is fairly straightforward. Evaluation is more difficult but necessary for a good answer. It is also best to discriminate between cortical and subcortical structures, and avoid dwelling on split-brain studies and lateralisation.

5 What do psychologists understand by the term 'homeostatic mechanisms'? Discuss physiological evidence that has been used to examine how mechanisms are involved in normal and abnormal functions of the nervous system.

(AEB, 'A', 1991)

Points: Organisation of the nervous system is peripheral to this question: concentrate on the hypothalamus and temperature, hunger or thirst. Include non-homeostatic mechanisms.

6 How may drugs affect the nervous system in terms of neural activity and what are the consequent effects upon behaviour?

(AEB, 'A', 1990)

Points: A question like this is either answered very badly, with common knowledge about alcohol and LSD, or answered extremely well, covering neural *and* behavioural effects.

7 Using psychological evidence, critically consider whether hypnosis should be regarded as an altered state of awareness.

(AEB, 'AS', 1991)

Points: It is easy to include material which is not relevant.

8 What is the purpose of sleep?

(AEB, 'A', 1984)

Points: Sleep is a popular topic and therefore answers must be of a high standard to get good marks. Ensure that you answer this particular question and not write a general essay on sleep.

9 Discuss the evidence that electrical and chemical activity is closely associated with sleep and dream states.

(AEB, 'A', 1987)

Points: See the points to question 8. 'Discuss the evidence' means that empirical work should be described *and* evaluated.

10 'Psychology has no contribution to make to our understanding of emotion. Physiology provides all the answers'. Discuss.

(AEB, 'AS', 1989)

Points: Describe *and* evaluate. Remember that stress and pain are emotional states.

11 Describe and discuss some physiological responses to states of stress.

(AEB, 'A', 1988)

Points: Material on emotion may be relevant, as stress is an emotional state, but it is important to state such connections explicitly.

12 (a) Discuss some of the major sources of psychological stress. (13 marks)
   (b) Evaluate, from a psychological viewpoint, some strategies which individuals use to cope with stress. (12 marks)

(AEB, 'AS', 1992)

Points: You should distinguish between stressors, stress responses and ways of coping. The question calls for more than descriptions of how to cope.

13 Environmental and technological catastrophes have been shown to produce considerable stress. A local authority is concerned about preparations for a disaster in its area of responsibility.
   Your task is to prepare a report for the council on the psychological effects of environmental stress caused by a neutral disaster (such as an earthquake or flood) or a technological disaster (such as a nuclear accident at a power station, or a major pollution spill into the local water supply). In your report you should:
   (a) review some psychological evidence on the behaviour of people in response to stressful events like those described above. This evidence could include the long-term effects as well as the short-term effects,
   (b) explain why you think these studies are relevant to the task,
   (c) evaluate these studies (i) for the methodology they used, and (ii) the conclusions they arrived at,
   (d) suggest how the council might prepare to cope with a disaster.

(Oxford and Cambridge, 'A')

Points: Beware of applying results from non-human studies to humans.

14 The local health authority wants to set up a support group for the relatives of people with severe pain.
   Your task is to prepare a report about pain and its control. In your report you should:
   (a) review some psychological studies or approaches that have contributed to our understanding of pain,
   (b) explain how these approaches and studies relate to the symptoms of pain experienced by the sufferer,
   (c) evaluate these studies or theoretical approaches in terms of the methodology they used or the conclusions they arrived at,
   (d) suggest some behavioural coping strategies for the sufferers and their relatives.

(Oxford and Cambridge , 'A')

Points: Marks are awarded for psychological knowledge, analysis, evaluation and making novel links between existing information and specific applications.

CHAPTER 8

ANIMAL BEHAVIOUR

Units in this chapter:

Chapter overview

The study of animal behaviour is divided between the laboratory (behaviourists who study learning and the effects of experience) and natural settings (where ethologists observe the survival value of behaviours). Animal psychology is sometimes termed 'comparative psychology' because animal data is used to make comparisons (similarities and differences) between species of animals, including humans. The degree to which it is applicable to human understanding is questionable, there are critical qualitative differences to be considered.

An historical view

Darwin (1871) introduced the idea that the comparative study of different species yields information about evolution. This aroused intense scientific interest and led to the formal study of animal behaviour. The first research was undertaken by psychologists in the form of behaviourism, for example, Watson and Pavlov. They used animals to pursue their understanding of *human* behaviour, arguing on the basis of evolutionary principles that all animal behaviour is the same, the differences being quantitative rather than qualitative.

In contrast, other psychologists have preferred to observe, rather than experiment with, animals. In about 1950 this led to the development of ethology, which regards laboratory-based work as unnatural and emphasises the genetic rather than learned aspects of behaviour.

Current views tend towards a middle position between genetic and environmental determinism.

8.1 PRINCIPLES OF EVOLUTION

Evolution provides psychologists with a means of explaining behaviours in terms of their different survival values.

Evolution is not a theory it is a fact: to evolve is to develop. However there are theories to explain the processes by which it occurs:

- **Lamarck**'s theory of evolution proposed that *acquired* characteristics are passed on from one generation to the next. This has been shown to be mistaken, though some learning experiences do affect offspring before birth.

- **Darwin**'s theory of **natural selection** proposed that all life forms have developed from a single source through **survival of the fittest**.

GENES

Evolution is the change of gene frequencies for a population. A **gene** is the basic unit of heredity; each gene is a set of instructions for making proteins. These combine to form features of the organism, such as eye colour. Even the simplest features are determined by more than one gene. Complex traits such as intelligence are determined by numerous genes **(polygenetic inheritance)**.

The basis of genes is **DNA**, located on long spiralling strands (the double helix) called **chromosomes**. The number of chromosomes varies from species to species, in humans there are 23 pairs. Each chromosome pair contains corresponding pairs of genes; one has come from the mother and one from the father. For each pair there may be a dominant gene **(Mendelian inheritance** of dominant and recessive genes) or the expression of the genes may depend on more complex factors such as **penetrance** – the interaction between genetic expression and environmental conditions. The act of **reproduction** passes on a set of genes from parent to child. Where reproduction is sexual two parents combine their two sets of chromosomes to form a new, unique combination. In simpler life forms reproduction is **asexual**, by cell division, so that genetically the 'offspring' remain identical except for **mutations**, which occur naturally at a rate of about one per 100,000 genes in each generation. Sexual reproduction offers vastly increased potential for genetic variation.

There is a critical balance to be struck:

- **Genetic stability:** too much change between generations may threaten survival. The offspring should be as near as possible to its parents who have adapted successfully to their environment and also to ensure that mating will be possible.

- **Genetic change:** the environment is changing constantly and organisms must adapt to the changes in order to survive. Therefore the species needs to continually try out new variations otherwise the gene pool will die out. Change occurs through new combinations and/or random mutations creating an entirely new feature. The rate of change is closely related to environmental change or stability.

A glossary of terms

genotype: the genetic make up of an organism, a purely theoretical notion,
phenotype: the actual expression of the genes, the external character of the organism which occurs through interaction between genotype and the environment,
species: a group of individuals who share a common and discrete gene pool,
genus: a group of related species.

NATURAL SELECTION

Darwin proposed natural selection (as opposed to artificial breeding, a means of deliberately selecting desirable traits) as the process through which species diversify:

- At any time a species occupies an **ecological niche**; only one species can occupy it at any one time (e.g. giraffes and elephants occupy different niches though they live side by side).

- A species is particularly **adapted** to its niche (environment).

- This adaptation has been achieved through **selective pressure**, the mechanism by which one species is favoured (survives) more than another.

- Survival is measured in terms of reproductive success and **survival of the fittest** is achieved by those individuals who are best adapted to their niche.

- **Fitness** is the degree to which the species 'fits' or is adapted to its environment.
- **Environmental change** means that this process is ongoing; as long as the environment remains the same there is no need for a species to adapt further.
- Only differences which are inherited can be naturally selected.
- Only those individuals who survive to reproduce matter. It is only their genes which natural selection acts upon.

Evidence is from:

- Comparing living species with each other and their fossil ancestors.
- Comparing closely related species living in different habitats; any differences reveal those behaviours which have been adaptive. Darwin's first observations were about the effects of geographical isolation of the different islands of the Galapagos.
- Studying the effects of environmental change, as in the case of industrial melanism.

Industrial melanism

One of the most popular examples of natural selection is the case of the peppered moth before and after the industrial revolution in Britain. Environmental change (surfaces blackened by soot) meant that the dark form of the moth had an adaptive advantage over the lighter variety because it was better camouflaged against moth-eating birds. The dark form first appeared in 1850 in the industrial north; by 1900 (about 50 generations) it had virtually replaced the lighter form. **Kettlewell (1955)** demonstrated this selective pressure at work by recording the frequency that the birds took the different types of moths on darker and lighter trees. He also noted that the moths preferred to rest on the appropriate background.

Similar selective pressures have occurred with insecticides – some strains of housefly are now resistant to all forms of insecticide. Similarly, bacteria are now developing strains resistant to antibiotics through mutation.

THE EVOLUTION OF BEHAVIOUR

Behaviour is a series of movements. The scientific study of behaviour is possible because it has repeatable, recognisable units occurring in members of the same species.

Behaviour has evolved according to the same principles as anatomy and physiology, however evidence is not as easily obtainable:

- *Fossil* records may provide evidence of certain anatomical features which imply certain behaviours.
- *Archaeology* supplies evidence of previous human activities. For example, encampments with animal bones and stone axes imply organised hunting or early agricultural practices.
- The best evidence is *interspecies comparisons*. A behaviour pattern shared by all species within a genus must be more ancient than those which differ. On this basis **Lorenz** concluded that the mallard was one of the most primitive ducks since it shows all the basic behaviour patterns common to ducks. The same behaviour may appear in different species because of:
  - *Homology:* the species share a common ancestor,
  - *Analogy:* they have evolved due to the same environmental pressures.
- *Cross-breeding:* can demonstrate the heritability of behaviour. For example, **Dilger (1962)** cross-bred two species of lovebirds. Each species had a different method of carrying nesting material. The hybrid offspring tried to combine the two methods and in the end failed to build the nest.
- *Universal human behaviours:* aggression, mother–child bond, language, incest taboo, gender differences, altruism, conformity, ethics, genocide, love, spite, territoriality and xenophobia. The fact that these are universal suggests a genetic basis and, it can further be argued, that they must have a survival value to have been naturally selected.

THE EVOLUTION OF CULTURE

1 **The analogy between cultural and genetic inheritance:** cultural behaviour is that which is passed on from one generation to the next. Cultural inheritance is analogous to genetic inheritance and leads to a process of evolutionary change. Those behaviours which are successful or adaptive will be imitated and be passed on to future generations. Thus they are selected and inherited. However the process is only analogous but not the same as genetic evolutionary change.

2 **The superiority of cultural transmission:** it is more powerful and flexible because it is considerably faster. **Brown (1986)** points out that rapid cultural evolution will make biological evolution irrelevant. For example, it took 200 million years for the first marine animals to evolve into amphibians, whereas it took 50 years of cultural evolution for man to move from flying in the air to space travel.

3 **Animal culture**, examples:
- **Ridley (1986)** describes observations of the Japanese macaque undertaken since 1952. The researchers left sweet potatoes on the beach for the monkeys, one of whom, Imo, 'invented' the idea of washing the sand off the potatoes in the sea. Soon other monkeys imitated her. Imo later invented wheat skimming, gathering handfuls of grain and washing them. This too soon passed into the troop's shared knowledge.
- Great tits and blue tits were first observed removing the foil tops of milk bottles and drinking the milk in 1921. Within the next ten years the habit spread throughout Britain. It is possible that more than one bird invented the habit, but it is likely that most learned through imitation. It was certainly not due to natural selection because the change was too rapid. **Sherry and Galef (1984)** demonstrated that birds learn by a combination of imitation, spontaneous discovery and learning from drinking from already opened bottles.

4 **Human culture:** in humans much of our behaviour is due to cultural rather than genetical determinants. This is not true for animals, where culture has a smaller role and genes play a concomitantly larger role in behavioural determination. This is the reason why some psychologists are hesitant to apply the same insights to humans as to animals.

The evolution of language

Cultural transmission occurs through learning (see 1.6 and 8.3) and language (see 4.1 and 4.3), which enables learning to be stored and transmitted across generations. Language has developed as follows:

- Certain necessary behaviours (intention movements, displacement activities and autonomic responses) have meaning for an observer, thus taking on communicative significance.

- These behaviours become ritualised in order to make them less ambiguous, they are now signals.

- Signals have obvious survival value in the mating process and inter- and intraspecies aggression, so species who develop communication will have an evolutionary advantage.

- Language develops out of sophisticated signals with speech coming later. **Chomsky (1957)** suggested that language is related to specific types of mental organisation not simply higher intelligence. Brain asymmetry may be a further clue.

- Symbolic representation began about 30,000 years ago. Written language seems to have developed from representational symbols first with emotional/mystical significance, then with informational value. True language is when we find symbols for the sounds of speech rather than concepts. Language probably started with the sophisticated use of gestures; speech probably developed later.

- **McNeill (1966)** notes that the innovators of linguistic evolution were and are children. When they acquire language they reformulate the language received from adults by inventing transformations. For every child, acquiring language is a process of reinventing transformational grammar and in doing so possibly improving it to become a better system. Each new transformation slightly changes the corpus of speech. The process is one of simplification because each new generation progressively produces transformations to make it simpler and more rule-driven, therefore reducing the time it takes to acquire.

8.2 ETHOLOGICAL EXPLANATIONS

Ethology is the study of behaviour from the point of view of biology, an interdisciplinary study. Ethologists emphasise:

- Precise **observation** of the behaviour of animals in their natural environment recorded as an **ethogram**, the details of all the behaviours of a species.

- The study of behaviour in terms of its **evolutionary** significance. Behaviours are explained in terms of their survival value and function.

- A greater interest in **phylogenesis** (how behaviour evolved in a particular species) more than **ontogenesis** (how behaviour develops in an individual). Phylogenesis is mainly determined by heredity, whereas ontogenesis is more influenced by experience. This explains why ethologists take more of a nativist view than, for example, behaviourists.

- Using argument rather than experimentation as a means of proof (since their method is one of observation). For example, if two species display the same behaviour and have a similar biological construction, that is taken as evidence that the behaviour is inherited.

- A reductionist and deterministic approach, in that all behaviour can be reduced to and largely explained by its evolutionary significance.

There have been several phases of ethology:

❶ *Pre-popular* ethology: **Whitman, Craig** and **Heinroth** all had similar ideas but made less impact.

❷ *Classical* ethology (1930s–1950s): **Lorenz** and **Tinbergen** brought ethology to a much wider audience. They had a major influence on subsequent work by, for example, **Bowlby, Eibl-Eibesfeldt** and **Desmond Morris**.

❸ *Modern* (1950s–1980s): the classical view was seen as oversimplified, particularly in relation to mammals and primates. The use of experiments which were as natural as possible was introduced, for example, **Harlow**.

❹ *Sociobiology* (1970s): approach to understanding social behaviour and structure in terms of genes not just individuals.

Tinbergen and other ethologists have listed four basic questions to be answered:

1 *Cause* – what mechanisms produce a behaviour, what 'triggers' a response?

2 *Function* – what are the useful consequences of a behaviour, its survival value?

3 *Ontogeny* – how does an individual learn the behaviour?

4 *Phylogeny* – how has the behaviour evolved within the species?

Lea (1984) identified four ways that ethology is used:

1 *Practically* – for example, in breeding endangered species.

2 *Methodologically* – the development of naturalistic observation techniques.

3 *Conceptually* – ideas adopted in psychological theories.

4 *Empirically* – to test the theoretical propositions of evolution.

CONCEPTS

❶ **Instinct (species-specific behaviour):** an inherited behaviour pattern common to all members of a species, made up of *fixed action patterns* which are *released* by *sign stimuli*. The key features are that such behaviour:

- tends to be stereotyped, i.e. always appears in the same form when displayed,
- appears in individuals reared in isolation,
- is fully developed in individuals who have been prevented from practising it.

The concept was originally used by philosophers in relation to animal behaviour and then introduced to human behaviour by Darwin and later, Freud. Behaviourists refer to reflexes rather than instincts.

Tinbergen introduced the term to ethology (1951, *The Study of Instinct*), some of his classic work was based on the behaviour of the three-spined stickleback (1952, *The curious behaviour of the stickleback*). He found that males reared in isolation would still attack other males in spring and their own image in a mirror.

The term 'instinct' became unfashionable because it implies some form of energy, which leads to a confusion over whether it is an explanation or a description of behaviour. Critics claimed it could only be the latter and it has now been replaced by the phrase **'species-specific behaviour'** to avoid the original connotations.

2 **Fixed action patterns (FAPs)**: units of innate species-specific behaviour (like morphemes are to language):
- exhibited in a repertoire and thus more complex that reflexes,
- independent of learning, but can be affected by experience,
- inevitable: triggered by a specific stimulus (sign stimulus),
- ballistic and inflexible: once launched the rest is inevitable,
- distinct: serve one function and occur in one circumstance.

All of these features can be related to the survival value (and evolutionary significance) of such behaviours.

Example:
- The egg retrieval behaviour of the greylag goose. When a goose sees an egg outside the nest the following behaviour is inevitable. The goose stands in the nest, faces the egg, extends its neck outwards until it is over the egg, then puts the underside of the beak on the far side of the egg and starts to roll it back, moving its bill from side to side to prevent it slipping away. If the egg does slip away (or is removed) the goose none-the-less continues back to the nest (ballistic and inflexible). Then, when it sees the egg again the sequence recommences until it is finally successful.

3 **Sign stimuli**: environmental features which lead an animal to produce an FAP, i.e. acts as a **releaser**.

Tinbergen and Perdeck (1950) demonstrated which features of a herring gull's beak act as the sign stimulus to elicit the begging response in their chicks. Using cardboard cut-outs they varied:
- spot colour: the red spot is most effective but chicks pecked at other colours,
- spot–beak contrast: pecking increased along with the degree of contrast,
- beak colour with no spot: red was the best.

Therefore, it is the redness and the contrast.

4 **Releasers and the innate releasing mechanism (IRM)**: releasers are certain features in the environment which trigger or release certain patterns of response (FAPs). The IRM is the inbuilt mechanism by which such stimuli are recognised; the inevitability of sign stimuli to trigger the IRM means that the term is virtually synonymous with releaser:
- all releasers are sign stimuli,
- not all sign stimuli are releasers, they may be moderated by environmental cues or hormones which mean that the response is prevented,
- true releasers are often not species-specific.

Examples:
- The egg acts as a releaser for the greylag goose's behaviour.
- The spot on a herring-gull: the chick's pecking behaviour 'releases' a regurgitation response in the parent.

5 **Super-releasers**: sign stimuli which are exaggerated:
- **Tinbergen (1948)** substituted an oystercatcher's egg with a gull's one, which is twice the size but otherwise similar. The female oystercatcher preferred this to her own, and even better was an absurdly outsized one. **Hinde (1982)** pointed out that sometimes the most effective sign stimulus is not the natural one but a caricature of it.

- The gaping mouth of the nestling thrush is brightly coloured. **Tinbergen and Kuenen (1939)** found that hearing the parent's call and/or shaking the nest led to a gaping response. The parent then feeds the young. The gape is imitated by cuckoo nestlings so as to be fed by the adopted parents. The cuckoo has a huge gape, which acts as a super-releaser.

6 **Action-specific energy (ASE)**: on occasion an FAP can occur in the absence of external stimulation (**vacuum activity**). This is explained in terms of the psychohydraulic model, which proposes that energy (ASE) is stored in a reservoir in-between demand. A sign stimulus triggers the IRM which releases ASE. When demand is non-existent this builds up until it 'overflows', triggering the IRM and the FAP in the absence of a sign stimulus. This can be likened to a cistern which fills to a certain level and then flushes automatically unless already flushed.

The model explains displacement activity as occurring when two mutually incompatible systems are released simultaneously which inhibits both of them, and the energy (ASE) from both overflows and triggers a third behaviour which has no relevance to the current situation.

7 **Environmental moderation**: it may be necessary for more than one sign stimulus to be present before the IRM is triggered.
Examples:
- The red underbelly of the male stickleback acts as a sign stimulus to release aggressive behaviour. However, this depends on a second sign stimulus of territory. It only occurs if the male is on home ground, otherwise it will flee.
- Changes in daylight trigger the release of certain hormones (see 7.3). Only then will a male bird respond to the sign stimulus of a female and engage in courtship displays.

8 **Nature and nurture**: some apparently innate behaviours depend on prior experience.
- **Thorpe (1963)** showed that only some aspects of the chaffinch song are innate. When chicks are reared in isolation they were only able to produce the basic song. The young seem to learn a dialect in their first year which then remains invariant through their life.
- **Lorenz's (1935)** classic work on imprinting goslings shows the interaction between nature and experience. The gosling has an instinct to find a mother but the actual mother-figure depends on what is available.

9 **Optimal behavioural strategies**: develop through selective pressure not conscious or deliberate action. Behaviour generally evolves as a trade-off between costs and benefits, which can be expressed as: **cost function** = the instantaneous level of risk incurred by, and the reproductive value available to, an animal in a particular internal state, activity and environment.

SOCIOBIOLOGY

Sociobiology was introduced by **Hamilton (1964)** and **Wilson (1975)**. It differs from classical ethology in:

- focusing particularly on social behaviour,
- taking the set of genes, rather than the individual, as the basic unit of evolution – genetic instead of biological determinism.

Key concepts

1 **Altruism**: behaviour which increases the survival potential of others at a possible risk to the altruist's survival (see also 2.6).

2 **The paradox of selfish altruism**: natural selection should favour selfish behaviour rather than altruism because the survival of the fittest individual is the basis of evolution. However, sociobiologists suggested that it is the survival of the gene rather than the individual which accounts for altruism. **Dawkins (1976)** described this in *The Selfish Gene*. The paradox is that what appears as an altruistic act is actually selfish at the gene level.

The classic example of altruism is parental care, which is easily explained even at an individual level. However, less clear is the frequent practice in insect communities where some individual members are sterile. These individuals contribute to the general well-being of the community, enabling other members to reproduce and thus ensuring the survival of their gene pool.

- Natural selection will favour altruism in two circumstances:
  - *kin selection* and *inclusive fitness*: when it is directed towards relatives,
  - *reciprocal altruism:* behaviours of low cost which are later reciprocated,
- *Co-operation* is sometimes altruistic, but more often mutually beneficial.
- **Ridley (1986)** adds manipulated behaviour, as when a parasite shapes the host's behaviour in such a way that the it enables the parasite's survival. He argues that if the definition of altruism is taken as 'one that increases the number of offspring left by the recipient, and decreases the number left by the altruist' then such parasitic behaviour is altruistic. This is to define it in terms of reproductive consequences rather than the process by which natural selection favours it.

③ Kin selection: natural selection will favour genes that promote altruistic behaviour towards individuals that are genetically related to the altruist.

In order for this to work, an individual must be able to recognise its relatives. In social insects this may be achieved through colony odour which is derived from their diet. **Ridley (1986)** describes a study where bees from two beehives, sharing the same source of food, showed less fighting; presumably because they mistook each other for members of the same hive.

Prejudice is a possible example of kin selection in humans. **Ardrey (1967)** suggested that the hatred existing between races is an example of an inborn biological tendency similar to the animal's desire to protect its territory against predators. A dislike of foreigners may be based on their potential threat to our way of life and survival.

④ Inclusive fitness: it is not just the survival of the fittest individual, but of all genetically-related individuals. Even if an animal has no offspring, its inclusive fitness may not be zero because its genes are passed on by close relatives.

Many animals have 'helpers' for child care. The Florida scrub jay parents are assisted by up to six helpers, 75% of whom are offspring of a previous brood, who therefore have a genetic interest. The red fox, jackal, African hunting dog, and mongoose all use helpers though they are not always genetic relatives.

⑤ Reciprocal altruism: a form of co-operation based on trust. The initial act is altruistic but it is based on a return favour. It would be naturally selected without any need for the animals to be related. This system only works in stable groups where members are recognisable and cheating can't take place without penalty.

Packer (1977) observed olive baboons. Two males may co-operate to fight off a single male so that one of the pair may mate with a female. The 'friend' has behaved altruistically in helping the other to mate. When another female comes into season, the roles seem to be reversed and the first male this time helps his friend.

⑥ Co-operation: where both participants benefit or stand to benefit:
- *Intraspecies co-operation:* may be altruistic, some of it may be based on kin selection, e.g. hunting or grooming.
- *Interspecies co-operation* (symbiosis) is usually reciprocal, e.g. the remora fish clings to sharks and other marine animals. It feeds on the leavings of their meals, and also cleans the host of external parasites. The tickbird or oxpecker clings to the hide of cattle or other big-game animals and removes ticks and maggots from their hide. When alarmed the birds hiss, alerting their hosts to possible danger. They also take blood from their hosts leaving sores which may be slow to heal.

CRITICISMS AND ALTERNATIVES

① Oversimplified picture:
- The extension to human behaviour is doubtful because genetic determinism has been overtaken by cultural transmission.
- Reductionist: it explains behaviour in terms of a single cause.

② An overemphasis on innate factors:
  ● Is the genetic basis any more than conjecture?
  ● Are there true behavioural universals?
  ● Such determinist arguments can be politically dangerous. A reliance on nature suggests that the differences we observe, such as those between men and women, or the need for territorial or racial aggression, are immutable and based on many millennia of evolution to produce the most adapted form. As regards humans in particular, the effects of cultural evolution and moral principles must not be overlooked.

③ Description rather than explanation:
  ● The energy concept underlying the hydraulic model is derived from physical science and mistakenly used by ethologists. As long as the concepts are merely descriptive, they can serve a useful purpose.
  ● Any suggestion of explanation tends towards reification. It is easy to slip into a sense that the 'strategies' described are intentional, which presupposes a god-like figure.

④ The main rival explanation is from the behaviourists, who focus on smaller units of inherited behaviour – reflexes – and play up the role of experience. The ethological approach might suggest that even learning itself is the result of natural selection since it is a highly adaptive form of behaviour.

8.3 IMPRINTING AND LEARNING

Learning has been covered fully in 1.6. In this unit the approach is ethological: focusing on the adaptive nature of learning and imprinting:

● *learning:* is relatively permanent behavioural change through experience,

● *maturation:* is change which is due to age rather than experience. This is an innate process,

● *imprinting:* is maturational (genetically programmed and takes place during critical periods) *and* influenced by experience (what is actually learned is determined by the environment),

● *learning as an adaptive strategy:* as with imprinting, the ability to learn is innate, the actual change is influenced by environment.

THE EVOLUTION OF LEARNING

Learning is the basis of cultural transmission, beyond that it has other adaptive features:

① **Analogy with genetic evolution:** learning is also made necessary by changing environments; a static environment could be coped with by an innate set of rules. In fact unchanging aspects *are* encoded in reflexes such as an antigravitational reflex.

  Intelligence is the ultimate form of adaptive learning which enables an animal to adapt to any change; perhaps the best test is not what an individual knows but how it behaves when it doesn't know the answer.

② **Instinctive behaviour:** predisposes the animal to certain forms of learning.

  For example, innate fears; it has been suggested that rats may have evolved a 'bait shyness', which results in their continued survival. The behaviour consists of a tendency to avoid unfamiliar foods and sample them tentatively. As humans have laid bait for centuries, those rats with this behaviour would be naturally selected.

  Another example shows that animals may inherit the tendency to form certain, adaptive associations. **Garcia and Koelling (1966)** demonstrated an innate predisposition in rats to avoid forming certain associations. Rats are conditioned to the sound of a bell, group 1 receive a shock plus saccharin water, group 2 receive the same water and an injection which makes them nauseous. When the bell rings, group 1 avoid any drink, group 2 avoid only saccharin water. Therefore group 1 forms an association between sound and shock but not taste and shock, whereas group 2 has a link between taste and nausea but not sound and nausea.

③ **One trial learning**: is an important survival trait. **Seligman (1970)** pointed out that, in the case of a particularly strong stimulus, learning should be immediate, e.g. falling on tarmac results in greater care in future; parents often say 'they only have to do it once'.

④ **Imprinting and maturation**: animals are preprogrammed to learn (or change) certain behaviours at certain ages (see below). These changes are ones that have important survival value.

LEARNING

In practice, distinctions between learning and inherited predispositions (nurture and nature) are not as clear as theory might suggest:

● Much learning takes place prior to hatching/birth, which can be mistaken for inherited behaviour. **Kuo (1932)** observed chicks inside the egg by placing a window on the eggshell; he claimed that their behaviour indicated that they were learning skills such as pecking before hatching.

● *Non-associative learning:* is behaviour change which is not mediated by higher order thinking and may appear to be instinctive (reflexive). *Habituation* is a process of becoming less sensitive to a stimulus, e.g. if the sea hare's siphon is prodded the animal withdraws it. However, this response is not indefinite, eventually it leaves the siphon out. After a rest, when prodding is resumed it will withdraw the siphon again. As an adaptive feature, habituation enables resources such as attention to be conserved (see 1.4). *Sensitisation:* is the reverse, i.e. becoming more sensitive. For example, if the sea hare is given an electric shock it then becomes more responsive to other stimuli generally. Again this is not a permanent change, but is also adaptive when the environmental cues suggest that the individual needs to pay greater attention.

● *Associative learning:* classical and operant conditioning (see 1.6).

MATURATION

The issue of whether certain behaviours develop as a result of accumulated experience or because of maturation has been explored in relation to Piaget's theory of cognitive development (see 3.1). Physical developments at puberty are examples of maturational changes.

Experimental evidence of restricted experience:

● **Spalding (1873)** reared swallows and **Grohmann (1939)** reared pigeons. Both were restricted in their wing movements but none-the-less were able to fly as normal when they reached the appropriate age, suggesting that maturation rather than experience determines when a bird can fly.

● **Gesell and Thompson (1929)** gave one member of a pair of MZ twins practice in climbing stairs, the other twin was later given the opportunity to climb stairs and caught up in two days. This indicates that certain behaviours can be achieved through practice rather maturation alone, but that it may be easier to learn certain things at an appropriate age, as with imprinting.

IMPRINTING

The concept comes from embryology, where there are short periods during development when the individual is especially vulnerable. For example, German measles only causes damage to hearing in the human fetus if it occurs during the third month of pregnancy.

Heinroth (1911) observed that the young of precocial species show a fairly indiscriminate attachment to moving objects. One of the classic studies of ethology is **Lorenz's (1935)** demonstration of such imprinting with goslings. Some goslings from a clutch of eggs were faced with Lorenz, rather than their mother, upon hatching. When the chicks were then shown their mother they chose Lorenz. In fact the goslings persisted in following Lorenz as if he were their mother.

The main features of imprinting:

- there is a *critical period:* only occurs at a specific developmental period,
- there is *rapid behavioural change,*
- *irreversible:* once set, behaviour doesn't change,
- *supra-individual:* is not tied to an individual but rather to a class of objects,
- *lasting:* it has repercussions on later behaviours.

Without these features, such behavioural changes would merely be learning:

- it may be based on any of the five sensory modalities, singly or together,
- it has important survival consequences,
- it is related to neural and developmental maturity, therefore it will occur more often in those animals who are *less* well developed at birth,
- there is supportive evidence from many other areas of psychology:
  visual perception, language, cognitive development, emotional development (attachment).

Critical or sensitive period

The intended meaning is that unless certain learning takes place at a particular time, it will never happen. To test this deprivation studies are used:

- The fact that such imprinting is very rapid suggests a specific readiness to make certain connections at specific periods of development.
- **Hess (1958)** exposed ducklings to a model at various ages from hatching to 32 hours old and found that imprinting was strongest when it occurred between 12 and 17 hours. He called this the critical age.
- **Marler and Mundinger (1971)** found that sparrows kept in isolation between the age of 8 to 90 days fail to develop adult birdsong, though they are able to produce a basic version. This suggests the role of experience in modifying innate behaviours during a critical period. However, **Schjelderup-Ebbe (1935)** found that domestic chickens reared away from others still crowed as normal when they reached maturity.
- **Bateson (1964)** showed that chicks placed in a cage with striped walls later preferred this to other patterns. This may be associated with neural changes in the visual cortex, and also with imprinting being a period of maturation (see 1.1).
- The critical period may also be associated with hormones. **Landsberg (1981)** found that peaks of testosterone production in young zebra finches coincided with key periods of imprinting. The hormones may have an organisational effect on brain development.
- **Sluckin (1965)** found that a young bird kept in isolation is still imprintable beyond the normal period and therefore proposed *sensitive* rather than critical periods. Learning may take place at other times but not as easily. It is probably best to see it as a period of heightened sensitivity to form certain connections.
- It is possible that animals reared in isolation have extended periods of sensitivity so that they remain more 'imprintable', which would make it hard to test the whole thing.

Irreversible

If imprinting is related to neural maturation then alterations which take place as a result of sensory stimulation would explain the relative irreversibility:

- What happens if an individual is exposed to more than one imprinting experience? **Hess (1958)** suggested that the former experience maintains dominance in the long run. **Sluckin and Salzen (1961)** imprinted young chicks on a green ball. After a short delay they were imprinted on a blue ball. The reverse was done with a second group. Three days later they were retested and showed a preference for their original colour. However, after another interval in isolation their preference changed once again to the second imprinting experience and this preference continued. This was performed under laboratory conditions and Hess claimed that this may affect performance.

- **Guiton (1966)** demonstrated how leghorn chicks, exposed to a pair of yellow rubber gloves used in feeding them during their first six weeks, became imprinted on them, even trying to mate with them. After this, the cocks were kept with other normal hens. Their behaviour reverted and later they would only mate with the hens and not the gloves. This suggests that imprinting has important effects, but that these can be reversed under suitable circumstances

- **Hinde (1966)** proposed that once imprinting has occurred, the organism is also programmed to avoid situations where imprinting might occur, e.g. being afraid of other potential mother-figures.

- Studies of attachment (see 3.1) in humans suggest that the degree of irreversibility depends on many things, such as the original imprinting experience and the quality of later experiences, which may well override the original experience.

Supra-individual

Lorenz's original experiment showed that the process is not tied to the individual species but rather a class of objects, in this case those that move. He later imprinted goslings with a cardboard box.

On the other hand, attachment – an example of imprinting – is to a particular individual. The offspring distinguish their particular parent from others of the same species, which is distinctly not supra-individual.

Lasting effects

The immediate effects of imprinting are to establish a bond between parent and offspring, for the purpose of protection, food and imitation of adult behaviour (e.g. birdsong as described above). There appear to be lasting effects in terms of reproduction. This may be related to ensuring that offspring mate with the right species (which assumes that they imprint on their own kind):

- **Lorenz (1935)** noted that Barbary doves imprinted on humans would often direct their subsequent sexual behaviour towards humans.

- **Schutz (1971)** raised mallard ducklings with other species of duck and found that later they preferred to mate with the species of their rearing (which was outbreeding) rather than their own kind. This was more evident in males than females, who seemed to select their own species regardless.

- **Harlow and Zimmerman (1959)** (see 3.1) found that monkeys reared with wire mothers generally failed to mate and then to be capable of mothering themselves.

Physiological basis

Immelman and Wolff (1980) (cited by **Gross, 1992**) identified changes in the young zebra finch's brain which might be related to imprinting. Around day 21 there is massive cell death in the hyperstriatum, followed by regeneration.

Aural imprinting

Visual imprinting takes place after hatching; aural imprinting is available before this time. **Hess (1972)** studied the reciprocal noises made by the female mallard and her young before hatching. It may be that this helps to time the hatching process.

Grier et al. (1967) exposed chick eggs to continuous sound stimulation of one second beeps for a period of six days before hatching; after hatching the chicks showed a preference for this sound rather than a higher pitched version.

Similar behaviour has been found in humans. **DeCasper and Spence (1986)** showed that infants who had been read *The Cat in the Hat* while in utero showed recognition after birth. **Hepper (1991)** reported the same was true for tunes from soap operas which the mothers had watched when pregnant. **DeCasper and Fifer (1980)** suggest that infant prenatal imprinting is an important part of the bonding process which occurs after birth.

Aural imprinting also takes place after hatching, as in birdsong.

Other senses

Some animals rely on smell. **Klopfer and Gamble (1966)** found that mother goats are sensitive to the smell of their offspring for about an hour after birth; in fact contact with any kid for a 5-minute period will mean that it is accepted as her own and she will allow it to suckle. This is shown in the practice of wrapping an orphaned lamb in the skin of a dead one so that the mother will suckle the adopted lamb.

Imprinting versus learning

Is imprinting really a special case? **McFarland (1993)** concludes that it is essentially the same as ordinary conditioning. **Bateson (1990)** suggests that the things which once made imprinting seem different are now seen as commonplace, as a result of changed views of learning:

- things which are imprinted can be learned at other times, though perhaps the learning is then less easy and less likely,
- the process of learning results in neurological changes that may be irreversible,
- not all imprinting is irreversible,
- there are predispositions for learning at certain times, which would have obvious evolutionary advantages.

8.4 SOCIAL BEHAVIOURS

Social behaviour is necessary in all animals for mating. In some species, individuals co-operate in parenting, obtaining food and protection. Communication facilitates these processes and is discussed more fully in 4.3.

SOCIAL ORGANISATION

Advantages of living in a group

- facilitates mating,
- food location, for example, insects share such information with the whole community,
- a larger group enables a more accurate equilibrium to be maintained between available food supplies and population numbers (**Wynne-Edwards**).
- tackling larger prey – an organised group hunts more effectively than a solitary animal,
- less vulnerable to predation:
  - safety in numbers, the predator will only take part of the group,
  - mutual protection, **Hall and DeVore (1965)** found that baboons protect their young when on the move by forming a circle around them,
  - a group can more easily confuse the prey,
  - a group can share the task of look-out. **Barnard (1979)** demonstrated that individual sparrows spent less time watching for predators and more time feeding in relation to increasing group size.

Solitary living

- safer because a group could be more easily spotted,
- may be necessary due to scarcity of food,
- requires mechanisms, such as mating calls, to locate a partner for reproduction.

Controlling group size

Groups maintain an optimal size in relation to factors such as food, e.g. **Chapman (1928)** varied the quantities of flour placed in a jar with flour beetles; the ratio of beetles to food remained constant: 44 beetles to every gram of flour.

Group size is often controlled either by variations in litter sizes or by how many group members are breeding. **Krebs and Boonstra (1979)** noted that only larger voles mate successfully when the population density is high; when the density falls the smaller ones are allowed to mate as well (see also **Calhoun (1962)** in 9.2).

Group members may keep track of group size through flocking; the 'morning (dawn) chorus' may serve the same purpose.

Group structures

Dominance hierarchies facilitate group interactions. They develop as a means of controlling food, aggression and mating. Examples are:

- *pecking-orders* as first studied in chickens by **Schjelderup-Ebbe (1922)**, a simple kind of social structure found throughout the animal kingdom,
- *matriline groups:* a group of sexually mature daughters and the dependent young of all of them, found in almost all primates.

THE PROCESS OF REPRODUCTION

The processes involved can be simply described or can be approached in terms of the survival value of the behaviours, i.e. an ethological approach. The process involves:

- finding a member of the right species and sex who is 'fit' in terms of survival,
- maximising the survival of the offspring, in terms of mate selection and later parenting.

Reproduction

1. **Sexual reproduction:** in terms of natural selection, sexual reproduction has advantages in terms of genetic variability, particularly in relation to environmental fluctuation. This is well illustrated by the freshwater hydra, which reproduces asexually in spring and summer when food is plentiful, but sexually in autumn when environmental conditions start to change.

2. **Cross-breeding:** a possible means of increasing genetic variability would be mating between species. However, this tends to be unsuccessful, as hybrid offspring are usually non-viable or infertile (e.g. the mule). Means of prevention are geographical separation, different reproductive organs and species-specific mating behaviour (e.g. bird calls or courtship displays).

   When interbreeding does occur there appears to be an adaptive link between intraspecies attraction and the 'new' species. **Bentley and Hoy (1974)** mated a pair of crickets from two closely-related species; when the hybrid female offspring were put on a y-maze they moved in the direction of the hybrid male's songs rather than those of either parental species. The evolutionary significance of such a link is that, for continuance of the new 'species', it should mate with its own kind rather than the ancestor.

3. **External and internal fertilisation:** a water environment makes external fertilisation possible; land animals require closer contact for mating.

4. **Control of the reproductive cycle:** the most common system in animals is through hormonal change directed by changes in day length. A classic study of the Barbary dove was conducted by **Lehrman (1964)**. At the beginning of the reproductive cycle the male's levels of testosterone are low, which leads to aggression towards females; this suppresses the release of female reproductive hormones. An increase in day length stimulates the production of testosterone and courtship behaviour (males injected with testosterone do this). The male's behaviour stimulates the female's pituitary to release gonadotropin, which causes the eggs to ripen. This triggers release of oestrogen, which in turn triggers nest building behaviour and the

eggs are laid. The nest building stimulates the release of progesterone in both parents which causes them to incubate the eggs. Finally this activity leads to production of prolactin, which leads to the production of a kind of milk in both parents to feed the young with.

Reproductive strategies

Trivers (1972) described the balance between time and resources as *parental investment*; there are a number of strategies (naturally favoured or selected):

1 **Number of offspring, the parents may have:**
- many eggs and devote little resource – the numbers alone should ensure that some survive,
- relatively few eggs and devote more energy to ensuring their survival.

2 **Combinations:**
- *Monogamy* (pair-bonding): a single male pairs with a single female. Rare in animals but common in birds. The male and female remain together for one or more mating seasons, both take part in care of offspring and tend to be similar in size.
- *Polygyny:* a single male mates with several females. Often organised as a harem, one male has exclusive rights to a group of females, as in deer. Many males die without mating at all while others do most of the mating. The male with the harem tends to be larger (presumably because larger males are more successful in fights over females) and females do most of the child care.
- *Polyandry:* one female mates with several males. The female develops bizarre characteristics normally associated with males, e.g. the Tasmanian native hen or the spotted sandpiper, who mates with more than one male and provides each with a clutch of eggs. Polyandry and polygyny sometimes co-occur.

3 **Sexual selection:** generally females select and males compete for their attention. This occurs at the most basic level between eggs and sperm. Large numbers of sperm compete to be the one to fertilise the egg, which is produced in small if not individual quantities:
- Male strategies: a male can potentially fertilise hundreds of females, and his gene pool is best served by ensuring that he does so to the maximum. Any adaptation in a male which enables him to copulate with more females will be strongly favoured by natural selection.
- *Intrasexual* selection: is the male strategy, to compete with rival males.
- Female strategies: females are limited in their mating by the rate at which they produce eggs and young. They therefore invest more in the outcome of each fertilisation and each time must select the 'fittest' mate. Natural selection will favour discrimination in females.
- *Intersexual* selection: is the female strategy, to select the best (fittest) in the opposite sex.

Darwin claimed sexual selection was the basis of sexual differences.

4 **Finding a mate:**
- Mobility of the animal influences the mate location, e.g. in plants the release of airborne spores is a method of transferring reproductive cells.
- In widely dispersed solitary animals, sound (e.g. bird call) or smell (pheromones, as in the female silk moth) are means of communicating readiness and, since such signals are species-specific, giving information to aid selection of a mate of the right species.
- Where an animal lives in a social group, the problem of finding the right mate is alleviated. Where dominance hierarchies exist, even the problem of competition between males is solved; in other cases there is competition, usually between rivals.

Sexual dimorphism and attraction

Sexual dimorphism is the difference between the sexes. Females usually do not need to compete with rivals, unlike males (see 'sexual selection' above), therefore they do not need:

- weaponry for psychological or physical advantage (see 'aggression', p.235),
- physical attributes to make them more attractive (appear 'fitter') to the opposite sex.

These are characteristics important in males to ensure reproductive success. However, this does not explain some of the bizarre characteristics found in males, such as the peacock's tail. It is hard to see how these might be judged as 'fitter' since they often threaten survival value in terms of safety and metabolic load. How have such features been naturally selected?

1. **Female choice:** Fisher (1930) proposed that because females mate with the most attractive males for the purpose of producing sons who will attract more females, the characteristics which she selects must be heritable. Initially these characteristics have some survival value but because females actively select mates with this feature it becomes exaggerated. This continues as long as the advantage it confers in terms of selection outweighs its disadvantages in terms of survival. Empirical evidence for this view is:
   - Andersson (1982) demonstrated this in practice by experimentally altering the tail length of long-tailed widow birds. He cut the tails of some males and stuck on either a longer or shorter tail; the number of nests on the territories of those with longer tails was higher.
   - Stags' antlers have little survival value, otherwise they would not be shed outside the breeding season and females would have them as well. Their value lies in ritualised fighting and intrasexual selection. Their disadvantage is in terms of the strain that their growth places on the stags' diet (needing massive calcium and phosphorus). Fossils of the extinct giant deer show that its antlers had reached a span of 3 metres. It is possible that the intrasexual advantage was offset by the cost and this led to their extinction.

2. **Handicapping theory:** Zahavi (1975) has proposed that females prefer males precisely because they carry a handicap and therefore must be robust individuals, e.g. if a male peacock can survive despite his tail he must be a robust individual. Critics of this view say that the same might then apply to males who have been injured but survived, but this 'handicap' would not be heritable and in fact might act detrimentally as those individuals who are injured might be less 'fit' individuals.

Courtship

The length of courtship varies from being non-existent to lasting for many months. The waved albatross spends most of the year in courtship activity. It serves to:

- Attract a mate, particularly for males.
- Provide the female with the opportunity to assess the male's fitness. Coyness gives the female time to do this.
- Provide examples of ritualised behaviour. They are essentially signals about the species of the displayer and the fitness of the individual. The value of extreme displays is related to natural selection in terms of female choice (see above).
- Appease or integrate aggressive responses to invasion of territory. Courtship displays often involve zigzagging (chaffinch, stickleback) which is thought to be a result of conflict between approach and fleeing.
- Close courtship may ensure that the male is the sole parent. When multiple copulation occurs it is the sperm from the last partner which are more likely to fertilise the egg.
- In some species a second male copulates after the dominant one (sneak copulation). In order to avoid this a male needs to ensure that he is the father, which may be another reason for close and prolonged courtship, and shared parental care.

Parental care

1. **Functions of parental care:**
   - The classic example of altruism: the parent seeks to ensure the maximal survival of its genes, those aspects of parental care which increase reproductivity will be naturally selected.

- Protection from prey and the elements: imprinting aims to ensure close contact between parents and offspring.
- Provision of food.
- Learning in the form of imitation or conditioning, e.g. food foraging, ability to become a good parent. **Harlow and Zimmerman (1959)** (see 3.1) found that monkeys reared with wire mothers generally failed to mate and and were themselves incapable of mothering.

2 **Factors which affect the amount of parental care:**
- Minimal courtship seems to be related to minimal parental care.
- Numbers of offspring: where there are few offspring parental defensive behaviour is stronger.
- Maturity at birth/hatching: where offspring are born relatively immature in terms of mobility and sensory development (altricial) they are totally dependent and require more parental care. Offspring born later (precocial–precocious) need less care.
- The presence of young elicits continued parenting behaviour, for example, **Rosenblatt (1969)** found that when young rats were removed from the nest the mother stopped nest building.

3 **Factors that affect which parent does the caring:**
- External versus internal fertilisation: where there is external fertilisation there is often paternal care (e.g. male stickleback); there is maternal care in the case of internal fertilisation. **Dawkins** has suggested that one sex leaves the other 'holding the baby'. When fertilisation is external the female can leave first; once the eggs are deposited the male has the last task of fertilising them. With internal fertilisation the female is obviously left holding the baby and thus left with care.
- Monogamy, polygyny and polyandry: in a similar way to external fertilisation, animals which are polygynous are more likely to have maternal care. Where a species is polyandrous, there would be paternal care and monogamous parents will be biparental.
- In animals where the females 'advertise' their receptive period (oestrus) the male can restrict his presence to those periods only. In species (such as humans) who are receptive throughout their menstrual cycle, the males remain with the females throughout the year and therefore are available for shared care. It is possible that this strategy of continuous sexual availability has evolved as a means of ensuring help with child rearing.
- If both parents are involved in care there is less need for the males to compete to ensure the survival of their offspring. They essentially do this after birth rather than prior to mating. Therefore monogamy results. This predicts the possibility in humans that, as men take an increasing parental role, monogamy should increase.

AGGRESSIVE AND AGONISTIC BEHAVIOURS

Agonistic behaviours are social conflicts of attack, threat, fight, flight and submission. Aggression occurs within a species (intraspecies) or between species (interspecies), in either case different rules apply and different motivations:

- Intraspecies: injury is rare and usually due to territory or mating disputes. **Darwin** predicted from the theory of natural selection that animals which are successful in competition will be selected and therefore they should be the more common. However, natural selection actually favours those that threaten successfully but avoid unrestrained battles, and thus are more likely to survive. Dominance hierarchies are another means of resolving disputes.

- Interspecies: either for predation (which ends in death) or competition over shared resources/territory. Even in predation there is a balance to be struck because it is not in the interest of the predator to wipe out all of its prey. Therefore optimal strategies for predator–prey relations will be 'fitter'. Where animals are competing for limited resources, this is usually resolved by dominance of one species over another.

Therefore there is high evolutionary value for animals who develop optimal aggressive behaviours and other strategies such as dominance hierarchies or interspecies dominance.

Three kinds of behaviour reduce the amount of aggressive fighting. It has been suggested that in humans we have lost the natural means of stopping aggression because we lack such behaviours (see also 2.7):

1 Ritualised fighting:

- The *initial stages* of an aggressive encounter enable an individual to size up their opponent and back down if necessary, **Clutton-Brock and Albon (1979)** observed fighting in deer on the island of Rhum. There are three stages: roaring matches, parallel walking and locking antlers. The initial stages enable the rivals to assess the opponent with respect to body size and condition. Most encounters (75%) stop before the third stage. They recorded a small percentage of males who received any serious injury. Such encounters lead to dominance relations.

- *Signals*: many behaviours which were once the first stages of an aggressive act have become a signal of threat, thus avoiding the need for anything further. There are many other signals which prevent aggressive escalation, such as appeasement, submission, dominance and displacement activities.

- **Maynard Smith (1982)** described a balance or *evolutionary stable strategy* (ESS) which must be struck between 'hawks' and 'doves' in a species. Too many hawks and they will kill each other off, too many doves and they are prey to the remaining hawks. Where the balance is right the hawks don't always win because they sometimes encounter another hawk, and the doves sometimes win because they encounter another dove and settle amicably.

2 Dominance: dominant individuals have priority over subordinate ones:

- **Schjelderup-Ebbe (1935)** made the first observations of *dominance hierarchies* in hens, and studies have continued to focus on them. When a group of hens is first placed together they fight amongst themselves, but they soon learn who is stronger and give way rather than risk injury. Dominance is maintained by pecking subordinate hens. The larger the group the more complicated the hierarchy.

- Dominance confers *feeding* and *mating advantages*, which make successful reproduction more likely, and therefore dominance hierarchies will have an evolutionary advantage.

- Dominance *reduces aggression* because individuals know their place and don't engage in aggressive encounters. In some species, the dominant male polices any fighting.

- Dominance is usually *established* through fighting, size and sometimes age.

3 Territory: a space which is exclusively used and defended by a solitary animal or family group:

- *The intruder usually flees:* **Tinbergen** demonstrated how this fight or flight reaction is related to territory. He let two male sticklebacks (A and B) set up territory in a fish tank, then put each in a test tube. If both tubes were placed in A's territory A attacks and B tries to flee, if the tubes were placed in the other's territory the reverse happened.

- Territories reduce the amount of *aggression* because the owner usually wins. Why? Possibly because owners are stronger and intruders are weaker members without a territory *or* the owner will fight harder because its worth more to him *or* there is an 'owner wins' convention. **Davies and Houston (1984)** tested this final hypothesis with the speckled wood butterfly, which defends sunspots underneath bits of wood. When an intruder lost a contest, they removed the owner and waited for the intruder to occupy the territory. They then reintroduced the original owner and found that the new owner won the contest. It seems that the intruder automatically backs down when meeting an 'owner'. The same is true for a group occupying a territory; **Yasukawa (1979)** formed two separate hierarchies of junco birds and placed one group in the others' cage. The intruders took their place at the bottom of the hierarchy with little fighting. If both groups were placed in a completely new cage they engaged in much more fighting and established a new hierarchy, thus showing how ownership of the territory settles disputes on the basis of owner wins.

- Territories are a means of managing *food* supplies:
  - There is a balance between territory size and food, too large a territory and the animal expends too much energy defending it.

- A sole occupancy enables some animals to husband their supplies. For example, sunbirds 'farm' the flowers in their territory in rotation so that they only return when the supply has been replenished.
- Not all animals find their food in their territory. For example, sea birds have cliff territories but search for food elsewhere.
- Territories are related to *reproduction*. For example, in sticklebacks the female will only mate with a male who has a territory. Such a system maintains a balance between community size and food supplies.
- The *boundaries* are probably not fixed but are 'fuzzy'. **Manning (1973)** claims that the fact that animals engage in threat displays or displacement activities on their borders is evidence of this, as they are in a state of conflict over whether to fight or flee.

8.5 THE USE OF ANIMALS IN RESEARCH

The three questions are:

1 In what ways are animals preferable to human subjects?
2 Can we generalise from animal to human behaviour?
3 What is ethical in terms of the use of animal subjects?

Animals make better subjects than humans

- They are cheaper.
- There are *fewer* ethical problems, some procedures would be impossible with human subjects.
- Animals produce the same behaviours as humans only in a less complex manner, therefore it is easier to study these behaviours in animals.
- They can be conditioned more successfully.
- They are less susceptible to experimental bias.
- Their life cycles are shorter, enabling successive generations to be followed. So that, for example, the effects of early experience or selective breeding can be seen.
- Instinctive behaviour can be studied in animals. This is not possible in humans because of cultural transmission, which largely masks the influence of biology.
- However, animals can't report what they are thinking, which makes assessment difficult in some areas of research.

Are the results of animal research applicable to humans?

1 Yes
- Some aspects of behaviour are unquestionably the same. For example, studying the functioning of nerves (the effects of drugs on behaviour is more complicated).
- The behaviourist view is that different species differ quantitatively rather than qualitatively. This is based on evolution and leads to the premise that research on certain 'building blocks' of behaviour such as stimulus–response (S–R) links in animals can justifiably be transferred to humans.
- The comparisons which can be made are at least useful. For example, the ethological approach to understanding the origins of some behaviours through the differences and similarities of closely related species.
- Even if data is not directly applicable to humans it may point the way or act as pilot research.

❷ No

- Simply because structures are the same doesn't mean they perform the same function.
- Humanists argue that humans are qualitatively different from animals. Certain (possibly unique) features of humans, such as consciousness and language, mean that it might never be appropriate to generalise from animals; **Koestler (1970)** coined the term 'ratomorphism' to describe generalisation from animals to man.
- Similarly, the effects of cultural transmission mean that the same rules do not apply to animal and human behaviour. In humans, culture plays by far the greater role, whereas in animals many behaviours are innately programmed and genetically driven. The higher up the phylogenetic tree the less genetics plays a role (see cultural evolution, 8.1).
- The danger of anthropomorphism – imputing human feelings to animals.

Ethics: do the ends justify the means?

(see also 'Ethics in Research', 10.4).
The issue is to weigh up costs (in terms of animal suffering) versus benefits:

- It may contribute directly to improving the life of animals as well as humans, e.g. protecting endangered species.

- It may cause a very low level of suffering, such as genetic engineering, but nonetheless raise ethical questions about humans interfering with nature.

- It is not just research which leads to questions of ethics. Keeping some animals as pets is unethical. **Herzog (1991)** points out that the owners of kittens and snakes place the interests of their pets ahead of the unfortunate animals that they must eat, and that this is not so very different from researchers who place the interests of sick animals or humans ahead of those animals used for research.

- In terms of suffering, we need some means of assessing this without being anthropomorphic. Do rats have the same feelings as primates? What about plant life?

- One can distinguish between different species of animals in terms of their awareness. Experiments with rats might seem preferable to those with monkeys. The potential for language is another means of dividing (or not dividing) humans from other animals (see 4.1).

- There has been a recent move to formulate a bill of rights for primates which would place them on a par with humans, on the basis that we have a moral obligation to other primates (**Singer, 1993**).

- Similar arguments are presented in relation to the monetary costs of scientific research, does the end justify the cost? The true value of any research can only be judged with hindsight. For example, Harlow's research with monkeys started with no notion that maternal deprivation could have such consequences.

- The issue is of where you draw the line. *Some* research is justifiable, but how much?

The facts about animal research

Coile and Miller (1984) examined a body of American psychological articles and found that only 7% had been primarily concerned with animals; the rest were based on human subjects.

The **Animals Act (1986)** has laid down strict guidelines for animal research. For example, research using animals usually requires a licence from the Home Office. In America, all work except that involving rats, mice and birds must be licensed by the government. In addition the **British Psychological Society (1985)** strongly advises psychologists to:

- 'avoid, or at least minimise, discomfort to living animals',
- discuss any such research with a Home Office inspector,
- be familiar with the unique requirements of the species they are studying,
- minimise the number of subjects used,
- consider the relative costs and benefits, and alternatives.

Alternatives

- Use naturalistic observation rather than experimental manipulation, though this hampers research into cause and effect.
- Computer simulations are becoming increasingly more realistic and possible.
- For some aspects of psychology, the use of *in vitro* techniques such as tissue cultures in test tubes, as in medical research, may be suitable.

An ethological conclusion

An American city council held a public meeting to decide whether they should give the animals kept in the city pound (who had been abandoned by their owners) to scientific research. At the meeting one woman spoke of how her baby's life had been saved by an operation which had been pioneered on dogs. She asked whether the audience would rather save children or dogs, to which they replied 'Dogs, dogs, dogs' (**Flanagan, 1988**). In terms of human evolution, this response does not bode well for our species. On the other hand, the laws of natural selection suggest that those humans with genes which favour their own species will be the ones who survive!

Chapter roundup

Related material in other chapters:
- cognitive psychology (Chapter 1), covers learning;
- social psychology (Chapter 2), aggression and altruism, plus social behaviour generally;
- developmental psychology (Chapter 3) examines attachment and early experience which draw on ethology; Piaget's theory of cognitive development uses the concept of maturation;
- communication (Chapter 4) includes teaching animals to speak, animal communication and its origins;
- intelligence, personality and assessment (Chapter 5) contains some of the most critical evidence in relation to the nature/nurture argument;
- biological psychology (Chapter 7) offers a biologically determined view of human nature;
- applied psychology (Chapter 9) considers crowding and territoriality in human behaviour;
- research and design (Chapter 10) includes a general discussion on the ethics of research.

Illustrative question

Discuss the nature/nurture issue in psychology, using appropriate evidence to support your answer.

(AEB, 'A', 1989)

Tutorial note

This is the question which meanders through the whole of psychology. Evidence can be taken from perception (Chapter 1), aggression (chapter 2), gender roles (Chapter 3), language (Chapter 4), intelligence and personality (Chapter 5), abnormal behaviour (Chapter 7). It seems particularly apt to present an answer in this chapter which focuses on the genetic origins of animal life and the more recent (in evolutionary terms) development of learning. I have chosen to present the answer mainly in terms of argument rather than empirical evidence, much of which can be found elsewhere in this book. An equally valid (and more traditional) answer could be based on the evidence from any of the topics listed above.

Suggested answer

By 'nature' we mean behaviour which is determined by our genes, such genetic determinism is associated with **nativists**, and also classical **ethologists**. At the other extreme is **behaviourism**, which takes the view that all changes in behaviour (development) can be explained in terms of experience (i.e. learning). Historically, this view was espoused by **empiricists** who suggested that a baby's mind was a tabula rasa (blank slate) at birth.

The issue can be approached: (1) from a philosophical position, 'which is it?' (2) from an empirical position, 'how can the relative contributions be assessed?' (3) from a pragmatic position, 'why does it matter?'

Ethologists use the analogy of a blueprint for genetic determination: 'behaviour is not contained somehow within a gene, waiting to leap out like Athena, fully armoured, from the head of Zeus. Rather, genes are blueprints, which code for a range of potential actions.' **(Barash, 1982)**. **Lorenz** noted the behavioural similarities in different species of ducks, and concluded that this could only be explained in terms of genetically coded behaviours inherited from a common ancestor.

Ethologists acknowledge, however, that much of behaviour is learned. Imprinting, an ethological concept, is an example of genetic and environmental determination: it is a predisposition to learn certain things at certain times. However *what* is learned is dependent on the environment. There is some debate about whether imprinting is a special kind of learning. All learning can be described in the same way: it is a means of adapting rapidly to changing environments, and has evolved to a greater or lesser extent in all animals.

The position of environmental determinism, as used by behaviourists, largely explains behaviour in terms of learning. However, this is not to the exclusion of inherited behaviour: reflexes (involuntary, unlearned responses which are important for the protection or survival of an individual) differ from fixed action patterns only perhaps in terms of complexity.

This suggests that learning and inheritance are not distinctly different, there are other arguments to support this. The notion of genotype *versus* phenotype has been described as meaningless by, for example, **Hebb,** who likened it to asking whether the width or length of a rectangle was more responsible for its area. Genotype – the inherited characteristics of an individual – can only be expressed through phenotype; they cannot exist separately. As soon as an organism begins to develop after fertilisation, the environment has an effect.

Culture (learned) and evolution (genetic) are different forms of the same process. They are both means of adapting to changing environments. They are both means of transmitting such adaptation across generations.

The extent of environmental or genetic influence may depend on what is being studied. In animals behaviour is much more genetically determined. Where cultural transmission occurs, as in humans, it accounts for much of behaviour. However, it depends on what behaviour is being discussed. For example, perception is a relatively lower order of mental activity and concomitantly more affected by biological determination. The same may be true of gender. Studies which focus on phylogenesis (as ethologists do) emphasise genetic determination, whereas descriptions of ontogenesis (of greater interest to the psychologist) would give greater evidence of experience.

Wherever you look the answer is a resounding 'both nature and nurture', but in what way do they interact?

Ideally it would be possible to provide empirical evidence by isolating nature and nurture, to sequester an individual from birth. Ethologists used this method when investigating species-specific behaviour such as birdsong. However, learning may take place even before hatching. The fledgling is certainly able to hear in the egg.

Alternatively the matter can be investigated by comparing situations of either constant environment or constant genetics to see what similarities and differences can be observed in behaviour, in the same way that one might experiment with varying length and width to see how the area changes.

In humans this is only possible through observing existent situations, such as looking at the correlation between genetic relationship (mother–son and sister–brother) and a trait such as intelligence. Heritability is the measure of the degree to which a characteristic is inherited. Other techniques use monozygotic twins and/or adopted children. The problems here are that no MZ twins are ever truly genetically identical. Adoption is not a guarantee of a completely different environment to the 'natural' one and in any event twins in such cases have shared experiences before birth and possibly after birth.

In animals it is possible to use selective breeding to demonstrate how genes might control behaviour. **Cooper and Zubek (1958)** created strains of maze-bright and maze-dull rats, which showed large differences in performance when tested in ordinary conditions. However, if both strains were reared in a restricted environment they both performed poorly. If they were raised in an enriched environment they both performed equally well. This demonstrates that simply controlling genetics or environment does not give a true picture.

A recent development in genetic research has been the mapping of genomes. The genome is the full complement of genes of an organism. It is clear that we will soon be able to identify whether an individual has the genes for certain behaviours. However, it must be recognised that possessing a particular gene does not automatically mean that the individual will develop that behaviour. For example, **Egeland *et al.* (1987)** located a defect on chromosome 11 which was associated with manic depressive illness. However, not all subjects with the defect had developed the illness. This is related to the penetrance of genes and to environmental triggers.

In what way is the issue of nature–nurture of practical importance? The nativist position suggests that behaviour is not within our control, it is predetermined by our genes. In the case of intelligence, Jensen has argued that certain races are genetically inferior, which has echoes of the eugenic practices of the Nazis. The idea that some abnormal behaviours are predestined favours the medical approach to their treatment. In a different direction, the position of linguistic determinism **(Chomsky)** favours the view that humans *are* uniquely different from animals.

In each of these areas, a person's moral views may influence the position they prefer to take rather than the evidence itself. Perhaps the greatest test is yet to come as the results of the Human Genome Project become known. Psychologists may be called on for advice about the likelihood that certain genes lead inevitably to certain behaviours. And even then we will have to decide whether such eugenics is acceptable.

Question bank

Allow 45 minutes for each question.

1 To what extent do evolutionary concepts contribute to our understanding of the behaviour of non-human animals?

(AEB, 'A', 1990)

Points: Many candidates answer questions in this section on the basis of a wealth of knowledge gleaned from wildlife programmes. This is by no means irrelevant, but a good answer requires evaluation skills, evidenced by making some theoretical sense out of the descriptive data. It is also tempting to be anthropomorphic (e.g. talk about animals falling in love) but this suggests a superficial level of understanding.

2 Use evidence to discuss how the behaviour of successfully adapted non-human animals has been determined by the interaction of genetic and environmental factors.

(AEB, 'A', 1987)

Points: A slightly different version of the nature/nurture question answered above, this time focusing on non-humans, whose behaviour is much more genetically determined.

3 Discuss the contribution that ethological studies have made to the understanding of mating behaviour in non-human animals.

(AEB, 'A', 1985)

Points: Questions referring to ethology seem to show that many candidates are not clear about what this is. This question would encompass both ethological and non-ethological material (as a means of assessing the contribution of the former) but the distinction between the two should be clear.

4 How do dominance and territoriality influence the social behaviour of non-human animals?

(AEB, 'A', 1989)

Points: Both dominance and territoriality affect mating and agonistic behaviours. Evaluation skills can be demonstrated by relating the description to its evolutionary significance.

5 Using examples, show what is meant by apparent altruistic and selfish behaviour in non-human species. Discuss how these behaviours may have potential survival value.

(AEB, 'A', 1991)

Points: A classic question on this area of the syllabus. Descriptive skills are clearly distinguished from evaluation skills (discuss...) yet many candidates do little more than describe, without comment on survival value.

6 Describe studies of imprinting in non-human animals and discuss how the imprinting process may be beneficial to animals.

(AEB, 'A', 1991)

Points: Candidates in examinations dwell too much on the original work by Lorenz rather than branching out to the many other classic studies. A good essay should consider more than visual imprinting, and comment on more than the immediate effects.

7 Discuss, using evidence from non-human animal studies, the effect of early deprivation on later behaviour.

(AEB, 'A', 1985)

Points: A question which sounds like one on attachment but is specifically about non-humans and therefore work from Bowlby, etc. is irrelevant.

8 Evaluate the usefulness of observational methods in studying animal behaviour.

(AEB, 'A', 1986)

Points: A good answer should consider different methods of studying animals as a means of evaluation.

APPLIED PSYCHOLOGY

Units in this chapter

Chapter overview

Applied psychology is the use of psychological theories and empirical data in day-to-day settings, for the benefit of humankind. Such information may be derived specifically for certain applications (as in the Applied Psychology Unit at Cambridge or a market research company) or may be drawn from academic research. The boundary between academic and applied psychology is by no means distinct. Everyday uses of psychological data appear throughout this book. However, there are some specialist applications which are examined in this chapter.

Jobs in psychology

- The *industrial* (or occupational) psychologist typically works for a particular company and is concerned with personnel selection, developing training schemes, maximising production, helping the flow of communication and industrial relations, advising management on, for example, decision-making and motivation to work, advising on sales techniques and market research strategies.
- The *educational* or school psychologist is described in detail in 9.3.
- The *clinical* psychologist is involved with the diagnosis and treatment of emotional and behavioural problems, e.g. mental illness, juvenile delinquents, criminals, drug addiction, mental retardation and marital problems.
- The *health* psychologist assists patients in adjusting and managing health problems, researches into the prevention and management of health and illness, and may train health workers.
- There are also legal and criminological psychologists.

9.1 ORGANISATIONAL PSYCHOLOGY

Organisational or industrial/organisational (I/O) psychology is concerned with:
- the study of behaviour in work settings,

- the application of psychological principles to changing work behaviour and conditions,
- to benefit both the worker and productivity levels.

An *organisation* is a structured system of diverse parts with a common goal; *work* is an effort directed to an end. As this is an application of psychology, many areas covered elsewhere in this book should be considered:

- interpersonal processes: group behaviour (2.8 and 2.9), social perception (2.1 and 2.2),
- critical life events: ageing, unemployment and retirement (3.5),
- communication (4.2),
- assessment and psychometric techniques (5.3),
- motivation (7.4) and stress (7.6).

AN HISTORICAL OVERVIEW

Work has its antecedents in hunting and gathering. The industrial revolution and, more recently, the computer revolution, have led to profound changes in social life related to patterns of employment.

① **Scientific principles**: were first introduced to the study of work behaviour at the turn of the century by **Taylor**, an engineer, who suggested that it was possible:

- To study jobs scientifically. He introduced the concept of *time-and-motion studies*. Work tasks are broken down into simple component movements and the movements timed to develop a more efficient method for performing the tasks. He found that production rates sometimes improved up to four times.
- To use financial incentives to introduce changes or increase productivity because, he thought, money is the prime motivator. He suggested that such increases benefited the workers as well as management.
- To apply scientific principles to calculating piece rates, and to selecting suitable workers for training and better management.
- To design tools and work systems to fit the requirements of the job and the characteristics of the worker (human engineering). For example, he experimented with different shovelling movements, shovel loads, shapes of shovel and was able to increase productivity.

② **Worker morale**: financial incentives are sometimes secondary to social and personal factors, particularly where jobs are repetitive and boring. There have been various movements offering means of improving the social life of the workers, e.g. the Co-operative movement (started in Britain in 1844), Marks and Spencer (1884), and the human relations movement (Mayo, 1933).

③ **Organisational research**: is hampered by difficulty in manipulating variables such that all extraneous influences are controlled. The *Hawthorne effect* **(Mayo, 1933)** was first observed in a study to assess the effect of lighting on productivity. The researchers found that any change they made led to improved productivity and realised that the improvements were not related to increased illumination but due to the fact that the workers benefited from the extra attention.

(In a later study productivity in fact fell when the changes being tested were related to more demanding production quotas; therefore the Hawthorne effect only occurs when workers feel the research is for their benefit.)

④ **Personnel selection**: first appeared with the Army Alpha and Beta tests for recruiting military personnel on the basis of their intelligence (see 5.4)

⑤ **Fair employment practices**: such as the Civil Rights Act (1964) in America and, in Britain, the Equal Pay Act (1970), the Sex Discrimination Act (1975) and the Race Relations Act (1976). These aim to ban discriminative practices and force organisations to take the task of hiring and firing more seriously.

PERSONNEL ISSUES

The cost to the organisation of employing the wrong person in a job is high, therefore much energy is devoted to improving the fit between people and jobs. **Schmidt *et al.* (1979)**

calculated that a cost $36,800 (approximately £20,000) per annum would be saved if the validity of selection methods increased from 0.3 to 0.5:

1 **Job analysis**: the systematic study of the tasks involved in and the qualities needed to perform a job. Job analysis includes wage evaluation and performance criteria for assessment. One tool for writing a job description is the Position Analysis Questionnaire (**PAQ; McCormick *et al.*, 1969**); a structured questionnaire to analyse jobs in terms of 187 elements arranged in six categories: information input, mental processes, work output, relationship with other persons, job context and other characteristics.

2 **Finding potential applicants**: newspaper advertisements, employment agencies, walk-ins (applicant-initiated). The effectiveness of each varies with level of job and research indicating how to reach the 'right' potential applicants.

3 **Screening applicants**: collecting appropriate information to determine suitability. Long- and short-listing:
- *Application forms*: standard forms or open-ended. Lower-level positions require less information and the form can be more specific. Weighted forms enable a score to be calculated for each applicant. Research indicates which factors are good predictors of job success and these are given more weight.
- References and resumés: are declining in use because they invariably are skewed in a positive direction.
- *Peer assessment*: recruitment within the organisation. Peers rate, rank or nominate each other.

4 **Selecting the employee**: generally involves face-to-face methods:
- *Personnel testing*: IQ, personality and aptitude tests and interest inventories (see 5.3 on reliability, validity and standardisation of psychological tests).
- *Situational exercises*: applicants are asked to perform tasks that approximate to actual work, such as role playing a management task or leaderless group discussion. A technique for selecting higher level workers, with good correlation with later job performance, i.e. validity (**Argyle, 1989**).
- *Interviews*: low validity because conducted haphazardly by inexperienced interviewers with inevitable biases (halo effects, attribution errors, too lenient/ severe, racial/sexual/ageist prejudices). Interviewers often do much of the talking and ask different questions of each candidate, which makes it difficult to compare applicants. Interviewees are often nervous and may succeed because they are good at self-presentation and/or intelligent rather than being in possession of job-related skills. The interview method can be improved by: structuring the interview, using a method of scoring/rating the applicant, asking questions which are job related, training the interviewers, using a panel of interviewers who discuss judgements (interviewing methods are covered in 5.3 and interviewee presentation in 2.1).
- *Multiple 'hurdles'*: at each stage some applicants are rejected, using a combination of tests and interviews, as well as involving different personnel in assessment.

5 **Making the decision**
- *Clinical approach*: subjective judgements, generally prone to error though better when handled by experienced decision-makers.
- *Statistical decision-making models*: each piece of information is weighted in relation to its value in predicting future job performance.
- *Assessment centres*: in a large organisation it may be feasible to have an expert department. The costs of such procedures are offset by their greater effectiveness.
- *Legal burden*: in the US the employer has a duty to show that their screening and selection methods are valid indicators of future performance. Any hiring of disproportionate numbers of a 'protected group' (based on the numbers who applied) may be investigated.

WORKER ISSUES

Traditionally most adults have spent most of their waking lives at work, which therefore had a major impact on their general life satisfaction. Changes in work habits and longer retirement mean that leisure is becoming an increasingly important factor. Motivation, job satisfaction and work stress are used to explain productivity levels and personal well-being. Other factors contribute as well: group dynamics, organisational health and work environments.

Motivation in the workplace

Motivation is the force that energises, directs and sustains behaviour (see 7.4 for a general discussion of motivation). Productivity depends on good motivation. What motivates people to work? And to work better? The following suggestions are not mutually exclusive. Individual differences mean that individuals vary as to what motivates them and it is necessary to match individual profiles to jobs and incentives which will satisfy needs:

1. Extrinsic motivation:
   - *Money*: **Warr (1982)** found that approximately 30% of people would continue working even if it were not financially necessary.
   - *Levels of need*, as suggested by **Maslow**: workers first need to satisfy lower-levels of need e.g. monetary incentives, and then the higher-levels of social, esteem and self-actualisation needs.
   - *Achievement*: **McClelland** suggests that people vary in terms of their desire for achievement, power and affiliation. This may be related to occupational choice in the first place. People high in the need to achieve (nAch) choose risky, entrepreneurial professions. **McClelland and Boyatzis (1982)** found that a combination of high need for power (nPower) and low need for affiliation (nAff) (need to form close relationships) may also be a good predictor of managerial success.

2. **Intrinsic motivation**: doing work for its own sake, i.e. because it gives pleasure. Examples are: the Protestant work ethic, voluntary work, commitment to a career. Extrinsic motivation may decrease intrinsic motivation, so pay might even decrease productivity!

3. **Reinforcement theory**: the behavioural model of operant conditioning suggests that organisations should reward and thus increase desirable behaviours (such as high productivity or ideas) and punish, and thus reduce, undesirable behaviours (lateness and absenteeism), as a means of motivating the workforce.

4. **Job design theories**: if the job itself is enlarged or reorganised this may increase motivation, for example:
   - *Job characteristics*: **Hackman and Oldham (1976)** proposed three dimensions for change:
     - meaningfulness: perceive work as meaningful,
     - responsibility: have a sense of responsibility towards their job,
     - knowledge of results: some idea of the results.
   - *Job enrichment*: a motivational programme which redesigns jobs so that workers have a greater role in the planning, doing and evaluating of their jobs. Failures of such methods may be due to poor implementation. **Janson (1971)** found that typists improved their production rates when they were asked to correct their own mistakes; this is less true for manual workers.

5. **Equity theory**: equity can be: (1) everyone paid equally; (2) those who are skilled or in higher levels of an organisation should be paid more; (3) those who do boring unpopular jobs should be paid more because others have intrinsic rewards:
   - **Adams (1965)** suggested that workers are motivated to reduce perceived inequities between work inputs (experience, education, effort) and outputs (pay, fringe benefits, status, interest).
   - **Vroom (1964)** proposed VIE theory: *V*alence (desirability of outcome), *I*nstrumentality (likelihood of receiving the benefit), *E*xpectancy (relationship between effort and achievement). Workers weigh the expected costs and benefits before they are motivated to take action.
   - **Argyle (1989)** reports that there are good correlations between instrumentality and productivity, but generally research indicates that workers don't seek rewards in a simple, rational way, such as both theories suggest.

6. **Goal-setting theory**: goals should be specific, quantified and achievable. A simple strategy to implement, and therefore popular, is incentive schemes (e.g. piecework).

Workers are paid in relation to productivity rates rather than time. **Guzzo et al. (1985)** found that they were more successful than other strategies in a meta-analysis of 13 studies. However, it is hard to study the effect of incentives alone since they are usually accompanied by a number of other changes.
- Group piecework: encourages co-operation and reduces conflicts.

7 **Organisational commitment**: loyalty to the organisation (or to the union):
- This is typified by Japanese organisational style, where motivation is aroused by a sense of responsibility to the employer and work group and a total commitment to productivity rather than job satisfaction. This is linked with a cultural tradition of duty and the family. Many firms are family dominated and work groups function like interdependent family units.
- Can be achieved through, for example, employee ownership, profit-sharing, benefits, social activities.

Job satisfaction

Job satisfaction is the feelings and attitudes concerning one's job; satisfaction leads to personal well-being and dissatisfaction decreases the desire to work.

1 **Causes of satisfaction**:
- The *job*: boredom can be reduced and satisfaction increased when jobs are rotated, modified or enriched, as described above.
- *Pay*: more often a matter of dissatisfaction. Satisfaction may be more dependent on relative than absolute pay. Pay can be based on knowledge rather than position; there can be performance-related bonuses for individuals (merit pay) or group productivity levels (gain-sharing), profit sharing and co-partnership.
- *Benefits*: schemes to benefit the employee aside from direct pay, such as medical insurance, pension schemes, child care.
- *Work relationships*: smaller workgroups experience more satisfaction. Satisfaction decreases in conditions where opportunities for interaction are reduced such as a noisy factory. Unpopular group members usually leave the group. Social interactions provide emotional support.
- *Industrial democracy*: increased participation tends to lead to greater satisfaction, though **Wall and Lischeron (1977)** found this was not true for all workers; e.g. nurses had low desire to take part in decisions.
- *Organisational structure*, e.g. size, fewer levels of hierarchy, participation, constructive supervision, praise, encouragement and pleasant social atmosphere.
- *Individual differences*: fit between the person (personality, knowledge, skills) and the job.
- Also: job security, status, promotion prospects, leadership style (see 2.9).

2 **Effects of job satisfaction**: it is difficult to ascertain whether certain features are actually causes or effects of job satisfaction. The safest claim is to say that these factors co-vary with satisfaction:
- *Productivity*: **Petty et al. (1984)** found correlations between job satisfaction and productivity of 0.31 for higher levels of workers and 0.15 for lower ones.
- *Physical and mental health*: **Cooper and Marshall (1976)** suggest that certain aspects of work, such as performing boring tasks and conflicts with other personnel, may be intervening variables which decrease both job satisfaction and health.
- *Life satisfaction*: work is still a major part of most people's lives and self-definition.
- *Absenteeism*: it is necessary, but difficult, to distinguish voluntary from involuntary absence, though short absences are likely to be voluntary. **Scott and Taylor (1985)** found little relationship between job satisfaction and voluntary absenteeism. It is hard to assess absenteeism at the managerial level because the hours of work are variable.
- *Staff turnover*: also voluntary and involuntary. Probably less a function of job satisfaction than of organisational commitment.

3 **Theories of job satisfaction**:
- **Herzberg (1966)** proposed a *two-factor theory* of motivation: job satisfaction and job dissatisfaction are distinct: *motivators* (e.g. type of work, promotion prospects) lead to satisfaction; *hygienes* (e.g. benefits, working conditions), if absent, lead to dissatisfaction. This theory is probably more applicable to white-collar workers.

- *Need-satisfaction*: a congruence between needs and rewards leads to satisfaction. **Hackman and Oldham (1976)** found that not everyone wants a demanding job.
- *Social information processing*: **Salancik and Pfeffer (1977)** suggested that certain social perceptions (e.g. comparisons with others, affiliation with co-workers, group norms and organisational climate) lead to satisfaction. **Thomas and Griffin (1983)** manipulated social cues and found that job satisfaction increased as predicted.

Work stress

Stress, the physiological and psychological reactions to environmental events, is covered generally in 9.4. The particular features of work stress are:

1 **Effects**: leads to absenteeism, high job turnover, poor performance (quantity and quality) and making errors. *Burnout*, where prolonged exposure to work stress leads to work failure, is a particular problem for human services professions (nurses, teachers, social workers, policemen), who feel their efforts fail to produce the desired results.

2 **Causes**: job uncertainty, organisational change, interpersonal conflicts, sexual harassment, punitive management, lack of control, work overload, underutilisation of skills, responsibility for others, difficult tasks, shift work (see 7.3), decision-making, dangerous, unpleasant or uncomfortable work environment, lack of support.

3 **Coping strategies**: individual strategies are covered in 9.4. The organisation can: improve person and job fit, fund employee training programmes, provide better sense of job control, improve work conditions and benefits, give personal support, offer flexitime, facilitate communication for complaints and better information about organisation change.

Organisational issues

The concepts of organisational health or climate are used to discuss the prevailing atmosphere which influences successful man management and higher quality productivity. Key considerations involve different ways of looking at the interactions within the organisation:

1 **Group processes**: inter- and intragroup interactions are a focus of study for I/O psychologists, drawing on social psychology to explain increased or decreased productivity: roles, norms, conformity, obedience, pro- and antisocial behaviour, problem-solving in groups (groupthink, group polarisation, brainstorming), leadership, power, group facilitation and influence. The details are discussed in Chapter 2.

   The use of work teams and group incentive schemes encourages co-operation and group cohesion, in turn reducing conflict, isolation and stress.

2 **Organisational structure**: the arrangement of positions in an organisation and the authority and responsibility relationships between them. To a large extent the structure varies with the demands of different organisations:

   - *Bureaucracy*: first proposed at the turn of the century in response to growth in the size of organisations which led to chaos. The six main characteristics are: division of labour, well-defined authority hierarchy, formal procedures, impersonality, merit-based employment decisions and written records. There are many such organisations, usually large, which provide a good service but may be negatively related to worker satisfaction.
   - *Line-staff structure*: the line (workers directly engaged in production) and staff (the specialised positions who support the line so that it can get on with the primary task, for example book-keeping, personnel, market research). An appropriate description of some organisations, e.g. a car factory or doctor's surgery, but where the organisation performs multiple functions it is not so easy to distinguish the line from the staff. The description can be used to understand conflicts between line and staff, such as having practical versus theoretical orientation.
   - *Matrix organisation*: a non-traditional approach where a team of workers is organised around a particular project, e.g. a film crew. It is characterised by

flexibility, collaboration among workers, group decision-making and de-emphasis on status. A project task force is a similar though more temporary arrangement.

- *Decentralised structure*: an increasing move away from traditional approach in large organisations, takes decision making away from the top level and aims to increase worker satisfaction.
- *Communication networks* (see 2.9) provide a means of describing structure in terms of links between workers.

3 Organisational development (OD): an organisation must have structures which will lead to adaptive change:

- *Training*: for example raft building or survival exercises on residential courses.
- *Work teams*: groups of workers discuss how to improve performance by looking at their interactions and other problems. **Galbraith (1973)** developed a set of rules to maximise their effectiveness. The team should: feel important, include some members with organisational power, have the necessary information, have authority, represent and inform workmates; decisions should be based on expertise, members should have good interpersonal skills and there should be adequate leadership.
- *Management by objectives (MBO)*: members from different levels in the organisation set performance goals, evaluate progress and then reset new goals which are both realistic and representative of management, individual and organisational needs.
- *Process consultation*: involves an expert in advising the organisation on how to solve problems after objectively studying them.
- *Quality circles*: a Japanese strategy. Small groups of volunteers meet to formally discuss and offer solutions for work-related problems.

4 Communication in the organisation: many organisations have hundreds or thousands of workers entailing complex communications: verbal, non-verbal, and written; upwards, downwards and laterally between hierarchy levels. Some considerations:

- *Downward* communications: appraisal interviews, instructions about job, communications from experts.
- *Upward* communications: employee suggestion schemes, grievance systems, open-door policies.
- *Noise*: physical or psychological distractions which interfere with the communication process; both are present in the office and factory.
- *Distortion* of information: censorship, exaggeration, filtering, are signs of an unhealthy organisation.
- *Technical language*: jargon may cause problems.
- Related to *power*: those who control the main sources of information have power, the grapevine is a powerful source within the organisation.
- The *organigram* is a way of displaying the formal communication links within an organisation. A *sociogram* can be used to show the informal links; *communication networks* are also useful (see 2.9).
- *Teleconferencing*: holding meetings over long distances using audio and visual links.

5 Organisational politics: the principles, aims and methods of those in control. Unions and management hold different sorts of power, which leads to conflicts requiring policies to promote good industrial relations:

- *Empowerment*: increased sense of power and control in the work environment has positive effects on production. For example, in the traditional British approach of *trade union representation*, shop stewards negotiate conditions. *Workers' councils* (elected representatives who control the organisation) are common in the Netherlands. In the US the *Scanlon Plan* has two main components: (1) committees composed of elected workers and a management member, have considerable powers of decision-taking; (2) committees share out profits.
- *Bargaining*: specialist negotiators are engaged in peace keeping when conflicts reach crisis proportions. Research is undertaken to facilitate methods. For example, **Morley and Stephenson (1969)** found that in a no-vision situation, bargaining results in the stronger case winning, but when face-to-face, things such as 'wanting to be liked' become more important.

- *Training*: workshops can help managers and workers resolve differences. For example, **Blake** *et al.* **(1964)** organised tasks to increase communication. Each side conveyed the image they held of the other side, which led to increased or at least open conflict. The next step was to gain insight into the opposition's position and understand the origins of conflict, and finally to uncover some common goals and plan future strategies.

SKILLS AND TRAINING

A **skill** is an organised pattern of mental and/or physical activity which is built up gradually, usually until it becomes automatic, accurate and effortless. A skill may be self-taught or the result of formal or informal training.

The following are skills: walking, speech, reading, driving a car, typing, playing golf. On the other hand: cabinet making, managing a company and being the captain of an aircraft are not skills in a psychological sense. Skills involve 'hierarchies' rather than 'sets', and therefore speech is a skill whereas managing a company involves a set of skills. The 'lay' use of the term 'skill' differs from the psychological one, e.g. distinguishing between skilled and unskilled labour, both of which involve skills in the psychological sense.

Training is the systematic development of knowledge or a skill required by a person in order to perform a task. The aim is to produce a specific set of (usually motor) behaviours. Education, on the other hand, aims to develop knowledge, moral values and understanding required throughout life, rather than in relation to a particular task. Therefore, training is seen as convergent and goal-oriented, as in the case of training a circus animal or toilet training. Often operant conditioning methods are suitable; involuntary reflexes may be classically conditioned. However, even aspects of divergent thinking, such as problem-solving or management techniques, have been the object of training schemes.

Theories of skill acquisition

Skill acquisition involves integrating activities into a hierarchical structure and being able to do these activities automatically, so that they require a minimum of mental resources (see 1.4):

- **Adams (1971)**: a closed-loop theory of motor learning: has described skill acquisition as a process of verbal–motor extrinsic feedback, which establishes an accurate perceptual trace, followed by motor only.
- **Fitts (1962)**: three-stage theory: describes skill learning as proceeding through three stages – cognitive, associative (practice) and autonomous (automatic).

Training techniques

① **Demonstration**: the novice is shown what to do.
② **Guidance**: 'error-free' training because the instructor follows the novice through the activity, giving verbal or physical guidance. In the case of verbal tasks, this is called 'prompting', and for perceptual detection tasks, 'cueing':
  - This may be more effective than feedback in the early stages of learning because it prevents errors.
  - It may be particularly important where errors early in learning could have safety consequences.
  - It may be boring, therefore guidance should be interspersed with practice and feedback. This also helps the trainer to re-assess the current objectives.
  - It may support performance rather than learning.
③ **Practice**
  - Practice is only effective after each component has been learned correctly. This is one of the problems for self-instruction.
  - *Massed and distributed practice:* with massed practice there is no or little rest permitted between tasks and it is generally less productive. The benefits of distributed practice can be related to: (1) memory, if practice intervals are too long learning may be forgotten; (2) warm-up, some tasks require re-orientation to a task which may take extra time; (3) psychological or physical fatigue, too short

rest periods lead to inhibitory carry-over (e.g. **McGeoch and Irion, 1952**). There is a difficulty in being precise about the difference between massed and distributed practice. For example, how long does the interval between practice sessions have to be to be distributed? Another difficulty is distinguishing between performance and learning. Massed practice may result in true levels of learning being masked.

- *Simulation:* an attractive solution but omits one component of the real situation – stress. It is therefore necessary for any simulation to be followed by on-the-job training.

4 **Feedback**: evaluating the performance (good or bad), or reporting on the type of error made (too hard or soft):

- *Continuous or at the end* of a block of time: if feedback is given after subsequent responses it may be disruptive.
- *Intrinsic or extrinsic:* which is not the same as internal or external. Intrinsic feedback is that which is available during the course of the normal task situation. Extrinsic feedback is supplied by other agents, such as the instructor, and will be absent after training.
- *Action versus learning* (concurrent versus terminal) feedback: forms of extrinsic feedback which are present during the course of performance (action) or after it (learning). When training subjects to apply a pressure, **Annett (1959)** found that continuous visual (action) feedback by the movement of an indicator was less effective than post-action feedback when comparing subjects after the training period. It seems that concurrent feedback acts as a prop during training, and, when removed, it becomes apparent that no learning has actually taken place. This may be because the trainee expects the prop to remain.
- *Cognitive versus proprioceptive* feedback: skilled activity is characterised by being able to anticipate stimuli and respond without the lag of normal reaction time. Therefore many skills bypass visual or cognitive feedback, which are slower. For example, typing or the 'inner game of tennis' approach to learning motor skills. This later technique involves bombarding the learner with hundreds of tennis balls so that they merely react rather than think. On the other hand **Fitts** and **Adams'** model involves a primary cognitive phase to skill learning. **Belbin and Belbin (1972)** taught the art of invisible mending by giving workers a large scale model so they could see clearly what they were doing; this was then transferred to the real thing.

Training concerns

1 **Transfer effects**: the transfer of learning or training refers to the influence of earlier learning on later learning:

- *Positive transfer*: occurs when learning task A has a positive effect on learning task B; when an old response is required by a new stimulus. At one time the study of Latin was justified as a means to acquire general skills which would then transfer to new learning situations. An example of the transfer of a motor skill would be learning to swim backstroke after breaststroke.
- *Negative transfer*: occurs when earlier learning interferes with later learning: a new response is required by an old stimulus or when there is some conflict between task 1 and 2, for example trying to play badminton using the same action as previously learned in tennis (which requires the whole arm not just a flick of the wrist). There may equally be some positive transfer in learning the new task such as ball sense. Negative transfer is more complicated since a new skill is learned and an old skill is unlearned.
- *Similarity*: tasks must be sufficiently similar for transfer effects to occur.

2 **Speed and accuracy trade-off**: the *measurement* of any skill is usually in terms of speed and accuracy. The *performance* of any skill is a trade-off of these attributes. Quick response versus waiting a short time to be sure that the response is correct:

- The *power law of practice*: once a task is performed correctly, practice initially leads to a large improvement in speed and accuracy but this tails off. This slower improvement may continue for many years; automaticity may take a long time.

3 **Part and whole training: Annett and Kay (1956)** concluded that if the elements of a task are highly independent the task is best learned as a whole, whereas if the tasks are interdependent, they should be split up and learned separately.

4 **Individual differences**: some training programmes will be more or less successful with different individuals:

- *Intelligence*: **Gropper (1968)** found that trainees in a low IQ group showed less benefit from longer demonstration units than those of high IQ.
- *Abilities*: there may be differences, particularly in learning motor tasks, in the time it takes different people to acquire skills depending on general skills such as manual dexterity, aiming, and tracking. Pre-assessment may make it easier to fit training schemes to trainees.
- *Age*: see 3.5 on ageing and the older worker.
- *Personality*: **Leith (1969)** found that unstructured and ambiguous training programmes were more successful with extroverts whereas the opposite was true for introverts.
- *Motivation*: the use of rewards, which may be extrinsic (such as financial) or intrinsic (a sense of personal achievement).

Training programmes

1 **Designing the programme**:
- task description,
- task analysis: defining the component skills or parts,
- psychological translation,
- sequences of training: designing a sequence of experiences each of which must be achieved before the next one is attempted,
- selection of suitable students, which might involve some pre-training and identifying suitable tests.

2 **Evaluating the programme**: not the same as validating a programme. Evaluation involves assessing the costs and benefits. **Riggio (1990)** suggests four levels at which training can be assessed:
- *reaction criteria*: impressions of the trainees, using interviews and questionnaires,
- *learning criteria*: trying to assess learning rather than performance in training, using tests,
- *behavioural criteria*: i.e. transfer of training to job performance. This requires *pretest–post-test* measures to compare performance before and after training,
- *results criteria*: assessing the value to the organisation – changes in the functioning of the organisation, evaluating cost effectiveness.

HUMAN FACTORS OR ERGONOMICS

Human factors (ergonomics or human engineering) is the study of the relationship between a person's physical and psychological requirements and the demands of particular work or machinery. Engineering is the design of machines for a particular job; human engineering is the design of machines with human needs in mind.

Examples: the flight control deck of an aircraft or a car; the shape of a chair which will ease back strain; the user-friendly software of a computer; the buttons on a video machine; optimal factory lighting to avoid eye strain and glare.

Therefore the scope of human factors research includes the design of:

- the human–machine interface,
- minimising human error and maximising safety,
- the demands of the technological revolution,
- work environments (see also 9.2 'Designing the environment').

The human–machine interface

1 **Who does what?** The first decision is what tasks to give the machine and what to leave to human intervention. Machines are good at repetitive, error-free work, humans are good at decision making (see 1.2).

2 Machine to human signals: can be visual (e.g. radar), tactile (a keyboard), auditory (a bell), olfactory (smell might indicate a leak). The aim is to maximise operator response time. Considerations for design:

- Visual displays: *digital* is good for precision but some figures can be confused (e.g. A/H and 3/8). *Analogue* is good for quick impressions, e.g. petrol gauge. *Check-reading* displays have a light for on or off.
- Information limits: too much information leads to overload.
- Arrangement of displays: preferably at eye level, and placed in a horizontal sequence because people read from left to right. Continuous-process technology, e.g. at a power plant or chemical works, involves a few people monitoring many gauges.
- Auditory signals: for getting attention. This works faster than a visual display and a visual signal might be missed, but in some (noisy) environments it is not suitable. *Synthetic speech* is useful for instructions, but it is not always clear, which may lead to misunderstandings.
- Coded information can help speed and ambiguity.

3 Human to machine feedback: controls, levers and knobs. Again speed is important, but so also are safety and correctness. Considerations for design include:

- Movements, which should mirror the machine actions they produce, e.g. a steering wheel. On a forklift the steering is reversed because most of the driving is done with driver facing backwards.
- Combine related controls, e.g. on-off and volume control on a radio,
- Mark the controls clearly for rapid identification. On aeroplanes the different knobs on levers are shaped differently so that the pilot can associate *tactile* sensation with the appropriate activity.
- A standardised placement of controls makes errors less likely.
- Controls should be spaced to avoid simultaneous pressing, e.g. keys on a keyboard, or to avoid accidental pressing e.g. cover on fire alarm.
- Voice or speech operated controls can be used when hands not free.

4 Engineering anthropometry: the design of equipment which fits the human shape, involves measuring physical characteristics such as arm length or hand shape.

Safety: accidents and errors

During the Second World War engineers realised that some accidents were due to poorly designed control systems. For example, many B-25 bombers landed on their bellies because experienced pilots operated the control for steering flaps instead of the one for landing gear which was placed next to it (**Riggio, 1990**).

Particular note is taken of large industrial plants where errors may lead to major disasters, e.g. Chernobyl or the chemical accident at Bhopal. One accident report stated that operators had to scan more than 1600 gauges, though another factor is operators being unaware of the seriousness of the system malfunction.

These disasters have led to increasingly careful design of the interface between humans and machines:

- design of human–machine interface with safety in mind (see above),
- task vigilance (see 1.4, absentmindedness),
- accident reports: analyses of major incidents and statistics of common problems. **Swain and Guttmann (1983)** classified the errors in terms of: omission (not doing something), commission (doing it incorrectly), sequence errors (doing it in the wrong order), and timing errors (doing it too slowly or quickly).

Information technology (IT)

Information processing is the organisation, manipulation and distribution of information; IT is the study of this process. The terms are essentially synonymous with 'computers' but shift the focus from the machine to the whole system of hardware, software and liveware (the human user).

343

1 **Hardware design**: the machines themselves. Examples of design considerations:
- ergonomically designed keyboards; the QWERTY keyboard remains the standard even though other arrangements may be more efficient,
- analogue data entry such as mouse, trackball, joystick, touch screen control,
- eye strain and VDU screens.

2 **Software design**: the programmes which run the machines. The ideal people to design user-friendly systems are Artificial Intelligence (AI) psychologists, who understand both human and machine behaviour. Psychological research, such as cognitive advances in understanding how people think, contribute to better designed systems. Microchip technology means that faster and cheaper systems can be produced, leading to increasing demands on software design. Examples: cash dispensers, information services over the telephone, word processors, programmable machines such as video recorders.

3 **Isolation**: the computer potentially enables most work to be performed in isolation:
- A work group may never meet but communicate entirely via desktop terminals (groupware). The ability to share information quickly should improve efficiency. However successful groupware must also allow for human interaction. **Siegel *et al.* (1986)** compared the ability of small groups to make decisions via a computer or face-to-face. The computer link resulted in greater equality, more shift from original opinions, a longer time spent on task, and fewer remarks made by the group members.
- Home links are increasing but work is best in terms of personal enjoyment when there are opportunities for face-to-face contact. Neighbourhood technology centres offer shared use of information technology in rural communities.

4 **Technophobia**: the introduction of automated machinery calls for thought in terms of social and emotional consequences:
- Workers, who naturally resist change because of fear of job loss and fear of the unknown. Management should involve workers in decisions to automate, provide suitable training and ensure compatibility. This applies to all levels of line and staff.
- Robots are progressively taking over many tasks previously done by humans because we are increasingly able to design systems better capable of decision making. Robots are quicker and more efficient, but will they cost too many jobs?

Workspace design

The workspace encompasses the environment and machinery. Curvilinear relationships exist between features of the environment and optimum performance; too much or too little results in reductions in activities. There are also differences according to the task that is being performed. (see also 9.2 for consideration of 'Design and the environment'):

1 **Lighting**: there are handbooks available giving levels appropriate for particular jobs. Considerations:
- glare of sunlight, overhead lights or computer screens,
- wall surfaces which don't reflect light,
- lighting may help with shift work (see 7.3).

2 **Temperature**: mental and physical activity is related to optimum temperatures:
- it is difficult to regulate temperature in large buildings such as warehouses,
- some tasks involve unavoidable hot or cold temperatures, e.g. meat packing or baking,
- regulating humidity or air currents may moderate temperature effects, management can also provide suitable clothing. **Enander (1987)** found decreases in manual dexterity, increases in errors but no effects on reaction time when subjects were exposed to moderate cold.

3 **Noise**: there are individual differences in ability to tolerate noise distractions; the effects of noise are very much task related:
- air conditioning noises can be stressful, producing a constant background hum,
- some workers like the radio on, particularly where work is boring,
- muzak – pleasant background noise to relax workers (and consumers),
- noise may interfere with machine or human communication,
- can be moderated with carpeting, wall and ceiling tiles.

④ **Vibration** and other motion:
  - vibrating machinery may lead to back and joint problems,
  - motion sickness, dizziness and disorientation may occur.

⑤ **Pollution**: for example chemicals in the atmosphere, asbestos in the building materials, fumes from copying machines or smoking:
  - **Evans and Jacobs (1981)** found decreases in attention, co-ordination and problem-solving when carbon monoxide levels were higher than normal. This is not only relevant for some work places but for urban environments generally,
  - atmospheric electricity (see below),
  - 'clean rooms' (free from dust or moisture) are required in the construction of computer circuitry; it is difficult to adapt such environments to human needs as well.

⑥ **Decoration**: a well decorated and maintained environment indirectly communicates 'caring' to the workers.

CONSUMER BEHAVIOUR

It is a major business concern to match a particular service or product to consumer needs, and thus keep ahead of the competition:

- *Marketing*: a series of processes where demand for a service or product is identified, supplied, anticipated or manipulated.
- *Market segmentation*: dividing the market into segments comprising similar kinds of people so that marketing efforts can be targeted more precisely.
- *Market research*: carried out by the organisation or a specialist firm to determine the market for a particular product and the best sales strategies to use. Genuine research should be distinguished from suggers or fruggers, who sell or solicit for charity under the guise of market research.
- *Market penetration* or *share*: the amount of demand in a particular market which is supplied by a particular organisation. A means of assessing the effectiveness of a marketing strategy.

Model of consumer behaviour

The marketing process starts before purchase and continues long after:

① Development and perception of want or need: advertising (informational and persuasive), marketing, display techniques (point-of-sale advertising), informal communications (from a friend).

② Pre-purchase decision-making: shop or mail order, method of payment, what shop? Determined by a combination of economic (prices), ethical (co-operative, charity, pro-animal rights), personalising (good service) or apathetic (convenient) factors.

③ The actual purchase of selected brand.

④ Evaluation of success leading to a decision to buy again and tell your friends about it. A combination of such things as satisfaction, post-decisional dissonance reduction and after sales service.

Market segmentation: demographics

Demographics are a set of figures used to describe market segments (or any population), e.g. age, sex, socio-economic status, most of which are straightforward to assess.

① **Individual differences**: the aim is to segment the market 'psychographically' (describe individual differences). In general empirical support has been disappointingly weak:
  - *Personality traits*: such as impulsiveness or dominance to product preference. **Westfall (1962)** found little relationship for car type.
  - *Personality types*: such as introvert/extrovert. **Cohen (1968)** found that compliant types were more likely to use mouthwash, drink wine, watch *Dr Kildare* and read *Readers' Digest*, though such associations are weak.

- *Self-image*: buyers prefer ads which are consonant with their self-perceptions. **Grubb and Hutt (1968)** found that car owners perceived themselves as similar to other people who owned the same brand of car.

2 **Age**: much advertising is directed specifically at children, who will then persuade their parents to buy a product, even when the product is not for children. Teenagers are a particularly attractive market segment. The increasing numbers of over 65s with spending power should lead to advertising changes in the future.

3 **Social class**: the Registrar General's classification scheme is based on occupation and used extensively in marketing investigations. Alternatives are to use the source of income, education, house type, dwelling area. Social class is associated with product usage, brand preference, store patronage choice of information sources, shopping frequency and innovative behaviour **(Foxall, 1980)**.

4 **Culture**: US products may fail in the UK because brand names, certain colours or packaging may have different connotations. The same is true between regional, ethnic, religious or age-based subcultures within the UK.

Market research: sampling

Many demographics are collected through sampling techniques (see 10.2). When assessing the results, the important questions to ask are: how was the sampling done, the size of the sample, the refusal rate and what questions were asked.

1 **Quota sampling**: interviewers aim to question people who are representative of the population in terms of age, sex, socio-economic status, etc.:
- This method makes assumptions about what is and is not representative.
- The area where the quota is selected, e.g. a shopping mall, means the sample is biased from the start.
- Biased by those people who refuse to take part, essentially a volunteer bias.

Examples:
- *Large-scale survey*: the Target Group Index (TGI) is a massive undertaking; 36,000 90-page questionnaires are sent out annually; 70% are returned, giving details of personal tastes and consumer habits which are put on a computer database and accessed for a fee. A typical Carling Black Label drinker is aged 18 to 24; likes to lie in the sun and to eat and drink on holiday; may well subscribe to satellite TV; likes to go to the pub for company as much as for drinking; prefers brand names to own-label, and is not interested in gardening or wholemeal bread. The profile for a Hellmann mayonnaise user is very different.
- *In-depth interview*: based on very small sample of, say, 20. Each person is asked why they choose each of the items in their larder, and then accompanied shopping to see how exactly they make their choices. Attitudinal rather than numerically-based.
- *Longitudinal survey*: panel samples. A large selection of families (8500) have a bar code reader at home which they use to record all purchases and transmit this data weekly via a modem to a computer. The panel is selected using quota sampling, though it is essentially a volunteer sample.
- BARB (Broadcasters Audience Research Board); reports TV viewing figures based on 4500 people meters in selected homes to keep a record of which family member is watching what programme. The assumption that if the TV is on, someone is watching it, may be wrong.

2 **Random sampling**: take every *n*th person from the electoral register. The National Readership Survey (NRS) is one of the largest, providing information about newspaper and magazine readers for potential advertisers. It samples 35,000 adults a year by picking addresses at random from the Post Office address file, randomly selecting one person from that address, and only interviewing that person. If the person is unavailable, no substitution is made and the interviewer calls again. There is a 63% response rate.

3 **Sample size**: where quota sampling is used, a sample of 1000 will only contain a few members from each representation group, e.g. white, middle-class, female, 20–25 age group, educated to degree level, etc.

④ **Questionnaire design**: see 10.2. The key concerns include: avoiding the use of leading questions, question order, closed questions, response set, social desirability bias.

Buyer's behaviour

Behavioural science is the attempt to make accurate predictions of what buyers will do on the basis of empirical data. The research is largely influenced by cognitive and social psychology, and sociology. It tends to be divided between pure academic interests and those funded by industry, resulting in mutual suspicion. The results can be contradictory, expensive to implement and lack predictive validity.

When designing marketing strategies the following should be considered:

① **Perception**: see 1.1. The selective, active nature of perception, the importance of context, individual preferences for the 'look' of the product or shop. Subliminal perception, and perceptual defence have important implications for visual advertising. **Foxall (1980)** reports a claim that Coca Cola put a subliminal advertising message into a normal film performance and increased sales by 57%. Replication has not been successful; the technique is banned by the Advertising Authority's code of practice.

② **Attention**: see 1.4. Catching a person's attention through novelty, prominence, interest or stimulation. The use of visual and auditory stimuli. Some attention-grabbing stimuli may have the contrary effect: they may be jarring therefore producing negative associations.

③ **Memory**: see 1.5. Memory can be improved through active organisation, the use of haunting melodies or memorable phrases, incomplete ads (e.g. 'Schhh... you know who'), which make you think longer and process more deeply. It is critical that people have an accurate memory for an advertisement; it may be influenced by many factors such as prejudice. **Allport and Postman (1966)** showed subjects a picture of a black and white man arguing. When asked who held the knife they generally, and incorrectly, said it was the black man. This shows that preconceptions alter your memory of images.

④ **Learning**: all consumer preferences are learned, see 1.6: conditioning and positive (or negative) reinforcement from advertising, group conformity or using a product. Persistent reinforcement leads to habits which are hard to break:
- Advertising may fail to affect learning significantly because of lack of audience involvement. One solution is to advertise the company's name through sponsorship of sport or research, areas where people do feel involvement.
- Learning may be more effective if the campaign is broken by gaps after a few weeks. Learning plateaus after initial exposure; an interval leads to some forgetting and therefore further exposure will be beneficial.
- Socialisation processes turn children into consumers. Understanding of these processes helps advertisers, and is important when framing consumer protection legislation.

⑤ **Attitudes**: one of the most important variables, see 2.3.
- The aim of learning is to create or strengthen a positive attitude.
- Attitude change is critical for innovation and competition between brands.
- Post-decisional dissonance is useful for understanding behaviour after purchasing.
- It should be remembered that attitudes and behaviour don't always correspond.
- Attitude measures (consumer surveys, opinion polls) draw on psychological theories.

⑥ **Intergroup processes**: conformity, reactance, compliance and group dynamics, refer to 2.8 and 2.9. Reference groups are social artefacts which provide individuals with information for comparison and social norms. Group affiliation influences brand choices, particularly the family group. The media is often blamed for moulding public opinion, but **Schram and Roberts (1971)** suggest that people rely on their social group to interpret media information. People come to the media seeking what they want not what the media intend.

⑦ **Communication**: non-verbal communication is the stronger channel, see 4.2. The *two-step flow hypothesis* uses the notion of formal and informal messages about products. Formal communications come from the mass media; these are picked up by relatively few influential individuals (*opinion leaders*) who disseminate information via informal channels to non-leader members of their social group.

- Effectiveness of the informal route: **Atkins (1962)** found that 80% of women exposed to word-of-mouth advertising tried a new supermarket, compared to 48% who said their choice was due to formal advertising.
- Key role of opinion leader: **Arndt (1968)** monitored the interest in a new food product among housewives in an apartment building: they were sent a leaflet plus coupons. Opinion leaders were more active as receivers and transmitters than non-leaders.

⑧ Motivation: see 7.4. This is not easy to investigate because people are usually unaware of their motives for buying and provide 'expected' answers rather than the real thing. Explanations can be framed in terms of a desire to avoid cognitive dissonance – Freud's suppressed motives, Maslow's hierarchy of needs, or **Lasswell's (1948)** *theory of triple appeal*. A successful ad should appeal to the id, ego and superego ('A Mars a day helps you work rest and play'). **Foxall (1980)** suggests that this theory may apply to a more moral generation, because many ads today are strictly aimed at the id.

⑨ Economics: the traditional view inversely links demand with cost, but in reality financial behaviour is influenced by more than money:

- People choose the more expensive item in a pair of similar versions of the same product. This may be due to linking quality with cost or social status. Boots the Chemist found its own brand items, which were lower priced than the competitors, weren't selling well. They raised the prices and increased sales. Price awareness is inversely related to socio-economic status (**Gabor and Granger, 1961**).

⑩ Evaluating effectiveness: does advertising and brand loyalty lead to increased sales? **Allison and Uhl (1964)** tested drinkers' ability to discriminate between brands of beer. If they were given the beers with no brand labels, they discerned no differences, whereas the presence of brand names biased their judgements, suggesting effective brand marketing.

9.2 ENVIRONMENTAL PSYCHOLOGY

Environmental psychology is a relatively recent development, which focuses on the interactions between people and their environment:

- how the environment affects behaviour (which can be contrasted with physiological explanations),
- how people affect the environment,
- the effects can be positive or negative – conducive or restricting to certain behaviours, e.g. a sunny room or a noisy environment, a well designed office or a prison,
- the subject combines material from many disparate disciplines such as social psychology, sociology, ethology, anthropology, human ecology, architecture, urban planning, human geography, demography, politics and ergonomics.

Other sections in this book underpin the material covered here, as it is built upon traditional psychology:

- interpersonal environment: see crowding and aggression (2.7 and 8.4), pro- and antisocial behaviour (2.6 and 2.7), prejudice (2.5),
- abnormal behaviour: see environmental causes (6.1 and 6.4),
- stress (7.6),
- sensory overload: see perception (1.1), attention (1.4).

RURAL AND URBAN ENVIRONMENTS

Agriculture was the beginning of urban life. Hunter–gathers had no fixed abodes but settled farming led to communities with increasingly complex interactions and the construction of permanent structures. The drift from rural areas to cities has always been the case; the town is the place of trade and education. This century we have seen the development of mega-cities (population of more than 4 million). Today there are more people living in New York City than were alive in the world 10,000 years ago.

The environment can be considered in terms of physical factors (such as weather, noise, pollution) and psychological ones (such as crowding and crime).

Differences in behaviour between urban and rural areas

Helping behaviour: **Korte and Kerr (1975)** found that 70% of the stamped postcards dropped in small rural towns around Boston were returned compared with 61% of those dropped in Boston itself.

Miller (1989) describes small town psychology as distinctly different from that of the urban dweller, and suggests that these differences have design implications for social interactions in rural areas. However, there are pockets of rural-type communities within cities.

Do urban environments create stress?

Many of the features of city life appear to be positively correlated with aggression and stress (see also 7.6 'Stress').

1 **Psychological overload**: too much noise and activity leads to overarousal and increased levels of stress. This overstimulation may be due to the presence of so many strangers, crowding, noise, etc. City dwellers learn to cope by filtering out irrelevant stimuli, (ignoring the presence of others) and seeking oases (city parks):
   - Evidence of arousal, e.g. **Schaeffer et al. (1988)** found that blood pressure increases in commuters.
   - Is it arousal *per se* or the fact that the city is an unpleasant environment? **Amato and McInnes (1983)** compared interpersonal behaviours (eye contact, smiling, speaking) in a shopping mall (pleasant and arousing) with a downtown construction site (unpleasant and arousing) and found that people were more friendly in the pleasant environment, suggesting that overload alone does not explain urban stress.
   - **Density–intensity hypothesis: Freedman (1975)** proposed that high-density situations only intensify what is happening already (see also 'Climate', p.350).

2 Noise:
   - May be most stressful if unpredictable. **Glass et al. (1969)** found that subjects made fewer errors on a clerical task when the background noise was predictable (see 7.6).
   - **Cohen et al. (1973)** compared two groups of children, one living on the highest and one on the lowest floors of an apartment building over a busy highway in New York. Noise is greater at the lower level. They found that those living on the lower levels performed less well on tests of auditory discrimination and reading ability despite being matched for factors such as social class. They concluded that exposure to loud, unpredictable noise was responsible.

3 Temperature:
   - **Cunningham (1979)** showed that people are less likely to agree to be interviewed when the weather is hot.
   - **Baron and Ransberger (1978)** looked at incidences of collective violence in the US between 1967 and 1971. They found that aggression indeed increased with temperature but only up to a point, indicating a curvilinear relationship between heat and aggression, with a peak in the low to mid-80s. (The Yerkes–Dodson law predicts a similar relationship between noise and performance.)
   - **Anderson and Anderson (1984)** correlated the number of aggressive crimes with temperature over a two-year period and found a positive correlation. For temperatures below 88°F. the rates were very similar; above this there was a marked increase.

④ **The physical environment**: many inner city areas are derelict, have inadequate public services and are dirty.

⑤ **The psychological environment**:
- multiracial problems and racial tensions,
- contrast between rich and poor,
- migration (see below).

Do urban environments lead to pathological behaviour?

Cities are not only associated with higher levels of stress, but also with pathological behaviours such as crime and mental illness. Why?

① **Population size**: the topic of density and crowding is considered in greater detail on p.351:
- **Whyte (1989)** found that an individual is more likely to be the victim of a criminal offence in the parking lot of a suburban shopping mall than in the middle of a large city.
- **Perry and Simpson (1987)** collected longitudinal data by monitoring the growth of Raleigh, North Carolina over a decade. They found that as the population increased, murder rates and those for aggravated assault decreased whereas rape incidences increased.

② **Migration**: crime rates increase in areas where there is a lot of population movement. Young people from rural areas move to the city seeking 'better lives'. At the same time some city dwellers move out, but only those who have adequate resources, leaving behind those who are aged or deprived.
- **Linsky and Straus (1986)** suggest that such movement entails the loss of stable interpersonal relationships and normative guidelines, which in turn leads to maladaptive social behaviour.
- This can be related to the social drift hypothesis of schizophrenia (see 6.4).

③ **Noise**:
- **Cohen (1980)** found that prolonged exposure to noise is correlated with increases in physical illnesses, higher mortality rates, mental illnesses and interpersonal conflict. It may be that individuals in such conditions are forced to expend more psychic energy in the course of adapting.

Other environmental influences

There are some more general factors which may be exacerbated in urban life.

① **Climate**:
- *Ion levels* (atmospheric electricity) as associated with thunderstorms are related to increases in suicides, industrial accidents and some types of crime. **Baron, Russell and Arms (1985)** increased the levels of negative ions in a laboratory and found that type A individuals behaved more aggressively, suggesting that the effect was an increase in general activation levels. The same may be true of other 'exciting' weather conditions such as wind or rainstorms. **Baron (1987)** found that negative ions had significant effects on certain cognitive activities, such as proof reading, memory span and decision making. However, such effects are not straightforwardly positive.
- *Seasonal affective disorder* (see 7.3): a depressive illness associated with winter darkness. It is treated with increased artificial lighting.

② **Pollution**: most commonly by cigarette smoke:
- **Rotton et al. (1979)** found that increased amounts of air pollution resulted in people feeling less happy.
- Passive smoking increases the likelihood of cancer in non-smokers (**Russell et al. (1984)**, see 9.4).

③ **Technophobia**: the fear of living in a technological society. The technological inventions around us have led an increasing sense of personal danger, e.g. cars, emissions from microwaves, the effects of VDU screens, exposure to high voltage electricity wires (also radiation phobia).

THE HUMAN ENVIRONMENT: CROWDING AND DENSITY

Much of the blame for urban stress and pathology is put on overcrowding, not least because of a classic study by **Calhoun (1962)**. He varied the population densities of rat communities and found that crowding led to pathological behaviour ('behavioural sink') not because of limited food and water, which was in plentiful supply, but presumably because of the stress.

He found increased levels of aggression, physical illness and cannibalism. Most notably many of the disordered behaviours were related to reproduction. 'Probers' are hyperactive and hypersexual males who constantly seek sexually receptive females and rape those they find. Females frequently died giving birth, became poor mothers, failed to build nests for young, to protect them from danger or to nourish them; 95% of the young died before reaching maturity. This suggests an innate mechanism to prevent overpopulation.

Similarly, **Dubos (1965)** found that the mass suicides of lemmings, when they run down to the sea, seem to occur when density reaches certain levels.

Density versus crowding

Density is the objective or physical measure; crowding is the subjective or psychological response. The same density may be acceptable at a football match but not in an airport. When does density lead to a sense of crowding and therefore a negative effect?:

❶ **Overload**: increased density leads to more sensory stimulation and physiological arousal; an excessive amount leads to stress.

❷ **Lack of control**: high-density situations lead to a sense of loss of control over your own behaviour. Predictability, stress and controllability are related:

- **Gardner (1978)** failed to find any negative effects of unpredictable noise in a study similar to **Glass et al.'s** (see p.349). He then realised that, on this occasion, subjects had been asked to sign a consent agreement indicating that they understood their rights as a subject. This was giving them a sense of control which they had previously lacked. When only half of the subjects were given consent forms he demonstrated that his hypothesis was correct: control cancelled out the effects of unpredictability.

❸ **Attributions**: density creates physiological arousal which is usually attributed to a psychological sense of crowding. If the arousal is attributed to something else, such as excitement (as at a football match or party) or anxiety over bad news, then crowding is not felt.

- **Worchel and Yohai (1979)** arranged for 5-person groups to sit either closely together or spaced apart. They were played a 'subliminal noise' (there was no noise) to test its influence on their performance. The experimenters expected that, if the subjects had an 'explanation' for their sense of arousal they would not feel 'crowded'. Those subjects who were sat close together and told that the noise would be stressful *did not* feel as crowded as those who expected relaxing effects. In other words they attributed the 'stress' to the sound rather than the density.

❹ **Interference**: if the crowd does not interfere with personal goals, a sense of crowding is diminished.

❺ **Staffing**: **Wicker (1979)** has described the concept of *optimal staffing* – too many or too few staff leads to decreased efficiency, for example, in a fast food restaurant, bar or airport. If a building is properly designed, the effects of density are diminished. Too few people and a place seems empty and threatening.

❻ **Cultural differences**: Asians in Hong Kong have lower levels of pathology than westerners living less densely in, for example, Los Angeles.

❼ **Social versus spatial density**: **Baum and Valins (1977)** suggested that there is a difference between the number of people present in a constant space (social density) and a ratio of available space and number of people (spatial density); social density causes more negative responses:

- **Baron et al. (1976)** found that where three people occupied the same size dormitory as two people (social density) they liked their room-mates less, felt less satisfied with living conditions, and did less well at college.

- **Ehrlich and Freedman (1971)** (cited in **Dobson** *et al.*, 1981) gave groups of people various games to play. The smaller the room, the more competitive the participants, indicating that spatial density also leads to aggression.

Control of crowding: personal space and territoriality

Personal space and the use of territories are a means of controlling density and social behaviour; they act as social organisers. There is a necessary balance between too much contact, leading to stress and aggression, and too little contact, leading to a sense of isolation.

Personal or body space is the most intimate territory. Some territories are an extension of body space, for example your car or house. **Altman (1975)** distinguished three other types of territory:

- *primary*: sense of ownership rather than simply frequency of use, such as your car parking space,
- *secondary*: maintenance of moderate control, established through regular use, e.g. where you sit in class, or stand at the local pub,
- *public*: yours only during use, e.g. telephone box.

1 **Settled territories** are related to dominance hierarchies, both of which lead to reduced aggression (see 8.4). **Sundstrom and Altman (1974)** studied the behaviour of delinquent boys in their institutional home. The two most dominant boys controlled the most desirable areas in the first five weeks of the study; at this time disruptive and aggressive behaviour was at a minimum. When these boys were transferred and replaced by two new members, fighting and disruptive behaviour increased dramatically until, after a few weeks, territories became re-established.

2 **Personal space**: is a means of organising social behaviour. It is a channel for nonverbal communication (see 4.2). You can threaten someone by standing too close or you can indicate liking. The degree of comfort or discomfort varies with:
   1 personal characteristics (age, sex, culture, personality),
   2 characteristics of the other person (nonverbal behaviours, similarity, sex),
   3 interpersonal relations (status, degree of friendship, family and cultural),
   4 situational factors (inside or outside, size of room such as a lift, task which might involve whispering).
   Middlemist, Knowles and Matter (1976) observed that men had more difficulty urinating in a public toilet when another user (confederate) stood in the next urinal, thus invading his personal space. **Henley (1977)** observed the behaviour of pavement encounters. A woman moved out of a man's way 63% of the time whereas a man moved out of a women's way 16% of the time. **Storms and Thomas (1977)** interviewed subjects from a distance of either 6 or 30 inches. If the interviewer behaved in an unfriendly fashion, the close contact situation was interpreted as invasion whereas when behaviour was friendly the subject evaluated the interviewer positively. **Felipe and Sommer (1966)** observed the reaction of students in a library when someone sat down next to them. Most built some kind of physical barrier or signalled with body posture, some actually left and one actually asked for more space.

3 **Defence** of personal space and territory:
   - territories are marked using signs: personal articles, such as clothing or books in a library; furnishings, such as decorating your room; fences or hedges around the garden,
   - considerations of territorial marking and defence are important in architectural and urban planning,
   - threatening behaviour, e.g. staring, or verbal requests,
   - aggressive attacks: there is generally a 'home field advantage' (a sporting phenomenon) which is related to the 'owner wins' convention found in animals (see 8.4).

HOW PEOPLE AFFECT THE ENVIRONMENT

From the beginning humans shaped their environment, for good and bad. We can observe environmental changes, but any larger causal inferences are only theoretical.

1. **Global warming**: as average annual temperatures world-wide increase, the polar ice caps melt; this raises the sea level and will lead to significant portions of land being submerged:
   - This may be due to the *greenhouse effect*. A result of various human activities, such as the burning of fossil fuels, which have led to increases in the levels of carbon dioxide and methane in the atmosphere. Increased levels of chloroflurocarbons (CFCs) cause holes in the earth's ozone layer, which in turn means that we are less protected from the sun's harmful rays.
   - An alternative explanation lies in natural climactic fluctuations (ice ages) which have occurred regardless of human activity.
   - The changes in sea level which are occurring are in some places due to land sinking as part of the ongoing continental movement.

2. **Pollution**: the discharge of industrial waste and sewage into rivers, seas, the air and burial underground.

3. **Depletion of resources**: such as overfishing, coal mining, cutting down trees. Animal research will help understanding of life-cycles and improve such 'farming' of the seas. Computer technology may reduce demands on paper in the future.

4. **Nuclear power**: is an alternative to depleting natural fuel resources and burning fossil fuels. However, there are other attendant risks. Those people who feel the risks are unacceptable may be accused of 'radiation phobia'. It is worth knowing that there are many natural sources of radiation, not least the sun itself, and therefore some exposure to radiation is natural. The main threat is of accidents such as at Chernobyl. The problem of designing accident-free systems is a concern for psychologists.

5. **Conservation**: not all human intervention is for the bad; some of it is to put right the wrongs we have collectively done. In other cases, such as saving endangered species, we may be unethically tampering with Mother Nature. Humans also conserve aspects for their own benefit, for example building sea walls to prevent the sea taking over.

   Attempts to change human behaviour are related to attitude change and persuasion generally (see 2.3 and the illustrative question about persuasion in Chapter 2):
   - education, prompts (signs) and advertising campaigns which say 'don't leave litter', 'save electricity, turn off the lights',
   - legislation, returning bottles, cans and paper.

DESIGNING THE ENVIRONMENT

Winston Churchill is credited with the saying that 'We shape our buildings – and they shape us'.

Interior decorators, office designers, architects and urban planners have the task of maximising the features of the environment to promote healthy behaviour.

The architect Lubetkin designed the Penguin House at London Zoo with a view to providing the correct environment in which the penguins would be more content. To this end his team scientifically researched the penguins' needs. The same approach is applied to human behaviour and the design of their environments.

1. **Housing projects**: the advent of the tower block was seen as progressive; in practice it led to social disasters. Various features of their design have been identified as responsible:
   - Few communal areas mean social networks don't develop.
   - Numerous stairwells make the supervision of children difficult.
   - Sterile, institution-like features such as concrete stairs, wall tiles, narrow hallways – features that were designed to prevent vandalism.
   - Lack of defensible spaces, particularly secondary territories.
   - **Yancey (1971)** studied the breakdown of the Pruitt-Igoe building with 3000 apartments in St Louis. The architecture won prizes but it was a social failure and ended up being demolished,
   - **Newman (1972)**, an architect and urban planner, compared two housing projects in New York, which were next door to each other. One was like the Pruitt-Igoe housing; the other, the Brownsville project, had many entrances, each used by

only a small number of families and anyone entering was overlooked by a number of windows. He interpreted this as leading to a sense of greater defensibility and a more positive attitude among residents.

2 **Individual housing**: architects have many issues to consider, such as:
- The placing of rooms which may dictate social relations in the family.
- Open plan versus isolation or decreased privacy.
- Windows, sound proofing versus cost.

3 **Institutional environments**:
- Provision of personal territory in, for example, a nursing home. Designers often concentrate more on open arrangements that encourage interaction while neglecting the fact that residents need somewhere of their own.
- School design reflects the teaching styles. For example open plan for team teaching versus individual classrooms for more traditional, teacher–directed activity.
- Promoting health: **Reddick (1985)** found evidence that health problems in elderly residents could be related to problems in their housing, such as poor heating, high steps between floors, and poor choice of colours.
- The design of play environments for children must take both the needs of the children and of safety into account.
- Football stadiums. As outbreaks of violence continue on the terraces the question is being tested as to whether redesigned stadiums with seating will significantly affect behaviour,

4 **Urban environments**:
- The provision of open spaces and floral displays are means of making the environment more pleasant, no longer the 'concrete jungle'.
- Moving traffic away from city centres to eliminate noise, dirt and pollution.
- Varying the landscape with buildings of different shapes and textures.
- Street lighting for safety and night-time activity.
- **Beer (1991)** suggests that urban planning has yet to take sufficient notice of the research produced by environmental psychologists.

5 **Roads**:
- Driver behaviours can be modified through research, for example the use of optical brakes and transverse bar patterns which become progressively closer together and affect drivers' judgements of speed. The Transport Research Laboratory suggests that these can reduce accidents by up to 57%.

6 **Furniture**: can be used to control or reflect activity:
- Arrangements of desks in a classroom, e.g. teacher-centred activity: desks in rows facing front.
- An official seated behind the desk confers power and domination, e.g. the bank manager or headmaster.
- A hollow square or round table for committee use, suggests equal partnership.

7 **Decor**: the police conduct interrogations in a bare room; a man woos a woman in a candlelit restaurant:
- Colours and moods, e.g. red is exciting, lively, either angry or passionate; blue is cool, leisurely, pleasant, secure. **Argyle (1988)** reports that children tested in blue, yellow, yellow–green and orange rooms scored 12 points more on an IQ test than those tested in white, black or brown rooms. **Kwallek and Lewis (1990)** found that subjects made more proof reading errors in a red office than in a white office.
- Lighting: the classic experiment on illumination comes from **Mayo (1933)** and the Hawthorne effect. Production levels of workers in the Hawthorne electrical components factory increased as illumination levels did. However, when they tried decreasing levels of illumination production didn't fall. This lead to the realisation that the workers' performance had been improving because of the extra attention they were receiving from researchers, not from better illumination *per se*.

8 **Working environments**: the environment can be designed to make conditions more conducive to feeling 'good'. It may also help to make workers more productive (see 9.1). The layout of supermarkets is aimed at promoting consumer behaviours.

9.3 EDUCATIONAL PSYCHOLOGY

Educational psychology is the application of relevant psychological knowledge to educational theory and practice. This is includes material covered elsewhere in this book:

① Cognitive factors:
- learning theories: conditioning, social learning, cognitive approaches (1.6) and cognitive developmental approach: Piaget, Bruner, Vygotsky (3.2),
- cognitive style, problem solving, concept formation (1.3),
- acquisition of skills, training, transfer of skills (9.1).

② Social factors:
- social interactions in the classroom: interpersonal perception (2.1 and 2.2), attitudes (2.3), prejudice (2.4), group dynamics and leadership (2.9), non-verbal communication (4.2),
- expectations and labelling (2.1 and 3.4),
- design of suitable learning environment (9.2),
- control and discipline: negative reinforcement (1.6), social skills training and behaviour modification (6.2).

③ Personal factors:
- coping strategies for exams: Section 1,
- individual differences: 5.1 (intelligence) and 5.2 (personality),
- developmental factors: 3.2 (cognitive development), 3.4 (socialisation, self-concept and influence of the school), and 4.1 (language acquisition),
- effects of motivation on learning and performance: see essay at end of this chapter,
- handicaps and learning disabilities (6.5),
- therapeutic interventions: counselling (6.2).

④ Assessment:
- assessment of ability and performance: 5.3 (psychometric techniques), 5.4 (intelligence tests) and 5.5 (personality tests),
- methods of assessing classroom behaviour: measuring attitudes (2.3), observation and other methods (10.1).

PROMOTING EFFECTIVE LEARNING

Matching learning to learner

Ideally the pupil:teacher ratio would be 1:1, then learning would fit the learner. Means of improving the fit include:

① *Tracking*: dividing the class into ability or interest groups, and setting appropriate work.

② *Programmed instruction*: computer- or book-based, any auto-instructional device. The learner works at their own pace without a teacher. Can be linear or branching, may include diagnostics and record of progress. An example is *precision teaching*: individual behavioural objectives are set in terms of accuracy and speed, which can be checked by daily exercises.

③ *Computer-assisted instruction (CAI)* (see 1.3), e.g. LOGO as a means of acquiring strategic rather than knowledge-based skills. Expert systems can be used for careers advice or for simulation (see training).

④ *Individualised instruction*: a subject is broken down into sequential units, each with an end of unit test. This system provides individual programming but requires a lot of support in development and management. **Bangert et al. (1983)** reviewed 51 studies of individualised learning and concluded that success was modest but, considering the effort involved, not significantly better than other methods.

⑤ *Learning styles*: **Dunn and Griggs (1988)** pointed out that some students, for example, work best in the mornings and prefer highly-structured regimes. If you have a profile of each learner you could tailor the classroom to individual learning style. This is possible on a limited scale. *Attribute-treatment interaction (ATI)* is a similar approach – matching certain personal attributes to teaching styles. For example, highly structured methods have been shown to benefit low ability or anxious students (**LeFrancois, 1991**).

6 *Mastery learning*: As there are fast and slow learners, **Bloom (1976)** suggested that aptitude should be regarded as a function of speed. If work is adapted to each individual's pace, they will ultimately all achieve a similar standard, i.e. given optimal conditions all students achieve mastery of the same material. To enable the class to continue working together, extra enriched work needs to be provided for the faster students. This approach increases motivation because of the inherent expectation that all learners will succeed.

Appropriate feedback

Feedback is an essential part of the learning process. The section on 'Training' (9.1) explored various possibilities: continuous/blocked, internal/external, intrinsic/extrinsic, concurrent/terminal, and cognitive/proprioceptive. For higher order thinking, other issues may be considered as well:

1 **Formative/summative**: assessment during or at the end of a period of instruction. **Bloom** emphasised the need for constant (formative) evaluation to help the learner stay on track. Summative feedback may act as an incentive.

2 **Positive/negative**: public examination boards aim at 'positive marking'. GCSEs are designed specifically to avoid anyone experiencing a sense of failure. **Bloom** suggested that no students should fail: students should be given an 'A' for completed or 'I' for incomplete. **Holt (1964)** described how students 'learn to fail' because of negative feedback.

TEACHING STYLES

A teaching style is an identifiable and related group of teaching activities. Teachers invariably use different styles in different situations. It may be a matter of instruction method (e.g. lecturing or questioning) or predominant relationship with students (e.g. authoritarian or democratic). Good teaching style aims to promote achievement, motivation, satisfaction and effective learning.

A teacher's style is derived from: the teacher's personality, personal philosophy, teacher training, textbooks and research.

1 **The two dimensions** along which style vary are:
   (a) teacher-centred/exposition learning/direct/authoritarian/formal/traditional
   (b) pupil-centred/discovery learning/indirect/democratic/informal/progressive
   ● Either put emphasis on: individual rather than group work; assessment; extrinsic movement and staying in your seat; a teacher lecturing from the front is authoritarian, does not solicit pupil's opinions.
   ● Or: group work and co-operation; subject integration; pupil freedom in choice of activity, motivation, and seating; lack of emphasis on assessment.
   ● **Flanders (1970)** concluded that most classrooms (two-thirds) are teacher-directed.

2 **Comparing effectiveness** is difficult because some styles are better in some situations, and different styles have different objectives:
   ● **Bennett (1976)** found that formal methods were related to higher academic achievement.
   ● **Horwitz (1976)** found that informal methods were associated with higher self-concepts, greater creativity and co-operation.
   ● **Holt (1964)** claimed that traditional teaching methods resulted in children learning to fail.
   ● See also, leadership styles, laissez-faire, democratic and authoritarian (2.9).

3 **Personal philosophy**: choice is a matter of general principles rather than empirical evidence, e.g. humanists (Rogers, Maslow) believe that teachers should be learning facilitators rather than didactic instructors, should emphasise social and personal development and de-emphasise performance. Behaviourists (Skinner) espouse programmed learning methods.

An effective lesson

Rosenshine and Stevens (1986) suggest the following for teaching a well-structured subject:

1 start lesson with brief review of prior learning,
2 state the lesson's goals,
3 present material in small steps, with short practices in between,
4 give explicit instructions,
5 ask students many questions,
6 provide systematic and immediate feedback, so that errors do not persist.

Classroom discipline

Wegmann (1976) described the many-faceted management activity involved in classroom discipline as a highly problematic series of interaction sequences, such as the physical location of the student, the right to speak, the 'explanation' as a tactic in maintaining discipline, the decision as to what should be taken 'seriously', and the significance of humour.

FACTORS AFFECTING EDUCATIONAL ACHIEVEMENT

① **Biological/genetic**: the potential range of intelligence for each person is innate, therefore educational performance is dictated by biological factors (see 5.1 for arguments for and against this view).

② **Experience**: early deprivation or enrichment, such as poverty, diet, bad housing, language development. These are discussed in 5.1 and deprivation in 3.1. Evidence from 'Language and thought' (1.3) should also be considered.

Experience of success and failure affect one's sense of self-esteem and self-efficacy (3.4), which in turn affect expectations and achievement.

③ **Gender and race**: there are obvious, learned differences, such as boys preferring certain sports while more girls are interested in domestic subjects. In single-sex schools girl do better in science subjects than their counterparts in mixed education. It has been thought that girls are better at languages and verbal intelligence, but the evidence is marginal (see 3.4).

④ **Cultural**: the attitudes, expectations and beliefs that a child has about school will be significantly determined by their culture, parents and peer-group subculture. **Hargreaves (1967)** demonstrated how low band pupils develop a subculture related to taking on deviant self-concepts.

⑤ **Parental involvement**: parents may join the PTA, attend meetings, or help out. Such involvement is beneficial. **Topping and Wolfendale (1985)** found it was related to helping early reading skills.

⑥ **The school**:
- The quality of the individual school, in terms of staff, buildings, financial arrangements.
- 'Labelling' (the self-fulfilling prophecy) differential treatment by teachers due to the stereotypes and expectations they have about, e.g. race or gender.
- **Keddie (1971)** criticised the common practice of explaining educational failure in terms of pupils' ethnic and social background. Instead she found that teachers rated pupils highest when they were readily involved in their lessons. High ability pupils don't question what they are taught whereas low ability ones tend to offer 'irrelevant' knowledge.

BEHAVIOUR PROBLEMS

The catch-all phrase 'disruptive behaviour' is much used in the classroom to refer to behaviour which disrupts the learning process for all pupils. **Westmacott and Cameron (1981)** suggest the starting point should be defining disruptive behaviours in precise terms rather than using labels which arouse stereotypes. DSM IV (see 6.5) includes 'disruptive behaviour disorders' as one of the major clusters of childhood disorders, which can be further subdivided:

Attention-deficit hyperactivity disorder

Defined as developmentally inappropriate inattention, impulsiveness and motor hyperactivity at home and school. More boys than girls are affected and the disorder tends to appear early. Normal children can't concentrate for as long as adults, and might be mistakenly called hyperactive.

Possible causes:

- May be chronic over-arousal, switching attention continually.
- Or under-arousal – the inability to maintain attention.

Treatment:

- *Drug therapy:* stimulant drugs work best.
- *Behaviour modification:* For example, working with children and parents to train the children to get attention for positive rather than negative reasons. However, such techniques are rarely studied with control groups and therefore are difficult to assess.
- *Diet:* some children respond to elimination of certain foods from their diet, such as chocolate or artificial additives.

Conduct disorder or delinquency

A delinquent is anyone who commits a crime or violates a legal code. It is a term applied to those under 18 and for non-serious crimes. Conduct disorder occurs when a child's conduct persistently violates the norms for interpersonal behaviour. The child may be physically aggressive, lie, steal or become involved in crime. The most extreme behaviour can be related to sociopathology (see 6.3), however delinquency generally is not a pathological disorder and most children transgress at some time. (A third category of disruption exists – oppositional defiant disorder. Such children are hostile and violent but not usually as antisocial as those covered here.)

Possible causes:

- *Adolescent storm and stress* (see 3.5): mindless vandalism and minor delinquency may be little more than rebellion coupled with a lack of social responsibility.
- *Discordant families:* discipline is either inconsistent or extremely severe or lax, lacking attention or affection (see 3.1).
- *Economic and social deprivation:* areas of high delinquency are characterised by high unemployment, poor housing and poor schooling. Deprivation covaries with illegitimate births, child abuse, drug dependence and venereal disease.
- *A genetic link* is supported by studies of adopted children. **Mednick (1978)** found that the criminal records of adopted sons are closer to those of the biological fathers, with whom they never lived.
- *Personality disorder:* sociopaths appear to be unable to experience high emotional arousal and are therefore less responsive to praise and punishment – factors which encourage socialisation. This underarousal may be inherited.
- *Academic underachievement:* **Hinshaw (1992)** reports that not only is delinquency clearly associated with school failure, but that such a link appears before formal schooling, suggesting a common cause and a need for early intervention.

Treatments:

- *Short, sharp shock.*
- *Achievement place:* a special children's home started in the US. Foster parents look after six to eight delinquent children sent by the courts in a regime of prosocial training. They have had some success, though they are undermined by children having to return to troubled homes. The cost is significantly less than a state institution.
- *Early intervention:* for example, programmes to promote social competence.

Bullying

Bullying is not included in the DSM list but is a major concern in schools, as the problem is more widespread than adults have acknowledged. It can be physical (hitting, pushing, taking money) or emotional (telling tales, teasing, social exclusion). At minimum it is distressing, for some pupils it has led to suicide. Empirical work:

- Prevalence: **Yates and Smith (1989)** conducted an anonymous questionnaire in South Yorkshire. Seven per cent of children said they were bullied several times a week, 10% were bullied sometimes, **Whitney** *et al.* **(1992)** report similar figures for secondary pupils but much higher levels (37%) for junior/middle school children.
- Effects of bullying: **Gillmartin (1987)**, using retrospective data, found a link between later relationship difficulties and having been bullied. This may possibly be due to loss of self-esteem.
- What happens to the bullies? **Olweus (1989)** found that former school bullies were four times more likely to have three or more court convictions by the age of 24.

Possible causes:

- Bullies have usually been bullied themselves and have learned aggression and control as a means of social interaction.
- Bullying is an extreme form of 'normal' childhood/adolescent teasing and interactions, which might be related to pecking orders and the formation of cliques as a means of establishing identity.

Interventions:

- *Nationwide campaign:* one was set up in Norway in 1982 as a response to two adolescent suicides. It consisted of advice for teachers and parents, and a video of bullied children for class discussion. One study **(Olweus, 1989)** found some improvement but another study **(Roland, 1989)** did not.
- *School monitoring:* supervision of corridors, treating incidents seriously, taking a public stand, student-directed 'bully courts', where children arbitrate on bullying incidents.
- *Classroom-based activities:* co-operative group work, role-playing,
- *Help-lines and support agencies:* Kidscape organisation (1986), was established to offer support to the victims and advice to schools. **Knox (1992)** reports success from school counselling.

School phobia

School phobia is an example of an emotional childhood disorder. A small number of persistent absentees are suffering from more than merely disliking school:

Possible causes:

- unrealistically high levels of aspiration,
- separation anxiety,
- depression or beginnings of more serious disorders.

Treatment:

- home tutoring, counselling and gradual re-introduction to school.

THE ROLE OF THE EDUCATIONAL PSYCHOLOGIST

The Educational Psychologist has two broad functions: advising over general educational policy and providing assessment and support for specific individuals' learning/behaviour problems. Overall their concern is to ensure effective learning.

Activities:

- assessment using psychometric tests, at home, school or in a specialist centre,
- direct treatment of emotional problems, using counselling or behavioural methods,
- working alongside parents, social workers, teachers to help individual problems,
- in-service training for schools,

- advice and development of school practices,
- advice for the national curriculum, e.g. criterion-referenced testing, development of norms and formative assessments,
- involvement in teacher training,
- research in developing new methods of teaching.

The training consists of a degree in psychology, a one-year teaching qualification, a minimum of two years teaching in school and then a training course in educational psychology. Educational psychologists are usually employed by an education authority to cover an area (Schools Psychological Service), but also are based in assessment centres, children's hospitals, further and higher education, and research.

ACQUISITION OF SKILLS: READING

The process of reading

Proficient readers use bottom-up and top-down processing:

Bottom up:
graphemes (letters) ➜ phonemes (sounds) ➜ words ➜ access memory for meaning

Top down:
contextual cues ➜ meaning ➜ expectations ➜ influence word and letter perception

When learning to read, an individual relies more on bottom-up processing. However, even proficient readers have to alternate between both strategies depending on such things as their familiarity with the words and whether they are reading for gist. The fact that there are different processes means that different models are necessary.

Some examples of models and research related to reading:

1. **A connectionist theory of reading: McClelland and Rumelhart (1981)** suggested that processing takes place simultaneously on three levels: feature, letter and word. Recognition at one level triggers expectations at the other levels, called **interactive activation**. For example, if you expect a certain word ('the man ran _____ the bank') this will influence letter perception and generate mistakes.

2. **Empirical evidence:**
   - *Word superiority effect*: **Reicher (1969)** exposed a letter string and then asked subjects what letter appeared in, for example, the third position. When the string is an actual word or if letter combinations are of familiar spelling patterns they perform better, demonstrating top down processing and interactive activation.
   - *Contextual cues*: **Tulving and Gold (1963)** gave subjects part of a sentence to read and very briefly exposed the final word. When the final word was consistent with the portion that was shown (e.g. 'the actress...performer') the time taken to perceive the end word was faster than if the word was irrelevant (e.g. 'the fish...performer'); the more of the sentence that was shown the more this effect increased.
   - *Expectation:* influences processing at a very early stage. **Carpenter and Dahneman (1981)** gave subjects a passage about fishing; the last line was 'some of the best bass guitarists...'. People spend longer than normal on the word guitarists and backtrack, which shows the immediate effects of expectations.
   - The processing of speech is similar to reading (see also 1.1 and 4.1).

3. **Eye movements:** can be studied using a computer to present a word and track the movements. Reading is not smooth but in *saccades*, a series of rapid eye movements separated by fixations which last about 200 milliseconds or longer depending on difficulty and matching of expectations. Generally people fixate on the beginning or middle of word and some of the time (10%) move backwards; each jump is equivalent to the '*perceptual span*', between 10 and 20 characters.

4. **Speed reading:** attempts to expand the bottleneck created by a limited perceptual span. Techniques aim to increase the number of words taken in at one fixation. The advice is to imagine a line down the centre of the page and move your eyes down that line, registering the whole line at one fixation. It may help to move your finger

down the imaginary line. The question is whether the result includes comprehension or just better skimming. However, since many texts contain little information this may be a useful technique for some types of reading.

Learning to read

The task consists of:
- learning the set of visual units (graphemes) and their corresponding sounds,
- matching words to already known to sounds, thus accessing their meaning.

There are cases of children learning to read at very early ages through special training regimes. However, most feel that the necessary skills depend on maturational factors.

① **Readiness**: the evidence suggests that some skills are prerequisite for reading; it is not always possible to be certain whether they are due to experience or maturation.

- **Visual and cognitive: letter discrimination: Gibson *et al*. (1962)** showed 4–8 year–olds a letter-like stimulus and several transformations of it (Fig. 9.1). The under 5's perceived them as being the same whereas the older children could detect the distinctive features – a skill necessary for reading. The most common confusions arise between b, h and d, and m and w. One of the factors may be learning that letters, unlike, for example, chairs, are not the same whichever way you view them.

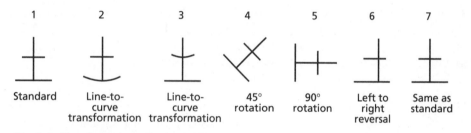

Fig. 9.1 Transformations of a letter–like stimulus

- **Cognitive: language skills**: to read a child must have some linguistic ability. By the age of five their word idiosyncrasies are few and they have a reasonable understanding of grammar (see 4.1).
- **Auditory and cognitive: sensitivity to sounds: Bryant and Bradley (1985)** tested 400 prereaders on their ability to categorise sounds, by asking them to detect the odd one out (e.g. bun, hut, gun). Four years later they tested reading ability and found high correlations between reading ability and earlier sound discrimination. They also found correlations between IQ and reading but these weren't as large, showing that sound sensitivity is an important factor.

② **Prereading skills**: certain activities help prepare children:
- stories, the concept of a story leads to interest in reading to self,
- rhyming and alliteration, trains sound discrimination,
- training visual skills to help discrimination,
- concepts of up, down, backwards and forwards, also for discrimination of similar but transformed letters,
- drawing is good for future writing and reading skills, starts the understanding that some 'marks' correspond to sounds,
- 'reading' picture books which have words,
- reading with a sympathetic peer or adult who acts as a model.

Topping and Wolfendale (1985) conducted research aimed at helping the parents of poor readers. The paired reading programme educates parents to concentrate on word-building, avoid constant corrections or attempts at word guessing. Parents should present reading, most importantly, as a pleasant and useful activity. This approach proved very successful.

Methods of teaching

- **Phonic method**: phonetic alphabet – teaching phonemes rather than letter 'names' – leads to 'sounding out' words. There was a vogue in the 1970s for the initial teaching alphabet (ITA) which consisted of a letter for every phoneme. Children used special books and later were changed over to traditional symbols and spelling.

- **Learn to form expectations**: 'what do you think the word might be?' Some reading tests use 'cloze procedure' as a means of testing the child's reading age; the child is asked to fill in the blank with an appropriate word, 'the cat sat on ____ mat'.
- **Whole word method**: 'Look and Say'. At one time this was the universal method and still has to be used for words not susceptible to 'sounding out', e.g. yacht, and may be a good starting place.
- **Word templates**: as reading skills progress words are recognised by their overall shape.

Assessment of reading ability

Assessment is through reading tests. They provide a *reading age*, which can be compared with chronological age to give an indication of progress.

- **Word lists**: e.g. the Burt Word Reading Test. Children are asked to read a set of 50 words which become progressively more difficult. Their age is derived from the point that they have reached when they have made their fifth mistake. The words are unrelated and sometimes obscure, making the task an artificial one.
- **Cloze (gap-fill) procedure**: e.g. Macmillan Group Reading Test. Children are given paragraphs with occasional missing words for them to fill in. The paragraphs and words become progressively more difficult. The task is more realistic and can be administered to a group.
- **Diagnostic tests**: e.g. Neale Analysis of Reading Ability. The child reads a set of graded passages aloud. The test provides information about accuracy, comprehension and speed. The test provides the means to analyse mistakes for deciding future strategies. Children must be fairly fluent readers to do this test.

Dyslexia

1. **Reading difficulty**: dyslexia is not another word for reading difficulty; it is difficulty which is out of proportion with the child's intellectual and emotional development. **Aaron (1987)** divided a set of poor-reading college students into dyslexics, who had IQs over 95 and 'nonspecific reading disabled', who had IQs under 85. The two groups differed in terms of certain skills; in particular the dyslexics had difficulties with decoding skills.

2. **Types of dyslexia**:
   - either developmental or acquired as the result of later brain damage (alexia),
   - auditory (phonological) dyslexia: difficulty sounding out,
   - visual (surface) dyslexia: can only sound out words,

   Japanese writing combines a system of graphemes with symbols which stand for entire words; different types of dyslexics find one or the other difficult.

   There is some evidence that the dyslexia observed in older children (over 11) may have a different cause to that in younger children. **Wadsworth et al. (1989)** found a high correlation between young twin pairs, suggesting a strong genetic component, but this was not true of an older group.

3. **Neurological explanations**:
   - Evidence from acquired dyslexics suggests damage to the posterior part of left hemisphere (auditory dyslexia) and to temporal/parietal region (visual dyslexia).
   - Autopsies on dyslexic boys who died in accidents showed thinner than normal cerebral cortex particularly around Wernicke's area.
   - **Witelson (1977)** has suggested that dyslexics have two right hemispheres, lacking language centres.
   - **Geiger and Lettvin (1987)** found that dyslexics were worse than normal readers at identifying letters presented in the foveal region whereas the opposite was true of their peripheral vision. They may need to develop an alternative reading strategy.

9.4 HEALTH PSYCHOLOGY

Health psychology first appeared in the 1970s. **Sarafino (1990)** identifies four concerns:

- to promote *health*,
- to prevent and treat *illness*,
- to research the causes of illness (related to epidemiology, the study of the frequency and distribution of disease),
- to improve health policies (related to public health).

Health psychology, as an application, draws on many areas covered elsewhere in this book:

- clinical psychology: the philosophy, assessment and treatment of mental illness (Chapter 6),
- biological psychology: drugs (7.1), stress (7.6) and pain (7.7),
- interpersonal issues: attitude change and compliance to medical requests (2.3 and 2.8), group dynamics (2.9), social perception and attribution (2.1 and 2.2),
- interpersonal communication: non-verbal behaviour (4.2),
- healthy development (Chapter 3),
- assessment and psychometric techniques (5.3).

LIFESTYLES AND HEALTH

Longevity and health have increased dramatically this century as a result of medical discoveries and changes in lifestyle, for example: diet, hygiene, medical care and attitudes.

Risk factors, as listed below, are not causes of death in themselves and their influence varies considerably from person to person.

1 Smoking: heart disease, cancer, stroke, generally more infections particularly respiratory ones:

- *Passive smoking*: The **American Surgeon General (1986)** concluded that involuntary smoking is a cause of disease, including lung cancer, in healthy non-smokers. The children of smokers are more likely to have increased respiratory infections and simply separating smokers and non-smokers does not fully solve the problem. **Russell *et al.* (1986)** tested the nicotine concentrations in the urine of non-smokers, which was 0.7% that of smokers, and therefore estimated that 1000 non-smokers may die per year in the UK (0.7% of the estimated number of smokers who die of smoking-related diseases). Intake of tar and carbon monoxide is likely, if anything, to be higher.

2 Alcohol: prolonged use may lead to cancer, liver cirrhosis, brain damage, fetal alcohol syndrome in the fetuses of pregnant women. Excessive bouts of drinking are related to both accidental (e.g. drunk driving) and non-accidental injuries (e.g. wife beating):

- **Smith and Kraus (1988)** found that accidents of various types, such as unintentionally firing a gun or a boating mishap, are related to drinking.
- **Press (1987)** recorded that over 50% of fatal car accidents involve drunk driving.
- There is the possibility that moderate drinking may be beneficial or related to healthy lifestyles. For example, **Friedman and Kimball (1986)** found a positive correlation between moderate drinking and *lower* illness rates.

3 Substance abuse: accidents, fetal harm (addiction), overdoses, related injuries because of shared needles: AIDS and hepatitis.

4 Stress: see 7.5 for evidence relating stress and illness, and stress and accidental injury.

5 Diet: too much or too little cholesterol, caffeine, sugar, salt, certain vitamins and fibre may lead to hardened arteries, hypertension, heart disease, stroke, cancer, diabetes, excess weight.

6 Lack of exercise: **Paffenbarger *et al.* (1986)** followed nearly 17,000 Harvard graduates for a period of 12 years and found that mortality rates were significantly lower amongst those who were physically active, regardless of hypertension, smoking or weight.

7 **Unhealthy living**: infrequent medical checks, unsafe practices (e.g. driving too fast and without seatbelt), exposure to the sun:

- **Belloc and Breslow (1965)** measured illness in terms of work absence and related this to good health practices, which were assessed on the basis of: amount of daily sleep (ideally 7–8 hours), eating breakfast, little eaten between meals, being near correct weight, never smoking, little alcohol intake and regular physical exercise. They found a clear positive correlation.
- Marriage has been related to better health (see 3.5).

HEALTH-RELATED BEHAVIOUR

Such behaviours can be approached via a number of strategies:

1 *Primary prevention*: public health advertising and education to encourage, for example, wearing seatbelts, using fluoride for teeth, good diets, the self-examination of breasts for lumps, regular medical check-ups and exercise. Genetic counselling and methods such as amniocentesis offer the opportunity of banishing genetically-determined problems.

2 *Secondary prevention*: to identify and treat problems through medical consultation, tests, and medication.

3 *Tertiary prevention*: action to contain or slow down problems related to serious injury or chronic/untreatable disease, for example, rehabilitation and/or medication.

Compliance with medical advice

It is difficult to assess the *extent* to which people do not follow health guidelines or patients do not take their medications, however it is clear that not everyone follows such advice. Why? The following considerations apply both to minor matters, such as consulting the doctor for a minor ailment, or cases of significant intervention, such as chemotherapy.

1 Failure to remember or misunderstanding information: for example, what the doctor advises or the correct dosage. This can be alleviated by the use of written information and community care by nurses.

2 Unpleasant side-effects: a person may consciously or unconsciously avoid or quit a treatment because of the effects. This must be weighed in terms of costs and benefits.

3 The seriousness of the illness: a more serious illness may make it more likely that someone will take advice. On the other hand, a person may repress the matter as a means of coping.

4 Doctor–patient relationship: a practitioner may fail to communicate information helpfully; good communication takes time. Professionals should be taught specific techniques for presenting medical information.

5 Personal beliefs: the particular orientation of a practitioner may not agree with the individual's own attitudes. For example, Scientologists refuse any medical intervention on principle. Some people support homeopathic methods or common-sense approaches.

Models of health-related behaviour

1 **Learning theory**: operant conditioning and social modelling offer a simple way to explain behaviour. The fact that punishment in terms of negative reinforcement is usually delayed (e.g. lung cancer) would explain why some people fail to take advice.

2 **Attitude change**: people resist changes to health behaviour because most long-standing habits are anchored in personality (see 2.3). Any change would involve the whole personality or way of life, for example reducing alcohol intake.

3 The **Health Belief model (Rosenstock, 1966**, modified by **Becker and Maiman, 1975)** aims to predict when a person will engage in health behaviour, i.e. comply with advice. A person's behaviour can be predicted from three groups of sociocognitive factors:

- perceived threat of disease X (a combination of perceived susceptibility/ seriousness and cues to action, e.g. article in newspaper, reminder from dentist),

- perceived benefits of treatment and barriers to action,
- personal variables (demographic – age, sex, race – and sociopsychological – personality, class).

This model has been used with some success and has been useful in generating research and designing questionnaires. A review of studies by **Haynes** *et al.* **(1979)** found a link between compliance and perceived vulnerability, severity of illness and costs/benefits.

④ The theory of reasoned action of **Fishbein and Ajzen (1975)** (see also 2.3) suggests that the combination of perceived facts and social norms leads to the formation of personal intentions and health behaviours. For example, smoking behaviour might be determined by 'smoking causes cancer' (a perceived fact) and 'my parents smoke' (a social norm) therefore 'I won't be so foolish' (an intention) which leads to refusing a cigarette from a friend (the behaviour).

Evaluation:
- suggests a direct link between actions and behaviour; however empirical evidence doesn't support this (see 2.3),
- limited to the effect of attitudes and social norms on behaviour.

⑤ Conflict theory: explains the fact that people are often irrational and change their attitudes with time. **Janis (1984)** suggested that health behaviour results from a challenge to action (stressor). Such challenges may be an illness, a television programme giving frightening statistics or a friend inviting you to join an exercise class. The challenge shakes complacency, leading to an assessment of alternatives and a decision about whether to act or not.

⑥ Cognitive Control: people differ in their desire to control (internal attributions) or to attribute their behaviour to external influences. Such attributions determine health behaviours particularly in relation to coping strategies. For example, Attribution therapy (see 2.2) aims to teach a person how to take control and thereby overcome the health problem:
- **Fradkin and Firestone (1986)** worked on alleviating the symptoms of pre-menstrual tension (PMT). If women were given an article emphasising the biological and therefore inevitable effects of PMT they continued to experience symptoms as before. However, a group who were given an article attributing PMT not to biology but instead to 'negative societal myths' later reported a dramatic decline in symptoms.
- **Langer** *et al.* **(1975)** described methods of cognitive control for patients facing surgery. When these patients were compared with a group of well-informed controls the ones trained in self-control were less anxious and requested fewer sedatives.

Moral issues

With increased knowledge comes increased responsibility and decisions to be made at all levels of society:

- *Personal responsibility*: since we know that certain risk factors are associated with certain health problems, should a person bear responsibility for their chosen lifestyle? For example, should smokers be refused certain costly medical treatments unless they give up smoking? What about sports injuries? **Knowles (1977)** proposed that we have a moral obligation to practice a healthy lifestyle.

- *Social responsibility*: medical care is funded by governments and/or insurance companies; to what extent is it reasonable that they refuse to cover certain individuals? Since resources will always be limited, decisions will have to be made on what treatments will be practised. For example, should we transplant all organs or stop other expensive treatments?

- *Financial interests*: many of these decisions are based on financial limitations. Beyond this, health care is big business. Many companies have vested interests in promoting health issues for commercial gain.

- *Genetic engineering*: as we identify the genes associated with particular characteristics we must decide on the extent to which unborn children can be 'engineered'. The fact that a person carries a particular gene does not always lead to its expression, for example the gene for breast cancer. Even where there is 100% certainty not everyone wishes to use this information, for example Huntington's chorea.

SUBSTANCE ABUSE

There are many distinctions related to substance abuse which can be made, such as:

- physical versus psychological dependence,
- social use of drugs versus maladaptive use, which constitutes a disorder,
- socially (culturally) acceptable drugs versus unacceptable ones,
- legally prescribed or available drugs versus illegal ones,
- addictions which are life threatening and those that aren't,
- use, misuse, abuse and addiction.

Substance or drug abuse has a long history, particularly as part of religious functions. It is the leading health problem in the US. The drugs abused include: solvents, nicotine, alcohol, stimulants, barbituates, hallucinatory and 'hard' drugs.

The main characteristics are:

- *improper* use of substances over a *prolonged* period (misuse),
- *impaired* psychosocial functioning (abuse),
- *loss of control* when using the substance (abuse),
- psychological or physiological *adaptation* to the drug (addiction).

This list takes into account the fact that some substances, such as cocaine, have no physical withdrawal symptoms. It also distinguishes between misuse, abuse and addiction.

Why are some substances addictive?

Solomon (1977) described the *addictive cycle*, which is created when a substance has a pleasurable effect and the additional reinforcing properties of tolerance and withdrawal symptoms. These properties are the characteristics of *physical dependence*:

- *tolerance or habituation:* the body increasingly adapts to the substance and needs larger doses to achieve the same effect. At some point these increases level off,
- *withdrawal:* symptoms such as anxiety, craving, hallucinations, nausea and headache which when use of the substance is discontinued.

Psychological dependence is characterised by:

- feeling a compulsion because of pleasant effects,
- many activities being centred around it,
- learning through repeated use.

Why do people become abusers?

1 **Biological:** the body's response to stress and pain is to produce endorphins – naturally occurring opiates. Therefore the effects of opiates can be biologically explained in terms of tension-reduction. Naloxone blocks opiate receptors and reduces the the effects of alcohol and narcotics.

2 **Genetic predisposition:** for example, a lack of naturally-occuring endorphins. Alcohol dependence is four times more likely in children whose parents are alcoholic. This is true even when the children have been adopted, which suggests more than social transmission.

3 **The addictive personality:** the majority of people who try potentially addictive substances do not go on to become dependent. The problem with any research is that it inevitably draws on existing users, so it is impossible to distinguish between factors which may be effects of use from those which may have caused it:
   - the idea of an oral-dependent personality has had only partial support,
   - alcohol abuse has been linked with antisocial personalities,
   - low social conformity, rebellion and impulsiveness have been linked with dependence generally.

④ **Social and environmental factors:**
- *family*: tension and poverty are associated with drugs. Use tends to run in families, which may be partly due to inherited factors but also modelling,
- *a desirable social image:* **McKennell and Bynner (1969)** found that smoking is associated with being attractive and tough,
- *peer influences and pressure,*
- *context:* abusers come to associate drug use with certain situations and emotions, which serves as a reminder for persistent use. **Wikler (1948)** observed that drug-dependent patients experienced withdrawal symptoms during group discussions when another patient described settings associated with drug use,
- *compensation for lack of social stimulation:* **Alexander et al. (1978)** kept a group of rats in isolated conditions while a second group had roomy, social conditions. Both were given morphine solution to drink. After they had habituated to the morphine only the isolated rats continued to prefer the morphine solution to water.

Treatments

The effectiveness of any treatment depends on individual differences. Most approaches combine several techniques, and must both stop the substance use *and* prevent relapse. They may take place under expert guidance or self-help, alone or with social support, in the community or in some institutional setting (see also 6.4 for abnormal treatments generally).

① **Self-help groups:** such as Alcoholics Anonymous, provide social support and an opportunity to make a public statement of intention. This has been shown to be important in attitude change (see 2.3). Such techniques are hard to assess because of the anonymity.

② **Psychotherapy:** group or individual psychotherapy seem to be equally effective; group therapy is more cost-effective.

③ **Therapeutic communities:** use the same approach as self-help groups with expert guidance and close supervision.

④ **Substitution therapy:** such as nicotine gum or replacing heroin with methadone, a longer-lasting, oral drug with no euphoric effects. The effectiveness may be due to several factors: the lack of euphoria may break the addiction cycle, and contextual dependency is lessened because methadone is oral and given by doctors. However, it is not very successful over the long-term.

⑤ **Abstinence-oriented therapy:** detoxification, quitting 'cold turkey', preferably with social support and medical supervision in case of severe withdrawal symptoms. Tends to have a high drop-out rate.

⑥ **Aversion therapy:** a behavioural technique. Negative affect is paired with the abused substance to recondition the patient. This may involve smoking a lot of cigarettes which causes sickness; taking a drug which, when mixed with alcohol, induces nausea; using electric shocks, imagining negative scenes, or using hypnosis.

⑦ **Self-management strategies:** or spontaneous remission, without benefit of formal treatment. According to the US Surgeon General, 95% of smokers have quit on their own. **Glasgow et al. (1985)** found that people stopped smoking mainly 'cold turkey', using oral substitutes, with a friend, using cognitive strategies or rewards for quitting and punishments for backsliding.

⑧ An example of a **cognitive strategy** is the use of attribution (see 2.2) – disassociating the substance from a particular context, such as in the case of US soldiers returning from Vietnam: 93% gave up opium without any professional help.

Prevention

A different approach is to prevent use developing into abuse, or to stop use altogether. The Government has a number of approaches to this:

① **Legislation:** outlawing drugs, which may prevent some usage but it means that the sources are not regulated thus allowing poor quality substances, spread of diseases like AIDS and association with crime.

② **Policing:** particularly focusing on those who sell the drugs and the Third World sources.

③ **Health promotion campaigns:** *advertising* and *social inoculation* against persuasion. **McGuire (1964)** has suggested that you can prepare people to resist temptation by giving them a set of strong counterarguments, in the same way that inoculations provide us with antibodies. **McAlister *et al.* (1980)** assessed this type of programme used in high schools and found that it reduced the likelihood to smoke by half.

Chapter roundup

Related material in other chapters:
- cognitive psychology (Chapter 1) includes learning and other cognitive processes relevant to education and personnel training;
- social psychology (Chapter 2) is the basis for much of organisational theory in terms of group processes. Environmental influences are used to explain many social behaviours, such as pro- and antisocial behaviours. Social behaviour also determines interactions in the classroom and health behaviours;
- developmental psychology (Chapter 3) covers some issues related to work, retirement and unemployment. It also includes theories of cognitive development which are critical to educational psychology;
- communication (Chapter 4) details non-verbal behaviours, such as personal space, which is a useful concept to environmental psychology, and communication networks, a concept used in organisational and educational psychology;
- intelligence, personality and assessment (Chapter 5). Personnel work and educational psychology draw on techniques of psychological assessment;
- abnormal psychology (Chapter 6) includes the application of psychology to the treatment of abnormal behaviour;
- biological psychology (Chapter 7) includes sections on motivation (as in motivating the worker), biological rhythms (which interact with environmental changes), stress and pain and ways of coping with them;
- animal behaviour (Chapter 8) examines territoriality, from an ethological view, as a means of controlling aggression environmentally;
- research and design (Chapter 10) includes details of research methods and ethical considerations.

Illustrative question

Discuss how motivation affects the performance of pupils in the classroom. Support your statements with empirical evidence wherever possible.

(NEAB, 'A', 1991)

Tutorial note

Several exam syllabi include 'the effect of motivation on learning' as an example of applied psychology. It is not a popular choice in exams and, when answered, candidates use their common sense rather than psychological evidence. This may be because such a topic relates to the 'lay' use of motivation rather than the more traditional psychological approach in terms of basic or higher needs.

The question is not simply about learning but classroom behaviour in general. It also emphasises the need for empirical support.

Questions on the application of academic psychology often require candidates to think on their feet, thus enabling a more able candidate to do well. In this chapter, however, the applications are predetermined and therefore a more thorough knowledge is expected plus a critical understanding of the issues.

Suggested answer

When trying to explain educational success and failure the two most common and powerful concepts are intelligence and motivation. The question also goes beyond educational success to classroom behaviour in general.

Pupils succeed because they want to or because they have been motivated to do so. This is described as intrinsic (internal) and extrinsic (external) motivation. Behaviourist approaches emphasise extrinsic motives and reinforcement (praise, reward and punishment, criticism). Humanists are concerned with intrinsic motives (the need to be autonomous, to develop competence, to actualise potential).

How effective is praise and reinforcement?
Hurlock (1925) gave 10–year–olds practice in a series of addition tests. Group 1 was a control group and taught separately; group 2 was praised irrespective of performance, group 3 was reproved for poor work and group 4 was ignored but present with others so they heard the other comments. After five days the praised group were doing significantly better. Interestingly the reproved group had initially improved but, after two days, their performance declined, suggesting that *any* attention was beneficial.

However, more recent work suggests that praise may not be effective. **Dweck (1975)** set up a retraining programme for children who had extreme difficulty with failure. Over a period of a month one group were given positive feedback (praise) while the other group were repeatedly told they were taking too long and should try harder. At the end, the second group showed greater task persistence. The programme had aimed to shift motivation from extrinsic to intrinsic, and suggests that intrinsic motivation is more powerful.

Brophy (1981) suggests that praise must be well regulated if it is to be effective. It should not be too frequent, should be contingent on specific behaviour not random and unsystematic, and a teacher should not praise mere participation but rather the quality of outcome.

There are occasions when learning takes place in the absence of reinforcement, that is incidental or latent learning. **Tolman and Honzik (1930)** allowed one group of rats to explore a maze, receiving no reinforcement. A second group was reinforced with food. Later testing of both groups, by presenting food, showed that the non-reinforced rats learned as well or even better than those who were always reinforced.

On the other hand, **Loftus and Loftus (1983)** set out to understand why people find video games so compelling and concluded that the fact that they involve variable and unpredictable reinforcement schedules leads to compulsive playing. The same could be true in the classroom.

What evidence is there to support the effectiveness of intrinsic motives?
White (1959) has argued that one of the most important intrinsic needs is competence; we are motivated to perform competently which results in feelings of confidence and worth from successful performance. In humans the competence motive is particularly important since we are born with so few competencies, such as feeding yourself and language. Curiosity and information-seeking behaviour are both derived from the competence motive.

Another intrinsic motive is the need for achievement (nAch) as outlined by **Murray (1938)**. Some people have a higher need to be successful than others. **Atkinson (1964)** proposed a modified model with nAch, fear of failure and certain contextual variables, such as incentives and perceptions of probability of success. Several experiments have shown that high-need achievers are more likely to take on tasks of moderate challenge and to attribute performance to internal factors. However, low-need achievers usually select tasks that are either very difficult or very easy, therefore failure can be attributed to external factors such as task difficulty, or success is explained by good luck. This work has had many practical applications, such as devising achievement programmes for use in schools to encourage learners to arrive at realistic goals and take responsibility for their successes or failures.

One of the key aspects of intrinsic motivation is an internal locus of control. Attribution theory and retraining programmes, such the one by Dweck, mentioned above, emphasise how using internal attributions can lead to success. **Diener and Dweck (1980)** used the concept of learned helplessness to show how some children may enter a cycle of failure. They found that 'helpless' children attributed failure to themselves and saw it as insurmountable, whereas success was unrelated to their ability. Mastery–oriented children emphasised motivational factors and viewed failure as surmountable.

deCharms (1976) used the terms 'pawn' for someone who sees themselves as largely controlled by external forces, and 'origin' for a person who regards their actions as caused by their own free choices and consequently assumes responsibility. deCharms conducted an experiment with black inner-city children aged 12–14 years, encouraging them to assume more control of their own activities and training their teachers to encourage them to be 'origins' rather than 'pawns'. The programme resulted in a change in their thinking about themselves from pawns to origins and a positive influence on their school achievement.

Self-esteem is part of the whole cycle of failure and helplessness. Repeated failure leads to lower self-esteem, lower confidence and reduced motivation to succeed because you don't believe you can, i.e. a self-fulfilling prophecy. A defence mechanism against failure is to attribute the cause to external forces. However, as indicated above, this perpetuates the cycle of failure, which in turn lowers motivation.

Coopersmith (1968) studied a group of 10–12–year–old boys and related self-esteem to a variety of behaviours. For example, those high in self-esteem tended to be active, expressive individuals who were successful academically and socially; those of medium self-esteem were similar but were uncertain about their self-worth and were particularly dependent on social acceptance; those of low self-esteem were sensitive to criticism, self-conscious, dwelt on their own difficulties and tried not to be noticed.

Lawrence (1971) has tried to improve the performance of backward readers by providing counselling as a means of improving their self-esteem and enabling them to tackle their failure. His programme achieved moderate success. **Project Headstart** is another example of an attempt to intervene in the cycle of failure and improve self-confidence.

Bandura (1986) also related self-esteem to competence, he called it self-efficacy, the sense we have of our personal effectiveness. We are unlikely to tackle things where we expect to fail, therefore self-efficacy is likely to influence motivation.

Bloom's (1976) system of mastery learning emphasised the potential of all learners to reach the same goals if they are given time. His expectation of universal success leads to raised feelings of self-efficacy and may explain why mastery learning is successful.

Aside from intrinsic or extrinsic motives, how else can students be motivated to learn?

Another angle to consider is the method of teaching. Ausubel and Bruner have suggested contrasting methods: expository and discovery teaching respectively, not mutually exclusive but appropriate for different situations and ages.

Ausubel (1968) claims that to learn is to fit facts into existing frameworks, so the most effective means of teaching is to provide students with the framework (advance organisers). Ausubel also described achievement motivation as having at least three components: cognitive drive (related to competence motives and task-interest), ego-enhancement (the learner's feelings about status, self-esteem and success) and affiliative (gaining others' approval). Such a framework combines many of the points already made.

Bruner (1966) also sees learning as a process of categorisation. However, he feels it is essential that the learner makes their own categories. He feels that schooling tends to destroy curiosity and the interest in learning children have when they first start school. The ill effects of schooling may also be due to reducing learning to a mechanistic activity through a system of rewards. It is also the case that extrinsic motivation can destroy intrinsic motivation.

A further aspect to consider is arousal. To become motivated to act an organism must first be aroused; no arousal, no action, no learning.

Yerkes and Dodson (1908) experimented with rats and found that as the level of motivation increases for a given task an optimum is reached beyond which performance deteriorates. In the classroom too much arousal is rarely a problem, there is usually too little. **Lefrancois (1991)** suggests that a teacher may manipulate arousal through intensity, meaningfulness, novelty and complexity of stimulation; through modulating their voice and introducing variety.

Anxiety is another means of increasing arousal, but in relation to learning tends to decrease performance especially on tests. **Hembree (1988)** summarised 562 studies on test anxiety and concluded that test anxiety causes poor performance, and is related to lower self-esteem and occurs in females more than males. **McKeachie (1984)** found that anxiety has a detrimental effect on learning as well.

Both competition and co-operation can be used to motivate classroom performance. Competition can be related to arousal, co-operation to affiliation. The need to affiliate is **Murray**'s term for the need to be with others, to socialise and to form friendships. **Maslow** describes the need for belongingness (love, affiliation and acceptance) and esteem (status) as an intermediate need, more important than the higher order cognitive ones such as curiosity and self-actualisation. Much of classroom behaviour will be driven by the social environment and the desire to create a good impression.

In summary, the following factors explain how motivation can be related to classroom performance:

● appropriate rewards,
● partial reinforcement schedules,
● intrinsic motives such as competence, need for achievement, fear of failure, curiosity,
● internal locus of control,
● optimum arousal,
● low anxiety,
● the social environment and the need to affiliate and gain esteem.

Question bank

Allow 45 minutes for each question.

1 The management team of a local college of further education wants to examine the way it takes decisions. It has discovered that many of the management decisions that are taken are ignored, or turn out to be inappropriate.

Your task is to prepare a report for the management team on the effectiveness of communication networks, and how the structure of power relationships in committees affects decision making. In your report you should:

(a) review some psychological studies on the effectiveness of communication structures, and on the way decisions are taken in groups.
(b) explain how these studies are relevant to this problem.
(c) evaluate these studies (i) for the methodology they used, and (ii) the conclusions they arrived at.
(d) suggest how the company management team could improve its decision making performance, and improve communication networks in the college.

(Oxford and Cambridge, 'A', specimen paper)

Points: This syllabus covers many different topic areas and uses a somewhat different format of examination question. Other examples shown below indicate a similar style. An answer to this question requires consideration of material from Social Psychology as well.

2 Describe and comment on the main techniques of training and retraining. Consider what factors are taken into account in evaluating their success.

(AEB, 'AS', 1990, 1992)

Points: A straightforward question, probably in an attempt to encourage students to study this area of the syllabus. Evaluation must be in terms of stated factors.

3 (a) Explain what psychologists mean by the term 'skill acquisition'. (5 marks)
(b) Discuss any **two** psychological theories of skill acquisition. (12 marks)
(c) How, according to **either** or **both** of these theories, can skill acquisition be made more efficient? (8 marks)

(AEB, 'AS', 1993)

Points: Use the distribution of marks to guide the time spent on each part of the question.

4 (a) Take any **one** motor skill and show how its performance can be measured.
  (6 marks)
  (b) Discuss the ways in which motor learning and the learning of verbal material differ. Make reference to empirical work in your answer. (14 marks)

(NEAB, 'A', 1991)

Points: Other areas of psychology can provide empirical work for your answer.

5 'Sudso', the wonder washing powder from the shores of sunny Cathay. A detergent company wants to introduce a new washing powder onto the market. It is not sure how to present it to customers.
  Your task is to prepare a report for the company on the psychological aspects of consumer behaviour. In your report you should:
  (a) review some psychological studies about the behaviour of consumers.
  (b) explain how these studies are relevant to selling this new washing powder.
  (c) evaluate these studies (i) for the methodology they used, and (ii) the conclusions they came to.
  (d) suggest how the company might encourage people to buy its new product.

(Oxford and Cambridge, 'A', specimen paper)

Points: Again this question can draw on other areas of psychology. Certainly reference should be made to Chapter 10 for evaluations of methods.

6 Discuss the consequences of the 'labelling' of pupils by teachers. Use empirical evidence to support your arguments.

(NEAB, 'A', 1992)

Points: This was not a popular choice in the examination despite the fact that 'labelling' is explicitly mentioned in the syllabus. Consider all those behaviours which lead to a person's self-concept, and then how that self-concept relates to behaviour.
  Consideration could be made of the self-fulfilling prophecy, self-concept, positive and negative effects, and a distinction between the causes and consequences of labelling.

7 In what ways do differences between people bring about differences in their performance on learning tasks?

(NEAB, 'A', 1990)

Points: A question which draws on many areas of psychology: cognitive, social, personality, abnormal and educational.

8 (a) Describe **two** types of delinquent behaviour. (4 marks)
  (b) Discuss **one** problem of defining anti-social behaviour. (6 marks)
  (c) Discuss, making reference to empirical studies, explanations for **one** of the delinquent behaviours you have described above. (10 marks)

(NEAB, 'A', 1992)

Points: Distinguish between delinquency, psychopathology and criminality. The explanations for delinquent behaviour can be drawn from many areas of psychology: aggression, social learning and learning theory, and maternal deprivation.

9 Discuss the role of educational psychologists in relation to the school. Discuss any **two** problems they may encounter in their work.

(NEAB, 'A', 1991)

Points: A straightforward question taken directly from the syllabus, but another one which few candidates were prepared for.

10 Discuss the contribution of psychology to our understanding of reading development in children.

(AEB, 'AS', 1993)

Points: Surprisingly, this is not a popular area of study, despite its importance and familiarity. General principles of learning can be made relevant along with specific information on reading.

11 (a) What are pre-reading skills? (5 marks)
(b) Discuss studies which investigate the importance of pre-reading skills. (15 marks)

(NEAB, 'A', 1989)

Points: Reference should be made to cognitive and language development.

12 A survey of a small Northern town revealed that the average diet of adults was poor. The people consumed too much fat, a substance which makes them more likely to develop a number of health disorders, including heart disease. The local Health Education Council invested a considerable amount of money in an advertising campaign to highlight the dangers of the local diet. A follow-up survey found that although most of the respondents recalled the campaign, very few had changed their eating habits.

Your task is to write a short report for the Health Education Council. In your report you should:
(a) review a number of studies in psychology that are relevant to this issue.
(b) explain why you think these studies are relevant.
(c) evaluate these studies (i) for the methodology they used, and (ii) the quality of the conclusions they arrived at.
(d) suggest how they might bring about some change in the diet of the people of the town with a more effective campaign.

(Oxford and Cambridge, 'A', specimen paper)

Points: Both health and consumer psychology will be useful here, plus other more traditional empirical work on attitudes.

13 (a) Discuss **two** problems of defining addiction. (8 marks)
(b) Outline **one** method used by psychologists to treat alcohol addiction. (4 marks)
(c) Evaluate the effectiveness of this treatment by reference to empirical evidence. (8 marks)

(NEAB 'A', 1993)

Points: Candidates tend to be weak on clear, comprehensive definitions of addiction which distinguish between psychological and physical aspects. They also lack specific knowledge of treatment programmes, methods of measuring addiction and other addictive substances aside from alcohol.

14 Consider the following statements:
(i) 'I have a cup of coffee and a cigarette in the morning before I can get going.'
(ii) 'After a hard day at work I always unwind with a bottle of wine in the evening.'
(iii) 'I enjoy having a relaxed day by smoking marijuana two or three times in the morning and afternoon.'

(a) Discuss problems of defining addiction using the above examples of human behaviour. (6 marks)
(b) Outline **two** treatment programmes that psychologists use to overcome addiction. (6 marks)
(c) With reference to **either** alcohol abuse or smoking, discuss the effectiveness of the treatment programmes you have outlined in your answer to (b) above. (8 marks)

(NEAB, 'A', 1991)

Points: General points on evaluating therapeutic treatments should be used for part (c).

RESEARCH AND DESIGN

Units in this chapter

Chapter overview

The whole of psychology is founded on the bedrock of research, without which our statements are nothing more than introspection and speculation. However, the theorist must be aware that research outcomes are **not** objective facts – they are probabilities whose determination may have been influenced by subtle experimental factors. Criticisms of realism and ethics apply not just to experimental methods, but to numerous other techniques as well. An understanding of research techniques is vital for a realistic assessment of the data used in psychology, and in fact in all sciences.

10.1 METHODS OF INVESTIGATION

Research is 'any honest attempt to study a problem systematically or to add to man's knowledge of a problem' (*Penguin Dictionary of Psychology*).

METHODS

For any method there is a compromise between conflicting advantages and disadvantages. The methods listed below are not necessarily exclusive, for example, you can have a cross-cultural observation.

❶ **Experiment, scientific:** the relationship between two things is explored by deliberately producing a change in one variable (the independent variable, IV) and recording what effect this has on the other variable (the dependent variable, DV). There is a tendency to use the term 'experiment' too loosely, a mistaken practice which detracts from the rigorous nature of a true experiment. The elements of the scientific method are discussed in more detail on p.378.

Advantages:
- determines a causal link,
- can be well controlled,
- can be replicated.

Disadvantages:
- artificial and therefore may not generalise to real-life,
- total control is never possible, many variables remain beyond the control of the experimenter,
- can be affected by, for example: experimenter bias, demand characteristics, volunteer bias, sample bias,
- some classes of subjects, such as children, react poorly under experimental conditions,
- in some cases it would be unethical to manipulate exposure to certain conditions, e.g. early deprivation in children.

2 Field experiment: an experiment conducted in the natural environment, where the subjects are unaware that they are participating in a psychology experiment. The independent variable is still manipulated.

Uses:
- where the research design calls for a natural setting (e.g. a library, street, bus).

Advantages:
- greater validity,
- avoids subject bias and demand characteristics.

Disadvantages:
- inevitably extraneous variables are harder to control,
- more time-consuming and expensive.

3 Natural experiment: where conditions may vary naturally, the effects of an independent variable can be noted without any intervention by the experimenter. It is still an experiment in the sense that a cause and effect are being identified. If a new teaching programme is being tested, a comparison might be made before and after.

Uses:
- where conditions vary naturally.

Disadvantages:
- subjects may be aware of being studied (possible Hawthorne effect),
- inevitable loss of control over extraneous variables,
- since we have not directly manipulated the independent variable we cannot truly claim cause and effect; a third variable may be involved, as with correlational studies.

4 Correlation: tests whether a systematic relationship exists between two (or more) variables. The reason for the relationship can only be supposed and is outside the reference of a correlational study. Therefore we cannot talk in terms of independent and dependent variables but only in terms of co-variables.

Strictly speaking, it is not a method but a technique of data analysis.

Uses:
- where experimental manipulation would be unethical or impossible,
- in suggesting avenues for experimental studies of causation,
- in enabling psychologists to predict an increase or decrease in one variable from another, without reference to the cause.

Disadvantages:
- establishes a relationship only, not a cause and effect,
- the relationship may be due to other extraneous variables, e.g. height and IQ are linked because diet influences both,
- correlations only deal with linear relationships. Relationships can be curvilinear, such as the Yerkes–Dodson effect, and may be overlooked by simply calculating the correlation coefficient.

5 Observation: behaviour is observed in its natural environment. All variables are free to vary and interference is kept to a minimum. No independent variable is manipulated but nevertheless a hypothesis may be tested.

In a sense, all research involves observation. It can be a technique for collecting data for experimental or correlational methods, or it is the overall design of the study. The elements of observation are discussed in more detail on p.379.

Uses:
- when behaviour is studied for the first time to establish possible relationships,
- good for working with young children, wild animals and uncooperative subjects,
- where there are ethical objections to manipulating variables, e.g. looking at the effects of death.

Advantages:
- gives a more realistic picture of spontaneous behaviour,
- is of high ecological validity,
- if the observer remains undetected most experimental effects are avoided, e.g. experimenter bias, demand characteristics, evaluation apprehension, etc.

Disadvantages:
- can't infer cause and effect,
- difficult to replicate,
- lack of controls, can't exclude effect of other variables,
- observer bias, observer sees what he 'wants' to see,
- disclosed observations lead to unnatural behaviour. Subjects behave differently because they know they're being watched; even non-participant observers, by their mere presence, can alter a situation,
- there are ethical objections to undisclosed observation or intervention of any kind,
- observer reliability can be questioned with more than one observer or the same observer on different occasions.

6 Survey: is a search for particular kinds of information, a technique to assess public opinion. It is an umbrella term covering questionnaires, attitude scales, opinion polls, interviews and the clinical method (for diagnosing mental and psychological problems). It ranges from the highly to the loosely structured and is presented in written or oral form. The results can be used for description or analysis (see 'Survey construction', p.379).

Uses:
- where large samples are needed to provide data sufficient to analyse or describe trends.

Advantages:
- good trade-off between time spent and amount of data gathered,
- access to information not available from direct observation,
- interviews can be adapted in the light of subject's previous answers.

Disadvantages:
- can draw conclusions about correlations but not cause and effect,
- relies on self-report, which is open to problems such as social desirability bias,
- limited choice answers may exclude information,
- open questions may be difficult to summarise,
- reliance on linguistic competence excludes certain subjects (e.g. children) and leads to misinterpretation by both experimenter and subject. Interviews may overcome some problems because uncertainties can be explained, but then experimenter bias is introduced,
- sampling technique is particularly critical,
- preconceptions about factors which are important leads to narrow-mindedness in the questions which are asked, therefore excluding possible areas of relevance.

7 Psychological Tests: designed and carefully tested to measure a factor or assess some ability. Reliability, validity and standardisation are key issues (see 5.3). They are generally used as a tool rather than a method of research in themselves. There is some degree of overlap between psychological tests and survey methods. They draw on some similar techniques but are designed to measure rather than sample.

Techniques include: questions, projective techniques, semantic differential, inventories, grids, checklists, sentence completion. Methods used include: personality tests, intelligence tests, tests of specific abilities, aptitude tests, achievement tests.

Advantages:
- provides large amount of information easily,
- presents uniform situation so that subjects can be compared.

Disadvantages:
- constructing valid and reliable tests is very difficult,
- culture bias, especially in intelligence tests,
- also 'designer bias', in the sense that any test is biased in the direction of the author's views.

8 Case Study: detailed account of a single individual: personal history, background, test results, ratings, interviews and so on; an idiographic technique.

Uses:
- psychotherapy, e.g. cases of multiple personality,
- for groups of people, events or institutions as well as individuals,
- to provide insights from an unusual perspective,
- very popular because of the realism involved.

Advantages:
- gives in-depth picture producing rich data,
- relates to real life,
- may be the only way to study atypical behaviours which occur only rarely.

Disadvantages:
- usually involves recall of earlier history, and is therefore unreliable,
- close relationship between experimenter and subject introduces bias,
- cause and effect difficult to establish,
- not associated with rigorous methodology, unstructured, unreplicable and unreliable,
- limited sample, lacks generalisability,
- time-consuming and expensive.

9 Cross-sectional: groups of individuals of different ages are compared at the same point in time.

Uses:
- provides a picture of development over time,
- comparing effect of some treatment with a control group,
- developmental, clinical and social psychology.

Advantages:
- quick and relatively inexpensive, particularly in comparison to the alternative of longitudinal studies,
- easily replicated,
- relatively easy to modify,
- avoids cross-generational problem (see longitudinal method below).

Disadvantages:
- subjects used may not be comparable, any differences should be due to age rather than social changes (= cohort effect),
- subject variables can never be matched perfectly,
- lacks cause and effect, says nothing about changes within an individual.

10 Longitudinal: one group of individuals studied over a long period of time, taking periodic samples of behaviour.

Uses:
- as for cross-sectional studies, but can draw conclusions on cause and effect,
- chiefly used in developmental psychology.

Advantages:
- repeated measures so subject variables are controlled.

Disadvantages:
- subjects may drop out or be 'lost', leaving a biased group,
- once started, can't modify the design,
- impossible to replicate because of societal changes,
- requires a large investment of time and money,
- sample used may be unrepresentative because of events specific to that generation, such as the Vietnam War (= cross-generational problem).

11 Cross-cultural: different cultures compared with regard to certain practices, e.g. child-rearing, literacy, taboos, language and thought. A kind of natural experiment in the sense that practices are found to vary naturally between cultures, so providing a chance to study independent and dependent variables which can't be manipulated on ethical or other grounds.

Uses:
- indicates universal and therefore innate behaviours,
- enables us to observe how some practices may be linked with certain outcomes,
- popular in developmental and social psychology, and anthropology.

Advantages:
- suggests cause and effect,
- rich data, provides interesting insights into our own practices.

Disadvantages:
- an outsider may not understand language or practices,
- an outsider may have cultural biases,
- researchers may have a hostile reception,
- practices may not be directly comparable,
- observations are only a sample of that culture's behaviour, they may not be typical,
- can't be certain that an observed practice is actually the cause,
- costly and time-consuming.

THE SCIENTIFIC METHOD

Science is knowledge gained through critical and systematic testing. The body of knowledge is thus intimately related to the method of acquiring it. Rigid scientific techniques are essentially the same that we all use in our everyday observations of the physical and psychological world. We make generalisations from the particular, we form hypotheses (expectations for the future), we note when our hypotheses are wrong and readjust our expectations accordingly.

The scientific or inductive method consists of the following steps:

1 simple, unbiased observation,

2 observations which lead to generalisations,

3 an hypothesis is formulated to express these generalisations,

4 a method is designed to test the hypothesis,

5 data is collected and analysed; the hypothesis proved or disproved,

6 knowledge/theory adjusted accordingly.

Essential features

1 Control: in order to be certain that the only change occurring is in the independent variable, the experimenter must seek to control as far as possible all extraneous variables, in particular those which might be thought to have an influence. Only then can we be certain that it was the independent variable which influenced the dependent one.

2 Proof: if you throw a coin five times and each time the result is heads, this does not *prove* that there are no tails (i.e. that the coin is double-headed). After twenty more throws of heads only, you can be more certain that there are no tails but the hypothesis is still not proven. If tails occurs, the theory can be proven to be wrong through *disproof*. **Popper** held that scientific theories cannot be proven to be true, but can be subjected to attempts to prove them false; that is they are *falsifiable*. We can state our degree of certainty or confidence (probability, expressed as significance levels) but never state that something is proven, only that it is likely.

3 Theory: facts are meaningless without a theoretical basis. They can be explained in terms of many different theories. The test of a 'good' theory is that it explains the facts and can generate further questions to test it. In other words that it has good explanatory and predictive power. Research and theory work together:
- data is organised into a theory as a means of attempting to explain interrelationships,
- theories generate hypotheses which can then be tested empirically,
- empirical evidence (data) is used to refine the theory.

④ **Replication**: if an experimental result is 'true' it should be possible to reproduce it. Therefore it is an expectation of any scientific research that the researcher provides sufficient detail for any one else to attempt to replicate the work, thus enhancing its validity.

OBSERVATIONAL METHODS

Observational methods cover a wide variety of techniques, and even underlie experimental methods, as experimenters in essence observe their subjects:

- *naturalistic observation*: behaviour observed in its natural setting, leaving things as you found them. This method is particularly used by ethologists,
- *controlled observation*: spontaneous behaviour is observed but in a situation which has to some extent been manipulated by the observer. For example, Ainsworth's strange situation,
- *indirect observation*: using archival data or social statistics,
- *content analysis*: frequency counts of certain words or behaviours in a communication are recorded,
- *participant observation*: the observer is part of the group being studied. This is very prone to observer bias,
- *non-participant observation*: the observer only watches. However, even the presence of an observer can lead to systematic biases. The use of one-way mirrors avoids these, but raises ethical questions,
- *undisclosed observation*: subjects unaware of observer's true role or presence. Used because observation would otherwise be impossible, but it is ethically questionable (such as **Festinger** *et al.*'s **(1956)** infiltration of Mrs Keech's group, see 2.3) or because an observer's role would interfere excessively with natural behaviour (such as sociological studies).

Recording techniques

- *grid* of behavioural categories: to tick occurrences of target behaviours,
- *rating* behaviour: score each individual in terms of degree, such as amount of interest shown,
- *codes*: a system of symbols or abbreviations is developed as a shorthand when time is limited,
- *diaries*: subjects and/or observers keep a diary of events, either at the time or at the end of the day. May be necessary in participant observation or to limit awareness of being observed,
- *sketches*: showing who is where.

Sampling techniques

- *event sampling*: a list of behaviours is drawn up and a frequency count kept of their occurrence,
- *time sampling*: observations are made at regular intervals, such as once a minute,
- *random observation*: periodic observations may produce biased data, a random number table can generate observation times to avoid such systematic bias,
- *point sampling*: observer concentrates on one individual until sufficient record has been made of their behaviour, then moves on to another.

Equipment: video recorders, cameras, tape recorders, paper, one-way mirrors, stopwatches (for time sampling).

SURVEY CONSTRUCTION

Surveys are self-report methods prone to particular problems and lack of control:

- People often don't actually know what they think and therefore are open to suggestion.
- Even if they do know, their responses are coloured by perceived social desirability or response bias.

- There is evidence that what people say and what they do are different, therefore a measure of what people say they do may not be representative of behaviour (see 2.3, 'Attitudes and behaviour').
- It is impossible to control for personal interpretations; any attempts to explain questions would create differential bias between subjects.

Designing a questionnaire

1. Select the general area of study and conduct research to produce a wide variety of relevant questions.

2. *Generate questions*: a top-down approach starts with subtopics, then broad questions which can be broken down into specific behaviours. For example, Freudian theory would suggest that smoking occurs in orally fixated subjects. Do you chew gum? Do you suck pens? Were you breast-fed? It may be best to work with a group because more varied ideas can be generated.

3. *Writing the questions*:
   - Open versus closed questions? For maximum information open questions are best, however this makes scoring and analysis of the data difficult. Closed questions can be binary forced-choice (yes/no, agree/disagree) or a multiple choice of answers. The use of 'don't know' allows an escape which may be quite genuine, forced 'yes' answers may bias your results.
   - Avoid: complexity, technical terms, negatives, ambiguity, emotive language and leading questions.
   - How many questions? Not too many or the respondent may become bored; too few and the information collected will be rather thin.

4. *Question order*: best to start with easy ones, saving difficult questions or ones which raise defences until the respondent has relaxed. Also, respondents may resist answering 'yes' or 'no' too many times in a row (response set).

5. *Standardised instructions*: need to be written.

6. *Trial run*: test it on a small sample and show it to experts for their critical comments.

7. *Redraft the questionnaire*: if necessary.

8. *Sampling techniques*: decide who and how to collect your data.

Designing an attitude scale

There are many approaches to the measurement of attitudes, for example: the Likert and Thurstone methods, the Bogardus social distance scale, the semantic differential technique, sociometry, and opinion polls (see 2.3). The Thurstone method is described here:

1. *Select a topic* and divide it into sub-areas.

2. *Write the statements*: write a pool of about 50 attitude statements. Positive and negative items should be roughly in balance, plus some extreme statements. It helps to work as a group, each person producing one example of each for each sub-area.

3. *Collate all statements*: type, duplicate and cut up them into slips.

4. *Rate the statements*: group members should now individually rate each statement on an 11-point scale, where 11 is highly unfavourable. The judgement is based on the contents of each item and not the student's own agreement or disagreement. The question is 'if a person agrees with this statement, where does that person stand on the continuum, in a favourable/very favourable/very unfavourable or neutral position?' At the end each person should record their rating on the back of each of their slips.

5. *Select the statements*: for each statement:
   - enter all ratings into a mathematical calculator,
   - calculate the mean and standard deviation for each statement,
   - decide on a minimum spread and exclude all items with scores above this,
   - assign an integer rating to each statement.

   As a group, select the best statement(s) from each rating category – the best are the ones with the greatest agreement (lowest spread) – ending up with 11 or, for a longer scale, 22 statements (2 from each category).

6 *Using the scale*: randomise the order of the statements and present on a sheet, with two columns – 'agree' and 'disagree'. Ask subjects to tick the appropriate column for each statement. Any other questions, such as age, sex, etc. should be included.

7 *Scoring the scale*: for all statements marked 'agree', add up the original mean values for these statements.

10.2 DESIGN CONSIDERATIONS

These are matters not just for experimental design, but also for observations, surveys and so on.

HYPOTHESES

A hypothesis is a provisional statement about what your research intends to prove or disprove. It is a formal, unambiguous statement of what you predict or expect.

The **null hypothesis (H_0)** is a statement of 'no difference/effect/relationship/change' between the variables being investigated.

The **alternate (alternative or experimental) hypothesis (H_1)** predicts that the independent variable will affect the dependent variable.

Since a hypothesis can never actually be proven (see p.378) it must be disproved; therefore the method is to be able to disprove or reject the null hypothesis, and thus accept the alternate hypothesis. This is as close to proof as you can have.

An **operationalised** hypothesis is one where the factors are described in terms of measurable features; for example, rather than 'hungry subjects' use 'subjects who have not eaten for 8 hours'. This minimises ambiguity.

A **one-tailed test** predicts the *direction* of this effect. The independent variable (IV) will increase or decrease some aspect of the dependent variable (DV).

A **two-tailed test** anticipates a *difference* but not a direction.

For example: one-tail hypothesis: boys will be more intelligent than girls.
two-tail hypothesis: boys and girls will differ in their intelligence.

SAMPLING

Sampling is a research technique used in:

● observational studies as a means of selecting observations,

● experimental studies as a means of selecting the subjects from the target population,

● see also 9.1, 'Market research'.

Sampling terms

● **population:** Total number of cases about which a specific statement can be made (also target population).

● **sample:** Part of a population selected such that it is considered to be representative of the population as a whole. A truly representative sample is an abstract ideal.

● **sampling population:** The population from which the sample is actually drawn. This in itself may be unrepresentative. Selecting a sample from one school or from the Monday morning shoppers is biased from the start.

● **biased sampling:** Some subjects have a greater or lesser chance of being selected than they should be given their frequency in the population. Leads to systematic errors.

● **probability sampling:** The events or elements are drawn according to some known probability structure. Random sampling is a special case.

- **random sampling**: Every member of the population has an equal chance of being selected. Achieved with random number tables or numbers drawn from a hat.

- **systematic or quasi-random sampling**: e.g. every 10th case. Often mistakenly called random sampling.

- **non-probability sampling**: Probability of each element or event is not known. As in opportunity sampling.

- **opportunity or accidental sampling**: The subjects you just happen to be able to get, chosen without regard to representativeness, e.g. 'the man on the street'; probably the most common method in practice. Invariably biased.

- **volunteer and self-selecting samples**: Subjects who become part of an experiment, either because they volunteer when asked or they become involved in a manipulated situation (such as being a helpful bystander).

- **quota and stratified sampling**: The population is divided into distinct parts or strata, and a specific number of samples taken from each strata. Popular in market research.

- **area, block, cluster sampling**: Selecting subjects from specific geographical regions, groups or classes. Saves time.

- **snowball sampling**: Each person in sample is asked to give names of other people who can be added to the sample. Useful when target population hard to identify, e.g. drug users.

- **vertical sampling**: From two or more socio-economic classes.

- **horizontal sampling**: From a single socio-economic class.

- **behaviour sampling**: Recording behaviour for specific time periods, chosen to represent overall patterns of behaviour.

Biased samples

The importance of an unbiased sample lies in the fact that:

- the researcher aims to be able to generalise from the study, therefore the sample must be representative of the target population,

- inferential statistics are based on the assumption that the sample is random.

In reality all samples are biased in some ways, most commonly:

- **small sample size** invariably leads to bias because only a small range of subjects are tested;

- **opportunity sampling** is the most common sampling practice. This has led to much of psychological theory being based on a target population of male college students. Developmental psychology has often used the children of college teachers/professors.

Some methods of obtaining a sample

- **wrong number technique**: for example, **Milgram (1970)**, who found that small town residents were more helpful than city-dwellers when someone ostensibly dialled the wrong telephone number.

- **lost-letter method**: used by **Benson *et al.* (1976)**, who left application forms with attached photograph in a public place. They found that the forms were posted to the applicant more often if the photograph was attractive.

- **pavement requests**: asking directions.

- **coin in the telephone box**: **Bickman (1974)** investigated the effects of appearance on the frequency of a coin being returned.

VARIABLES

A variable is a thing that changes. In any research there are two kinds of variables:

1 **Experimental** variables, the ones we are studying:
- The *independent variable* (IV) is the one which is specifically manipulated so that we can observe its effect on the *dependent variable* (DV).
- Theoretically the independent variable is independent of any changes in other variables. It is sometimes called the treatment, experimental or controlled variable.
- The *dependent variable* is usually the one we are measuring or assessing.
- *Intervening variable* is an internal variable which cannot be assessed directly, but it is assumed that changes in the IV, which are seen to affect the DV, do so via the intervening variable.

2 **Extraneous** variables, the ones which are outside our current interest. Any variable other than the independent or dependent variable. These can be:
- *Random variables*, which are unsystematic.
- *Confounding variables*, also called constant or systematic errors.
- Systematic errors may be responsible for the observed (and systematic) changes in the dependent variable rather than the IV. Unsystematic errors create background 'noise' but should not bias the results.
- One source of extraneous influence may be from the participants themselves: *experimenter and subject variables* are those aspects of the behaviour which can bias the results (see p.384).

MEASURING VARIABLES

Operational definitions are necessary in order to make a variable measurable. Such a definition is based on the set of operations or objective components which constitute the behaviour which is varying. Scales of measurement may be:

- *Discontinuous/discrete*: measurements are separate or distinct, as in nominal or ordinal scales. For example the number of children in a family; you might have a mean of 2.4 children, but that figure cannot exist.

- *Continuous*: measurements reflect uninterrupted changes, made along a continuum, as in interval or ratio scales. Even if the scale is in discrete units, such as using centimetres for height, the underlying variable is nonetheless continuous.

Levels of measurement represent progressively greater amounts of information; examples given are for means of recording temperature, nominal is the lowest level.

nominal: e.g. Winter, Spring, Summer, Autumn,
ordinal: e.g. hot, warm, cool, cold,
interval: e.g. Fahrenheit scale,
ratio: e.g. absolute zero scale.

1 **Nominal**: named categories.
The simplest scale. A system for identifying, classifying and naming observations. No magnitude is represented; it is strictly qualitative. The frequency of observations belonging to each category are recorded, e.g.
- grid technique in observational studies comparing sex (male/female) with conformity (high/low).

Appropriate statistics: mode, chi-squared.

2 **Ordinal**: ordered, ranked, positional.
Observations are ordered along some dimension or placed in terms of relative position, compared to others in the group. Limited because the true magnitude is not expressed, only the relative magnitude, e.g.
- pleasantness rankings,
- 5-point Likert scale 'agree–disagree',
- race results, 1st, 2nd, 3rd etc.,
- IQ data and most psychological scales.

Appropriate statistics: medians, percentiles, non-parametric. Quasi-legitimate use of mean, standard deviation and parametric statistics if assume underlying normal distribution. This is done because many ordinal scales are treated as interval scales. Standardising is an attempt to make the intervals on psychometric tests equal.

3 **Interval**: intervals are constant – of equal size.
Reflects precise statements about the differences between observed magnitudes. The intervals are specified but arbitrary, the zero point is not a true zero. It is the simplest true quantitative scale, e.g.
● measurements of time, minutes, seconds.
Appropriate statistics: any.

4 **Ratio**: true zero point, intervals constant.
Rare in psychological measurement, e.g.
● scale to measure weight or height.

EXPERIMENTER AND EXPERIMENTAL BIASES

A bias is a prejudice; it is a confounding variable. There are numerous ways the research can be biased: sample, volunteer, social desirability and observer biases. Experimental results may be subtly and unconsciously affected by investigator and subject expectations.

Investigator biases

1 *Experimenter bias*: an experimenter has expectations about the outcome of an experiment and may unwittingly communicate these to the subject, or even lower organisms, so affecting the results.

2 *Interviewer bias*: an interviewer or tester contaminates responses through, for example, leading questions or subtle reinforcement of 'right' or 'wrong' answers. **Greenspoon (1955)** (the **Greenspoon effect**) was able to alter subjects' behaviour by using subtle reinforcement techniques. Saying 'mm-hmm' or 'uh-huh' after responses led to increased or decreased production of plural words in random word generation. **Loftus *et al.* (1978)** showed that they could manipulate a subject's answers by asking a question either as 'a headlight' or 'the headlight'.

Subject biases

1 *Demand characteristics*: some features of an experiment 'invite' subjects to behave in particular ways. One example is the subject's attempts (not necessarily conscious) to guess what the experiment is about, and do (or not do) what is expected of them. **Orne (1962)** tested this by telling subjects they were participants in an experiment investigating sensory deprivation. In fact subjects were not deprived at all, yet they displayed the classic symptoms; in other words they did what they were expected to do.

2 *Hawthorne effect*: anything new causes improved behaviour, first observed by **Mayo (1933)** (see 9.1).

3 *Volunteer bias*: volunteers are atypical subjects, they are usually more highly motivated and perform better than randomly selected subjects.

4 *Response bias*: a preference for making any particular response rather than another, independent of the relevant response, usually in order to give socially acceptable answers.

Psychological explanations

1 **The experiment as a social situation**: for social reasons, people like to appear in a good light and may adjust their behaviour, even when performing anonymously, in line with what they perceive as socially acceptable behaviour. This is true in face to face behaviour and also when answering questions on paper. **Asch's** classic conformity study (see 2.8) demonstrated how reluctant subjects are to disagree with a group of strangers; people prefer to behave socially rather than antisocially.

2 **The subject as a willing participant**: **Orne (1962)** says that the picture of the subject as an automaton is a foolish ideal. More realistically the subject should be seen as a true participant and this naturally involves the subject's active search for clues.

③ Evaluation apprehension: a subject is aware of being 'tested' and wants to appear normal and create a good impression; they may feel that a psychologist can 'read their mind'. In order to dissipate anxiety and uncertainty, the subject tries to discern what the experimenter really wants.

④ The experimenter's expectations: there are pressures on a researcher to produce useful results. Even in double-blind situations (where neither subject nor experimenter knows the purpose of the research) the experimenter is not 'expectation-free'.

⑤ The self-fulfilling prophecy: Rosenthal and Jacobsen (1966) provided empirical evidence for the notion that things frequently turn out as one expected, not because the expectations were correct but because the expectations caused alterations in behaviour. The communication of such expectations is quite subtle and Rosenthal first showed it with rats **(Rosenthal and Fode, 1963)**.

⑥ The effect of set: research in many areas of psychology shows how ambiguous data is resolved on the basis of expectations. For example, perceptual set **(Bruner and Mintern, 1955)** and memory **(Brown and Lenneberg, 1954)**.

⑦ Attribution of likely cause: when subjects are faced with a request to evaluate their 'state', they seek the most likely explanation, as predicted by attribution theory. We label our physical sensations according to environmental cues **(Schachter and Singer, 1962)**. This is particularly relevant in explaining the effect of placebos.

CONTROLS

Control is the regulation of various treatments so that causal factors may be unambiguously identified. Essentially it is a matter for experimental research, but it is applicable to other areas as well. For example, regulating observer bias or order effects in correlational studies. It can be:

① a means of **providing a baseline** against which to measure the effect of the experimental variable,

② a technique of **eliminating extraneous variables** in order to observe the effect of the IV on the DV.

Control: providing a baseline

The techniques used to achieve this are:

● *Related measures*, where the pairs of subjects are related – either repeated measures or matched subjects (see below). All things being equal, repeated measures is the preferred design because it controls for personal variables, and the statistics are more powerful because, even with small groups, the amount of variance is reduced.

● *Independent measures*: comparison is made between two unrelated groups of subjects.

① Repeated measures (or own control): the same subject is tested before and after treatment, therefore all subjects are exposed to the IV and tested on the DV:

Advantages
● good control for irrelevant subject variables,
● related measures statistics are more sensitive,
● needs fewer subjects.

Disadvantages
● order effects,
● subjects guess purpose of the experiment.

Statistical tests
● related *t*-test, Wilcoxon test, sign test.

② Matched pairs: where repeated measures (test–retest) are not possible, subject variables are controlled by matching pairs of subjects on key extraneous attributes. Only the experimental group is exposed to the IV, the control group receives no treatment. Pairs of subjects, one from each condition, are compared on the DV.

Advantages
● no order effects or other problems of repeated measures design,

- some subject differences are inevitably present,
- can use related design statistics which are more powerful.

Disadvantages
- matching is difficult, time-consuming and may waste subjects,
- some subject variables inevitably present.

Statistical tests
- as for repeated measures.

③ **Independent measures**: subjects in groups not pairs. One group receives the experimental treatment, the other doesn't. Their performance on the DV is compared.

Advantages
- avoids order effects and other problems of repeated measures.

Disadvantages
- lacks control of subject variables,
- needs more subjects,
- statistics less powerful,
- lack of homogeneity of variance may prevent the use of the parametric test.

Statistical tests
- independent *t*-test, Mann–Whitney test, chi–squared test.

④ **Single sample or subject**: test one sample and compare their mean performance with that of a known or hypothetical population; or test one subject repeatedly and compare performance. Not a related subjects design, since scores are not paired.

Statistical tests
- one sample *t*-test, one sample proportions test, chi-squared $1 \times N$.

Control: eliminating extraneous variables

❶ **Experimenter and subject variables, removing bias**:
- *Single-blind* technique: used in almost all experiments so that subjects are unaware of the experimental conditions or aim, thus preventing their expectations interfering with performance. They may still be influenced by experimenter bias.
- *Double-blind* technique: neither the experimenter or the subject knows the 'crucial' aspects of the experiment. Avoids experimenter bias and demand characteristics.
- *Placebos*: a control for the effects of expectations because subjects think they are receiving the experimental treatment when they are not. Subjects receive a 'treatment', which appears the same as the real thing but does not have its critical effects. The technique was first introduced in pharmacological research to distinguish between the psychological and physiological properties of a drug. Examples from psychology include Schachter and Singer's work with suproxin (see 7.5) or Storms and Nisbett's attribution retraining of insomniacs using the pill which they thought would relax them (see 2.2).
- *Undisclosed observation*: field or natural experiment, the subject has no expectations because she is unaware of being part of an experiment.
- *Random allocation*: eliminates any bias in placing subjects in experimental and control groups/conditions.

❷ **Order effects** from repeated measures. When subjects are tested on two (or more) conditions (A and B) their performance may be improved or depressed by certain order effects, such as practice, fatigue or boredom:
- *Counterbalance*: by giving half the subjects condition A first while the other half get condition B first. Therefore some subjects receive AB, others BA. An alternative method is ABBA: each subject is given two A conditions and two B conditions, and a mean calculated for each. A *counterbalance check* can be used to see if the counterbalancing worked.
- *Equivalent measures*: where a subject is re-tested. The test must be given in two equivalent forms created by taking one test and randomly placing equivalent items in form A or form B. These forms can then be counterbalanced.
- *Independent subjects*: not as good from a statistical point of view.

3 Environmental conditions may vary randomly or systematically, such as noise or temperature:
- *Systematic elimination*: where conditions vary systematically it should be possible to eliminate or balance them.
- *Random* variables: at best can assume the effects will be equally spread across all conditions.

4 Treatment variables: a subject's behaviour may improve because of *aspects* of the IV rather than the IV itself. For example, if a new teaching technique is investigated, extra time with the teacher rather than the technique itself may account for changes in the experimental group as compared with the control group:
- *Counterbalance*: to ensure both groups get, in the above case, the same amount of time with the teacher.
- *Placebo*: both groups think they are receiving the same treatment.

GENERALISABILITY

All research data is used at some time to make generalisations about humans or animals. There are some important qualifications to consider when doing this:

1 *Sampling bias*: true random sampling is rare. A lot of experiments use volunteers drawn from psychology departments. Statistical analyses assume unbiased sampling, otherwise claims of significance may be invalid.

2 *Biased data*: to perceive effects of the IV ideally we must eliminate all other 'noise' or extraneous variables. But the choice of such controls is necessarily dependent on knowledge and intuition and some experimental bias is inevitable. Experimenter bias is also unavoidable, researchers quite naturally have expectations.

3 *Publishing bias*: research whose findings is in line with current political correctness is often more likely to be published. People want evidence to support the beliefs they already hold.

4 *Validity*: the more you control an experimental situation, the less like reality it becomes. The more a study has ecological validity, the more likely that extraneous variables enter the equation. Validity is a question of balance.

5 *Reliability*: a true test of scientific 'proof' is replication (see 'The scientific method', p.378). Psychology never finds 100% agreement between similar studies. This is due to problems in repeating standardised procedures exactly, and the fact that people are not perfectly consistent.

Does this mean that it is not possible to generalise from empirical data? It certainly means that anyone using such data must understand the underlying qualifications, but in the absence of any better methods, it is the only option.

10.3 STATISTICAL ANALYSES

A statistic is:
- a number(s) used to represent facts or data (e.g. **numerical statistics**),
- the collection, classification and analysing of data (e.g. **graphical statistics**),
- procedures or formula based on probabilities (**inferential statistics**).

Descriptive statistics are any methods which are not based on probabilistic calculations, they include numerical and graphical methods.

Numerical statistics can be measures of central tendency ('averages') or of dispersion (spread or distribution).

Graphical statistics are methods of visually displaying data.

Inferential statistics involve *inferences* being drawn from sample data to the population as a whole.

NUMERICAL STATISTICS: MEASURES OF CENTRAL TENDENCY

Representing data by giving the most typical or central value. The 'average' is a loose term, mistakenly used. The correct terms are:

1 Mean (or arithmetic mean): represented by $\bar{x}$, can be calculated from grouped frequencies and class interval data (use the mid-interval value for each class).

2 Median (the middle or central value in an ordered list): place all values in order, find the mid-point. If the mid-point lies between two numbers work out the mean of these values.

   To calculate for *grouped frequencies/class intervals*: using the frequency table, find the position of the $(n/2)$th value, e.g.

Interval	1–10	11–20	21–30	31–40
Frequency	2	6	9	5

   $n = 22$, $^n\!/_2 = 11$, the 11th case lies in 21–30 class.

Estimate of the median (mid-interval) = 25.5 or, to be more exact takes $^3\!/_9$ of the interval ($= 24.3$) because 11th is three cases into the group.

3 Mode – modal group (the most common): place values in order and find the value or values occurring most frequently. With grouped frequency/class interval data this information is shown automatically.

Which one to use:

mean: symmetrical distributions and/or no extreme values,
median: skewed distributions and/or data with extremes,
mode: bimodal distributions and/or nominal data.

NUMERICAL STATISTICS: MEASURES OF DISPERSION

1 Range: distance between lowest and highest value. Most accurate if you add 1 to the difference, to account for possible measurement error.

2 Semi-interquartile range: place all values in order, find mid-point (Q2), then halve again to get Q1 and Q3, giving four equal groups, e.g.

5	8	9	12	15	16	18	18	21	29	34
		Q1			Q2			Q3		

   then subtract (Q3 − Q1) and divide by 2 = (21 − 9) ÷ 2 = 6.

3 Mean deviation, variance and standard deviation: are all measures of the mean difference of all scores (x's) from the mean:
   - mean deviation: calculate the mean ($\bar{x}$). Calculate each deviation (d) by subtracting the mean from each value ($x - \bar{x}$); sum all deviations, ignoring minus signs: $\Sigma|d|$; and divide by n.
   - variance (s^2): square each value (x^2) and add them up: $\Sigma(x^2)$. Sum all values (x's), square this and divide by n: $[\Sigma(x)^2]/n$. Find the difference and divide by $n-1$.
   - standard deviation (s): find the square root of the variance (s^2).

Which one to use:

range: symmetrical distributions, simple to measure, affected by extreme values.

semi-interquartile range: reasonably simple, less affected by extremes (more stable).

mean deviation: takes account of all data, simple to calculate, can't be used for population parameters.

standard deviation (variance): as mean deviation but slightly more difficult to calculate (though scientific calculators do it for you) and can be used to estimate population parameters.

DISTRIBUTIONS

❶ Frequency distribution: is a display of the frequency of each score, giving a picture of mean and spread.

❷ Normal distribution: the theoretically expected distribution when a sample is drawn from an infinite population in which all events are equally likely to occur and the variables are continuous. It is one of the critical assumptions underlying the use of parametric statistics.

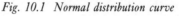

Fig. 10.1 *Normal distribution curve*

A normal distribution is bell-shaped, symmetrical and unimodal. The mean, median and mode all have the same value.

It is extremely common. Many different variables are normally distributed, such as: psychological (intelligence), physical (life of light bulb) and biological (height).

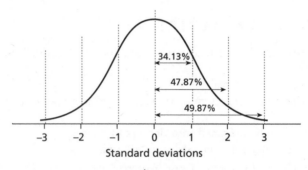

Fig. 10.2 *Number of standard deviations from the mean*

The standard normal curve is completely defined by its mean and standard deviation.

We can work out the area (or number of people/observations) between a given value and the mean, as in Fig. 10.2.

A **z-score** (or **standard score**) is a score calculated from a set of data taking the mean and standard deviation into account, therefore enabling comparisons to be made between different sets of data because they are all 'set' to the same mean and standard deviation. The formula for calculating the z-score is $z = (x - \bar{x})/s$.

❸ Uniform or rectangular distribution: all classes have the same frequency or probability, producing a rectangular graph. One might think this describes the normal distribution, but a uniform distribution is formed when only one contributing variable is involved, e.g. one dice thrown. A normal distribution occurs when many factors are involved in producing the observed behaviour e.g. polygenetic inheritance.

❹ Skewed distribution: lopsided, asymmetrical, negative or positive (right-hand tail longer). An example of negative skew might come from a test which is too difficult (floor effect), positive skew from a test which is too easy (ceiling).

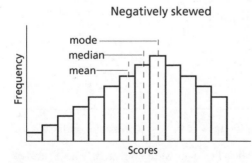

Fig. 10.3 *Negatively skewed distribution*

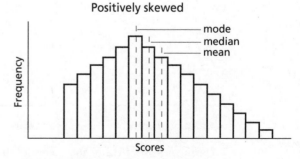

Fig. 10.4 *Positively skewed distribution*

A population whose distribution is skewed requires non-parametric statistics.

The median may be the best measure of central tendency as it is least affected by extreme values. The same can be said for semi-interquartile range or deviation measures.

⑤ **Bimodal distribution**: two points reasonably remote from each other that show a clear concentration of scores. Two humps not necessarily of equal size, such as might be produced by attitude measurements where people are polarised for or against, or shoe size in an adult population.

⑥ **Percentiles**: the percentile represents the percentage scores in a sample that lie below it, e.g. the 20th percentile is the point where 20% of the scores lie below.

Related to interquartile range, it is used in charts of normal development giving 10th and 90th percentiles for weight and height so that abnormal development can be detected.

⑦ **Class intervals**: a grouped frequency distribution (as used in the median), used when list of values is long, more understandable if data grouped in equal intervals, such as 0–9 years, 10–19 years, etc.

GRAPHICAL STATISTICS

① **Graphical statistics for all frequency data**: nominal, ordinal, interval, discrete and continuous:
- *tables*: can use class intervals,
- *bar chart*: visual representation of frequencies of nominal, ordinal or interval data; discrete units,
- *pie chart*: frequency translated into degrees of a circle,
- *pictogram*: frequency represented by suitable pictures.

② **Graphical statistics for ordinal and interval data only**:
- *histogram*: differs from a bar chart in that the area of the bars *must* be proportional to the frequencies represented,
- *frequency polygon*: mid-point of each bar joined to show continuous change, not suitable for discrete data,
- *line graph*: suitable for continuous data,
- *curved lines*: a sketch of an approximate line may be the best way to represent the data rather than using a jagged line graph, useful for skewed, bimodal or normal data,
- *ogive*: a line of cumulative frequency where frequencies are progressively added to each other,
- *scattergram*: for correlations, each pair of values is plotted against each other to show if a consistent trend is present (the 'line of best fit' is a precisely calculated line and not just the line that appears to represent the data).

Examples

① Scattergrams (one dot = one person)

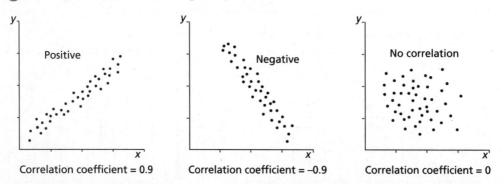

Correlation coefficient = 0.9   Correlation coefficient = –0.9   Correlation coefficient = 0

② **Using nominal data**: for example, the following data were collected from a study into the types of play which were observed in different age groups:

TYPES OF PLAY	Frequency observed in each age group		
	Age 1 year	Age 2 years	Age 3 years
solitary (S)	16	8	4
parallel (P)	3	9	7
co-operative (C)	1	3	9
TOTAL	20	20	20

Pictogram

	S	P	C
1	𝕏𝕏𝕏𝕏𝕏𝕏𝕏𝕏	𝕏𝕏	𝕏
2	𝕏𝕏𝕏𝕏	𝕏𝕏𝕏𝕏𝕏	𝕏𝕏
3	𝕏𝕏	𝕏𝕏𝕏𝕏	𝕏𝕏𝕏𝕏𝕏

𝕏 represents 2 children

Piechart: Example of an angle calculation:

For S1 $\dfrac{16}{20} = \dfrac{x}{360}$ (because there are 360 degrees in a circle)

$x = 16 \times 360 \div 20 = 288°$

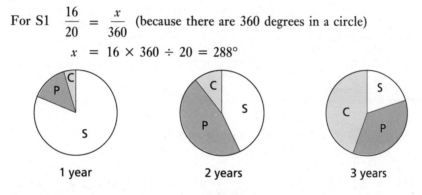

1 year   2 years   3 years

❸ **Using ordinal data**: for example, subjects were asked to rate a speaker on a scale of 1 to 5 (where 5 was highly intelligent) after they had read a biography of the speaker containing either the word 'warm' or 'cold'.

Rating	Number of subjects		To calculate the mean	
	WARM	COLD		
1	0	0	1×0	1×0
2	5	6	2×5	2×6
3	12	23	3×12	3×23
4	26	21	4×26	4×21
5	21	10	5×21	5×10
Total			255	215
n			64	60
mean ($\bar{x}$)			3.98	3.58

Histogram with **frequency polygon**

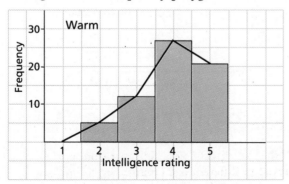

Histogram with **sketch**

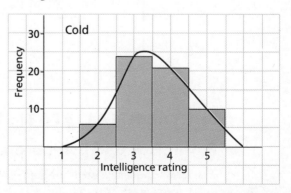

2 × 2 contingency table (for chi-square analysis)

	Warm	Cold
Low rating	5	6
High rating	47	31

4 **Using interval data:** for example, determining the effects of predictable (condition 1) versus unpredictable (condition 2) noise on a proof reading task.

Score	Condition 1	Condition 2	To calculate the mean (using mid-interval values)		Cumulative frequency 1	2
0–4	2	1	2 × 2	2 × 1	2	1
5–9	3	1	7 × 3	7 × 1	5	2
10–14	7	4	12 × 7	12 × 4	12	6
15–19	9	7	17 × 9	17 × 7	21	13
20–24	13	10	22 × 13	22 × 10	34	23
25–29	11	14	27 × 11	27 × 14	45	37
30–34	6	11	32 × 6	32 × 11	51	48
35–39	6	8	37 × 6	37 × 8	57	56
40–44	1	3	42 × 1	42 × 3	58	59
45–49	2	1	47 × 2	47 × 1	60	60
n	60	60	1,395	1,595		
Mean ($\bar{x}$)			23.25	26.58		
Standard deviation (s)			10.24	9.22		

Histogram

This is constructed from the total in each interval.

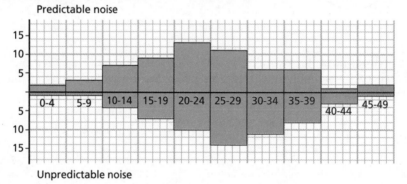

Predictable noise

Unpredictable noise

Ogives

These are constructed from the cumulative frequency values.

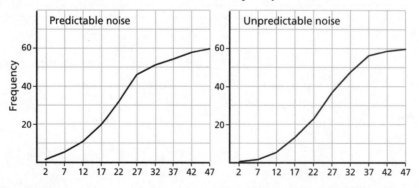

INFERENTIAL STATISTICS: CONSIDERATIONS

Parametric and non-parametric tests

The term 'parametric' stems from the term 'parameters', which are the descriptive measures of a *population* rather than those of a *sample* (which are called statistics). Only samples which have been *randomly* drawn from a population are parameters. Where selection is not random, the use of non-parametric statistics is necessary:

- *Parametric* procedures are preferred over non-parametric ones because they have greater statistical *power*, i.e. they are more likely to detect statistically significant effects. This sensitivity is because they use all the data rather than comparative data such as ranks.

- *Non-parametric* tests are simpler to compute, have fewer assumptions and can be used more widely but are not as powerful as parametric tests.

The *assumptions* of a parametric test are that the samples:

1 Are drawn from a *normal distribution*: you can't actually prove that an underlying distribution is normal, but you can be reasonably certain if:
- the sample is drawn from a well-known normal distribution, e.g. IQ scores,
- sketch out the sample's distribution to see if it looks normal,
- can be checked using the chi-squared goodness of fit test.

2 Have equal or known (homogenous) *variance*: this is similarly impossible to prove:
- it is not particularly important when using a test of related measures because they should have similar variance,
- can be checked using the *F*-test (variance-ratio).

3 Are measured using an *interval* or ratio scale: some essentially ordinal measurements are accepted as interval or at least taken as approximating to equal intervals (e.g. rating scales and standardised scores). Ranked data are most definitely not ordinal.

BUT parametric tests are *robust*: even quite marked departures from the basic assumptions can be tolerated without undermining the meaning of the result, *except*:

- Where the sample size and variances are different. Care is particularly important where the samples are independent.

- Where the sample is small. It may be non-normal despite the population being normal (or vice versa).

Conclusion: The advice is therefore, that you can use parametric statistics unless:

- data is in the form of ranks,

- the sample is small,

- distribution is obviously non-normal,

- there are obviously large differences in variances.

Significance

Levels of significance are related to certainty. In an experiment any changes observed in the DV are either due to:

1 the effect of the IV, or

2 chance factors (random extraneous variables).

At what point would you accept that the explanation is (1) and not (2)?

100% due to IV	and	0% due to chance ?
99%		1% ?
95%		5% ?
90%		10% ?

Saying '99%' means that in 99 out of 100 cases, the results would be due to the IV and not chance. This can also be stated as: the probability (p) of the result being due to chance is less than 0.01 or $p < 0.01$.

How do you decide?

1 **High or low** significance?
- 0.1% level $(p \leq 0.001)$ very highly significant, 'stringent'
- 1% level $(p \leq 0.01)$ highly significant
- 5% level $(p \leq 0.05)$ significant
- 10% level $(p \leq 0.10)$ somewhat significant, 'low, lenient'

2 How **important** is the research?
- 1% level used where research may affect human health, should take few if any chances,

- **5% level** generally used in psychological research because is a good compromise between type I and type II errors (see below),
- **10% level** rather thin but worth reporting because follow-up studies might prove worthwhile; also acceptable when replicating a previous study.

3 **Type I and Type II errors**
- **Type I error**: at the 10% level (too low/easy/lenient): runs the risk of rejecting a null hypothesis which is in fact true (accepting the alternate hypothesis which is false).
- **Type II error**: at the 1% level (too high/hard/stringent): runs the risk of accepting a null hypothesis which is in fact false (rejecting an alternate hypothesis which is true).

Observed and critical values

The data are used to calculate an *observed value* using an inferential statistical test. The *critical value* is listed in a *table of significance* and found using the following information:

- calculate the *degrees of freedom* (df) which is one less than the total number of data items (n-1) (a mathematical concept that the last number of a set of numbers is completely determined by the (n-1) numbers and their mean),
- whether the hypothesis was one- or two-tailed,
- the level of significance decided on at the outset,
- the critical value can then be located and compared with the observed value to determine significance.

INFERENTIAL TESTS: TWO SAMPLE DIFFERENCE TESTS

The aim of these tests is to compare two samples of data and determine whether they came from the same or a different population, i.e. whether the samples are significantly different in terms of their mean and standard deviation. A simplified contingency table (N.B. all tests can be used with data of higher levels):

Data level	Sample related	Sample independent	Parametric?
nominal	sign test	chi-square	no
ordinal	Wilcoxon	Mann–Whitney	no
interval	related *t*-test	independent *t*-test	yes

Related samples

1 **Related *t*-test**: the most powerful of the related samples tests.
2 **Wilcoxon matched pairs signed ranks test**: must be used if $n<8$; shouldn't be used where $n>25$. (The Wilcoxon Rank Sum test is a test for related samples and equivalent to the Mann–Whitney test). Nearly as powerful and easier to calculate.
3 **Sign test**: for testing the difference rather than the magnitude of difference.

Independent samples

Tests of independent samples tend to be less sensitive than those of related ones because subject variables tend to obscure the effects of the IV:

1 **Independent *t*-test**: the most powerful of the unrelated samples tests.
2 **Mann–Whitney test**: must be used if $n<8$; shouldn't be used where $n>20$, unless a correction is applied. Nearly as powerful and easier to calculate.
3 **Chi-square (χ^2) test**: observed frequencies placed in a contingency table of any number of rows × columns (R × C, to remember this order, think *R*oman *C*atholic). The frequency in each cell must always be greater than four in each cell. Chi-square is also a test of association and goodness of fit.

INFERENTIAL TESTS: TESTS OF CORRELATION

A test of correlation determines whether two factors vary systematically. However, this is not evidence that one factor has *caused* the other to vary.

The statistic (number) produced is called the *coefficient* of correlation, it is always within the range $+1.0$ to -1.0. The degree of correlation which is 'acceptable' varies with the number of subjects (called degrees of freedom): if there are ten subjects, 0.63 would be highly correlated; for twenty subjects, 0.45 would be high.

Types of correlation:

positive: both factors increase/decrease together, the coefficient is positive.

negative: as one factor increases the other decreases, coefficient is negative.

perfect: $+1.0$ or -1.0, significance is determined by sign not magnitude.

zero: the relationship is random.

linear: detected by tests of correlation (as below); simple correlation.

non-linear or curvilinear the relationship between two variables is not linear, it is described by a quadratic or higher order equation, can use tests of goodness of fit to a predicted curve.

Tests of correlation:

1 **Pearson's product-moment of correlation (*r*):** for interval/parametric data,

2 **Spearman's rank correlation (rho):** for ordinal/non-parametric data,

3 **Chi square:** a test of association with nominal data.

10.4 ETHICAL CONSIDERATIONS

Ethics is that which is deemed acceptable in human behaviour in pursuit of certain goals or aims; it is not simply a question of 'right' but of balance between ends and means.

The particular issue of animal research is discussed in 8.5. We must also consider the rights of the research subject, in terms of informed consent, and the responsibilities of a researcher as a professional.

Ethical guidelines for psychologists are produced by the British Psychological Society (BPS) and the American Psychological Association (APA), for example:

● *Ethical Principles for Conducting Research with Human Participants* (BPS, 1990),

● *Casebook of Ethical Principles for Psychologists* (APA, 1987),

● *Guidelines for the Use of Animals in Research* (BPS, 1985),

● *Code of Conduct for Psychologists* (BPS, 1985).

Responsibilities of a scientist

One definition of a profession is that it is a body of practitioners who govern themselves, with the right and duty to stop 'unprofessional' members from practising. For example, the British Medical Association 'strikes off' a doctor for malpractice; the same is true for the BPS. Therefore psychologists are obliged to behave professionally.

Most scientists believe that it is not sufficient to conduct research in a vacuum; the scientist has a moral obligation to society to form opinions about the usefulness and ethics of his research and its ultimate applications. It is impossible to stop human attempts to extend the body of knowledge but we have a duty to maintain control over its uses.

Means and ends

Both American and British professional bodies recognise that research involves a balance between the interests of the subject and the humane or scientific value of the research. The aim of psychological research is to seek greater understanding of behaviour in order to 'ameliorate the human condition and enhance human dignity'.

When considering the balance, it should be remembered that retrospective analyses are biased:

1 **The ends are unanticipated**: much important knowledge has been gained unintentionally, 'understanding grows because we examine situations in which the end is not known' **(Milgram, 1974)**. Many people find this very hard to accept, however, if all scientific research had to be justified in terms of its outcomes or purpose very little would be undertaken and few discoveries made.

2 **The means are unanticipated**: the results of many psychology studies seem obvious *in retrospect*, but at the time the research was planned, the effect on the subjects was not expected. In the case of Milgram's classic study of obedience, the subjects' behaviour and resulting stress was a surprise to all involved.

A summary of ethical guidelines

When conducting research, investigators should strive to follow these guidelines:

1 **Designing research**:
- The investigator should weigh anticipated costs and benefits.
- Leave things as they were prior to any research.
- Any experimental manipulations should be positive; research creating anxiety and stress should be avoided.
- Any research likely to involve deception, stress, involuntary participation or invasion of privacy should be checked with colleagues and should be used only when it is the sole option. Subjects, when debriefed, should be offered the option of withholding their data.
- Research involving animals requires extreme caution and should be avoided unless specifically necessary.
- Cross-cultural research should take local cultural practices into account.

2 **Briefing**: informed consent and the right to withdraw:
- Wherever possible the investigator should inform subjects of objectives and, later, results of the research.
- Consent: permission must be obtained from all subjects; where young children are involved parents must be informed.
- Subjects should be reminded of their right to withdraw at any time.

3 **Conducting the research**:
- If experimental effects or stress are greater than expected the investigator should stop the research immediately.
- Investigators should maintain the highest standards of safety.

4 **Debriefing**: subjects should be:
- Offered the chance to withhold their data.
- Be given the results of the research.

5 **After the research**:
- All investigators should report their findings honestly.
- All investigators should provide a sufficiently detailed account for others to use their data.
- Confidentiality: all personal data should be treated as confidential, as stated in the Data Protection Act. This is particularly true where data is taken from observation or using records.

6 **Professional standards**:
- All research should pay regard to the public image of psychological studies.
- All psychologists have a duty to monitor the work of their peers and students, and to encourage any infringements to be 're-evaluated'.

Drawbacks and alternatives

In a sense it might appear to be easy to apply such guidelines and continue to produce useful research, however:

- Informed consent may render results quite different. For example, **Gardner (1978)** (9.2) produced a different set of results on the effects of unpredictable noise when he gave the subjects the right to withdraw and thus, unintentionally, gave them the sense of control.

- In order to avoid undisclosed observation, role play might be used but even then this may not avoid subject distress. For example, in **Zimbardo**'s study many subjects suffered a great deal, despite it only being a 'game' and the fact that they could withdraw at any time.
- An alternative to manipulating behaviour would be to ask people to say how they would behave. However research on the consistency between attitudes and behaviour (see 2.3) suggests that this would be unreliable.
- Where interventions are positive and natural, the question remains about the control group. Is it unethical to withhold treatments from a control group as in the case of testing a new educational method or psychotherapeutic intervention?
- The use of naturally occurring cases avoids many problems of experimental manipulation. Because these are infrequent, this means that important decisions might be based on extremely limited and biased samples.

A look at commonly cited studies

When discussing the ethics of particular studies it is important to make explicit points, to present both pros and cons and base criticism on *informed* knowledge of the study. The studies mentioned below are selected for some of the issues they raise:

1 **Milgram (1963) study of obedience**: is criticised for the psychological conflict subjects experienced in causing pain to another 'subject' and the deception. However:
  - There is an important distinction between intending to do harm and the case where the researchers cannot, and in this case did not, anticipate the outcome. (They did, however, repeat the same experiment in a number of variations, knowing the distress that was caused).
  - Milgram has argued (**Tarvis, 1974**) that the purpose of an experiment is not to confirm or disconfirm history but to understand it. We know that people die of cancer, so why study it?
  - Milgram took extraordinary lengths after the research to check on the subjects' well-being; 84% of the subjects said they were glad they participated and 75 % found the experience enlightening.

2 **Harlow (1958 onwards) research on maternal deprivation in monkeys**: again, the psychological distress caused was totally unanticipated and has had important consequences for the treatment of humans and animals in care.

3 **Watson and Rayner (1920) conditioned emotional response**: in this case the result was physical and psychological harm, one of the few examples in psychological research of deliberate harm being done.
  - The researchers did intend to restore Little Albert to his initial fearless state and, in the end, the patient and his mother did use their right to withdraw.
  - The experiment gave strong evidence of CERs, a finding of great value and sufficient for a trial of one to remain as the standard.
  - It also provides another sort of evidence: distorted reports of the original research appear everywhere and remind us that it is important to consult the original text of any research, rather than someone else's version, in order to evaluate a piece of research fairly (**Cornwell and Hobbs, 1976**).

4 **Piliavin *et al.* (1969) study of helping behaviour**: the subjects were unable to give consent or to be debriefed yet they undoubtedly suffered distress. The question is whether it is possible to collect certain sorts of evidence except in this way, and whether the potential understanding justifies the method.

5 **Burt (1955) intelligence and heredity**: now infamous for invented data that went on to be widely used to argue in favour of an inherited view of intelligence. In fact it seems that he invented some co-workers and their data (see, for example, **Joynson, 1989**). The question is, why did he do it?

6 **Curtiss (1977) and the case of 'Genie'.** A *Horizon* programme presented some details of this case, including the fact that Genie's mother eventually sued the psychologists involved in her treatment for their extensive testing. Case studies are a popular and memorable source of documenting extreme cases (as with S.B., who recovered his sight, and H.M., who had a memory disorder). How human is a human who treats a damaged creature as a specimen?

Other important studies which might be considered are: **Schachter and Singer** (deception), **Jouvet** (animal experiments and sleep deprivation), **Bexton** *et al.* (physical and psychological deprivation), **Lashley** (removing parts of animals' brains), **Sherif** (children's emotions manipulated), **Asch** (social pressure), **Bandura** (children exposed to violence), **Riesen** (animals reared in darkness).

Chapter roundup

Related material in other chapters:
- All chapters include empirical work worthy of discussion in terms of techniques and ethics;
- cognitive psychology (Chapter 1), considerations of perceptual and mental sets;
- social psychology (Chapter 2), includes details useful for considering the experiment as a social situation, such as the effects of person perception and conformity;
- communication (Chapter 4) covers non-verbal communication, the means of conveying subtle cues;
- intelligence, personality and assessment (Chapter 5) provides details of psychometric techniques;
- abnormal psychology (Chapter 6) explores ethical issues related to psychotherapeutic interventions;
- biological psychology (Chapter 7) includes stress, an issue related to the effects of some experimental interventions;
- animal behaviour (Chapter 8) examines the ethics of animal research.

Illustrative question 1

(NEAB, 'A', 1993)

In a longitudinal study of intelligence two groups of children, aged six at the outset, were given a series of tests and an Intelligence Quotient (IQ) was obtained for each child.

Group 1 consisted of children from Chinese families who had migrated recently from China to England; Group 2 comprised children from white English families born in England. Each group consisted of 100 children.

Each group was tested three times; at the start of the study, three months later, and at the end of two years. One psychologist carried out the first assessment; a different psychologist carried out the assessments on occasions two and three.

Figures 1 and 2 show the distribution of the IQs of Group 1 and Group 2 when first tested.

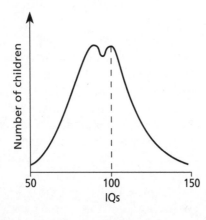

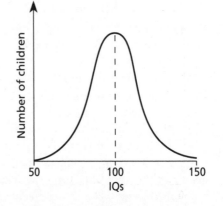

Fig. 1 distribution of IQs for Group 1   **Fig. 2** distribution of IQs for Group 2

(a) Name and describe the distribution of scores for Group 1 in Figure 1. (2 marks)

answer: A bimodal distribution.

(b) Name the distribution of scores for Group 2 in Figure 2. (1 mark)

answer: A normal (or Gaussian) distribution.

(c) Approximately two thirds of the children in Group 2 had IQs between 85 and 115 points. Given the mean score (X) = 100, which of the following values is most likely to be the Standard Deviation: 5, 15, 25 or 35? (1 mark)

answer: 15

(d) How many children in Group 2 could reasonably be expected to show IQs of between 70 and 130? (1 mark)

answer: 95 or 95%.

(e) Analysis of the test data gave the following mean IQs:

Table 1

	Group 1	Group 2
First testing (Age 6 years 0 months)	97	100
Second testing (Age 6 years 3 months)	105	105
Third testing (Age 8 years 0 months)	104	101

(i) Apart from the cultural experience of the Chinese prior to immigration, give **two** reasons for the difference in mean IQs between Group 1 and Group 2 on the first occasion of testing. (2 marks)

answer: e.g. experience taking tests, tester bias, large error scores, effects of recent immigration, cultural differences (any two).

(ii) Give **three** reasons for the changes in mean IQs between the first and second testing. (3 marks)

answer: e.g. practice effect, different experimenter used on each occasion, unreliable test, cultural adjustment by group 2 (any three).

(iii) Give **one** suggestion for the difference in mean IQs between Group 1 and Group 2 on the third occasion of testing. (1 mark)

answer: e.g. the Chinese may have a greater aptitude for intelligence tests or a greater commitment to learning; may be due to error in score (any 1).

(iv) Figures 3 and 4 show the distribution of the IQs for the number of children in each of the groups on the third occasion of testing.

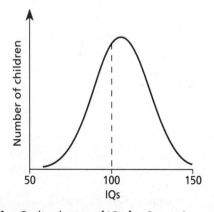 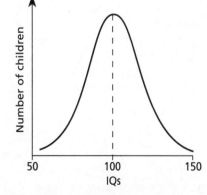

Fig. 3 distribution of IQs for Group 1   **Fig. 4** distribution of IQs for Group 2

If you had the individual scores for all the children, what statistical procedure would you use to determine whether there was a significant difference in the mean IQ between the two groups? Briefly justify your choice. (2 marks)

answer: Since the data (IQ scores) is approximately interval (quasi-interval) and should be normally distributed and with similar variance, we should use a parametric test. The test is comparing samples which are unrelated. Therefore the test to use is an independent *t*-test.

(f) The results of the third testing of Group 2 were compared with a national sample of 100,000 British children. State **two** reasons which might account for any obtained differences in mean IQ. (2 marks)

answer: e.g. different IQ tests used, tests standardised on different populations, the larger sample produces a lower error score.

(g) Outline how you would go about establishing split-half reliability of IQ tests. (2 marks)

answer: Obtain a set of IQ scores, randomly divide the test items into two halves, and correlate the score on each half for each subject. The coefficient obtained is a measure of the test's reliability.

(h) How might characteristics of testers affect the test results? (3 marks)

answer: e.g. different expectations/prejudices about performance, different degree of tolerance as to what is a correct answer, provide a different test condition (atmosphere).

Illustrative question 2

(AEB 'A', 1992)

A group of researchers decided to investigate whether there was an association between people's age and their ability to tell the difference between music played to them on record, cassette and compact disc. They placed an advertisement in a newspaper asking for volunteers who would be interested in participating in the study. There were 218 respondents. For the purpose of the study the researchers divided respondents into two age groups: those under the age of 40 and those aged 40 and over.

Having first carried out a pilot study, the researchers began testing the discriminative listening skills of the two age groups. The procedure that the researchers used was as follows: participants were asked to which type of music they would prefer to listen in this investigation: rock, jazz or classical. One of the researchers then played each participant a single recording of their preferred type of music three times: once from a record, once from a cassette and once from a compact disc. The order of presentation of the three formats was randomised for each participant.

After hearing the three presentations each participant was asked to identify which of the presentations was from a record, which was from a cassette and which was from a compact disc. Participants' responses were recorded as being correct (all three formats correctly identified) or incorrect (less than three formats correctly identified). The researchers analysed these data using a chi-squared test.

The results were as follows:

Table 1: *number of participants who were correct/incorrect*

Age of participants	Correct	Incorrect
Under 40 years	85	35
Over 40 years	55	43

The chi-squared analysis produced a value of 4.47.
The relevant line (df=1) of the statistical table for chi-squared interpretation was:

Table 2

Significance level	0.1	0.05	0.01	0
Chi-squared value	2.71	3.84	6.64	10.83

(a) State an appropriate null hypothesis for the above study. (1 mark)

answer: There is no significant association (difference) between the conditions (the age of the participants and their ability to discriminate between the media used); any relationship which occurs will be due to chance.

(b) What is an independent variable? (1 mark)

answer: The one which is deliberately manipulated/controlled by the experimenter to create a difference between the experimental and control conditions.

(c) What is a dependent variable? (1 mark)

answer: The variable which is measured in order to assess the effect of the IV.

(d) What was the dependent variable in the above study? (1 mark)

answer: The subjects' identification of the media (record/cassette/CD).

(e) Identify the target population in the above study. (1 mark)

answer: The total readership of the newspaper for that particular issue.

(f) Identify the sample in the above study. (1 mark)

answer: The people who responded to the advertisement, a self-selected sample of 218 people.

(g) What is meant by the term 'pilot study'? (1 mark)

answer: A preliminary, usually smaller-scale study prior to the main study.

(h) Give **two** reasons why a pilot study was used here. (2 marks)

answer: e.g. to try out standardised instructions and procedures, becoming familiar with the techniques to be used, testing scoring procedures, determining whether any changes need to be made.

(i) Identify one possible uncontrolled variable in the study and describe the effect it may have had. (3 marks)

Tutorial note: 1 mark for naming the possible effect plus 1 mark for explaining how this would be important, another mark if this description is detailed.

answer: e.g. the fact that the sample were volunteers, no means of assessing hearing ability, no control of subjects' familiarity with the different media, no control for variations in the music played to each subject. In each case the main problem is that such effects would be systematic rather than randomly distributed between the age groups, for example, older persons might well have poorer hearing or have a preference for classical rather than rock music.

(j) Describe how you would have dealt with this uncontrolled variable. (3 marks)

Tutorial note: The answer to this is entirely dependent on the previous answer; 1 mark for a common sense solution, full marks for an answer which shows an awareness of 'good practice'.

answer: e.g. give all subjects a hearing test and eliminate any whose hearing is worse than the set standard to ensure equivalence between groups.

(k) Give two reasons why a chi-squared test was used to analyse the results of the above study. (2 marks)

answer: e.g. nominal data, parametric criteria not satisfied, independent samples (not related), the expected frequencies were high enough (any two).

(l) What is meant in Table 2 by the phrase 'significance level'? (2 marks)

answer: The probability that the results can be attributed to chance factors or random error rather than the IV. ('the level of probability' would be given 1 mark).

(m) State the significance level of those given in Table 2 at which researchers are most likely to make a type 1 error. (2 marks)

answer: A type 1 error is more likely to be made at the 10% level of significance.

(n) Explain the reasoning behind the decision you have made in question (m) above. (2 marks)

answer: A type 1 error is the rejection of a true null hypothesis. When the significance level is too low (or liberal) we are more likely to accept a false hypothesis, thus rejecting the true null hypothesis because we tolerate a greater 'amount' of chance factors.

(o) Explain whether the null hypothesis would be retained or rejected. (3 marks)

answer: The null hypothesis would be rejected at the 5% level (1 mark) because the observed value of chi-squared is 4.47 (1 mark) which is greater than the critical value of 3.84 (1 mark).

(An alternative answer is to accept the null hypothesis at the 1% level because the critical value for this is 6.64.)

TEST RUN

In this section:

Test Your Knowledge Quiz

Test Your Knowledge Quiz Answers

Progress Analysis

Mock Exam

Mock Exam Suggested Answers

- This section should be tackled towards the end of your revision programme, when you have covered all your syllabus topics, and attempted the practice questions at the end of the relevant chapters.

- The Test Your Knowledge Quiz contains short-answer questions on a wide range of syllabus topics. You should attempt it without reference to the text.

- Check your answers against the Test Your Knowledge Quiz Answers. If you are not sure why you got an answer wrong, go back to the relevant unit in the text: you will find the reference next to our answer.

- Enter your marks in the Progress Analysis chart. The notes below will suggest a further revision strategy, based on your performance in the quiz. Only when you have done the extra work suggested should you go on to the final test.

- The Mock Exam is set out like two real exam papers. These contain a wide spread of topics and question styles, as used by the examination boards. You should attempt the papers under examination conditions, in the time allowed, and without reference to the text.

- Compare your answers to our Mock Exam Suggested Answers. We have provided tutorial notes to each question showing what must be included for a good answer, and pitfalls to avoid.

TEST YOUR KNOWLEDGE QUIZ

1 What is perceptual set?

2 How did Turing propose that you could test whether a machine can think?

3 What are 'fuzzy boundaries'?

4 How does Kahneman's capacity theory differ from Allport's?

5 How can explanations of forgetting be separated into two types?

6 Give an example of a secondary reinforcer.

7 What is a 'confirmatory bias'?

8 What is 'attribution retraining'?

9 What four methods are used to measure attitudes?

10 What explanation is given by 'social exchange theory' for attraction?

11 Why did Tajfel use the term 'minimal group'?

12 What is the bystander effect?

13 What view of aggression do ethologists take?

14 Distinguish between conformity, obedience and compliance.

15 Fiedler's contingency theory states that style is contingent on what?

16 List three effects the media may have.

17 What is probably the most important feature of a caregiver in establishing attachment?

18 Why is Piaget's approach structuralist?

19 What are the two most significant differences between Piaget and Bruner's accounts?

20 What are the three major orientations which have offered explanations of moral development?

21 What is the categorical self?

22 What was Coleman's view of adolescence?

23 Chomsky proposed a transformational grammar, what do these rules transform?

24 What are 'metalinguistics'?

25 How can research in NVC help mental patients?

26 What age, according to the Gardners', did Washoe's finally reach linguistically?

27 What is the main drawback of the factorial approach?

28 What do MZ and DZ stand for?

29 According to Freud, which part of the personality embodies innate desires?

30 What is concurrent validity?

31 What is IQ?

32 What are projective techniques?

33 What phrase was put forward by Szasz as a way to better describe mental illnesses?

34 Why is Rogers' theory of personality called 'self-theory'?

35 What is the 'hello–goodbye' effect?

36 What is aetiology?

37 What is the difference between 'normal' depression and pathological depression?

38 How can mental retardation be determined genetically?

39 What is the main function of the ANS?

40 What region of the brain is associated with sleep?

41 What is the dominant 'zeitgeber' in all organisms?

42 What is the difference between extrinsic and intrinsic motivation?

43 What two factors contribute to emotion?

44 What are the three stages of GAS?

45 What hormones influence the experience of pain?

46 What does 'fitness' mean?

47 What is a 'super-releaser'?

48 What term describes change which is due to age rather than experience?

49 In what way can aggression be a non-adaptive strategy?

50 What other incentives aside from pay are offered to increase worker motivation?

51 What is the difference between density and crowding?

52 What is a 'learning style'?

53 How are health and attitude change linked?

54 What is the 'word superiority effect'?

55 What is 'observer bias'?

56 How does a one-tailed test differ from a two-tailed test?

57 Define 'demand characteristics'.

58 Which measure of central tendency is most suitable when the distribution of data is skewed?

59 Which type of error describes the rejection of a true hypothesis and with what significance level is it associated?

60 What is debriefing?

TEST YOUR KNOWLEDGE QUIZ ANSWERS

1   The tendency to perceive things on the basis of prior expectations. (1.1)

2   If a machine is capable of deception. (1.2)

3   The distinction between one concept and another is not all-or-nothing; items within a class do not all possess the properties of the class. (1.3)

4   Kahneman's has a central processor whereas Allport proposes several, independent processors. (1.4)

5   As failures of access or availability. (1.5)

6   Money or anything which might be reinforcing but is not a primary need. (1.6)

7   The tendency to select explanations which confirm already existing views. (2.1)

8   The use of attribution principles to change maladaptive behaviours through taking internal control. (2.2)

9   Physiological measures, observed behaviour, opinion polls and attitude scales. (2.3)

10 Relationships are a matter of costs and rewards, relationships are formed and will continue if the the ratio of cost:reward is sufficient (2.4)

11 Group membership was based on very little, only being an over or under estimator. (2.5)

12 The observation that certain conditions lead to a lack of helping. (2.6)

13 It is an innate and adaptive behaviour to ensure the survival of the species. (2.7)

14 Conformity tends to involve group norms and a change in behaviour and attitudes; obedience is generally to one person and suggests external rather than internal changes; compliance is seen as a response to an explicit order/request and again not internalised. (2.8)

15 The favourability of the situation. (2.9)

16 Increasing violence, increasing prosocial behaviour and perpetuating social stereotypes. (2.10)

17 Sensitivity and responsiveness to a child's signals. (3.1)

18 It emphasises the relation among the phenomena, i.e. the structure. (3.2)

19 The role of language and the sequential character of stages rather than the more accumulative nature of modes. (3.2)

20 Learning, psychodynamic and cognitive-development theories. (3.3)

21 The various different 'selves' e.g. gender, roles, etc. (3.4)

22 He thought it was normally tension-free but an accumulation of problems, some perhaps pre-existing adolescence, may lead to difficulties. (3.5)

23 Surface structure into deep structure and vice versa. (4.1)

24 Using language to talk about language, word play. (4.1)

25 Using social skills training patients can learn more appropriate non-verbal behaviours. (4.2 and 6.4)

26 Two years. (4.3)

27 It is subjective and tends to reify factors. (5.1)

28 Monozygotic and dizygotic (identical and non-identical twins). (5.1)

29 The id. (5.2)

30 A means of demonstrating the trueness of a test by correlating it with another measure thought to demonstrate the ability. (5.3)

31 Intelligence Quotient, mental age divided by chronological age multiplied by 100. (5.4)

32 Methods of assessing personality where the subject's performance is assessed in terms of how they have projected themselves onto their response. (5.5)

33 Problems in living. (6.1)

34 The concept of self, self-unity and self-esteem are fundamental to psychological health. (6.2)

35 The tendency for patients to initially exaggerate their unhappiness to convince the therapist that their need for help is genuine; and the opposite tendency to exaggerate well-being at the end as a means of showing appreciation. (6.2)

36 The science or philosophy of causation, the inquiry into origin or cause of anything but especially diseases. (6.4)

37 A matter of degree and duration. (6.4)

38 Down syndrome and phenylketonuria (PKU) are two examples. (6.5)

39 Control of the endocrine system (hormones and arousal). (7.1)

40 Reticular activating system (RAS), raphe system. (7.2)

41 Light. (7.3)

42 External rewards versus feelings of satisfaction. (7.4)

43 Physiological and cognitive. (7.5)

44 Alarm, resistance, collapse. (7.6)

45 Endorphins. (7.7)

46 The extent to which an organism is adapted to its environment so that survival is most likely. (8.1)

47 An exaggerated sign stimulus. (8.2)

48 Maturation. (8.3)

49 Any species which fights to the death will soon die out. (8.4)

50 Possibilities include: benefits, job enrichment, promotion prospects, factors which increase the 'meaningfulness' of the job, a sense of fair pay, realistic goals, organisational commitment.

51 Density is the objective measure, crowding is the subjective experience; density does not always lead to a sense of crowding. (9.2)

52 The preferred pattern of working of each individual. (9.3)

53 Health workers need to find ways to encourage people to adopt more positive *attitudes* to changing their lifestyles and their health. (9.4)

54 The effect of top-down processing, known words or common letter-patterns generate an expectation that certain letters will appear. (9.3)

55 The extent to which an observer interprets what he sees in terms of pre-existing expectations. (10.1)

56 The former states the direction of the anticipated difference. (10.2)

57 The features of a situation which invite a person to behave in certain ways. (10.2)

58 The median. (10.3)

59 A type 1 error at the 10% level. (10.3)

60 Subjects are told any necessary information about the research after the study has been conducted; they may also be able to provide useful information. (10.4)

PROGRESS ANALYSIS

Place a tick next to those questions you got right.

Question	Answer	Question	Answer	Question	Answer	Question	Answer
1		16		31		46	
2		17		32		47	
3		18		33		48	
4		19		34		49	
5		20		35		50	
6		21		36		51	
7		22		37		52	
8		23		38		53	
9		24		39		54	
10		25		40		55	
11		26		41		56	
12		27		42		57	
13		28		43		58	
14		29		44		59	
15		30		45		60	

My total mark is: _____ out of 60

If you scored 1–15

You need to do some more work. The Mock Exam is intended as a test of exam technique. It will be wasted if your basic syllabus coverage is insufficient. Make a realistic assessment of your understanding of each chapter. This will give you a further revision plan to work from. You will need to attempt the Test Your Knowledge Quiz one more time before you are ready to go on to the Mock Exam.

If you scored 16–30

You need to do a little more work. The Mock Exam is intended as a test of exam technique. It will not be really useful until you have filled in the gaps in your knowledge. If you have time, go through the unit list at the beginning of each chapter and revise all those that look unfamiliar. If you don't think you have time to do this, look through the questions at the end of each chapter, and the notes on points to include. You should then attempt the Test Your Knowledge Quiz again.

If you scored 31–45

You are just about ready to attempt the Mock Exam. First, however, you should look through the questions at the end of each chapter, and the notes on points to include. This will be a good guide to which syllabus areas are still unfamiliar. If you do not think you have time to do this, go over those chapters whose reference is given in the Quiz answers for the questions you got wrong. You should then be ready to go on to the Mock Exam.

If you scored 46–60

Congratulations. You have sufficient grasp of the syllabus topics to get real value out of attempting the Mock Exam under exam conditions. First, however, you should go back to the specific chapter referred to in the Test Your Knowledge Quiz answers for each question you got wrong. Reassure yourself that there is no real gap in your knowledge.

MOCK EXAM

PAPER 1

Time allowed: 3 hours

Answer **four** questions.
Answer **one** question in Section A.
Answer **three** questions from Sections B, C & D, but not more than **two** from any one section.

Mark allocations are shown in brackets.

Section A: perspectives on psychology

1   Discuss the use of animals in psychological research and consider the ethical issues raised by such research. *(AEB 1992)*   (25 marks)

2   What do psychologists mean by the term 'reductionism'? Discuss the controversy relating to reductionism in a psychological context. *(AEB 1991)*   (25 marks)

3   Describe and evaluate the contributions of **either** the psychoanalytic approach **or** the behaviourist approach to the understanding of behaviour. *(AEB 1993)*
                                                                         (25 marks)

Section B: cognitive psychology

4   Describe and discuss how sensory processes relate to perception. *(AEB 1991)*
                                                                         (25 marks)

5   Describe and evaluate two theories which attempt to explain the production and comprehension of language. *(AEB 1991)*   (25 marks)

6   (a) Describe one or more computer models of thought.   (10 marks)
    (b) Discuss the usefulness of computer models to an understanding of human thought. *(AEB 1993)*   (15 marks)

7   Discuss applications of psychological research on memory and describe the studies upon which these applications are based. *(AEB 1992)*   (25 marks)

Section C: social psychology

8   Critically discuss attributional approaches in social psychology. *(AEB 1990)*
                                                                         (25 marks)

9   Describe and evaluate the attempts of psychologists to explain the formation AND breakdown of friendships. *(AEB 1992)*   (25 marks)

10 'Power and leadership arise from the interaction of social influences.' Describe and discuss psychological research which focuses on this statement. *(AEB 1991)*
                                                                         (25 marks)

11 (a) Discuss one or more of the social–psychological theories of aggression.
                                                                         (12 marks)
    (b) Consider the implications that social–psychological theories of aggression might have for the reduction of aggressive behaviour. *(AEB 1993)*   (13 marks)

Section D: comparative psychology

12 (a) Briefly describe the main principles upon which any **one** form of learning theory is based.   (8 marks)
    (b) Consider how **one** form of learning theory has been applied to the areas of **either** educational **or** clinical psychology, and how successful it has been. *(AEB 1992)*   (17 marks)

13 Describe and critically assess the role of evolutionary concepts in understanding the behaviour of non-human animals. *(AEB 1993)* (25 marks)

14 Describe attempts to teach 'language' to non-human animals and consider the extent to which these attempts have been successful. *(AEB 1992)* (25 marks)

15 (a) Describe any two types of social organisation found in non-human animals.
(10 marks)

(b) Consider the selective advantage of these arrangements to the animals concerned. *(AEB 1993)* (15 marks)

PAPER 2

Time allowed: 3 hours

Answer **four** questions.
Answer the question in Section A.
Answer **three** questions from Sections B, C & D, but not more than **two** from any one section.

Mark allocations are shown in brackets.

Section A: experimental design and research methods

1 A psychotherapist wanted to assess the effectiveness of a technique for treating people suffering from animal phobias.

Research into reaction-time had already shown that phobics took longer to respond to words related to their phobia than to neutral words. In view of this, the psychotherapist reasoned that effective therapy should result in a reduction in reaction-time to phobia-related words.

To test this idea, the psychotherapist selected 10 clients who had phobias about animals whose skin was covered in hair or fur. Reaction times of each client were tested by asking them to read aloud a list of words. One list (the experimental list) contained both neutral and phobia-related words, for example:

record apple monkey window table candle rainbow hamster
curtain rabbit picture paper

This list was extended to 40 words in total. The other list (the control list) consisted of 40 neutral words.

Before therapy began, the 10 clients were given standardised instructions in which they were asked to read aloud the two lists as quickly as possible. The time taken to complete each list was recorded. Half the clients read the experimental list first and then the control list, the other half read the control list first followed by the experimental list.

When the course of psychotherapy was completed, the reaction-times of the 10 clients to the two lists were tested in the same way as before. The psychotherapist was then able to compare reaction-times measured before and after treatment. Since the data met the requirements for a parametric test, it was decided to use a related *t*-test to analyse the results. The significance level chosen was $P \leqslant 0.05$.

(a) The psychotherapist was confident enough to use a one-tailed hypothesis for this investigation. What is meant by a one-tailed hypothesis? (1 mark)

(b) In this study
(i) name **one** independent variable. (1 mark)
(ii) what is a dependent variable? (1 mark)

(c) Had the data not fulfilled the criteria for a parametric test, what non-parametric test of differences could be used in this investigation? (1 mark)

(d) One of the criteria that data need to fulfil before a parametric test is employed is that both sets of data to be compared should have 'similar variance'. Suggest **one** way in which you would check if both sets of data had a similar variance. (1 mark)

(e) Suggest **one** way in which it can be established whether or not a sample of data is normally distributed. (1 mark)

(f) Half of the clients read the experimental list first and then the control list, the other half read the control list first followed by the experimental list. What is the reason for this procedure? (1 mark)

(g) The control lists used in this investigation may appear to be redundant. However, there are good reasons for their inclusion. Briefly explain **one** such reason.

(2 marks)

(h) Comparing clients' reaction-times for the control list and the experimental list, would you expect reaction-times to be:
(i) the same or different before the course of psychotherapy? (1 mark)
(ii) the same or different after the course of psychotherapy? (1 mark)

(i) The psychotherapist decided to use the $P \leqslant 0.05$ level of significance for this investigation. What is meant by the expression $P \leqslant 0.05$ level of significance?

(1 mark)

(j) Explain why a 0.05 rather than a 0.01 level of significance was chosen as an appropriate level for this investigation. (1 mark)

(k) The psychotherapist ensured that all the words chosen for this study were of two syllables and of similar length. Suggest **one** reason why this was done. (2 marks)

(l) In the example from the experimental list you will see that phobia-related words such as rabbit or hamster do not appear at the top of the list. What could be wrong with putting phobia-related words at the top of the list? (2 marks)

(m) Each client received standardised instructions before their reaction-times were tested.
(i) What is meant by the term standardised instructions? (1 mark)
(ii) Briefly explain why standardised instructions were used. (1 mark)

(n) It is important that control lists used before and after the course of psychotherapy show reliability.
(i) What is meant by reliability in this context? (2 marks)
(ii) How would you test for reliability in this investigation? (2 marks)

(o) The measurements employed in this investigation could be challenged as lacking in validity. What does the term validity mean in this context? *(AEB 1991)* (2 marks)

Section B: bio-psychology

2   Describe both physiological and alternative explanations of emotion. Discuss their relative contribution to our understanding of emotion. *(AEB 1991)*   (25 marks)

3   Discuss psychological explanations which have contributed to an understanding of the role of homeostatic mechanisms in behavioural functions.
(AEB 1990)   (25 marks)

4   'Not simply the absence of waking, sleep is a special activity of the brain, controlled by elaborate and precise mechanisms. Not simply a state of rest, sleep has its own specific, positive functions'. (Hobson, 1989). Discuss this view in the light of psychological research. *(AEB 1992)*   (25 marks)

5   Critically consider the influence that drugs have been shown to have on behaviour. *(AEB 1993)*   (25 marks)

Section C: developmental psychology

6   Use psychological studies to discuss functions of play that may be related to social and cognitive development in children. *(AEB 1991)*   (25 marks)

7   (a) Distinguish between sociability and attachment. (5 marks)
(b) Describe and evaluate psychological research which has investigated factors which influence the development of sociability. *(AEB 1992)*   (20 marks)

8   Critically consider the view that the self **develops** as a result of socialisation processes. *(AEB 1993)*   (25 marks)

9   (a) What is meant by the term adolescence?   (4 marks)
    (b) Discuss **one** psychological study concerned with adolescence.   (7 marks)
    (c) Critically consider whether adolescence must inevitably be a period of 'storm
        and stress'. *(AEB 1993)*   (14 marks)

Section D: individual differences

10 Discuss **two** theories of intelligence. What are the implications of these theories
    for intelligence testing? *(AEB 1991)*   (25 marks)

11 Describe and critically contrast the trait and type approaches to personality.
    (AEB 1993)   (25 marks)

12 (a) Distinguish between neuroses and psychoses.   (4 marks)
    (b) Discuss some of the difficulties in diagnosing mental disorders.   (10 marks)
    (c) Discuss the influence of either genetic or neurochemical or environmental
        factors on mental illness. *(AEB 1993)*   (11 mark)

13 What assumptions are made by the medical approach to normality and
    abnormality? Discuss ethical and practical implications of this approach.
    (AEB 1991)   (25 marks)

MOCK EXAM
SUGGESTED ANSWERS

Paper 1

1   **Animal research**: covered in: 8.5 'The use of animals in research' and 10.4
    'Ethics'.

    * Both parts of the question must be answered: coverage of specific studies using
       animals and a more general analysis of ethical issues. Both aspects can be
       covered separately or at the same time. 'Rote' lists of ethical issues and/or animal
       studies would gain little credit, as would uninformed arguments against the use of
       animals.

2   **Reductionism**: covered in: Chapter 7 'Philosophical background' and illustrative
    question for that chapter. Examples of reductionist approaches include: computer
    analogies (1.2), behaviourist learning theory (1.6), Freudian theory (5.2),
    biological explanations of behaviour (Chapter 7). The alternatives are numerous,
    but most obviously the Gestalt (1.1) and humanist (5.2) approaches.

    * A good answer would cover a variety of reductionist approaches and offer some
       alternatives by way of comparison.

3   **Psychoanalysis or behaviourism**: both approaches are considered in the
    following sections: learning (1.7), early development (3.1), social development
    (3.3), personality theory (5.2), treatment (6.2) and diagnosis (6.3) of abnormal
    behaviour, and motivation (7.4). Criteria for evaluation are given in Section 1, p.21.

    * Poor answers go little further than Skinner, Pavlov and learning or Freud and
       abnormal behaviour. Both psychoanalysis and behaviourism have made
       contributions to almost every area of psychology and a good essay should reflect
       this wider appreciation. A competent essay must also cover both description **and**
       evaluation.

4   **Perception**: covered in 1.1.

    * All senses (visual, auditory, tactile, etc.) are relevant to this reductionist question
       (can we reduce perception to its physiological components?). The 'straightforward'

answer to the question is a description of the sensory process. Evaluation skills are tested by discussing the interaction between sensations and cognitive processes (bottom up and top down processing), looking at: illusions, expectations, organisation, etc.

5   **Language**: covered in theories of language (4.1) and reading (9.3).

   * This is not an essay about language and thought, though some of the same material could be made relevant. A theory of language explains linguistic behaviour in terms of a set of principles such as behaviourism or linguistic universals. Criteria for evaluation are given in Section 1, p.21; in this essay evaluation might be achieved through comparing one theory with another.

6   **Computer models**: covered in 1.2.

   * The more current approach to subdividing questions focuses the candidates attention on the two tasks of describing and discussing. Descriptions will probably be of the General Problem Solver. Evaluation ('discuss') should be related to the reference point given, i.e. for 'understanding human thought'. Therefore the answer should look at the arguments for and against computers as models of thought.

7   **Memory**: covered in memory (1.5) and applications in ergonomics (9.1), education (9.3) and student revision (Section 1)

   * This question requires no reference to theoretical models of memory. Instead you should outline the applications of memory research *and*, for each, give one or more studies related to this. A list of applications and relevant research will be adequate but a good answer should go even further, and evaluate ('discuss') this material.

      (The examiner's report for this question noted how many candidates wrote general essays on memory and ignored the specific reference to applications, and thus gained very few marks: ANSWER THE QUESTION).

8   **Attribution**: covered in 2.2.

   * A straightforward question *if* this is a topic you know. A good answer requires both competent description of attribution theories and evaluation of such theories by comparing them and in terms of their individual merit (see criteria for evaluation in Section 1, p.21).

9   **Friendship**: covered in 2.4 and social development (3.4).

   * The question is about friendship rather than love or sexual attraction. Candidates must write about both formation and breakdown of friendships, even though the latter is less well covered by the theorists and empiricists. Criteria for evaluation are given in Section 1, p.21.

10   **Leadership**: covered in conformity, obedience and compliance (2.8), group dynamics (2.9) and organisational psychology (9.1).

   * While material on social influence (conformity, obedience and compliance) is relevant, it does not constitute a sufficient answer as there is a large body of research (and related theories) which is specifically about power and leadership. A good answer must evaluate both research and theory as suggested in Section 1, p.21.

11   **Aggression**: covered in aggression (2.7) and social behaviours in animals (8.5).

   * The question specifically excludes the biological theories of aggression. The first part requires both description and evaluation of social aggressive theories; the second part focuses on ways of reducing aggressive behaviour, but expressly from the standpoint of the theory. Essays which are limited to Bandura's work would gain less than half marks, no matter how well they are done.

12   **Learning theory**: covered in human learning (1.6) or animal learning (8.3); evaluating effectiveness of educational practices (9.3) or therapy (6.2) based on learning theory.

* An answer based on classical or operant conditioning will be the wisest choice as much more information is available, particularly when answering part (b). However any theory is acceptable. A good answer should do more than describe the work of Pavlov and Skinner; you should work from the position of general principles of the theory.

13 **Evolution**: covered in Chapter 8, evolutionary concepts underlie the ethological approach to understanding animal behaviour.

   * A good answer should describe such concepts and explain their relationship with ethological understanding of non-human behaviour. Evaluation (see Section 1, p.21) is the final component of the essay.

14 **Animal language**: covered in 4.3.

   * A good answer should go beyond a description of the basic attempts and provide appropriate details of the research as well as an evaluation of the methods and conclusions. Different kinds of animals, primates and marine mammals might be worthy of consideration. The crucial question to address is what constitutes language?

15 **Social organisation**: covered in 8.4.

   * The first part is a straightforward description of (probably) the two main types of social organisation. The term 'consider', used in part (b), asks for knowledge and understanding; in this question evaluation skills will be demonstrated by an awareness of the strengths and limitations of the evolutionary approach.

Paper 2

1 **Research and design**,
   (a) The key word is 'direction'.
   (b) (i) The time when clients were assessed, or the presence/absence of phobic-related words in the lists. (ii) The time taken to react to the lists.
   (c) Wilcoxon signed ranks, or sign test (data is related).
   (d) Compare variances (standard deviations), or distributions of data, or use an F-test.
   (e) Plot the scores as a frequency distribution; or compare mean, median and mode (which should be similar); use chi-square goodness of fit test.
   (f) Counterbalancing; or to avoid order effects such as practice, boredom, etc.
   (g) Provides a baseline for comparing reaction times to the experimental lists, or distracts subjects from real purpose of the research.
   (h) (i) different, (ii) the same.
   (i) The likelihood of the event occurring by chance is equal to, or less than, 5 cases in one hundred.
   (j) The 0.01 level is too stringent for this type of research, while the 0.1 is too lenient; 0.05 provides a compromise between type 1 and 2 errors (see 10.3, for discussion of these). It is not sufficient to say that 0.05 is the most usually selected.
   (k) To exclude any extraneous or confounding variables; for 2 marks the term used must be explained.
   (l) Neutral words at the start of the test may disguise the purpose of the research; or might prevent the subject beginning in an emotional state; or assists relaxation. For 2 marks you must give the reason and an explanation.
   (m)(i) Exactly the same instructions are given to each subject. (ii) They prevent any extraneous variables distorting the results.
   (n) (i) The pre- and post-therapy scores are similar/consistent. (ii) Correlate these two scores and look for a high, positive coefficient of correlation.
   (o) That the test measures what it sets out to measure, that it is a true measure of degree of phobia.

2 **Emotion**: covered in 7.5.

   * A good essay will describe a minimum of two accounts (one physiological, the other not) and then evaluate them through comparisons such as how well each one explains the empirical evidence (other ways of evaluating are given in Section 1, p.21).

3   **Homeostasis**: covered in motivation (7.4).

   *   It is important to be able to distinguish between psychological and physiological models of motivation, as only the former are required for this answer. However physiological accounts are relevant when evaluating the psychological ones. 'Discuss' calls for description and evaluation (see Section 1, p.21).

4   **Sleep**: covered as a state of consciousness (7.2) and a biological rhythm (7.3).

   *   The answer should focus on the quotation and not be a general report about sleep theories and research. The best approach is to identify specific points in the quotation and discuss these. In this way you are almost forced to go beyond description only (of how sleep is controlled) and analyse the functions which have been suggested, which includes both REM and NREM sleep.

5   **Drugs**: covered in 7.1.

   *   This question is either poorly answered by someone who has a largely anecdotal knowledge of drugs, or is extremely well done by drawing on a range of substances and detailing their effects. Evaluation is demonstrated by an understanding of the neurophysiological mechanisms and models which account for behaviour and a critical account of any empirical work.

6   **Play**: covered in 3.4.

   *   A straightforward question for a candidate who has prepared an essay on play, but more commonly Piaget's general work on cognitive development is offered and gains few marks. Even though the question refers to cognitive development any discussion of this must be in terms of how play is important. Evaluation is demonstrated through critical presentation of any empirical work and by contrasting alternative explanations.

7   **Sociability and attachment**: covered in 3.1.

   *   The distinction between sociability and attachment is not one which many candidates have thought about. Making the distinction should help with part (b) which is only concerned with sociability. Sociability is not the same as socialisation and work on attachment can be made relevant but is not sufficient for a good answer. Criteria for evaluating research are described in Section 1, p.21.

8   **Self development**: covered in 3.4.

   *   There is a distinction to be made between social factors and socialisation; both are relevant to this question but a good answer is particularly concerned with socialisation, a more interactive process. Any empirical or theoretical evidence presented should be critically evaluated and can be compared with alternative explanations for the development of self.

9   **Adolescence**: covered in 3.5.

   *   Adolescence can be defined by age and/or psychological and physical changes which take place; it is worth mentioning the vagueness of the term and its cultural specificity. For part (b) only one study is required and this should be crisply described and evaluated in terms of its methodology, value, etc. The time spent on part (c) should reflect the fact that over half of the marks are from here. A selection of empirical and theoretical positions should be described and evaluated (as described in Section 1, p.21).

10 **Intelligence**: covered in the concept of intelligence (5.1) and intelligence tests (5.4)

   *   The two theories of intelligence should be described and evaluated (see Section 1, p.21). The implications for intelligence testing might be dealt with in conjunction with each theory or as a completely separate section. In either case, both parts of the question should be clearly answered. Many candidates make the mistake of writing anything about intelligence rather than answering the specific question. It is possible to turn such a general approach into something of value by inserting a few sentences, placed appropriately, to link the answer to the question.

11 **Personality theories**: covered in 5.2.

* A standard answer to this would probably describe Eysenck's and Freud's theories with some evaluation of both. A good essay will make some attempt to explain the terms 'trait' and 'type' and will explicitly contrast the two approaches rather than just set them down.

12 **Diagnosis and causes of mental illness**: covered in 6.3 and 6.4.

* All parts of this question require description and evaluation (see Section 1, p.21). The distinction between neuroses and psychoses is vague, which is partly why the classification schemes no longer use it; this point could be raised by way of evaluation. The rest of the question is straightforward though candidates should beware of the choice in part (c). It is valuable to discuss more than one mental illness and even to use evidence relating to a different cause than the one selected *if* this is explicitly given as a means of evaluation.

13 **The medical model**: covered in the concept of abnormality (6.1), models and treatments (6.2), diagnosis and classification (6.3) and ethical issues (6.6)

* The topic of abnormality, and ethical/practical implications of approaches is a large one and this essay limits the discussion to the medical model; a point overlooked by some students. However, it may be useful to use other models as a means of evaluating the medical approach. A good answer will go beyond a simplistic view of the medical model as bad. It is also important to address all three parts of the question.

BIBLIOGRAPHY

Aaron, P.G. (1987) Developmental dyslexia: Is it different from other forms of reading disability? *Annals of Dyslexia, 37*, 109-25.

Abernethy, E.M. (1940) The effect of changed environmental conditions upon the results of college examinations, *Journal of Psychology, 10*, 293-301.

Abrahamson, L.Y., Seligman, M.E.P. & Teasdale, J.D. (1978) Learned helplessness in humans: Critique and reformulation. *Journal of Abnormal Psychology, 87*, 49-74.

Adams, J.A. (1971) A closed-loop theory of motor learning. *Journal of Motor Behaviour, 3*, 111-49.

Adams, J.S. (1965) In L. Berkowitz (Ed.) *Advances in experimental social psychology (Vol. 2)*. New York: Academic Press.

Adamson, R.E. (1952) Functional fixedness as related to problem-solving. *Journal of Experimental Psychology, 44*, 288-91.

Adorno, T.W., Frenkel-Brunswick, E., Levinson, D., & Sanford, N. (1950) *The authoritarian personality*. New York: Harper.

Agnew, H.W., Jr., Webb, W.B. & Williams, R.L. (1964) The effects of stage four sleep deprivation. *Electroencephalography and Clinical Neurophysiology, 17*, 68-70.

Ahrens, R. (1954) Beitrag zur entwicklung des physiognomie und minikerkennes. *Zeitschrift fur Experimentelle und Angewandte Psychologie, 2*, 412-54.

Ainsworth, M.D.S. (1967) *Infancy in Uganda: Child care and the growth of love. Baltimore*: John Hopkins University Press.

Ainsworth, M.D.S. (1973) The development of mother-infant attachment. In B.M. Caldwell & H.N. Ricciutti (Eds.) *Review of child development research*, (Vol. 3), Chicago: University of Chicago Press.

Ainsworth, M.D.S. (1979) Attachment as related to mother-infant interaction. In J.G. Rosenblatt, R.A. Hinde, C. Beer & M. Busnel (Eds.) *Advances in the study of behaviour* (Vol. 9). Orlando, Fl.: Academic Press.

Ainsworth, M.D.S. (1989) Attachments beyond infancy. *American Psychologists, 44*, 709-16.

Ainsworth, M.D.S., Bell, S.M. & Stayton, D.J.(1974) Infant/mother attachment and social development as a product of reciprocal responsiveness to signals. In M.P.M. Richards (Ed.) *The integration of the child into a social world.* Cambridge: Cambridge University Press.

Ainsworth, M.D.S., Blehar, M.C., Waters, E. & Wall, S. (1978) *Patterns of attachment: A psychological study of the strange situation*, Hillsdale, NJ: Lawrence Erlbaum.

Alderfer, C. (1972) *Existence, relatedness and growth: Human needs in organisational settings*. New York: Free Press.

Alexander, B.K., Coambs, R.B. & Hadaway, P.F. (1978) The effect of housing and gender on morphine self-administration in rats. *Psychopharmacology, 58*, 175-9.

Allen, M.G. (1976) Twin studies of affective illness. *Archives of General Psychiatry, 33*, 1476-78.

Allen, M.G., Greenspan, S.I. & Pollin, W. (1976) The effect of parental perceptions on early development in twins. *Psychiatry, 39*, 65-71.

Allison, R.I. & Uhl, K.P. (1964) Influence of beer brand identification on taste perception. *Journal of Marketing Research, 1*, 36-9.

Allport, D.A. (1980) Attention and performance. In G. Claxton (Ed.) *Cognitive psychology: New directions*. London: Routledge & Kegan Paul.

Allport, D.A., Atonis, B., & Reynolds, P. (1972) On the division of attention: A disproof of the single channel hypothesis. *Quarterly Journal of Experimental Psychology, 24*, 225-235.

Allport, F.H. (1924) *Social psychology*. Boston: Houghton Mifflin.

Allport, G.W. (1935) Attitudes. In C. Murchison (Ed.) *Handbook of social psychology*. Worcester, MA: Clark University Press.

Allport, G.W. (1937) *Personality: A psychological interpretation*. New York: Holt.

Allport, G.W. (1961) *Pattern and growth in personality*. New York: Holt, Rinehart & Winston.

Allport, G.W. (1965) *Letters from Jenny*. New York: Harcourt, Brace and World.

Allport, G.W. & Postman, L. (1966) The basic psychology of rumour. In E. Maccoby *et al.* (Eds.) *Readings in social psychology*. New York. Holt.

Allyon, J. & Azrin, N. (1968) *The token economy*. New York: Appleton-Century-Crofts.

Altman, I. (1975) *The environment and social behaviour*. Monterey, CA: Brooks/Cole Publishing Co.

Amato, P.R. & McInnes, I.R. (1983) Affiliative behaviour in diverse environments: A consideration of pleasantness, information rate, and the arousal-eliciting quality of settings. *Basic and Applied Social Psychology, 4*, 109-22.

Amsterdam, J.D., Winokur, A., Dyson, W., Herzog, S., Gonzalez, F., Rott, R. & Koprowski, H. (1985) Borna disease virus. *Archives of General Psychiatry, 42*, 1093-6.

Anand, B.K., Chhina, G.S. & Singh, B. (1961) Some aspects of electroencephalographic studies in Yogis. *EEG Clinical Neurophysiology, 13*, 452-6.

Anastasi, A. (1968) *Psychological testing* (3rd edition), London: Macmillan.

Anderson, C.A. & Anderson, D.C. (1984) Ambient temperature and violent crime: Tests of linear and curvilinear hypotheses. *Journal of Personality and Social Psychology, 46*, 91-7.

Anderson, J.R. (1983) *The architecture of cognition*. Cambridge, MA: Harvard University Press.

Andersson, M. (1982) Female choice for extreme tail length in widow bird. *Nature, 299*, 818-9.

Andrew, R.J. (1963) The origin and evolution of the calls and facial expression of primates. *Behaviour, 20*, 1-107.

Animals Act (1986) *Halsbury's statutes* (4th edition) *Current statutes service, Issue 9*, Vol. 2. London: Butterworth.

Anisfeld, E., Casper, V., Nozyce, M. & Cunningham, N. (1990) Does infant crying promote attachment? An experimental study of the effects of increased physical contact on the development of attachment. *Child Development, 61*, 1617-27.

Annett, J. (1959) Learning a pressure under conditions of immediate and delayed knowledge of results. *Quarterly Journal of Experimental Psychology, 11*, 3-15.

Annett, J. & Kay, H. (1956) Skilled performance. *Occupational Psychology, 30*, 112-7.

Anstey, E. (1977) A 30-year follow-up of the CSSB procedure, with lessons for the future. *Journal of Occupational Psychology, 50*, 149-59.

Antelman, S.M., Rowland, N.E. & Fisher, A.E. (1976) Stress related recovery from lateral hypothalamic aphagia. *Brain Research, 102*, 346-50.

Ardrey, R. (1967) *The territorial imperative*. London: Collins.

Argyle, M. (1978) *The psychology of interpersonal behaviour* (3rd edition). Harmondsworth, Middlesex: Penguin.

Argyle, M. (1987) *The psychology of happiness*. London: Methuen.

Argyle, M. (1988) *Bodily communication* (2nd edition). London: Routledge.

Argyle, M. (1989) *The social psychology of work* (2nd edition). Harmondsworth, Middlesex: Penguin.

Argyle, M., Alkema, F. & Gilmour, R. (1972) The communication of friendly and hostile attitudes with verbal and nonverbal signals, *European Journal of Social Psychology, 1*, 385-402.

Argyle, M. & Henderson, M. (1984) The rules of friendship. *Journal of Social and Personal Relationships, 1*, 211-37.

Arlin, P.K. (1977) Piagetian operations in problem finding. *Developmental Psychology, 13*, 297-8.

Armsby, R.E. (1971) A re-examination of the development of moral judgement in children. *Child Development, 42*, 1241-8.

Arndt, J. (1968) A test of the two-step flow in diffusion of a new product. *Journalism Quarterly*, 45.

Arnhoff, F.N. & Damianopoulos, E.N. (1962) Self-body recognition: An empirical approach to the body image. *Merill-Palmer Quarterly, 8*, 143-8.

Aronfeed, J. (1963) The effects of experimental socialisation: Paradigms upon two moral responses to transgression. *Journal of Abnormal and Social Psychology, 66*, 437-8.

Aronson, E., Bridgeman, D.L. & Geffner, R. (1978) The effects of a cooperative classroom structure on student behaviour and attitudes. In D. Bar-Tal & L. Saxe (Eds.) *Social psychology of education*. New York: Wiley.

Aronson, E. & Linder, D. (1965) Gain and loss of esteem as determinants of interpersonal attractiveness. *Journal of Experimental Social Psychology, 1*, 156-72.

Aronson, E. & Mills, J. (1959) The effects of severity of initiation on liking for a group. *Journal of Abnormal and Social Psychology, 59*, 177-81.

Aronson, E. & Osherow, N. (1980) Co-operation, prosocial behaviour and academic performance: Experiments in the desegregated classroom. In L. Bickman (Ed.) *Applied social psychology annual, Vol. 1*. Beverly Hills, CA: Sage Publications.

Aronson, E., Willerman, B. & Floyd, J. (1966) The effect of a pratfall on increasing interpersonal attractiveness, *Psychonomic Science, 4*, 227-8.

Aronson, L.R. & Cooper, M.L. (1979) Amygdaloid hypersexuality in male cats re-examined. *Physiology and Behaviour, 22*, 257-65.

Arvey, R.D. & Campion, J.E. (1982) The employment interview: A summary and review of recent research. *Personnel Psychology, 35*, 281-322.

Asch, S.E. (1946) Forming impressions of personality. *Journal of Abnormal and Social Psychology, 41*, 258-90.

Asch, S.E. (1951) Effects of group pressure on the modification and distortion of judgements. In H. Guetzkow (Ed.), *Groups, leadership and men*. Pittsburgh: Carnegie Press.

Asch, S.E (1952) *Social psychology*. Englewood Cliffs, NJ: Prentice Hall.

Asch, S.E (1956) Studies of independence and submission to group pressure: 1: A minority of one against a unanimous majority. *Psychological Monographs, 70(9)*, (Whole no. 416).

Aschoff, J. & Wever, R. (1976) Human circadian rhythms: A multioscillatory system. *Federation Proceedings, 35*, 2326-32.

Atchley, R.C. (1985) *Social forces and ageing: An introduction to social gerontology*. Belmont, CA: Wadsworth.

Atkins, K.L. (1962) Advertising and store patronage. *Journal of Advertising Research*, December.

Atkinson, J.W. (1964) *An introduction to motivation*. Princeton, NJ: Van Nostrand.

Atkinson, R.C. (1975) Mnemotechnics in second-language learning. *American Psychologist, 30*, 821-828.

Atkinson, R.C. & Shriffrin, R.M. (1968) Human memory: a proposed system and its control processes. In K.W. Spence & J.T. Spence (Eds.) *The psychology of learning and motivation, Vol. 2*. London: Academic Press.

Atkinson, R.C. & Shiffrin, R.M. (1971) The control of short-term memory. *Scientific American, 224*, 82-90.

Ausubel, D.P. (1963) *The psychology of meaningful verbal learning*. New York: Grune & Stratton.

Ausubel, D.P. (1968) *Educational psychology: A cognitive view*. New York: Holt, Rinehart & Winston.

Ausubel, D.P. (1977) The facilitation of meaningful verbal learning in the classroom. *Educational psychologist, 12*, 162-78.

Ax, A.F. (1953) The physiological differentiation between fear and anger in humans. *Psychosomatic Medicine, 15*, 433-42.

Axline, V. (1947) *Play therapy*. New York: Ballantine Books.

Ayerhoff, F. & Abelson, F.P. (1976) ESP and ESB: Belief in personal success at mental telepathy. *Journal of Personality and Social Psychology, 34*, 240-7.

Azrin, N.H., Sneed, T.J. & Foxx, R.M. (1974) Dry-bed training: Rapid elimination of childhood enuresis. *Behaviour Research and Therapy, 11*, 147-56.

Back, K.W., Festinger, L., Hymovitch, B., Kelley, H.H., Schachter, S. & Thibaut, J.W. (1950) The methodology of studying rumour transmission. *Human Relations, 3*, 307-12.

Backman, C.W. & Secord, P.F. (1959) The effect of perceived liking on interpersonal attraction, *Human Relations, 12*, 379-84.

Baddeley, A.D. (1966) The influence of acoustic and semantic similarity on long term memory for word sequences. *Quarterly Journal of Experimental Psychology, 18*, 302-9.

Baddeley, A.D. (1982) Domains of recollection. *Psychological Review, 89*, 708-29.

Baddeley, A.D. (1986) *Working memory*. Oxford: Oxford University Press.

Bagley, C. & Verma, G.K. (1979) *Racial prejudice: The individual and society*. Farnborough: Saxon House.

Bahrick, H.P. (1984) Semantic memory content in permastore: Fifty years of memory for Spanish learned in school. *Journal of Experimental Psychology: General, 113*, 1-35.

Bahrick, H.P., Bahrick, P.O., & Wittinger, R.P. (1975) Fifty years of memory for names and faces: A cross-sectional approach. *Journal of Experimental Psychology: General, 104*, 54-75

Bales, R.F. (1950) *Interaction Process Analysis: A method for study of small groups*. Reading, MA: Addison-Wesley.

Bandura, A. (1977) Self-efficacy: Toward a unifying theory of behaviour change. *Psychological Review, 84*, 191-215.

Bandura, A. (1986) *Social foundations of thought and action: A social cognitive theory*. Englewood Cliffs, NJ: Prentice-Hall.

Bandura, A. (1989) Perceived self-agency in the exercise of personal agency. *The Psychologist, 2*, 411-24.

Bandura, A., Cioffi, D., Taylor, C.B. & Brouillard, M.E. (1988) Perceived self-efficacy in coping with cognitive stressors and opioid activation. *Journal of Personality and Social Psychology, 55*, 479-88.

Bandura, A. & Huston, A.C. (1961) Identification as a process of incidental learning. *Journal of Abnormal and Social Psychology, 63*, 311-8.

Bandura, A. & McDonald, F.J. (1953) Influence of social reinforcement and behaviour of models on children's moral judgements, *Journal of Abnormal and Social Psychology, 47*, 274-81.

Bandura, A., Ross, D., & Ross, S.A. (1961) Transmission of aggression through imitation of aggressive models. *Journal of Abnormal and Social Psychology, 63*, 575-82.

Bandura, A., Ross, D., & Ross, S.A. (1963) Imitation of film-mediated aggressive models. *Journal of Abnormal and Social Psychology, 66*, 3-11.

Bangert, R.L., Kulik, J.A. & Kulik, C.C. (1983) Individualised systems of instruction in secondary schools. *Review of Educational Research, 53*, 143-58.

Barash, D.P. (1982) *Sociobiology and behaviour* (2nd edition). New York: Elsevier.

Bard, P. (1929) The central representation of the sympathetic system. *Archives of Neurology and Psychiatry, 22*, 230-46.

Bard, P. (1934) On emotional expression after decortication with some remarks on certain theoretical views. *Psychological Review, 41*, 309-29.

Barnard, C.J. (1979) "Birds of a feather". *New Scientist, 13 August*

Baron, R.A. (1974) Aggression as a function of victim's pain cues, level of prior anger arousal, and exposure to an aggressive model, *Journal of Personality and Social Psychology, 24*, 117-24.

Baron, R.A. (1983) The control of human aggression: A strategy based on incompatible responses. In R.G. Geen & E.I. Donnerstein (Eds.), *Aggression: Theoretical and empirical reviews* (Vol. 2). New York: Academic Press.

Baron, R.A. & Byrne, D. (1991) *Social psychology: Understanding human interaction* (6th edition). London: Allyn & Bacon.

Baron, R.A. & Ransberger, V.M. (1978) Ambient temperature and the occurrence of collective violence: The "long hot summer" revisited. *Journal of Personality and Social Psychology, 36*, 351-60.

Baron, R.A., Russell, G.W. & Arms, R.L. (1985) Negative ions and behaviour: Impact on mood, memory and aggression among Type A and B persons. *Journal of Personality and Social Psychology, 48*, 746-54.

Baron, R.M., Mandel, D.R., Adams, C.A. & Griffen, L.M. (1976) Effects of social density in university residential environments. *Journal of Personality and Social Psychology, 34*, 434-446

Baron-Cohen, S. (1990) Autism: A specific cognitive disorder of "mind-blindness". *International Review of Psychiatry, 2*, 81-90.

Bartlett, F.C. (1932) *Remembering*. Cambridge: Cambridge University Press.

Bartholomew, K. (1990) Avoidance of intimacy: An attachment perspective. *Journal of Social and Personal Relationships, 7,* 141-78.

Bates, E., O'Connell, B. & Shore, C. (1987) Language and communication in infancy. In J.D. Osofsky (Ed.) *Handbook of infant development* (2nd edition). New York: Wiley.

Bates, E., Thal, D., Whitsell, K., Fenson, L. & Oakes, L. (1989) Integrating language and gesture in infancy. *Development Psychology, 25,* 1004-19.

Bateson, G., Jackson, D.D., Haley, J. & Weakland, J. (1956) Toward a theory of schizophrenia. *Behavioural Science, 1,* 251-64.

Bateson, P.P.G. (1964) An effect of imprinting on the perceptual development of domestic chicks. *Nature, 202,* 421-2.

Bateson, P.P.G. (1990) Is imprinting a special case? *Philosophical Transactions of the Royal Society, London, 203,* 125-31.

Baum, A. & Valins, S. (1977) *Architecture and social behaviour: Psychological studies of social density.* Hillsdale, NJ: Lawrence Erlbaum

Baumrind, D. (1971) Current patterns of parental authority. *Developmental Psychology Monographs, 4* (1,2)

Bavelas, A.(1950) Communication patterns in task-oriented groups, *Journal of the Acoustic Society of America, 22,* 725-30.

Baxter, L.A. (1984) Trajectories of relationship disengagement. *Journal of Social and Personal Relationships, 7,* 141-78.

Beaman, A.L., Barnes, P.J., Klentz, B. & McQuirk, B. (1978) Increasing helping rates through information dissemination: teaching pays. *Personality and Social Psychology Bulletin, 4,* 406-11.

Beck, A.T. (1988) Cognitive approaches to panic disorder: Theory and therapy. In S. Rachman & J.D. Maser (Eds.) *Panic: Psychological perspectives.* Hillsdale, NJ: Lawrence Erlbaum.

Beck, A.T., Ward, C.H., Mendelson, M., Mock, J.E. & Erbaugh, J.K. (1962) Reliability of psychiatric diagnoses II: A study of consistency of clinical judgements and ratings. *American Journal of Psychiatry, 119,* 351-7.

Bee, H.L. & Mitchel, S.K. (1980) *The developing person: A life-span approach.* New York: Harper & Row.

Beecher, H.K. (1956) Relationship of significance of wound to pain experienced. *Journal of the American Medical Association, 161,* 1609-13.

Beer, A.R. (1991) Urban design: The growing influence of environmental psychology. *Journal of Environmental Psychology, 11,* 359-71.

Belbin, E. & Belbin, R.M. (1972) *Problems in adult retraining.* London: Heinemann.

Bell, G. & French, R. (1950) Consistency of individual leadership position in small groups of varying membership, *Journal of Abnormal and Social Psychology, 45,* 764-5.

Belloc, N.B. & Breslow, L. (1972) Relationship of physical health status and health practices. *Preventative Medicine, 1,* 409-21.

Belsky, J. (1984) The determinants of parenting: A process model. *Child Development, 55,* 83-96.

Belsky, J. (1988) Infant day-care and socio-emotional development: The United States. *Journal of Child Psychology and Psychiatry, 29,* 397-406.

Bem, D.J. (1972) Self-perception theory. In L. Berkowitz (Ed.) *Advances in experimental social psychology* (Vol. 6). New York: Academic Press.

Bem, S.L. (1974) The measurement of psychological androgyny. J*ournal of Consulting and Clinical Psychology, 42,* 155-62.

Bem, S.L. (1983) Gender schema theory and its implications for child development: Raising children in a gender-aschematic society, *Signs: Journal of Women in Culture and Society, 8,* 598-616.

Bengston, V.L., Cuellar, J.B. & Ragan, P.K. (1977) Stratum contrasts and similarities in attitudes toward death. *Journal of Gerontology, 32,* 76-88.

Bennett, N. (1976) *Teaching styles and pupil progress.* London: Open Books.

Benson, P.L., Karabenick, S.A. & Lerner, R.M. (1976) Pretty pleases: The effects of physical attractiveness, race and sex on receiving help, *Journal of Experimental and Social Psychology, 12,* 409-15.

Bentley, D. & Hoy, R.R. (1974) The neurobiology of cricket song. *Scientific American, 231* (2), 34-44.

Benton, D. & Cook, R. (1991) Vitamin and mineral supplements improve intelligence scores and concentration. *Personality and Individual Differences, 12(11),* 1151-8.

Berko, J. (1958) The child's learning of English morphology. *Word, 14,* 150-77.

Berkowitz, L. (1962) *Aggression: A social psychological analysis.* New York: McGraw-Hill.

Berkowitz, L., Cochran, S., & Embree, M.C. (1981) Physical pain and the goal of aversively stimulated aggression. *Journal of Personality and Social Psychology, 40,* 687-700.

Berlin, B. (1972) Speculations on the growth of ethnobiological nomenclature. *Language in Society, 1,* 51-86.

Berlin, B. & Kay, P. (1969) *Basic colour terms: Their universality and evolution.* Berkeley, CA: University of California Press.

Berndt, T.J. (1982) The features and effects of friendship in early adolescence. *Child Development, 53,* 1447-60.

Bernstein, B. (1961) Social class and linguistic development. In A.H. Halsey, J. Flaud & C.A. Anderson (Eds.), *Education, economy and society.* London: Collier-Macmillan Ltd.

Bernstein, B. (1971) A socio-linguistic approach to socialisation: with some reference to educability. In D. Hymes and J.J. Gumperz (Eds.) *Directions in sociolinguistics.* New York: Holt, Rinehart & Winston.

Bettleheim, B. (1967) *The empty fortress.* New York: The Free Press.

Bexton, W.H., Heron, W., & Scott, T.H. (1954) Effects of decreased variation in the sensory environment, *Canadian Journal of Psychology, 8,* 70-6.

Bickman, L. (1974) Clothes make the person. *Psychology Today, 8(4),* 48-51.

Birren, J.E., Butler, R.N., Greenhouse, S.W., Sokoloff, L. & Yarrow, M.R. (Eds.) (1963) *Human ageing: A biological and behavioural study.* Publication number (HSM) 71-9051.

Birdwhistell, R.L. (1970) *Kinesics and context.* Philadelphia: University of Philadelphia Press.

Blackmore, S.J. (1992) Psychic experiences: Psychic illusions. *Skeptical Inquirer, 16,* 367-76.

Blake, R.R., Mouton, J.S. & Sloma, R.L. (1964) An actual case history of resolving intergroup conflict in union-management relations. In R.R. Blake, H.A. Shepard & J.S. Mouton, *Managing intergroup conflict in industry.* Houston, TX: Gulf.

Blakemore, C. (1988) *The mind machine.* London: BBC Publications.

Blakemore, C. & Cooper, G.F. (1970) Development of the brain depends on the visual environment. *Nature, 228,* 477-8.

Block, A.R., Kremer, E. & Gaylor, M. (1980) Behavioural treatment of chronic pain: The spouse as discriminative cue for pain behaviour. *Pain, 9,* 243-52.

Bloom, B.S. (1976) *Human characteristics and school learning.* New York: McGraw-Hill.

Bodmer, W.F. (1972) Race and I.Q.: The genetic background. In K. Richardson & D. Spears (Eds.) *Race, culture and intelligence.* Harmondsworth, Middlesex: Penguin.

Bogardus, E.S. (1925) Measuring social distance, *Journal of Applied Sociology, 9,* 299-308.

Borke, H. (1975) Piaget's mountains revisited: Changes in the egocentric landscape. *Developmental Psychology, 11,* 240-3.

Botwinick, J., West, R. & Storandt, M. (1978) Predicting death from behavioural test performance. *Journal of Gerontology, 33,* 755-62.

Bouchard, T.J. & McGue, M. (1981) Famial studies of intelligence: A review. *Science, 22,* 1055-9.

Bower, G.H. (1970) Imagery as a relational organiser in associative learning. *Journal of Verbal Learning and Verbal Behaviour, 9,* 529-33.

Bower, G.H. (1975) Cognitive psychology: An introduction. In W. Estes (Ed.) *Handbook of learning and cognitive processes* (Vol. 1). Hillsdale, NJ: Lawrence Erlbaum.

Bower, G.H., Clark, M., Lesgold, A., & Winzenz, D. (1969) Hierarchical retrieval schemes, in recall categorised word lists, *Journal of Verbal Learning and Verbal Behaviour, 8,* 323-43.

Bower, T.G.R. (1981) Cognitive development. In M. Roberts & J. Tamburrini (Eds.) *Child Development 0-5.* Edinburgh: Holmes McDougall.

Bower, T.G.R. & Wishart, J.G. (1972) The effects of motor skill on object permanence. *Cognition, 1(2),* 28-35.

Bowlby, J. (1946) *Forty-four juvenile thieves*. London: Balliére, Tindall & Cox.

Bowlby, J. (1951) *Maternal care and mental health*. Geneva: World Health Organization.

Bowlby, J. (1953) *Child care and the growth of love*. Harmondsworth, Middlesex: Penguin.

Bowlby, J. (1969) *Attachment and Loss. Vol. 1: Attachment*. London: Hogarth Press.

Bowlby, J. (1973) *Attachment and Loss. Vol. 2: Separation, anxiety and anger*. London: Hogarth Press.

Bowlby, J. (1980) *Attachment and Loss. Vol. 3: Loss, sadness and depression*. London: Hogarth Press.

Brackbill, Y., McManus, K. & Woodward, L. (1985) *Medication in maternity: Infants exposure and maternal information*. Ann Arbor, MI: University of Michigan Press.

Brady, J.V. (1958) Ulcers in executive monkeys. *Scientific American, 199*, 95-100.

Braine, M.D.S. (1963) The ontogeny of English phrase structures: The first phase. *Language, 39*, 1-13.

Bransford, J.D. & Johnson, M.K. (1972) Contextual prerequisites for understanding: Some investigations of comprehension and recall. *Journal of Verbal Learning and Verbal Behaviour, 11*, 717-26.

Brehm, J.W. (1956) Post-decision changes in desirability of alternatives. *Journal of Abnormal and Social Psychology, 52*, 384-9.

Breland, K. & Breland, M. (1961) The misbehaviour of organisms. *American Psychologist, 16*, 661-4.

British Psychological Society (1985) A code of conduct for psychologists. *Bulletin of the BPS, 38*, 41-3.

British Psychological Society (1990) *Ethical principles for conducting research with human participants*. Leicester: The British Psychological Society.

Broadbent, D.E. (1958) *Perception and communication*. Oxford: Pergamon.

Bromhall, H.S. & Winefield, A.H. (1990) A comparison of the affective well-being of young and middle-aged unemployed men matched for length of unemployment. *British Journal of Medical Psychology, 63*, 43-52.

Bromley, D.B. (1988) *Human ageing: An introduction to gerontology*. (3rd edition). Harmondsworth, Middlesex: Penguin.

Brophy, J.E. (1981) Teacher praise: A functional analysis. *Review of Educational Research, 51(1)*, 5-32.

Brown, G.W. and Harris, T. (1978) *Social origins of depression: A study of psychiatric disorders in women*. London: Tavistock.

Brown, R. (1970) *Psycholinguistics*. New York: Free Press.

Brown, R. (1973) *A first language: The early stages*. Cambridge, MA: Harvard University Press

Brown, R. (1986) *Social psychology: The second edition*. New York: The Free Press.

Brown, R., Cazden, C. & Bellugi, U. (1969) The child's grammar from I-III. In J.P. Hill (Ed.) *Minnesota Symposia on Child Psychology*, vol. 2. Minneapolis: University of Minnesota Press.

Brown, R. & Fraser, C. (1963) The acquisition of syntax. In C.N. Cofer & B. Musgrave (Eds.) *Verbal behaviour and learning: Problems and processes*. New York: McGraw-Hill.

Brown, R. & Kulik, J. (1977) Flashbulb memories. *Cognition, 5*, 73-99.

Brown, R. & Lenneberg, E.H. (1954) A study of language and cognition, *Journal of Abnormal Social Psychology, 49*, 454-62.

Brown, W.J. & Cody, M.J. (1991) Effects of a prosocial television soap opera in promoting women's status. *Human Communication Research, 18*, 114-42.

Browne, K. (1989) The naturalistic context of family violence and child abuse. In J. Archer & K. Browne (Eds.) *Human aggression: Naturalistic approaches*. London: Routledge.

Bruner J.S. & Mintern, A.L.C. (1955) Perceptual identification and perceptual organisation. *The Journal of General Psychology, 42*, 444-5.

Bruner, J.S. (1966) *Toward a theory of instruction*. Cambridge MA: Harvard University Press.

Bruner, J.S. (1983) *Child's talk*. New York: Norton.

Bruner, J.S., Goodnow, J.J. & Austin, G.A. (1956) *A study of thinking*. New York: Wiley

Bruner, J.S. & Kenney, H. (1966) *The development of the concepts of order and proportion in children*. New York: Wiley.

Bruner, J.S. & Minturn, A.L. (1955) Perceptual identification and perceptual organisation, *The Journal of General Psychology, 53*, 21-8..

Bryan, J.H. & Test, M.A. (1967) Models and helping: naturalistic studies in helping behaviour, *Journal of Personality and Social Psychology, 6*, 400-7.

Bryant, B., Harris, M. & Newton, D. (1980) *Children and minders*. London: Grant McIntyre.

Bryant, P.E. & Bradley, L. (1985) *Children's reading problems*. Oxford: Basil Blackwell.

Bryant, P.E. & Trabasso, T. (1971) Transitive inferences and memory in young children. *Nature, 232*, 456-8.

Buck, R. (1984) *The communication of emotion*. New York: Guilford.

Bull, R. (1983) *Body movement and interpersonal communication*. New York: John Wiley & Sons.

Burchinal, M., Lee, M. & Ramey, C. (1989) Type of day-care and preschool intellectual development in disadvantaged children. *Child Development, 60*, 128-37.

Burman, B. & Margolin, G. (1989) Marriage and health. *Advances, 6*, 51-8

Burns, R.B. (1966) Age and mental ability: re-testing with thirty-three years' interval. *British Journal of Educational Psychology, 36*, 116.

Burt, C. (1949) The structure of the mind: A review of the results of factor analysis. *British Journal of Educational Psychology, 19*, 176-99.

Burt, C. (1955) The evidence for the concept of intelligence. *British Journal of Educational Psychology, 25*, 158-77.

Burton, R.V. (1976) Honesty and dishonesty. In T. Lickona (Ed.) *Moral development and behaviour*. New York: Holt, Rinehart & Winston.

Butler, R.N. (1963) The life review: An interpretation of reminiscence in the aged. *Psychiatry, 26*, 65-76.

Byrne, D. & Clore, G.L. (1970) A reinforcement model of evaluative responses. *Personality: An International Journal, 1*, 103-8.

Byrne, D. & Nelson, D. (1965) Attraction as a linear function of proportion of positive performance. *Journal of Personality and Social Psychology, 1*, 659-63.

Calhoun, J.B. (1962) Population density and social pathology. *Scientific American, 206(2)*, 139-48.

Calhoun, J.B. (1971) Space and the strategy of life. In A.H. Esser (Ed.) *Environment and behaviour: The use of space by animals and men*. New York: Plenum.

Campbell, H.J. (1973) *The pleasure areas*. London: Methuen.

Cannon, W.B. (1927) The James-Lange theory of emotion: A critical examination and an alternative. *American Journal of Psychology, 39*, 106-24.

Cannon, W.B. (1929) *Bodily changes in pain, hunger, fear and rage: An account of recent researches into the function of emotional excitement*. New York: Appleton-Century-Crofts.

Cannon, W.B. (1929) Organisation for physiological homeostasis. *Physiological Reviews, 9*, 399-431.

Cannon, W.B. (1942) "Voodoo" death. *American Anthropologist, 44*, 169-81.

Cannon, W.B. & Washburn, A.L. (1912) An explanation of hunger. *American Journal of Psychology, 29*, 441-54.

Carlyle, T. (1841) *On heroes, hero-worship, and the heroic*. London: Fraser.

Carmichael, L., Hogan, P. & Walter, A. (1932) An experimental study of the effect of language on the reproduction of visually perceived forms. *Journal of Experimental Psychology, 15*, 73-86

Carpenter, P.A. & Dahneman, M. (1981) Lexical retrieval and error recovery in reading: A model based on eye fixations. *Journal of Verbal Learning and Verbal Behaviour, 20*, 137-160

Carroll, J.B. & Casangrande, J.B. (1958) The function of language classifications in behaviour. In E.E. Maccoby, T.M. Newcombe & E.L. Hartley (Eds.), *Readings in social psychology* (3rd edition). New York: Holt, Rinehart & Winston.

Carskadon, M.A. & Dement, W.C. (1975) Sleep studies on a 90 minute day. *Electroencephalography and Clinical Neurophysiology, 22*, 11-21.

Carson, R.C. (1991) Dilemmas in the pathway of the DSM-IV. Special Issue: Diagnoses, dimensions, and DSM-IV: The science of classification. *Journal of Abnormal Psychology, 100(3)*, 302-7.

Caserta, M.S. & Lund, D.A. (1992) Bereavement stress and coping among older adults: Expectations versus the actual experience. *Omega Journal of Death and Dying, 25*, 33-45

Cattell, R.B. (1963) Theory of fluid and crystallised intelligence: A critical experiment. *Journal of Educational Psychology, 54*, 1-22.

Cattell, R.B. (1965) *The scientific analysis of personality*. Harmondsworth, Middlesex: Penguin.

Cattell, R.B. & Nesselrode, J.R. (1967) Likeness and completeness theories examined by 16 personality factor measures on stable and unstable married couples. *Journal of Personality and Social Psychology, 7*, 351-61.

Ceraso, J. (1967) The interference theory of forgetting. *Scientific American, 217*, 117-24.

Cerletti, U. & Bini, L. (1938) L'Electroshock. *Archivio Generale di Neurologica e Psichiatria e Psicoanalisi, 19*, 266-8.

Chandler, M.J. (1973) Egocentrism and antisocial behaviour: the assessment and training of social perspective taking skills. *Developmental Psychology, 9*, 326-332.

Chellin, A. (1985) *Marriage, divorce and remarriage*. Cambridge, MA: Harvard University Press.

Cherlin, A.J., Furstenberg, F.F., Chase-Lansdale, P.L. & Kiernan, K.E. (1991) Longitudinal effects of divorce on children in Great Britain and the United States. *Science, 252*, 1386-9.

Cherry, E.C. (1953) Some experiments on the recognition of speech with one and two ears. *Journal of the Acoustical Society of America, 25*, 975-9.

Chesney, M.A. & Rosenman, R. (1980) Type A behaviour in a work setting. In C.L. Cooper & R. Payne (Eds.) *Current concerns in occupational stress*, Chichester: Wiley.

Chiriboga, D.A. & Thurnher, M. (1980) Marital lifestyles and adjustment to separation. *Journal of Divorce, 3*, 379-90.

Chomsky, N. (1957) *Syntactic structures*. The Hague: Mouton.

Chomsky, N. (1959) Review of Skinner's *Verbal Behaviour*. *Language, 35*, 26-58.

Chomsky, N. (1965) *Aspects of a theory of syntax*. Cambridge, MA: MIT Press.

Christiansen, K.O. (1977) A review of studies of criminality among twins. In S.A. Mednick & K.O. Christiansen (Eds.) *Biosocial bases of criminal behaviour*. New York: Gardner Press.

Christie, R. & Cook, P. (1958) A guide to the published literature relating to the authoritarian personality, *Journal of Psychology, 45*, 171-99.

Chukovsky, K. (1963) *From two to five*. Berkeley, CA: University of California Press.

Cialdini, R.B. (1985) *Influence: Science and practice*. Glenview, IL: Scott, Foresman.

Cialdini, R.B., Vincent, J.E., Lewis, S.K., Catalan, J., Wheeler, D. and Darby, B.L. (1975). Reciprocal concessions procedure for inducing compliance: The door-in-the-face technique. *Journal of Personality and Social Psychology, 31*, 206-15.

Clare, A. (1980) *Psychiatry in dissent*. London: Tavistock.

Clare, John in J. Reeves (Ed.) *Selected poems of John Clare*. London: Heinemann, 1954.

Clark, H.H. & Clark, E.V. (1977) *Psychology and language: An introduction to psycholinguistics*. San Diego: Harcourt Brace Jovanovich.

Clark, R.D. III & Word, L.E. (1972) Why don't bystanders help? Because of ambiguity? *Journal of Personality and Social Psychology, 24*, 392-400.

Clarke, A.C. (1952) An examination of the operation of residual propinquity as a factor in mate selection. *American Sociological Review, 27*, 17-22.

Clarke, A.M. & Clarke, A.D.B. (1976) *Early experience: Myth and evidence*. New York: Free Press.

Clarke-Stewart, A. (1973) Interactions between mothers and their young children: Characteristics and consequences. *Monographs for the Society of Research in Child Development, 38* (serial no. 153).

Clausen, J.A. (1975) The social meaning of differential physical maturation. In D.E. Drugastin & G.H. Elder (Eds.) *Adolescence in the life cycle*. New York: Halsted Press.

Clayton, P.J., Halikes, J.A. & Maurice, W.L. (1971) The bereavement of the widowed. *Diseases of the Nervous System, 32*, 597-604.

Cline, V.B., Croft, R.G. & Corrier, S. (1973) Desensitisation of children to television violence. *Journal of Personality and Social Psychology, 27*, 360-5.

Clulow, C.F. (1990) Divorce as bereavement: Similarities and differences. *Family and Conciliation Courts Review, 28*, 19-22.

Clutton-Brock, T.H. & Albon, S.D. (1979) The roaring of red deer and the evolution of honest advertisement. *Behaviour, 69*, 145-70.

Cogan, R., Cogan, D., Waltz, W. & McCue, M. (1987) Effects of laughter and relaxation on discomfort thresholds. *Journal of Behavioural Medicine, 10*, 139-44.

Cohen, C.E. (1981) Person categories and social perception: Testing some boundaries of the processing effects of prior knowledge. *Journal of Personality and Social Psychology, 40*, 441-52.

Cohen, J.B. (1968) The role of personality in consumer behaviour. In H.H. Kassarjian & T.S. Robertson (eds.) *Perspectives in consumer behaviour*. Scott Foresman.

Cohen, S. (1965) *Folk devils and moral panic*. London: Paladin.

Cohen, S. (1980) Aftereffects of stress on human performance and social behaviour: A review of research and theory. *Psychological Bulletin, 87*, 578-604.

Cohen, S., Glass, D.C. & Singer, J.E. (1973) Apartment noise, auditory discrimination and reading ability in children. *Journal of Experimental Social Psychology, 9*, 407-22.

Coile, C. & Miller, N.E. (1984) How radical animal activists try to mislead humane people. *American Psychologist, 39*, 700-1.

Colby, A. & Kohlberg, L. (1987) *The measurement of moral judgement*: Vol. 1: *Theoretical foundations and research validation*. Cambridge: Cambridge University Press.

Colby, A., Kohlberg, L., Gibbs, J., & Lieberman, M. (1983) A longitudnal study of moral judgement. *Monographs of the Society for Research in Child Development, 48*, nos. 1-2.

Colby, K.M., Hilf, F.D., Weber, S., & Kraemer, H.C. (1972) Turing-like indistinguishability tests for the validation of a computer simulation of paranoid processes. *Artificial Intelligence, 3*.

Cole, P.M. (1986) Children's spontaneous control of facial expression. *Child Development, 57*, 1309-21.

Coleman, J.C. (1961) *The adolescent society*. London: Methuen.

Coleman, J.C. (1980) *The nature of adolescence*. London: Methuen.

Collins, A.M. & Quillian, M.R. (1969) Retrieval time from semantic memory. *Journal of Verbal Learning and Verbal Behaviour, 8*, 240-8.

Collins, B.E. & Raven, B.H. (1969) Group structure: Attraction, coalitions, communication and power. In G. Lindzey & E. Aronson (Eds.) *The handbook of social psychology* (2nd ed., Vol. 4). Reading, MA: Addison-Wesley.

Collins, J.L. (1982) Self-efficacy and ability in achievement behaviour. Cited in N. Hayes *Principles of social psychology*. Hillsdale, NJ: Lawrence Erlbaum.

Collins, L.J., Ingoldsby, B.B., & Dellman, M.M. (1984) Sex-role stereotyping in children's literature: A change from the past. *Childhood Education, 60 (4)*, 278-85.

Colquhuon, W.P. (1970) Circadian rhythms, mental efficiency, shift work. *Ergonomics, 13 (5)*, 558-60.

Comstock, G. & Strasburger, V.C. (1990) Deceptive appearances: Television violence and aggressive behaviour. Conference: Teens and television (1988, Los Angeles, California). *Journal of Adolescent Health Care, 11*, 31-44.

Condry, J. & Condry, S. (1976) *Sex differences: A study in the eye of the beholder*. *Child Development, 47*, 812-9.

Conrad, R. (1964) Acoustic confusions in immediate memory. *British Journal of Psychology, 55*, 75-84.

Cooley, C.H. (1902) *Human nature and the social order*. New York: Scribner.

Cooper, C.L. & Marshall, J. (1976) Occupational sources of stress: A review of the literature relating to coronary heart disease and mental ill-health. *Journal of Occupational Psychology, 49*, 11-28.

Cooper, R.M. & Zubek, J.P. (1958) Effects of enriched and restricted early environments on the learning ability of bright and dull rats. *Canadian Journal of Psychology, 12*, 159-64.

Coopersmith, S. (1968) Studies in self-esteem. *Scientific American, 218(2)*, 96-106.

Cornwell, D. & Hobbs, S. (1976) The strange saga of Little Albert, *New Society, March*, 602-4.

Cottrell, N.B., Wack, K.L., Sekerak, G.J. & Rittle, R. (1968) Social facilitation of dominant responses by the presence of an audience and the mere presence of others. *Journal of Personality and Social Psychology, 9*, 245-50.

Cowen, E.L. & Bobrove, P.H. (1966) Marginality of disability and adjustment. *Perceptual and Motor Skills, 23*, 869-70.

Cox, T. (1975) The nature and management of stress. *New Behaviour, September 25*, 493-5.

Craik, F.I.M. & Lockhart, R.S. (1972) Levels of processing: A framework for memory research, *Journal of Verbal Learning and Verbal Behaviour, 11*, 671-84.

Creighton, S. (1984) *Trends in child abuse 1977-1982*. London: NSPCC.

Crick, F. & Mitchison, G. (1986) The function of REM sleep. *Nature, 304*, 111-4.

Crisp, A.H., Callander, J.S., Halek, C. & Hsu, L.G. (1992) Long-term mortality in anorexia nervosa: A 20-year follow-up of the St. George's and Aberdeen cohorts. *British Journal of Psychiatry, 161*, 104-7.

Crittenden, P.M. (1988) Distorted patterns of relationship in maltreating families: The role of internal representation models. *Journal of Reproductive and Infant Psychology, 6*, 183-99.

Cross, H.A., Halcomb, C.G. & Matter, W.W. (1967) Imprinting or exposure learning in rats given early auditory stimulation. *Psychonomic Sciences, 7*, 233-4.

Crossman, E.R.F.W. & Szafran, J. (1956) Changes with age in the speed of information intake and discrimination. *Experimentia Supplement, 4*, 128-35.

Crow, T.J. (1984) A re-evaluation of the viral hypothesis: Is psychosis the result of retroviral integration at a site close to the cerebral dominance gene? *British Journal of Psychiatry, 145*, 243-53.

Crue, B.L. Jr. & Carregal, E.J.A. (1975) Pain begins in the dorsal horn - with a proposed classification of the primary senses. In B.L. Crue, Jr. (Ed.) *Pain: Research and treatment*. New York: Academic Press.

Crutchfield, R.S. (1955) Conformity and character. *American Psychologist, 10*, 191-8.

Cullingford, C. (1984) *Children and television*. Aldershot: Gower.

Cumberbatch, G. (1987) *The portrayal of violence on British television*. London: BBC publications.

Cumberbatch, G., Jones, I. & Lee, M. (1988) Measuring violence on television. Special Issue: Violence on television. *Current Psychology Research and Reviews, 7*, 10-25.

Cumming, E. & Cumming, J. (1957) *Closed ranks: An experiment in mental health*. Cambridge, MA: Harvard University Press.

Cumming, E. & Henry, W.E. (1961) *Growing old: The process of disengagement*. New York: Basic Books.

Cunningham, M.R. (1979) Weather, mood and helping behaviour: Quasi-experiments with the sunshine Samaritan. *Journal of Personality and Social Psychology, 37*, 1947-56.

Curtiss, S. (1977) *Genie: A psycholinguistic study of a modern-day 'wild child'*. London: Academic Press.

Damon, W. (1977) *The social world of the child*. San Francisco: Jossey-Bass.

Danner, F.W. & Day, M.C. (1977) Eliciting formal operations. *Child Development, 48*, 1600-6.

Darley, J.M. & Batson, C.D. (1973) "From Jerusalem to Jericho": A study of situational and dispositional variables in helping behaviour. *Journal of Personality and Social Psychology, 27*, 100-8.

Darley, S.A. & Katz, I. (1973) Heart rate changes in children as a function of test versus game instructions and test anxiety. *Child Development, 44*, 784-9

Darwin, C.A. (1871) *The descent of man and selection in relation to sex*. London: John Murray.

Darwin, C.A. (1872) *The expression of emotions in man and the animals*. John Murray: London.

Darwin, C.A. (1877) A biographical sketch of an infant. *Mind, 2*, 385-99.

Davies, N.B. & Houston, A.I. (1984) Territory economics. In J.R. Krebs & N.B. Davies (Eds.) *Behavioural ecology*. Oxford: Blackwell Scientific Publications.

Davis, K. (1947) Final note on a case of extreme isolation. *American Journal of Sociology, 52*, 432-7.

Davis, M.H. & Harvey, J.C. (1992) Declines in major league batting performance as a function of game pressure: A drive theory analysis. *Journal of Applied Social Psychology, 22*, 714-35.

Dawkins, R. (1976) *The selfish gene*. Oxford: Oxford University Press.

Dawkins, R. & Krebs, J.R. (1978) Animal signals: information or manipulation? In J.R. Krebs & N.B. Davies (Eds.) *Behavioural ecology*. Oxford: Blackwell Scientific Publications.

Dawson, D. & Campbell, S.S. (1991) Time exposure to bright light improves sleep and alertness during simulated night shifts. *Sleep, 14*, 511-6

Dearborn, W.F. & Rothney, J. (1941) *Predicting the child's development*. Cambridge, MA: Sci-Art Pub.

Deaux, K. (1984) From individual differences to social categories: An analysis of a decade's research on gender. *American Psychologist, 39*, 105-16.

deBono, E. (1970) *Lateral thinking: A textbook of creativity*. London: Ward Lock Educational.

DeCasper, A.J. & Fifer, W.P. (1980) Of human bonding: Newborns prefer their mothers' voices. *Science, 208*, 1174-6.

DeCasper, A.J. & Spence, M.J. (1986) Prenatal maternal speech influences newborns' perception of speech sounds. *Infant Behaviour and Development, 9*, 133-50.

deCharms, R. (1976) *Enhancing motivation: Change in the classroom*. New York: Halsted.

DeFleur, M.L. & Westie, F.R. (1958) Verbal attitudes and overt acts: An experiment on the salience of attitudes. *American Sociological Review, 23*, 667-73.

Delgado, J.M.R. (1969) *Physical control of the mind*. New York: Harper & Row.

Dell, G.S. (1986) A spreading-activation theory of retrieval in sentence production. *Psychological Review, 93*, 283-321.

DeLongis, A., Coyne, J.C., Dakof, G., Folkman, S. & Lazarus, R.S. (1982) The impact of daily hassles, uplifts and major life events to health status. *Health Psychology, 1*, 119-36.

Dement, W. (1960) The effect of dream deprivation. *Science, 131*, 1705-7.

Dement, W. (1972) *Some must watch while some must sleep*. San Francisco: W.H. Freeman.

Dement, W. & Kleitman, N. (1957) The relation of eye movements during sleep to dream activity: An objective method for studying dreaming. *Journal of Experimental Psychology, 53*, 339-46.

Dennis, W. (1960) Causes of retardation amongst institutional children: Iran. *Journal of Genetic Psychology, 96*, 47-59.

Deregowski, J. (1972) Pictorial perception and culture. *Scientific American, 227*, 82-8.

Dermer, M. & Thiel, D.L. (1975) When beauty may fail. *Journal of Personality and Social Psychology, 31*, 1168-76.

Deutsch, J.A. & Deutsch, D. (1963) Attention: Some theoretical considerations, *Psychological Review, 70*, 80-90.

Deutsch, J.A., Young, W.G. & Kalogeris, T.J. (1978) *The stomach signals satiety. Science, 201*, 165-7.

Deutsch, M. & Collins, M.E. (1951) *Interracial housing: A psychological evaluation of a social experiment*. Minneapolis, MN: University of Minnesota Press.

Deutsch, M. & Krauss, R.M. (1960) The effects of threat upon interpersonal bargaining. *Journal of Abnormal and Social Psychology, 61*, 181-9.

Deutsch, M. & Solomon, L. (1959) Reactions to evaluations by others as influenced by self-evaluations. *Sociometry, 22*, 93-112.

deVilliers, P.A. & deVilliers, J.G. (1979) *Early language*. Cambridge, MA: Harvard University Press.

DeVries, R. (1969) Constancy of generic identity in the years three to six. *Monographs of the Society for Child Development, 34* (Serial No. 127).

Diamond, M. (1982) Sexual identity, monozygotic twins reared in discordant sex-roles and a BBC follow up. *Archives of Sexual Behaviour, 11*, 181-6.

Dicara, L.V. & Miller, N.E. (1968) Changes in heart rate instrumentally learned by curarised rats as avoidance responses. *Journal of Comparative and Physiological Psychology, 65*, 8-12.

Diener, C.I. & Dweck, C.S. (1980) An analysis of learned helplessness: II. The processing of success. *Journal of Personality and Social Psychology, 39*, 940-52.

Diener, E., Fraser, S.C., Beaman, A.L. & Kelem, R. (1976) Effects of deindividuation on stealing among Halloween trick or treaters. *Journal of Personality and Social Psychology, 33*, 178-83.

Dilger, W.C. (1962) The behaviour of lovebirds. *In Psychobiology: Readings from Scientific American*. San Francisco: W.H. Freeman & Co.

Dipboye, R.L. & Wiley, J.W. (1978) Reactions of male raters to interviewee self-presentation style and sex; extensions of previous research. *Journal of Vocational Behaviour, 13*, 192-203.

Dobson, C.B., Hardy, M., Heyes, S., Humphreys, A. & Humphreys, P. (1981) *Understanding psychology*. London: Weidenfeld & Nicolson.

Dollard, J.R., Doob, L.W., Miller, N.E., Mowrer, O.H. & Sears, R.R. (1939) *Frustration and aggression*. New Haven, CN: Yale University Press.

Doms, M. & Avermaet, E. Van (1981) The conformity effect: A timeless phenomenon? *Bulletin of the British Psychological Society, 34*, 383-5.

Donaldson, M. (1978) *Children's minds*. London: Fontana.

Douglas, J.W.B. & Ross, J.M. (1964) Age of puberty related to educational ability, attainment and school leaving age. *Journal of Child Psychology and Psychiatry, 5*, 185-96.

Dove, A. (1968) The chitling test. *Newsweek, July 15*.

Dowd, J.J. (1981) Conversation and social exchange: Managing identities in old age. *Human Relations, 34*, 541-53.

Dreyfus, H.L. (1979) *What computers can't do*, (2nd edition). New York: Harper Row.

Duberman, L. (1973) Step-kin relationships. *Journal of Marriage and the Family, 35*, 283-92.

Dubos, R. (1965) *Man adapting*. New Haven, CN: Yale University Press.

Duck, S.W. (1973) *Personal relationships and personal constructs: A study of friendship formation*. London: Wiley.

Duck, S.W. (1982) A topography of relationship disengagement and dissolution. In S.W. Duck (Ed.) *Personal relationships 4: Dissolving personal relationships*. London: Academic Press.

Duck, S.W. (1984) A perspective on the repair of personal relationships: Repair of what, when? In S.W. Duck (Ed.) *Personal relationships 5: Dissolving personal relationships*. London: Academic Press.

Duck, S.W. (1992) *Human relationships* (2nd edition). London: Sage Publications.

Duck, S.W. & Pond, K. (1989) Friends, Romans, countrymen: Lend me your retrospective data : Rhetoric and reality in personal relationships. In C. Hendrick (Ed.) *Review of social psychology and personality (10): Close relationships*. Newbury Park, CA: Sage.

Duncan, S.L. (1976) Differential social perception and attribution of intergroup violence: Testing the lower limits of stereotyping of blacks. *Journal of Personality and Social Psychology, 34*, 590-8.

Duncker, K. (1945) On problem solving. *Psychological Monographs, 58* (whole no. 270).

Dunn, R. & Griggs, S.A. (1988) *Learning styles : Quiet revolution in American secondary schools*. Reston, VA: National Association of Secondary School Principles.

Durkin, K. (1985) *Television, sex roles and children*. Milton Keynes: Open University Press.

Dutton, D.G. & Aron, A.P. (1974) Some evidence for heightened sexual attraction under conditions of high anxiety. *Journal of Personality and Social Psychology, 30*, 510-7.

Dweck, C.S. (1975) The role of expectations and attributions in the alleviation of learned helplessness. *Journal of Personality and Social Psychology, 31*, 674-85.

Dworksky, J.P. (1981) *Introduction to child development*. St Paul, MN: West Publishing Co.

Dyck, P.J., Lambert, E.H. & O'Brien, P. (1976) Pain in peripheral neuropathy related to size and rate of fibre degeneration. In M. Weisenberg & B. Tursky (Eds.) *Pain: New perspectives in therapy and research*. New York: Plenum Press.

Eagly, A.H. (1978) Sex differences in influenceability. *Psychological Bulletin, 85*, 86-116.

Eakins, B.W. & Eakins, R.G. (1978) *Sex differences in human communication*. Boston: Houghton Mifflin.

Eccles, J.S., Midgley, C., Wigfield, A., Buchanan, C.M. et al. (1993) Development during adolescence: The impact of stage-environment fit on young adolescents' experiences in schools and in families. *American Psychologist, 48*, 90-101.

Edwards, W. (1961) Probability learning in 1000 trials. *Journal of Experimental Psychology, 62*, 385-94.

Egan, D.W. & Greeno, J.G. (1974) Theories of rule induction: Knowledge acquired in concept learning, serial pattern learning and problem solving. In W.G. Gregg (Ed.), *Knowledge and cognition*. Hillsdale, NJ: Lawrence Erlbaum.

Egeland, B., Gerhard, D.S., Pauls, D.L., Sussex, J.N., Kidd, K.K., Allen, C.R., Hostetter, A.M. & Housman, D.E. (1987) Bipolar affective disorders linked to DNA markers on chromosome 11. *Nature, 325*, 783-87.

Egeland, B., Jacobitz, D. & Sroufe, L.A. (1988) Breaking the cycle of abuse. *Child Development, 59*, 1080-8.

Egeland, B. & Sroufe, L.A. (1981) Attachment and early maltreatment. *Child Development, 52*, 44-52.

Ehrlich, D., Guttman, I, Schînbach, P. & Mills, J. (1957) Post-decision exposure to relevant information. *Journal of Abnormal and Social Psychology, 54*, 98-102.

Eibl-Eibesfeldt, I. (1970) *Ethology: The biology of behaviour*. New York: Holt, Rinehart & Winston.

Ekman, P. & Friesen, W.V. (1969) Non-verbal leakage and clues to deception. *Psychiatry, 32*, 88-106.

Ekman, P. & Friesen, W.V. (1971) Constants across cultures in the face and emotion. *Journal of Personality and Social Psychology, 17*, 124-9.

Ekman, P. Friesen, W.V. & Tomkins, S.S. (1971) Facial affect scoring technique: A first validity study. *Semiotica, 3*, 37-58.

Ekman, P., Levenson, R.W. & Frieson, W.V. (1983) Autonomic nervous system activity distinguishes among emotions. *Science, 221*, 1208-10.

Elder, G.H. Jr. (1980) *Family structure and socialisation*. New York: Arno Press.

Ellis, A. (1962) *Reason and emotion in psychotherapy*. New York: Lyle Stuart.

Ellis, G.T. & Sekgra, F. (1972) The effect of aggressive cartoons on the behaviour of first-grade children. *Journal of Psychology, 81*, 37-43.

Empson, J. (1989) *Sleep and dreaming*. London: Faber and Faber.

Enander, A. (1987) Effects of moderate cold on performance of psychomotor and cognitive tasks. *Ergonomics, 30*, 1431-45.

Erikson, E.H. (1963) *Childhood and society* (2nd edition). New York: Norton.

Erikson, E.H. (1980) *The life cycle completed: A review*. New York: Norton.

Erikson, M. (1968) The inhumanity of ordinary people. *International Journal of Psychiatry, 6*, 278-9.

Erlenmeyer-Kimling, L. & Jarvik, L.F. (1963) Genetics and intelligence: A review. *Science, 142*, 1477-9.

Eron, L.D. (1987) The development of aggressive behaviour from the perspective of a developing behaviourism. *American Psychologist, 42*, 435-42.

Eron, L.D., Huesmann, L.R., Lefkowitz, M.M. & Walder, L.O. (1972) Does television violence cause aggression in children? *American Psychologist, 27*, 253-63.

Ervin-Tripp, S. (1964) An analysis of the interaction of language, topic and listener. *American Anthropologist, 66*, 94-100.

Evans, C. (1984) *Landscapes of the night: How and why we sleep*. New York: Viking.

Evans, G.W. & Jacobs, S.V. (1981) Air pollution and human behaviour. *Journal of Social Issues, 37*, 95-125.

Eysenck, H.J. (1947) *Dimensions of personality*. London: Routledge & Kegan Paul.

Eysenck, H.J. (1952) The effects of psychotherapy: An evaluation. *Journal of Counselling Psychology, 16*, 319-24.

Eysenck, H.J. (1954) *The psychology of politics*. London: Routledge Kegan Paul.

Eysenck, H.J. (1963) Biological basis of personality, *Nature, 199*, 1031-4.

Eysenck, H.J. (1973) *The inequality of man*. London: Temple Smith.

Eysenck, H.J. & Eysenck, S.B.G. (1975) *Manual of the Eysenck personality questionnaire*. London: Hodder & Stoughton.

Eysenck, M.W. & Keane, M.J. (1990) *Cognitive Psychology*. Hove, Sussex: Lawrence Erlbaum.

Fabrega, H. (1992) Diagnosis interminable: Toward a culturally sensitive DSM-IV. *Journal of Nervous and Mental Disease, 180*, 5-7.

Fagot, B.I. (1985) Beyond the reinforcement principle: another step toward understanding sex role development, *Developmental Psychology, 21*, 1097-1104.

Fantz, R.L. (1961) The origin of form perception. *Scientific American, 204*(5), 66-72.

Felipe, N.J. & Sommer, R. (1966) Invasions of personal space. *Social problems, 14*, 206-14.

Festinger, L. (1957) *A theory of cognitive dissonance*. Stanford, CA: Stanford University Press.

Festinger, L. & Carlsmith, J.M. (1959) Cognitive consequences of forced compliance. *Journal of Abnormal and Social Psychology, 58*, 203-10.

Festinger, L., Riecken, H.W. & Schachter, S. (1956) *When prophecy fails*. Minneapolis, MN: University of Minnesota Press.

Festinger, L., Schachter, S. & Back, K. (1950) *Social pressure in informal groups: A study of human factors in housing*. New York: Harper.

Fidell, L.S. (1970) Empirical verification of sex discrimination in hiring practices in psychology. *American Psychologist, 25*, 1094-8.

Fiedler, F.E. (1965) Engineer the job to fit the manager. *Harvard Business Review, 43*, 115.

Fiedler, F.E. (1971) Validation and extension of the contingency model of leadership effectiveness: A review of empirical findings. *Psychological Bulletin, 76*, 128-48.

Fink, M. (1980) A neuroendocrine theory of convulsive therapy. *Trends in Neurosciences, 3*, 25-7.

Fink, M. (1985) Convulsive therapy: Fifty years of progress. *Convulsive therapy, 1*, 204-16.

Fishbein, H.D. (1984) *The psychology of infancy and childhood: Evolutionary and cross-cultural perspectives*. Hillsdale, NJ: Lawrence Erlbaum.

Fishbein, M. & Ajzen, I. (1975) *Belief, attitude, intention, and behaviour: An introduction to theory and research*. Reading, MA: Addison-Wesley.

Fisher, R.A. (1930) *The genetical theory of natural selection* (2nd edition, 1958). Oxford: Oxford University Press.

Fishkin, J., Keniston, K. & Mackinnon, C. (1973) Moral reasoning and political ideology. *Journal of Personality and Social Psychology, 27*, 109-19.

Fitts, P.M. (1962) Factors in complex skills training. In R. Glaser (Ed.) *Training research and education*. Pittsburgh: University of Pittsburgh.

Flanagan, D. (1988) *Flanagan's version: A spectator's guide to science on the eve of the 21st century*. New York: Knopf.

Flavell, J.H. (1977) *Cognitive Psychology*. Englewood Cliffs, NJ: Prentice-Hall.

Floody, O.R. (1968) Hormones and aggression in female animals. In B.B. Suare (Ed.) *Hormones and aggressive behaviour*. New York: Plenum Press.

Foa, U.G. (1961) Convergences in the structure of interpersonal behaviour. *Psychological Review, 68*, 341-53.

Fodor, E.N. (1972) Delinquency and susceptibility to social influence among adolescents as a function of level of moral development. *Journal of Social Psychology, 86*, 257-60.

Fogelman, K. (1976) *Britain's sixteen year olds*. London: National Children's Bureau.

Folkard, S., Hume, K.I., Minors, D.S. Waterhouse, J.M. & Watson, F.L. (1985) Independence of the circadian rhythm in alertness from the sleep/wake cycle. *Nature, 313*, 678-9.

Fonagy, P. & Higgitt, A. (1984) *Personality theory and clinical practice*. London: Methuen.

Forsyth, D.R. (1987) *Social Psychology*. Monterey, CA: Brooks/Cole Publishing Co.

Fouts, R.S. (1973) Acquisition and testing of gestural signs in four young chimpanzees. *Science, 180*, 978-80.

Fox, N. (1977) Attachment of Kibbutz infants to mother and metapelet. *Child Development, 48*, 1228-39.

Foxall, G.R. (1980) *Consumer behaviour*. London: Routledge.

Fradkin, B. & Firestone, P. (1986) Pre-menstrual tension, expectancy and mother-child relations. *Journal of Behavioural Medicine, 9*, 245-59.

Fraiberg, S. (1975) The development of human attachments in infants blind from birth. *Merrill-Palmer Quarterly, 21*, 315-334.

Frank, F. (1966) Perception and language in conservation. In J.S. Bruner (Ed.) *Studies in cognitive growth*. New York: Wiley.

Freedman, J.L. (1975) *Crowding and human behaviour*. San Francisco: W.H. Freeman.

Freedman, J.L. & Fraser, S.C. (1966) Compliance without pressure: The foot-in-the-door technique. *Journal of Personality and Social Psychology, 4*, 195-202.

Freeman, D. (1984) *Margaret Mead and Samoa: The making and unmaking of an anthropological myth*. Cambridge, MA: Harvard University Press.

Freud, A. & Dann, S. (1951) An experiment in group upbringing. *Psychoanalytic Study of the Child, 6*, 127-68.

Freud, S. (1900) The interpretation of dreams. In J. Strachey (Ed. and trans.) *The complete psychological works: The standard edition* (vol. 4). New York: Norton, 1976.

Freud, S. (1901) *Psychopathology of everyday life*. London: Hogarth Press. Republished 1976 Harmondsworth, Middlesex: Penguin.

Freud, S. (1909a) Analysis of phobia in a five-year-old boy. In J. Strachey (Ed. and trans.) *The complete psychological works: The standard edition* (vol. 10). New York: Norton, 1976.

Freud, S. (1909b) Notes upon a case of obcessional neurosis. In J. Strachey (Ed. and trans.) *The complete psychological works: The standard edition* (vol. 10). New York: Norton, 1976.

Freud, S. (1920) *Beyond the pleasure principle*. (1975 edition) New York: Norton.

Freud, S. (1940) An outline of psychoanalysis. *International Journal of Psychoanalysis, 21*, 27-84.

Friedman, L.A. & Kimball, A.W. (1986) Coronary heart disease mortality and alcohol consumption in Framington. *American Journal of Epidemiology, 124*, 481-9.

Friedman, M. & Rosenman, R.H. (1959) Association of specific overt behaviour pattern with blood and cardiovascular findings. *Journal of the American Medical Association, 169*, 1286-96.

Friedman, M. & Rosenman, R.H. (1974) *Type A behaviour and your heart*. New York: Knopf.

Friedrich, L.K. & Stein, A.H. (1973) Aggressive and prosocial television programmes and the natural behaviour of preschool children. *Monographs of the Society for Research in Child Development, 38*, no. 4.

Fujinaga, T., Kasuga, T., Uchida, N. & Saiga, H. (1990) Long-term follow-up study of children developmentally retarded by early environmental deprivation. *Genetic, Social and General Psychology Monographs, 116*, 37-104.

Furman, W., Rahe, D.F. & Hartup, W.W. (1979) Rehabilitation of socially withdrawn preschool children through mixed-age and same-age socialisation. *Child Development, 50*, 915-22.

Furnham, A. & Walsh, J. (1991) Consequences of person-environment incongruence: Absenteeism, frustration and stress. *Journal of Social Psychology, 131*, 187-204.

Furth, H.G. (1966) *Thinking without language*. New York: Free Press.

Gabor, A. & Granger, C. (1961) On the price consciousness of consumers. *Applied Statistics, 10*.

Gaertner, S.L. & Bickman, L. (1971) Effects of race on elicitation of helping behaviour: The wrong number technique. *Journal of Personality and Social Psychology, 20*, 218-22.

Gagné, R.M. (1985) *The conditions of learning* (3rd edition). New York: Holt, Rinehart & Winston.

Gainotti, G. (1972) Emotional behaviour and the hemispheric side of lesion. *Cortex, 8(1)*, 41-55.

Galbraith, J. (1973) *Designing complex organisations*. Reading, MA: Addison-Wesley.

Gallup, G.G. (1977) Self-recognition in primates. *American Psychologist, 32*, 329-38.

Galton, F. (1883) *Inquiries into the human faculty and its development*. London: Macmillan.

Gannon, L.R., Haynes, S.N., Cuevas, J. & Chavez, R. (1987) Psychophysiological correlates of induced headaches. *Journal of Behavioural Medicine, 10*, 411-23.

Garcia, J. & Koelling, R.A. (1966) Relation of cue to consequence in avoidance learning. *Psychonomic Science, 4*, 123-4.

Gardner, B.T. & Gardner, R.A. (1969) Teaching sign language to a chimpanzee. *Science, 165*, 664-72.

Gardner, B.T. & Gardner, R.A. (1980) Two comparative psychologists look at language acquisition. In K. Nelson (Ed.) *Children's language*, (Vol. 2). New York: Gardner Press.

Gardner, G.A. (1978) The effects of human subject regulations on data obtained in environmental stressor research. *Journal of Personality and Social Psychology, 36*, 317-49.

Gardner, H. (1983) *Frames of mind: The theory of multiple intelligence*. New York: Basic Books.

Gardner, R.A. & Gardner, B.T. (1978) Comparative psychology and language acquisition. In K. Salzinger & F. Denmark (Eds.) *Psychology: The state of the art. Annals of the New York Academy of Sciences, 309*, 37-76.

Garvey, C. (1977) *Play*. London: Fontana.

Gauld, A. & Stephenson, G.M. (1967) Some experiments relating to Bartlett's theory of remembering. *British Journal of Psychology, 58*, 39-50.

Geiger, G. & Lettvin, J. (1987) Dyslexia. *The New England Journal of Medicine, 316,* 1238-43.

Geis, F.L., Brown, V., Jennings (Walstedt), J. & Porter, N. (1984) Television commercials as achievement scripts for women. *Sex Roles, 10,* 513-25.

Gelman, R. & Shatz, M. (1977) Appropriate speech adjustments: The operation of conversational constraints on talk to two-year-olds. In M. Lewis & L.A. Rosenblum (Eds.) *Interaction, conversation and the development of language.* New York: Wiley.

Genshaft, J.L. & Hirt, M. (1974) Language differences between black children and white children. *Developmental Psychology, 10,* 451-456.

Gershon, E.S. (1983) The genetics of affective disorders. In L. Grinspoon (Ed.) *Psychiatry update.* Washington, DC: American Psychiatric Press, Inc.

Gerson, R.P. & Damon, W. (1978) Moral understanding and children's conduct. In W. Damon (Ed.) *New Directions in child development: Frontiers and possible futures.* New York: Cambridge University Press.

Gesell, A. & Thompson, H. (1929) Learning and growth in identical twins: An experimental study by the method of co-twin control. *Genetic Psychology Monographs, 6,* 1-123.

Gewirtz, J.L. (1965) The cause of infant smiling in four child-rearing environments in Israel. In B.M. Foss (Ed.) *Determinants of infant behaviour* (Vol. 3). London: Methuen.

Gibson, E.J., Gibson, J.J., Pick, A.D. & Osser, H.A. (1962) A developmental study of the discrimination of letter-like forms. *Journal of Comparative and Physiological Psychology, 55,* 897-906.

Gibson, E.J. & Walk, R.D. (1960) The 'visual cliff'. *Scientific American, 202 (4),* 64-71.

Gibson, J.J. (1966) *The senses considered as perceptual systems.* Boston: Houston Mifflin.

Gibson, J.J. (1979) *The ecological approach to visual perception.* Boston: Houston Mifflin.

Gilbert, G.M. (1951) Stereotype persistence and change among college students. *Journal of Personality and Social Psychology, 46,* 245-54.

Gilchrist, J.C. & Nesburg, L.S. (1952) Need and perceptual change in need-related objects. *Journal of Experimental Psychology, 44,* 369-76.

Giles, H. & Powesland, P.F. (1975) *Speech style and social evaluation.* London: Academic Press.

Gilligan, C. (1982) *In a different voice: Psychological theory and women's development.* Cambridge, MA: Harvard University Press.

Gillmartin, B.G. (1987) Peer group antecedents of severe love-shyness in males. *Journal of Personality, 55,* 467-89.

Girodo, M. & Wood, D. (1979) Talking yourself out of pain: The importance of believing that you can. *Cognitive Therapy and Research, 3,* 23-33.

Glasgow, R., Klesges, R.C., Mizes, J.S. & Pechacek, T.F. (1985) Quitting smoking: Strategies used and variables associated with success in a stop-smoking contest. *Journal of Consulting and Clinical Psychology, 53,* 905-912.

Glass, D.C., Singer, J.E. & Friedman, L.W. (1969) Psychic cost of adaptation to an environmental stressor. *Journal of Personality and Social Psychology, 12,* 200-10.

Glueck, S. & Glueck, E. (1950) *Unravelling juvenile delinquency.* New York: Commonwealth Fund.

Goddard, S.J. & Cross, J. (1987) A social skills training approach to dealing with disruptive behaviour in a primary school. *Maladjustment and Therapeutic Education, 5,* 24-9.

Godden, D.R. & Baddeley, A.D. (1975) Context-dependent memory in two natural environments, *British Journal of Psychology, 66,* 325-31.

Godden, D.R. & Baddeley, A.D. (1980) When does context influence recognition memory? *British Journal of Psychology, 71,* 99-104.

Goffman, E. (1959) *The presentation of self in everyday life.* Garden City, NY: Doubleday.

Goffman, E. (1968) *Asylums - essays on the social situation of mental patients and other inmates.* Harmondsworth, Middlesex: Penguin.

Gold, D.R., Rogacz, S., Bock, N., Tosteson, Tor-D. et al (1992) Rotating shift work, sleep and accidents related to sleepiness in hospital nurses. *American Journal of Public Health, 82,* 1011-14.

Goldberg, P.A. (1968) Are women prejudiced against women? *Transaction, April,* 28-30.

Goldberg, S. (1983) Parent-infant bonding: Another look. *Child Development, 54,* 1355-82.

Goldfarb, W. (1943) The effects of early institutional care on adolescent personality. *Journal of Experimental Education, 12,* 106-29.

Goldstein, A. (1980) Thrills in response to music and other stimuli. *Physiological Psychology, 8,* 126-9.

Goldwater, B.C. & Collis, M.L. (1985) Psychologic effects of cardiovascular conditioning: A controlled experiment. *Psychosomatic Medicine, 47,* 174-81.

Goldwyn, E. (1979) The fight to be male. *Listener, May 24,* 709-12.

Goodall, J. (1968) The behaviour of free-living chimpanzees in the Gombe Stream Reserve. *Animal Behaviour Monographs, 1,* 161-311.

Goodall, J. (1978) Chimp killings: Is it the man in them? *Science News, 113,* 276.

Goodwin, D.W., Powell, B., Bremer, D., Hoine, H. & Stern, J. (1969) Alcohol and recall: state-dependent effects in man. *Science, 163,* 1358.

Gould, S.J. (1981) *The mismeasure of man.* Harmondsworth, Middlesex: Penguin.

Gould, S.J. (1982) A nation of morons. *New Scientist, 6 May,* 349-52.

Gray, J.A. & Wedderburn, A.A.I. (1960) Grouping strategies with simultaneous stimuli. *Quarterly Journal of Experimental Psychology, 12,* 180-184.

Green, R. & Berkowitz, L. (1967) Some conditions facilitating the occurrence of aggression after the observation of violence. *Journal of Personality, 35,* 666-76.

Greene, D. & Lepper, M.R. (1974) Effects of extrinsic rewards on children's subsequent interest. *Child Development, 45,* 1141-5.

Greenfield, P.M. (1984) *Mind and media: The effects of television, video games and computers.* Aylesbury: Fontana.

Greenfield, P.M. (1991) Language, tools and brain: The ontogeny and phylogeny of hierarchically organised sequential behaviour. *Behavioural and Brain Sciences, 14,* 531- 95.

Greenfield, P.M. (1993) *Chimp talk.* Horizon programme on BBC, 21 June.

Greenspoon, J. (1955) The reinforcing effect of two spoken sounds on the frequency of two responses. *American Journal of Psychology, 68,* 409-16.

Gregory, R.L. (1990) *Eye and brain,* London: Weidenfeld & Nicolson.

Gregory, R.L. & Wallace, J. (1963) *Recovery from early blindness.* Cambridge: Heffer.

Greist, J.H. (1992) An integrated approach to treatment of obsessive compulsive disorder. *Journal of Clinical Psychiatry, 53 (4, supplement),* 38-41.

Grier, J.B., Counter, S.A. & Shearer, W.M. (1967) Prenatal auditory imprinting in chickens. *Science, 155,* 1692-3.

Griggs, R.A. & Cox, J.R. (1982) The elusive thematic-material effect in Wason's selection task. *British Journal of Psychology, 73,* 407-20.

Grohmann, J. (1938) Modifikation oder funktionsreifung? Ein beitrag zur klÑrung der wechselseitigen beziehungen zwischen instinkthandlung und erfahrung. *Zeitschrift Fur Tierpsychologie, 25,* 132-44.

Gropper, G.L. (1968) Programmed visual presentations for procedural learning. *Audio-Visual Communication, 16,* 33-5.

Gross, R.D. (1992) *Psychology: The science of mind and behaviour* (2nd edition) London: Hodder & Stoughton.

Grossman, S.P. (1964) Some neurochemical aspects of the central regulation of thirst. In M.J. Wayner (Ed.) *Thirst.* New York: Pergamon.

Grubb, E.L. & Hupp, G. (1968) Perception of self, generalised stereotypes and brand selection. *Journal of Marketing Research, 5.*

Guilford, J.P. (1967) *The nature of human intelligence.* New York: McGraw-Hill.

Guiton, P. (1966) Early experience and sexual object choice in the brown leghorn. *Animal Behaviour, 14,* 534-8.

Gulevich, G., Dement, W.C. & Johnson, L. (1966) Psychiatric and EEG observations on a case of prolonged (264 hours) wakefulness. *Archives of General Psychiatry, 15,* 29-35.

Guthrie, E.R. (1935) *The psychology of learning.* New York: Harper & Brothers.

Guthrie, E.R. (1938) *Psychology of human conflict.* New York: Harper.

Gwinner, E. (1986) Circannual rhythms in the control of avian rhythms. *Advances in the Study of Behaviour, 16,* 191-228.

Hackman, J.R. & Oldham, G.R. (1976) Motivation through the design of work: Test of a theory. *Organizational Behaviour and Human Performance, 16,* 250-79.

Hall, C.S. & Lindzey, G. (1970) *Theories of personality* (2nd edition). London: John Wiley & Sons, Inc.

Hall, G. S. (1904) *Adolescence.* New York: Appleton-Century-Crofts.

Hall, J. & Watson, W.H. (1970) Individual and group decision-making. *Human Relations, 23,* 299-317.

Hall, K.R.L. & DeVore, I. (1965) Baboon social behaviour. In I. DeVore (Ed.) *Primate behaviour.* New York: Holt.

Hamblin, R.L. (1958) Leadership and crisis. *Sociometry, 21,* 322-35.

Hamilton, W.D. (1964) The genetical theory of social behaviour (I and II). *Journal of Theoretical Biology, 7,* 1-32.

Harari, H. & McDavid, J.W. (1973) Teachers' expectations and name stereotypes. *Journal of Educational Psychology, 65,* 222-5.

Hargreaves, D. (1967) Social relations in a secondary school. London: Routledge and Kegan Paul.

Harlow, H.F. (1949) Formation of learning sets. *Psychological Review, 56,* 51-65.

Harlow, H.F (1958) The nature of love. *American Psychologist, 13,* 673-85.

Harlow, H.F (1959) Love in infant monkeys. *Scientific American, 200(6),* 68-74.

Harlow, H.F. & Harlow, M.K. (1962) Social deprivation in monkeys. *Scientific American, 207(5),* 136-46.

Harlow, H.F, Harlow, M.K. & Suomi, S.J. (1971) From thought to therapy: Lessons from a primate laboratory. *American Scientist, 59,* 74-83.

Harlow, H.F. & Zimmerman, R.R. (1959) Affectional responses in the infant monkey. *Science, 130,* 421-32.

Harrell, R.F., Woodyard, E. & Gates, A.I. (1955) *The effect of mothers' diets on the intelligence of the offspring.* New York: Public Teachers' College, Columbia University.

Harter, S. (1983) Developmental perspectives in self-esteem. In P.H. Mussen (Ed.) *Handbook of child psychology. Vol. 4: Socialisation, personality and social development.* New York: Wiley.

Hartland, J. (1991) *Language and thought.* Leicester: BPS Books.

Hartmann, P. & Husband, C. (1981) The mass media and racial conflict. In S. Cohen & J. Young (Eds.) *The manufacture of news.* London: Constable.

Hartmann, E., Milofsky, E., Valliant, G., Oldfield, M., Falke, R. & Ducet, C. (1984) Vulnerability to schizophrenia. *Archives of General Psychiatry, 41,* 1050-6.

Hartshorne, H. & May, M.A. (1928) *Studies in the nature of character: Studies in deceit (Vol. 1); Studies in self-control (Vol. 2); Studies in the organisation of character (Vol. 3).* New York: Macmillan.

Hartup, W.W. (1983) Peer relations. In P.H. Mussen (Ed.) *Handbook of child psychology. Vol. 4: Socialisation, personality and social development.* New York: Wiley.

Hatfield E. & Traupmann, J. (1981) Intimate relationships: A perspective from equity theory. In S.W. Duck & R. Gilmour (Eds.) *Personal relationships 1: Studying personal relationships.* London: Academic Press.

Havighurst, R.J., Neugarten, B.L. & Tobin, S.S. (1968) Disengagement and patterns of ageing. In B.L. Neugarten (Ed.) *Middle age and ageing.* Chicago: University of Chicago Press.

Hawkins, L.H. & Armstrong-Esther, C.A. (1978) Circadian rhythms and night shift working in nurses. *Nursing Times, May 4,* 49-52.

Hayes, K.J. & Hayes, C. (1952) Imitation in a home-raised chimpanzee. *Journal of Comparative Physiological Psychology, 45,* 450-9.

Hayes, N. & Orrell, S. (1987) *Psychology: An introduction.* London: Longman.

Haynes, R.B., Taylor, D.W. & Sackett, D.L. (1979) *Compliance in health care.* Baltimore, MD: Johns Hopkins University Press.

Hazan, C. & Shaver, P.R. (1987) Romantic love conceptualised as an attachment process. *Journal of Personality and Social Psychology, 52,* 511-24

Heather, N. (1976) *Radical perspectives in psychology.* London: Methuen.

Hebb, D.O. (1949) *The organisation of behaviour.* New York: Wiley.

Heider, E. (1972) Universals in colour naming and memory, *Journal of Experimental Psychology, 93,*10-20.

Heider, F. (1958) *The psychology of interpersonal relations.* New York: Wiley.

Heider, F. & Simmel, M. (1944) An experimental study of apparent behaviour. *American Journal of Psychology, 57,* 243-59.

Heim, A. (1970) *The AH6 group tests of high level intelligence.* Windsor: NFER-Nelson.

Heinroth, O. (1911) BeitrÑge zur biologie, insbesondere psychologie und ethologie der anatiden. *Verhandlungen des internationalen Ornithologenkongresses,* Berlin

Held, R. & Hein, A. (1963) Movement-produced stimulation in the development of visually guided behaviour. *Journal of Comparative and Physiological Psychology, 56,* 607-13.

Hembree, R. (1988) Correlates, causes, effects and treatment of test anxiety. *Review of Educational Research, 58,* 47-77.

Henley, N.M. (1977) *Body politics: Power, sex and nonverbal communication.* Engelwood Cliffs, NJ: Prentice-Hall.

Hepper, P.G. (1991) An examination of fetal learning before and after birth. *Irish Journal of Psychology, 12,* 95-107.

Herman, J.H., Ellman, S.J. & Roffwarg, H.P. (1978) The problem of NREM recall re-examined. In A.M. Arkin, J.S. Antrobus & S.J. Ellman (Eds.) *The mind in sleep.* New York: Wiley.

Herman, L.M., Morrel-Samuels, P. & Pack, A.A. (1990) Bottlenosed dolphin and human recognition of veridical and degraded video displays of an artificial gestural language. *Journal of Experimental Psychology General, 119,* 215-30.

Herriot, P. (1970) *An introduction to the psychology of language.* London: Methuen.

Herrman, L. & Hogben, L. (1932) The intellectual resemblance of twins. *Proceedings of the Royal Society of Edinburgh, 53,* 105-29.

Hersey, P. & Blanchard, K.H. (1976) Leadership effectiveness and adaptability description (LEAD). In J.W. Pfeiffer & J.E. Jones (Eds.), *The annual handbook for group facilitators* (Vol. 5). La Jolla, CA: University Associates.

Herzberg, F. (1966) Grapevine - Here to stay but not beyond control. *Personnel, 43,* 62-6.

Herzog, H.A. (1991) Conflicts of interest: Kittens and boa constrictors, pets and research. *American Psychologist, 46,* 246-8.

Hess, E.H. (1958) Imprinting in animals. *Scientific American, 198,* 81-90.

Hess, E.H. (1965) Attitude and pupil size. *Scientific American, 212,* 46-54.

Hess, E.H. (1972) "Imprinting" in a natural laboratory. *Scientific American, 227,* 24-31.

Hess, E.H. (1972) Pupilmetrics. In N. Greenfield & R. Sternbach (Eds.) *Handbook of psychophysiology.* New York: Holt, Rinehart & Winston.

Heston, L.L. (1966) Psychiatric disorders in foster home reared children of schizophrenic mothers. *British Journal of Psychiatry, 112,* 819-25.

Hetherington, E.M. (1989) Coping with family transitions: Winners, losers and survivors. *Child Development, 60,* 1-14.

Hewitt, J. (1972) Liking and the proportion of favourable evaluations. *Journal of Personality and Social Psychology, 22,* 231-5.

Hilgard, E.R. (1977) *Divided consciousness: Multiple controls in human thought and action.* New York: Wiley-Interscience.

Hill, C.T., Rubin, Z. & Peplau, L.A. (1976) Break-ups before marriage: The end of 103 affairs. *Journal of Social Issues, 32(1),* 147-67.

Hill, K.P. (1980) *Decision making in child abuse cases: Retrospective study of 200 cases of non-accidental injury to children in Nottinghamshire.* Unpublished thesis, CCETSW, London.

Himmelweit, H.T., Oppenheim, A.N. & Vince, P. (1958) *television and the child: An empirical study into the effects of television on the young.* London: Oxford University Press.

Hinde, R.A. (1966) *Animal behaviour* (1st edition). New York: McGraw-Hill

Hinde, R.A. (1982) *Ethology.* Oxford: Oxford University Press and London: Fontana Paperback.

Hinshaw, S.P. (1992) Academic underachievement, attention deficits and aggression: Comorbidity and implications for intervention. *Journal of Consulting and Clinical Psychology, 60*, 893-903.

Hinton, J. (1967) *Dying*. Baltimore: Penguin.

Hobson, J.A. & McCarley, R.W. (1977) The brain as a dream state generator: an activation-synthesis hypothesis of the dream theory. *American Journal of Psychiatry, 134*, 1335-48.

Hobson, R.P. (1986) The autistic child's appraisal of expressions of emotion. *Journal of Childhood Psychology and Psychiatry, 27*, 321-42.

Hobson, R.P. (1990) On acquiring knowledge about people and the capacity to pretend: response to Leslie (1987). *Psychological Review, 97*, 114-21.

Hock, R.R. (1992) *Forty studies that changed psychology*. Englewood Cliffs, NJ: Prentice Hall.

Hockett, C.F. (1958) *A course in modern linguistics*. New York: Macmillan.

Hodges, J. & Tizard, B. (1989) Social and family relationships of ex-institutional adolescents. *Journal of Child Psychology and Psychiatry, 30 (1)*, 77-97.

Hoeffer, B. (1981) Children's acquisition of sex-role behaviour in lesbian-mother families. *American Journal of Orthopsychiatry, 51*, 536-44.

Hoffman, L.W. (1989) Effects of maternal employment in the two-parent family. *American Psychologist, 44*, 283-92.

Hoffman, M.L. (1970) Moral development. In P.H. Mussen (Ed.) *Carmichael's manual of child psychology* (Vol. 2). New York: Wiley.

Hofling, K.C., Brontzman, E., Dalrymple, S., Graves, N. & Pierce, C.M. (1966) An experimental study in the nurse-physician relationship. *Journal of Mental and Nervous Disorders, 43*, 171-8.

Hohmann, G.W. (1966) Some effects of spinal cord lesions on experienced emotional feelings. *Psychophysiology, 3*, 143-156.

Hokanson, J.E. (1970) Psychophysiological evaluation of the catharsis hypothesis. In E.I. Megargee & J.E. Hokanson (Eds.) *The dynamics of aggression: Individual, group and international analyses*. New York: Harper & Row.

Holmes, G. (1939) The cerebellum of man. *Brain, 62*, 21-30.

Holmes, T.H. & Rahe, R.H. (1967) The social readjustment rating scale. *Journal of Psychosomatic Research, 11*, 213-8.

Holstein, C. (1976) Irreversible, stepwise sequence in the development of moral judgement: A longitudinal study of males and females. *Child Development, 47*, 51-61.

Holt, J. (1964) *How children fail*. Harmondsworth, Middlesex: Penguin.

Hopson, B. & Scally, M. (1980) Change and development in adult life: Some implications for helpers. *British Journal of Guidance and Counselling, 8(2)*, 175-87.

Horn, J.L. & Donaldson, G. (1980) Cognitive development in adulthood. In O.G. Brim, Jr. & J. Kagan (Eds.) *Constancy and change in human development*. Cambridge, MA: Harvard University Press.

Horne, J.A. & Minard, A. (1985) Sleep and sleepiness following a behaviourally "active" day. *Ergonomics, 28*, 567-75.

Horney, K. (1924) On the genesis of the castration complex in women. *International Journal of Psychoanalysis, V*, 50-65.

Horwitz, R.A. (1976) Psychological effects of the open classroom. *Review of Educational Research, 49*, 71-86.

House, R.J. (1971) A path-goal theory of leader effectiveness. *Administrative Science Quarterly, 1*, 321-38.

Hovland, C.I. (1957) *The order of presentation in persuasion*. New Haven, CN: Yale University Press.

Hovland, C.I., Janis, I.L. & Kelley, H.H. (1953) *Communication and persuasion*. New Haven CN: Yale University Press.

Hovland, C.I., Lumsdaine, A.A. & Sheffield, F.D. (1949) *Experiments in mass communication*. Princeton, NJ: Princeton University Press.

Howarth, C.I. & Gillham, W.E.C. (1981) *The structure of psychology: An introductory text*. London: George Allen & Unwin.

Howes, C. (1990) Can the age of entry into child care and the quality of child care predict adjustment into kindergarten? *Developmental Psychology, 26*, 292-303.

Howitt, D. & Cumberbatch, G. (1974) Audience perceptions of violent television content. *Communication Research, 1*, 204-223.

Hubel, D.H. & Wiesel, T.N. (1962) Receptive fields, binocular interaction and functional architecture in the cat's visual cortex. *Journal of Physiology, 160*, 106-54.

Hudson, L. (1966) *Contrary imaginations*. London: Methuen.

Hughes, M. (1975) *Egocentrism in preschool children*. Edinburgh University: unpublished doctoral thesis.

Hull, C.L. (1943) *Principles of behaviour*. New York: Appleton-Century-Crofts.

Hurlock, E.B. (1925) An evaluation of certain incentives used in school work. *Journal of Educational Psychology, 16*, 145-59.

Hutt, C. (1966) Exploration and play in children. *Symposia of the Zoological Society of London, 18*, 61-81.

Hutt, C. & Bhavnani, R. (1972) Predictions from play. *Nature, 237*, 171-2.

Hyman, R. & Honorton, C. (1986) A joint communiqué: The psi Ganzfeld controversy. *Journal of Parapsychology, 50*, 351-64.

Illsley, R. & Thompson, J. (1975) Women from broken homes. In E. Butterworth & D. Weir (Eds.) *The sociology of modern Britain*. London: Fontana.

Imperato-McGinley, J., Guerro, L., Gautier, T. & Peterson, R.E. (1974) Steroid 5-reductase deficiency in man: An inherited form of male pseudohermaphroditism. *Science, 186*, 1213-6.

Insko, C.A. (1965) Verbal reinforcement of attitude. *Journal of Personality and Social Psychology, 2*, 621-3.

Jacobs, P.A., Brunton, M. & Melville, M.M. (1965) Aggressive behaviour, mental abnormality and XXY male. *Nature, 208*, 1351-2.

Jaffe, J., Stern, D.N. & Perry, J.C. (1973) 'Conversational' coupling of gaze behaviour in pre-linguistic human development. *Journal of Psycholinguistic Research, 2*, 3.

Jahoda, M. (1958) *Current concepts of positive mental health*. New York: Basic Books.

Jahoda, M. (1979) The impact of unemployment in the 1930s and the 1970s. *Bulletin of the British Psychological Society, 32*, 309-14.

James, W. (1884) What is an emotion? *Mind, 9*, 188-205.

James, W. (1890) *Principles of psychology*. New York: Holt.

Janicak, P.G., Davis, J,M, Gibbons, R.D., Ericksen, S., Chang, S. & Gallagher, P. (1985) Efficacy of ECT: A meta-analysis. *American Journal of Psychiatry, 142*, 297-302.

Janis, I.L. (1982) *Victims of groupthink* (2nd edition). Boston, MA: Houghton-Mifflin.

Janis, I.L. (1984) The patient as decision maker. In W.D. Gentry (Ed.) *Handbook of behavioural medicine*. New York: Guilford.

Janis, I.L. & Gilmore, J.B. (1965) The influence of incentive conditions on the success of role-playing in modifying attitudes. *Journal of Personality & Social Psychology, 1*, 17-27.

Janson, R. (1971) Job enrichment in the modern office. In J. Maher (Ed.) *New perspectives in job enrichment*. New York: Van Nostrand.

Jemmott, J.B., III, Borysenko, M., McClelland, D.C., Chapman, R., Meyer, D. & Benson, H. (1985) Academic stress, power motivation and decrease in salivary secretory immunoglobulin: A secretion rate. *Lancet, 1*, 1400-2.

Jenkins, J.G. & Dallenbach, K.M. (1924) Oblivescence during sleep and waking. *American Journal of Psychology, 35*, 605-12.

Jenner, D.A., Reynolds, V. & Harrison, G.A. (1980) Catecholamine excretion rates and occupation. *Ergonomics, 23*, 237-46.

Jenness, A. (1932) The role of discussion in changing opinion regarding matter of fact. *Journal of Abnormal and Social Psychology, 27*, 279-96.

Jensen, A.R. (1969) How much can we boost IQ and scholastic achievement? *Harvard Educational Review, 39*, 1-123.

Johnson, W., Emde, R.N., Pannabecker, B., Stenberg, C. & Davis, M. (1982) Maternal perception of infant emotion from birth through to 18 months. *Infant Behaviour and Development, 5*, 313-22.

Johnston, W.A. & Heinz, S.P. (1978) Flexibility and capacity demands of attention, *Journal of Experimental Psychology, 5*, 168-75.

Johnston, W.A. & Wilson, J. (1980) Perceptual processing of non-targets in an attention task, *Memory and Cognition, 8*, 372-7.

Jones, D.N., Pickett, J., Oates, M.R. & Barbor, P. (1987) *Understanding child abuse* (2nd edition). London: Macmillan.

Jones, E.E. & Harris, V.A. (1967) The attribution of attitudes. *Journal of Experimental Social Psychology, 3*, 1-24.

Jones, E.E. & Nisbett, R.E. (1971) The actor and observer: Divergent perceptions of the causes of behaviour. In E.E. Jones, D.E. Kanouse, H.H. Kelley, R.E. Nisbett, S. Valins & B. Wiener (Eds.) *Attribution: Perceiving the causes of behaviour.* Morristown, NJ: General Learning Press.

Jones, E.E., Rock, L., Shaver, K.G., Goethals, G.R. & Ward, L.M. (1968) Pattern of performance and ability to attribution: An unexpected primacy effect. *Journal of Personality and Social Psychology, 9,* 317-40.

Jones, E.E. & Sigall H. (1971) The bogus pipeline: A new paradigm for measuring affect and attitude. *Psychological Bulletin, 76,* 349-64.

Jones, G.V. (1982) Tests of the dual-mechanism theory of recall. *Acta Psychologica, 50,* 61-72.

Jones, M.C. & Bayley, N. (1950) Physical maturing among boys as related to behaviour. *Journal of Educational Psychology, 41,* 129-48.

Jordan, H.A. (1969) Voluntary intragastric feeding. *Journal of Comparative and Physiological Psychology, 68,* 498-506.

Jouvet, M. (1967) Mechanisms of the states of sleep: A neuropharmological approach. *Research Publications of the Association for the Research in Nervous and Mental Disorders, 45,* 86-126.

Joynson, R.B. (1989) *The Burt affair.* London: Routledge.

Julien, R.M. (1992) *A primer of drug action* (6th edition). New York: W.H. Freeman & Co.

Kacmar, K.M., Delery, J.E., & Ferris, G.R. (1992) Differential effectiveness of applicant impression management tactics on employment interview decisions. *Journal of Applied Social Psychology, 22,* 1250-72.

Kagan, J. (1972) Do infants think? *Scientific American, 226,* 74-82.

Kagan, J., Kearsley, R.B. & Zelazo, P.R. (1978) *Infancy: Its place in human development.* Cambridge, MA: Harvard University Press.

Kahneman, D. (1973) *Attention and effort.* Englewood Cliffs, NJ: Prentice-Hall.

Kahneman, D. & Tversky, A. (1972) Subjective probability: A judgement of representativeness. *Psychology Review, 93,* 136-53.

Kalat, J.W. (1988) *Biological psychology* (3rd edition). Belmont, CA: Wadsworth Publishing Co.

Kamarck, T.W., Manuck, S.B. & Jennings, J.R. (1990) Social support reduces cardiovascular reactivity to psychological challenge: A laboratory model. *Psychosomatic Medicine, 52,* 42-58.

Kamin, L.J. (1977) *The science and politics of IQ.* Harmondsworth, Middlesex: Penguin.

Kandel, D.B. (1978) Similarity in real-life adolescent friendship pairs. *Journal of Personality and Social Psychology, 36,* 306-12.

Kanner, L. (1943) Autistic disturbances of affective contact. *Nervous Child, 2,* 217-50.

Kaplan, R.M., Atkins, C.J. & Reinsch, S. (1984) Specific efficacy expectations mediate exercise compliance in patients with COPD. *Health Psychology, 3,* 223-42.

Karlins, M., Coffman, T.L. & Walters, G. (1969) On the fading of social stereotypes: Studies in three generations of college students. *Journal of Personality and Social Psychology, 13,* 1-16.

Kasl, S.V. & Mahl, G.F. (1965) Relationship of disturbances and hesitations in spontaneous speech to anxiety. *Journal of Personality & Social psychology, 1,* 425-433.

Katz, D. & Braly, K. (1933) Racial stereotypes of one hundred college students. *Journal of Abnormal and Social Psychology, 28,* 280-90.

Kaye, K. (1984) *The mental and social life of babies.* London: Methuen.

Keddie (1971) Classroom knowledge. In M. Young (Ed.) *Knowledge and control.* London: Collier Macmillan.

Kelley, H.H. (1950) The warm-cold variable in first impressions of people. *Journal of Personality, 18,* 431-9.

Kelley, H.H. (1967) Attribution theory in social psychology. *Nebraska Symposium on Motivation, 15,* 192-241.

Kelley, H.H. (1971) Attribution in social interaction. In E.E. Jones, D.E. Kanouse, H.H. Kelley, R.E. Nisbett, S. Valins & B. Wiener (Eds.) *Attribution: Perceiving the causes of behaviour.* Morristown, NJ: General Learning Press.

Kellogg, W.N. & Kellogg, I.A. (1933) *The ape and the child.* New York: McGraw-Hill.

Kelly, G.A. (1955) *The psychology of personal constructs, 1 and 2.* New York: Norton.

Kelman, H. & Lawrence, I., (1972) Assignment of responsibility in the case of Lt. Calley: Preliminary report on a national survey. *Journal of Social Issues, 28,* 177-212.

Kendell, R.E. (1991) Relationship between the DSM-IV and the ICD-10. Special Issue: Diagnoses, dimensions, and DSM-IV: The science of classification. *Journal of Abnormal Psychology, 100(3),* 297-301.

Kendler, K.S. (1983) Overview: A current perspective on twin studies of schizophrenia. *American Journal of Psychiatry, 140,* 1413-25.

Kendrick, D.T. & Cialdini, R.B. (1977) Romantic attraction: Misattribution versus reinforcement explanations. *Journal of Personality and Social Psychology, 35,* 381-91.

Kennard, M.A. (1938) Reorganisation of motor function in the cerebral cortex of monkeys deprived of motor and premotor areas in infancy. *Journal of Neurophysiology, 1,* 477-96.

Kent, G. (1985) Memory of dental pain. *Pain, 21,* 187-94.

Kerckhoff, A.C. & Davis, K.E. (1962) Value consensus and need complementarity in mate selection. *American Sociological Review, 27,* 295-303.

Kernis, M.H., Brockner, J. & Frankel, B.S. (1989) Self-esteem and reactions to failure: The mediating role of overgeneralisation. *Journal of Personality and Social Psychology, 57,* 707-14.

Kettlewell, H.B.D. (1955) Selection experiments on industrial melanism in the Lepidoptera. *Heredity, 9,* 323-42.

Kettlewell, H.B.D. (1956) Further selection experiments on industrial melanism in the Lepidoptera. *Nature, 175,* 934.

Kiecolt-Glaser, J.K. & Glaser, R. (1986) Psychological influences on immunity. *Psychosomatics, 27,* 621-4.

Kihlstrom, J.F. (1985) Hypnosis. *Annual Review of Psychology, 36,* 385-418.

Kimmel, D.C. (1990) *Adulthood and Ageing* (3rd edition). New York: John Wiley & Sons.

Kintsch, W. & Keenan, J. (1973) Reading rate and retention as a function of the number of propositions in the base structure of sentences. *Cognitive Psychology, 5,* 257-74.

Kintsch, W. & van Dijk, T.A. (1983) Toward a model of text comprehension and production. *Psychological Review, 85,* 363-94.

Klaus, M.H. & Kennell, J.H. (1976) *Maternal-infant bonding.* St Louis: Mosby.

Klein, R. & Armitage, R. (1979) Rhythms in human performance: 1.5 hour oscillations in cognitive style. *Science, 204,* 1326-7.

Kleinhesselink, R.R. & Edwards, R.W. (1975) Seeking and avoiding belief-discrepant information as a function of its perceived refutability. *Journal of Personality and Social Psychology, 31,* 787-90.

Kleinke, C.L. (1977) Compliance to requests made by gazing and touching experimenters in field settings. *Journal of experimental Social Psychology, 13,* 218-23.

Kleitman, N. (1963) *Sleep and wakefulness* (revised and enlarged edition). Chicago: Chicago University Press.

Kleitman, N. (1969) The basic rest-activity cycle in relation to sleep and wakefulness. In A. Kales (Ed.) *Sleep: Physiology and pathology.* Philadelphia: Lippincott.

Klopfer, P.H. & Gamble, J. (1966) Maternal 'imprinting' in goats: The role of the chemical senses. *Zeitschrift Fur Tierpsychologie, 23,* 588-92.

Klüver, H. & Bucy, P.C. (1939) Preliminary analysis of functions of the temporal lobes in monkeys. *Archives of Neurology and Psychiatry (Chicago), 42,* 979-1000.

Knowles, J.H. (1977) The responsibility of the individual. In J.H. Knowles (Ed.) *Doing better and feeling worse: Health in the United States.* New York: Norton.

Knox, J. (1992) Bullying in schools: Communicating with the victim. *Support for Learning, 7,* 159-62.

Koestler, A. (1970) *The ghost in the machine.* London: Pan Books.

Kohlberg, L. (1966) A cognitive-developmental analysis of children's sex-role concepts and attitudes. In E.E. Maccoby (Ed.) *The development of sex differences.* Stanford, CA: Stanford University Press.

Kohlberg, L. (1969) Stage and sequence: The cognitive-developmental approach to socialisation. In D.A. Goslin (Ed.) *Handbook of socialisation theory and practice.* Skokie, IL: Rand McNally.

Kohlberg, L. (1978) Revisions in the theory and practice of moral development. *Directions for Child Development, 2,* 83-8.

Köhler, W. (1925) *The mentality of apes.* New York: Harcourt Brace.

Koluchova, J. (1972) Severe deprivation in twins: A case study. *Journal of Child Psychology and Psychiatry, 13,* 107-14.

Koluchova, J. (1976) The further development of twins after severe and prolonged deprivation: A second report. *Journal of Child Psychology and Psychiatry, 17,* 181-8.

Koluchova, J. (1991) Severely deprived twins after 22 years observation. *Studia Psychologica, 33,* 23-8.

Korf, R.K. (1985) Macro-operators: A weak method for learning. *Artificial Intelligence, 26,* 35-77.

Korte, C. & Kerr, N. (1975) Response to altruistic opportunities in urban and nonurban settings. *Journal of Social Psychology, 95,* 183-4.

Kosslyn, S.M. (1980) *Image and mind.* Cambridge, MA: Harvard University Press.

Kraepelin, E. (1896) *Lehrbuch der psychiatrie* (5th edition). Leipzig: Barth.

Krafft-Ebing, R. von (1931) *Psychopathia sexualis.* New York: Physicians & Surgeons Book Co.

Krebs, C. & Boonstra, R. (1979) Viability of large and small sized adults in fluctuating vole populations. *Ecology, 60 (3),* 567.

Krebs, J.R. & Dawkins, R. (1984) Animal signals: mind-reading and manipulation. In J.R. Krebs & N.B. Davies (Eds.) *Behavioural ecology.* Oxford: Blackwell Scientific Publications.

Kroodsma, D.E. & Miller, E.H. (Eds.) (1982) *Acoustic communication in birds.* New York: Academic Press.

Kübler-Ross, E. (1969) *On death and dying.* London: Tavistock/Routledge.

Kuhn, H.H. (1960) Self attitudes by age, sex and professional training. *Sociological Quarterly, 1,* 39-55.

Kuo, Z.Y. (1932) Ontogeny of embryonic behaviour in Aves, IV: The influence of embryonic movements upon the behaviour after hatching. *Journal of Comparative Psychology, 14,* 109-22.

Kwallek, N. & Lewis, C.M. (1990) Effects of environmental colour on males and females: A red or white or green office. *Applied Ergonomics, 21,* 275-8.

LaBerge, D. (1983) Spatial extent of attention to letters and words, *Journal of Experimental Psychology: Human Perception and Performance, 9,* 371-9.

Labov, W. (1970) The logic of non-standard English. In F. Williams (Ed.) *Language and poverty.* Chicago: Markham.

Labov, W. (1973) The boundaries of words and their meanings. In C.J.N. Bailey and R.W. Shuy (Eds.) *New ways of analysing variations in English.* Washington, DC: Georgetown University Press.

Laing, R.D. (1965) *The divided self.* Harmondsworth, Middlesex: Penguin.

Laird, J.D. (1974) Self-attribution of emotion: The effects of facial expression on the quality of emotional experience. *Journal of Personality and Social Psychology, 29,* 475-86.

Lamb, M.E. (1981) The development of father-infant relationships. In M.E. Lamb (Ed.) *The role of the father in child development.* New York: Wiley.

Lambert, H.H. (1978) Biology and equality: A perspective on sex differences. *Signs: Journal of Women in Culture and Society, 4,* 97-117.

Landsberg, J.W. (1981) Hormones and filial imprinting. *In Proceedings of the 7th International Ornithological Congress,* 837-41. Berlin, 1978.

Landy, D. & Sigall, H. (1974) Beauty is talent: Task evaluation as a function of the performer's physical attractiveness. *Journal of Personality and Social Psychology, 29,* 299-304.

Langer, E.J. & Abelson, R.P. (1974) A patient by any other name ...: Clinical group difference in labelling bias. *Journal of Consulting and Clinical Psychology, 42,* 4-9.

Langer, E.J., Blank, A. & Chanowitz, B. (1978) The mindlessness of ostensibly thoughtful action. *Journal of Personality and Social Psychology, 36,* 635-42.

Langer, E.J., Janis, I.L. & Wolfer, J.A. (1975) Reduction of psychological stress in surgical patients. *Journal of Experimental Social Psychology, 11,* 155-65.

Lanzetta, J.T., Cartwright-Smith, J. & Kleck, R.E. (1976) Effects of nonverbal dissimulation on emotional experience and autonomic arousal. *Journal of Personality and Social Psychology, 33,* 354-70.

LaPiere, R.T. (1934) Attitudes vs. action. *Social Forces, 13,* 230-7.

Lashley, K.S. (1950) In search of the engram. *Symposia of the Society for Experimental Biology, 4,* 454-82.

Laswell, H.D. (1948) *The analysis of political behaviour.* London: Routledge & Kegan Paul.

Latané, B. & Darley, J.M. (1970) *The unresponsive bystander: Why doesn't he help?* New York: Appleton-Century-Crofts.

Latané, B. & Nida, S.A. (1981) Ten years of research on group size and helping. *Psychological Bulletin, 89,* 308-24.

Lawrence, D. (1971) The effects of counselling on retarded readers. *Educational Research, 13,* 119-24.

Lawrence, D. (1978) *Counselling students with reading difficulties.* London: Good Reading Ltd.

Lazar, I. & Darlington, R. (1982) Lasting effects of early education: A report from the Consortium for Longitudinal Studies. *Monographs of the Society for Research in Child Development, 47,* nos. 2-3.

Lazarus, R.S. & McCleary, R.A. (1951) Automatic discrimination without awareness: A study of subception. *Psychological Review, 58,* 113-22.

Lea, S.E.G. (1984) *Instinct, environment and behaviour.* London: Methuen.

Leathers, D.G. (1986) *Successful nonverbal communication.* Cambridge: Cambridge University Press.

Leavitt, J.J. (1951) Some effects of certain communication patterns on group performance. *Journal of Abnormal and Social Psychology, 46,* 38-50.

Lee, J.A. (1973) *The colours of love: An exploration of the ways of loving.* Ontario: New Press.

Lefrancois, G.R. (1991) *Psychology for teaching.* Belmont, CA: Wadsworth Publishing Co.

Lehrman, D.S. (1964) The reproductive behaviour of ring doves. *Scientific American, 211,* 48-54.

Leith, G.O.M. (1969) Personality and learning. In W.R. Dunn and C. Holroyd (Eds.) *Aspects of educational technology, II.* London: Methuen.

LeMasters, E.E. (1957) Parenthood as crisis. *Marriage and Family Living, 19,* 352-5.

Lenneberg, E.H. (1967) *The biological foundations of language.* New York: Wiley.

Lepper, M.R., Greene, D. & Nisbett, R.E. (1973) Undermining children's intrinsic interest with extrinsic reward: A test of the overjustification hypothesis. *Journal of Personality and Social Psychology, 28,* 129-37.

Lerner, M.J. (1980) *The belief in a just world: A fundamental delusion.* New York: Plenum.

Lerner, M.J. & Miller, D.T. (1978) Just world research and the attribution process: Looking back and looking ahead. *Psychological Bulletin, 85,* 1030-51.

Leslie, A.M. & Firth, U. (1990) Prospects for a neuropsychology of autism: Hobson's choice. *Psychological review, 97,* 122-31.

Lester, B.M., Kotelchuck, M., Spelke, E., Sellers, M.J. & Klein, R.E. (1974) Separation protest in Guatemalan infants: Cross-cultural and cognitive findings. *Developmental Psychology, 10,* 79-85.

Lethem, J., Slade, P.D., Trou, J.D.G. & Bentley, G. (1983) Outline of a fear-avoidance model of exaggerated pain perception-I. *Behaviour Research and Therapy, 21,* 401-8.

Levine, J.D., Gordon, N.C. & Fields, H.L. (1978) The mechanism of placebo analgesia. *Lancet, September 23,* 654-7.

Levison, D.J., Darrow, D.N., Klein, E.B., Levinson, M.H. & McKee, B. (1978) *The seasons of a man's life.* New York: Knopf.

Lewin, K., Lippett, R. & White, R.K. (1939) Patterns of aggressive behaviour in experimentally created "social climates". *Journal of Social Psychology, 10,* 271-99.

Lewis, M. & Brooks-Gunn, J. (1979) *Social cognition and the acquisition of self.* New York: Plenum.

Lewis, M. & Rowe, D. (1994) Good news, bad news. *The Psychologist, 7,* 157-60.

Levy, Y., Amir, N. & Shalev, R. (1992) Linguistic development of a child with a congenital localised L.H. lesion. *Cognitive Neuropsychology, 9,* 1-32.

Likert, R. (1932) A technique for the measurement of attitude. *Archives of Psychology, 22,* 1-55.

Lindemann, E. (1944) Symptomatology and management of acute grief. *American Journal of Psychiatry, 101,* 141-8.

Linsky, A. & Straus, M. (1986) *Social stress in the United States: Links to regional patterns in crime and illness.* Dover, MA: Auburn House.

Litt, M.D. (1988) Self-efficacy and perceived control: Cognitive mediators in pain tolerance. *Journal of Personality and Social Psychology, 54*, 149-60.

Littenberg, R., Tulkin, S. & Kagan, J. (1971) Cognitive components of separation anxiety. *Developmental Psychology, 4*, 387-8.

Liublinskaya, A.A. (1957) The development of children's speech and thought. In B. Simon (Ed.) *Psychology in the Soviet Union*. Stanford, CA: Stanford University Press.

Loftus, E.F. & Loftus, G.R. (1980) On the permanence of stored information in the human brain. *American Psychologist, 35*, 409-20.

Loftus, E.F., Miller, D.G. & Burns, H.J. (1978) Semantic integration of verbal information into visual memory, *Journal of Experimental Psychology, 4(1)*, 19-31.

Loftus, G.R. & Loftus, E.F. (1983) *Mind at play: The psychology of video games*. New York: Basic Books.

Logan, G.D. & Zbrodoff, N.J. (1979) When it helps to be misled: Facilitative effects of increasing the frequency of conflicting stimuli in a Stroop-like task, *Memory and Cognition, 7(3)*, 166-73.

Lorenz, K.Z. (1932) Betrachtunngen über das erkennen der arteigen triebhandlungen der vögel. *Journal of Ornithology, 80*, 50-98.

Lorenz, K. (1935) Der kumpan in der umwelt des vogels. *Journal of Ornithology, 83*, 137-213.

Lorenz, K.Z. (1937) The companion in the bird's world. *Auk, 54*, 245-73.

Lorenz, K.Z. (1952) *King Solomon's Ring: New light on animal ways*. New York: Thomas Y. Crowell.

Lorenz, K.Z. (1958) The evolution of behaviour. *Scientific American, 199(6)*, 67-78.

Lovaas, O.I. (1987) Behavioural treatment and abnormal education and educational functioning in young autistic children. *Journal of Consulting and Clinical Psychology, 55*, 3-9.

Lovaas, O.I., Freitas, L., Nelson, K. & Whalen, C. (1967) The establishment of imitation and its use for development of complex behaviour in schizophrenic children. *Behaviour Research and Therapy, 5*, 171-81.

Love, R.E. & Greenwald, A.C. (1978) Cognitive responses to persuasion as mediators of opinion change. *Journal of Social Psychology, 104*, 231-41.

Luce, R.D. & Raffia, H. (1957) *Games and decisions*. New York: Wiley.

Luchins, A.S. (1957) Primacy-recency in impression formation. In C. Hovland (Ed.) *The order of presentation in persuasion*. New Haven, CN: Yale University Press.

Luchins, A.S. (1942) Mechanisation in problem solving. The effect of Einstellung, *Psychological Monographs, 52*, 248.

Ludwig, A.M. (1975) Sensory overload and psychopathology. *Diseases of the Nervous System, 36*, 357-60.

Lugaresi, E., Medori, R., Montagna, P., Baruzzi, A., Cortelli, P., Lugaresi, A.., Tinuper, P., Zucconi, M. & Gambetti, P. (1986) Fatal familial insomnia and dysautonomia with selective degeneration of the thalamic nuclei. *New England Journal of Medicine, 315*, 997-1003.

Luria, A.R. (1969) *The mind of a mnemonist*. London: Jonathan Cape.

Luria, A.R. & Yudovich, F.I. (1956) *Speech and the development of mental processes in the child*. Harmondsworth: Penguin.

Lykken, D.T. (1957) A study of anxiety in the sociopathic personality. *Journal of Abnormal and Social Psychology, 55*, 6-10.

Lykken, D.T., Tellegen, A. & DeRubeis, R. (1978) Volunteer bias in twin research: The rule of two-thirds. *Social Biology, 25*, 1-9.

Lynch, M. & Roberts, J. (1982) *Consequences of child abuse*. London: Academic Press.

Maccoby, E.E. (1980) *Social development: Psychological growth and the parent-child relationship*. San Diego, CA: Harcourt Brace Jovanovich.

Macintosh, H.G. & Hale, D.E. (1976) *Assessment and the Secondary School Teacher*. London: Routledge and Kegan Paul.

MacKinnon, D. (1938) Violations of prohibitions. In H.A. Murray (Ed.) *Explorations in personality*. New York: Oxford University Press.

Mackworth, N.H. (1950) Researches in the measurement of human performance. *MRC Special Report Series, No. 268*. H.M.S.O.

Maclean, P.D. (1970) The limbic brain in relation to psychoses. In P. Black (Ed.) *Physiological correlates of emotion*. New York: Academic.

Mandler, G. (1967) Organisation and memory. In K.W. Spence & J.T. Spence (Eds.) *The psychology of learning and motivation*, (Vol. 2). London: Academic Press.

Mann, L. (1981) The baiting crowd in episodes of threatened suicide. *Journal of Personality and Social Psychology, 41*,703-9.

Mann, R.D. (1959) A review of the relationships between personality and performance in small groups. *Psychological Bulletin, 56*, 241-70.

Manning, A. (1973) *An introduction to animal behaviour*. London: Edward Arnold.

Manstead, A.R. & McCulloch, C. (1981) Sex-role stereotyping in British television advertisements. *British Journal of Social Psychology, 20*, 171-80.

Marañon, G. (1924) Contribution a l'etude de l'action emotive de l'adrenaline. *Revue Francaise Endocrinologie, 2*, 301-25.

Marcia, J.E. (1970) Identity in adolescence. In J. Adelson (Ed.) *Handbook of adolescent psychology*. New York: Wiley.

Marler, P. (1959) Developments in the study of animal communication. In P.R. Bell (Ed.) *Darwin's biological work: Some aspects reconsidered*. Cambridge: Cambridge University Press.

Marler, P. (1976) Social organisation, communication and graded signals: The chimpanzee and the gorilla. In P.P.G. Bateson & R.A. Hinde (Eds.) *Growing points in ethology*. Cambridge: Cambridge University Press.

Marler, P. & Mundinger, P. (1971) Vocal learning in birds. In H. Moltz (Ed.) *The ontogeny of vertebrate behaviour*. New York: Academic Press.

Marquis, D.P. (1931) Learning in the neonate: The modification of behaviour under three feeding schedules. *Journal of Experimental Psychology, 29*, 263-82.

Marr, D. (1982) *Vision: A computational investigation in the human representation and processing of visual information*. Oxford: W.H. Freeman.

Marsh, Rosser & Harre (1978) *Rules of disorder*. London: Routledge & Kegan Paul.

Marshall, G.D. & Zimbardo, P.G. (1979) Affective consequences of inadequately explained physiological arousal. *Journal of Personality and Social Psychology, 37*, 970-88.

Marslen-Wilson, W. & Tyler, L.K. (1980) The temporal structure of spoken language understanding. *Cognition, 8*, 1-71.

Maslow, A. (1954) *Motivation and personality*. New York: Harper & Row.

Mason, M.K. (1942) Learning to speak after six and one-half years silence. *Journal of Speech Disorders, 7*, 295–304.

Masterson, J.F. (1967) *The psychiatric dilemma of adolescence*. Boston: Little Brown.

Matarazzo, J.D. & Wiens, A.N. (1977) Black Intelligence Test of Cultural Homogeneity and Wechsler Adult Intelligence Scale scores of Black and White police applicants. *Journal of Applied Psychology, 62*, 57-63.

Mayall, B. & Petrie, P. (1977) *Minder, mother and child*. Windsor: NFER.

Mayall, B. & Petrie, P. (1983) *Childminding and day nurseries: What kind of care?* London: Heinemann Educational Books.

Maynard Smith, J. (1982) *Evolution and the theory of games*. Cambridge: Cambridge University Press.

Mayo, E. (1933) *The human problems of an industrial civilisation*. New York: Macmillan.

McAlister, A., Perry, C., Killen, J., Slinkard, L.A. & Maccoby, N. (1980) Pilot study of smoking, alcohol and drug abuse prevention, *American Journal of Public Health, 70*, 719-21.

McArthur, L.Z. (1972) The how and what of why: Some determinants and consequences of causal attribution. In E.T. Higgins, C.P. Herman & M.P. Zanna (Eds.) Social cognition: *The Ontario symposium* (Vol. 1). Hillsdale, NJ: Lawrence Erlbaum.

McCaul, K.D., Gladue, B.A. & Joppa, M. (19920 Winning, losing, mood, and testosterone. *Hormones and Behaviour, 26*, 486-504.

McClelland, D.C. & Boyatzis, R.E. (1982) Leadership motive pattern and long-term success in management. *Journal of Applied Psychology, 67*, 737-43.

McClelland, D.C., Atkinson, J., Clark, R. & Lowell, E. (1953) *The achievement motive*. New York: Appleton-Century-Crofts.

McClelland, J.L. (1981) Retrieving general and specific information from stored knowledge of specifics, *Proceedings of Third Annual Meeting of the Cognitive Science Society*, 170-2.

McClelland, J.L. & Rumelhart, D.E. (1981) An interactive activation model of context effects in letter perception. Part 1. An account of basic findings, *Psychological Review, 88*, 375-407.

McClintock, C.G. (1971) Menstrual synchrony and suppression. *Nature, 229*, 244-5.

McClintock, C.G. & McNeel, S.P. (1966) Reward level and game playing behaviour. *Journal of Conflict Resolution, 10*, 98-102.

McConnell, J.V. (1962) Memory transfer through cannibalism in planarians. *Journal of Neuropsychiatry, 3* (Supplement 1), 42-8.

McCormick, E.J., Jeanneret, P.R. & Mecham, R.C. (1969) *Position analysis questionnaire*. West Layfayette, IN: Occupational Research Centre, Purdue University.

McFarland, D. (1993) *Animal behaviour*. Harlow: Longman.

McGarrigle, J. & Donaldson, M. (1974) Conservation accidents. *Cognition, 3*, 341-50.

McGeoch, J.A. & Irion, A.L. (1952) *Psychology of human learning* (2nd edition). London: Longman.

McGeoch, J.A. & McDonald, W.T. (1931) Meaningful relation and retroactive inhibition. *American Journal of Psychology, 43*, 579-88.

McGhee, P.E. (1979) *Humor: Its origin and development*. San Francisco: W.H. Freeman.

McGinnies, E. (1949) Emotionality and perceptual defence. *Psychological Review, 56*, 244-51.

McGregor, D. (1960) *The human side of enterprise*. New York: McGraw-Hill.

McGuire, W.J. (1964) Inducing resistance to persuasion: Some contemporary approaches. In L. Berkowitz (Ed.) *Advances in experimental social psychology*. (Vol. 1). New York: Academic Press.

McGuire, W.J. (1968) Personality and susceptibility to social influence. In E.F. Borgatta & W.W. Lambert (Eds.) *Handbook of personality theory and research*. Chicago: Rand McNally.

McGurk, H. & MacDonald, J. (1976) Hearing lips and seeing voices. *Nature, 264*, 746-8.

McKay, D.G. (1973) Aspects of the theory of comprehension, memory and attention. *Quarterly Journal of Experimental Psychology, 25*, 22-40

McKeachie, W.J. (1984) Does anxiety disrupt information processing or does poor information processing lead to anxiety? *International Review of Applied Psychology, 33*, 187-203.

McKennell, A.C. & Bynner, J.M. (1969) Self images and smoking behaviour among school boys. *British Journal of Educational Psychology, 39*, 27-39.

McNeill, D. (1966) The creation of language, *Discovery, 27(7)*, 34-8.

McRobbie, A. (1978) *Women take issue*. Hutchinson.

Mead, M. (1928) *Coming of age in Samoa*. New York: Morrow.

Mead, M. (1935) *Sex and temperament in three primitive societies*. New York: Morrow.

Mead, M. (1949) *Male and female*. New York: Morrow.

Meddis, R. (1979) The evolution and function of sleep. In D.A. Oakley & H.C. Plotkin (Eds.) *Brain, behaviour and evolution*. London: Methuen.

Mednick, S.A. (1978) Berkou's fallacy and high risk research. In L.C. Wynne, R.L. Cromwell & S. Matthysse (Eds.) *The nature of schizophrenia*. New York: Wiley.

Melhuish, E.C. (1990) Research on day care for young children in the United Kingdom. In E.C. Melhuish & P. Moss (Eds.) *Day care for young children: International perspectives*. London: Routledge.

Meltzoff, A. & Moore, M. (1983) New born infants imitate adult facial gestures. *Child Development, 54*, 702-9.

Melzack, R. (1973) *The puzzle of pain*. New York: Basic Books.

Melzack, R. & Wall, P.D. (1965) Pain mechanisms: A new theory. *Science, 150*, 971-9.

Melzack, R. & Wall, P.D. (1982) *The challenge of pain*. New York: Basic Books,

Menzies, R. (1937) Conditioned vasomotor responses in human subjects. *Journal of Psychology, 4*, 75-120.

Messner, S.F. (1986) Television violence and violent crime: An aggregate analysis. *Social Problems, 33(3)*, 218-235

Middlemist, R.D., Knowles, E.S. & Matter, C.F. (1976) Personal space invasions in the lavatory: Suggestive evidence for arousal. *Journal of Personality and Social Psychology, 33*, 541-6.

Miles, L.E.M., Raynal, D.M. & Wilson, M.A. (1977) Blind man living in normal society has circadian rhythms of 24.9 hours. *Science, 198*, 421-3.

Milgram, S. (1963) Behavioural study of obedience. *Journal of Abnormal and Social Psychology, 67*, 371-8.

Milgram, S. (1970) The experience of living in cities: A psychological analysis. *Science, 167*, 1461-8.

Milgram, S. (1974) *Obedience to authority*. New York: Harper & Row.

Miller, G.A. (1956) The magic number seven, plus or minus two: Some limits on our capacity for processing information, *Psychological Review, 63*, 81-93.

Miller, D.I. (1989) The ecological psychology of the small town. *Psychology A Journal of Human Behaviour, 26*, 11-14.

Miller, G.A. & McNeill, D. (1969) Psycholinguistics. In G. Lindzey & E. Aronson (Eds.), *The handbook of social psychology, Vol. III*. Reading, MA: Addison-Wesley.

Miller, N.E. (1941) The frustration-aggression hypothesis. *Psychological Review, 48*, 337-42.

Miller, N.E. & Bugelski, R. (1948) Minor studies in aggression: the influence of frustration imposed by the ingroup in attitudes expressed towards the outgroups. *Journal of Psychology, 25*, 437-42.

Milner, B. (1959) The memory defect in bilateral hippocampal lesions. *Psychiatric Research Reports, 11*, 43-58.

Minard, R.D. (1952) Race relations in the Pocahontas coalfield. *Journal of Social Issues, 8*, 29-44.

Mintz, A. (1951) Non-adaptive group behaviour. *Journal of Abnormal and Social Psychology, 46*, 150-9.

Mischel, H. (1974) Sex bias in the evaluation of professional achievements. *Journal of Educational Psychology, 66(2)*, 157-66.

Mischel, W. (1968) *Personality and assessment*. New York: Wiley.

Mischel, W. & Peake, P.K. (1982) Beyond déjà vu in the search for cross-situational consistency, *Psychological Review, 89*, 730-55.

Mita, T.H., Dermer, M. & Knight, J.(1977) Reversed facial images and the mere exposure hypothesis, *Journal of Personality and Social Psychology, 35*, 597-601.

Money, J. & Ehrhardt, A.A. (1972) *Man and woman, boy and girl*. Baltimore, MD: John's Hopkins University Press.

Moniz, E. (1937) Prefrontal leucotomy in the treatment of mental disorders. *American Journal of Psychiatry, 93*, 1379-85.

Mor, V., McHorney, C. & Sherwood, S. (1986) Secondary morbidity among the recently bereaved. *American Journal of Psychiatry, 143*, 158-63.

Moray, N. (1959) Attention in dichotic listening: Affective cues and the influence of instructions, *Quarterly Journal of Experimental Psychology, 11*, 56-60.

Moreno, J.L. (1953) *Who shall survive?* (2nd edition). New York: Beacon.

Morley, I. & Hosking, D. (1984) Decision making and negotiation: leadership and social skills. In M. Gruneberg & T. Wall (Eds.) *Social psychology and organisational behaviour*. New York: Wiley.

Morley, I.M. & Stephenson, G.M. (1969) Interpersonal and interparty exchange: A laboratory simulation of an industrial negotiation at plant level. *British Journal of Psychology, 60*, 543-5.

Morris, C.D., Bransford, J.D. & Franks, J.J. (1977) Levels of processing versus transfer appropriate processing, *Journal of Verbal Learning and Verbal Behaviour, 16*, 519-33.

Morris, D. (1967) *The naked ape*. London: Jonathan Cape.

Morris, D. (1969) *The human zoo*. London: Jonathan Cape.

Morris, D. (1977) *Manwatching*. London: Jonathan Cape.

Mosher, F.A. (1962) Strategies for information gathering. Paper read at Eastern Psychological Association. Report in J.S. Bruner (1964) The course of cognitive growth. *American Psychologist, 19*, 1-15.

Mowrer, O.H. (1950) *Learning theory and personality dynamics*. New York: Ronald Press.

Moynahan, E.O. (1973) The development of knowledge concerning the effects of categorisation upon free recall. *Child Development, 44*, 238-45.

Murray, H.A. (1938) *Explorations in personality*. New York: Oxford University Press.

Murstein, B.I. (1972) Physical attractiveness and marital choice. *Journal of Personality and Social Psychology, 22(1)*, 8-12.

Myers, D.G. & Bishop, G.D. (1970) Discussion effects on racial attitudes. *Science, 169*, 778-89.

Navon, D. (1977) Forest before trees: The precedence of global features in visual perception. *Cognitive Psychology, 9*, 353-83.

Neisser, U. (1976) *Cognition and reality*. San Francisco: W.H. Freeman.

Neisser, U., Norick, R. & Lazar, R. (1963) Searching for ten targets simultaneously. *Perceptual and Motor Skills, 64*, 644-65.

Nelson, K. (1973) Structure and strategy in learning to talk. *Monographs for the Society for Research in Child Development, 38* (serial no. 149).

Nelson, K. (1987) What is in a name? Reply to Seidenberg and Petitto. *Journal of Experimental Psychology General, 116*, 293-6.

Neugarten, B.L. (1968) Adult personality: Toward a psychology of the life-cycle. In B.L. Neugarten (Ed.) *Middle age and ageing*. Chicago: University of Chicago Press.

Newcomb, M.D. (1990) Social support by any many other names: Towards a unified conceptualisation. *Journal of Social and Personal Relationships, 7*, 479-94.

Newcomb, T.M. (1961) *The acquaintance process*. New York: Holt, Rinehart & Winston.

Newcomb, T.M. (1971) Dyadic balance as a source of clues about interpersonal attraction. In B.I. Murstein (Ed.) *Theories of attraction and love*. New York: Springer.

Newell, A. & Simon, H.A. (1963) GPS, a program that simulates human thought. In E.A. Feigenbaum & J. Feldman (Eds.) *Computers and thought*. New York: Wiley.

Newell, A. & Simon, H.A. (1972) *Human problem solving*, Englewood Cliffs, NJ: Prentice Hall.

Newman, H.H., Freeman, F.N. & Holzinger, K.J. (1928) Twins: *A study of heredity and environment*. Chicago: University of Chicago Press.

Newman, O. (1972) *Defensible space*. New York: Macmillan.

Newson, J. and Newson, E. (1976) Day to day aggression between parent and child. In N. Tutt (Ed.) *Violence*. London: HMSO.

Nisbett, R.E., Caputo, C., Legant, P. & Marecek, J. (1973) Behaviour as seen by the actor and as seen by the observer. *Journal of Personality and Social Psychology, 27*, 154-64.

Noble, G. (1975) *Children in front of the small screen*. Pye survey. London: Constable

Nobles, W.W. (1976) Extended self: Rethinking the so-called Negro self-concept. *Journal of Black Psychology, 2*, 99-105.

Norman, D.A. (1968) Toward a theory of memory and attention. *Psychological Review, 75*, 522-36.

Norman, D.A. (1980) Twelve issues for cognitive science, *Cognitive Science, 4*, 1-32.

Norman, D.A. & Bobrow, D.G. (1975) On data-limited and resource-limited processes, *Cognitive Psychology, 7*, 44-64.

Novak, M.A. & Harlow, H.F. (1975) Social recovery of monkeys isolated for the first years of life. I: Rehabilitation and therapy. *Developmental Psychology, 11*, 453-65.

Novak, R.D., Smolensky, M.H., Fairchild, E.J. & Reves, R.R. (1990) Shiftwork and industrial injuries at a chemical plant in southeast Texas. *Chronobiology International, 7*, 155-64.

O'Connell, J.C. & Farran, D.C. (1982) Effects of day care experience on the use of intentional communicative behaviours in a sample of socio-economically depressed infants. *Developmental Psychology, 18*, 22-9.

O'Connor, R. (1969) Modification of social withdrawal through symbolic modelling. *Journal of Applied Behaviour Analysis, 2*, 15-22.

Ochiai, M. & Mizuno, K. (1979) About the relationship between the developmental stages of number and liquid conservation and the transformational capacities of active and passive sentences. *Japanese Journal of Educational Psychology, 27*, 228-37.

Oden, B.G., Clohisy, D.J. & Francois, G. (1982) Interanimal transfer of learned behaviour through injection of brain RNA. *Psychological Record, 32*, 281-90.

O'Leary, K.D., Kaufman, K.F., Kass, R.E. & Drabman, R.S. (1974) The effects of loud and soft reprimands on the behaviour of disruptive students. In A.R. Brown & C. Avery (Eds.) *Modifying children's behaviour: A book of readings*. Springfield, IL: Thomas.

Olds, J. & Milner, P. (1954) Positive reinforcement produced by electrical stimulation of the septal area and other regions of the rat brain. *Journal of Comparative and Physiological Psychology, 47*, 419-28.

Olsen, J.M. & Ross, M. (1988) False feedback about placebo effectiveness: Consequences for the misattribution of speech anxiety. *Journal of Experimental Social Psychology, 24(4)*, 275-91.

Olweus, D. (1989) Bully/victim problems among schoolchildren: Basic facts and effects of a school based intervention program. In K. Rubin & D. Pepler (Eds.) *The development and treatment of childhood aggression*. Hillsdale, NJ: Lawrence Erlbaum.

Orne, M.T. (1962) On the social psychology of the psychology experiment - with particular reference to demand characteristics and their implications. *American Psychologist, 17 (11)*, 776-83.

Ornstein, R. (1986) *The psychology of consciousness* (2nd revised edition). Harmondsworth, Middlesex: Penguin.

Osborn, A.F. (1957) *Applied imagination*. New York: Scribner.

Osgood, C.E., Suci, G.J. & Tannenbaum, P.H. (1957) *The measurement of meaning*. Urbana, IL: University of Illinois Press.

Osgood, C.E. & Tannenbaum, P.H. (1955) The principles of congruity in the prediction of attitude change, *Psychological Review, 62*, 42-55.

Oswald and Adam, K. (1980) *The man who had not slept for 10 years*. British Medical Journal, 281, 1684-5.

Packer, C. (1977) Reciprocal altruism in *Papio anubis. Nature, 265*, 441-3.

Palmer, J.D. (1989) Comparative studies of tidal rhythms: VIII. A translocation experiment involving circalunidian rhythms. *Marine Behaviour and Physiology, 14*, 231-43.

Paffenbarger, R.S., Hyde, R.T., Wing, A.L. & Hsieh, C. (1986) Physical activity, all-cause mortality and longevity of college alumni. *New England Journal of Medicine, 314*, 605-13.

Papert, S. (1980) *Mindstorms: Children, computers, and powerful ideas*. New York: Basic Books.

Parke, R.D. (1981) *Fathers*. Cambridge, MA: Harvard University Press.

Parkes, C.M. (1987) *Bereavement: Studies of grief in adult life*. (2nd edition). Madison: International Universities Press.

Parten, M.B. (1932) Social participation among preschool children. *Journal of Abnormal and Social Psychology, 27*, 243-69.

Patterson, F.G. & Linden, E. (1981) *The education of Koko*. New York: Holt, Rinehart & Winston.

Pavlov, I.P. (1927) *Conditioned Reflexes*. London: Oxford University Press.

Penfield, W. (1955) The permanent record of the stream of consciousness. *Acta Psychologica, 11*, 47-69.

Pepperberg, I.M. (1983) Cognition in the African Grey parrot: Preliminary evidence for auditory/vocal comprehension of the class concept. *Animal Learning and Behaviour, 11*, 179-185.

Pepperberg, I. (1990) Referential mapping: A technique for attaching functional significance to the innovative utterances of an African Grey parrot *(Psittacus erithacus). Applied Psycholinguistics, 11*, 23-44.

Perrin, S. & Spencer, C. (1980) The Asch effect: A child of its times? *Bulletin of the British Psychological Society, 32*, 405-6.

Perry, J.D. & Simpson, M.E. (1987) Violent crimes in a city: Environmental determinants. *Environment and Behaviour, 19*, 77-90.

Pessin, J. (1933) The comparative effects of social and mechanical stimulation on memorising. *American Journal of Psychology, 45*, 263-70.

Peterson, C. & Seligman, M.E.P. (1980) Helplessness and attributional style in depression. *Symposium on the Development of Metacognition, the Formation of Attributional Styles, and the Formation of Self Instruction*.

Peterson, L.R. & Peterson, M.J. (1959) Short-term retention of individual verbal items. *Journal of Experimental Psychology, 58*, 193-8.

Petitto, L. & Seidenberg, M.S. (1979) On the evidence for linguistic abilities in signing apes. *Brain and Language, 8*, 162-3.

Pettigrew, T.F. (1959) Regional difference in anti-negro prejudice. *Journal of Abnormal and Social Psychology, 59*, 28-56.

Pettigrew, T.F., Allport, G.W. & Barnett, E.O. (1958) Binocular resolution and perception of race in South Africa. *British Journal of Psychology, 49,* 265-78.

Petty, M.M., McGee, G.W. & Cavender, J.W. (1984) A meta-analysis of the relationship between individual job satisfaction and individual performance. *Academy of Management Review, 9,* 712-21.

Petty, R.E. & Cacioppo, J.T. (1981) *Attitudes and persuasion: Classic and contemporary approaches.* Dubuque, IA: Wm. C. Brown.

Petty, R.E. & Cacioppo, J.T. (1986) The elaboration likelihood model of persuasion. In L. Berkowitz (Ed.) *Advances in experimental social psychology.* (Vol. 19). New York: Academic Press.

Phares, E.J. & Wilson, K.G. (1972) Responsibility and attribution: Role of outcome severity, situational ambiguity and internal-external control, *Journal of Personality, 40,* 392-406.

Phelps, L. & Branyan, J. (1990) Academic achievement and nonverbal intelligence in public school hearing-impaired children. *Psychology in the Schools, 27,* 210-7.

Philips, H.C. (1987) The effects of behavioural treatment on chronic pain. *Behaviour Research and Therapy, 25,* 365-77.

Philips, H.C. & Jahanshahi, M. (1986) The components of pain behaviour report. *Behaviour Research and Therapy, 24,* 117-25.

Phillips, K. (1991) Biofeedback. In M. Pitts & K. Phillips (Eds.) *The psychology of health: An introduction.* London: Routledge.

Piaget, J. (1926) *The language and thought of the child.* New York: Harcourt Brace Jovanovich.

Piaget, J. (1932) *The moral judgement of the child.* Harmondsworth: Penguin.

Piaget, J. (1950) *The psychology of intelligence.* San Diego, CA: Harcourt Brace Jovanovich.

Piaget, J. (1951) *Play, dreams and imitation in childhood.* London: Routledge & Kegan Paul.

Piaget, J. (1967) *The child's conception of the world.* Totowa, NJ: Littlefield Adams.

Piaget, J. (1970) Piaget's theory. In P.H. Mussen (Ed.) *Carmichael's manual of child psychology* (Vol. 1). New York: Wiley.

Piaget, J. & Inhelder, B. (1956) *The child's conception of space.* London: Routledge & Kegan Paul.

Piliavin, I.M., Rodin, J. & Piliavin, J.A. (1969) Good Samaritanism: An underground phenomenon, *Journal of Personality and Social Psychology, 13,* 1200-13.

Platt, S. (1986) Recent trends in parasuicide ("attempted suicide") and unemployment among men in Edinburgh. In S. Allen *et al.* (Eds.) *The experience of unemployment.* Basingstoke: Macmillan Education.

Pollack, C.P., Green, J. & Smith, G.P. (1989) Blood glucose prior to meal request in humans isolated from all temporal cues. *Physiology and Behaviour, 46,* 529-34.

Posner, M.I. (1992) Attention as a cognitive and neural system. Current Directions in Psychological Science, 1, 11-14.

Posner, M.I. & Snyder, C.R.R. (1974) Attention and cognitive control. In R.L. Solso (Ed.) *Information processing and cognition: The Loyola Symposium.* Hillsdale, NJ: Lawrence Erlbaum.

Postman, L. & Crutchfield, R.S. (1952) The interaction of need, set, and stimulus structure in a cognitive task. *American Journal of Psychology, 65,* 196-217.

Premack, D. (1971) Language in chimpanzee? *Science, 172,* 808-22.

Press, A. (1987) The menace on the road. *Newsweek, December 21,* 42-3.

Pritchard, R.M. (1961) A collimator stabilising system for the retinal image. *Quarterly Journal of experimental Psychology, 13,* 181.

Pylyshyn, Z.W. (1980) The "casual power" of machines. *Behavioural and Brain Sciences, 3,* 442-4.

Quattrone, G.A. (1982) Overattribution and unit formation: When behaviour engulfs the person. *Journal of Personality and Social Psychology, 42,* 593-607.

Quinton, D. & Rutter, M. (1976) Early hospital admissions and later disturbance of behaviour: An attempted replication of Douglas's findings. *Developmental Medicine and Child Neurology, 18,* 447-59.

Rabbie, J.M. & Horwitz, M. (1960) Arousal of ingroup-outgroup bias by a chance win or loss. *Journal of Personality and Social Psychology, 13,* 269-77.

Rabbitt, P.M.A. (1965) An age decrement in the ability to ignore irrelevant information. *Journal of Gerontology, 20,* 233-8.

Rabkin, J.G. (1980) Stressful life events and schizophrenia: A review of the research literature. *Psychological Bulletin, 87,* 408-25.

Rahe, R.H. & Arthur, R.J. (1977) Life change patterns surrounding illness experience. In A. Monat & R.S. Lazarus (Eds.) *Stress and coping.* New York: Columbia University Press.

Reason, J.T. (1979) Actions not as planned. In G. Underwood & R. Stevens (eds.) *Aspects of consciousness.* London: Academic Press.

Reddick, J. (1985) The interdependence of health and housing for the elderly. *Journal of Housing for the Elderly, 2,* 77-82.

Redfern, P.H. (1989) "Jet-lag": Strategies for prevention and cure. *Human Psychopharmacology Clinical and Experimental, 4,* 159-68.

Reed, S.K. (1972) *Psychological processes in pattern recognition.* New York: Academic Press.

Reeves, A.G. & Plum, F. (1969) Hyperphagia, rage and dementia accompanying a ventro-medial hypothalamic neoplasm. *Archives of Neurology, 20,* 616-24.

Reichard, S., Livson, F. & Peterson, P.G. (1962) *Ageing and personality.* New York: Wiley.

Reicher, G.M. (1969) Perceptual recognition as a function of meaningfulness of stimulus material, *Journal of Experimental Psychology, 81,* 274-280.

Richter, C.P. (1957) On the phenomenon of sudden death in animals and man. *Psychosomatic Medicine, 19,* 191-8.

Ridley, M. (1986) *Animal behaviour: A concise introduction.* Oxford: Blackwell Scientific Publications.

Riggio, R.E. (1990) *Introduction to industrial/organisational psychology.* London: Scott Foresman/Little.

Ringness, T.A. (1961) Self-concept of children of low, average and high intelligence. *American Journal of Mental Deficiency, 65,* 453-61.

Robertson, J. & Robertson, J. (1967-73) *Young children in brief separation.* A film study.

Robins, L.N. (1966) *Deviant children grow up.* Baltimore, MD: Williams & Wilins.

Robins, L.N., Davis, D.H. & Goodwin, D.W. (1974) Drug use by the U.S. Army enlisted men in Vietnam: A follow-up on their return home. *American Journal of Epidemiology, 99,* 235-49.

Robson, K.S. (1967) The role of eye-to-eye contact in maternal-infant attachment. *Journal of Child Psychology and Psychiatry, 8,* 13-25.

Rogers, C.A. & Franz, C. (1962) *Racial themes in Southern Rhodesia.* New Haven: Yale University Press.

Rogers, C.R. (1951) *Client-centred therapy: Its current practices, implications and theory.* Boston: Houghton-Mifflin.

Rogers, C.R. (1959) A theory of therapy, personality and interpersonal relationships, as developed in the client-centred framework. In S. Koch (Ed.) *Psychology: A study of science* (Vol. 3). New York: McGraw Hill.

Rogers, C.R. (1961) *On becoming a person.* Boston: Houghton Mifflin.

Roland, E. (1989) Bullying: The Scandinavian research tradition. In E. Roland & E. Munthe (Eds.) *Bullying: An international perspective.* London: David Fulton.

Rosch, E. (1975) Cognitive reference points, *Cognitive Psychology, 7,* 532-47.

Rose, S.A. & Blank, M. (1974) The potency of context in childrens' cognition: An illustration through conservation. *Child Development, 45,* 499-502.

Rosenberg, G.B. & Langer, J. (1965) A study of postural-gestural communication. *Journal of Personality and Social Psychology, 2,* 593-7.

Rosenberg, M.J., Nelson, C. & Vivekanathan, P.S. (1968) A multidimensional approach to the structure of personality impression. *Journal of Personality and Social Psychology, 9,* 283-94.

Rosenblatt, J.S. (1969) The development of maternal responsiveness in the rat. *Journal of Orthopsychiatry, 39,* 36-56.

Rosenblum, L.A. & Harlow, H. (1963) Approach-avoidance conflict in the mother surrogate situation. *Psychological Reports, 12,* 83-5.

Rosenhan, D.L. (1973) On being sane in insane places. *Science, 179,* 250-8.

Rosenhan, D.L. & Seligman, M.E.P. (1989) *Abnormal Psychology* (2nd edition). London: Norton.

Rosenshine, B. & Stevens, R. (1986) Teaching functions. In M.C. Wittrock (Ed.) *Handbook of research on teaching* (3rd edition). New York: Macmillan.

Rosenthal, R. & Fode, K.L. (1963) The effect of experimenter bias on the performance of the albino rat. *Behavioural Science, 8 (3),* 183-9.

Rosenthal, R. & Jacobsen, L. (1966) Teacher expectations. *Psychological Reports, 19,* 115-8.

Rosenthal, R. & Jacobsen, L. (1968) *Pygmalion in the classroom.* New York: Holt, Rinehart & Winston.

Ross, L., Greene, D. & House, P. (1977) The false consensus phenomenon: An attributional bias in self-perception and social perception processes. *Journal of Experimental Social Psychology, 13,* 279-301.

Rothbart, M.K. & Maccoby, E.E. (1966) Parents' differential reactions to sons and daughters. *Journal of Personality and Social Psychology, 4,* 237-43.

Rotter, J.B. (1966) Generalised expectancies for internal versus external control of reinforcement. *Psychological Monographs, 30 (1),* 1-26.

Rotton, J., Frey, J., Barry, T., Milligan, M. & Fitzpatrick, M. (1978) The air pollution experience and physical aggression. *Journal of Applied Social Psychology, 9,* 397-412.

Rubin, K.H. (1973) Decentration skills in institutionalised and non-institutionalised elderly. *Proceedings of the 81st Annual Convention of the American Psychology Association, 8,* 759-60.

Rubin, Z. (1973) *Liking and loving: An invitation to social psychology.* New York: Holt, Rinehart & Winston.

Ruble, D.N. & Brooks-Gunn, J. (1982) The experience of menarche. *Child development, 53,* 1557-66.

Rumbaugh, D.H., Gill, T.V. & Glaserfeld, E.C. (1973) Reading and sentence completion by a chimpanzee. *Science, 182,* 731-3.

Russeck, M. (1971) Hepatic receptors and the neurophysiological mechanisms controlling feeding behaviour. In S. Ehrenpreis (Ed.) *Neurosciences research* (Vol. 4). New York: Academic Press.

Russell, M.A., Jarvis, M.J., & West, R.J. (1986) Use of urinary nicotine concentrations to estimate exposure and mortality from passive smoking in non-smokers. *British Journal of Addiction, 81,* 275-81.

Russell, M.J., Switz, G.M. & Thompson, K. (1980) Olfactory influences on the human menstrual cycle. *Pharmacology, Biochemistry and Behaviour, 13,* 737-8.

Russo, N.F., Feller, L. & Patrick, H. (1982) Sex role stereotypes in television advertising: Strategy for change in the 80s. *Academic Psychology Bulletin, 4,* 117-35.

Rutter, M. (1981) *Maternal deprivation reassessed* (2nd edition). Harmondsworth, Middlesex: Penguin.

Rutter, M., Graham, P., Chadwick, D.F.D., & Yule, W. (1976) Adolescent turmoil: Fact or fiction? *Journal of Child Psychology and Psychiatry, 17,* 35-56.

Rutter, M., Tizard, J. & Whitmore, K. (1970) *Education, health and behaviour.* London: Longman.

Saarinen, T.F. (1987) *Centering of mental maps of the world: Discussion paper.* Department of Geography & Regional Development, University of Arizona, Tucson.

Sachs, J., Bard, B. & Johnson, M.L. (1981) Language learning with restricted input: Case studies of two hearing children of deaf parents. *Applied Psycholinguistics, 2,* 33-54.

Saegart, S., Swap, W. & Zajonc, R.B. (1973) Exposure, context, and interpersonal attraction. *Journal of Personality and Social Psychology, 25,* 234-42.

Salancik, G.R. & Pfeffer, J. (1977) Who gets power and how they hold on to it: A strategic-contingency model of power. *Organizational Dynamics, 5,* 3-21.

Samuel, J. & Bryant, P. (1984) Asking only one question in the conservation experiment. *Journal of Child Psychology and Psychiatry, 25 (2),* 315-8.

Saper, B. (1991) The JAP joke controversy: An excruciating psychosocial analysis. *Humor International Journal of Humor Research, 4,* 223-39.

Sarnoff, I. & Zimbardo, P.G. (1961) Anxiety, fear and social affiliation, *Journal of Abnormal and Social Psychology, 62,* 356-63.

Savage-Rumbaugh, E.S. (1991) Language learning in the bonobo: How and why they learn . In N.A. Krasnegor, D.M. Rumbaugh, R.L. Schiefelbusch & M. Studdert-Kennedy (Eds.) *Biological and behavioural determinants of language development.* Hillsdale, NJ: Lawrence Erlbaum.

Savage-Rumbaugh, E.S., Rumbaugh, D.M. & Boysen, S. (1978) Symbolic communication between two chimpanzees (Pan troglodytes). *Science, 201,* 641-4.

Scarr, S. & Weinberg, R.A. (1983) The Minnesota adoption studies: Genetic difference and malleability. *Child Development, 54,* 260-7.

Schachter, S. (1951) Deviation, rejection and communication, *Journal of Abnormal and Social Psychology, 46,* 190-207.

Schachter, S. (1959) *The psychology of affiliation.* Stanford, CA: Stanford University Press.

Schachter, S. & Latané, B.T. (1964) Crime, cognition and the autonomic nervous system. In D. Levine (Ed.) *Nebraska symposium on motivation.* Lincoln, NB: University of Nebraska Press.

Schachter, S. & Singer, J.E. (1962) Cognitive, social and physiological determinants of emotional state. *Psychological Review, 69,* 379-99.

Schaeffer, M.H., Street, S.W., Singer, J.E. & Baum, A. (1988) Effects of control on the stress reactions of commuters. *Journal of Applied Social Psychology, 18,* 944-57.

Schafer, R., Berg, I. & McCandless, B. (1951) Report on survey of current psychological testing practices. *Supplement to newsletter, Division of Clinical Abnormal Psychology, American Psychological Association, 4,* no. 5.

Schaffer, H.R. & Emerson, P.E. (1964) The development of social attachments in infancy. *Monographs of the Society for Research in Child Development, 29(3)* Serial No. 94.

Schaie, K.W. (Ed.) (1983) *Longitudinal studies of adult psychological development.* New York: Guilford Press

Schank, R.C. & Abelson, R.P. (1977) *Scripts, plans, goals and understanding.* Hillsdale, NJ: Lawrence Erlbaum.

Schank, R.C. (1975) *Conceptual information processing.* Amsterdam: North-Holland.

Scheerer, M., Rothmann, E. & Goldstein, K. (1945) A case of "Idiot Savant": An experimental study of personality organisation. *Psychological Monographs, 58* (no. 4), 668-9.

Schein, E.H. (1956) The Chinese indoctrination programme for prisoners of war: A study of attempted "brainwashing", *Psychiatry, 19,* 149-72

Schiff, M., Duyne, M., Dumaret, A., Stewart, J., Tomkiewicz, S. & Fenigold, J. (1978) Intellectual status of working-class children adopted early into upper-middle class families. *Science, 200,* 1503-4.

Schinke, S.P., Schilling, R.F. II, Barth, R.P., Gilchrist, L.D. & Maxwell, J.S. (1986) Stress-management intervention to prevent family violence. *Journal of Family Violence, 1,* 13-26.

Schjelderup-Ebbe, T. (1935) Social behaviour of birds. *In A handbook of social psychology.* Worcester, MA: Clark University Press.

Schmidt, F.L., Hunter, J.E., McKenzie, R.C. & Muldrow, T.W. (1979) Impact of valid selection procedures on workforce productivity. *Journal of Applied Psychology, 64,* 609-26.

Schmitt, B., Gilovich, T.K., Goore, N. & Joseph, L. (1986) Mere presence and social facilitation: One more time. *Journal of Experimental Social Psychology, 22,* 242-8.

Schram, E.W. & Roberts, D.F. (1971) *The process and effects of mass communication.* University of Illinois Press.

Schultz, N.R., Kaye, D.B. & Hoyer, W.J. (1980) Intelligence and spontaneous flexibility in adulthood and old age. *Intelligence, 4,* 219-31.

Schusterman, R.J & Gisiner, R. (1988) Artificial language comprehension in dolphins and sea lions: The essential cognitive skills. *Psychological Record, 38,* 311-48.

Schutz, F. (1971) Prägung des sexualverhaltens von enten und gänsen durch sozialeindrücke während der jugendphase. Described in D. McFarland (1993) *Animal behaviour.* Harlow: Longman.

Scott, K.D. & Taylor, G.S. (1985) An examination of conflicting findings on the relationship between job satisfaction and absenteeism: A meta-analysis. *Academy of Management Journal, 28,* 599-612.

Searle, J. (1980) Minds, brains and programs. *Behavioural and Brain Sciences, 3,* 417-57.

Secord, P.F., Dukes, W.F. & Bevan, W. (1959) Personalities in faces. I: An experiment in social perceiving. *Genetic Psychology Monographs, 49,* 231-79.

Segal, M.W. (1974) Alphabet and attraction: An unobtrusive measure of the effect of propinquity in a field setting. *Journal of Personality and Social Psychology, 30,* 654-7.

Segal, S.J. & Fusella, V. (1970) Influence of imaged pictures and sounds on detection of visual and auditory signals, *Journal of Experimental Psychology, 83,* 458-64.

Segall, M.H., Campbell, D.T. & Herskovits, M.J. (1963) Cultural differences in the perception of geometrical illusions. *Science, 139,* 769-71.

Segraves, R.T. (1985) Divorce and health problems. *Medical Aspects of Human Sexuality, 19,* 152-64.

Seidenberg, M.S. & Petitto, L.A. (1987) Communication, symbolic communication, and language: Comment on Savage-Rumbaugh, McDonald, Sevcik, Hopkins and Rupert (1986). *Journal of Experimental Psychology General, 116,* 279-87.

Selfe, P. (1987) *Work out sociology.* Basingstoke: Macmillan.

Seligman, M.E.P. (1970) On the generality of the laws of learning. *Psychological Review, 77,* 406-18.

Seligman, M.E.P. (1975) *Helplessness: On depression, development and death.* San Francisco: W.H. Freeman.

Seligman, M.E.P. (1978) Comment and integration. *Journal of Abnormal Psychology, 87,* 165-79.

Selye, H. (1956) *The stress of life.* New York: McGraw-Hill.

Shaffer, D.R. (1993) *Developmental psychology: Childhood and adolescence* (3rd edition). Pacific Grove, CA: Brooks/Cole Publishing Co.

Shaffer, L.H. (1975) Multiple attention in continuous verbal tasks. In P.M.A. Rabbit & S. Dornic (Eds.) *Attention and performance* (Vol. V). London: Academic Press.

Shakespeare, R. (1982) *The psychology of handicap.* London: Methuen.

Shallice, T. (1967) Temporal summation and absolute brightness threshold. British *Journal of Mathematical and Statistical Psychology, 20,* 129-62.

Shapiro, C.M., Bortz, R., Mitchell, D., Bartel, P. & Jooste, P. (1981) Slow-wave sleep: A recovery period after exercise. *Science, 214,* 1253-4.

Shatz, M. & Gelman, R. (1973) The development of communication skills: Modifications in the speech of young children as a function of the listener. *Monographs for the Society for Research in Child Development, 38,* 1-38.

Shaw, M.E. (1932) Comparison of individuals and small groups in the rational solution of complex problems. *American Journal of Psychology, 44,* 491-504.

Shaw, M.E. (1954) Some effects of problem complexity upon problem solution efficiency in different communication nets. *Journal of Experimental Psychology, 48,* 211-7.

Shayer, M. & Wylam, H. (1978) The distribution of Piagetian stages of thinking in British middle and secondary school children: II. *British Journal of Educational Psychology, 48,* 62-70.

Sheldon, W.H., Stevens, S.S. & Tucker, W.B. (1940) *The varieties of human physique: An introduction to constitutional psychology.* New York: Harper.

Sheldon, W.H., Dupertuis, C.W. & McDermott, E. (1954) *Atlas of men: A guide for somatotyping the adult male at all ages.* New York: Harper.

Shepard, R.N. (1967) Recognition memory for words, sentences and pictures. *Journal of Verbal Learning and Verbal Behaviour, 6,* 156-63.

Sherif, M. (1936) *The psychology of social norms.* New York: Harper & Row.

Sherif, M., Harvey, O.J., White, B.J., Hood, W.R. & Sherif, C.W. (1961) *Intergroup co-operation and conflict: The Robbers Cave experiment.* Norman, OK: University of Oklahoma Press.

Sherif, M. & Hovland, C.I. (1961) *Social judgement: Assimilation and contrast effects in communication and attitude change.* New Haven, CN: Yale University Press.

Sherrington, C.S. (1900) Experiments on the value of vascular and visceral factors for the genesis of emotion. *Proceedings of the Royal Society, 66,* 390-403.

Sherrington, R., Brynjolfsson, J., Petursson, H., Potter, M. *et al.* (1988) Localisation of a susceptibility locus for schizophrenia on chromosome 5. *Nature, 336,* 164-7.

Sherry, D.F. & Galef, B.G. (1984) Cultural transmission without imitation: Milk bottle opening by birds. *Animal Behaviour, 32,* 937-8.

Shields, J. (1962) *Monozygotic twins brought up apart and brought up together.* London: Oxford University Press.

Shields, S.A. (1983) Development of autonomic nervous system responsivity in children: A review of the literature. *International Journal of Behavioural Development, 6,* 291-319.

Shiffrin, R.M. & Schneider, W. (1977) Controlled and automatic human information processing: II. Perceptual learning, automatic attending, and a general theory. *Psychological Review, 84,* 127-90.

Shontz, F.C. (1975) *The psychological aspects of physical illness and disability.* New York: Macmillan Co.

Siann, G. (1985) *Accounting for aggression - perspectives on aggression and violence.* London: Allen & Unwin.

Siegal, M. & Cowen, J. (1984) Appraisals of intervention: The mother's versus the culprit's behaviour as determinants of children's evaluations of discipline techniques. *Child Development, 55,* 1760-6.

Siegel, J., Dubrovsky, V., Kiesler, S. & McGuire, T.W. (1986) Group processes in computer-mediated communication. *Organizational Behaviour and Human Decision Processes, 37,* 157-87.

Silverman, I. (1971) Physical attractiveness and courtship. *Sexual Behaviour, 1,* 22-5.

Simon, H.A. & Reed, S.K. (1976) Modelling strategy shifts on a problem solving task, *Cognitive Psychology, 8,* 86-97.

Sinclair-de-Zwart, H. (1969) Developmental psycholinguistics. In D. Elkind and J. Flavell (Eds.), *Studies in cognitive development.* New York: Oxford University Press.

Singer, L.M., Brodzinsky, D.M., Ramsay, D., Steir, M. & Waters, E. (1985) Mother-infant attachments in adoptive families. *Child Development, 56,* 1543-51.

Singer, P. (1993) *The great ape project.* Fourth Estate.

Sinson, J.C. & Stainton, C.L. (1990) An investigation into attitudes (and attitude change) towards mental handicap. *British Journal of Mental Subnormality, 36,* 53-64.

Skeels, H. & Dye, H.B. (1939) A study of the effects of differential stimulation on mentally retarded children. *Proceedings and Addresses of the American Association on Mental Deficiency, 44,* 114-36.

Skinner, B.F. (1938) *Science and behaviour.* New York: Macmillan.

Skinner, B.F. (1948) *Walden two.* New York: Macmillan.

Skinner, B.F. (1953) *Science and human behaviour.* New York: Macmillan.

Skinner, B.F. (1957) *Verbal behaviour.* New York: Appleton-Century-Crofts.

Skinner, B.F. (1971) *Beyond freedom and dignity.* London: Pelican Books.

Skinner, B.F. (1989) The origins of cognitive thought. *American Psychologist, 44,* 13-18.

Skodak, M. & Skeels, H. (1949) A final follow-up study of 100 adopted children. *Journal of Genetic Psychology, 75,* 85-125.

Slobin, D.I. (1979) *Psycholinguistics* (2nd edition). Glenview, IL: Scott Foresman.

Sluckin, W. (1965) *Imprinting and early experiences.* London: Methuen.

Sluckin, W. & Salzen, A. (1961) Imprinting and perceptual learning. *Quarterly Journal of Experimental Psychology, 13,* 65-77.

Smith, C. & Lloyd, B. (1978) Maternal behaviour and perceived sex of infant: Revisited. *Child Development, 49,* 1263-5.

Smith, G.S. & Kraus, J.F. (1988) Alcohol and residential, recreational, and occupational injuries: A review of the epidemiological evidence. In J. Breslow, J.E. Fielding & L.B. Lave (Eds.) *Annual review of public health* (Vol. 9). Palo Alto, CA: Annual Reviews.

Smith, J.C., Glass, G.V. & Miller, T.I. (1980) *The benefits of psychotherapy.* Baltimore: Johns Hopkins Press.

Smith, P.K., Dalgleish, M. & Herzmark, G. (1981) A comparison of the effects of fantasy play tutoring and skills tutoring in nursery class. *International Journal of Behavioural Development, 4,* 421-41.

Smith, V.L. & Ellsworth, P.C. (1987) The social psychology of eyewitness accuracy: Misleading questions and communicator expertise. *Journal of Applied Psychology, 72,* 294-300.

Snarey, J.R. (1985) Cross-cultural universality of social-moral development: A critical review of Kohlbergian research. *Psychological Bulletin, 97,* 202-32.

Snyder, F.W. & Pronko, N.H. (1952) *Vision with spatial inversion.* Wichita, KS: University of Wichita Press.

Snyder, M. (1979) Self-monitoring processes. In L. Berkowitz (Ed.) *Advances in experimental social psychology* (Vol. 6). New York: Academic Press.

Snyder, M., Tanke, E.D. & Bersheid, E. (1977) Social perception and interpersonal behaviour: On the self-fulfilling nature of social stereotypes. *Journal of Personality and Social Psychology, 35,* 656-66.

Sokolov, E.N. (1960) In M.A.B. Brazier (Ed.) *The central nervous system and behaviour.* New York: Josiah Macey Jr. Foundation.

Solomon, R.L. (1977) An Opponent theory of acquired motivation: The affective dynamics of addiction. In J. Maser & M. Seligman (Eds.) *Psychopathology: Experimental models.* San Francisco: Freeman.

Solso, R.L. (1974) Theories of retrieval. In R.L. Solso (Ed.) *Theories of cognitive psychology.* Potomac, MD: Lawrence Erlbaum.

Solso, R.L. (1991) *Cognitive Psychology.* London: Allyn & Bacon.

Spalding, D. (1873) Instinct: with original observations on young animals. *Macmillan's Magazine, 27,* 282-93. Reprinted in *British Journal of Animal Behaviour, 2,* 1-11.

Spearman, C. (1904) General intelligence, objectively determined and measured. *American Journal of Psychology, 15,* 201-93.

Speisman, J.C., Lazarus, R.S., Mordkoff, A.M. & Davidson, L.A. (1964) The experimental reduction of stress based on ego defence theory. *Journal of Abnormal and Social Psychology, 68,* 397-8.

Sperling. G. (1960) The information available in brief visual presentations, *Psychological Monographs, 74* (Whole no. 498), 1-29

Sperry, R.W. & Gazzaniga, M.S. (1967) Language following surgical disconnection of the hemispheres. In F. Darley (Ed.) *Brain mechanisms underlying speech and language.* New York: Grune & Stratton.

Spitz, R.A. & Wolf, K.M. (1946) Anaclitic depression. *Psychoanalytic Study of the Child, 2,* 313-42.

Staats, A.W. & Staats, C.K. (1958) Attitudes established by classical conditioning, *Journal of Abnormal and Social Psychology, 57,* 37-40.

Staats, A.W. & Staats, C.K. (1963) *Complex human behaviour.* New York: Holt Rinehart & Winston.

Stanton, H.R. & Litwak, E. (1955) Toward the development of a short-form test of interpersonal competence. *American Sociological Review, 20,* 668-74.

Stass, J.W. & Willis, F.N. Jr. (1967) Eye contact, pupil dilation and personal preferences. *Psychonomic Science, 7,* 375-6.

Stein, A.H. & Friedrich, L.K. (1975) Impact of television on children and youth. In E.M. Hetherington, J.W. Hagen, R. Kron & A.H. Stein (Eds.) *Review of child development research* (Vol. 5). Chicago: Chicago University Press.

Sternbach, R.A. (1968) *Pain: A psychophysiological analysis.* New York: Academic Press.

Sternberg, R.J. (1985) *Beyond IQ: A triarchic theory of human intelligence.* Cambridge: Cambridge University Press.

Steuer, F.B., Applefield, J.M. & Smith, R. (1971) Televised aggression and interpersonal aggression of preschool children. *Journal of Experimental Child Psychology, 11,* 442-7.

Stevenson, K.M., Leung, P. & Cheung, K.M. (1992) Competency-based evaluation of interviewing skills in child sexual abuse cases. *Social Work Research and Abstracts, 28,* 11-6.

Stewart, J.E. III (1980) Defendant's attractiveness as a factor in the outcome of criminal trials: An observational study. *Journal of Applied Social Psychology, 10,* 348-61.

Stoner, J.A.F. (1968) *A comparison of individual and group decisions involving risk.* Unpublished master's thesis, Massachusetts Institute of Technology.

Storms, M.D. & Nisbett, R.E. (1970) Insomnia and the attribution process, *Journal of Personality and Social Psychology, 16,* 319-28.

Storms, M.D. & Thomas, G.C. (1977) Reactions to physical closeness. *Journal of Personality and Social Psychology, 35,* 412-8.

Stouffer, S.A., Suchman, E.A., DeVinney, L.C., Starr, S.A., & Williams, R.M. (1949) *The American soldier: Adjustment during army life,* Vol. 1. Princeton, NJ: Princeton University Press.

Stroop, J.R. (1935) Studies of interference in serial verbal reactions. *Journal of Experimental Psychology, 18,* 643-62.

Stroymeyer, C.G. (1970) Eidetikers. *Psychology Today, November,* 76-80.

Sundstrom, E. & Altman, I. (1974) Interpersonal relationships and personal space: Research review and theoretical model. *Human ecology, 4,* 47-67.

Swain, A. & Guttmann, H. (1983) *Handbook of human reliability analysis with emphasis on nuclear power plant applications.* Washington, DC: Nuclear Regulatory Commission.

Syvia, K. (1977) Play and learning. In B. Tizard & D. Harvey (Eds.) *The biology of play.* London: SIMP/Heinemann.

Sylva, K. (1992) The impact of pre-school education on later educational motivations and attributions. *Educational and Child Psychology, 2,* 9-16.

Sylva, K., Roy, C. & Painter, M. (1980) *Child watching at playgroup and nursery school.* London: Grant McIntyre.

Szasz, T.S. (1960) *The myth of mental illness.* London: Paladin.

Szasz, T.S. (1974) *Ideology and insanity.* Harmondsworth, Middlesex: Penguin.

Tait, P.E. (1990) The attainment of conservation by Chinese and Indian children. *Journal of Visual Impairment and Blindness,* 84 380-2.

Tajfel, H., Billig, M.G., Bundy, R.P., & Flament, C. (1971) Social categorisation and intergroup behaviour. *European Journal of Social Psychology, 1,* 149-78.

Talland, G.A. (Ed.) (1968) *Human ageing and behaviour.* New York: Academic Press.

Tarvis, C. (1974) The frozen world of the familiar stranger, A conversation with Stanley Milgram. *Psychology Today, June,* 71-80.

Taylor, L.K., Cook, P.F., Green, E.E. & Rogers, J.K. (1988) Better interviews: The effects of supervisor training on listening and collaborative skills. *Journal of Educational Research, 82,* 89-95.

Tedeschi, J.T., Schlenker, B.R. & Bonoma, T.V. (1971) Cognitive dissonance: private ratiocination or public spectacle? *American Psychologist, 26,* 685-95.

Teitelbaum, P. & Stellar, E. (1954) Recovery from the failure to eat produced by hypothalamic lesions. *Science, 120,* 894-5.

Terrace, H.S. (1979) *Nim.* New York: Knopf.

Tesser, A. (1978) Self-generated attitude change. In L. Berkowitz (Ed.) *Advances in experimental social psychology* (Vol. 11). New York: Academic Press.

Thibaut, J.W. & Kelley, H.H. (1959) *The social psychology of groups.* New York: Wiley.

Thigpen, C.H. & Cleckley, H. (1957) *The three faces of Eve.* New York: McGraw-Hill.

Thomas, J. & Griffin, R. (1983) The social information processing model of task design: A review of the literature. *Academy of Management Review, 8,* 672-82.

Thomson, D.M. & Tulving, E. (1970) Associative encoding and retrieval: Weak and strong cues. *Journal of Experimental Psychology, 86,* 255-62.

Thompson, R.A., Cicchetti, D., Lamb, M.E. & Malkin, C. (1985) Emotional responses of Down's syndrome and normal infants in the strange situation: The organisation of affective behaviour in infants. *Developmental Psychology, 86,* 255-62.

Thorndike, E.L. (1898) Animal intelligence: An experimental study of the associative processes in animals. Psychological Review, *Monograph Supplement, 2* (Whole no. 8).

Thorndike, E.L. (1913) *The psychology of learning.* New York: Teachers College.

Thorpe, W.H. (1963) *Learning and instinct in animals* (2nd edition). London: Methuen.

Thurstone, L.L. (1931) *The measurement of social attitudes.* Chicago, IL: University of Chicago Press.

Thurstone, L.L. (1938) Primary mental abilities. *Psychometric Monographs,* number 1.

Tinbergen, N. (1948) Social releases and the experimental method required for their study. *Wilson Bulletin, 60,* 6-52.

Tinbergen, N. (1951) *The study of instinct.* London: Oxford University Press.

Tinbergen, N. (1952) The curious behaviour of the stickleback. *Scientific American, 187 (6),* 22-6.

Tinbergen, N. & Kuenen, D.J. (1939) Uber die auslösenden und die richtunggebenden reizsituationen der sperrbewegung von jungen drosseln. *Zeitschrift Fur Tierpsychologie, 3,* 37-60.

Tinbergen, N. & Perdeck, A.C. (1950) On the stimulus situation releasing the begging response in the newly hatched herring gull chick (*Larus a. argentatus* Pont.) *Behaviour, 3,* 1-38.

Tizard, B. & Hodges, J. (1978) The effect of early institutional rearing on the development of eight-year-old children. *Journal of Child Psychology and Psychiatry, 19,* 99-118.

Tizard, B. & Rees, J. (1975) A comparison of the effects of adoption, restoration to the natural mother, and continued institutionalisation on the cognitive development of 4-year-old children. *Child Development, 45,* 92-9.

Tolman, E.C. & Honzik, C.H. (1930) Introduction and removal of reward and maze learning in rats. *University of California Publications in Psychology, 4,* 257-75.

Tolstrup, K. (1990) Incidence and causality of anorexia nervosa seen in a historical perspective. *Acta Psychiatrica Scandinavia, 82,* 1-16.

Topping, K. & Wolfendale, S. (Eds.),(1985) *Parental involvement in children's reading.* London: Croom Helm.

Torgersen, S. (1983) Genetic factors in anxiety disorders. *Archives of General Psychiatry 40,* 1085-9.

Torrance, S. (1986) Breaking out of the Chinese room. In M. Yazdani (Ed.), *Artificial intelligence: Principles and applications.* London: Chapman & Hall.

Travis, L.E. (1925) The effect of a small audience upon eye-hand co-ordination. *Journal of Abnormal and Social Psychology, 20,* 142-6.

Treisman, A.M. (1964) Verbal cues, language, and meaning in selective attention, *American Joumal of Psychology, 77,* 206-19.

Treisman, A.M. & Riley, J.G.A. (1969) Is selective attention, selective perception or selective response?: A further test, *Journal of Experimental Psychology, 79,* 27-34.

Trevarthen, C. (1974) Conversations with a two-month-old. *New Scientist, 62,* 230-5.

Trimble, M.R. & Thompson, P.J. (1986) Neuropsychological and behavioural sequelae of spontaneous seizures. *Annals of the New York Academy of Sciences, 462,* 284-92.

Triplett, N. (1897) The dynamogenic factors in pacemaking and competition, *American Joumal of Psychology, 9,* 507-33.

Trivers, R.L. (1972) Parental investment and sexual selection. In B. Campbell (Ed.) *Sexual selection and the descent of man.* Chicago: Aldine.

Tronick, E.Z. (1989) Emotions and emotional communication in infants. *American Psychologist, 44,* 112-9.

Tuddenham, R.D. (1958) The influence of an avowedly distorted norm upon individual judgement. *Journal of Psychology, 46,* 329-38.

Tulving, E. (1962) Subjective organisation in free recall of unrelated words. *Psychological Review, 69,* 344-54.

Tulving, E. (1968) Theoretical issues in free recall. In T. Dixon and D. Horton (Eds.) *Verbal behaviour and general behaviour theory.* Englewood Cliffs, NJ: Prentice-Hall.

Tulving, E. (1972) Episodic and semantic memory. In E. Tulving & W. Donaldson (Eds.) *Organisation of memory.* London: Academic Press.

Tulving, E. (1974) Cue-dependent forgetting. *American Scientist, 62,* 74-82.

Tulving, E. (1979) Relation between encoding specificity and levels of processing. In L.S. Cermak & F.I.M. Craik (Eds.) *Levels of processing in human memory.* Hillsdale, NJ: Lawrence Erlbaum.

Tulving, E. (1989) Memory: Performance, knowledge, and experience, *The European Journal of Cognitive Psychology, 1,* 3-26.

Tulving, E. & Gold, C. (1963) Stimulus information and contextual information as determinants of tachistiscopic recognition of words. *Journal of Experimental Psychology, 66,* 319-27.

Tulving, E. & Pearlstone, Z. (1966) Availability versus accessibility of information in memory for words. *Journal of Verbal Learning and Verbal Behaviour, 5,* 381-91.

Tulving, E. & Psotka, J. (1971) Retroactive inhibition in free recall: Inaccessibility of information available in the memory store. *Journal of Experimental Psychology, 87,* 1-8.

Turing, A. (1950) Computer machinery and intelligence, *Mind, 59,* 433-60.

Turner, C.W., Hesse, B.W. & Peterson-Lewis, S. (1986) Naturalistic studies of the long-term effects of violence. *Journal of Social Issues, 42,* 51-73.

Turner, J.C. & Helms, D.B. (1989) *Contemporary adulthood* (4th edition). Fort Worth, FL: Holt, Rinehart & Winston.

Turner, R.J. & Wagenfeld, M.O. (1967) Occupational mobility and schizophrenia. *American Sociological Review, 32,* 104-13.

Tversky, A. & Kahneman, D. (1973) Availability: A heuristic for judging frequency and probability. *Cognitive Psychology, 4,* 207-32.

Tyerman, A. & Spencer, C. (1983) A critical test of Sherif's Robbers' Cave experiment: Intergroup competition and co-operation between groups of well-acquainted groups and individuals. *Small Group Behaviour, 14(4),* 515-31.

Tyler, L.E. (1965) *The psychology of human differences* (3rd edition). New York: Appleton-Century-Crofts.

Underwood J. (1957) Interference and forgetting. *Psychological Review, 64,* 49-60.

Valins, S. (1966) Cognitive effects of false heart-rate feedback. *Journal of Personality and Social Psychology, 4,* 400-8.

Valzelli, L. (1973) The "isolation syndrome" in mice. *Psychopharmalogia, 31,* 305-20.

Vaughn, B., Egeland, B., Sroufe, L.A. & Waters, E. (1979) Individual differences in infant-mother attachments at twelve and eighteen months: Stability and change in families under stress. *Child Development, 50,* 971-5.

Veitch, R. & Griffith, W. (1976) Good news, bad news: Affective and interpersonal effects. *Journal of Applied Social Psychology, 6,* 69-75.

Venkatesan, M. (1966) Consumer behaviour: conformity and independence. *Journal of Marketing Research, 3.*

Vernon, P.E. (1950) *The structure of human abilities.* London: Methuen.

Vernon, P.E. (1958) Education and the psychology of individual differences. *Harvard Educational Review, 28,* 91-104.

Vertes, R.P. (1986) A life-sustaining function for REM sleep: A theory. *Neuroscience and Biobehavioural Reviews, 10,* 371-6.

Von Wright, J.M., Anderson, K. & Stenman, U. (1975) Generalisation of conditioned G.S.R.s in dichotic listening. In P.M.A. Rabbit & S. Dornic (Eds.) *Attention and performance* (Vol. V). London: Academic Press.

Von Frisch, K. (1967) *The dance language and orientation of bees.* Cambridge, MA: Belknap.

Vroom, V.H. (1964) *Work and motivation.* New York: John Wiley & Sons.

Vroom, V.H. & Yetton, P.W. (1973) *Leadership and decision-making.* Pittsburgh: University of Pittsburgh Press.

Vygotsky, L.S. (orig. 1934 reprinted 1962) *Thought and language.* Cambridge, MA: MIT Press.

Vvgotsky, L.S. (1967) Play and the role of mental development in the child. *Soviet Psychology, 5,* 6-18.

Vygotsky, L.S. (1978) *Mind in society: The development of higher psychological process.* Cambridge, MA: Harvard University Press.

Vygotsky, L.S. (1987) The development of scientific concepts in childhood. In R.W. Rieber and A.S. Carton (Eds.) *The collected works of L.S. Vygotsky.* (Vol. 1). New York: Plenum Press.

Wadsworth, S.J., Gillis, J.J., DeFries, J.C. & Fulker, D.W. (1989) Differential genetic aetiology of reading disability as a function of age. *Irish Journal of Psychology, 10,* 509-20.

Walker, L.J., deVries, B. & Trevethan, S.D. (1987) Moral stages and moral orientations in real-life and hypothetical dilemmas. *Child Development, 58,* 842-58.

Wall, T.D. & Lischeron, J.A. (1977) *Worker participation.* London: McGraw-Hill.

Wallas. G. (1926) *The art of thought.* London: Cape.

Wallerstein, J. & Kelly J. (1985) *Surviving the breakup.* London: Grant McIntyre.

Wallston, B.S. & Wallston, K.A. (1978) Locus of control and health: A review of the literature. *Health Education Monographs, 6,* 107-11.

Walster, E. (1965) The effect of self-esteem on romantic liking. *Journal of Experimental Social Psychology, 1,* 184-97.

Walster, E. (1966) The assignment of responsibility for an accident. *Journal of Personality and Social Psychology, 3,* 73-9.

Walster, E., Aronson, V., Abrahams, D. & Rottman, L. (1966) The importance of physical attractiveness in dating behaviour, *Journal of Personality and Social Psychology, 4,* 508-16.

Walster, E. & Festinger, L. (1962) The effectiveness of 'overheard' persuasive communication. *Journal of Abnormal and Social Psychology, 65,* 395-402.

Walster, E., Walster, G.W. & Bersheid, E. (1978) *Equity theory and research.* Boston, MA: Allyn & Bacon.

Warr, P.B. (1978) A study of psychological well-being. *British Journal of Psychology, 69,* 111-21.

Warr, P.B. (1982) A national study of non-financial employment commitment. *Journal of Occupational Psychology, 55,* 297-312.

Warren, R.M. & Warren, R.P. (1970) Auditory illusions and confusions. *Scientific American, 223,* 30-6.

Wason, P.C. (1966) Reasoning. In B.M. Foss (Ed.) *New horizons in psychology.* Harmondsworth, Middlesex: Penguin.

Watson, J.B. (1913) Psychology as the behaviourist views it. *Psychological review, 20,* 158-77.

Watson, J.B. & Rayner, R. (1920) Conditioned emotional reactions. *Journal of Experimental Psychology, 3,* 1-14.

Waugh, N.C. & Norman, D. (1965) Primary memory. *Psychological Review, 72,* 89-104.

Weatherly, D. (1961) Anti-semitism and expression of fantasy aggression. *Journal of Abnormal and Social Psychology, 62,* 454-7.

Weatherly, D. (1964) Self-perceived rate of physical maturation and personality in late adolescence. *Child Development, 35,* 1197-1210.

Webb, W.B. & Agnew, H.W. (1971) Stage 4 sleep: Influence of time course variables. *Science, 174,* 1354-6.

Webb, W.W. (1985) A further analysis of age and sleep deprivation effects. *Psychophysiology, 22,* 156-61.

Wechsler, D. (1944) *The measurement of adult intelligence* (3rd edition). Baltimore, MD: Wilkins & Wilkins.

Wechsler, D. (1958) *The measurement and appraisal of adult intelligence* (4th edition). Baltimore, MD: Wilkins & Wilkins.

Wechsler, D. (1989) *Manual for the Wechsler preschool and primary scale of intelligence - Revised.* New York: Psychological Corporation.

Wechsler, D. (1974) *Wechsler intelligence scale for children.* New York: Psychological Corporation.

Wegmann, H., Klein, K.E., Conrad, B. & Esser, P. (1983) A model for prediction of resynchronization after time-zone flights. *Aviation, Space, and Environmental Medicine, 54,* 524-527.

Wegmann, R.G. (1976) Classroom discipline: An exercise in the maintenance of social reality. *Sociology of Education, 49,* 71-9.

Wehr, T.A., Sack, D.A. & Rosenthal, N.E. (1987) Sleep reduction as a final common pathway in the genesis of mania. *American Journal of Psychiatry, 144,* 201-4.

Weigel, R.H., Vernon, D.T.A., & Tognacci, L.N. (1974) Specificity of the attitude as a determinant of attitude behaviour congruence. *Journal of Personality and Social Psychology, 30,* 724-8.

Weinberg, R.S., Gould, D. & Jackson, A. (1979) Expectations and performance: An empirical test of Bandura's self-efficacy theory. *Journal of Sport Psychology, 1,* 320-331.

Weiner, B. (1980) *Human motivation.* New York: Holt Rinehart & Winston.

Weinstein, C.F. & Mayer, R.F. (1986) The teaching of learning strategies. In M.C. Wittrock (Ed.) *Handbook of research on teaching* (3rd edition). New York: Macmillan.

Weisman, A.D. & Kastenbaum, R. (1968) *The psychological autopsy: A study of the terminal phase of life.* New York: Behavioural Publications, Inc.

Weiss, M.R. & Friedrichs, W.D. (1986) The influence of leader behaviours, coach attributes and institutional variables on performance and satisfaction of collegiate basketball teams. *Journal of Sport Psychology, 8,* 332-46.

Weitzman, E.D., Czeisler, C.A., Coleman, R.M., Spielman A.J., Zimmerman, J.C. & Dement, W. (1981) Delayed sleep phase syndrome. *Archives of General Psychiatry, 38,* 737-46.

Weizenbaum, J. (1966) ELIZA-A computer program for the study of natural language communication between man and machine. *Communications of the Association for Computing Machine, 11,* 145-72.

Weizenbaum, J. (1976) *Computer powerand human reason.* San Francisco: W.H. Freeman.

Welford, A.T. (1958) *Ageing and human skill.* Oxford: Oxford University Press for the Nuffield Foundation.

Wells, G.L., Liepe, M.R. & Ostrom, T.M. (1979) Guidelines for empirically assessing the fairness of a lineup. *Law and Human Behaviour, 3,* 285-93.

Wender, P.H., Kety, S.S., Rosenthal, D., Schulsinger, F., Ortmann, J. & Lunde, I (1974) Psychiatric disorders in the biological and adoptive families of adopted individuals with affective disorders. *Archives of General Psychiatry, 30,* 121-8.

Wernick, R.I. (1983) Stress inoculation in the management of clinical pain: Applications to burn pain. In D. Meichenbaum & M.E. Jaremko (Eds.) *Stress reduction and prevention.* New York: Plenum.

Westfall, R. (1962) Psychological factors in predicting brand choice. *Journal of Marketing, 26.*

Westmacott, E.V.S. & Cameron, R.J. (1981) *Behaviour can change.* London: Macmillan Education.

White, D. (1975) The growth of conscience. *New Society, December 4th,* 538-40.

White, G.L., Fishbein, S., & Rutstein, J. (1981) Passionate love and the misattribution of arousal. *Journal of Personality and Social Psychology, 41,* 56-62.

White, R.W. (1959) Motivation reconsidered: The concept of competence. *New Society, December 4,* 538-40.

Whitney, I., Nabuzoka, D. & Smith, P.K. (1992) Bullying in schools: Mainstream and special needs. *Support.for Learning, 7,* 3-7.

Whorf, B.L. (1956) *Language, thought and reality.* Cambridge, MA: MIT Press.

Whyte, W.H. (1989) *City: Rediscovering the center.* New York: Doubleday.

Wicker, A.W. (1979) Attitudes versus actions: The relationship between verbal and overt behavioural responses to attitude objects. *Journal of Social Issues, 25,* 41-78.

Wicklegren, W.A. (1974) Single trace fragility theory of memory dynamics. *Memory and Cognition, 2,* 775-80.

Wiegman, O., Kuttschreuter, M. & Baarda, B. (1992) A longitudinal study of the effects of television viewing on aggressive and prosocial behaviours. *British Journal of Social Psychology, 31,* 147-64.

Wiesel, T.N. (1982) Postnatal development of the visual cortex and the influence of environment. *Nature, 299,* 583-91.

Wikler, A. (1948) Recent progress in research on the neurophysiologic basis of morphine addiction. *American Journal of Psychiatry, 105,* 329-88.

Williams, F.T. (1993) The ageing population. In *Medical schools and poor patients: Report on the conference.* Irvine, CA: University of California.

Williams, R.L. (1973) Black intelligence test of cultural homogeneity (BITCH). *Newsweek. 19 December, 109.*

Williams, T.M. (1985) Implications of a natural experiment in the developed world for research on television in the developing world. Special Issue: Television in the developing world. *Journal of Cross Cultural Psychology, 16(3),* 263-287.

Wilson, B.J., Linz, D., Donnerstein, E. & Stipp, H. (1992) The impact of social issue television programming on attitudes towards rape. *Human Communication Research, 19,* 179-208.

Wilson,E.O. (1975) *Sociobiology: The new synthesis.* Cambridge, MA: Harvard University Press.

Winch, R.F. (1958) *Mate selections: A study of complementary needs.* New York: Harper.

Winfree, A.T. (1986) Benzodiazepines set the clock. *Nature, 321,* 114-5.

Winter, D.G. (1973) *The power motive.* New York: Free Press.

Witelson, S.F. (1977) Developmental dyslexia: Two right hemispheres and none left. *Science, 195,* 309-11.

Wolfe, J.B. (1936) Effectiveness of token-rewards for chimpanzees. *Comparative Psychology,* monograph 12, no. 60.

Wolff, P.H. (1969) The natural history of crying and other vocalisations in early infancy. In B.M. Foss (Ed.) *Determinants of infant behaviour* (Vol. 4). London: Methuen.

Wolpe, J. (1958) *Psychotherapy by reciprocal inhibition.* Stanford, CA: Stanford University Press.

Wood, D.J., Bruner, J.S. & Ross, G. (1976) The role of tutoring in problem-solving. *Journal of Child Psychology and Psychiatry, 17,* 89-100.

Woods, P.A., Higson, P.J. & Tannahill, M.M. (1984) Token-economy programmes with chronic psychotic patients: The importance of direct measurement and objective evaluation for long-term maintenance. *Behaviour Research and Therapy, 22,* 41-53.

Worchel, S. & Yohai, S. (1979) The role of attribution in the experience of crowding. *Journal of Experimental Social Psychology, 15,* 91-104.

Word, C.O., Zanna, M.P. & Cooper, J. (1974) The nonverbal mediation of self-fulfilling prophecies in interracial interaction, *Journal of Experimental Social Psychology, 10,* 109-20.

Worthington, A.G. (1969) Paired comparison of scaling brightness judgements: A method for measuring perceptual defence. *British Journal of Psychology, 60,* 363-8.

Yancey, W.L. (1971) Architecture, interaction and social control: The case of large-scale housing projects. In J.F. Wohlwill & D.H. Carson (Eds.) *Environment and the social sciences: Perspectives and applications*. Washington DC: American Psychological Association.

Yarrow, L.J. (1963) Research in dimensions of early maternal care. *Merrilll-Palmer Quarterly, 9*, 101-14.

Yasakawa, K. (1979) A fair advantage in animal confrontations. *New Scientist, 1 November*.

Yates, C. & Smith P.K. (1989) Bullying in two English comprehensive schools. In E. Roland & E. Munthe (Eds.) *Bullying: An international perspective*. London: David Fulton.

Yelsma, P. & Athappilly, K. (1988) Marital satisfaction and communication practices: Comparisons among Indian and American couples. *Journal of Comparative Family Studies, 19*, 37-54.

Yerkes, R.M. & Dodson, J.D. (1908) The relation of strength stimulus to rapidity of habit-formation. *Journal of Comparative Neurological Psychology, 18*, 459-82.

Zahavi, A. (1975) Mate selection – a selection for handicap. *Journal of Theoretical Biology, 53*, 205-14.

Zajonc, R.B. (1965) Social facilitation, *Science, 149*, 269-74.

Zajonc, R.B. (1968) Attitudinal effects of mere exposure.

Journal of Personality and Social Psychology (Monograph), 9, 1-29.

Zajonc, R.B., Heingarter, A. & Herman, E.M. (1969) Social enhancement and impairment of performance in the cockroach. *Journal of Personality and Social Psychology, 13*, 83-92.

Zajonc, R.B. & Markus, G.B. (1975) Birth order and intellectual development. *Psychological Review, 82*, 74-88.

Zeigler, H.P. & Karten, H.J. (1974) Central trigeminal structures and the lateral hypothalamus syndrome in the rat. *Science, 186*, 636-7.

Zillman, D. (1983) Arousal and aggression. In R.G. Geen & E.l. Donnerstein (Eds.) *Aggression: Theoretical and empirical reviews* (Vol. 1). New York: Academic Press.

Zimbardo, P.G. (1960) Involvement and communication discrepance as determinants of opinion conformity. *Journal of Abnormal and Social Psychology, 60*, 86-94.

Zimbardo, P.G. (1969) The human choice: Individuation reason and order versus deindividuation, impulse and chaos. *Nebraska Symposium on Motivation, 17*, 237-307.

Zimbardo, P.G. (1975) Transforming experimental research into advocacy for social change. In M. Deutsch & H.A. Hornstein (Eds.) *Applying social psychology*. Hillsdale, NJ: Lawrence Erlbaum.

APPENDIX: PERSPECTIVES IN PSYCHOLOGY

Several examinations have a section entitled 'Perspectives in Psychology' which specifically examines the issues raised throughout this book:

Major Approaches

Approach	Unit	Topics
BIOLOGICAL physiological	2.7	aggression
	3.4, 3.5	social development: gender, adolescence, ageing
	3.5, 7.6	life events and stress
	6.2	treatment of mental illness (e.g. drugs, ECT)
	7.1, 7.2, 7.3	biological psychology (e.g. effect of drugs, homeostasis, etc.)
	7.4	motivation (e.g. Cannon)
	7.5	emotion (e.g. Cannon–Bard theory)
	7.6	stress (e.g. Selye)
genetic	4.1	language acquisition (Chomsky)
	5.1	intelligence (e.g. Jensen)
	7.2	sleep (evolutionary theory)
	6.4	causes of mental illness (e.g. schizophrenia, manic depression)
	8.1, 8.2	evolution and adaptiveness (ethological approach)
BEHAVIOURAL	1.3	thought and problem-solving (e.g. Watson, Thorndike)
	1.6	learning (e.g. Pavlov, Skinner)
	1.6, 2.7	social learning (e.g. Bandura on aggression)
	3.3, 3.4	moral and social development (e.g. gender)
	4.1	language acquisition (Skinner)
	5.2	personality (trait and type e.g. Catell and Eysenck)
	6.2	treatment of mental illness (e.g. behaviour therapy)
	7.4	motivation (e.g. Hull)
	7.5	emotion (e.g. James–Lange theory)
	7.6	stress (e.g. Watson)
COGNITIVE	1.1	perception (e.g. top-down processing)
	1.2	computer analogies (e.g. Newell and Simon)
	1.3	thought (e.g. prototypes)
	1.4	attention (e.g. Broadbent)
	1.5	memory (e.g. McClelland)
	1.6	learning (e.g. Piaget, Bruner, Ausubel)
	2.1, 2.2, 2.3, 2.5	social cognition (e.g. cognitive dissonance, attribution, prejudice)
	3.2	cognitive development (e.g. Piaget, Bruner)
	3.3	moral development (e.g. Kohlberg)
	3.3, 3.4, 3.5	social development (e.g. gender, play, adolescence, ageing: Erikson)
	3.2, 4.1	language acquisition (e.g. Piaget)
	5.2	personality (e.g. Kelly)
	6.2	treatment of mental illness (e.g. personal construct therapy)
	6.4	causes of mental illness (e.g. a learned response)
	7.4	motivation (e.g. Murray)
	7.5	emotion (e.g. cognitive labelling or appraisal theories)

PSYCHOANALYTIC	1.5	memory and forgetting (Freud)
	3.3	moral development (Freud)
	3.3, 3.4, 3.5	social development (gender, play, adolescence)
	5.2	personality (Freud and neo-Freudians)
	6.2	treatment of mental illness (psychoanalysis)
	7.4	motivation (Freud)
HUMANISM	5.2	personality (e.g. Rogers)
	6.2	treatment of mental illness (psychotherapy and counselling)
	7.4	motivation (e.g. Maslow)
ETHOLOGICAL	8.4	social behaviour (kin selection, e.g. Dawkins)
	2.7, 8.4	aggression (e.g. Lorenz)
	3.1	attachment (e.g. Bowlby)
	3.4	play (naturalistic studies e.g. Sylva)
	4.3	origins of communication (e.g. manipulation hypothesis)
	7.2	sleep as an adaptive process (evolutionary theory)
	8.3	imprinting and learning (e.g. Tinbergen)
CROSS-CULTURAL	1.1	perception (visual illusions)
	3.1	attachment (e.g. kibbutzim)
	3.3, 3.4, 3.5	social development (gender, adolescence, ageing: Mead)

Key debates/philosophical issues

Freewill versus determinism	5.2	freewill (e.g. Rogers)
	1.6	environmental determinism (e.g. Skinner)
	3.1, 5.2	biological determinism (e.g. Bowlby, Freud)
Reductionism	1.2	artificial intelligence (computer analogies)
	1.6	behaviourism (SR units)
	5.2	Freud (psychological constituents)
	7.1	biological explanations (e.g. neurons)
Structuralism	3.1	Piaget's theory of cognitive development (stages)
	5.2	Freud's theory of personality (id, ego, superego)
Functionalism	8.1, 8.2	ethological explanations
Nature versus nurture	1.1	perception
	1.3	language and thought (effects of deprivation)
	2.7	aggression
	3.1	early development (deprivation)
	3.4	gender roles
	4.1	language
	4.2	function of non-verbal communication
	5.1	intelligence
	5.2	personality
	6.4	causes of mental illness
Objectivity versus subjectivity	10.1	scientific method versus diary/introspection
Nomothetic versus idiographic	3.1, 3.2	development (e.g. Rutter versus Piaget)
	5.2	personality (e.g. Eysenck versus Allport or Freud)
	10.1	psychological enquiry (e.g. survey versus case study)
Major concepts	7.1, 7.2, 7.4, 7.5	e.g. mind/body, consciousness, motivation, emotion
Psychological enquiry	10.1	scientific, observation, survey, correlation, case study,
	5.3, 5.4, 5.5	psychometrics (attitudes, intelligence, personality)
Psychometrics	2.3	attitudes
	5.1, 5.4	intelligence
	5.2, 5.5	personality
Ethics of social and behaviour change	6.2	treatment of abnormal behaviour
	8.5	use of animals in research
	10.4	research ethics
Historical perspectives, covered in:	Chapter 1	cognitive psychology
	Chapter 2	social psychology
	Chapter 3	developmental psychology
	Chapter 5	intelligence and personality
	Chapter 6	abnormal psychology
	Chapter 8	animal behaviour

INDEX